005.43
T366u

UNIX® Administration Guide for System V

Rebecca Thomas, PhD.
Rik Farrow

D1310360

Prentice Hall
Englewood Cliffs, New Jersey 07632

Library of Congress Cataloging-in-Publication Data

Thomas, Rebecca (date)
    UNIX administration guide for system V / Rebecca Thomas, Rik
Farrow.
    p.   cm.
        Includes index.
    ISBN 0-13-942889-5
    1. UNIX System V (Computer operating system)   I. Farrow, Rik,
(date)   II. Title.
    QA76.76.063T46   1989
    005.4'3—dc19   88-15723
                                                                   CIP

Editorial/production supervision: *Sophie Papanikolaou*
Cover design: *Diane Saxe*
Manufacturing buyer: *Mary Ann Gloriande*

E-Mail: uunet! uworld! beccat

DEC, PDP, and VAX are registered trademarks of Digital Equipment Corp.
Microsoft and XENIX are registered trademarks of Microsoft, Inc.
Teletype is a registered trademark of Teletype Corp.
Workbench is a registered trademark of AT&T/Bell Labs.
UNIX is a registered trademark of AT&T.

The publisher offers discounts on this book when ordered
in bulk quantities. For more information, write:
            Special Sales/College Marketing
            Prentice-Hall, Inc.
            College Technical and Reference Division
            Englewood Cliffs, NJ 07632

Printed in the United States of America

10   9   8   7   6   5   4   3   2

ISBN   0-13-942889-5

PRENTICE-HALL INTERNATIONAL (UK) LIMITED, *London*
PRENTICE-HALL OF AUSTRALIA PTY. LIMITED, *Sydney*
PRENTICE-HALL CANADA INC., *Toronto*
PRENTICE-HALL HISPANOAMERICANA, S.A., *Mexico*
PRENTICE-HALL OF INDIA PRIVATE LIMITED, *New Delhi*
PRENTICE-HALL OF JAPAN, INC., *Tokyo*
SIMON & SCHUSTER ASIA PTE. LTD., *Singapore*
EDITORA PRENTICE-HALL DO BRASIL, LTDA., *Rio de Janeiro*

Dedication

To Fran, Tink, and Linda, without whose support and understanding throughout the years, this book would not have been possible.

RT

To my family for their loving assistance and to all the people who have to struggle with the UNIX system.

RF

Contents

Acknowledgments

To begin with, we want to recognize each other. If either of us had known how long this project would take or the amount of work required, we probably would not have attempted it. Becca had just completed the first revision of A *User Guide to the UNIX System* and was in no mood to write another book. Rik, however, had just acquired a Motorola 68000 system that ran System V and was raring to go. Rik created an outline, based on the Installation Notes he had written for his UNIX system, and convinced Becca that there was a place for a system administration book, and that together they could write it. We estimated it would take six months.

Becca, the established author, wrote the proposal and a sample introduction. Her old friend, Joe Campbell, provided friendly advice and jazzed up the proposal. The search for a publisher ended when we met (by phone) Patricia Henry of Prentice Hall, our first editor. Pat was both helpful and encouraging, and we might not have finished without her.

Writing the book took two and a half years. Although we both had administered and worked with UNIX systems for years, it is just not the same as working at Bell Labs or being a graduate student at Berkeley. We lacked the support structure and the breadth of experience that would have given us the confidence to proceed quickly. Instead, we were in the position of most users, with one difference. We were dedicated to discovering what a user needed to know to be a good system administrator, and we spent our lives explaining it to people.

Part of writing a good book is the review process. We were fortunate to know several people that represented different audiences, and Prentice Hall provided us with many technical reviewers. We would like to thank all of our reviewers, and apologize to any of you that we miss here. In particular, thanks to Jim Wright and his class at Purdue University for their in-depth reviews. Gary Donnelly (of UniTech) gave us helpful suggestions for appealing to a non-technical audience. Gary Wilson (of Campbell, California) provided us with more suggestions about organization, and Jim Knutson (of Austin, Texas) helped with the technical accuracy, as did some others. King Ables, also of Texas, was especially helpful with his detailed reviews, and willingness to help in the project.

Our most important reviewer by far was Peggy Mooney. Peggy had been an English teacher before she started raising a family. When she reentered the job market, she decided to work with computers. She was faced with the UNIX system at her first job, and hunted down Rik whom she discovered had written her UNIX system's documentation. Peggy represented an important member of our audience— an intelligent person with some computer experience and a desire to learn. Peggy not only forced us to explain things in terms she could understand, she was also our style editor. Where other reviewers sent us several pages of notes, Peggy sent us heavily marked-up xeroxed copies of every page, which showed us where our explanations were unclear or our English muddy. Her support kept us going.

We also sought out live audiences for instant feedback. Bruce Stewart and Steven List of Benetics arranged our first one-day seminar on system administration. Bruce also reviewed Becca's chapters. John Donnelly and Judith DesHarnais arranged for us to give seminars at the Usenix conventions. (Becca has also taught at UniForum.) Ray Swartz arranged for us to meet Chuck Jaffee of ARIX Systems. We designed and taught a five day hands-on course for ARIX Systems, which gave us much practical experience in working with small groups of people with widely varying backgrounds.

We also received help in other forms. Santa Cruz Operations gave us versions of XENIX to experiment with, and Microport sent us a PC version of System V. UNIXWORLD magazine not only supported Becca, but also supplied us with information and many anecdotes about what happens when "ordinary" people collide with the UNIX system. Special thanks goes to Paul Fertal and Dave Flack of UNIXWORLD. Rik thanks the people of the now-defunct Morrow Designs, especially Bob Groppo, Len Edmonsun, and Kevin Mankin, and the Sherrill-Lubinski Company, both for work and exposure to BSD systems. Opus Systems supplied both hardware and answers to specific technical questions. Thanks also to the production staff at Prentice Hall's College Book Division, in particular Ed Moura (our final editor) and Sophie Papanikolaou (the production editor). There are many other Prentice Hall employees and contractors who are unknown to us, but equally important in producing this book.

Finally, we want to thank our personal support groups. Rik might have quit if it hadn't been for his wife, Rose Moon, and her calming influence. Their two children, Jasmine and Canyon, were also helpful, especially Canyon, who, at age ten, learned how to startup and shutdown UNIX systems, use **vi**, and play **robots**. Becca thanks her personal assistants Starry Bush and Elizabeth Selandia, and most of all, her three cats: Beetle Bailey, Gray Matter, and Nubbins always made sure that they were central to any operation, be it editing, connecting modems, or testing scripts.

Rik Farrow
Rebecca Thomas

1

Introduction

WHAT IS SYSTEM ADMINISTRATION?

When we started researching system administration, we talked to many people at U.C. Berkeley to find out what they thought system administrators did. They either didn't know or couldn't tell us. They could answer specific questions about using commands, but they had no overall picture of what they were doing.

Part of the reason for this situation is that system administration is a large, complex, and somewhat vague topic. At Berkeley, in particular, were many highly experienced programmers who were actively modifying the UNIX system. These system programmers, called "gurus," had designed and set up the system so that it would function as smoothly as possible. Therefore, while the system administrators we talked to were quite capable of handling the day-to-day tasks for maintaining many large UNIX systems, they didn't have experience setting up a system from scratch. Their systems had been set up and configured by expert system programmers—the gurus.

At the time of our research (1982), the UNIX system was gaining in popularity in arenas outside universities and the Bell System (AT&T today), where it was originally designed. Most people using these new UNIX systems didn't have the services of systems programmers or experienced UNIX system administrators to help them. Instead, all they had was their vendor's installation notes and the UNIX documentation.

Oh, their trials and vexations were mighty indeed! Someone at a university or within the Bell System merely had to find the right person to get an answer to their questions. The new UNIX system user (on the outside), by comparison, might as well have been in Africa or on an island in the South Pacific. Even the "traditional" method for isolated users seeking information, Usenet (a UNIX network dedicated to communicating by posting messages and software), was virtually unknown and unavailable to the new population of users.

Since 1980, over a hundred books have described various aspects of the UNIX system. These books form an invaluable aid to the novice computer user becoming acquainted with the UNIX system. People can learn what the UNIX system does and how to use it.

However, system administration requires a much broader knowledge of the UNIX system. The administrator must both set up the system (as the gurus do) and solve any problems that may arise while using the system. The documentation that comes with new UNIX systems is hopelessly inadequate for this task.

One goal of this book is to guide you, the system administrators, into understanding what's necessary to accomplish your job. We arranged the chapters in the order that we use to teach system administration. Each topic is explored in depth. The discussions are a mix of the information found in UNIX documentation, hints from experienced administrators, and our own research.

Although we encourage you to read this book cover to cover, its material is arranged so that it works in a stand-alone fashion—individual sections can be read and used separately. The nature of the topic makes for somewhat heavy reading, and its breadth prevented us from including more humor and lightness. You'll enjoy using it more if you try anything that you find interesting.

We would also like to add a word of caution at this point. The UNIX system is not stamped out like coins from a coin press. Each vendor's version is apt to be different, sometimes in small ways, other times with vast differences. To write this book, we used computers running System V releases of the UNIX system, and tested the examples on a variety of computers also running System V and XENIX releases. However, we are not claiming infallibility. We strongly recommend that you check everything that we suggest. The bumper sticker adage comes immediately to mind —"Question Authority." Don't believe what we are telling you unless you know that it's correct. Try to disprove us, and you will do what we want to accomplish with this book. You will learn to be an expert system administrator.

So, onward. Please don't just sit back and read. Explore your UNIX system. This guidebook must be experienced to be enjoyed. You don't get to Africa by watching *The African Queen*, and you won't learn system administration by only reading a book. Good luck!

Overview to Chapter 1

In this chapter we've put some of the general background that will help you administer UNIX systems. A bit of history will help you separate XENIX from BSD from System V. We survey the general duties of the system administrator, including how to organize a system logbook. Next, we introduce the system administrator's assistants, the daemons that perform background tasks. The "clock daemon" in particular serves many administrative functions, and will be described. We lay out the common UNIX directories and guide you through the megalithic UNIX documentation. We end with some useful commands and a short list of terms with which every system administrator should feel comfortable.

EVOLUTION OF THE UNIX SYSTEM

During the mid to late sixties, a group of computer scientists worked together on a project called Multics. This experimental operating system was a joint project of Massachusetts Institute of Technology, AT&T Bell Labs, and General Electric Co. (GE). The scientists were designing an operating system for a specific computer, the GE 635, an advanced (for its day) mainframe computer. The new operating system was to be designed with flexibility and interactive use in mind. Along with interactive use, the architects wanted to make this system secure, yet still facilitate file and information sharing.

Unfortunately, the development of this complex system met with many delays, and Bell Labs left the project. Ken Thompson and Dennis Ritchie had been exposed to Multics, via a preliminary version at Bell Labs. Thompson had written a game, "Space Travel," on a GE 635 running Multics. Ken Thompson and Dennis Ritchie rewrote the game so it could be used on a minicomputer, a PDP-7 to which they had access. Their efforts were complicated by the primitive environment on the PDP-7. They needed to perform all their development work on a GE 635 running GECOS, a batch-oriented operating system, and move the finished programs for execution to the PDP-7 using paper tape.

The aggravations involved convinced Ken Thompson to create a simple file system and some utilities for the PDP-7. This primitive operating system and utilities were given the name UNIX the following year (1970). The meaning of the name has never been revealed officially, although UNIX could be a play on the name Multics.

This first version of the UNIX system, primitive as it was, still met with attention. Thompson, Ritchie, and associates were able to get a more advanced minicomputer, a PDP-11, in exchange for a promise to add text-processing capabilities to the system. UNIX development was now an official project recognized by Bell Labs. A second version was implemented with document-processing features and used by Bell Lab's patent licensing organization.

In 1973, the UNIX system was rewritten in the high-level C language, facilitating its maintenance and portability to other machines. Other groups within Bell Labs had begun using the UNIX system (now Version 4), and some universities had acquired it for use in teaching operating system design. Despite the fact that the system was not formally supported, its popularity grew. The UNIX system was unlike other operating systems of the day, because it was small, was written in a high-level language, encompassed some new useful ideas, and was not kept secret.

In time, versions 5 and 6 arrived. When needed, users would add utilities, which later became part of the official distribution. Bell Labs still had not officially released any version of the UNIX system to the commercial world because of uncertainties about the legality of selling computer products. Under a 1956 consent decree, AT&T was limited in the businesses that they could engage in and the patents they could license. This uncertainty prevented the UNIX system from becoming a commercial product, yet (probably) enhanced its evolution. Most of the hundreds of programs in today's UNIX versions became part of the UNIX system before it was officially released. By comparison, only a comparative handful of utilities have been added since its official release.

Version 7 of the UNIX system became the first official external release in the spring of 1978. All other variants of the UNIX system can trace their heritage back to Version 7 as a common ancestor. After Version 7, the genealogy becomes much more complicated. Although there are many other branches that could be mentioned, Figure 1.1 identifies three major ones that diverge at this point—the commercial AT&T releases, BSD (Berkeley Software Distribution), and XENIX (from Microsoft Corporation).

Figure 1.1 Evolution of the UNIX system.

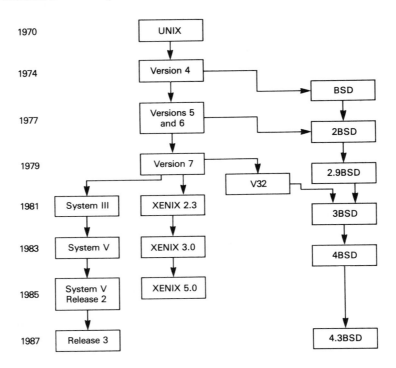

Berkeley

The University of California, Berkeley campus became involved with the UNIX in 1973, when Professor Fabry heard the first paper presented on it. Professor Fabry acquired Version 4 the next year. (During most of the seventies, universities were able to get source licenses to the UNIX system essentially for free.) In 1975, Ken Thompson visited the University of California, his alma mater, on a sabbatical. He helped install Version 6 on a PDP-11/70. The same year, two graduate students also arrived at Berkeley: Bill Joy and Chuck Haley. These graduate students were to play an important role in the development of the UNIX system at Berkeley.

Joy and Haley took over a Pascal system that Thompson had put together. Later that same year, they worked to produce the editor **ex**, starting from an editor named **em**. When Thompson left at the end of the year, they began taking an interest in the internal operations of the kernel.

Mainly because of interest in the Pascal compiler, Bill Joy put together a software distribution that he called the "Berkeley Software Distribution." Later, Joy expanded the editor **ex** to work with CRT terminals that provided addressable cursors and produced **vi**. Joy also wrote the C shell, so named because of its C programming language-style syntax. In 1978, an update of the distribution was made, named the "Second Berkeley Distribution," which was quickly shortened to 2BSD. There were many releases of 2BSD, and some PDP-11 computers may still be running the most recent version, 2.9BSD.

Also in 1978, the Berkeley systems group acquired a VAX-11/780. The VAX initially ran the VMS operating system (from DEC), but the staff had grown accustomed to using the UNIX system. So Professor Fateman obtained a copy of 32/V, a Version 7 port of the UNIX system for the VAX. Joy and a graduate student named Ozalp Babaoglu added virtual memory to 32/V (allowing programs larger than the available memory to run). Joy also ported the utilities that were part of 2BSD to what was then called "Virtual VAX/UNIX." In December 1979, this composite system, part 2BSD and Version 7, was distributed as 3BSD.

The Defense Advanced Research Project Agency (DARPA) provided the funding and impetus to the next distribution, 4BSD. 4.1BSD was released shortly afterward, with some important performance tune-ups. Release 4.2BSD (1983) included the Fast File System. A major modification to the UNIX file system structure, under the Fast File System, each file system is subdivided into cylinder groups, and the operating system creates and writes files so that they are limited to one cylinder group. This approach attempts to keep the disk blocks that make up a file in the same physical region of a disk, thus speeding up access and preventing fragmenting of files. 4.2BSD also supported connecting computers on the Ethernet network. Sun Microsystems added the Network File System (NFS) to 4.2BSD at a later date.

Release 4.3BSD (1987) consists mainly of tune-ups to 4.2. The less drastic changes in this release (contrasting with earlier releases) may be a sign that BSD and AT&T versions of the UNIX system may eventually converge.

XENIX

The XENIX system is based on Version 7. Microsoft released XENIX 2.3 in 1980 as an UNIX implementation for microcomputers. Although based on Version 7, some utilities were borrowed from 4.1BSD. XENIX 3.0 incorporated some new features from AT&T's System III, and XENIX 5.0 is intended to conform to the System V Interface Definition. The stated intention of Microsoft and the Santa Cruz Operation is that XENIX and UNIX systems will merge, with XENIX vendors providing support to microcomputer-based UNIX systems.

AT&T

Interestingly enough, AT&T did not formally release a version of the UNIX system until 1982, years after XENIX and 4.1BSD had been released. The first commercial release was named System III. (We don't know what happened to Systems I and II, or even if they really existed.) System III was based primarily on Version 7. Important Berkeley innovations, such as the C shell and screen editing capabilities, were not incorporated into this AT&T release. Instead, some features of the Version 6 Programmer's Workbench were included.

After this point, the pace at AT&T seems to pick up. In 1983, System V was released. System V included some important Berkeley utilities (like **vi**) and the screen-oriented software libraries (**curses**). The **init** program, used to start up processes that allow UNIX system access, underwent further modifications, so it's significantly different from the original Version 7 program.

Release 2 of System V followed soon (1984), and Release 3 has also come out (1987). With Release 2, AT&T introduced their own version of the terminal-capability database **termcap** file, called **terminfo**, which consists of many files, one to describe each terminal. Other changes in Release 2 include minor changes in the file system hierarchy, and the addition of Streams and the Remote File System, AT&T's response to the Berkeley vendor's Network File System.

Newcomers to the UNIX system often wonder what happened to AT&T System I, or 1.0BSD. There was a System IV inside AT&T, but it was never released externally. We don't know about System I and II. And the first release of BSD was just called the "Berkeley Software Distribution," so there was no 1.0BSD. There are many versions of the UNIX system that have been created and never released, plus countless versions developed by other vendors. Best not to get too worried about it.

And in the Future...

The future of the UNIX system, in some shape or form, has been assured by the acceptance of the System V Interface Definition by some major players. In particular, the U.S. government has started using the System V Interface Definition when requesting bids for both software and computer systems. IBM has announced support for System V on some of its mainframes. The IEEE P1003 Portable Operating System Environment standards committee has issued a report describing an interface essentially identical to System V, Release 2. And Microsoft, Santa Cruz Operation, and AT&T have announced the convergence of XENIX with UNIX System V on Intel microprocessors.

While these different groups appear to be lining up behind the UNIX system, what they are really supporting is the System V Interface Definition (SVID). The Interface Definition spells out exactly what services the operating system will perform and exactly how to request these services. The SVID does not require that the environment be a System V variant from AT&T. Vendors of BSD systems have already produced operating systems that provide both a Berkeley style and a SVID interface that is software selectable. IBM's support for SVID on its mainframes will probably not include other System V utilities.

Here's what we think the future will bring. There will be more and more multiuser computers running variants of System V. Berkeley versions won't disappear, although more features of BSD will cross over into AT&T versions. System V will become something like (shudder) COBOL. COBOL owes much of its success to its acceptance by the U.S. government, the type of support the UNIX system is beginning to get today. Menu-driven system administration packages will become better and more popular. These new programs won't replace system administrators, but will make their lives easier.

This text focuses on System V not out of prejudice or a judgment that System V is superior to BSD. Both variants have their adherents, who are willing to debate the topic heatedly. We simply found that it was easier to obtain computers which happened to run System V while we were developing the material for this book. We also feel that System V will be more prevalent than BSD in the business world. We wanted to cover BSD with the same depth, but found that we were writing two different versions of the same book. Users of other versions of the UNIX system will still find this book helpful despite the differences.

THE SYSTEM ADMINISTRATOR

The system administrator is one of the users of a system, and something more. The administrator wears many hats, as knowledgeable user of UNIX commands, as an operator of system hardware, and as a problem solver. The administrator is also called upon to be an arbitrator in human affairs. A multiuser computer is like a vast imaginary space where many people work and utilize the resources found there. The administrator must be the village elder in this space and settle the disputes that may arise with, hopefully, the wisdom of Solomon.

It is possible, and in fact we have seen, systems where there is no system administrator. Essentially, every user with some system experience is entrusted with system administration duties. And as you might expect, these systems are administered in a somewhat haphazard fashion. The bright side to this picture is that when something goes wrong, there's nobody to blame! With no one designated as responsible, no one has the agreement to take care of business. This "hands-off" style of system administration doesn't work very well. Only the single-user workstation can have a system administrator group that's identical to the user group.

Choosing a System Administrator

The persons chosen as system administrators must be responsible. Commonly, the most experienced UNIX system user inherits the role of system administrator. Although experience is certainly important, consistent reliability is even more important. A veteran programmer might not be as good a choice as the user who is totally organized, highly dependable, just, and consummately tactful. The programmer becomes the advisor, and the system administrator the doer.

Most system administrators have other jobs to perform. System administration is generally an additional duty on top of their other responsibilities. Most UNIX systems require attention only part of the time, unless the installation is large or involves many computers. One solution is to hire a reliable student with a background in the UNIX system to work part-time as the administrator. Just make certain that anyone that you use as a system administrator keeps a logbook.

Qualities of a System Administrator

The system administrator must allocate resources fairly. No user or group of users can be allowed to bully the rest of the user population with unfair activities. The administrator must also be a capable problem solver. Once a system has been properly configured, much of the administrator's work will involve fixing things that don't work, or have stopped functioning.

The administrator must also prevent security problems. By carefully arranging file and directory access permissions, controlling system access, and keeping a careful watch on the system, the administrator can avoid many problems that would otherwise occur. Security results from a well-administered system.

Finally, the administrator must reliably maintain the system. Primarily, maintaining the system means backing up the file systems. Of all the tasks that must be performed by the system administrator, backing up ranks as the single most important task. The information in the computer system's disk memory may represent many years of work and creativity, and a simple mistake or failure could make those data unrecoverable. A carefully designed and implemented backup strategy guards against such losses, whether they are trivial or catastrophic.

Table 1.1 outlines the majority of the system administrator's system duties.

TABLE 1.1 SYSTEM ADMINISTRATION DUTIES

System startup and shutdown
File system backup and file recovery
Maintenance of file system integrity and free space
Changing configuration files for:
        Adding or removing user accounts
        Activating/deactivating access ports
        Setting up and maintaining communications
        Setting up and maintaining the line printer system
        Startup and shutdown scripts
        Setting up files to run commands at selected times
Monitoring system accounting and activity
Balancing users' needs
Reading **root's** mail
Teaching users UNIX basics
Establishing and maintaining security
Installing hardware and software
Purchasing supplies and new equipment
Correcting errors and problems

THE IMPORTANCE OF BEING ROOT

The UNIX system's special *superuser* identity is immune from restrictions placed upon other users by the system. Any UNIX account with a user-id of zero (**0**) confers *superuser* privilege on the user of this account. In all systems we've seen, an account named **root** exists which has superuser privilege. The user of this account can access any file and run any command, including system-related ones that require superuser privilege (actually, system calls used by this command are privileged). This privileged mode of access allows the superuser to perform administrative tasks that would be difficult, if not impossible, without the privilege.

Superuser privileges allow a user to back up any file or file system, examine a file system for possible security violations, and create new file systems or device files. Also, users that have gotten themselves into untenable positions, such as removing access permissions for all (including themselves) in their home directory, can be helped by the superuser.

On the other hand, this very power can be very dangerous. A person working with superuser privileges can read any file, which might include salary information, other people's mail, and so on. The superuser can also redirect the output of a command to a file system device, destroying the beginning of that file system. Perhaps the most famous example of a dangerous command is **rm —rf *** when executed by a superuser in the root directory. This command will start removing every file in the file system hierarchy (directories will be spared after **/bin/rmdir** has been removed), making restoration of files basically a complete reinstallation of the UNIX system.

The point is that the superuser account is both necessary and dangerous. Novice users should not be entrusted with the superuser account password, ever. And experienced users should work as superuser only when mandatory. System administrators should do everything that they can while working with their ordinary user identity. All System V system status reporting commands (like **ps** or **lpstat)** can be run by ordinary users. And scripts can be developed and (mostly) tested while working as an ordinary user. Once administrators know exactly what needs to be done, they can use the **su** command to become **root** to do what's necessary with superuser privileges, then return to their login identity and relinquish the power—and danger—of **root**.

Because of the dangers involved in using superuser privileges, it is wise to create shell scripts to perform administrative tasks. Once a script has been written and debugged, it can be relied upon to carry out the same set of instructions time after time without making mistakes.

USING A LOGBOOK

A logbook is a very helpful tool that can make your life easier. The manuals and the installation notes describe your UNIX system in its delivered state. The changes that you and others make to your system's configuration won't appear in any documentation unless you take the time to put them there.

There are other equally powerful reasons for keeping a logbook. For example, it lets you avoid the nuisance of someone from work interrupting you at home. By recording routine procedures, other users don't need to interrupt your holiday with such routine questions as "Hey, how do you start up the computer?" You want to explain in your logbook some ordinary routine procedures in terms that other people can understand. The two most important procedures are starting up the system (with some advice on how to deal with the file system check done by **fsck)** and how to perform routine backups. Even with uninterruptible power supplies, you can't be certain that a system won't have to be rebooted while you're not available. And backups must be done routinely, whether you are present or not.

Another motivation is present when there is more than one administrator. It's quite possible for one person to undo the changes that someone else has laboriously installed. It is also very nice to know who has been doing what; for example, was something done by a fellow administrator or by someone who broke into your system? Table 1.2 lists some useful information you can include in your logbook.

Some files contain encrypted passwords, such as the system password file (**/etc/passwd**). But even more important, other files contain *unencrypted* passwords, such as the **Systems** or **L.sys** file used with the UUCP system. It is especially

TABLE 1.2 ITEMS TO INCLUDE IN A SYSTEM LOGBOOK

Reference Materials
  Listings of configurations files (without passwords) and scripts
  File system backup procedures
  Startup and shutdown procedures
  Any procedures (like adding users) done in a special way
  The hardware configuration
  Information about entries in the device directory (**/dev**)

Diary Section
  Times that changes occurred
  Name of person making changes
  Description of changes and reasons for changes
  When the system was started or stopped
  When backups were performed
  When and what errors are reported

important to edit out these passwords (and system-access telephone numbers) before printing a copy of these configuration files for the logbook. To be useful, the logbook must be accessible, and system crackers might find even encrypted passwords helpful, so remove them before recording the password file.

After you have written up a procedure, such as system startup, for the logbook, have someone else try it. You may discover that something which is obvious to you is nonsense to the intended user. Often, the step that you perform without thinking (e.g., typing or *not* typing a return at a prompt) will stump a less experienced user. So test your procedures on likely individuals.

Get a three-ring binder for the logbook. Print out the scripts and (edited) configuration files for it. Use tab separators to break the logbook into these sections: the system diary, configuration files, hardware log, and device directory.

Hardware Log

Don't overlook recording the manufacturers' names for your system's configuration and any hardware that has been added to it. For example, you may have an AT&T 3B2/310 with an expansion module and tape archiver. Writing down exactly what type of system you have can help you, or someone else, get telephone assistance from a vendor.

Also, and perhaps more obvious, record the physical connections. Generally, a computer's connections make the back of a stereo system look trivial indeed. And most people cringe at the thought of hooking up a stereo system! We suggest that you create sketches of your computer's connections, carefully labeling what each connection is and what you are using it for. For example, the long skinny one on the left goes to the outboard disk, where the console is connected, and so on. Every serial port should be labeled, and the cable that goes to it given a matching label. If you ever have to move (or repair) your computer system, you will be very thankful for this written record.

Also label any cables that can be connected two different ways so that there is no doubt which way to plug it in. These cables are often "ribbon" cables that connect disk drives or tapes, and plugging them incorrectly can prevent a system from working, and even worse, damage the hardware. Put "THIS SIDE UP" on a label and stick it on the ribbon cable. Even if the manufacturer didn't see fit to prevent you from connecting it wrong, you can now label it correctly, while the system is (still) working.

Finally, create a table that helps you locate both ends of each serial cable. You have already labeled the end of the serial cable connected to the serial port. Now you want to create a table in your logbook that describes the location of the other end of the cable, for instance, "tty01 Chuck Jaffee Cubicle 9.1" or "tty14 Laser Printer Computer Room." Except in very small systems, serial cables will quickly disappear into holes in the wall or above ceiling tiles, and reappear somewhere else. It is much easier to log the destination of the cables than to have to play guessing games later. You can do this easily by walking around to all the terminals, logging in, and entering the **tty** command to find out which port they are connected to. You can also use a blueprint or floor plan and map out your cable locations. Don't forget to log your modem and printer connections.

The System Device Directory

The device directory in UNIX systems, **/dev**, holds from 30 to several hundred entries, each making a potential connection between some piece of hardware and the file system. The hardware, the *devices*, range from the connections to terminals, printers, and modems, to the memory inside the computer, and to storage devices like the disks and tapes. There are also several subdirectories in later System V releases that contain still more entries (**/dev/dsk**, **/dev/rdsk**, and **/dev/mt**, for example). Make a long listing of each of these directories by using the command **ls −l**, and redirect this listing to a file. Then edit this file by adding comments that identify your device files. You also want to label any "spare" disk partitions, along with their sizes. And mark each serial port device (files such as **/dev/tty13**) with its physical connection; for example, **/dev/tty11** is connected to the laser printer. Figure 1.2 is an abbreviated example of a commented device directory listing.

Figure 1.2 Sample device name listing with comments.

a. Example of redirecting a long listing to a file:

```
$ ls -l /dev /dev/dsk /dev/rdsk /dev/mt /dev/rmt >/tmp/devfiles
```

b. Part of an edited listing suitable for a logbook; we suggest that you add more blank lines to make your listing easier to read.

```
/dev:
***Connected to modem
crw-rw-rw-   1 root        sys         5,  1 Apr 12  1986 tty1
***Connected to printer
crw--w--w-   1 root        sys         5,  0 Mar 18  1986 tty0
***The "generic" tty, a synonym for the user's terminal
crw-rw-rw-   1 root        sys         2,  0 Aug 13 14:08 tty
***The system tty, usually same as the console
crw--w--w-   4 root        sys         0,  0 Aug 19 19:08 systty
***The "virtual" console used by the init program
crw--w--w-   4 root        sys         0,  0 Aug 19 19:08 syscon
***The dedicated console port
crw--w--w-   4 root        sys         0,  0 Aug 19 19:08 console
***The null device, used for unwanted output (a bit bucket)
crw-rw-rw-   1 root        sys         1,  2 Jun 26 20:36 null
***The system's memory (physical addresses)
cr--------   1 root        sys         1,  0 Mar 18  1986 mem
***The system's memory as mapped by kernel (virtual addresses)
cr--------   1 root        sys         1,  1 May 26 14:41 kmem
***System V's special error logging device driver
cr--------   1 root        sys         3,  0 Mar 18  1986 error
***The disk directory for "block" devices
dr-xr-xr-x   2 root        sys            656 Jan 26  1987 dsk/
/dev/dsk:
***The root file system
br--------   1 root        sys         0,  0 Aug 11 19:09 c0d0s0
***The swap device
br--------   2 root        sys         0,  1 Apr 10  1986 c0d0s1
br--------   2 root        sys         0,  1 Apr 10  1986 swap
***/usr file system
br--------   2 root        sys         0,  2 Aug 19 19:02 c0d0s2
br--------   2 root        sys         0,  2 Aug 19 19:02 usr
***/u (first user) file system
br--------   2 root        sys         0,  3 Mar 18  1986 c0d0s3
***Partitions 4-7 are spare, 30242 blocks total
br--------   1 root        sys         0,  4 Mar 18  1986 c0d0s4
br--------   1 root        sys         0,  5 Mar 18  1986 c0d0s5
br--------   1 root        sys         0,  6 Aug 13  1986 c0d0s6
br--------   1 root        sys         0,  7 Aug 19 19:02 c0d0s7
```

Some of the information that you will gather in your device file listings can be gleaned from section seven of your *Administrator Reference Manual*, Special Files(7). Entries in this section should describe the device file naming conventions (and the minor device numbers) used by the vendor of your system. There is no guarantee that this has been done, or has been completed correctly. Of course, the *Administrator Reference Manual* will not describe how your system uses particular device files.

Why keep this information in your logbook? For one thing, you want a written record of how device files are used. Beyond that, you can also replace a device file using the information in the listings. Figure 1.3 shows how the **/etc/mknod** command was used to replace a device file that had been deleted by accident.

Figure 1.3 Replacing a missing device file.

```
# /etc/mknod /dev/dsk/c0d0s5 b 0 5
# □
```

In Figure 1.3 the device special file, **/dev/dsk/c0d0s5**, has been created with the **mknod** (make node) command. The three arguments for this command appear in the long listing information for the file shown in Figure 1.2. The first character in the long listing determines the type of the file (**b**lock, in this case), and the two numbers before the date, the major and minor device numbers, make up the last two arguments to **mknod**. You can use **mknod** to create any missing special device file. Note that BSD versions contain a shell script named **/dev/MAKEDEV** that is used to create or replace missing device special files. By changing directory to **/dev**, the superuser can use this script to make just one special device file, or all the device files.

Running Notations or the System Diary

Your system diary notes, in chronological order, everything you do as a system administrator. Routine tasks, such as system startup, shutdown, and file system backup, should be documented here. Even more important, write in the log error messages, especially those from **fsck**. This running commentary on your system is of utmost importance to administering your system.

The notes that you take will often be mundane and relatively unimportant. Maintaining the logbook is tedious and time-consuming. But this is a small price to pay when you need to use these notes. For example, you might solve a mysterious problem with the LP or UUCP system. Then, six months later, the same problem shows up again. Looking up the solution in your diary is much easier than having to remember it or to recreate the solution from scratch. You might also notice a pattern of strange occurrences that alone mean nothing, but together indicate a problem that could get worse.

Error Messages.   Error messages from the file system check program, **fsck**, cannot be saved in a disk file contained in the file system being checked. It would be nice if **fsck** would keep a file recording all its reports and activities. After all, computers are supposed to reduce drudgery, not increase it. However, writing to a file system while it is being checked will cause that file system to appear damaged to **fsck**. But you must keep a record of what **fsck** does. Once **fsck** has completed repairing a damaged file system, it will be your responsibility to replace lost files from backups. If you don't write down the names of any files that **fsck** removes, you don't know which files to replace! Writing down error messages, although tedious, also helps you to detect patterns of file system damage.

It's important to record any error messages that appear on the system console. The System V **errlog** daemon will record certain kernel error messages in a file. However, recovering these error messages from the logfile requires a special configuration file, **/etc/master**, that may not be present on your system. And, if the system has failed, the logfile will be inaccessible anyway, while the system is down.

Keeping a diary of error messages provides you with a history of how your computer has been operating. You can easily observe if a certain disk partition is constantly short on free space. Or, if the number of errors reported for a particular disk drive has increased over time. You log these errors by writing down the error message from the console, your name, and the time that you observed the error.

Log-Keeping Script. For the more routine forms of log keeping, you can use a simple script that we call **logger**. This script simply copies its standard input (what you type) to a designated logfile, where it is date-stamped. This script can be incorporated into other system maintenance scripts to provide automatic logging of events such as file system backup or adding a new user. Figure 1.4 shows the **logger** script.

Figure 1.4 A simple logging script.

a. Listing of the **logger** script:

```
:
# logger [file] - copies date and standard input
# or file into LOGFILE
PATH=/bin:/usr/bin
LOGFILE=/etc/logfile
date >> $LOGFILE
cat >> $LOGFILE
exit 0
```

b. Using **logger** to add a note interactively:

```
# logger
Added user account for Shirley MacLaine - Rik
<Control-D>
# □
```

c. Using **logger** in a backup shell script:

```
logger <<!
Incremental backup completed successfully.
!
```

Adding the **logger** script to your other command scripts makes some logging automatic. Print out a copy of the logfile each day for your log book. You can setup the **cron** daemon to do this for you. You will also want to truncate the logfile periodically. An example of printing and archiving the logfile with **cron** appears later in this chapter.

CONFIGURATION FILES AND SCRIPTS

Simply by amending configuration files and shell scripts, you can change the behavior of the UNIX system. Configuring some operating systems requires cognoscenti to poke bytes in the appropriate places. These bytes "do something" in a mysterious way within the operating system.

While things work faster this way (for the operating system, that is), things are a lot tougher for the humans involved. Such questions arise as "Was that really the right byte to change, and was that the appropriate value?" Then, after doing it, you can wonder if you did it right or not. Of course, if it's something terribly unsubtle, you'll know soon enough. Things will stop working.

The UNIX system is a lot nicer. You aren't expected to poke bytes in mysterious locations. Instead, you edit text files or give commands. These commands are interpreted by the system, which then implements the command action. This book shows how to edit configuration files correctly and how to use configuration commands intelligently. You will also learn how to create your own scripts or commands to perform those administrative tasks that aren't done by existing commands or scripts.

Configuration Files

Configuration files are readable text files containing tables of formatted information. You can edit or examine these files using an editor like **vi**, or other editors that have a plain-text, ASCII, or nondocument mode. (Standard word processors add nonprinting characters to setup margins, underlining, or centering. These special characters will foil the programs that interpret the configuration file.) The catch is that you must follow the format of the file that you are editing. An incorrectly formatted entry line might be ignored by the program that is interpreting it, or it could cause the program to ignore the rest of the configuration file. For instance, the **login** program will ignore badly formatted lines in the **/etc/passwd** file, while the **getty** program stops interpreting the **/etc/gettydefs** file after it encounters the first mistake in format. Before editing a configuration file, you can make a backup copy of it to protect yourself. For example, **cp /etc/passwd /etc/opasswd** creates a backup copy of the password file before you edit it. Table 1.3 lists some of the configuration files that we will be discussing.

TABLE 1.3 SOME UNIX SYSTEM CONFIGURATION FILES

File	Description
/etc/passwd	User account database
/etc/group	Group database
/etc/inittab	Table that directs the **init** program
/etc/ttys	BSD table that directs the **init** program
/etc/checklist	List of file systems to be checked by **fsck**
/etc/gettydefs	Line conditions used by **getty**
/usr/lib/cron/cron.allow	List of users that can use **cron**
/usr/lib/uucp/Dialcodes	Phone number abbreviations used with UUCP

UNIX configuration files end each entry in a file with a newline. This line-by-line style is consistent throughout most of the UNIX system. However, other aspects of format, like the field (column) separators, are not consistent. You can examine these files using the **pg** command, or an editor like **view**, the read-only version of **vi**. You can feel comfortable poking around with **view**, because you can't harm anything.

Shell Scripts

Shell scripts play an equally important role in system administration. A script is a file containing a list of UNIX commands. Scripts are interpreted by programs known as shells, or command line interpreters. The most common UNIX shells are the Bourne, Korn, and C shells. The original shell, the Bourne shell (**/bin/sh**), was written by Steve Bourne. The C shell (**/bin/csh**), so named because of its C programming language-like syntax, was authored years later by Bill Joy. Most recently, David Korn wrote the Korn shell (**/bin/ksh**). The Korn shell attempts to combine the best features of both previous shells.

All of the scripts in this book are written for the Bourne shell, partly because the C and Korn shells are not available on all UNIX systems. However, the Korn shell will run Bourne shell scripts without problems (although some scripts can be rewritten to work faster under the Korn shell).

The C shell will not run many Bourne shell scripts without problems. The solution is easy enough (unless you have spent your life learning C shell programming and wish to convert all the Bourne shell scripts into C shell scripts). The C shell will automatically invoke a Bourne shell to interpret a script if the script contains any character besides a pound sign (#) as its first character. We like to use a colon (:) as the first character. The colon is a null command for the Bourne shell—it does nothing, so it has no impact on Bourne shell scripts. Every script in this book starts with a colon on a line by itself so that the C shell will recognize the script as a Bourne shell script.

Why use scripts? Simple. Scripts can reliably carry out a list of commands without requiring the operator to enter and possibly mistype long and complicated command lines, or puzzle over command syntax. Once a procedure is crystallized in a script, it is easy to repeat. For instance, the **/etc/rc** script performs a medley of tasks that are necessary when the system changes from single-user to multiuser operation. The **/usr/bin/spell** command is actually a shell script containing many other commands. This script filters out **nroff** formatting directives and converts all text to single words, one per line, and then sorts the list before comparing them to words in the dictionary.

Using an editor, you can edit or modify the actions of scripts, the same way that configurations files can be changed. Once again, only editors such as **ed**, **vi**, or **emacs** can be used, or text processors that don't add nonprinting characters to files. The formatting rules are those for the Bourne shell programming language. If you are unfamiliar with Bourne shell programming, you may wish to study one of the books listed in the bibliography that teach you how to write Bourne shell programs. We have made an effort to explain most of the scripts that are used in this book, and to keep things simple. You are encouraged to add your own elaborations where you see fit.

Table 1.4 lists some of the scripts used in UNIX systems. We suggest that you examine these scripts, at least briefly, at this point.

TABLE 1.4 SOME UNIX SYSTEM SCRIPTS

File	Description
/etc/rc	Runs commands for multiuser operation
/etc/mvdir	Lets superuser move a directory
/etc/profile	Provides default environment for Bourne shell
/etc/shutdown	Shuts down system
/bin/basename	Returns filename part of pathname
/usr/bin/spell	Checks spelling
/usr/bin/man	Formats and displays on-line manual entry
/usr/lib/acct/runacct	Creates accounting reports
/usr/lib/uucp/uudemon.poll	Polls UUCP sites (HoneyDanBer)
/usr/spool/lp/model/dumb	Interfaces ordinary printers

DAEMON PROCESSES

Daemons are processes that run unattended within your UNIX system. Contrary to the popular connotation of the word "demon," "a guardian spirit" better defines a daemon than, say, a "devilish spirit" (see Webster's Unabridged Dictionary). Daemons in the UNIX system perform routine tasks that don't require supervision.

Daemon processes run unattached to any user's terminal session. Thus, when a user starts a daemon, the daemon process continues after the user logs off. While this ability is actually undesirable for most user processes, it is appropriate for system administration tasks. You want the daemon to continue working after you have logged off. All the daemons that are part of the UNIX system work as the system administrator's assistants. Table 1.5 lists some of the daemons found in UNIX systems.

TABLE 1.5 SOME UNIX SYSTEM DAEMONS

---

init

The **init** process starts during system startup, and continues until the UNIX system is halted. **init** is process number one, and is responsible for initiating user log-in processes and launching the other daemons.

cron

The **cron** daemon is the clock watcher. **cron** wakes up every so often (usually once a minute), checks the time, and starts processes when they appear in **cron**'s configuration file(s). **cron** starts when the system goes multiuser.

lpsched

lpsched is the Line Printer Scheduler Daemon. This daemon sleeps until a user makes a request for printing with the **lp** command. Then the daemon wakes up and starts an interface program to handle the print request, and continues to schedule printing requests until all have been satisfied. It then goes back to sleep.

errdemon

The **errdemon** records system-wide errors. This process gets launched when the system goes multiuser. **errdemon** waits for the kernel to write error messages to **/dev/error**, and then copies these messages to **/usr/adm/errfile**.

uucico

uucico stands for UNIX to UNIX copy-in copy-out (no wonder it's abbreviated). This daemon wakes when one user either sends mail to another user on a remote machine, or invokes **uucp**, **uux**, or **uuto** to request file transfers. The **cron** daemon may also start **uucico** periodically. **uucico** terminates after processing any pending UUCP requests.

sendmail

A BSD daemon that listens to a socket (often connected to Ethernet) and handles incoming mail messages.

You might have noticed that most of these daemons respond to user requests or other outside events. Part of the nature of daemons is that they are not continually active, but merely stand by in a state of readiness to carry out their duties. They are activated by timers (**cron**), user requests (**lpsched** and **uucico**), or other system events (**errdemon**).

The **init** process is covered in Chapter 5. The **lpsched** and **uucico** daemons are discussed in Chapters 6 and 8, respectively. The **cron** daemon gets used or mentioned throughout UNIX system administration and provides a good example of how files are used to configure your system. So we'll discuss it now.

Scheduling Tasks with cron

The **cron** process, also known as the "clock daemon," runs commands at specified dates and times. **cron** itself begins during system startup in the transition from single-user to multiuser mode by the **/etc/rc** script (**/etc/rc.d/cron** Release 3 and later).

There are two versions of the **cron** daemon at present. The "old" version is used by XENIX, BSD, and pre- System V, Release 2 AT&T systems. The "new" **cron** appears exclusively in AT&T Release 2 (and later). The two **cron**s differ in the names of their configuration and log files, and how they receive notification that their configuration files have changed. The new **cron** can also perform routine tasks for any user.

The cron Table File. The **cron** process gets its instructions for executing programs from a "cron table" file. A copy of this file is read into memory after **cron** starts up. **cron** examines this copy once a minute and executes any commands scheduled to run. If the disk copy of the cron table file is changed, **cron** will read the updated version into memory. The newer version of **cron** relies on a slightly different mechanism before it recognizes any changes.

In UNIX system releases prior to System V Release 2 (including BSD and XENIX) the cron table file had pathname **/usr/lib/crontab**. It was owned by the **root** account and could be changed only by the superuser. (Ordinary users can use the **at** command, if available, to schedule a program to be started once.)

In SVR2 and later AT&T UNIX versions, ordinary system users can create, change, or delete their own personal cron table file using a command with the same name—**crontab**. The **crontab** command also notifies the **cron** daemon that a cron table file has changed. The old version of **cron** checked every time it woke up to see if the cron table file had changed. The new version won't notice any changes to this file unless the **crontab** command is used, or the **cron** daemon is stopped and restarted.

The cron table files (after Release 2) are located in the spool directory, **/usr/spool/cron/crontabs**. They are named after the user who installs them. Thus the cron table file for user **beccat** would have full pathname **/usr/spool/cron/crontabs/beccat**. Although this file would be owned by **root**, it can be updated by an ordinary user since the **crontab** command is set-user-id owned by **root**, which gives the user temporary superuser privilege while running the command.

Figure 1.5 shows the contents of the **crontabs** spool directory on one of our systems.

Figure 1.5 Contents of a sample **crontabs** spool directory.

```
$ ls -al /usr/spool/cron/crontabs
total 6
drwxr-xr-x    2 root      sys           208 Oct 25 17:41 .
drwxr-xr-x    4 root      sys            64 May 13 19:29 ..
-r--r--r--    1 root      sys            32 Sep 19 06:56 adm
-r--r--r--    1 root      users          54 Oct 25 17:36 rik
-r--r--r--    1 root      sys           402 Oct 25 16:15 root
-r--r--r--    1 root      sys           309 Aug 23 12:08 uucp
$ □
```

Cron table files from most UNIX systems have the same internal format—six fields, each separated by spaces or tabs. Table 1.6 defines these fields and the other special characters recognized by **cron**.

TABLE 1.6 THE CRON TABLE FILE FORMAT

a. Six fields separated by spaces or tabs:

Field	Description
Minute	Time within the hour, from 0 to 59
Hour	Twenty-four-hour format, from 0 to 23
Day-of-month	The day of the month, from 1 to 31
Month	The calendar month, from 1 to 12
Day-of-week	Sunday is 0, Monday is 1, to Saturday, 6
Command	Command line using Bourne shell syntax

b. Special characters recognized by **cron**:

Character	Interpretation
-	Range of values indicated by a dash
*	Asterisk means all possible values, wildcard
,	Commas separate multiple values
%	Represents a newline in command
#	Begins a comment

The first five fields indicate when **cron** will execute the command line that is named in the last field. The first five fields must match the current time and date before the command will be executed. (Or, if you set the date ahead with the **date** command, **cron** will execute all the commands between the time it last woke up and the new time.)

The last field contains the shell command line. **cron** starts a Bourne shell to interpret and execute this line, which may contain redirection, pipes, and even more than one command, if separated by semicolons. (In 4.3BSD, a new field, the log-in name for the account that the shell script is to be run by, was added after the day-of-week field and before the shell command line. Essentially, an **su** command to the log-in name is performed before the shell command line is executed. This additional field makes 4.2BSD cron table files incompatible with 4.3BSD.)

Figure 1.6 shows an example of a simple cron table file. We use tabs as field separators in the file so that it is easier to read.

Figure 1.6 A simple cron table file.

```
#Min      Hour     Day      Month    Day      Command
#of       of       of       of       of
#Hour     Day      Month    Year     Week
#---------------------------------------------------------------------------
5         0        15       *        *        echo "Clean fan filters" | mail root
0         *        *        *        *        /bin/date >/dev/console
30        2        *        *        1-6      /usr/lib/acct/dodisk
1,20,40   17-7     *        *        *        /usr/1bin/autologout >/dev/null
1,20,40   8-16     *        *        0,6      /usr/1bin/autologout >/dev/null
25        1        *        *        *        /usr/bin/lp /etc/logfile 2>/dev/null
27        1        *        *        *        /bin/mv /etc/logfile /etc/ologfile
```

The lines beginning with a pound sign (#) are comment lines. We have added several comment lines that help us remember what the different fields are. The first entry in our example mails the message "Clean fan filters" to the **root** account at 5 minutes, the "5" in the first column, after midnight (the zero hour) of the fifteenth day of each calendar month. The second entry displays the date on the system console every hour, on the hour. The asterisks are "wildcards" and mean match all time values for this column. The third entry runs the **dodisk** accounting script at 2:30 A.M. every morning, Monday through Saturday. The fourth and fifth entries execute the **autologout** script every 20 minutes after 5 P.M. and before 8 A.M. on weekdays and all day on the weekends. (The **autologout** script logs out inactive users.) Notice that the hour-of-day values may range from before to after midnight, as in **17—7** (from 5 P.M. to 7 A.M.). The last two entries print the logfile (created by the **/etc/logger** script) for the system logbook at 1:25 A.M. daily, and archive the logfile 2 minutes later.

Use **cron** intelligently by scheduling wisely. If you arrange your cron table file so that many commands are started at the same time, you may bog down your system. This is especially true on smaller systems. In Figure 1.6, none of the commands are scheduled to run at the same time. If several commands are scheduled to start at exactly the same minute, **cron** will reliably start these commands, one after another, as fast as it can. It will be as if a large group of users sprang into action at the same instant. You may already have noticed that your system bogs down every hour, on the hour. The solution is to reschedule events so that commands aren't all started at the same minute.

The crontab Command

The **crontab** command (part of the new **cron**) enables users to create, change, display, or remove their own cron table file. The superuser should use this command also, instead of editing the cron table file directly, since any changes made by editing a cron table file won't be noticed until **cron** is started again. (Pre-Release 2 of System V, XENIX, and BSD users must edit the **/usr/lib/crontab** file with an editor, and **cron** will notice that the file has been updated.) Figure 1.7 shows the command line syntax.

Figure 1.7 Syntax for the **crontab** command.

> **crontab** [*file* | −r | −l]

When **crontab** is invoked with a *file* argument, that file is copied into the **crontabs** spool directory, **/usr/spool/cron/crontabs**. The file is given the name of the user (account) who ran **crontab**. If no arguments are specified, the **crontab** command copies the standard input (until an end-of-file, generally the control-D, is typed) to the cron table file.

You invoke the **crontab** command with the −l (list) option to display the contents of your cron table file. The −r option is used to remove the cron table file. In each case, the cron table file for the user invoking the command is affected.

Figure 1.8 shows an example of creating, listing, and deleting a simple one-line cron table file.

Figure 1.8 Using the **crontab** command.

```
$ who am i
beccat      tty02      Sep 1 14:16
$ crontab
0    *    *    *    *         /bin/date >/dev/tty02
<control-D>
warning: commands will be executed using /bin/sh
$ crontab -l
0    *    *    *    *         /bin/date >/dev/tty02
$ ls -l /usr/spool/cron/crontabs/beccat
-r--r--r-- 1 root   users    34 Oct 25 17:32 /usr/spool/cron/crontabs/beccat
$ crontab -r
$ crontab -l
crontab: can't open your crontab file
$ □
```

Figure 1.8 first shows the creation of a one-line cron table file that redirects the output of the **date** command on the hour to the **/dev/tty02** terminal. The "warning" is just a reminder that **cron** uses the Bourne shell to interpret commands. The **ls −l** long listing shows that the cron table file installed by user **beccat** is owned by **root** but maintains the same group ownership as the user who installed it.

If you wish to enter several entries or update an existing cron table file, it's more appropriate to use the *file* argument as shown in Figure 1.9.

Figure 1.9 Using the **crontab** command.

```
$ crontab -l >/tmp/crontab
[edit /tmp/crontab]
$ crontab /tmp/crontab
$ crontab -l
0 * * * * /bin/date >/dev/tty02
7 2 * * * /bin/find /usr1/beccat -name core -exec rm -f {} \;
$ □
```

The standard output of the **crontab −l** command was copied to a temporary file for editing. In the next step (not shown) we appended an entry to execute **/bin/find** at 2:07 A.M.. Then we installed the updated cron table file using **/tmp/crontab** as the filename argument. Finally, we listed the contents of the updated cron table file.

The cron Log File

System V Release 2 **cron** notes each command it executes in a logfile with pathname **/usr/lib/cron/log**. The old **cron**'s logfile had the pathname **/usr/lib/cronlog**. Figure 1.10 shows a few entries taken from the beginning of such a logfile on one of our systems.

Figure 1.10 A sample **cron** logfile.

```
$ ls -l /usr/lib/cron/log
-rw-r--r-- 1 root    root      9490 Oct 25 18:00 /usr/lib/cron/log
$ cat /usr/lib/cron/log
! *** cron started ***   pid = 20 Sat Oct 25 11:09:37 1986
>   CMD: /usr/lbin/autologout >/dev/null
>   root 92 c Sat Oct 25 11:20:00 1986
<   root 92 c Sat Oct 25 11:20:02 1986
>   CMD: /usr/lbin/autologout >/dev/null
>   root 206 c Sat Oct 25 11:40:00 1986
<   root 206 c Sat Oct 25 11:40:03 1986
. . .
$ □
```

First **cron** notes its process-id number and the date and time it started. Then every command it runs gets a three-line entry. The first line names the command; the second, the starting time; and the third, the ending time. Also, the particular cron table file that was executed is noted (**root** in this example) followed by the process-id number of the shell running the command. Note that the ending time entry of a long running command might come after the starting time for a different command (they can interleave).

This logfile will grow forever or until you run out of disk space, unless it's archived routinely. Archive the logfile by copying the old file to an "old" name, and copying nothing (from **/dev/null**) to truncate the original logfile. These changes can be done while **cron** is running. In fact, you can use **cron** to truncate its own logfile. Or, you can add commands to truncate the logfile to the **/etc/rc** script (or **/etc/rc.d/cron**) during system start up.

Figure 1.11 Truncating the **cron** logfile.

a. Commands used with the old **cron** (pre-Release 2 version):

```
cp /usr/lib/cronlog /usr/lib/OLDcronlog
cp /dev/null /usr/lib/cronlog
```

b. Commands used with Release 2 and later version of System V:

```
cp /usr/lib/cron/log /usr/lib/cron/OLDlog
cp /dev/null /usr/lib/cron/log
```

For Release 2 System V **cron**, the standard output and standard error of any commands executed by **cron** get mailed to the user whose cron table file started the command (unless the output is redirected to a file). Pre-Release 2 System V, XENIX, and some BSD versions of **cron** write the output of commands that are not redirected into the **/usr/lib/cronlog** file.

Controlling crontab Command Use

New versions of **cron** support two files that allow or deny users access to run the **crontab** command. Users whose log-in names are listed in the **/usr/lib/cron/cron.allow** file are allowed to run the **crontab** command. If this file exists but contains no entries, no users will have the ability to schedule jobs with **crontab**. Figure 1.12 shows a sample **cron.allow** file.

Figure 1.12 A sample **cron.allow** file.

```
$ ls -l /usr/lib/cron/cron.allow
-rw-r--r-- 1 root    sys     25 Oct 25 16:29 /usr/lib/cron/cron.allow
$ cat /usr/lib/cron/cron.allow
```

```
root
sys
adm
uucp
beccat
rik
$ □
```

Alternatively, you can choose to *deny* some user access to the **crontab** command. To deny access, list the users in the **/usr/lib/cron/cron.deny** file by log-in name. If this file exists and contains no entries, all users will be able to use **crontab**.

Only one of these two files should be used. Pick the one that's appropriate for your site. Obviously, **cron.allow** is safer in that you must list a user explicitly to allow them access. However, if you have a large community of users and wish to deny access to only a few, it makes more sense to work with the **cron.deny** file instead.

TOUR OF THE FILE SYSTEM

When we talk about the UNIX file system, we mean one of two things. The file system is, first, an impeccably organized structure on disk and in memory. In Chapter 4 we discuss the parts of this structure and how to create and maintain file systems.

The organization of directory and file names is the second meaning for file system. We will often use the term *hierarchy* to describe this organization. Although UNIX systems vary widely, most UNIX systems have a similar hierarchy. The basic directory layout is like a signature that you can use to recognize UNIX systems. This hierarchy includes the directories and files shown in Figure 1.13.

Figure 1.13 The file system hierarchy.

a. The logical layout of the hierarchy:

```
/          : the root directory
¦
--------bin          : directory for basic commands
       dev          : devices directory
       etc          : configuration and administrative directory
       lib          : C compiler library directory
       lost+found : found files directory
       tmp          : directory for temporary files
       unix         : kernel (the operating system program) file
       usr          : second major branch directory
       ¦
       --------adm          : accounting processing directory
              bin          : directory for more user commands
```

```
lib             : administrative commands directory
¦
--------spell          : spelling directory
        uucp           : UUCP configuration dir.
spool        : spooling directories
¦
--------lp             : Line Printer Spooling
        uucp           : UUCP Spool directories
        uucppublic  : UUCP public dir.
tmp          : another temporary directory
```

b. Viewing the hierarchy as an inverted tree:

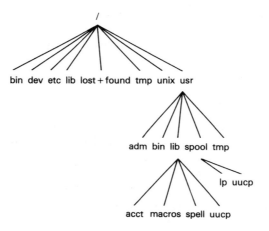

Notice that the root directory (*/*) is also the *root* of the file system hierarchy (viewing it as an upside-down tree). You can reach seven directories directly from the root directory, namely, **/bin**, **/dev**, **/etc**, **/lib**, **/lost+found**, **/tmp**, and **/usr**. This organization is not an accident. Files found in these directories must be present when the UNIX system is booted and running in single-user mode. You will always find **sh** and **date** in **/bin**, and **init** and **fsck** in **/etc**.

A second major branch in the hierarchy —the **/usr** directory—holds the names of still other directories. It forms an important subsection of the hierarchy. On many systems, the **/usr** hierarchy is a second file system that gets mounted (attached to the root directory of the file system) when the system goes multiuser. Thus, the files and directories in **/usr** aren't essential for system startup. You will find **spell**, document-processing, system accounting, and communication programs here.

What's important about the hierarchy? It makes working with UNIX systems easier. You can rely on things being similar from system to system. Also, you get acquainted with where to find things. Each directory is like a folder or file cabinet, and certain other files and directories will be contained there. So, rather than searching for a configuration file or a command, you know right where to look. You can recognize an experienced administrator by how familiar he or she is with the file system hierarchy.

Let's take a look at some of the different types of directories. Fitting directories into logical categories is a good way to learn how the directories are used.

Command Directories

UNIX systems contain four major command directories: **/bin**, **/usr/bin**, **/etc**, and **/usr/lib**. Two of these directories bear the abbreviation *bin*. *bin* is short for binary, an old term used for executable programs (as opposed to shell scripts). **/bin** and **/usr/bin** contain most of the commands available to users of UNIX systems. Locally added commands belong in the **/local/bin**, **/usr/lbin**, or **/usr/local/bin** directory.

Two other directories hold administrative commands. The **/etc** and **/usr/lib** directories contains utilities that are used by system administrators. These directories are not in the search path of ordinary users. Also, **/etc** contains system configuration files.

Temporary Directories

You use temporary directories for scratch files. Scratch files are like scratch paper—something you intend to discard within a couple of days. Some programs use temporary directories for scratch files. **vi** uses **/tmp** for its edit buffers and the C compiler may use **/usr/tmp** while compiling.

You want to establish the habit of using temporary directories for scratch files. In this book we suggest that you prevent ordinary users from writing in system directories, mainly for security reasons. However, you, working as the superuser, can write in any directory, regardless of permissions set for that directory. So it is especially important that you use **/tmp** for temporary files. The root directory, in particular, is an inappropriate place for temporary files. Like the entranceway to your home or the reception area of an office, you want to keep the root directory clean and free of nonessential clutter.

Other temporary directories exist in UNIX systems. The file system check (**fsck**) command uses the **lost+found** directory. **fsck** creates a temporary name for files or directories that it finds in the **lost+found** directory. The system administrator is responsible for discovering the real name for these files, or removing them. The UUCP system uses **/usr/spool/uucppublic** as a temporary repository for files transferred between systems.

Spooling Directories

Spooling is a technique for collecting files and work for later processing. A printer spooler queues up requests waiting for the printer. The spool directories contain temporary files, the work and data files that will be processed at a later time. The programs that use the spool directories are supposed to remove their work files when they are finished with them.

The LP system uses several directories located within **/usr/spool/lp**. Requests for files to be printed, and in some cases, copies of the files, are kept here. The LP system will always remove files when it has completed its requests.

The UUCP system uses many temporary directories, all starting with **/usr/spool/uucp**. The UUCP system is much more complex than the LP system, and the process of removing temporary files is also more complicated. Special shell scripts are responsible for removing old UUCP work and data files. We have devoted two entire chapters to the mechanisms of the LP system and UUCP.

Configuration Directories

The **/etc** directory contains files used to configure your entire UNIX system. These files (and scripts) affect startup and shutdown, assign user- and group-ids, mount or check file systems, and enable/disable ports.

You configure the UUCP system with files in the **/usr/lib/uucp** directory. This out-of-the-way directory will become familiar to you when you set up or reconfigure the UUCP system.

Libraries

The *lib* abbreviation stands for library. The **/lib** directory contains parts of the C compiler. It may also contain an additional directory for the Pascal compiler. The **/usr/lib** directory contains, besides administrative commands and the UUCP configuration directory, libraries for the C compiler. It also contains the font and macro directories for **troff** and **nroff**.

Devices

The **/dev** directory is the repository for device files. Device files are special—they do not contain any data. Instead, they contain the major and minor device numbers that identify devices, like disks or printers, to the operating system. All the device files belong in this directory, or in a subdirectory of it.

With Release 2 of System V, disk and tape device files are placed in subdirectories. The **/dev/dsk** directory is for file systems and **/dev/mt** tapes. The **/dev/rdsk** and **/dev/rmt** directories parallel the **/dev/dsk** and **/dev/mt** directories, but contain the corresponding *raw* (character-interface) device files. Raw devices are used in formatting, making and checking file systems, and in some backup operations.

User Account Directories

Wise system administrators isolate users' directories in their own portion of the file system hierarchy. Besides being good for organization, putting users in their own file systems serves other purposes as well. The users in a file system share the same pool of free disk space. If users share the same file system with the root or **/usr** file systems, they compete for free space with the rest of the system files.

User directory hierarchies are generally mounted as subdirectories of the root directory. Traditional names are **/usr1**, **/usr2**, or **/a** and **/b**. Some system administrators prefer to use more descriptive names, such as **/acct** for accounting group or **/mrkt** for a marketing or sales force. These names are not set in concrete and vary widely according to local custom.

Suggestions for Organizing File Systems

There are some simple guidelines for the effective use of file systems. While the reasons for these suggestions will be discussed later, it's good to start off knowing the best way to organize your file systems.

The first suggestion has already been mentioned. That is, separate user accounts and system files in different file systems. You don't want users and the system competing for the same free disk space. Also, you will degrade your system performance by putting too much file system activity on the same disk drive or controller.

Second, keep directories small. The optimal size for a directory stands at less than 64 entries. A small directory size speeds up file access and will improve system performance. When you examine the UNIX system hierarchy, only the **/bin** and **/usr/bin** directories are very large.

The third point is to create shallow, rather than deep, directory hierarchies. Long pathnames are difficult to type. Although this is only a nuisance to you, think what happens when the UNIX system must access a file with a long pathname. Each directory in the pathname must be searched for the name of the next directory in the pathname. For example, the system must search twice as many directories before accessing the file **/u/bob/mail/april/received/ray/apr2487** compared to **/u/bob/ray/apr2487**. It's the number of directories in the pathname that is significant, not the length of the directory names.

USING UNIX DOCUMENTATION

UNIX documentation has a well-earned reputation for terseness. Terse documentation is useful when you want to find something in a hurry—you don't have to wade through pages of explanatory material to find the answers that you know are there. UNIX documentation is designed as reference for experienced users.

Where does a beginning or novice user look for information? Elsewhere. If you are starting to work with the UNIX system, the best place to start is with one of the excellent books listed in the bibliography. These books are geared toward teaching people, rather than serving as reference works (like the UNIX documentation). Once you are grounded in the basics, UNIX documentation begins to make some sense. The old saw that the documentation becomes clear after you already comprehend the material is unfortunately too true.

If you are starting to work with a new UNIX system, the best place to look (for administration tips) is the vendor's *Installation Guide*. The *Installation Guide* (it may be called something else) is often the only literature that contains information pertinent to your system. If you are lucky, the vendor hasn't disguised it so it blends in with the standard UNIX documentation. Otherwise, you can use the list of standard documentation that appears later (Table 1.10) to pick out the vendor's additions. For AT&T 3B2 computers, the *Administrator Guide* is the place to start.

Of course, your vendor's documentation may be obtuse as well, depending on the market for which the computer is intended. This book is written to supplement vendor and UNIX system documentation for people who really want to learn about system administration. You can start here (after installing your system) and use the documentation provided with your system for the particulars necessary for dealing with your vendor's flavor of the UNIX system.

Another problem with UNIX documentation is its organization. While alphabetical order is great when you know what you're looking for, it doesn't help when you're trying to learn about something. We've never heard of anybody trying to read the reference manuals from beginning to end. What a crazy endeavor that would be. UNIX system documentation doesn't tell you where to get started.

Finding the Right Manual

In the not-too-distant past, UNIX documentation arrived in three volumes (very ponderous ones at that). Volume 1 contained reference materials (labeled sections 1 through 8). Volumes 2a and 2b contained papers and tutorials. (Some BSD systems, such as SUN Microsystem's, still use this organization, although there are many more volumes of tutorials and reference sections.) Today, UNIX systems are delivered with as few as a single volume, to more than a dozen. Although the organization of the volumes has changed significantly, the contents have changed less drastically. The three giant volumes were split into many smaller ones. Out-of-date material was updated, and some new sections were added. For example, most vendors use the original paper on **fsck**, written by Kowalski, although they usually rewrite portions of it (and leave out the original author's name).

All UNIX documentation is divided into three parts —reference materials, papers, and tutorials. The papers are written for (and by) experienced UNIX programmers. Often, the author of a major UNIX utility like **make** or **awk** would write a paper to document the new program.

We also found the AT&T "tutorials" heavy going, and like to steer people toward the books listed in the bibliography. (Note, though, that AT&T has provided some new tutorial materials, published through Prentice-Hall, which appear to be a vast improvement over the original papers.)

We'll focus on discussing the standard reference documentation here. Your reference documentation will (hopefully) correspond exactly to what's on your system. That is, it will correctly and completely describe how commands work, how files are formatted, and other specific details. UNIX systems vary, with vendors making small or large changes to commands and functionality. XENIX offerings correspond fairly closely to the AT&T UNIX system, yet small differences emerge throughout. BSD shares a common heritage with XENIX, but has diverged further from System V.

Reference Sections. Originally, eight reference sections comprised the documentation. These have been further subdivided, making the volumes smaller and forcing users to look in more volumes before finding the desired entry. The eight sections, including subdivisions, are listed in Table 1.7. The six corresponding reference sections used in the XENIX system are also listed. Note that XENIX uses letters rather than numbers to designate different sections.

TABLE 1.7 THE REFERENCE SECTIONS

UNIX	XENIX	Description
1	C	User commands
	CT	Text processing commands (XENIX only)
	CP	Programming commands (XENIX only)
1M	M	Administrative commands
2	S	System calls and system error messages
3	S	C language subroutines
4	F	File formats
5		Miscellaneous files and typesetting macros
6		Games
7		Special files (device file naming)
8		System maintenance (special instructions, sometimes) (Administrative commands on BSD systems)

In System V these sections are no longer contained in a single volume. Instead, they are spread out in three volumes. Table 1.8 illustrates the new order.

TABLE 1.8 AT&T REFERENCE VOLUMES

Volume name	Sections
User Reference Manual	User Commands (1) and Games (6)
Administrator Reference Manual	Administrative commands (1M), Device files (7), and Procedures (8)
Programmer Reference Manual	System calls (2), Subroutine libraries (3), File formats (4), and Miscellany (5)

Paralleling each of the reference manuals is a *guide*. The guide contains papers and tutorials about some of the materials in the corresponding reference work. For example, the *Administrator Guide* contains a paper on the **fsck** program, which also has a manual page entry in section 1M of the *Administrator Reference Manual*.

How do you determine which of these three volumes contains the entry desired? If looking for a command, your best bet is to start with the *User Reference Manual*. Most UNIX commands are documented there. Only commands meant for a clearly administrative purpose, such as **mkfs** or **fsck**, will be found in the *Administrator Reference Manual*.

The *Programmer Reference Manual* will often contain entries that are mentioned by the other reference manuals. How you use these cross-references is explained next.

Parts of a Reference Entry. All entries in sections 1 through 8 follow a similar format commonly known as a "manual page" format. The entry's name and section number appear at the top of the page. The name of the vendor may also appear in parentheses at the center if the entry did not derive from the regular UNIX distribution, but instead came from the vendor.

The name of the entry and a short description appear again in the **NAME** section. The short description appears in the *Permuted Index* (discussed below). Several other sections follow, describing the entry in more detail. Table 1.9 lists the section headings and what you will find in each section.

Most reference entries are well written, and every word counts. It is as if the person who wrote the documentation summarizes whole paragraphs of information into a single sentence. You may discover what you are looking for only by careful reading of the entire entry.

If you are having trouble using a command, look first in the Examples section. Examples bring the dry explanations to life. You may have left out a space after an option, or missed an important argument. The examples themselves are often helpful (e.g., look at the **find** command entry in the *User Reference Manual*, AT&T Section 1 or XENIX C).

The listing of options will many times be what you are looking for. The options often have been named according to a mnemonic scheme, to make them easy to remember. Unfortunately, the UNIX documentation doesn't always use the mnemonic in the explanation of the option (apparently because it was obvious to the author of the entry).

The **FILES** and **SEE ALSO** sections can provide more information about the entry. Sometimes, if you aren't certain about what you are looking for, you can follow the thread to related entries mentioned in the **SEE ALSO** section until you find the desired entry.

TABLE 1.9 SECTION HEADINGS IN THE REFERENCE SECTIONS

NAME

Command, function, or file name and a brief description that is used in the Permuted Index.

SYNOPSIS

How to use the command. Command names appear in bold typeface, optional arguments are enclosed in square brackets [*option*], and nonoptional arguments are neither bold nor bracketed. The full pathname, showing the directory where this command or file is found, is used in the synopsis.

DESCRIPTION

The long explanation of command usage and arguments to the command. Each option recognized by the command is listed in a bold typeface possibly followed by an option argument in italics. Sometimes, other commands or files relevant to this entry will be mentioned in the description section.

EXAMPLE

An optional section with command examples. Don't skip it. Often, this section provides the clearest information about how to use the command. Sometimes, useful and not immediately obvious uses for the command will appear here.

FILES

Files used by a command or related to the entry. When the files mentioned in this section are not present, or have incorrect permissions, the command will not work correctly. These files also provide further clues as to what this command does or how it works.

SEE ALSO

Related documentation entries. This section shows you where to look next if this entry isn't what you were looking for. Sometimes similar commands that are somewhat similar in purpose will be listed. Also, related Files Formats (section 4) and System Calls (section 2) will be listed here.

DIAGNOSTICS

Explanations of error messages (not always present). Unfortunately, this section usually says something like "The diagnostics produced are intended to be self-explanatory." No wonder this section is often missing.

BUGS

Known problems, or suggested improvements. Usually just a comment about how the command could have been better designed, there will occasionally be a note explaining why this command doesn't do what you want it to do.

Using the Permuted Index

The *Permuted Index* may appear useless and unfathomable at first. Yet, it can be very helpful in finding commands or files when all you have is an idea or purpose in mind. And UNIX commands have funny names. Since many entries are identified by strange combinations of letters, such as **awk**, **egrep**, or **dc**, the *Permuted Index* is your only hope of finding something. The *Permuted Index* also can help you discover commands that you never knew existed in your UNIX system.

The *Permuted Index* is sorted alphabetically down the *middle* column by keyword. The keyword is a word from the **NAME** section that best describes the purpose of this command, file, or function. The keyword will be located in the middle of the Permuted Index entry. And the entry continues until the ellipses (dots), and then wraps around to the beginning of the line. The name of the manual entry appears at the end of the line, followed by a dot and the section number. In the example that follows, the description from the **NAME** entry is "hex: translate object files into ASCII formats." The key word is *hex* (in the middle column), and the manual section is *hex.1*.

Figure 1.14 A sample Permuted Index entry.

```
ASCII formats  hex:  translate object files into . . . hex.1
```

You may want to look for a command that is a desk calculator, that will translate characters, or search for a pattern in a file. Try looking for these. Although it easiest to ask someone who knows more than you do about the UNIX system, the *Permuted Index* can help you find out more when you can't ask.

Using the man Command

The **man** command (actually a Bourne shell script) can display reference documentation entries. We say *can* because smaller UNIX systems won't have on-line copies of the documentation. UNIX Reference sections take about 4 megabytes (if they are unformatted) of disk space. For this reason, a UNIX desktop system won't have on-line manuals unless it also has a large hard disk. (Moreover, we have heard rumors that AT&T is no longer including the on-line manual pages in the standard distribution after Release 3.)

Using the **man** command at the terminal rather than referring to the printed materials has certain advantages. One, it saves paper, so not everyone needs to have three volumes of the reference manuals on their desktop. Secondly you don't have to go thumbing through several volumes looking for an entry.

man has its disadvantages, too. First, it's notoriously slow. It first finds all the related manual entries (unless you have specified otherwise), and then must format them using **nroff** or **troff**. Larger UNIX systems avoid the awesomely slow formatting step by having pre-formatted manual pages (called **catman**) available. (**catman** takes up even more space than the unformatted **man** pages.) The second problem is that **man** does not provide facilities for perusing the entry screenful by screenful. Once the beginning of the entry has scrolled off your screen, you have to start again from the beginning.

You can get around this second shortcoming by redirecting the output of the **man** command to a file in the **/tmp** directory. Then you can use an editor, and peruse the entry at your leisure. Alternatively, you can pipe the output of **man** into a screenful perusal filter program, such as **pg** or **more**. The BSD **man** command already pipes its output through **more**.

TABLE 1.10 LIST OF AT&T UNIX DOCUMENTATION

Volume name	Contents
User Reference Manual	User commands (section 1) and games (section 6)
User Guide	Tutorials on basics, such as editing, using the shell, etc.
Administrator Guide	Some advice, and revised papers describing fsck, LP System, Activity package, system startup
Administrator Reference Manual	Administrative commands (Section 1M) and special files (Section 7) and system maintenance procedures (Section 8); use system-specific documentation instead of generic Section 8 (unless revised by your vendor)
Error Messages	Available only for DEC and 3B processors unless vendor supplied
Programmer Reference Manual	System calls (Section 2), subroutine libraries (Section 3), file formats (Section 4), and miscellany (Section 5)
Programmer Guide	Papers on the C Compiler and programming tools
Graphics Guide	Graphics software for special terminals (Tektronix 401X)
Support Tools Guide	More papers on programming tools
Release Description	Bugs and problems
Operator Guide	Only available for DEC and 3B processors unless vendor supplied

A HANDFUL OF TOOLS

Before completing this introduction, we wanted to bring to your attention several utilities that will often be used in this book. These commands are not administrative utilities per se—they just happen to be ones useful for performing administrative duties. These tools, along with those familiar to all users, such as the shell and the **ls** command, make up the administrator's toolkit.

The grep Command

First on our list is **grep**. **grep** is an acronym for "**g**rab **r**egular **e**xpression and **p**rint," because that's what it does. **grep** picks out the lines that match the given regular expression. Figure 1.15 shows several examples.

Figure 1.15 Using **grep**.

a. Finding password file entry containing the string, **rik**:

```
$ grep rik /etc/passwd
rik:Hufw96A/ANUzE:100:50:Rik Farrow:/u/rik:/bin/ksh
$ □
```

b. Finding password-free entries:

```
$ grep '^[^:]*::' /etc/passwd
sync::20:10:The sync command:/:/bin/sync
$ □
```

c. Finding which file contains a function:

```
$ grep picDraw *.c
draw.c: int picDraw(lines, col, raster)
$ □
```

In the first example, the regular expression is literally the argument **rik**, and only lines in the file **/etc/passwd** that contain this string are printed. In the second example, a much more complicated match argument is used. The quoted argument translates as "match the first pair of colons only if it is not preceded by another colon."

The **grep** command is a favorite among programmers because it can quickly find the files containing particular functions or variables. The third example shows how **grep** is used to discover which file the function **picDraw()** is defined in. **grep**, and its related commands, **fgrep** (fast **grep**) and **egrep** (extended **grep**), make searches for the given expression.

The find Command

The second tool we'll discuss seems more closely related to system administration. The **find** command locates files that match the given criteria. **find** traverses directory hierarchies and checks each file it comes across. The selection criteria allow you to pick out files by permissions, access or modification dates, size, ownership, type, name, or number of links. Figure 1.16 provides some examples.

Figure 1.16 Using **find** to pick out files.

a. Searching for the files that haven't been accessed in over six months (180 days), and getting the opportunity to remove the file:

```
$ find /u/rik -atime +180 -ok rm {} \;
/u/rik/Usenix/Summer/outline: rm ? y
$ □
```

b. Searching for large directories (over two blocks):

```
$ find / -type d -size +2 -print
/bin
/usr/bin
```

```
/usr/lost+found
/usr/include/sys
/etc
/lost+found
/u/rik/Course/Day3
/u/rik/Course/Day5
$ □
```

The first example in Figure 1.16 shows how **find** can be used to locate old files and interactively remove them. The second example selects directories that are larger than two blocks. Remember to include the **-print** argument, or **find** will spend a lot of time doing something and never report anything.

The sed Command

The next utility in the toolkit we'll mention is **sed**. **sed** stands for **stream editor**, and uses a syntax similar to **ex**. **sed** is a master at performing text file conversions. Without invoking an interactive editor, you can change words, add indentation to lines, remove blank lines, or simply print selected lines. **sed** is often used as a *filter*, a program that is used in a pipeline to remove or transform part or all of its input. Figure 1.17 gives some examples of using **sed**.

Figure 1.17 Using **sed**, the master stream editor.

a. **Removing blank lines from a file:**

```
$ sed '/^$/d' file1 > file2
$ □
```

b. **Adding indentation to all lines in a file:**

```
$ sed 's/^/    /'file1 > file2
$ □
```

c. **Filtering the output of another command:**

```
$ find /u/rik -mtime +90 -print : sed '/Book/d' > oldfiles
$ □
```

The first two examples in Figure 1.17 depict **sed** being used to make changes in a file. The third example shows how **sed** can be combined with other commands in a pipeline. In this example, pathnames that include the name **Book** are being excluded from the output. You can use the **grep** command to exclude pathnames instead of **sed**.

The awk Command

The fourth utility to be included in the toolkit is **awk**. **awk** is an acronym for the names of its authors (Aho, Weinberger, and Kernighan), so you will simply have to remember the name by what it does. **awk** can perform many of the same tasks as **sed**, but with several differences. First, **awk** is much slower, so you will want to use **sed** instead of **awk** wherever possible. Second, although **awk** uses regular expressions for selecting lines, it uses a programming-style language for acting on the selected lines. And most important, **awk** can perform arithmetic.

You will usually be using **awk** for its calculating abilities. You can often use the **awk** utility for tasks that you'd have to write a C program to do. Figure 1.18 illustrates some ways that **awk** can be used.

Figure 1.18 Using **awk** for some calculations.

a. Produce the sum of the characters of all the files in a directory:

```
$ ls -l ¦ awk '{ s += $5 } END { print "Total characters:", s }'
Total characters: 209449
$ □
```

b. Create a list of home directories, including only nonsystem users:

```
$ awk -F: '/usr[0-9]/ { print $6 }' /etc/passwd > /tmp/HOMES
$ □
```

c. Print a bar graph representing disk usage by users:

```
$ cat bgraph
BEGIN {
x="XXXXXXXXXXXXXXXXXXXXXXXXXXXXXXXXXXXXXXXXXXXXXXXXXXXXXXXXXXXXXX"
scale = 100
max = 60
print "Each X represents", scale, "blocks, with a max of", max, "X's."
}
{
bar = $1 / scale
if (bar > max) bar = max
print "Directory", $2, "contains", $1, "blocks."
print substr(x,0,bar)
}
$ du -s `cat /tmp/HOMES` ¦ awk -f bgraph
Each X represents 100 blocks, with a max of 60 X's.
Directory /u/rik contains 3039 blocks.
```

```
XXXXXXXXXXXXXXXXXXXXXXXXXXXXXX
Directory /u/beccat contains 4202 blocks.
XXXXXXXXXXXXXXXXXXXXXXXXXXXXXXXXXXXXXXXXXXX
Directory /u/rose contains 37 blocks.

Directory /u/canyon contains 112 blocks.
X
$  □
```

awk is an interpretive programming language with quite amazing power. Even if you are not much of a programmer, you can certainly make use of some of **awk**'s more basic capabilities. In the first example in Figure 1.18, we use **awk** to add up all the numbers that appear in the fifth column (**$5**) of an **ls −l** long listing and print out the sum (the character count) at the end. The second example changes the field separator to a colon, and prints out the sixth field, the home directory, of lines in the password file that match the regular expression, which selects lines containing the strings **usr1**, **usr2**, etc. This way the home directories of all user accounts are printed.

The final example shows an **awk** program in the file **bgraph**. This program converts the output of the **du** command into a visual display, showing the relative magnitudes of the disk usage for the user accounts.

We have barely touched on the capabilities of the utilities in the toolkit. We aren't going into a tutorial on how to use these tools. You can learn about these commands, and others, from the books listed in the bibliography. What we wanted to do here is to point out to you several tools that we have used over and over again in system administration, and that we have found in the shell scripts delivered with the system and written by other administrators. The UNIX system is loaded with useful utilities because of its heritage as a programmer's environment. Learn enough to take advantage of these tools, and you'll get this heritage to work for you.

SOME BASIC TERMINOLOGY

In this section we define some of the terms that you will need to know for administering a UNIX system. Some of these terms, especially the *kernel* and *process*, have proven confusing to many people. Properly, a glossary belongs in the back of a book. But you must at least be introduced to these words before continuing. If you are already familiar with them, skip ahead, please.

Kernel. The kernel, or operating system "program," gets loaded into the computer during startup and stays in memory. The kernel manages the system's hardware, that is, the memory, disks, and communications. System calls pass requests to the kernel. The UNIX kernel was deliberately designed to be simple and perform only essential tasks. User programs perform auxiliary tasks using the system call interface.

System call.   A system call is a request made to the kernel. The **chmod** system call, for example, requests to change the permissions on a file. To read from or write to a file, or to discover the current time, a program needs to request help from the kernel. When people talk about System V compatibility, they mean that the system calls are guaranteed to work as stated in the System V Interface Definition. Thus, a software developer is assured that a program can reliably make requests from the kernel, and that the kernel will behave in a well-defined way.

Process.   A process is a program after it has been invoked by the kernel. A program is a list of machine codes and data saved as a file. The kernel loads a program into memory as the result of an **exec** (execute) system call. The kernel not only loads the program into memory and arranges its data, it also assigns ownership to the process and protects it from other processes. The process may freely read or write its own data, but must make system calls to read or write to the file system, or do anything beyond manipulating its memory space.

Shell.   The shell is a program designed to interact with people (users). Shell programs interpret lines typed by users and start other programs. The three most popular shells are the Bourne and Korn shells from AT&T and the C shell from the Berkeley UNIX system. Shells also interpret programs called shell scripts.

File.   A file is a collection of data stored on a disk. Files may have one or more names that refer to the same collection of data. The data may be a program, numbers, text, or anything that may be represented as numbers. Files have additional properties, including a set of access permissions, individual and group owner identification, date-time stamps showing the last time the file was read or written to.

Inode.   The inode, or information node for a file, contains all the information about a file, except the file's name and the actual data in the file. The owner, group owner, number of directory entries (links), permissions, file type, file size, list of the disk blocks that contain the data in the file, and three dates are part of the inode.

Directory.   A directory file contains the names of other files. The root directory of a file system is the starting point for the file system hierarchy, and has the names of other directories within it. Each directory may have the names of ordinary files or still more directories. More than one name can refer to the same collection of data (file).

Device file.   A device file contains device information. Disk partitions and other computer hardware can be referred to through the file system by using the device file. Device files contain no data, but have instead two special numbers, the major and minor device numbers, which uniquely identify the device to the kernel.

Device driver. The device driver is the part of the kernel that controls a particular type of device. For each different type of device (computer hardware) in a system, there is a device driver. For example, the disk controller and the communications controller each require a device driver that understands how to work that device. Writing device drivers requires intimate knowledge of both the device itself and the way that the rest of the kernel works with device drivers.

Major device number. The major device number identifies the device driver. There is a unique major device number for each device driver. The long listing of a device file displays the major device number first, followed by the minor device number.

Minor device number. The minor device number provides information to the device driver about which specific device to access. For example, a communications driver may be capable of handling 32 ports, and the minor device number will indicate which one of the ports is indicated.

Block devices. Block devices work with block-sized groups of data. Typically, a block is a multiple of 512 bytes, generally 1024 bytes on System V implementations. Disk and tape devices store data in blocks, so all reading and writing are also in block-size pieces. Block devices use the block buffers in the kernel as a cache, or temporary holding place, for data that has been read or will be written.

Character devices. Character devices work with any number of bytes of data, from one byte at a time, to large blocks of data. Devices, such as terminals, modems, or printers are character devices. You sometimes would use the character device interface to a block device (like a file system or tape drive) with programs that manage their own block buffers, such as **fsck** and **dd**. Using the character device interface with these programs can be much more efficient.

QUICK REFERENCE GUIDE — A Directory Hierarchy Summary

/	The beginning of the file system
/bin	Command directory with the essential utilities
/dev	Device files for terminals, memory, disks, tape, etc.
/etc	Etcetera; miscellaneous system administration files and commands
/lost +found	Files and directories found by **fsck**
/lib	Library containing files used by C compiler
/tmp	For temporary files created by users and programs
/usr	Beginning of **usr** subdirectory; no files, only directories

/usr/adm	Administration; logfiles and record keeping
/usr/adm/sa	System activity; reports collected from activity counters
/usr/adm/acct	System accounting; connect time and command usage
/usr/adm/acct/nite	Nightly (or daily) accounting records
/usr/adm/acct/sum	Summaries of past daily accounting runs
/usr/adm/acct/fiscal	Monthly accounting summaries
/usr/bin	More user commands
/usr/dict	Spelling dictionaries and support utilities
/usr/etc	Administrative commands on some BSD systems
/usr/games	Games and educational programs
/usr/include	Header files included by C programs
/usr/include/sys	Header files for system programs, such as **fsck** or the kernel
/usr/lib	Library of administrative commands and directories
/usr/lib/acct	System accounting programs and scripts
/usr/lib/font	Typesetting fonts for **troff**
/usr/lib/help	Help text files for use with **help**
/usr/lib/lex	Files and programs for use with **lex** (programming tool)
/usr/lib/libp	Library for Pascal compiler
/usr/lib/macros	Macros (command definitions) for **nroff** or **troff**
/usr/lib/me	Me macro package for **nroff** or **troff**
/usr/lib/ms	Ms macro package for **nroff** or **troff**
/usr/lib/sa	System activity programs
/usr/lib/tabset	Tab setting information for **nroff** or **troff**
/usr/lib/term	Terminal information for **nroff** or **troff**
/usr/lib/terminfo/*	Directories for terminfo database
/usr/lib/uucp	Commands and configuration files for UUCP
/usr/lbin	Locally produced commands and scripts for general use
/usr/lost+found	**lost+found** directory for **/usr** file system
/usr/mail	Mailboxes for users
/usr/man	Online manuals in **troff** input format (use **man** macros)
/usr/man/a_man	Administrative manual entries
/usr/man/local	Locally added manual sections
/usr/man/u_man	User manual entries
/usr/news	User community news, accessed by the **news** command
/usr/preserve	Used to save text edited by **vi** after system crash or hangup
/usr/pub	Public information, like ASCII character tables
/usr/spool	Directories for queuing up work to be performed later
/usr/spool/lp	Configuration files, requests, and temporary files for the LP system
/usr/spool/uucp	Request, status, and logfiles for the UUCP system
/usr/src	Source code: uncompiled programs for utilities and the system
/usr/tmp	Second temporary directory

2

Account Management

INTRODUCTION

When you began using the UNIX system, you learned early on that you access the system by logging into an account. The account probably had a name that was a variation of your own personal name, say **robin**. Then you noticed that other people, say Pete and Roger, had their own accounts, too. Those other accounts might have been set up somewhat differently from yours—maybe a different shell prompt or the ability to access a different part of the system.

Now as system administrator you must manage the accounts belonging to Pete, Roger, and other users on your system. And you're not only confronted with the potentate **root** account, but also other system-related accounts, such as **lp** and **uucp**.

In this chapter you'll learn about the different types of UNIX accounts, and how to create and remove them. As background you'll first learn about the password and group files, groups, and the working environment—all necessary for knowing how to set up accounts properly.

ACCOUNTS

An account consists of all the information needed for a person (known as a user) to log in to a UNIX system. Some of the information is mandatory, such as an entry in the system *password file*, **/etc/passwd**. Other information is optional, but considered helpful, such as a shell startup file to customize the working environment for the account user.

44

Types of Accounts

Accounts can be classified by how they're used and by the level of access to the UNIX system they provide. We'll be using particular terms for describing accounts in this chapter (and book). First let's look at the terms for classifying accounts by usage.

Classification by Usage. People accessing the system will have accounts for their personal use, which we'll call *user accounts*. Accounts used for system-related functions will be called *system accounts*. These include the **root** account used for setting up and maintaining the system, and accounts not generally used for system access, but rather for establishing file ownership, such as **lp** and **uucp**.

Classification by Access. Another way to classify accounts is by how much system access they provide. Most user accounts provide access to a personal work area—we'll refer to these as *ordinary accounts*. Some accounts provide privileged access to the UNIX system—so we'll call these *privileged accounts*. The **root** account is a good example of a privileged account. Other accounts restrict system access compared to ordinary accounts—let's denote these as *restricted accounts*. Restricted accounts are used for increasing the security of your UNIX system.

Account Management Overview

The account management discussed in this chapter includes establishing new accounts, changing existing accounts, and deactivating or removing obsolete ones. You'll find that the details of account management remain constant from one UNIX system to the next. Thus the principles you learn in this chapter can generally apply without much change to any UNIX-based operating system.

Adding a new user account can often be automated with a shell script or executable program. Look on your system for commands with names like **mkuser**, **newuser**, or **adduser**. If one is available, you should use such a program for creating new user accounts. These programs simplify the task of account management and may also prevent you from using illegal parameters when creating the accounts.

You may also find programs that remove accounts, such as **deluser**, **rmuser**, etc. However, we recommend deactivating an account instead of removing it completely, so account removal programs may not be the best choice.

Programs that add or remove accounts aren't as flexible as a manual approach. For instance, system accounts may have special requirements not foreseen by an automated program. Thus, you need to know all the steps for creating and removing accounts manually.

Adding, changing, and removing accounts all involve manipulation of the system password and perhaps the group file, too. So let's learn about these important system databases.

THE PASSWORD FILE

The password file defines UNIX accounts. An account exists by virtue of an entry in this file along with a home directory and startup program.

General Characteristics of the Password File

Figure 2.1 lists the characteristics of the password file, whose full pathname is **/etc/passwd**. Each account on your UNIX system must have an entry in this file.

Figure 2.1 Characteristics of the password file.

- The database that describes accounts.
- A human-readable ASCII text file.
- Readable by all system users, writable by none (except the superuser).
- Each line entry corresponds to an account.
- Each line consists of seven colon (:)-separated fields.

Conveniently, **/etc/passwd** is human-readable ASCII text, so you can manipulate it easily with UNIX commands that process text, such as an editor. This file must be readable by all system users for proper operation of some UNIX commands, such as **ls** or **find**. These commands need to associate an account user-id number (obtained from the inode for a file) with the name of the account (obtained from the **/etc/passwd** file).

The password file must not be writable by any user except for its owner (generally **root**). Otherwise, that user could set up a privileged account—a security breach. The **/etc/passwd** file should be either mode 444 or 644 and owned by **root**. As a safety precaution, the System V **passwd** command changes the mode to 444. *Note*: When you're logged in as superuser you can always override "read-only" permission and force writing to the password file. The group owner is generally the same as the default group of the **root** account. Figure 2.2 shows the correct ownership and permissions for a typical password file.

Figure 2.2 Recommended permissions and ownership for **/etc/passwd**.

```
$ ls -l /etc/passwd
-r--r--r--   1 root      sys        1352 Aug 14 12:55 /etc/passwd
$ □
```

Contents of the Password File

Each entry line in **/etc/passwd** defines an account. The line consists of seven fields separated from each other by a colon (:). Figure 2.3 shows a sample password file entry for a typical user account. The names of the fields are depicted below the entry.

Figure 2.3 A typical user account password file entry.

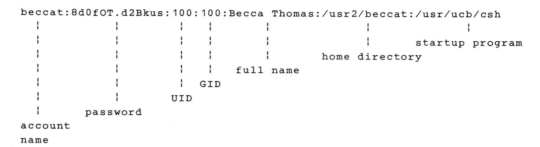

```
beccat:8d0fOT.d2Bkus:100:100:Becca Thomas:/usr2/beccat:/usr/ucb/csh
   ¦           ¦         ¦   ¦       ¦                    ¦            ¦
   ¦           ¦         ¦   ¦       ¦                    ¦        startup program
   ¦           ¦         ¦   ¦       ¦                    ¦
   ¦           ¦         ¦   ¦       ¦                home directory
   ¦           ¦         ¦   ¦       ¦
   ¦           ¦         ¦   ¦   full name
   ¦           ¦         ¦ GID
   ¦           ¦        UID
   ¦       password
account
name
```

Now let's discuss the contents of these fields in more detail.

Account Name.   The account, log-in, or user name identifies the account to the system. Thus, the name should be descriptive, such as a variation of a person's name for a user account. For instance, we use **beccat** and **rik** for our personal accounts. The names of system accounts should describe the function, such as **rje** for "remote job entry," or name the command used as a startup program, such as the **sync** account, which would execute the **/bin/sync** command after log-in. Generally, there is more variation for the names of system accounts compared to user accounts.

The name consists of up to eight characters. You can use any letter of the alphabet and the decimal digits. Nonprinting characters and punctuation are not recommended. *Caution*: The first character of the account name shouldn't be a capital letter. If so, when you attempt to log into that account, some of the older versions of the **getty** program assume that you're using a terminal that can handle only uppercase letters, such as a Teletype 33. From that point on, all system output will be in uppercase letters. Newer **getty** programs cause your terminal driver to go into uppercase mode only if all letters of the account name are capitalized. Thus, you could capitalize the first letter if you're interacting with the new **getty** program.

Encrypted Password.   This field either contains a valid encrypted password, or a character string that's not a valid password, or is left blank. A valid password would be a particular string consisting of 13 characters from the character set (.), (/), **A** to **Z**, **a** to **z**, and **0** to **9**. Certain other characters may be appended to provide password aging.

Any characters in this field not in the limited character set listed above would make the password invalid. For instance, administrators often use an asterisk (∗) to make an invalid password. Also, the character string must have been created by the UNIX **passwd** command or the **/usr/lib/makekey** program, or copied from another password field, whose contents was created using **passwd**. If the password is invalid, users can't log into this account. But if you already have superuser privilege, you can use **su** to change user identity to the account.

Providing an invalid password is useful if you need to prevent log-in access to an account. You would do so after an account was deactivated, which means that the account is no longer in active use on the system, but the password file entry is retained. Also, certain system accounts, such as **lp** and **uucp**, that denote ownership of files and aren't meant for system access have invalid passwords. Some administrators may elect to allow access to such accounts so that operators could maintain the LP and UUCP systems without needing superuser privilege.

If the password field is blank (or null), anyone can log in if they know the account name. This situation isn't secure—(almost) *every* account should have a password—either valid or invalid. One exception would be an account that runs a dedicated program, such as **sync**, which after it's run, logs the user off immediately. Make sure that the dedicated program can't provide a shell, else the user would have access to the system.

User-id Number Field.   The user-id (or UID) number identifies the account to the UNIX system. For instance, file ownership is denoted by the user-id, not the account name—impersonal, but efficient. Generally, this number should be unique; that is, every account should have a different user-id.

If two accounts do have the same user-id when you list their files with the **ls** −**l** command, all files would appear to be owned by one account—the one that occurs first in the password file. For instance, let's say that not only the **root** account (which uses the Bourne shell as the startup program), but also the **rootcsh** account (which uses the C shell) have user-id zero (0). And since the entry for **root** occurs first in the password file, then any files created by a user of either account would appear to be owned by **root** according to the **ls** −**l** command output. But the **rootcsh** account would own them as well.

Often, UUCP access accounts share the same user-id with the UUCP administrative account since they don't own any files on the system. All UUCP files are owned by the UUCP administrative account, **uucp**. And all UUCP accounts—both administrative and access accounts—may have the same user-id on your system. However, it's more secure if your UUCP access accounts have user-ids distinct from that of the **uucp** account.

The user-id can range from zero (reserved for superuser privileges) up to some large number, whose value depends on the system. For instance, the XENIX **mkuser** program uses an upper limit of 30,000. Beware, large user-id numbers give the user superuser privileges on XENIX systems—so keep the user-id to less than 30,000 if you add an account manually.

If you wish to use large user-id numbers, edit **/etc/passwd** to create a test account first. That is, create a "dummy" account with the large user-id and see if you can log in. If so, make sure that it acts as an ordinary account, not a privileged account. That is, see if you can write to files like **/etc/passwd** that only the superuser should be able to write to.

We recommend that you reserve user-ids zero through some limit like 99 for system accounts and use numbers larger than that limit for user accounts. This way you'll keep the system accounts separate from user accounts. Rarely would you need more than 100 different system accounts—but if you do, simply use a greater limiting value in the first place.

The user-ids for new user accounts are generally assigned sequentially using the next higher available number. And some programs that add user accounts can determine the next available user-id for you. The user-ids for system accounts have more variation, and other system accounts may dictate their values.

Group-id Number Field.   The group-id (or GID) number defines membership in a *default group*. An account may be a member of other groups as well, and these additional associations are defined in the group file (discussed below).

Group-id numbers can range from zero to some large value like 30,000. As with user-ids, we like to use group-ids in the range 0 to 99 for system-related groups and group-ids 100 and above for groups used by user accounts. You'll find great variation on the usage of group-ids from one UNIX system to the next. For instance, the XENIX system **mkuser** program allows group-ids for user accounts to range from 50 to 30,000.

Comment Field.   The use for this field varies from one installation to another. Generally, a brief description of the account usage is placed here for a system account or the person's full name for a user account. This way you could use a cryptic or short account name, with the comment field containing the real name as a "handle."

Also, the System V line printer spooler interface program for your printer may print the contents of this field at the beginning of a listing. The Berkeley **finger** command gets information from this field, too. Thus you'd want the comment field to contain a descriptive identifier for the account.

Home Directory Field.   This field contains the full pathname for the home directory for the account. The home directory is the initial working directory after logging in.

On many earlier UNIX systems, home directories often had **/usr** as their parent directory. But we feel that a different parent directory, such as **/usr2**, would be better, especially if you have a large user population. That way, you'll reduce your backup chores. When you backup **/usr2**, you get just the user account files. If you backup **/usr**, you get system files, too. The directory name **/usr2** is less ambiguous to communicate verbally than, say, **/user**, since UNIX users are familiar with the **usr** spelling.

Often, the home directories for user accounts are kept on a separate file system, which is mounted when the system goes into multiuser operation. And if you have many users, you may need to use several different file systems, like **/usr2**, **/usr3**, and so forth. This approach is useful if you're using a backup utility that saves an entire file system, such as System V **volcopy**, XENIX **backup**, or the Berkeley **dump** program.

Startup Program Field.   This field contains the full pathname for the program that's invoked by the **login** process as the last step in the log-in sequence. Generally, for user accounts it's a general-purpose shell, such as the Bourne, C, or Korn shell. However, for some system accounts it could be a special-purpose shell script, UNIX command, or application program. Note that if this field is left blank, most UNIX systems use the Bourne shell as a default case. Table 2.1 lists some of the more common startup programs with a brief description.

TABLE 2.1 SOME COMMON STARTUP PROGRAMS

Pathname	Usage
/bin/sh	Bourne shell (general-purpose shell)
/bin/rsh	Restricted Bourne shell (for security)
/bin/ksh*	Korn shell (general-purpose shell)
/usr/ucb/csh*	C shell (general-purpose shell)
/bin/vsh	Visual shell (XENIX systems)
/usr/lib/uucp/uucico	UUCP file transfer daemon (UUCP access)
/bin/sync	Update the file system (special purpose)
/bin/red	Restricted line editor (for security)

*The pathnames used for these shells vary from system
to system.

If you wish to restrict your users to operating certain application programs, make that application the startup program. For instance, your secretary might use a word-processing package, and your accountant would access an accounting program. For more security, make sure that access to a shell is prohibited.

Other examples might include giving system operators access only to system administration functions, such as backup and restore, system startup and shutdown, and so forth. You'll have to adjust ownerships and permissions so that the operator account will own the necessary files.

Password File Example

Figure 2.4 shows a typical password file on a small system. You may wish to inspect the password file on your system, comparing it to this example.

Figure 2.4 A typical password file.

```
root:kPabRrowAt1Po:0:3::/:/bin/sh
rootcsh:kPabRrowAt1Po:0:3::/:/bin/csh
daemon:**NO-LOGIN**:1:12::/:
bin:**NO-LOGIN**:2:2::/bin:
sys:**NO-LOGIN**:3:3::/usr/src:
```

```
adm:**NO-LOGIN**:4:4::/usr/adm:
uucp:**NO-LOGIN**:5:5::/usr/lib/uucp:
nuucp:POCHBwE/mB51k:6:5::/usr/spool/uucppublic:/usr/lib/uucp/uucico
sync::20:1::/:/bin/sync
rje:**NO-LOGIN**:68:8::/usr/rje:
lp:**NO-LOGIN**:71:2::/usr/spool/lp:
beccat:AS1doX.rOFqjo:100:100::/usr2/beccat:
rik:H6ofxJZJnmj9g,/.uA:101:100::/usr2/rik:/bin/csh
```

Examine the system accounts, such as **daemon**, **bin**, **sys**, **adm**, **uucp**, located near the beginning of the file. UNIX systems need these accounts to establish correct file ownership for some system files, not for system access. So the entries for these accounts have an impossible password, such as ****NO-LOGIN**** (12 instead of 13 characters, or the asterisk makes it invalid), so users can't log in to these accounts. You're likely to find some of these same accounts on your system.

As you examine your password file, you might be concerned with the following: What user-ids and group-ids are used for your system accounts? Are these identification numbers consistent, grouped logically, or randomly? Are any of the password fields blank?—they shouldn't be, except for an account such as **sync**. What's the home directory? Is it the root directory? Some other directory? Examine the startup program—is it a shell or special utility?

Look for your user accounts. They should be separated from your system accounts—generally all grouped at the end of the password file. Here again, you might ask: What user-ids and group-ids are used for the user accounts? Are these identification numbers consistent, grouped logically, or randomly? Do these accounts all have passwords?—they should. Are the account names descriptive? If not, is the person's name in the comment field? What are the home directories? Do they all branch from the same parent directory? Larger systems may have several parent directories. What shells are used for these accounts on your system? Are any of the user accounts restricted accounts?

We show two ordinary user accounts in the example, **beccat** and **rik**, which have user-ids 100 and 101, respectively. They both belong to the same default group, which has a group-id of 100. The **beccat** account doesn't have a startup program specified, so it uses the Bourne shell and the **rik** account uses the C shell. Also note that the encrypted password for the **rik** account uses password aging since there are more than 13 characters and the 14th is a comma.

ACCOUNT GROUPS

Account groups allow two or more accounts to share access to files while excluding file access to other accounts. Consult the example in Figure 2.5 for four user accounts in two groups.

Figure 2.5 Example for specifying default groups.

```
beccat:AS1doX.rOFqjo:100:100:Becca Thomas:/usr2/beccat:
rik:H6ofxJZJnmj9g,/.uA:101:100:Rik Farrow:/usr2/rik:/bin/csh
robin:vIeHMHqtyTcaw:102:200:Robin Williams:/usr2/robin:
lauren:8X./q8Ig3mnQa:103:200:Lauren Bacall:/usr2/lauren:
```

Users **beccat** and **rik** both belong to the same default group (group-id 100), while users **robin** and **lauren** belong to a different default group (with group-id 200).

Here are some examples of how files may be shared by accounts that belong to the same group: If **rik** enables group permissions (with **chmod**) for one of his files, then **beccat** can access that file. Similarly, **robin** and **lauren** can provide for each other to access files one or the other of them owns, all the while keeping others from reading or writing. Group permissions are handy for departments where a boss may want to edit the letter his secretary typed but wants no one other than himself and his secretary to be able to access the file.

However, files can't be accessed by members of *different* groups, even if group permissions have been enabled. Such users would be in the "other" category. Remember the order of file permissions evaluation—user, group, then others. Members of different groups aren't the file owner, nor the group owner, but in the "other" user category.

One way to allow different groups to access your files is to define additional group associations using the group file. Once this is done, users permitted to do so can change their group association so that they can access the requisite files.

THE GROUP FILE

The group file gives names to default groups and defines additional groups besides those defined in the password file. First let's learn about the general properties of the group file.

General Characteristics of the Group File

Figure 2.6 lists the characteristics of the system group file, whose full pathname is **/etc/group**.

Figure 2.6 Characteristics of the group file.

- Database used to describe groups.
- Human-readable ASCII text file.
- Readable by all users, writable by none (except the superuser).
- Each line entry corresponds to a group.
- Associates a name with a group-id number.
- Defines additional groups.

Many attributes of the group file are similar to those of the password file, such as both being human-readable text, readable by all users, writable by no users (except, of course, a user with superuser privilege). Each line in the group file describes a group just like each line in the password file describes an account. The entry either associates a group name with an existing default group (defined in the password file) or defines a new group and gives a name for it.

Contents of the Group File

A group file entry looks somewhat different from a password file entry. Both files have fields separated by colons (:), but the group file contains only four fields. Figure 2.7 shows a sample group file entry. The names of the fields are depicted below the entry.

Figure 2.7 A typical group file entry.

```
users::100:robin,lauren
  ¦    ¦ ¦         ¦
  ¦    ¦ ¦     account names
  ¦    ¦ GID
  ¦ password
group
name
```

Now let's discuss the contents of the fields in the group file.

Group Name Field.   The group name consists of up to eight characters. Use letters and numbers—just as you would in an account name. Don't use punctuation or nonprinting (control) characters. Here, unlike the account name in **/etc/passwd**, you could capitalize letters of a group name. But conventionally, all lowercase letters are used.

Encrypted Password Field.   Most UNIX systems don't have a way to add a password to the group file with a simple utility or program. So most systems don't use group passwords. You could use an editor and copy a valid password from the password file to the group file, if desired. Be sure you know the (unencrypted) password, though.

Here are the steps you could use to install a group password: You could change the password for an account on your system or create a "dummy" user account and install a password with the **passwd** command. Note the characters that make up the encrypted password for the "dummy" account. Then use an editor to place these *same* characters into the password field of the group file entry.

We don't recommend using group passwords because it's actually easier to gain unauthorized access to a group if a password is installed! That's right. If no password or an invalid one is used with a group, there's no way a system "cracker" can change to this group unless he or she can become superuser. Only users listed in the account name field of **/etc/group** can change to the group. However, if a password is installed and the "cracker" guesses it, he or she has access to the group with the password. And here's another reason for not using group passwords: it's human nature that system users aren't as likely to protect a group password as they would the password for their personal account.

Group-id Number Field.   The group-id (or GID) can range from zero to some maximum value, which depends on your UNIX implementation. We recommend using group-ids below some value, like 50 or 100 for system-related groups and group-ids above that range for user-related groups—just to keep things more organized.

Account Names Field.   This field contains the account names that belong to the group separated from one another by a comma (,). Additional group associations are defined for accounts by specifying their account names in this field.

Group File Example

Figure 2.8 shows a sample group file from a small UNIX system.

Figure 2.8 A sample group file.

```
root::0:root
other::1:other,root
bin::2:bin,root
sys::3:sys,root
adm::4:adm,root
uucp::5:uucp,root
mail::6:root
rje::8:rje
daemon::12:daemon,root
users::100:beccat,rik,robin
docum::200:lauren,robin,beccat
```

Compare this group file with the one on your system. Are any of the group names the same? If so, do they have the same group-id? What's in the password field? Is it left blank, or does it contain an impossible password, or a valid one? What accounts associate with each group?

In our example the first nine entries associate a group name with a group-id. Although not essential, names are easier to remember than numbers. In this example, the group file defines names for the group-id numbers 0 through 6, 8, and 12.

The last two user-account groups (with group-ids 100 and 200) happen to be default groups defined in the password file. These particular group file entries define additional group memberships for some user accounts. In the example shown, the group **users**, with group-id 100, lists the default members (**beccat** and

rik) and then an account from a different default group (**robin,** who's in the **docum** group), which allows that account to become a member of the **users** group. Similarly, the **docum** group, with group-id 200, lists the default members (**robin** and **lauren**) and an account from a different default group (**beccat** from the **users** group).

As we have seen, different users (accounts) can belong to the same group by assignment through **/etc/passwd.** System users can *potentially* belong to the same group by definition in the group file. However, a user can belong to only one group at a time. To change group association from one group to another, use the **newgrp** command.

THE newgrp COMMAND

The **newgrp** command acts somewhat differently from most commands the Bourne shell executes. When you run this command you create a new instance of the Bourne shell, which overwrites the current one. This new shell is almost identical to the old one—the primary difference is that both the real and effective group-ids have been changed if the **newgrp** command is successful. If not successful, the overwriting still occurs, but the group-ids don't change.

If the Bourne shell was your log-in shell process (the first shell obtained after you log on), the new shell will become your new log-in shell process. When you exit this shell you'll be logged out of the account. Of course, using **newgrp** doesn't change the password file, so when you log in again you'll belong to the default group specified by your account entry in **/etc/passwd.**

All environment variables retain their values, but variables not marked for export are either reset to a default value or are lost. System V Release 2 Bourne shell function definitions are also forgotten. As an example, let's say that you had changed your primary prompt string (defined by the **PS1** variable) to a value other than the default (**$** followed by one space character), but didn't mark the variable for export to the environment. Then after executing **newgrp,** your prompt string would be reset to a dollar sign (**$**) followed by a space. This change happens even if you weren't able to change to the new group successfully.

Part a of Figure 2.9 shows the general command line syntax for changing to another group, *group,* which can either be the group name or group-id number. The group association is changed back to the original default group by omitting the *group* argument. Use the dash (−) argument if you wish the shell startup files to be executed to change your environment to be the same as if you had actually logged into the system as the new group.

As an example, let's say that **beccat** wishes to access files owned by account **robin.** Files owned by **robin** wouldn't be accessible to **beccat** even if group permissions were enabled and permissions for others not enabled (mode 660 or **rw- rw----**) because the files don't have the same group ownership. However, since the group file shown in Figure 2.8 allows **beccat** to change group association to the group that **robin** belongs to by default, namely **docum**, the files may be accessed after that change in group identity.

Part b shows the command line used to change from the group **users** to **docum**. The change is verified by running the **id** command before and after. This command reports the real user- and group-id of the user running it (and effective user or group-id if it's different from the real ones).

Figure 2.9 Using the **newgrp** command.

a. General command line format:

    $ newgrp [−] [group]

b. A specific example:

```
$ id
uid=100(beccat) gid=100(users)
$ newgrp docum
$ id
uid=100(beccat) gid=200(docum)
$ □
```

If you invoke **newgrp** from a C shell, a new instance of this shell is spawned that doesn't overwrite the original one. Thus, both the new child shell and the old parent shell are still present. You'll be interacting with the child shell while the parent waits. This new child shell will have the new group association if the command succeeded. When you exit from the child shell, you return to the parent C shell with the previous group association without logging out.

You won't create a child shell if you use the **exec newgrp** command form instead of **newgrp** from the C shell. Then the child shell with the new group association overwrites the original C shell. Note, that specifying **exec** isn't necessary for the S.C.O. XENIX **newgrp** command. Here the C shell is overwritten without it.

THE WORKING ENVIRONMENT

Every account has an initial *working environment*. You'll learn what an environment is and how to set it up manually in this section. Later in this chapter you'll learn about setting up an environment automatically when a user logs into an account.

We'll be using the term "working environment" in a broad sense to mean all the parameters that can be changed for an account. These parameters consist of many elements, such as environment variables, like **PATH**, the file creation mask value (**umask**), the terminal settings, such as **tab3** versus **tabs**, and others. Let's discuss the shell variables that make up the working environment first.

Local shell variables are known only to the instance of the shell where they were defined. You can mark such variables for export so that they are placed in the execution environment of the shell, where they can be passed onto any program that the shell runs. Such variables are known as environment variables.

Environment variables are useful from the shell level. For instance, we often use an environment variable to abbreviate a long pathname, such as **LIB** for **/usr/lib/uucp**. After defining **LIB** this way and placing it in the environment, I can invoke **/usr/lib/uucp/uucico** as simply **$LIB/uucico**.

The environment variables may contain information accessed by a shell script and compiled programs that you run, such as the home directory of your account (in **HOME**), the list of directories to search to execute a command (in **PATH**), and so forth.

You mark environment variables differently depending on the shell you're using. Part a of Figure 2.10 shows how this is done with the Bourne or Korn shell, and part b shows a specific example. Part c shows the general approach with the C shell, and part d shows how the example in part b would be recoded for the C shell.

Figure 2.10 Defining environment variables.

a. General format when using the Bourne or Korn shell:

```
$ NAME = string     # define NAME to be string
$ export NAME       # mark environment variable
```

b. A specific example:

```
$ TERM=tvi950
$ export TERM
$ □
```

c. General format when using the C shell:

```
% setenv NAME value    # define and export in one step
```

d. A specific example:

```
% setenv TERM tvi950
% □
```

Note: By convention, environment variables are named with all capital letters.

In Appendix A we discuss the most important environment variables. Also, we provide a table in that appendix that lists the typical environment variables provided after you log into an account. And look there to see information on how you might change these variables to customize the working environment of a new account.

Besides the environment variables used by any program, the C shell also recognizes other local variables for customizing its operation. The **set** command defines these variables. And the complementary **unset** command removes the variable definition. Figure 2.11 shows the syntax and some examples for using both commands. Some variables aren't assigned a value—just defined—so you'd specify only the name of the variable on the **set** command line.

Figure 2.11 Defining and undefining C shell variables.

a. Defining to have (optional) value *string*:

```
% set name [ = string ]
```

b. A specific example:

```
% set ignoreeof
%  □
```

c. Undefining the C shell variable:

```
% unset name
```

d. A specific example for undefining a variable:

```
% unset ignoreeof
%  □
```

You can pass the values of these variables to subshells spawned by the C shell even though the variables aren't in the execution environment of this shell. You'd place the variable definition in the **.cshrc** shell startup file to do this. Since this file is executed by any subshell when it starts up, the variable would be defined for that subshell.

In Appendix B we discuss the most important C shell variables that are used for customizing the working environment of an account that uses this shell.

ADDING A NEW ACCOUNT

Now that you know about the password file, the group file, groups, and the working environment, you're ready to learn about account management. First let's see how to add a new account manually to the UNIX system. Later we discuss using a program or shell script for automating the process. Figure 2.12 shows six steps for adding a new account to your UNIX system.

Figure 2.12 Steps for adding an account.

- Select contents for fields of the password file.
- Update the password file.
- Install a password.
- Update the group file.
- Create a home directory with the correct ownership.
- Customize the working environment.

Choose Password File Contents

First you need to select the appropriate contents for the fields of the password file entry for the account. Let's discuss guidelines for selecting the account name, user- and group-id numbers, home directory, and shell (startup program).

Account Name Field.   The account name should be descriptive so that you can tell by inspection the purpose of the account. Generally, use some form of the person's name for a user account and a functionally descriptive name for a system account. Your site may use a particular convention for user account names, such as first name and last initial. Or your site may allow users to choose their own "handle." In this case their personal name should be included in the comments field. In any case you should be consistent with the established procedure.

User-id Field.   Then choose the next-higher user-id that's available for a user account. Figure 2.13 shows a command line for displaying the password file entry that has the greatest user-id.

Figure 2.13 Displaying the password file entry with the largest user-id.

```
$ sort -nt: +2 -3 /etc/passwd ¦ tail -1
guest:Xy/cqY,p2tsg3:122:120:guest account:/usr2/guest:/bin/sh
$ □
```

Here the **−n** option specifies a numeric sort, and the **t:** argument tells **sort** to treat the colon as the field separator. The **+2 −3** arguments causes the password file to be sorted on the third field only. The **tail −1** command displays the last line from the output of the **sort** command, which is the entry with the largest user-id.

User-ids for system accounts vary more than those for user accounts, so if you are setting up a system account, examine your password file and choose a user-id consistent with similar accounts. For example, let's say that your password file was like the one shown in Figure 2.4 and you wish to add a system account that would run the UNIX **tty** command as the startup program. Since you already have a similar account, named **sync**, you would probably place the **tty** account next so that it would have user-id 21.

Group-id Field. Examine both the password and group file to see what group would be appropriate for the new account. If the new account should share files with another account, either (1) it should be in the same default group, or (2) it should be allowed to change to the group to which the other account belongs. In the first case the new account would be given the same group-id as the other account. In the second case the new account would also be listed in the *account names* field of the group file entry used by the other account.

If the new account shouldn't share files with another account, it shouldn't be in the same group—either by default or potentially via the group file. And if the new group shouldn't share files with any other account, it should have a group-id number not used by any other account. A good example would be a public access "guest" account. You'd probably want to create a unique **guest** group for this account.

Home Directory Field. The home directory for a system account is generally determined by the type of account. If not, the root directory (**/**) is usually appropriate. User accounts often share the same parent directory for their home directory. There are exceptions; for instance, large systems may have user accounts spread out over different file systems. For instance, some accounts might be on a file system mounted as **/usr2** and others on a file system mounted as **/usr3**. The user account home directory commonly uses a basename the same as the account name.

The Startup Program Field. The startup program is chosen based on the purpose of the account. Generally, system accounts require specific programs to function. If the account is used only to denote file ownership and not to access the system, no program is specified. You'd probably choose a general-purpose shell for a user account, such as the Bourne, C, or Korn shell. You should ask your account user for a preference. Restricted accounts, such as general dial-up guest accounts, should use either a restricted (Bourne or Korn) shell or better yet, a "change root" environment.

The Bourne shell was the original shell distributed with the AT&T UNIX system, and is named after its author, Steve Bourne. The C shell is distributed with the Berkeley UNIX system and is so named because of its "C" language-like syntax. Users generally write shell scripts using the Bourne shell, but prefer using the C shell interactively since it provides command aliases and history. The Korn shell, named after its author David Korn, provides the best of both shells—it's a more powerful Bourne shell language superset for writing shell scripts and has command aliases and a history mechanism for interactive use. The Korn shell is still not generally distributed to binary licensees. Some vendors have ported it to various UNIX systems, such as XENIX, and are licensing it. You can purchase the source code for several thousand dollars from AT&T.

Update the Password File

The next step is to add the new account entry to the password file. You'll need superuser privilege to do this, since only the superuser should be able to write to this file. Change to the **/etc** directory to avoid typing full pathnames. Then try to create a directory named **ptmp**. The presence of the **/etc/ptmp** file (or directory) prevents another user from changing their password while you're editing the password file. And if **/etc/ptmp** already exists because someone is changing their password, you won't be able to create the directory with the same name.

Before editing the password file, create a backup copy just in case you mess up the original. You could call the duplicate **opasswd**, which is the name the **passwd** command uses for its backup copy. After you've finished editing **passwd** remove **ptmp**. Figure 2.14 shows these steps.

Figure 2.14 Adding an entry to the password file.

```
# cd /etc
# mkdir ptmp
# cp passwd opasswd
# [ edit password file ]
# rmdir ptmp
# □
```

If you're adding a user account entry, you'll probably append it to the end of the password file. In any case it's a good idea to keep the password file entries sorted in user-id order. This way system accounts occur at the beginning, separated from the users accounts, which would be at the end of the file.

System V provides the **pwck** command for checking the password file entries for inconsistencies. It validates the number of fields, account name, user- and group-id, and whether the home directory and startup program exist. Part a of Figure 2.15 shows the general command line syntax for using **pwck** and part b shows an example. Here *filename* could be any copy of the password file, or **/etc/passwd** will be used if no file argument is named.

Figure 2.15 Using the **pwck** command.

a. General command line format:

/etc/pwck [*filename*]

b. Sample usage:

```
# /etc/pwck

rje:**NO-LOGIN**:68:8:0000-rje(0000):/usr/rje:
        Login directory not found

beccat:Lp/InNt97ecc4:100:100:Becca Thomas:/usr2/beccat:/bin/csh
        Optional shell file not found

guest:vIeMHHqytTacw:104:200:/usr2/guest:/bin/srh
        Too many/few fields
# □
```

Here, there's no home (log-in) directory for the **rje** account. This account was never set up, but the password file entry was supplied by the UNIX system vendor. The pathname for the **beccat** account startup program isn't correct—the C shell isn't in the **/bin** directory on this system. Finally, **pwck** notes that the entry for the **guest** account has the wrong number of fields—it doesn't bother to check validity of the fields—note the typo in the startup program.

Install a Password

Most UNIX accounts should have a password. A possible exception is a system-related account that runs a dedicated command that doesn't have a shell escape, such as **/bin/sync**. Otherwise, accounts without a password are a security hazard.

We've seen UNIX systems that have system accounts, which are used for file ownership and not intended for system access, without a password. Since these accounts generally leave the startup program field blank—anyone could log into such an account and get a Bourne shell with the privileged access of the account! For instance, if the **bin** account is set up this way, an unauthorized user could have easy access to any file on the UNIX system owned by **bin**—that is, most of the commands and perhaps the command directories, too.

Some administrators leave the password field blank after creating a user account so that the new user can install a password. This approach isn't safe, as an unauthorized user could gain access before the password was installed. Leaving the password blank, but enabling password aging, to force the new user to supply a password, isn't any better. An unauthorized user could choose a password, then have access to the system, and furthermore even "lock out" the legitimate user of this account.

We recommend that you install a password and communicate it verbally (don't write it down) to the person authorized to use the account. Passwords should be chosen with care. They should be hard to guess, but easy to remember, like a clever "vanity" automobile license plate. The System V **passwd** command imposes some requirements on password selection, such as requiring a minimum of six characters with at least two alphabetic characters and one numeric or special character.

Update the Group File

You assign an account membership in a default group using the *group-id* field of the password file. Additional (potential) group memberships require adding the new account name to the list of account names of the appropriate group(s) in the group file. *Note*: It's redundant (but a good bookkeeping practice) to add the new account name to the group file account name list for the default group—the password file entry is sufficient.

You may even need to create an entirely new group for the new account, which could be done by defining a new default group in the password file. You still need to add the group to the group file, if you wish to associate a name with the new group or allow other accounts to become members of the new group. As with the password file, you can use any text editor to update the group file. But you'll need superuser privilege since **/etc/group** is read-only for all users.

Groups provide another way for unauthorized users to gain access to your system. If an account doesn't require file access to a group, you should assign it a group-id number that's not used by any other account.

System V provides a **grpck** command for verifying all entries in the group file. It checks the number of fields, group name, group-id numbers, and whether any names in the *account names* field appear in the password file. Part a of Figure 2.16 shows the general command line syntax for using **grpck** and part b shows an example. Here *filename* could be any copy of the group file, or **/etc/group** will be used if no file argument is named.

Figure 2.16 Using the **grpck** command.

a. General command line format:

/etc/grpck [*filename*]

b. Sample usage:

```
# /etc/grpck

rje:*VOID*:8
        Too many/few fields


daemon:*VOID*:12:
        Null login name


users::100:donna
        donna - Logname not found in password file
#
```

Here the **rje** group entry has too few fields—there should be a colon after the group-id number. The next message is a warning, not an error, since a group can exist without placing any names in the *account name* field. The last example shows a case where the account for **donna** was removed from the password file, but not from the group file.

Create a Home Directory

Change to the parent directory for the desired home directory. Create the new home directory with the **mkdir** command. Because the directory will then be owned by **root** and have the superuser's group association, you'll need to change individual and group ownership to that for the new account to allow the new user to create files in their work area. You use the **chown** (change owner) and **chgrp** (change group) commands to accomplish this. Figure 2.17 shows that the syntax for both commands is similar.

Figure 2.17 General syntax for using the **chown** and **chgrp** commands.

chown *newowner file...*
chgrp *newgroup file...*

Figure 2.18 shows the steps for creating a home directory and changing ownership for a typical user account. This example assumes that the home directory name matches the log-in name—the typical case. After changing ownership you'll need to make sure that the permissions on the new directory are appropriate—mode 755 is a typical value.

Figure 2.18 Creating a new home directory.

```
# cd /usr2
# mkdir billp
# chown billp billp
# chgrp users billp
# chmod 755 billp
# □
```

Customizing the Working Environment

Customizing the working environment is optional in one sense because the startup shell program provides an initial working environment. However, it's a minimal "bare-bones" environment and in practice you'll probably need to enhance and customize it for the particular needs of the new account.

You learned about the shell environment earlier in the section "The Working Environment." Initializing or changing shell variables is one way to customize your environment. You might add other commands to set up the account appropriately. One important command would be **stty**, which sets up low-level parameters for the new user to communicate with their terminal. Another one might be **umask**, to set the user file creation mask to a value that restricts access to newly created files. See a UNIX user guide for more information about these commands.

In this section we discuss how you provide a custom environment automatically for your users. The details depend on the shell that's used for the startup program, but the general principle is the same for most shells: Edit the shell startup files to add commands that you want. We'll discuss these files for the popular Bourne, C, and Korn shells. As an example, you might add C and Korn shell aliases and Bourne or Korn shell functions that make navigating around the UNIX system easier for less experienced users.

The Bourne Shell Startup Files.   When the Bourne shell starts up, it executes commands in two files. First, it runs commands in **/etc/profile**, then those in a file named **.profile** that occurs in the home directory of the account. The commands in **/etc/profile** customize all accounts on the system that use the Bourne shell as the startup program; **.profile** customizes the individual account in whose home directory it occurs. A directive in **.profile**, you'll be glad to hear, overrides those in **/etc/profile**. Table 2.2 is a table summarizing the Bourne shell startup files.

TABLE 2.2 SUMMARY CHART OF THE TWO BOURNE SHELL STARTUP FILES

/etc/profile	**/usr2/santa/.profile**
Read first after log-in. Use for customizing all accounts on your system.	Read second after log-in. Use for customizing a particular account.
`TZ=PST8PST; export TZ` `cat /etc/motd`	`TERM=tvi950; export TERM` `stty erase '^h'`

Guidelines for the functionality you might specify in the Bourne shell startup files are listed in Table 2.3.

TABLE 2.3 COMMANDS APPROPRIATE FOR THE BOURNE SHELL STARTUP FILES

- Changing terminal modes with **stty**.
- Setting an appropriate file creation mask with **umask**.
- Resetting the command search path by reinitializing **PATH**.
- Resetting the shell prompt, by changing **PS1**, and perhaps **PS2**.
- Setting the terminal type by initializing the **TERM** environment variable.
- Setting the time zone by initializing the **TZ** environment variable. Generally, do this in **/etc/profile** for general system use. Some application programs may need particular environment variables.
- Setting other shell variables and placing them in the environment.
- Display System V.2 shell function and local variable definitions with the **set** command.
- Display environment variable definitions with the **env** command.
- Record and display your current log-in time and previous log-in time to make sure that the account wasn't used unexpectedly.
- Display system status information, such as who is on the system with the **who** command, or all processes currently running with **ps −ef**.

Part a of Figure 2.19 shows a typical **/etc/profile** file and part b a **.profile** file example.

Figure 2.19 Sample Bourne shell startup files.

a. A sample **/etc/profile** file:

```
trap "" 1 2 3              # trap SIGHUP, SIGINT, and SIGQUIT signals
TZ=PST8PDT                 # set the time zone
export TZ                  # mark variable for export
cat /etc/motd              # display message of the day
if mail -e; then           # if there's mail
     echo "you have mail"  # say so
fi
trap : 1 2 3               # reset signals
```

b. A sample **.profile** file:

```
stty erase '^h' kill '^x'                 # set erase and line kill
stty intr '^c' quit '^u'                  # set interrupt and quit chars
umask 077                                 # set file creation mask
MAILPATH=/usr/mail/$LOGNAME:/etc/motd     # set mail path
PATH=/bin:/usr/bin:/usr/lbin              # command search path
TERM=adm3a                                # a hardwired terminal
export MAILPATH PATH TERM                 # mark for the environment
```

The Korn Shell Startup Files.   Like the Bourne shell, the Korn shell reads and runs commands in the **/etc/profile** and the **.profile** file in the user's home directory. Just as with the Bourne shell, you can place commands to customize the environment of all accounts in **/etc/profile**.

And you can define environment variables in the **.profile** file for export to the execution environment of the Korn shell. Most important, you'll define **ENV**, which is the pathname of the Korn shell-specific startup file, which we'll call the **ENV** file. Generally, users elect to use a pathname like **$HOME/.kshrc** for this file, but any pathname in their account directory tree could be used.

The **ENV** file contains commands for setting up the execution environment of the Korn shell. Now the question becomes: Which definitions and commands do I put in **.profile** and which in the **ENV** file? Of course, commands and definitions that are recognized only by the Korn shell would be put in the **ENV** file.

If you only use the Korn shell as your startup program, you might as well place all the commands in one place, namely the **ENV** file. Part a of Figure 2.20 shows a minimal **.profile** and part c illustrates an accompanying **ENV** file.

But you could elect to use the Bourne shell as the startup program and then "exec" the Korn shell from **.profile**. In this case the Bourne shell would read both the **/etc/profile** and **.profile** startup files to get environment information and the Korn shell would follow directions in the **ENV** file. Part b of Figure 2.20 shows a minimal **.profile** for invoking the Korn shell. And the **ENV** file in part c is still appropriate for this case.

Figure 2.20 The Korn shell startup files.

a. A **.profile** file that defines the **ENV** file:

```
ENV=$HOME/.kshrc         # Korn shell-specific startup file
export ENV               # mark for the environment
```

b. A **.profile** file that invokes the Korn shell after defining the **ENV** file:

```
ENV=$HOME/.kshrc         # Korn shell-specific startup file
export ENV               # mark for the environment
exec /usr/lbin/ksh       # invoke the Korn shell
```

c. A typical Korn shell **ENV** startup file:

```
# Commands to set environment
stty erase '^h' kill '^x'        # set erase and line kill
stty intr '^c' quit '^u'         # set interrupt and quit chars
umask 077                        # set file creation mask
# Environment variables:
CDPATH=.:$HOME:$HOME/Book        # directory list for cd
```

```
EDITOR=/usr/bin/vi                  # editor for history list
HISTSIZE=200                        # size of history list
PS1='${PWD}) '                      # primary prompt
SHELL=/usr/1bin/ksh                 # use Korn subshells
TERM=adm3a                          # a hardwired terminal
# Korn shell specific settings:
set -o allexport                    # export all variables
set -o monitor                      # monitor background jobs
set -o trackall                     # create full pathname aliases
# Define some aliases:
alias bye='tput clear;exit'         # clear screen and log out
alias h='fc -1 '                    # display history list
# Define functions:
function expr {                     # replacement for expr
    integer result                  # local integer variable
    let result="$*"                 # do arithmetic
    echo $result                    # output result
}
```

We discuss the Korn shell environment variables in Appendix A. The **set −o allexport** command exports all variable definitions to the environment so that you don't have to use **export**. The **set −o monitor** directive causes the Korn shell to show progress of background tasks. The **set −o trackall** command causes the Korn shell to store the full pathnames of commands it runs so that they can be invoked more quickly the next time. We show a couple of "alias" definitions and one "function" definition. You should refer to the Bibliography for works that discuss the powerful Korn shell in more depth.

The C Shell Startup Files.   Commands in the **.login** and **.cshrc** startup files are executed when you log into an account that runs the C shell as the startup program. These files must be located in the home directory for the account. First it executes commands in **.cshrc**; then it executes those in **.login**. The execution order **.cshrc**, then **.login**, is counterintuitive from the names. Additionally, commands in **.cshrc**, but not those in **.login**, execute *each time* you start up a C shell.

Some UNIX implementations, such as XENIX, have modified the C shell so that it recognizes a general system-wide startup file **/etc/cshrc** (analogous to the **/etc/profile** file for the Bourne shell). This file is not standard, but if available on your system, **/etc/cshrc** would be a convenient location for customizing the C shell for general system purposes, such as setting the time zone environment variable, **TZ**. The C shell first runs **/etc/cshrc** and then **.cshrc**, so definitions in the latter can override those in the former.

Table 2.4 summarizes the role of the three startup files recognized by the C shell and provides sample commands appropriate for each file.

TABLE 2.4 SUMMARY CHART OF THE THREE C SHELL STARTUP FILES

/etc/cshrc	/usr2/santa/.cshrc	/usr2/santa/.login
Read first after log-in. Use for system-wide variables. Not recognized on all systems.	Read second after log-in and each time a subshell is started up.	Read third after log-in. Use for commands that need to be executed once.
`setenv TZ PST8PST` `cat /etc/motd`	`set history = 500` `alias h 'history¦tail -22'`	`setenv TERM tvi950` `stty erase '^h'`

Place commands you'd want to execute only once during each session, such as setting the terminal with **stty**, in **.login**. Most other commands for customizing the C shell are placed in **.cshrc**, such as defining command aliases and enabling the history function. Also, you might wish to define a different prompt for a subshell than the startup shell. Figures 2.21 and 2.22 show sample **.login** and **.cshrc** files. If you use the **.login** file shown, create **.login_time** first.

Figure 2.21 A sample **.login** file.

```
# .login csh script (last updated: 08/22/86)
# Customize using programs:
stty intr '^c' erase '^h' kill '^x' quit '^u' echoe
umask 022
# Set environment variables:
setenv JOBNO ON
setenv TERM ansi
setenv TZ PST8PDT
# Set other variables:
set prompt = "$LOGNAME \!) "
# Display and record log-in time:
echo "Your previous log-in time was: `cat .login_time`"
echo "Your current  log-in time  is: `date¦tee .login_time`"
```

Figure 2.22 A sample **.cshrc** file.

```
# .cshrc (last updated: 08/22/86)
# Set local variables:
set history = 20
```

```
set ignoreeof
set noclobber
set prompt = "$LOGNAME \!)) "
set time = 10
# Set wordlist variables:
set cdpath = (. ~ ~/Letters ~/Vendors ~/Clients)
set mail = (/usr/mail/$LOGNAME 3600 /etc/motd)
# Define aliases:
alias cd        'cd \!*;dirs;ls'
alias ls        "ls -CF"
alias pwd       'echo $cwd'
alias rm        "rm -i"
```

After you've installed the shell startup files, you'll need to change their ownership to the account owner if you want the new account user to edit them. Note that execute permission is not necessary. Figure 2.23 shows some examples. Part a is for the Bourne shell startup file and part b the C shell startup files. As a system administrator, you'll need to find or create prototype startup files. We placed them in **/usr/lib** for this example.

Figure 2.23 Installing shell startup files.

a. For the Bourne shell:

```
# cp /usr/lib/.profile /usr2/billp/.profile
# cd /usr2/billp
# chown billp .profile
# chgrp users .profile
# chmod 600 .profile
# □
```

b. For the C shell:

```
# cp /usr/lib/.login /usr2/billp/.login
# cp /usr/lib/.cshrc /usr2/billp/.cshrc
# cd /usr2/billp
# chown billp .login .cshrc
# chgrp users .login .cshrc
# chmod 600 .login .cshrc
# □
```

Changing an Account

Occasionally, you may have need to change an old account so that it can be used by a different person. You'll want to change the account name in both the password and group files. Also change the contents of the comment field in the password file. The files owned by the old account may be left on the system as is since the ownership is determined by the user-id and group-ids, which the new user will inherit.

REMOVING AN ACCOUNT

In this section we recommend a method for removing an account from your system. Suppose that a user leaves your installation or migrates to another system at your site. You'll either assign their account to another user or remove it. Also, but less likely, you might wish to remove a system account that's no longer needed.

Generally, you wouldn't want to erase the user account entry from the **/etc/passwd** file, but "deactivate" it. Suppose that you did erase the account entry. Then that user-id might well be assigned to another user. And then, files owned by the old user that were restored from a backup tape would be owned by the new user. Your best bet is to deactivate the account until you are certain that all backup tapes containing the files of the former user have been recycled.

Figure 2.24 shows four steps for deactivating an account on your system. Generally, they are the reverse of the steps used for adding an account, except that files are archived before their removal and the password entry "deactivated," but not removed.

Figure 2.24 Four steps for deactivating an account.

- Place an invalid password in password file.
- Remove the account name from group file.
- Back up files owned by the account.
- Erase files the files on the working disk that were archived.

Update the Password File

Log in as superuser and then use the steps for updating the password file shown in Figure 2.14. Edit **/etc/passwd**, placing an invalid password in the encrypted password field for the account. For instance, you could place the date that the account was deactivated here. The "password" shown below is invalid because it contains fewer than 13 characters, and also because it contains the asterisk (*) character, which never occurs in valid passwords. Figure 2.25 shows an example.

Figure 2.25 A deactivated account entry.

```
billp:**08/26/86**:103:100:Bill Potts:/usr2/billp:/bin/sh
```

Also, you might move the deactivated account entry to the end of the password file. In this way, UNIX system programs that scan the password file won't spend extra time searching through inactive accounts to locate active ones. After about six months or so you could remove the old account entry completely and "recycle" the user-id for a new account.

Update the Group File

You can completely delete the account name from entries in the group file. If the group-id number is unique, you would have to maintain it in the group file as a "placeholder" on the system. This step ensures that files remaining or restored to the system can't be shared between the deactivated account and any active ones.

Archive Files

The next step is to back up any files owned by the old account. Figure 2.26 shows an example for doing so.

Figure 2.26 Archiving files used by the old account.

```
# NAME=billp
# find / -user $NAME -print > /tmp/${NAME}files
# cat /tmp/${NAME}files | cpio -ocvB >/dev/rmt/0m
# lp /tmp/${NAME}files
# □
```

Here you set the **NAME** variable to the old account name. Then you use the **find** command shown above to locate all files on the system owned by the account. Store this list in a file. You could print this list for a hard-copy record. The next command line backs up the files using "cpio" format.

Remove the Files

Now you're ready to dispose of the files that you backed up. You can start with the list of files created in Figure 2.26. Move files (with **rm**) on this list you wish to keep on the system disk either to a spare partition, say **/Using**, or to another user account. Then edit the file list, deleting names of files you decided to keep on the system. Then you can use the two **rm** command lines shown in Figure 2.27 to actually remove the remaining files from the system. Here we've set **HDIR** to be the home directory of the old account. The first **rm** command removes the home directory tree of the old account, and the second removes all other files (listed in **/tmp/${NAME}files**) on the system owned by the old account.

Figure 2.27 Removing the files owned by the deactivated account.

```
# HDIR=/usr2/billp
# rm -fr $HDIR
# grep -v $HDIR /tmp/${NAME}files | xargs rm -fr
# rm /tmp/${NAME}files
# □
```

The **xargs** command combines **rm** **—fr** with arguments read from the pipeline to execute **rm** as long as there are file names piped to **xargs**.

HELPFUL UTILITIES FOR ACCOUNT MANAGEMENT

Appendix C lists two utilities you should find helpful for account management. The **finger** program displays information in the comment field of the password file for one or more account names. The **newuser** shell script automates adding a user account.

QUICK REFERENCE GUIDE

This section lists some procedures in summary form for your reference.

Steps for Adding an Account

- Select contents for fields of the password file.
- Update the password file.
- Install a password.
- Update the group file.
- Create a home directory with the correct ownership.
- Customize the working environment.

Steps for Deactivating an Account

- Place an invalid password in password file.
- Remove the account name from group file.
- Back up files owned by the account.
- Erase the files on the working disk that were archived.

3

File System Backup

INTRODUCTION TO BACKUP STRATEGIES

You arrive at work Monday morning and your boss wants to see you urgently. She says that she lost a valuable file while working over the weekend. Could you restore it in time for the 10 A.M. weekly planning meeting? No problem, you say. You did a backup of the user file system last Friday before leaving work. You check the table of contents—sure enough, the file was saved. So you restore it in a few minutes. Your boss still has time before the meeting to add the few changes that were lost. Furthermore, she sees that you're a competent system administrator.

Another scenario. There was a sudden power surge that crashed your hard disk. You realize that you can't boot the system. So you format the disk, mount the distribution tape, and restore the UNIX system. Then you take your last full system backup and add all those files. Finally, you restore any files added or changed since the last full monthly backup from your weekly partial and daily incremental backups. And your company is back in business with minimal fuss. Whew! Thank goodness you had all the backups you needed—but what if you didn't?

Incidents like these happen all too often. You should be prepared for any event—from the loss of a single file to the destruction of your entire working disk—at any time. You can be prepared if you are backing up your system regularly. In this chapter you'll learn about backup schemes that work for any size system—from microcomputers to mainframes. First we discuss backup strategies and common backup media, then how to back up your system with the **dd**, **tar**, **cpio**, and **volcopy** utilities commonly available on System V.

What Is a Backup?

Information is stored on your computer system in files. These files stand ready and waiting for you on your working hard disk. However, you need to keep duplicate copies of these files elsewhere—on reliable external media. These copies are your *backups*. You *back up* a file so that you can *restore* it if the copy on the working disk gets lost, corrupted, or otherwise unusable. If your system is backed up properly you can restore any file or the entire contents of your working disk completely.

We'll often use the term "tape" to refer to any backup media, whether it be nine-track or cartridge tape, removable disk packs, or floppy disks. So, mentally substitute your particular medium for the word "tape" while reading this chapter.

Types of Backups

Data are generally written to a backup tape in one of two formats—file-by-file or image copy. As we'll see later, the **tar** and **cpio** utilities write the data file-by-file, whereas the **dd** and **volcopy** programs create a byte-for-byte image copy of the working disk. File-by-file data are written more slowly, but file restoration is easier. Conversely, image data are written more quickly, but restoration of individual files take more than one step and thus more time.

We'll also divide backups into other categories that reflect the amount of data archived. A *full backup* is a copy of your entire working disk, which includes the root file system and any other file systems you may have. Of course, this is the safest (most complete) backup approach, but is also the most time and media consuming. Luckily, you don't have to back up your entire disk on a daily basis if you supplement your last full backup with other, less extensive ones.

A *partial backup* is a complete copy of any given file system or a directory tree, such as **/usr**. And on systems with smaller disks (say, 5 or 10 megabytes), one file system could take up the entire disk. Larger disks generally contain more than one file system.

When making a partial backup you should include any system configuration files that occur on the root file system if you're not backing up that file system. You'd do partial backups of the file systems or directory trees that change most frequently, such as those containing your user account files, on a regular basis.

An *incremental backup* is a copy of files that have been added or changed since a particular time—generally since the last backup. These backups are generally quick and take less media. However, they do have their drawbacks. For instance, it may be difficult to locate a particular file in a series of incremental backups. For this reason you'll need to keep a table of contents of the files contained in each incremental backup.

The Ideal Backup

Now that we have some of the terminology out of the way let's look at some of the characteristics of an ideal backup scheme.

Easy to Use. Ideally, backing up files should be so easy that you don't have to think about it. Just mount a tape or insert a floppy and type one word. That's the goal.

Would you bother to do a backup late Friday afternoon before leaving for an exciting weekend if you had to spend an hour fussing with UNIX commands and files? Probably not. What would happen Monday morning when your boss wanted that file she lost over the weekend? Oops. Time to find another job.

So make backing up simple and painless. How do you do that? You design shell scripts that drive the necessary backup utility programs. These scripts can also decide which files you should back up. You'll see several examples of such shell script fragments in this chapter. Most are not complete applications (that's why we call them fragments) because they lack error detection and recovery. But they do show you how to encapsulate the backup utilities. You can take these sample shell scripts and customize them for your own particular needs.

Minimal Time. You'll want to design a backup scheme that minimizes the operator, real, and CPU time to do the backup operation or restore the files to your working disk. However, generally there's a trade-off involved here. Often, a simple quick-and-dirty backup scheme means a lengthly restoration process. Most likely you'll be backing up files more frequently than you'll be restoring them. You hope.

Labeling of Backups. You should use a consistent labeling scheme for identifying your backup tapes. Probably one of the most frustrating experiences is trying to find a file in a pile of poorly labeled tapes.

Verification of Backups. Don't wait until you need to restore a file to see if backups are good. What is needed is an automated procedure, like "read after write" verification, to check that backups are readable. That is, you should be able to read any file on the backup medium after writing it.

One technique would be to restore the last file on a backup tape, then compare it to the copy on the working disk. Restoring the last file is generally the most rigorous test, since you have to read to the end of the data on the tape to access it. Thus, you test the readability of the entire tape. Alternatively, as a minimum, you should be able to list the table of contents of the backup media for a file-by-file backup.

Tolerance of Media Failure. You need to have more than one backup copy of important data because your backup medium itself may get damaged. And for "disaster recovery" you really need to keep a copy off-site. Some institutions, such as banks and the government, require off-site storage of backups just in case the computer room or tape vault is destroyed.

You should retire old media (before they wear out) into permanent archives that can be kept "forever." Then use new media to do your regular backups.

Easy Restoration of Files.   When restoring files, the file pathname or name of the file system should be enough information to restore the file or file system. The file should be easy to locate on the backup medium.

Utilities that make image copies save entire file systems, not individual files. If you use such utilities, you'll need an easy way to restore individual files, not just file systems. For example, you restore the file system onto a spare disk partition and copy individual files onto your working partitions.

Portability of Backups.   If you ever need to restore your files onto a different computer system, you'll need portable backups. Perhaps your system is down and you need to continue working on another system. If you have many different systems at your facility, you'll want portable backups so that they can be moved around with ease.

Binary data generally aren't portable between different machine architectures. For instance, the lengths and byte order of integers may be different. Be aware that some backup utilities create table of contents header information in binary format to save space (but only a few bytes, generally). However, if the same information is written in ASCII character format, it will be portable.

How to Do Backup and Restoration

Let's consider some general guidelines for backing up and restoring your files.

When to Do Backups.   Ideally, you want to back up and restore when the file system is quiescent—not being used for anything else. This situation is always the case during single-user mode. In practice, though, you may not be able to bring the system down to single-user mode for backing up or restoring files.

Just be aware that files that change could corrupt your backup. For instance, if you were backing up a large database when a user was updating it, the associated index file may not point to the correct data. So at least attempt to back up when system activity is at a minimum. Get the cooperation of your users either by requesting a pause in their activities, or by having the affected users log out or quit working on files until the backups are done.

Techniques for Backups.   The techniques to use for backing up and restoring files depend on your hardware (disk and tape) configuration. Later, as we cover the backup utilities, we'll discuss the three common system configurations— floppy-based systems, cartridge tape or removable disk pack-based systems, and reel-to-reel tape systems.

If you're working in a facility with a number of machines, you may backup over the network. You might designate one machine on this network as the *backup server*. It would be the common destination for all backups and would have the necessary tape drives for archiving the data.

It's important to label your backup medium clearly. You should note items such as date, type of backup, blocking factor, file system, or provide a list of files. For tape, specify the density, reel number, etc. Also specify the format if the backup medium is formatted.

How Often to Do Backups.   Several factors dictate how often you should back up. You should back up more frequently if your system has a lot of file system activity.   For instance, if your site does a lot of data entry, you may wish to back up data entered that morning at lunch time and data entered in the afternoon at closing time.

The more valuable the data, the more often you should back up. If you can't afford the time to recreate the data or if it's not possible, then you should back up more often.

We can't give a pat recipe for how often to back up your system—your particular requirements will dictate that.   However, we would recommend that you do incremental backups every day, partial backups weekly, and a full system backup every month.   You may need to back up more or less often according to your specific needs.

Restoring Files.   We want to caution you when restoring files.   Be careful not to overwrite more recent files or file systems with older versions during the restoration.   For instance, if you need to retrieve individual files from an entire file system, you should restore the file system onto a *spare* disk partition and copy over the files that are missing or corrupted.   If you restore the entire file system to its original partition you may overwrite more recent files with older files.

Backup Media

The backup medium you use on your system largely determines the appropriate backup method.   Let's look at each type of common media in turn.

Floppy Diskette.   Five-and-one-quarter-inch floppy drives are common on smaller computer systems because of their low cost, generally only a few hundred dollars.   However, the cost per megabyte of storage is high.   As an estimate, assume that a high-quality 360-kilobyte-capacity diskette costs about $2; then the storage costs over $5 per megabyte. If you purchase premium-quality diskettes that can store 1.2 megabytes (on the IBM PC/AT) at $5, the cost drops to just over $4 per megabyte.   Still high compared to tape media, as we'll see below.

Floppy drives are slow.   And backups using them are the slowest and least convenient of techniques.   You have to feed diskettes one at a time, so substantial backups require considerable operator time.

Floppy diskette formats are generally not the same from one manufacturer to the next.   Thus, backups made on one machine type are generally not portable to another.   The 360-kilobyte and 1.2-megabyte IBM PC formats could be considered de facto standards since so many IBM personal computers use them.   However, other manufacturers generally have their own proprietary formats that are incompatible.

Reel-to-Reel Tape.   This medium is on the other end of the spectrum from floppy disks. One-half-inch nine-track tape uses different industry standard formats depending on the density—NRZI for 800 bpi (bits per inch), PE for 1600 bpi, and GCR for 6250 bpi. The 1600-bpi format is by far the most common on UNIX-based machines. Thus, backups made on this medium are generally portable from one machine to another.

However, the tape drives are moderately expensive, with the inexpensive units starting at about $4,000. Generally, they cost $10,000 and up, so they come as standard equipment only with larger supermicro-, mini-, and mainframe computers. But you can purchase drives that interface to smaller machines—even personal computers. Here the cost per megabyte of storage is low. A 2400-foot tape can store about 45 megabytes at 1600 bpi. If the tape costs about $25, then the storage cost is about 50 cents per megabyte.

Because backups using reel-to-reel tape are fast, they minimize operator time. They usually require no operator intervention except for loading and unloading the tape. Often you must thread the tape manually through the mechanism, although some drives will auto-load the tape.

The drives can either move the tape from reel to reel in a start/stop or streaming mode. With the older start/stop technology, the motors start up the tape, the data are transferred, and brakes stop the tape. A streaming drive moves the tape continuously past the read/write mechanism at constant speed. If the tape has moved too far, the drive can back it up to the correct spot. However, if the system can keep the tape moving, the streaming tape is considerably faster than the start/stop drive.

Cartridge Tape.   Cartridge tape systems steer the middle ground—they are a compromise between floppy and reel-to-reel systems. The drives are less expensive than reel-to-reel drives, usually $1000 to $3000. Thus, you often see these drives as standard equipment on medium-sized machines, supermicros, especially. These drives come in both start/stop and streamer models.

The cost per megabyte of storage is low. For instance, a 450-foot tape recorded at 6400 bpi costs about $35 to give a storage cost of about $1 per megabyte—much less than floppy diskettes and only about twice that of reel-to-reel tape.

Cartridge tapes come in three widths—0.15, ¼, and ½ inch. Manufacturers use widely differing formats for cartridge tapes. However, IBM 3480 format is rapidly becoming a standard for the ½-in.-tape.

Disk Packs.   Removable disk packs most often appear on larger minicomputers. However, they are becoming extinct—especially as nine-track tape systems come down in price. The drives are more expensive than self-contained fixed disks (so-called Winchester disks), and the disk packs themselves are not cheap, either.

They range from about $400 to $500 for a five-platter pack, which can store 50 to 80 megabytes, to $1000 dollars for a 12-platter pack, which stores from 100 to 300 megabytes. Thus the storage cost is moderately high—ranging from about $4 to $10 per megabyte.

The drives back up fast and the disk packs easily remove from the drive in a few seconds. Thus backing up to this type of medium minimizes operator time.

Summary Table.   Table 3.1 tabulates in summary form some of the costs discussed above. Of course, these prices will change, but they do give you an idea of the relative costs of the different media.

TABLE 3.1 A SUMMARY OF MEDIA COSTS

Medium	Unit Cost (dollars)	Capacity (megabytes)	Storage Cost (dollars/megabyte)	Relative Speed
Floppy disks (low capacity)	2	0.36	5.55	slowest
Floppy disks (high capacity)	5	1.20	4.17	slow
Nine-track tape (2400 ft, 1600 bpi)	25	45.00	0.56	fast
Cartridge Tape (450 ft, 6400 bpi)	35	34.50	1.01	fast
Disk Packs (5-platter)	400	80.00	5.00	very fast
Disk Packs (12-platter)	1000	300.00	3.33	fastest

BACKING UP WITH dd

You'll find the **dd** program useful for making an *image copy* of any media. An image copy is an exact byte-for-byte copy. You can duplicate tapes, disk partitions (or entire disks), and floppy diskettes quickly and easily with this utility.

Figure 3.1 shows the general command line syntax for using **dd**.

Figure 3.1 General command line syntax for **dd**.

dd [**if** = *input-file*] [**of** = *output-file*] [*option* = *value*]

The **dd** command line consists of a sequence of *option* = *value* pairs. The **if** = and **of** = keys are used to designate specific input and output files, respectively. If

if = *input-file* is omitted, input for **dd** is taken from its standard input file. Similarly, if **of** = *output-file* is omitted, output from **dd** is sent to its standard output file. Several *option* = *value* pairs may follow on the command line to specify buffer sizes, starting offsets, transfer block counts, and data conversions.

Copying a Boot Partition.   Figure 3.2 shows a sample command line for using **dd** to back up a boot partition from one device to another.

Figure 3.2 Using **dd** to back up a boot partition.

```
$ dd if=/dev/boot0 of=/dev/boot1 bs=152b count=4
4+0 records in
4+0 records out
$ □
```

Here, **if** = **/dev/boot0** specifies partition **/dev/boot0** as the *input file* and **of** = **/dev/boot1** names partition **/dev/boot1** as the *output file*. The **bs** = **152b** directive says to use 152 (512-byte) blocks as the record size (for both the input and output file). The last argument, **count** = **4**, means to transfer four records of that size ($4 \times 152 \times 512 = 311,296$ characters in all). After completion, **dd** reports the number of full and partial records input and output, four full records of 152×512 bytes in both cases.

Copying a Tape Volume.   Figure 3.3 shows a command line for duplicating a tape using **dd** to copy the contents of one tape from one tape device to another. Of course, this approach requires two tape drives, one for the source and one for the destination tape.

Figure 3.3 Using **dd** to copy a tape volume.

```
# dd if=/dev/rmt/0m of=/dev/rmt/1m
```

Note the use of the raw (character interface) devices for the input and output devices. Duplications are generally faster with the raw device compared to the block device.

Backing Up Your Boot Diskette.   Many floppy-based systems offer a boot diskette from which you can boot the operating system. This boot floppy may also contain a minimal set of utilities, such as a shell and file system check program. After booting from the floppy, you load the rest of the system onto your hard disk.

This floppy may be useful if you can't bring up your system from the hard disk. For instance, let's say that one of the vital programs, such as the kernel, Bourne shell, or **/etc/init**, was lost or corrupted. You'd boot from the floppy, restore the lost file, then reboot from the hard disk.

Conventional utilities used for backing up files and file systems can't duplicate your boot diskette. However, the **dd** command, which can make an exact copy of any device file, can. Of course, **dd** can be used to make a copy of *any* diskette.

Figure 3.4 shows one approach for backing up your boot floppy with **dd**. Note that only one floppy drive is needed. Make sure that the floppy is formatted before you begin. Since **dd** copies everything, including blank space, you'll need enough space on your working hard disk to accommodate the entire image of your floppy diskette—generally 360 kilobytes or 1.2 megabytes, depending on the drive capacity and diskette format.

Figure 3.4 Backing up your boot floppy with **dd**.

```
# dd if=/dev/floppy of=/tmp/floppy
360+0 records in
360+0 records out
# ls -l /tmp/floppy
-rw-r--r--   1 root       sys       368640 Sep 25 11:16 /tmp/floppy
[ remove original floppy and insert a formatted one ]
# dd if=/tmp/floppy of=/dev/floppy
360+0 records in
360+0 records out
# rm /tmp/floppy
# □
```

The first **dd** command line copies the contents of the floppy device to a temporary file, **/tmp/floppy**. This version of **dd** calls the input and output statistics records instead of blocks—the same thing. 360+0 means 360 full and 0 partial records (1-kilobyte blocks). The long listing of the temporary file shows that it contains 368,640 characters, which corresponds to 360 1-kilobyte blocks. After you copy the floppy contents onto the hard disk, remove the floppy from the drive and insert a blank formatted floppy. The second **dd** command copies the contents of the temporary file to diskette. Finally, the temporary file is removed when you're done making the copy.

Speeding Up dd

You can speed up the copy process significantly if you tell **dd** to use blocking. Figure 3.5 shows a comparison of the speed without then, with optimal blocking (defined using **bs = 9k**). Here we're reading the floppy and discarding the result by writing to the "null" device, **/dev/null**. The UNIX **time** program reports the time spent in user mode, kernel mode, and the total time spent in execution of the command. Note the dramatic difference.

Figure 3.5 Speeding up **dd** with blocking.

```
# time dd if=/dev/fd048ds9 of=/dev/null
360+0 records in
360+0 records out
0.4u 3.7s 1:40 3%
# time dd if=/dev/rfd048ds9 of=/dev/null bs=9k
20+0 records in
20+0 records out
0.3u 0.9s 0:34 2%
# □
```

The second **dd** command is significantly faster (34 real seconds compared to over a minute and a half) because it buffers entire tracks of data at a time. Each track contains 9 kilobytes—two heads times nine 512-byte sectors per head). In this example, we used the same blocking that the XENIX **tar** command uses by default for our particular diskette. Note that for this technique to work you must use the "raw" (character) device to avoid the block I/O system. You can use this type of approach to copy any media more quickly.

Verifying Backups

You can use **dd** to verify formatted media and backups by a quick check for read errors. Instruct **dd** to read the entire backup volume. If it gets to the end without a read error, then presumably the medium or backup is good. However, as we discuss in more detail later, you might want to do more extensive tests of your backups, such as checking the table of contents of the tape against the list of files backed up or actually restore a file from the tape.

Data Conversions with dd

Besides backups, you may find **dd** useful for converting data. Some of the conversions supported include EBCDIC-to-ASCII and ASCII-to-EBCDIC codes, mapping to all lower or uppercase alphabetic characters, and swapping each pair of bytes. The latter would be useful, say, for transferring data between two machines that use 16-bit-long integers, but one has the most significant byte first and other last in the integer word.

BACKING UP AND RESTORING WITH tar

The **tar** (for tape archiver) program is generally available on most UNIX systems—whether AT&T or Berkeley derived. This program backs up data, file by file, retaining the hierarchical directory structure, so files may be restored with their original pathnames. And you may backup relative to the current directory, so files can be moved around the UNIX directory tree.

AT&T appears to be phasing out **tar** in favor of **cpio**, which was first distributed with System III. However, the POSIX (Portable Operating System for Computer Environments) standard describes a data interchange format based on both **tar** and **cpio** formats.

Every file backed up by **tar** consists of a header block, followed by one or more blocks that contain the file data. Before we delve into using **tar**, let's discuss the format of header block.

The tar Header

A 512-byte header precedes every file backed up by **tar**. This header contains identifying information necessary for recovering the file from the backup. Table 3.2 shows the structure of this header. All data are stored as printable ASCII characters with numerical quantities represented by octal numbers. Thus, the header is portable from one machine to another.

TABLE 3.2 STRUCTURE OF THE **tar** HEADER BLOCK

Field	Size (bytes)
pathname	100
permissions mode	8
user-id	8
group-id	8
file size	12
modification time	12
checksum	8
link flag	1
link pathname	100

The end of the file in a **tar** archive is padded so that it occurs on an even block boundary. Thus, as a worst case, almost two additional 512-byte blocks (one for the header and one for the trailer) can be required on your backup medium for each file archived. As a best case, only 512 bytes extra will be needed. So, figure on 768 bytes (¾ kilobytes) of padding on the average.

Guidelines for Full and Partial Backups on Diskettes with tar

In this section we discuss specifically backing up your entire working disk onto floppy diskettes using **tar**. However, the general principles covered apply to any backup medium, whether tape or disk.

You'll either need a version of **tar** that can continue the backup across a diskette boundary or you'll have to be sure that you don't overflow any given diskette. As distributed from AT&T, **tar** doesn't continue a backup across diskette boundaries. However, the XENIX version of **tar** does, and many other Unix system vendors support this feature, too. Check your system documentation on **tar** for details—generally an option would be available for telling **tar** the diskette capacity.

If your version of **tar** doesn't cross diskette boundaries, you'll need to archive groups of files that will fit on one diskette. Generally, you select directories that are small enough to fit on one complete floppy and back up the entire directory tree onto the floppy. We'll discuss this backup type after we've covered the *full* backup.

If your **tar** program does continue the backup across diskette boundaries, then follow the steps outlined in the remainder of this section. Files will be backed up in one of two ways. One, the file is split into *extents* with one extent stored on one diskette and the next part on the following diskette in a series. This way the file can be larger than the capacity of a diskette. Two, the file must reside all on a given diskette. In the latter case the file must be smaller than the diskette capacity.

Before you start backing up, find out how many diskettes are required since *they must be already formatted.* You'll first determine the space occupied by all the files on your working disk and the capacity of your backup diskette. Then you need to take into account the extra diskette space the **tar** backup requires. Once you've figured out the total blocks you need, simply divide this total by the blocks each diskette can hold to ascertain the number of diskettes you'll need.

As a simple example, let's say that you need to back up a small file system containing about 200 files that occupy 1400 (512-byte) blocks onto a diskette that can hold 720 (512-byte) blocks. At first you might think you'll only need 1400/720 = 1.9 or 2 diskettes. But you'll actually need more. Why? The **tar** program requires one extra block per file to store the identifying header. Also since **tar** writes each file to an even block boundary in the archive, you may need another block per file. Let's assume that we're using a blocking factor of 1, so additional padding at the end of the backup won't be necessary. Now, as a worst case, 200 files require 400 blocks (header and padding) in addition to the 1400 blocks for data to give 1800 blocks. So 1800/720 = 2.5 or 3 diskettes will be required to back up this small file system.

In Appendix D we discuss a more extensive example for computing the number of floppy diskettes required to back up the root file system. We show you three ways to determine the allocated disk space, and then how to sum up a number of files for the file system to be backed up. Then you'll see how to determine the capacity of your floppies. A simple division plus a "fudge factor" should give you a good estimate for the required number of floppies.

Performing a Full System Backup with tar

The basic command for backing up the entire working disk with **tar** is shown in Figure 3.6. Here the special device name of the floppy drive, **/dev/floppy**, is specified after the **f** option.

Figure 3.6 A *full* backup using **tar** onto a generic floppy device, **/dev/floppy**.

```
# cd /
# tar cvf /dev/floppy .
```

The **c** key tells **tar** to create a new backup "tape," overwriting any previously existing files. The **v** (verbose) option causes **tar** to display the name of each file on the
standard error output as it is written to the tape. In Appendix E we list all the
keys and options recognized by the System V **tar** command.

Note that we first changed to the root directory (/), then used the directory
argument, dot (for the current directory). It's best to back up files using a pathname relative to the current directory, rather than an absolute pathname (one that
begins with slash, /). If you use an absolute pathname, the files have to be restored
to their original location in the directory hierarchy—you can't restore them elsewhere.

The **tar** command will descend the file system hierarchy starting with the
directory you specify on the command line. All files and subdirectories of that
directory will be backed up. Note that directories aren't stored on the backup tape,
only ordinary files. While restoring files, **tar** will create directories as necessary.

You may wish to redirect the list of files to a disk file to have an on-line table
of contents. To do so, use **2>** *pathname* with the Bourne shell or **>&** *pathname*
with the C shell. Note that this file will also be included with your full backup.

Using Blocking to Speed Up tar.   You can significantly speed up **tar** by
using blocking. The **tar** command recognizes a **b** option for specifying a *blocking
factor*, which can range from 1 to 20 512-byte blocks. The data will be read or
written in chunks equal to this blocking factor. Specify the "raw" (character)
name for the backup device when you use blocking to avoid the UNIX block I/O
system. Figure 3.7 shows the results when backing up the same files using a blocking factor of 1 and 20, with and without the raw device.

Figure 3.7 Comparing speed using different blocking factors with the block and the character
backup floppy diskette device.

```
# time tar cvbf 1 /dev/flpa
. . .
2:14.1r  11.3u  1:31.6s
# time tar cvbf 20 /dev/flpa
. . .
4:24.0r  1.6u  4.6s
# time tar cvbf 1 /dev/rflpa
. . .
3:57.2r  0.5u  2.1s
# time tar cvbf 20 /dev/rflpa
. . .
53.8r  11.8u  11.4s
# □
```

This **time** command displays the total elapsed time ("real" time), time spent in user
mode, and time spent in kernel mode (or "system" time). The best time 53.8r, or

about 54 seconds elapsed time, was obtained using the "raw" (character) device, **/dev/rflpa**, with a blocking factor of 20. The worst time (4 min 24 sec) was obtained using the block device, **/dev/flpa**, with the same blocking factor.

Using Default Devices with tar. You can generally use a shortcut to avoid typing the **f** *devicename* argument. Without this argument the **tar** command will attempt to use its default tape device, **/dev/mt0** or **/dev/mt/0m** (on Release 2 and later versions of System V). Figure 3.8 shows how you can link your floppy device to the default device name and thus abbreviate the **tar** command line.

Figure 3.8 Abbreviating the **tar** command line by linking to the default device.

```
# tar cvbf 20 /dev/rflpa .
. . .
# ln /dev/rflpa /dev/mt0
# tar cvb 20 .
. . .
# □
```

Careful: If you wish to use an actual "raw" device (like **/dev/rflpa**) as the default device (**/dev/mt0**), you're mixing up character and block device designations. But there appears no simple way around this inconsistency.

Using Default Devices with XENIX tar. The XENIX 5 system from Santa Cruz Operation also allows the use of floppy diskette default device names, but their approach is different. This system uses the file **/etc/default/tar** to determine the default device to use.

Figure 3.9 shows the contents of this file from one of our systems. The first field is a string of the format **archive***n* = *devicename*, the second a blocking factor, and the third the volume size in kilobytes. The blocking factor is the number of 512-byte blocks that **tar** uses for each read and write operation.

The devices are named according to their format. Here, **ss** means single-sided and **ds** double-sided format. The low-density floppies use 48 tracks per inch (TPI) and 9 sectors per track, and high-density floppies are formatted 96 TPI with 15 sectors per track.

Figure 3.9 Contents of **/etc/default/tar**.

```
# cat /etc/default/tar
#        device              blocking    total capacity
                                         (1-kilobyte blocks)

archive0=/dev/rfd048ds9        18            360
archive1=/dev/rfd148ds9        18            360
archive2=/dev/rfd096ds15       10           1200
```

```
archive3=/dev/rfd196ds15              10              1200
archive4=/dev/rfd048ss9               18               180
archive5=/dev/rfd048ds8               16               320
archive6=/dev/rfd048ss8               16               160
archive7=./tarfile                     1                 0
archivef=/dev/null                     1                 0
#  □
```

The first entry in this file (**archive0**) will be used as the device if you omit the **f** *devicename* argument on the command line when you invoke **tar**. This device has a capacity of 360 kilobytes and uses a default blocking of 18 512-byte blocks.

If you wish to use a different device listed in this file, you simply use a numerical argument—**1** through **7**, which corresponds to **archive1** through **archive7**, such as **tar cv 2**. Of course, you could specify **0** for **archive0**, but that's unnecessary, since **archive0** is chosen by default.

Specify **7** to write the backup to another part of your working disk, namely to the ordinary file named **tarfile** in your current directory. If you specify the **f** key letter, then the **archivef** entry is looked up, but since it has value **/dev/null**, the device specified after this option on the command line is used. That's how you can specify other devices using the **f** key.

Assigning Devices with XENIX System.   Assignable devices prevent simultaneous use of the same backup device. The XENIX **assign** *device* command line attempts to assign *device* to the current user. After assignment this user has exclusive access to the backup device. Devices can be unassigned with the **deassign** command or perhaps by logging out of the account. Figure 3.10 shows an example. Here *all* floppies are assigned by specifying **/dev/fd**.

Figure 3.10 Assigning and deassigning devices.

```
# assign /dev/fd
[ Perform back up operation ]
# deassign /dev/fd
#  □
```

See your XENIX reference manual page entry ASSIGN(C) for options, recommended ownerships, permissions, and **/etc/atab** file setup for using this command.

Archiving Files Across Floppy Boundaries with XENIX tar.   XENIX **tar** allows files to cross floppy boundaries. If you specify a device with the **f** argument, you would also need to use the **k** option to specify the size of the floppy diskette. By default, files will be split into "extents"—part will be on one floppy, part on another. If you don't wish a file to be split, also specify the **e** option.

When there's not enough room on the current floppy diskette for a given file, **tar** will prompt for a new one. Part a of Figure 3.11 shows a sample command line for backing up your entire file system using the XENIX **tar** command where you specify a device not listed in **/etc/default/tar**.

Figure 3.11 Full backup using XENIX **tar**.

a. One command for a full backup:

```
# cd /
# tar cvfk /dev/flpa 350 .
...
# □
```

b. An equivalent command line:

```
# cd /
# tar cvkf 350 /dev/flpa .
...
# □
```

We change to the root directory and specify the directory argument as dot (.) to store files with pathnames relative to the current directory. The option letter **k** has argument 350, the capacity of the floppy in kilobytes, which corresponds to 700 512-byte blocks. And the device name for the floppy is **/dev/flpa**. The arguments to the **f** and **k** key letters *must* be given in the same order as the key letters themselves. If you switch these key letters, you must switch the corresponding arguments as shown in part b of this figure.

Note that the XENIX 5 **tar** command allows you to recover a file even if it's been split across a floppy boundary. Also, whole files on later floppies in a series may be recovered individually without starting with the first diskette in a series.

Problems When Backing Up Across Floppy Boundaries. You can get into real trouble if you back up your files across floppy boundaries and a diskette in your series has a read error. Here it may be impossible to use **tar** to recover files from any of the diskettes in the series after the one that had the error. This problem is one reason for checking your diskettes for read errors after your backup is complete. See "Restoring Files Using tar" for a program that enables you to skip to a specified file and read the data off the diskette in spite of read error messages from **tar**.

Making a Partial Backup Using tar

To make a *partial backup* of one or more file systems with **tar**, you first mount the file system and then change to the mount point directory. You then instruct **tar** to back up the contents of the current directory. If you're using a tape medium, make sure that it has greater capacity than the file system you're backing up—remember the extra space used by the header and trailer blocks.

If you're using floppies and your **tar** program won't let you cross floppy boundaries, you'll need to back up groups of files that will all fit on one floppy. Also check to see if your **tar** command has an option (like **B**) that looks at the length of each file and refuses to back it up if it won't fit on the current diskette.

Generally, you'll want to back up file systems whose contents change frequently, such as file systems with user's home directories. We recommend that you place user accounts on their own file system. If that's not possible, at least place them in their own directory tree.

Some system administrators place user accounts in the **/usr** directory. This approach is undesirable since you must back up the entire **/usr** tree, which contains many files that don't belong to user accounts. We place all accounts on a separate file system mounted on **/users**. You may prefer to name such a file system **/usr1** or **/usr2**, which may be less ambiguous because we all know that "user" is spelt "usr." Some systems with many users may use several file systems, which would be mounted on directories like **/usr1**, **/usr2**, etc. If you do keep user accounts in **/usr**, specify subdirectories on the **tar** command line, such as **/usr/beccat**, **/usr/rik**, to back up each user account separately.

For the examples in this section we'll mount a small file system containing three files onto the **/Dbase** directory. Figure 3.12 shows a long directory listing for these files. Note the modification times, as this information will be important when we discuss incremental backups below.

Figure 3.12 Sample files used in examples below.

```
# ls -l /Dbase
total 3
-rw-r--r--    1 beccat    users          38 Sep 22 17:00 sep22.dta
-rw-r--r--    1 beccat    users          38 Sep 23 17:00 sep23.dta
-rw-r--r--    1 beccat    users          38 Sep 24 15:08 sep24.dta
# □
```

Figure 3.13 shows us using **tar** to make a backup of the file system mounted on the **/Dbase** directory. Note that in this and later examples we'll assume that the actual backup device has been linked to the default device, so we won't show the **f** *devicename* argument.

Figure 3.13 Using **tar** to back up the **/Dbase** directory.

```
# cd /Dbase
# tar cv . 2>/tmp/tbl.contents
```

```
# cat /tmp/tbl.contents
a ./sep22.dta 1 blocks
a ./sep23.dta 1 blocks
a ./sep24.dta 1 blocks
# □
```

This technique also suits backup of any directory in order to copy its contents onto a given diskette. Just change to that directory and "create" a new tape using the **c** key.

You'll probably want a list of files for each floppy that **tar** writes. You can get **tar** to list the files as it copies them with the verbose (**v**) option. The file list is placed on the standard error output for listing on your terminal screen. If you redirect standard error to a file, you've got a handy list of what **tar** has backed up for you, diskette by diskette. *Note*: The **a** preceding each pathname in the table of contents indicates that the file backed up was appended to end of the tape.

Verifying Your Backups

One approach to verifying the integrity of your backup is to list the files on each floppy diskette. You would use the **tar** command with the **t** (for table) key to do this. You can get more information about the files on the diskette by using the **v** (verbose) option along with the **t** key. Figure 3.14 shows some results on our System V example system using the **t** key first without and then with the **v** option.

Figure 3.14 Listing the files on the backup diskette.

```
# tar t
Tar: blocksize = 9
./sep22.dta
./sep23.dta
./sep24.dta
# tar tv
Tar: blocksize = 9
rw-r--r--100/100        38 Sep 22 17:00 1986 ./sep22.dta
rw-r--r--100/100        38 Sep 23 17:00 1986 ./sep23.dta
rw-r--r--100/100        38 Sep 24 15:08 1986 ./sep24.dta
# □
```

The fields shown in the long listing are the file permissions, user and group-id numbers, file sizes in bytes, modification time, and pathname to which the file will be restored.

With our version of **tar**, the message **Tar: blocksize** = *number* is displayed on the standard error output, whereas the list of files is printed on the standard output. The "blocksize" is the blocking factor used for the I/O operation.

> The XENIX 5 **tar tv** command shows a slightly different display. Here the
> message **tar: buffer size** = *number* is written to the standard error, where
> *number* is the size of a buffer used for I/O.

To verify your backups, you would compare the listings you get with the **t** key
to the table of contents obtained when you did the backup itself. Consistent results
tell you that the file header is intact but do not necessarily ensure that the file contents are correct.

To verify the backups more rigorously, restore a file from the backup medium.
Choose the last file on a diskette because read errors are more likely to occur on
the denser inner tracks where the last few files are stored. Also, read errors on
other parts of the diskette would prevent you from reaching the last file to restore
it. Later, we'll show you an actual example of this verification technique.

The **dd** utility will also scrutinize your backup diskettes for read errors. You
would copy the diskette contents to **/dev/null**, a method that speeds up the
verification. If **dd** is unable to read a block on the diskette, it will report a message,
such as **dd read error: I/O error**, and the disk device driver will also report an I/O
error on the virtual console terminal. This message probably means a defect in the
media. If you get such a message, you should use a different diskette and make
another backup.

Using tar for Incremental Backups

An incremental backup saves only the files that have been added or changed since
the last time a backup was performed. We'll discuss ways to perform an incremental backup with **tar** using the update (**u**) key option, and two methods using the **find**
command. Although our examples use floppy media, the same examples can be
applied in principle to other backup media.

Using the Update Key with tar.   You can use the **tar** command directly
for an incremental backup since **tar** can update the backup device. That is, any
files that have been added or changed since the last backup will be written to the
end of any data already on the diskette.

Both System V and XENIX **tar** commands can update tapes. However, this
update process is notoriously slow because **tar** must scan the entire backup tape *for
each file* prior to backup. Thus, this method is practical for updating only a small
number of files. Figure 3.15 shows a sample command line using the update (**u**)
key letter.

Figure 3.15 Using the update key of **tar**.

```
tar uvf /dev/floppy .
```

The **u** key of **tar** keeps a backup diskette up to date. It copies any file which either is not already on the diskette, or has been changed since it was last written there. It won't copy a file that's already backed up and hasn't been changed on the working disk.

On the surface this plan of attack seems handy and efficient, but **tar** takes its sweet time checking to see if the file is already present, and if so, when it was written. You can run into trouble if the size of the group of files you're backing up surpasses the available diskette space.

If you go this route, use the **v** option to display the name of each file on the standard error output as it is added to the diskette. Redirect this list to a file, print it out, and keep the listing with the diskette so that you know what's been added. This listing would be especially useful when you need to locate a particular file.

Figure 3.16 shows an example on our system of an incremental backup using the **u** option. It's important to note that for this example these commands were run on September 24th at 15:47 (3:47 P.M.).

Figure 3.16 Example of an incremental backup using the update key of **tar**.

```
# touch sep24.dta
# ls -l
total 3
-rw-r--r--    1 beccat    users         38 Sep 22 17:00 sep22.dta
-rw-r--r--    1 beccat    users         38 Sep 23 17:00 sep23.dta
-rw-r--r--    1 beccat    users         38 Sep 24 15:47 sep24.dta
# tar uv .
a ./sep24.dta 1 blocks
# □
```

First we used the **touch** program to update the file named **sep24.dta**. Without any options, the **touch** command changes the modification time of a file to be the current date and time. We're using it here to simulate updating a file. The long directory listing shows that the modification time is now Sep 24 15:47, as opposed to the value Sep 24 15:08 it was before (see Figure 3.12).

Now, when **tar uv** operates, it checks all the files in the current directory (denoted by the dot, .), but it only backs up the file that has changed since the last backup, namely **sep24.dta**.

> The **tar** program doesn't let you update blocked tapes. Thus you'll need to specify a blocking factor of 1 to override the default blocking used with XENIX **tar**. So you'll need to change the command line shown in Figure 3.16 to **tar uvb 1 .**.

Using find —mtime to Locate Files for an Incremental Backup with tar. As a generally more useful alternative technique, you can use the **find** command to generate the list of files that you wish **tar** to back up. There are two common approaches. One is to use the **—mtime** option to locate files modified within a certain number of days in the recent past. Figure 3.17 shows one general command line.

Figure 3.17 Listing files modified within a certain time.

```
# find . —type f —mtime —days —print > filelist
```

This command line causes **find** to locate all ordinary files (**—type f**) starting with the current directory (denoted by .) that have been modified (**—mtime**) within the past *days* days, and store their names in a file named **filelist**. If you're doing daily incremental backups, you'd want *days* to be 1 (one) so that all files modified within the last day will be located.

One disadvantage of this method is that you'll need to run the **find** command at the same time every day so that it won't miss files. It could include too many files in its listing, but that's okay—compared to missing them. You could use **cron** to execute a shell script that runs this **find** command the same time every day.

Also, **filelist** may include files that you don't want to back up, like temporary files or system logs. So you may need to edit out the "junk files." You could automate this procedure for files that have known names, such as **core**, **a.out**, etc. Examining your file list does force you to take a hard look at your files before they become "moldy oldies."

Figure 3.18 shows an example. The **find** command locates files in the **/Dbase** directory that are less than one day old. The shell places the output of the command **cat sep24.list** on the **tar** command line. Note that this example is being run at 15:55 hours on September 24th.

Figure 3.18 An incremental backup with **tar** using **find** to locate the files to back up.

```
# cd /Dbase
# find . -type f -mtime -1 -print >sep24.list
# ls -l
total 4
-rw-r--r--    1 beccat    users         38 Sep 22 17:00 sep22.dta
-rw-r--r--    1 beccat    users         38 Sep 23 17:00 sep23.dta
-rw-r--r--    1 beccat    users         38 Sep 24 15:47 sep24.dta
-rw-r--r--    1 beccat    users         37 Sep 24 15:55 sep24.list
# tar cvf /dev/flpa `cat sep24.list`
./sep23.dta
./sep24.dta
./sep24.list
# tar tf /dev/flpa
```

```
Tar: blocksize = 20
./sep23.dta
./sep24.dta
./sep24.list
# □
```

Note that **sep24.list** is also backed up since it was created in the current directory. Some versions of **tar** may not back up this file since it's in use (open).

This example shows that if you were to back up these files at this time of day you would have backed up **sep23.dta** twice if it was backed up yesterday. It's included in the output since **sep23.dta** is not 24 hours old. However, if you waited until right after 17:00 hours, only the **sep24.dta** file would be reported by **find**, as desired.

You might find a shell script useful for encapsulating the commands in Figure 3.18. Figure 3.19 shows an example. Part a shows the invocation command line. After verifying that the arguments are correct, the shell process running the script first changes to the directory specified as the first *directory* argument. Then it locates and archives all files modified in the number of days specified by the second *days* argument. The shell script is listed in part b of the figure.

Figure 3.19 A shell script for backing up incrementally with **tar**.

a. Invoking the **tarbackup1** script:

tarbackup1 *directory days*

b. Listing of the shell script:

```
    :
    # @(#) tarbackup1  Incremental Backup Script
    DEVICE=/dev/floppy
    USAGE="Usage: $0 directory days"
    case $# in
    2)  if [ ! -d "$1" ]; then
            echo "ERROR: \"$1\" not a directory"
            echo $USAGE
            exit 1
        fi
        cd "$1"
        find . -type f -mtime -"$2" -print > /tmp/tarlist
        tar cvf $DEVICE `cat /tmp/tarlist`
        lp /tmp/tarlist
        rm /tmp/tarlist ;;
    *)  echo $USAGE
        exit 2 ;;
    esac
```

You may wish to modify **tarbackup1** so that you can edit out superfluous files named in **/tmp/tarlist** before the backup is performed. We show some sample code for this purpose in Figure 3.23.

  Using find —newer to Locate Files for an Incremental Backup with tar. For the second approach using **find** you'd create a "time-stamp" file immediately after doing a backup. Then you would use the —**newer** option of **find** to locate any files created or modified since that time-stamp file was created. Figure 3.20 shows the basic approach.

Figure 3.20 A second way to use **find** to locate files for an incremental backup.

find . —type f —newer LAST.DONE —print >filelist

This command line causes **find** to locate all ordinary files starting with the current directory that have a modification time more recent (—**newer**) than the "time-stamp" file named **LAST.DONE** and store their names in a file named **filelist**.

  Figure 3.21 shows a **tar** incremental backup using **find** to locate files as shown in Figure 3.20.

Figure 3.21 Incremental backup with **tar** using **find** to locate the files to back up.

```
# touch 09231700 DONE.YESTERDAY
# ls -l
total 3
-rw-r--r--   1 beccat    users          0 Sep 23 17:00 DONE.YESTERDAY
-rw-r--r--   1 beccat    users         38 Sep 22 17:00 sep22.dta
-rw-r--r--   1 beccat    users         38 Sep 23 17:00 sep23.dta
-rw-r--r--   1 beccat    users         38 Sep 24 15:47 sep24.dta
# find . -type f -newer DONE.YESTERDAY -print > filelist
# touch DONE.TODAY
# tar cvf /dev/floppy `cat filelist`
./sep24.dta
./filelist
# mv DONE.TODAY DONE.YESTERDAY
# □
```

For our simulation we used **touch** with an argument to create **DONE.YESTERDAY** to have modification time September 23rd at 17:00 hours. This would correspond to the time that the previous backup operation was done on that date. At 15:55 on September 24th the **find** command located **sep24.dta** as being more recent than the time-stamp file, **DONE.YESTERDAY**.

  Note that the filename **filelist** is also stored in the file named **filelist** since it was created in the same directory as the files to be archived and it's more recent than **DONE.YESTERDAY**. This way your table of contents (contained in **filelist**) will be backed up along with the other files. Of course, you could redirect the output to a file in another directory to avoid including the listing file in your backup.

Then we create another dummy "time-stamp" file, named **DONE.TODAY**, *before* we use **tar**. This file is renamed to **DONE.YESTERDAY** *after* the backup operation. If you simply updated **DONE.YESTERDAY** at the end of the backup, you'd miss any files created or changed during the course of the backup operation, which can take a long time.

One advantage this technique has over the one discussed previously is that you don't have to run the **find** command at the same time each day to do a daily incremental backup. You could wait an arbitrary length of time and just locate all the files added or changed since the last backup.

Note that if all the files listed in **filelist** won't fit on one floppy and your **tar** program won't continue the backup to another diskette, you'll have to divide this list up manually. And if the list of names is so large that it overflows the shell input buffer (generally 5120 characters), you'll have to divide the list, too. You could use the **split** command to do this easily.

Figure 3.22 shows a simple example. The file **filelist** is divided into a number of 100 line files, **xaa** and **xab**, with the remaining lines in **xac**. Since the average file on our system is about three blocks long—100 files shouldn't overflow a diskette that holds 360 blocks. Consult the split(1) manual page for other options.

Figure 3.22 Using **split** to divide a file.

```
# split -100 filelist
# ls
filelist
xaa
xab
xac
# □
```

Our second approach also lends itself to using a shell script. Figure 3.23 shows an example. Part a shows the invocation command line. The shell process running the script first changes to the directory specified as the *directory* argument. Then it locates and archives all files that have a more recent modification time than the time-stamp file, **DONE.YESTERDAY**. The script is listed in part b of the figure. Here you're given the option to modify the file list with **vi**, if desired.

Figure 3.23 A shell script for backing up incrementally with **tar**.

a. Invoking the **tarbackup2** script:

tarbackup2 *directory*

b. Listing of the shell script:

```
:
# @(#) tarbackup2  Incremental Backup Script
DEVICE=/dev/floppy
USAGE="Usage: $0 directory"
case $# in
1)  if [ ! -d "$1" ]; then
        echo "ERROR: \"$1\" not a directory"
        echo $USAGE
        exit 1
    fi
    cd "$1"
    touch DONE.TODAY
    listing=`date +%m%d`.list
    find . -type f -newer DONE.YESTERDAY -print > /tmp/$listing
    echo "Do you wish to edit the file list (y/n)? \c"
    read answer
    case "$answer" in
    Y|y)  vi /tmp/$listing ;;
    *)        ;;
    esac
    tar cvf $DEVICE `cat /tmp/$listing`
    mv DONE.TODAY DONE.YESTERDAY
    lp /tmp/$listing
    rm /tmp/$listing ;;
*)  echo $USAGE
    exit 2 ;;
esac
```

We used the **date** command to give the listing file a more useful name. The **+%m%d** argument directs **date** to output the month and the day of the month, which will become the filename prefix. The **.list** suffix denotes this as a "listing" file. For instance, **0923.list** would be created on September 23rd.

Restoring Files Using tar

Sooner or later you'll need to restore files from your backup tape. If you archived the files with an absolute pathname (starting with /), they'll be restored with their original full pathnames. If you saved the files with a relative pathname, you could either start from the directory you archived them from or from a different directory, if desired. Figure 3.24 shows the general form of the command line you'd use for either case.

Figure 3.24 General command format for restoring files.

tar xvf *devicename pathname...*

Here the **x** key tells **tar** to extract the named files from the backup tape. If you specify *pathname* to be a directory, all files and subdirectories of that directory are restored. If you specify an ordinary file, only that file will be retrieved. If no *pathname* argument is supplied, *all* files are retrieved from the backup tape. Note that any writable files on the working disk with the same pathname as files on the backup tape will be overwritten.

If you've been using the **u** or **r** keys with **tar**, files will be appended to the end of a given tape. You can have more than one file with the same pathname on a given medium (they'll probably differ in other ways, such as in size or perhaps modification time). During restoring, files with the same pathname will overwrite each other until only the last file on the backup diskette with a given pathname will appear on your working disk.

The example shown in Figure 3.25 serves a double purpose. First, it illustrates a technique for verifying that a backup was done correctly. Second, it shows an example of restoring a single file from a backup.

Figure 3.25 Restoring a file from a backup tape.

```
# ls -l
total 3
-rw-r--r--    1 beccat    users         38 Sep 22 17:00 sep22.dta
-rw-r--r--    1 beccat    users         38 Sep 23 17:00 sep23.dta
-rw-r--r--    1 beccat    users         38 Sep 24 15:47 sep24.dta
# mv sep24.dta temp
# tar xvf /dev/flpa ./sep24.dta
Tar: blocksize = 9
x ./sep24.dta, 38 bytes, 1 tape blocks
# ls -l
total 4
-rw-r--r--    1 beccat    users         38 Sep 22 17:00 sep22.dta
-rw-r--r--    1 beccat    users         38 Sep 23 17:00 sep23.dta
-rw-r--r--    1 beccat    users         38 Sep 24 15:08 sep24.dta
-rw-r--r--    1 beccat    users         38 Sep 24 15:47 temp
# cat sep24.dta
This data was entered September 24th.
# cat temp
This data was entered September 24th.
# rm temp
# □
```

The first **ls −l** command lists the three files in the current directory. We use **mv** to rename the last file as a safety precaution so that the restoration step that follows won't overwrite it. The next long directory listing shows that both the restored file, **sep24.dta**, which was backed up in Figure 3.13, and the file **temp** appear to be the same (except for their modification times since we updated the former in Figure

3.16). The **cat** display shows that these files contain the same text. Finally, the temporary file is removed.

Figure 3.26 shows an interactive simple shell script for extracting one or more files from a tape. Just type the word **restore** to invoke the script, and answer the prompts.

Figure 3.26 A Bourne shell script for restoring files from a **tar** tape.

```
:
# @(#) tarrestore Restore one or more files
DEVICE=/dev/floppy
echo "Do you wish to see a table of contents first (y/n)? \c"
read answer
case "$answer" in
Y|y)  tar tvf $DEVICE | pg -cnsp\
        "Press RETURN for next screen" ;;
*)      ;;
esac
#
echo "Name one or more files to be restored:"
echo "Type a RETURN on a line by itself to end the list."
while read FILE
do
    if [ -z "$FILE" ]; then
        break
    fi
        FILELIST="$FILELIST $FILE"
done
if [ -z "$FILELIST" ]; then
    exit
fi
tar xvf $DEVICE $FILELIST
```

To customize this script, change **/dev/floppy** in the assignment to the **DEVICE** variable to the name of your particular backup device.

Read Errors When Extracting Tapes.   Often, read errors on a tape prevent you from restoring a file. Since **tar** stops working when it encounters an I/O error, a read error on one file will deny you access to later files on the tape.

Lest this gruesome possibility unnerve you from using **tar**, we present a C program named **tarskip** (named such since it skips read errors when reading tar tapes) for you that will let you recover files on a given diskette or a series of diskettes in spite of read errors. It was originally published in the Wizard's Grab-bag column in the September 1985 issue of UNIXWORLD magazine.

Figure E.2 in Appendix E lists the **tarskip** program. Figure 3.27 shows the command line format for using **tarskip**.

Figure 3.27 Command line format for using **tarskip** to recover files.

tarskip *pathname* [*tardevice*] | **tar xvf** −

Assume you have a diskette that has reported read errors and you wish to access a file on it. You would specify the pathname of the file after the read error on the command line shown in Figure 3.27. The read error would be ignored and after the specified pathname was located (in the header to the file) all data on the diskette would be sent to the standard output. These data are piped to the **tar xvf** − command, which extracts files from its standard input (specified by the dash argument) and writes them to your working disk. Of course, this technique assumes that the pathname in the header can be read. Figure 3.28 shows an actual example.

Figure 3.28 Using the **tarskip** program to extract a tape.

```
# tarskip ./sep24.dta /dev/floppy ¦ tar xvf -
Tar: blocksize = 9
x ./sep24.dta, 38 bytes, 1 tape blocks
#
```

Of course, you'll need to type in **tarskip.c** and compile it before using. Figure 3.29 illustrates a command line for producing a program named **tarskip**. The −**O** flag invokes an optimizer for more efficient code and −**s** strips the symbol table to yield a smaller program.

Figure 3.29 Compiling the **tarskip** program.

```
# cc -O -s -o tarskip tarskip.c
#
```

BACKING UP AND RESTORING WITH cpio

In this section we discuss backing up and restoring files with the UNIX **cpio** command. Although we'll be using tape as the backup medium in our examples, the general principles covered apply to any backup medium.

The **cpio** acronym stands for **c**opy **i**nput to **o**utput. When backing up files with **cpio**, you present a list of files to its standard input and it writes the file archive, which includes an identifying header followed by the file data, to its standard output.

Advantages of Using cpio. We think the primary advantage is the flexible syntax of the **cpio** command. It acts like a filter program—taking its input information from the standard input file and delivering its output to the standard output file. To manipulate the input and output of this backup utility, you use the use the shell to specify redirection and pipelines.

Also, like **tar**, it can archive individual files, not just whole file systems, like **volcopy**. This behavior means that you can restore individual files easily.

Backups made by **cpio** are generally smaller than ones created by **tar** because the header is shorter and there's no padding to an even block boundary. However, this advantage diminishes with larger files.

Some Disadvantages of Using cpio.   Some would consider the complicated **cpio** command line syntax a disadvantage. It's certainly more involved than, say, using **tar**. Using **cpio** is like driving with a stick shift compared to an automatic transmission—it takes more learning how, but increases your options and give you more control.

However, when using shell scripts, which hide "ugly" command line details, the flexible behavior outweighs the awkward syntax. Later we'll present some shell scripts for this purpose.

File links are not handled efficiently, since **cpio** doesn't record that two files are linked. Thus, multiple copies of a linked file are written to tape—one for each link name. However, **cpio** does restore the links when files are retrieved off the tape.

The **cpio** utility is designed so that it can write a file across a media boundary, but not all implementations support this feature. And if so, files can also be read across boundaries for restoration. **cpio** will prompt you for the device name of the next media volume when it comes to a boundary. This behavior means that you could change tape drives, say, during a backup or restore procedure.

Also, people complain that doing a large backup with **cpio** is slow compared to using a utility, like AT&T **volcopy** or BSD **dump**, both of which can archive an entire file system at once. However, the ability of **cpio** to manipulate files individually gives a real speed advantage when backing up and restoring a moderate number of files.

Reading from or writing to tape is less efficient with **cpio**—the maximum block size for I/O is 5120 bytes, compared to 10,240 for **tar** and even larger for **volcopy**.

Operating Modes.   The **cpio** program operates in one of three modes— copy-in, copy-out, and pass mode. Use the *copy-out* mode when creating a backup tape and the complementary *copy-in* mode when recovering files from that tape. You also use the copy-in mode when listing the table of contents of a backup tape, although no files are restored. The *pass mode* is generally used to copy files and directory trees from one place to another in your directory hierarchy. However, it can also be used for backing up files, as you'll see later.

Backing Up with Copy-Out Mode

Use copy-out mode for full, partial, or incremental backups. The difference among these occurs in the list of files you send to the standard input of **cpio**. In practice, you'll probably use the **find** command to create the file lists in all three cases.

The list of files for **cpio** to back up can be generated using either **echo**, keyboard input, **ls**, or **find**. We find **echo** convenient when only one file is named, keyboard input when only a few files are specified, **ls** when all files are in one directory, and **find** if a directory tree is involved.

Note that you can't update a tape with **cpio**—unless you have a device that doesn't rewind-on-close, or a utility that will position the tape for you. No-rewind-on close devices are often named like the rewind device, but with an "n" prefix— like **/dev/nrmt/0m** versus **/dev/rmt/0m**. If the tape always rewinds to the beginning, then each time you use **cpio**, you'll overwrite whatever is already on the tape. This property makes **cpio** less attractive for archiving just a few files—it's not an efficient use of backup media.

Performing File System Backups with cpio. You would back up a file system by first changing to the mount point directory. That is, change to the root directory (**/**) for a full backup of all file systems and the mount point for a particular file system for a partial backup. And if you only wish to back up the root file system, you'll have to unmount all other file systems. Then use **find** to locate all the files in the file system and pipe this list into the standard input of **cpio** running in copy-out mode.

Copy-out mode is specified by using the **−o** option on the **cpio** command line. In this mode several other options can be used as well. Appendix E tabulates all the options recognized by **cpio**. Part a of Figure 3.30 shows the general command line syntax to use for this mode, and part b shows an actual example that mirrors the syntax statement in part a. Here, **lettersmailed** contains a short list of files containing letters your office mailed yesterday.

Figure 3.30 Copy-out mode command line syntax.

a. General command line syntax:

cpio −o[*option...*] < *namelist* > *archive*

b. A sample command line:

```
# cpio -ovB < lettersmailed > /dev/rmt/0m
...
# □
```

In part a, *namelist* is the list of files to be backed up. The newline character must separate the file names in *namelist*. Thus, a list created using **echo** won't work, since space characters would separate the names. Most commonly, this filename list results from running a command, such as **ls** or **find**, but it could be contained in an ordinary file. In fact, if you need to be selective about the files you back up, then save your list of filenames on disk so that you can edit it. And redirect the input of **cpio** to come from the edited file list.

The *archive* argument is the device filename of the backup device. Redirecting the output to the device activates it so that you can write to it. Note that *archive* could name an ordinary file. However, you wouldn't generally use an ordinary file for backing up since you'll want to write the **cpio** output to external media. However, you could use an ordinary file to transport a "cpio" archive, say, to another machine via the UUCP system.

We'll be using a small file system for illustrating partial backups. This file system will be mounted on the **/Dbase** (for database) directory. Figure 3.31 shows a long directory listing of the three files in this file system. Here we mounted the file system, **/dev/dsk/2s0**, onto the **/Dbase** directory. Then we change to this mount point directory and display a long directory listing.

Figure 3.31 Files in our sample file system.

```
# mount /dev/dsk/2s0 /Dbase
# cd /Dbase
# ls -l
total 114
-rw-r--r--   1 beccat    users       13701 Oct  3 17:00 oct03.dta
-rw-r--r--   1 beccat    users       39646 Oct  4 17:00 oct04.dta
-rw-r--r--   1 beccat    users        3165 Oct  5 10:45 oct05.dta
# □
```

Figure 3.32 shows four ways to generate filenames for **cpio**. In parts a, c, and d, we supply the filenames to **cpio** through a pipeline, and in part b, the filenames are obtained directly from keyboard input. This last approach works because **cpio** reads from its standard input, which is the keyboard, unless it's redirected or connected to a pipeline.

Since you'll do the backup operation from the mount point directory, the files will be stored with a relative pathname (relative to the current directory, dot). This way restoration is more flexible—you could restore them in any directory on your working disk. If you use names beginning with a slash (/), the files can't be moved; they'll be restored to their original location in the directory hierarchy.

Figure 3.32 Four ways to generate filenames for backing up with **cpio**.

a. Using **echo**:

```
# echo oct03.dta ¦ cpio -o >/dev/rmt/0m
# □
```

b. Using keyboard input:

```
# cpio -o >/dev/rmt/0m
oct03.dta
oct04.dta
<control-D>
# □
```

c. Using **ls**:

```
# ls * ¦ cpio -o >/dev/rmt/0m
# □
```

d. Using **find**:

```
# find . -print ¦ cpio -o >/dev/rmt/0m
# □
```

In these examples we specified **/dev/rmt/0m** as the *archive* argument. This System V Release 2 (and later versions) tape device filename stands for the "raw" (character) device using device number 0 (zero) at a medium density (1600 bpi).

Part a shows the **echo** command, which is appropriate for naming one file at a time. Part b's keyboard input is good for a modest number of files—until you grow tired of typing filenames. Part c's **ls** command can name all files in a given directory. Part d's **find** command locates all files starting with the current directory (denoted by .). Note that all ordinary file and directory names are sent to **cpio**, which can back up directories (actually writes a header without data blocks) as well as ordinary files. The **−print** argument is necessary, else **find** wouldn't send any names into the pipeline. In all cases, the list of filenames is supplied to the standard input of **cpio**.

Some Options to Use with Copy-Out Mode.   Use the **v** (verbose) option if you wish **cpio** to report the filenames on your terminal screen (the standard error output) as they are archived. You could capture this list by redirecting the standard error output to a disk file. Figure 3.33 shows some examples.

Figure 3.33 Displaying or storing the filenames as they are archived.

```
# ls ¦ cpio -ov >/dev/rmt/0m
oct03.dta
oct04.dta
oct05.dta
111 blocks
# ls ¦ cpio -ov >/dev/rmt/0m 2> `date +%m%d`.list
# cat 1005.list
oct03.dta
oct04.dta
oct05.dta
111 blocks
# □
```

Here the filename for the listing file has a prefix that's the output of the **date +%m%d** command, which displays the current month followed by the day of the month, and a suffix (**.list**) that categorizes the file type. For instance, on March 6th the file would be named **0306.list**.

Normally, **cpio** writes the archive to its standard output in 512-byte records. If you specify the capital **B** option, it increases the record size to 5120 bytes, which would speed up the transfer to a "raw" (character) backup device significantly. Figure 3.34 shows another example for backing up the files in **/Dbase**. We compared the time it takes with and without specifying the **B** option.

Figure 3.34 Illustrating the speed improvement obtained by using larger records.

```
# time ls ¦ cpio -ov >/dev/rmt/0m
oct03.dta
oct04.dta
oct05.dta
111 blocks
45.6r 39.2u 5.9s
# time ls ¦ cpio -ovB >/dev/rmt/0m
oct03.dta
oct04.dta
oct05.dta
111 blocks
7.3r 6.3u 0.7s
# □
```

Even with a few files the speed improves dramatically. However, it's not 10 times, as might be expected even though the buffer size was increased 10-fold. It's more like six times faster, which is still a substantial improvement. So you'll probably want to use the **B** option with **cpio** and write to the "raw" (character interface) device. We'll see later that you'll also want to use the **B** option when restoring files from the "raw" device.

The **cpio** program will prompt you for another tape if it fills up the current one. The program will print "If you want to go on, type device/file name when ready." You should then change your backup tape and type the special filename of the backup device, as in **/dev/rmt/0m**. The **cpio** program will then attempt to continue writing to the device you specify. If you mistype the device name or the device can't be written to, you'll be prompted again—it's a fairly robust retry mechanism.

You could specify a different device than the one you started with. This feature might be useful, say, for continuing the backup onto a different disk or tape drive while changing the medium on the drive used previously.

The cpio Archive Header. The **cpio** program outputs an identifying header to the tape immediately before each file it archives in copy-out mode. This header contains all the information needed for restoring the file correctly. If you specify the **c** option, the header uses ASCII characters, which make the backup more portable from one machine to another. Table 3.3 shows the structure of the ASCII header.

TABLE 3.3 THE ASCII **cpio** HEADER STRUCTURE

Field	Size (bytes)	Example
magic number	6	070707
device number	6	000000
inode number	6	007400
mode	6	100444
user-id	6	000000
group-id	6	000003
number of links	6	000001
raw device number	6	027722
modification time	11	03743071476
length of pathname	6	000014
size of file	11	00000002501
pathname	256	/etc/passwd

All numerical information is stored as its octal value. The magic number is always 070707, and is used to identify the beginning of each header. Another "header" is stored at the end of the tape, but it contains the string **TRAILER!!!** instead of a pathname. The ASCII header contains 6 bytes for a "magic number," 6 bytes for the device number, and 64 bytes of information that comes from the inode of the file, plus *up to* 256 characters for a pathname. **cpio** archives generally squeeze more data on a backup tape than those created by **tar**, because (1) **tar** pads its header up to 512 bytes, but **cpio** doesn't, and (2) **tar** pads the last block of a file, whereas **cpio** doesn't.

Note that, unlike **tar**, **cpio** can "back up" special device files and directories. However, no data are stored—only headers for these file types. In these cases the contents of the file size field is zero. And for character and block special files the "raw device field" is defined to be the ID of the device, which is a combination of major and minor device numbers.

Using find to Create Filename Lists.   If you need to archive a directory tree, use the **find** command to generate the list of files. This command will descend the directory tree and name each file it encounters. Figure 3.35 shows a simple example. Here we've created a directory in **/Dbase** named **Test** to have a subdirectory for our example. We placed a copy of **oct05.dta** into this directory.

Figure 3.35 Using **find** to locate all files in a directory tree.

```
# find . -print
.
./oct03.dta
./oct04.dta
./oct05.dta
./Test
./Test/oct05.dta
# □
```

If you wish **find** to report the names of files in a directory before the directory name itself, use the **−depth** option. Otherwise, the directory name is reported first. You'll find this option useful if you don't have write permission for a directory. If you archive a directory without write permission, then you can't restore its contents unless you have superuser privilege. However, when you use **−depth** all the files in the directory would be restored before the directory itself. Figure 3.36 shows the same example as Figure 3.35 except that the **−depth** option is used.

Figure 3.36 Using **find** with the **−depth** option to locate all files in a directory tree.

```
# find . -depth -print
./oct03.dta
./oct04.dta
./oct05.dta
./Test/oct05.dta
./Test
.
# □
```

Note that neither Berkeley systems nor AT&T UNIX versions before Release 2 of System V support the **−depth** option for **find**.

Alternatively, you can avoid backing up directories by using the **−type f** argument with **find**. This argument causes **find** to list only ordinary files. However, you can still run into a stone wall when restoring files if an unwritable directory exists—it would prevent you from restoring files into it. The solution? Enable write permission for the directory or work with superuser privilege. Figure 3.37 shows a backup of the directory tree using **find** to locate names of ordinary files.

Figure 3.37 Backing up a directory tree with **find** and **cpio**.

```
# cd /Dbase
# find . -type f -print ¦ cpio -ocvB >/dev/rmt/0m
oct03.dta
oct04.dta
oct05.dta
Test/oct05.dta
120 blocks
# □
```

Figure 3.38 shows a simple shell script for backing up all files in a directory tree. Part a shows the invocation command line. The *directory* argument would be the starting point for the directory tree. The root directory (/) is used if this argument is omitted. You could use this script for backups of your file systems—start at the root directory for a full backup or at the mount point for the desired file system for a partial backup of a file system. The script itself is listed in part b of this figure.

Figure 3.38 Shell script for backing up all ordinary files in a directory tree with **cpio**.

a. Syntax for invoking the shell script:

cpiobackup1 [*directory*]

b. Listing of **cpiobackup1**:

```
    :
# @(#) cpiobackup1  Back up directories with cpio.
DEVICE=/dev/rmt/0m
USAGE="Usage: $0 [directory]"
case $# in
0)  cd /
    break ;;
1)  if [ ! -d "$1" ]; then
        echo "ERROR: \"$1\" not a directory"
        echo $USAGE
        exit 1
    fi
    cd "$1"
    break ;;
```

```
*)   echo $USAGE
     exit 2 ;;
esac
#
listing=`date +%m%d`.list
find . -print > /tmp/$listing
cpio -ocavB  </tmp/$listing >$DEVICE
lp /tmp/$listing
rm /tmp/$listing
```

If you specify zero or one argument, the backup operation is performed. If more than one argument, the script prints a usage message and exits. You may need to customize this shell script for your site by replacing **/dev/rmt/0m** with your particular backup device name.

Using find to Create a cpio-Archive. The **find** command recognizes a −**cpio** *devicename* "action" argument. This argument causes **find** to write the located file onto *devicename* in cpio-format transferring the data in 5120-byte records. However, since the headers aren't written in ASCII format, the backup fails to be as portable.

Figure 3.39 shows how to back up the files depicted in Figure 3.37 using the −**cpio** action argument to the **find** command. Here using **time** on each approach reveals only a little difference in speed between the two approaches.

Figure 3.39 Indirect and direct method for backing up files with **find** and **cpio**.

```
# cd /Dbase
# time find . -type f -cpio /dev/rmt/0m -print
./oct03.dta
./oct04.dta
./oct05.dta
./Test/oct05.dta
8.4r 5.3u 2.0s
# time find . -type f -print | cpio -ovB >/dev/rmt/0m
oct03.dta
oct04.dta
oct05.dta
Test/oct05.dta
7.0r 5.4u 1.4s
# □
```

Because of this (albeit small) gain in speed and since you get a portable ASCII header from piping the output of **find** into **cpio**, we'd advise against using the −**cpio** argument of **find**. Also, we've heard reports that the −**cpio** option to find doesn't work correctly on some implementations.

> When the **−cpio** *devicename* argument is used with the XENIX **find** command, the **−depth** option is used by default.

Incremental Backups Using cpio. Figure 3.40 shows a simple shell script using **cpio** for an incremental backup. We're using the preferred method of locating files with the **−newer** option of **find**. The shell script hides the "ugly" **cpio** command line—all you have to type is "cpiobackup2" followed by the starting directory. If you don't specify a starting directory, the script will start at the root directory (/).

Figure 3.40 A shell script for doing an incremental backup starting with any directory.

a. Syntax for invoking the shell script:

cpiobackup2 [*directory*]

b. Listing of the shell script:

```
    :
# @(#) cpiobackup2  Incremental Backup Script
DEVICE=/dev/rmt/0m
USAGE="Usage: $0 [directory]"
case $# in
0)  DIR=/
    break ;;
1)  if [ ! -d "$1" ]; then
        echo "ERROR: \"$1\" not a directory"
        echo $USAGE
        exit 1
    fi
    DIR="$1"
    break ;;
*)  echo $USAGE
    exit 2 ;;
esac
#
cd $DIR
touch DONE.TODAY
LOGFILE=/etc/backup/`date +%m%d`.log
echo "Backing up $DIR directory onto $DEVICE"
echo "Log file is $LOGFILE"
```

```
date >$LOGFILE
find . -newer DONE.YESTERDAY -print |
cpio -ocavB >$DEVICE 2>>$LOGFILE
mv DONE.TODAY DONE.YESTERDAY
```

Figure 3.41 shows what happens when the script runs. The long listing of
DONE.YESTERDAY tells us that this file was last updated at 5 P.M. on October
4th—immediately after backing up files for that day. The **cpiobackup2** script
backed up all the files in the **/Dbase** directory. The contents of the
/etc/backup/1005.log file announces first the date and time of the backup, October
5th at 5:23 P.M., and then the files archived, **oct05.dta** and **Test/oct05.dta**, as
expected. Finally, the modification time of **DONE.YESTERDAY** shows us that
cpiobackup2 won't redo the backing up that it has just accomplished for us since
oct05.dta and **Test/oct05.dta** are older (not newer) than **DONE.YESTERDAY**.

Figure 3.41 Using the **cpiobackup2** script.

```
# ls -l /DONE.YESTERDAY
-rw-r--r--    1 root        sys              Oct  4 17:00 /DONE.YESTERDAY
# cpiobackup2 /Dbase
Backing up /Dbase directory onto /dev/rmt/0m
Log file is /etc/backup/1005.log
# cat /etc/backup/1005.log
Mon Oct 5 17:23:15 PDT 1986
oct05.dta
Test/oct05.dta
20 blocks
# ls -l /DONE.YESTERDAY
-rw-r--r--    1 root        sys              Oct  5 17:23 /DONE.YESTERDAY
# □
```

Since incremental backups can contain several versions of the same file, you may
need to locate the most recent. Or you may simply want to know in which backup
a file is. You can use the UNIX **grep** pattern search command to find the file you
want. Keep the log from each backup in a particular directory as we've done by
using the shell script shown above. Then use **grep** with the −l option to locate the
logfile that contains the desired file by using its pathname as the pattern to search
for. Figure 3.42 shows an example.

Figure 3.42 Locating a particular file in an incremental backup log.

```
# cd /etc/backup
# grep -l oct05.dta *.log
1005.log
# □
```

When you've recycled your backup tapes containing the incremental backups, it would be time to erase the corresponding logfiles.

Restoring Files with Copy-In Mode

Use **cpio** in the *copy-in* mode (−**i** option) to restore files from your backup. Several other options are recognized in this mode, too. Appendix E tabulates all options for the **cpio** utility. Part a of Figure 3.43 shows the general command line syntax, and in part b a particular file is restored.

Figure 3.43 Using **cpio** copy-in mode.

a. General command line format:

cpio −**i**[*option...*] [*pattern...*] <*archive*

b. Restoring a specific file:

```
cpio -icvdmB Test/oct05.dta </dev/rmt/0m
```

Here, *archive* is usually the device name of the backup device, such as **/dev/rmt/0m**. Redirecting from a tape device means that the shell opens the device for reading, which activates the device—it reads the tape, returning characters ultimately to **cpio**. The *archive* argument could also name an ordinary file that was in "cpio" archive format. Such archive files wouldn't normally be used for backing up your system. However, they are useful for transferring directory trees over UUCP links, for instance.

If an ordinary user (not the superuser) restores a file, it will be owned by that user. This behavior is a security feature; for instance, an ordinary user can't restore a file that's set-user-id owned by **root** without the ownership reverting to the user running **cpio**. If the superuser restores a file, the original ownership, which is recorded on the backup tape, will be retained.

Restoring All Files on Your Backup Tape.   The *pattern* argument specifies the files you wish restored. If you don't specify this argument on the command line, **cpio** restores every file that's on the backup tape. Figure 3.44 shows an example.

Figure 3.44 Restoring all files and directories.

```
# cd /Dbase
# cpio -icvdumB </dev/rmt/0m
oct03.dta
oct04.dta
```

```
oct05.dta
Test
Test/oct05.dta
#
```

Some Options to Use with Copy-In Mode. Now let's discuss briefly the options used in this last example. As mentioned before, the −i specifies copy-in mode—so you can extract files from the tape.

We used the **c** option because ASCII headers were created during the backup. If you omit this option when the headers are in ASCII format, you'll get an "Out of phase" error message. And if the backup doesn't use ASCII headers and you specify the **c** option when extracting, you'll get the same error message. The ASCII header format isn't necessary if you're always backing up the same machine, since portability would not be an issue. You can save some space on the backup tape by not using ASCII headers.

The **d** option tells **cpio** to create directories as necessary. If you use this option when extracting, you don't need to back up any directory files. However, any directories created would be owned by the user running **cpio** with permissions determined by the current **umask** setting.

The **u** option means to copy *unconditionally*, that is, force overwriting of any files on the working disk by older files on the tape. If the file on the backup tape predates the one on the disk, you'll probably want to retain the more current files on the disk. Be sure to *omit* the **u** option in this case.

The **m** option causes **cpio** to maintain the modification times of the extracted files. That is, the restored file will be given the modification time stored in the header for the file, which is the same modification time that the file had when it was backed up. This way you retain the "history" of your file updates.

As in copy-out mode, the capital **B** option causes transfers in larger 5120-byte records. You should use this option with the "raw" character device, such as **/dev/rmt/0m**, for maximum restoration speed.

Restoring Selected Files. Use the *pattern* argument if you need to select particular files to restore. As an example, let's say that you had deleted the contents of the **/Dbase** directory (but not the directory itself) and you only wished to restore the ordinary files whose names began with "oct." Your first inclination might be to use the command shown in Figure 3.45 to do this.

Figure 3.45 Restoring files selectively.

```
# cpio -icvdumB oct* </dev/rmt/0m
No match.
#
```

What happened? Nothing was restored! The shell tried to expand the **oct*** argument, but didn't find any files in the current directory that matched (whose name started with "oct") because they had been deleted. So no file names are passed onto **cpio**.

You can quote the *pattern* argument to prevent wildcard expansion by the shell. Then the pattern will be passed onto **cpio**, which is smart enough to interpret the wildcard characters (like the shell would). You must use single, not double quotation marks. Figure 3.46 shows an example.

Figure 3.46 Restoring specified files, quoting the pattern argument.

```
# cpio -icvdumB 'oct*' </dev/rmt/0m
oct03.dta
oct04.dta
oct05.dta
120 blocks
# □
```

Our version of **cpio** reported 120 blocks, even though the extracted files occupy only 114 blocks. The **cpio** utility reports the total number of blocks on the backup tape rounded up to the nearest 10 blocks.

After you've selected the options to use, it's an easy matter to write a simple shell script for restoring files. Figure 3.47 shows one possibility. Part a of this figure lists the command line syntax. You must specify a directory argument first on the command line. Simply use a dot (.) for the current directory. The remaining arguments, if any, specify the particular files desired. If no more arguments are given, all files will be extracted from the tape. You can use wildcards when naming files, but remember to quote the wildcard characters or expressions.

Figure 3.47 A shell script for restoring files.

a. Syntax for invoking the shell script:

cpiorestore1 *directory* [*file ...*]

b. Listing of the shell script:

```
:
# @(#) cpiorestore1  Restore files
DEVICE=/dev/rmt/0m
USAGE="Usage: $0 directory [file...]"
case $# in
```

```
0)   echo $USAGE
     break ;;
1)   if [ ! -d "$1" ]; then
        echo "ERROR: \"$1\" doesn't exist or is not a directory"
        echo $USAGE
        exit 1
     fi ;;
*)   cd "$1"
     shift
     cpio -icvdmB $* < $DEVICE ;;
esac
```

At least one argument must be given, else the script will print a "usage" message and exit. If the first argument names a nonaccessible directory, the script says so, prints the correct command line to use, and exits. Otherwise, the shell running the script changes to the desired directory, shifts the directory argument, and attempts to extract all remaining file arguments. Any extraction problems will be reported by **cpio**. Change the backup device assigned to **DEVICE** if you're not using **/dev/rmt/0m**. Figure 3.48 shows an example using this script.

Figure 3.48 Using the **cpiorestore1** shell script.

```
# cpiorestore1 /Dbase 'oct*'
oct03.dta
oct04.dta
oct05.dta
120 blocks.
# □
```

Listing the Table of Contents.   You also employ copy-in mode for listing the files on the backup tape. In this case, use the **t** option and omit the **d, u,** and **m** options, as they have no effect.

Figure 3.49 shows two examples. In part a, **t** is used to name the files and directories on the tape. In part b, we add the **v** (verbose) option to get a "long" listing—similar to output of the **ls −l** command.

Figure 3.49 Listing files on a backup tape.

a. Listing the filenames:

```
# cpio -ictB <dev/rmt/0m
120 blocks
oct03.dta
oct04.dta
```

```
oct05.dta
Test/oct05.dta
# □
```

b. Listing files in "long" format:

```
# cpio -icvtB </dev/rmt/0m
120 blocks
100644 beccat   13701   Oct   3 17:00:00  1986   oct03.dta
100644 beccat   39646   Oct   4 17:00:00  1986   oct04.dta
100644 beccat    3165   Oct   5 10:45:41  1986   oct05.dta
100644 beccat    3165   Oct   5 15:30:33  1986   Test/oct05.dta
# □
```

The long format displays the mode of the file (in octal), the file owner, the size in bytes, the modification time, and the pathname used to store the file on the backup tape.

Figure 3.50 shows a simple shell script for creating a table of contents. Simply type "cpiotoc" for a long listing of the files on your backup tape.

Figure 3.50 Shell script for listing the files on a backup tape.

a. Syntax for invoking the shell script:

cpiotoc

b. Listing of the **cpiotoc** shell script:

```
:
# @(#) cpiotoc  List a table of contents
DEVICE=/dev/rmt/0m
USAGE="Usage: $0"
case $# in
0)   cpio -icvtB < $DEVICE
     exit 0 ;;
*)   echo $USAGE
     exit 1 ;;
esac
```

Verifying Your Backup. When you back up your files, save the standard error output of **cpio** in a disk file as discussed above. When your backup operation is complete, create another file containing the table of contents of the tape. Then compare the contents of these two files—they should contain the same filenames and block count.

Figure 3.51 shows an example. The first **cpio** command backs up the files to device **/dev/rmt/0m** and writes a log onto the standard error output, which is redirected to the ordinary file **/tmp/backup.log**. We break up this first long command line between the **find** and **cpio** command by entering a backslash (\) just before typing RETURN. The Bourne shell issues a secondary prompt (>) telling you that it's waiting for more input.

We used **−type f** with **find** to locate only ordinary files since we can use the **d** option with copy-in mode so that directories will be created as needed during restoration. However, any directories created will be subject to the current file creation mask, **umask**, value. Thus, directories would be created mode 777 if the **umask** is 0000, or mode 755 if the **umask** is 022, or mode 700 if the **umask** is 077. If you do back up directories onto the tape, they'll be restored with the modes recorded on the backup tape.

The second **cpio** command line reads the backup tape, writing the file list to standard output and the block count to standard error. We combine standard error with standard output and write both to the ordinary file, **/tmp/tbl.contents**, by using the construction **>/tmp/tbl.contents 2>&1**, which means first associate standard output with the **/tmp/tbl.contents** file, and then associate standard error with the same file.

For illustration, we show the contents of the log and table-of-contents files with **cat**. They have the same contents, except that the block count is last in the log file, but comes first in the table-of-contents file.

Figure 3.51 Verifying your backup.

```
# cd /Dbase
# find . -type f -print |\
> cpio -ocvB >/dev/rmt/0m 2>/tmp/backup.log
# cpio -ictB </dev/rmt/0m >/tmp/tbl.contents 2>&1
# cat /tmp/backup.log
oct03.dta
oct04.dta
oct05.dta
Test/oct05.dta
120 blocks
# cat /tmp/tbl.contents
120 blocks
oct03.dta
oct04.dta
oct05.dta
Test/oct05.dta
#  □
```

Comparing the backup log and table-of-contents files can be tedious at best. Figure 3.52 lists a shell script that backs up a directory and automatically compares the block counts obtained from the backup log and table-of-contents files. Any discrepancy is reported to the operator.

Figure 3.52 A backup shell script with automatic verification.

```
:
# @(#) cpiobackup3   cpio Directory backup with verify
DEVICE=/dev/rmt/0m
REWINDTIME=60     # Time to rewind tape (in seconds)
TMPDIR=/usr/tmp
trap "/bin/rm -f $TMPDIR/$$[ab]; exit" 0 2 3 15
USAGE="Usage: $0 [directory]"
case $# in
0)   cd /
     break ;;
1)   if [ ! -d "$1" ]; then
          echo "ERROR: \"$1\" not a directory"
          echo $USAGE
          exit 1
     fi
     cd "$1"
     break ;;
*)   echo $USAGE
     exit 2 ;;
esac
#
find . -type f -print |
cpio -ocavB >$DEVICE 2>$TMPDIR/$$a
# read tape to verify:
sleep $REWINDTIME     # wait for tape to rewind
echo "$0: Verifying files on backup tape.\n" >&2
cpio -ictB < $DEVICE >$TMPDIR/$$b 2>&1
# Compare block counts:
NUMWROTE=`grep blocks $TMPDIR/$$a`
NUMREAD=`grep blocks $TMPDIR/$$b`
if [ "$NUMWROTE" = "$NUMREAD" ];then
    echo "$0: No errors." >&2
else
    echo "$0: Verification error." >&2
    echo "Block counts don't match." >&2
fi
echo "Wrote to tape:  $NUMWROTE" >&2
echo "Read from tape: $NUMREAD"  >&2
lp $TMPDIR/$$b    # Get a hardcopy of the Table of Contents
```

For an even more rigorous test, try to restore the last file on your backup tape. We discussed this approach to verify backups made with **tar** in the preceding section. If you can restore the last file, you know that you can read the entire tape since the system must read all the intermediate data on the tape before reaching the last file. First determine what the last file is. Then rename the copy on the working disk so that it won't get overwritten. Next use the copy-in mode to restore the file to the working disk. If it's identical to the file you just renamed, you've verified your backup tape. Figure 3.53 shows an example.

Figure 3.53 Verifying your backup by extracting the last file on the tape.

```
# cpio -ictB < /dev/rmt/0m ¦ tail -1
120 blocks
Test/oct05.dta
# cd /Dbase
# mv Test/oct05.dta Test/temp
# cpio -icvdmB Test/oct05.dta < /dev/rmt/0m
Test/oct05.dta
120 blocks
# cmp Test/oct05.dta Test/temp
# sum Test/oct05.dta
18747 7 Test/oct05.dta
# sum Test/temp
18747 7 Test/temp
# rm Test/temp
# □
```

First, we determined the name of the last file on the backup tape using **tail** to limit the output to the last line. *Note:* The block count of the entire tape was displayed first, before the filename. Then we moved to the directory from which that file was backed up. We renamed **Test/oct05.dta** so that the extracted file wouldn't overwrite it. Then we extracted the last file on the tape. Finally, we used the **cmp** command to compare the two files. We know the files to be identical since **cmp** didn't display any output. For an alternative approach that shows some output, we compared the checksum and block counts of the two files using the **sum** command.

Archiving Files Using Pass Mode

In pass mode **cpio** copies files between directories on your working disk. You would copy between file systems for backup purposes. You can copy files between file systems with **cp**, but you can't retain the original modification times as you can with **cpio**. It's true that the **mvdir** command is more efficient than **cpio** for relocating directory trees within a file system. But you'll need to use **cpio** for moving directories between file systems.

Generally, pass mode is not considered for backups since the destination must be a directory on a mounted file system, not an external backup tape. However, we've found it convenient for, say, daily disk-to-disk copies that precede a weekly backup to tape. However, if both disks use the same controller, and it goes bad, your backups could get corrupted. Pass mode backups between machines using distributed file systems are convenient, fast, and relatively safe. Of course, if the local area network connecting the machines goes down, you lose access to your backup files.

Pass mode is specified by using the —p option on the **cpio** command line. Several other options can be used as well in this mode. All options for **cpio** are tabulated together in Appendix E.

Part a of Figure 3.54 shows the general command line syntax to use for pass mode. Part b shows a simple example. Here we create a subdirectory (named **Subdir**) in the current directory (**/Dbase**) and copy all ordinary files (whose names aren't capitalized) to the directory. The two **ls** —l commands show that the —m option to **cpio** retained the modification times of the files. You can use an approach like this example to move files anywhere in the directory hierarchy for which you have write permission.

Figure 3.54 Using pass mode with **cpio**.

a. General command line syntax:

cpio —p[*option...*] *directory* < *namelist*

b. An example of directory copy:

```
# cd /Dbase
# mkdir Subdir
# ls [a-z]* ¦ cpio -pdumv Subdir
Subdir/oct03.dta
Subdir/oct04.dta
Subdir/oct05.dta
112 blocks
# ls -l [a-z]*
-rw-r--r--    1 beccat    users       13701 Oct   3   1986 oct03.dta
-rw-r--r--    1 beccat    users       39646 Oct   4   1986 oct04.dta
-rw-r--r--    1 beccat    users        3165 Oct   5   1986 oct05.dta
# ls -l Subdir
total 114
-rw-r--r--    1 beccat    users       13701 Oct   3   1986 oct03.dta
-rw-r--r--    1 beccat    users       39646 Oct   4   1986 oct04.dta
-rw-r--r--    1 beccat    users        3165 Oct   5   1986 oct05.dta
# □
```

In the general command line format statement above, *directory* signifies the full or relative pathname of the destination directory for the copy and *namelist* the list of files to be transferred. Newlines must separate the file names in *namelist*. Usually, *namelist* comes from the output of the **ls** or **find** command, but you could write the names in an ordinary file or enter them from the keyboard.

Partial Backup to a Spare Partition. We just saw an example using **cpio** in pass mode to copy files from one directory to another. You can use a similar technique to do a partial backup to a mounted spare disk partition. You may find this approach useful if your backup medium is a removable disk pack or a disk on a remote machine connected by a LAN. The main advantage is that it's so easy to recover files. Just mount the partition with the backup and restore the files with **cp**, or if you wish to retain the modification time, use the —**m** option with the pass mode of **cpio**.

Figure 3.55 shows the setup we use on one of our workstations. Here we mount our small sample file system, **/dev/dsk/2s0**, onto the **/Dbase** directory, and the spare partition, **/dev/dsk/1s0**, onto the **/Backup** directory. Then we show a long listing of all the source files before we invoke **cpio**.

Figure 3.55 Setup for partial backup using **cpio** in pass mode.

```
# mount /dev/dsk/2s0 /Dbase
# mount /dev/dsk/1s0 /Backup
# cd /Dbase
# ls -l
total 115
drwxr-xr-x   2 beccat    users          48 Oct  8 16:18 Test/
-rw-r--r--   1 beccat    users       13701 Oct  3 17:00 oct03.dta
-rw-r--r--   1 beccat    users       39646 Oct  4 17:00 oct04.dta
-rw-r--r--   1 beccat    users        3165 Oct  5 10:45 oct05.dta
# ls -l Test
total 7
-rw-r--r--   1 beccat    users        3165 Oct  5 15:30 oct05.dta
# ls /Backup
# □
```

Figure 3.56 shows the transfer of files. We use **find** to locate all files in our source file system by starting with the mount point directory, **/Dbase**. This list of files is piped into **cpio** set up to copy them with pass mode to the **/Backup** directory.

Figure 3.56 Using **cpio** in pass mode to transfer files between file systems.

```
# find . -type f -print ¦ cpio -pdumv /Backup
/Backup/oct03.dta
/Backup/oct04.dta
/Backup/oct05.dta
```

```
/Backup/Test/oct05.dta
# □
```

The **v** (verbose) option of **cpio** will report the names of the destination files. Because the names all begin with the directory **/Backup**, we can see that the directory tree was copied to another directory. The **d** option causes directories to be created as necessary. The destination files will have the same modification time as the source files since we used the **m** option. Other attributes, such as permission modes and ownership, are also retained.

The long listing in Figure 3.57 reveals that modification times have remained the same.

Figure 3.57 Listings of destination files.

```
# cd /Backup
# ls -l
total 115
drwxr-xr-x    2 root      sys            48 Oct  9 08:55 Test
-rw-r--r--    1 beccat    users       13701 Oct  3 17:00 oct03.dta
-rw-r--r--    1 beccat    users       39646 Oct  4 17:00 oct04.dta
-rw-r--r--    1 beccat    users        3165 Oct  5 10:45 oct05.dta
# ls -l Test
total 7
-rw-r--r--    1 beccat    users        3165 Oct  5 15:30 oct05.dta
# □
```

Since the superuser did the backup, **root** owns the **Test** directory, which wasn't copied but rather created. Thus, to avoid changing ownership (and permission modes because of the **umask** setting), you should have **find** locate directories in your source partition for copying by **cpio** to the destination partition.

Incremental Backup to a Spare Partition.   Just as you can use **cpio** in pass mode to back up an entire file system to a larger spare partition, you can do incremental backups to a spare partition. We'll outline the approach that we use on one of our workstations.

Our 20-megabyte working disk contains both system and user files, and our 10-megabyte disk stores our backups. Every evening after bringing the system down to single-user mode, we do an incremental backup of our user files from the working disk to the spare hard disk. Since the backups flow repeatedly with the same relative pathnames to the same disk, the most recent backup constantly overwrites the earlier one. This way the space required on the backup disk is not as great as you'd first think since, in practice, files are frequently overwritten again and again. Of course, you should occasionally review the files on the backup disk to discard junk and temporary files. Figure 3.58 lists the backup shell script that we use.

Figure 3.58 The incremental backup Bourne shell script.

a. Syntax for invoking the shell script:

cpiobackup4

b. Listing of the shell script:

```
:
# @(#) cpiobackup4  An incremental backup using pass mode
cd /
mount /dev/dsk/1s0 /Backup
rm -f /tmp/listing
touch DONE.THISTIME
find `cat config.files` /users -newer DONE.LASTTIME -print >/tmp/listing
cat /tmp/listing | cpio -pdumv /Backup
mv DONE.THISTIME DONE.LASTTIME
umount /dev/dsk/1s0
date >>backup.log
lp /tmp/listing
rm /tmp/listing
```

First the shell process running the script changes to the root directory. Then it mounts our spare partition, **/dev/dsk/1s0**, onto the directory **/Backup**. The **find** command searches areas of the working disk that are updated frequently for files more recent than our time-stamp file, **DONE.LASTTIME**. The search includes files and directories listed in **config.files** and the directory containing all the user accounts, **/users**. To save time we don't search the entire disk because many of the areas, such as **/bin**, **/usr/bin**, and the like, don't change from day to day.

We touch **DONE.THISTIME** to create a time-stamp file before we use the **find** command. This approach ensures that any files created or changed during the backup operation will be archived next time the script is run. The list of files is piped to the standard input of the **cpio** command operating in pass mode. As these files will transfer to the spare file system, they keep their pathnames the same as on the working disk except for the **/Backup** directory prefix. Then the time-stamp file is renamed, the spare disk unmounted, and the current date and time written to a backup logfile, **/backup.log**. Finally, the script prepares a hard copy of the files that it backed up.

The file **config.files** lists configuration files (and some directories containing them) in our root file system. Note that **/usr** is contained in our root file system. We've reproduced the list in Figure 3.59. Note that to save space in the figure we listed the files in two columns. However, the actual filenames in **config.files** are listed one name per line. Most files in the root file system don't change, but the configuration files, which are crucial for system operation, must be backed up if they've changed.

Figure 3.59 Some System V Release 2 configuration files.

```
/.cshrc                              /etc/profile
/.exrc                               /etc/rc
/.login                              /etc/shutdown
/.logout                             /usr/lib/cron/at.allow
/.mailrc                             /usr/lib/cron/at.deny
/.newsrc                             /usr/lib/cron/cron.allow
/.profile                            /usr/lib/cron/cron.deny
/etc/bcheckrc                        /usr/mail
/etc/brc                             /usr/lib/uucp/L-devices
/etc/checklist                       /usr/lib/uucp/L.cmds
/etc/gettydefs                       /usr/lib/uucp/L.sys
/etc/group                           /usr/lib/uucp/USERFILE
/etc/inittab                         /usr/spool/cron/crontabs
/etc/motd                            /usr/spool/lp
/etc/passwd
```

Technically, the files whose names begin with a dot (.) aren't system configuration files. They are files that modify the working environment of the superuser account. You want to archive them if they're changed.

Restoration from a Spare Partition.   Let's see how easy it is to recover a file from our spare partition. Assume that we lost **/Dbase/oct03.dta** on the **/dev/dsk/2s0** partition. Figure 3.60 shows the steps we would use to restore this file.

Figure 3.60 Restoring a file from a Spare Partition.

```
# mount /dev/dsk/2s0 /Dbase
# cd /Dbase
# ls
Test
oct04.dta
oct05.dta
# mount /dev/dsk/1s0 /Backup
# cd /Backup
# echo oct03.dta | cpio -pdumv /Dbase
Dbase/oct03.dta
27 blocks
# cd /Dbase
# ls -1
total 115
drwxr-xr-x    2 beccat    users          48 Oct  8 16:18 Test/
-rw-r--r--    1 beccat    users       13701 Oct  3 17:00 oct03.dta
-rw-r--r--    1 beccat    users       39646 Oct  4 17:00 oct04.dta
-rw-r--r--    1 beccat    users        3165 Oct  5 10:45 oct05.dta
# □
```

After mounting the partition on **/Dbase**, we noted the absence of **oct03.dta**. Then we mounted the backup partition onto **/Backup**. We changed to this directory and used **cpio** to "pass" the file to the **/Dbase** directory. The long listing shows the restoration of this file with its original modification time, ownership, and permissions, as desired.

BACKING UP AND RESTORING WITH volcopy

The name **volcopy** stands for **volume copy**. A volume is a unit of block-oriented media, such as a file system on a disk partition, or a reel of tape. The **volcopy** utility backs up or restores entire file systems. Perhaps your system sends its backups to a nine-track tape or a removable disk pack. If so, **volcopy** would be a fast backup approach if your file systems fit on one tape or disk pack volume.

Some Advantages of Using volcopy.   The **volcopy** utility can back up file systems faster than either **tar** or **cpio** for several reasons: It creates a byte-for-byte image of the file system, which is faster than copying individual files, after adding an identifying header to each one. Since **volcopy** deals with "raw" character devices, it bypasses the UNIX block I/O system. And **volcopy** can choose a transfer buffer size that's best suited for the tape or disk being used. For tapes, the optimum buffer size depends on the particular tape drive and the recording density. For disks, it depends on the largest unit of data the controller and disk driver can handle—from disk blocks up to entire tracks (or cylinders).

As another feature, **volcopy** help prevent errors since it checks the labels on tapes and disks before backing up or restoring data. The labels have been previously written with the **labelit** command. For instance, as we'll see later, without your explicit override, **volcopy** refuses to write to a tape or disk partition that wasn't labeled as required by the command line you used to invoke **volcopy**.

Some Disadvantages of Using volcopy.   You can't recover individual files directly with **volcopy**. It restores only entire file systems. To restore an individual file, you must restore the file system on a spare disk partition, and then copy the file to the destination file system.

Also, you can't store more than one file system on a given backup tape with **volcopy**—unless you have a device that doesn't rewind on close, or a utility that will position the tape for you. Devices that don't rewind are often named like the device that does rewind on close, but with an "n" prefix—like **/dev/nrmt/0m** versus **/dev/rmt/0m**. If the tape always rewinds to the beginning, then each time you use **volcopy**, you'll overwrite whatever is already on the tape.

Furthermore, if there's a problem during a restoration like a power failure, or if **volcopy** gets interrupted, the file system being restored will probably be corrupted. However, you should be able to restart the restoration procedure again.

Labels and the labelit Utility

You must label your disks and tapes before **volcopy** can use them. So before discussing this backup utility, let's learn about disk and tape labels, and about **labelit**, which creates these labels.

Labels on Disks. The label for a disk partition is stored in the superblock of a file system. The label consists of two consecutive sets of characters, each set being 6 bytes long. The name of the file system is in the first 6 bytes and the volume name in the second 6. Figure 3.61 diagrams the disk label schematically. This example represents the root file system on volume named **0s0**.

Figure 3.61 A schematic diagram of the disk label for the root file system.

r	o	o	t			0	s	0			

Usually, the file system name of a mountable file system will be the same as the basename of its mount point directory. For instance, let's say you have a file system that you mount on **/usr**. Then its file system name would be **usr**. However, the root file system (which is always mounted) generally has the name **root**, not **/**.

The volume name of a fixed disk partition generally takes the device name of the partition. Thus the file system on the partition with device name **/dev/dsk/2s0** would probably use **2s0** as its volume name. Removable disk packs should use a volume name that won't be used for any other pack. Wise installations often use part of the serial number of the disk pack for the pack's volume name.

Labels on Tapes. Tape labels contain more information than disk labels. As you can see in Table 3.4, the tape label advises us of seven particulars of the tape, and it takes only 28 bytes to do so. The first column of the table is the field name, the second the data type used for storing the field information, and the third column is the length of the field. Note that the length of the long int (integer)-type field is almost always 4 bytes (or 32 bits).

TABLE 3.4 TAPE LABEL STRUCTURE USED BY **labelit** AND **volcopy**

Field name	Data type	Length (bytes)
magic	char	8
volume	char	6
total-reels	char	1
reel number	char	1
time	long int	4
length	long int	4
density	long int	4

labelit places the label at the beginning of the tape. It fills in only the first two fields—*magic* and *volume*. **volcopy** will complete the remaining fields. The *magic* field contains the string "Volcopy." The contents of the *volume* field will be the volume name specified on the **labelit** command line. But you also specify a file system name, such as **usr**, when you invoke **labelit** to create or change a tape label. Where is that stored?

Figure 3.62 shows the three 512-byte blocks that **labelit** writes at the beginning of a tape. The 28-byte tape label itself is written at the beginning of the first 512-byte block, which is padded to the end with 484 NULL characters. The second 512-byte block, which corresponds to the "boot block" of the file system, is blank (filled with NULLs). The third 512-byte block, which corresponds to the "superblock" of the file system, is a copy of the superblock for the file system specified on the **labelit** command line. This third (superblock) block contains the file system and volume name.

Figure 3.62 A schematic diagram of the information **labelit** writes to tape.

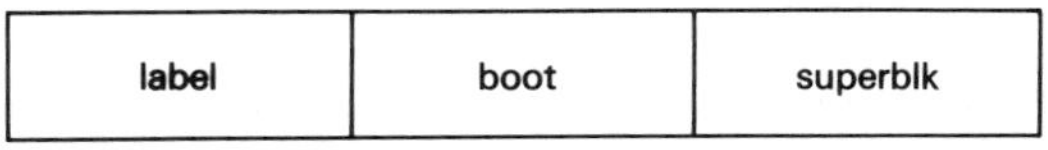

label	boot	superblk

Using the labelit Utility.   You use **labelit** to create or update a label on disk-based file systems or magnetic tape. It can also read the label on these devices. We will discuss using **labelit** to label file systems when we discussed the UNIX file system.

A file system should be unmounted when you label it. Why? Because **labelit** writes directly to the disk. And when you unmount the file system, the memory copy of the superblock replaces the superblock on the disk to keep the disk superblock up to date, overwriting the changes made by **labelit**. And how would you label the root file system, which is always mounted? You'd bring the system down to single-user mode, then enter **sync** to update the superblock, run the **labelit** command to label the root file system, and without typing anything else, reset the system. After booting up and running **fsck**, you should find the root file system labeled, as desired.

Figure 3.63 shows some **labelit** command lines. Part a depicts the general command line syntax. Parts b and c show sample command lines for labeling a fixed disk and tape, respectively.

Figure 3.63 Using the **labelit** command.

a. General command line syntax for the **labelit** command:

/etc/labelit *special* [*fsname volume* [**−n**]]

b. Labeling a fixed disk:

```
# /etc/labelit /dev/dsk/2s0 Dbase 2s0
```

c. Labeling a tape:

```
# /etc/labelit /dev/mt/0m Dbase 101186 -n
```

The *special* argument gives the device name of the physical disk partition or tape, such as **/dev/dsk/2s0** or **/dev/mt/0m**. The *fsname* argument gives the file system name, such as **root** or **usr**. The *volume* argument gives the volume name of the disk or tape, such as **p0001** or **t0001** for disk pack **0001** or tape **0001**, respectively.

If you omit the *fsname* and *volume* arguments, **labelit** will report all the label information that has been stored on device *special*. Figure 3.64 shows an actual example.

Figure 3.64 Reporting the label on a disk.

```
# /etc/labelit /dev/dsk/2s0
Current fsname: Dbase, Current volname: 2s0, Blocks: 3000, Inodes: 320
FS Units: 1Kb, Date last mounted: Wed Oct  8 16:20:05 1986
# □
```

Here the **labelit** program reports that partition **/dev/dsk/2s0** has file system name **Dbase** (for database partition) and volume name **2s0**. Next comes the total capacity of the partition, in both block and inode counts. The next field tells us that the file system uses 1-kilobyte-size blocks. The "Date last mounted" is actually the last time that the superblock was updated, which should be when it was unmounted.

Figure 3.65 shows how to label the tape to be used for backing up the file system depicted in Figure 3.64.

Figure 3.65 Labeling a tape.

```
# /etc/labelit /dev/rmt/0m Dbase 101186 -n
Skipping label check!
NEW fsname = Dbase, NEW volname = 101186 -- DEL if wrong!!
# □
```

You need the **−n** option to label a previously unlabeled tape. Without this argument, **labelit** complains "tape not labeled." The "DEL if wrong!!" message tells you have a 10-second grace period in case you've made a mistake. Press your interrupt character to abort the command.

Now let's look at the new label. Figure 3.66 shows the result.

Figure 3.66 Examining the new tape label.

```
# labelit /dev/rmt/0m
Volcopy tape volume: 101186, reel 0 of 0 reels
Written: Wed Dec 31 16:00:00 1969
Current fsname: Dbase, Current volname: 101186, Blocks: 0, Inodes: -16
FS Units: 512b, Date last mounted: Wed Dec 31 16:00:00 1969
# □
```

Don't be concerned by the negative inode count (-16) or the strange date (Wed Dec 31 16:00:00 1969). New tapes have no inodes, so the contents of this field is meaningless. The date results from all zeros in the field corresponding to "Date last mounted."

Figure 3.67 shows an example of relabeling a disk pack. That is, the pack already has a label but needs a new, updated one.

Figure 3.67 Relabeling a disk pack.

```
# /etc/labelit /dev/dsk/4s0 Dbase 101186
Current fsname: Dbase, Current volname: p0001, Blocks: 3000, Inodes: 320
FS Units: 1Kb, Date last mounted: Wed Oct  8 16:20:05 1986
NEW fsname = Dbase, NEW volname = 101186 -- DEL if wrong!!
# □
```

Here we changed the volume name from **p0001** to **101186**, which is the current date. You may find the date useful as the volume name of removable disk pack—especially if you back up daily.

Backing Up and Restoring File Systems with volcopy

Now that you have labels under control, let's move on to **volcopy**. Part a of Figure 3.68 depicts the general command line for using **volcopy** to either back up or restore a file system. Part b shows a specific example—backing up the **Dbase** file system by copying the contents of the **/dev/rdsk/2s0** partition onto the tape that has device name **/dev/rmt/0m** and volume name **101186**.

Figure 3.68 Using the **volcopy** command.

a. General command line format:

volcopy [*options*] *fsname special1 volume1 special2 volume2*

b. A specific example:

```
# volcopy Dbase /dev/rdsk/2s0 2s0 /dev/rmt/0m 101186
```

We'll discuss the *options* later as they depend on the particular task you're doing. The *fsname, special,* and *volume* arguments are analogous to those used by **labelit** discussed above. The **1** stands for the special or volume name for the source device and the **2** for the destination.

Backing Up from Disk to Disk. Larger minicomputers generally depend on removable disk packs as a backup medium. But even if you work on a smaller computer, you can use **volcopy** to back up partitions of your fixed working disk on to a disk pack.

Figure 3.69 shows an example. After **mkfs** creates a file system on the disk pack, it's labeled with **labelit**, and **volcopy** backs up a partition of the working disk onto the pack.

Figure 3.69 Backing up from working disk to disk pack with **volcopy**.

```
# mkfs /dev/rdsk/4s0 3500
Mkfs: /dev/rdsk/4s0?
(DEL if wrong)
bytes per logical block = 1024
total logical blocks = 1750
total inodes = 320
gap (physical blocks) = 7
cylinder size (physical blocks) = 4000
# labelit /dev/rdsk/4s0 Dbase 101186
Current fsname: , Current volname: , Blocks: 3500 Inodes: 320
FS Units: 1Kb, Date last mounted: Sat Oct 11 14:32:03 1986
NEW fsname = Dbase, NEW volname = 101186 -- DEL if wrong!!
# volcopy Dbase /dev/rdsk/2s0 2s0 /dev/rdsk/4s0 101186
/dev/rdsk/4s0 less than 48 hours older than /dev/rdsk/2s0
To filesystem dated:   Sat Oct 11 14:32:03 1986
Type 'y' to override:     y
From: /dev/rdsk/2s0, to: /dev/rdsk/4s0? (DEL if wrong)
  END: 3000 blocks.
# tail -1 /etc/log/filesave.log
/dev/rdsk/2s0;Dbase;2s0 -> /dev/rdsk/4s0;Dbase;101186 on Sat Oct 11 14:40:37 1986
# □
```

First we made a file system on the disk pack that was larger than the disk partition we're backing up. Then we labeled the pack with a label that dated the backup. Finally, we invoked **volcopy** to back up the partition.

First, **volcopy** queried us "override?" because our disk pack's file system was less than 48 hours older than the partition we were backing up. We answered **y** to override. The **volcopy** utility checks to make sure that a needless second copy isn't made by an inexperienced operator. 48 hours would be an appropriate limit if you're alternating between two disk packs—using one per day.

Then **volcopy** printed a message giving us another chance to abort (by typing our interrupt character). This last query gives you another chance, if, say, you've switched around the source and destination arguments on the command line by mistake.

Because we didn't abort, **volcopy** performed the backup and reported the number of blocks copied and logged the operation into **/etc/log/filesave.log**, as the **tail −1** command shows.

Note that if the file system name of the destination disk pack differs from that of the source disk partition, you'd get a warning query message with a chance to override. Also, if the volume names don't match, you'll be prompted to override as well. These and other checks made by **volcopy** really assist you to make foolproof backups if you're paying attention. Be careful, because you can destroy an entire file system with an incorrectly set up **volcopy** command line—analogous to a file copy, where copying the wrong way is disastrous.

If you're using **volcopy** interactively, you may prefer to have the program ask you explicitly if you wish to go ahead with the specified backup. You'd invoke **volcopy** with the −**a** option to begin a verification sequence that requires your response instead of the 10-second delay used without this option. Figure 3.70 illustrates use of this option.

Figure 3.70 Backing up from working disk to disk pack with query to continue.

```
# volcopy -a Dbase /dev/rdsk/2s0 2s0 /dev/rdsk/4s0 101186
/dev/rdsk/4s0 less than 48 hours older than /dev/rdsk/2s0
To filesystem dated:  Sat Oct 11 14:32:03 1986
From: /dev/rdsk/2s0, to: /dev/rdsk/4s0? (y or n) y
   END: 3000 blocks.
# □
```

Here the query about the age of the disk pack and the go-ahead for the backup operation was combined into the "From: to:? (y or n)" query.

Figure 3.71 illustrates a simple shell script that prompts for all the command line parameters and then executes **volcopy**. You may find it useful if you don't use **volcopy** often enough to remember the command line syntax. If you wish to run a backup by **cron**, you'll need to design a noninteractive shell script.

Figure 3.71 A shell script for running **volcopy** for fixed disk to disk pack backup.

a. Syntax for invoking the shell script:

disktopack

b. Listing of the **disktopack** shell script:

```
:
# @(#)  disktopack  Backup from working disk to disk pack
#
echo 'Enter file system name of the source (e.g., usr): \c'
read fsname
echo 'Enter source disk device name (e.g., 1s0 or /dev/rdsk/1s0): \c'
read reply
special1=/dev/rdsk/`basename $reply`
echo 'Enter source volume label (e.g., 1s0): \c'
read volume1
echo 'Enter destination disk device name (e.g., 4s0 or /dev/rdsk/4s0): \c'
read reply
special2=/dev/rdsk/`basename $reply`
echo 'Enter destination volume label (e.g., p0001): \c'
read volume2
/etc/volcopy $fsname $special1 $volume1 $special2 $volume2
```

Backing Up from Disk to Tape. Larger supermicros, many minicomputers, and most mainframes generally back up onto nine-track tape. You'll need to specify two options with **volcopy**—the tape density and length. Use the option **-bpi**-*density* to specify the tape recording density, *density* (in bits per inch or bpi), and **-feet***size* to specify the length of the tape in feet, *size*. **volcopy** stores the length and density information in the last eight bytes of the tape label at the beginning of the tape.

volcopy considers the tape density and length to determine the number of tape reels you'll need. It also uses the density to determine the internal buffer size that's optimal for the copy. If you also specify the **−buf** option, the data will be "double buffered"—that is, both the input from the source device and the output to the destination will be buffered separately, thereby speeding up operation.

Figure 3.72 show the steps for backing up a disk partition onto tape.

Figure 3.72 Backing up from working disk to tape with **volcopy**.

```
# labelit /dev/rmt/0m Dbase 101186 -n
Skipping label check!
NEW fsname = Dbase, NEW volname = 101186 -- DEL if wrong!!
# volcopy -bpi1600 -feet2400 Dbase /dev/rdsk/2s0 2s0 /dev/rmt/0m 101186

Reel 101186, 2400 feet, 1600 BPI
You will need 1 reels.
(        The same size and density is expected for all reels)
From: /dev/rdsk/2s0, to: /dev/rmt/0m? (DEL if wrong)
```

```
Writing REEL 1 of 1, VOL = 101186
  END: 3000 blocks.
# □
```

First we labeled a new tape using the −n option with **labelit**. Then we invoked **vol-copy** to make a copy on a 2400-foot tape recorded at a density of 1600 bpi. The backup required only one reel.

Figure 3.73 shows a handy shell script that combines the **labelit** and **volcopy** steps shown in Figure 3.72.

Figure 3.73 A shell script for using **volcopy** to backup from working disk to tape.

a. Syntax for invoking the shell script:

disktotape

b. Listing of the **disktotape** shell script:

```
:
# @(#)  disktotape  Backup from working disk to tape backup
#
echo 'Enter file system name (e.g., usr): \c'
read fsname
echo 'Enter source device name (e.g., 1s0 or /dev/rdsk/1s0): \c'
read reply
special1=/dev/rdsk/`basename $reply`
echo 'Enter source volume label (e.g., 1s0): \c'
read volume1
special2=/dev/rmt/0m                              # assume default tape device
echo 'Enter tape volume label (e.g., t0001): \c'
read volume2
echo 'Enter length of tape in feet (e.g., 2400): \c'
read size
echo 'Enter density of tape in bpi (e.g., 1600): \c'
read den
/etc/labelit $special2
if test  $? -gt 0                                # if not already labeled
then
    /etc/labelit $special2 $fsname $volume2 -n  # label it
    if test $? -gt 0
    then
        exit 1                                  # exit on error
    fi
fi
/etc/volcopy -bpi$den -feet$size $fsname $special1 $volume1 $special2 $volume2
```

Restoring from Disk Pack to Fixed Disk Partition.   The restore procedure is the inverse of the backup. Figure 3.74 shows the command to use if you were restoring from the backup made in Figure 3.69.

Figure 3.74 Restoring from disk pack.

```
# volcopy Dbase /dev/rdsk/4s0 101186 /dev/rdsk/2s0 2s0
From: /dev/rdsk/4s0, to: /dev/rdsk/2s0? (DEL if wrong)
  END: 3000 blocks.
# □
```

Restoring from Tape to Fixed Disk Partition.   Again, the restore procedure is the inverse of the backup. Figure 3.75 shows the command to use if you were restoring from the backup made in Figure 3.72.

Figure 3.75 Restoring from backup tape.

```
# volcopy Dbase /dev/rmt/0m 101186 /dev/rdsk/2s0 2s0

Reel 101186, 2400 feet, 1600 BPI
From: /dev/rmt/0m, to: /dev/rdsk/2s0? (DEL if wrong)

Reading REEL 1 of 1, VOL = 101186
  END: 3000 blocks.
# □
```

You don't have to specify the −**bpi***density* or −**feet***size* arguments since **volcopy** determines this information from the tape label.

Restoring a Single File.   As we stressed earlier, **volcopy** will restore an entire file system, but not an individual file. So in this section we discuss how you restore a single file.

For our example, let's say you just restored the file system containing the desired file onto the **/dev/dsk/2s0** disk partition. Then you can use the commands shown in Figure 3.76 to restore the file to the working disk with the correct pathname.

Figure 3.76 Restoring a single file.

```
# mount /dev/dsk/2s0 /Backup
mount: warning! <Dbase> mounted as </Backu>
# cd /Backup
```

```
# ls
Test
oct03.dta
oct04.dta
oct05.dta
# echo oct03.dta ¦ cpio -pdumv /Dbase
/Dbase/oct03.dta
27 blocks
# □
```

First, mount the **/dev/dsk/2s0** file system, say on the **/Backup** directory. Note that we received a warning message from **mount** because the file system name (**Dbase**) doesn't agree with the mount directory (**/Backup**). Then we changed directories to the mount point directory and listed the files. The file named **oct03.dta** is the one we wish to restore. So we use **cpio** in pass mode to copy it over. Since we used the **m** option the file modification time isn't changed.

QUICK REFERENCE GUIDE

Using **dd** for image copy duplication:

General command line syntax:

dd if = *input.file* **of** = *output.file* [*options*]

Example: Duplicating a media partition:

```
# dd if=/dev/boot0 of=/dev/boot bs=152b count=4
```

Example: Backing up a boot floppy:

```
# dd if=/dev/floppy of=/tmp/floppy
[ remove original and insert a formatted diskette ]
# dd if=/tmp/floppy of=/dev/floppy
# rm /tmp/floppy
```

Using **find** to locate files for backups:

General command line syntax:

find *pathname-list criteria-list action*

Example: Locate all files in a directory:

```
# cd Srcdir
# find . -print
```

Example: Locate all files that have been added or changed in the last *day* days:

find . **—mtime** *—day* **—print**

Example: Locate all files that have been added or changed since the last backup:

find . **—newer LAST.DONE —print**

Using **tar**:

General command line syntax for creating a backup:

tar cvf *devicename* [*file...*]

Example: Full system backup:

```
# cd /
# tar cvf /dev/mt/0m .
```


General command line syntax for listing files on backup:

tar tvf *devicename*

General command line syntax for restoring files:

tar xvf *devicename* [*pathname...*]

Example: Restoring all files from a tape:

```
# tar xvf /dev/mt/0m
```

Using **cpio**:

General command line syntax for performing a backup:

cpio −o[*option...*] < *namelist* > *archive*

Example: Backing up all files in a directory (tree):

```
# cd Srcdir
# find . -print | cpio -ocavB > /dev/rmt/0m
```

General command line syntax for restoring files:

cpio − i [*option . . .*] [*pattern*] < *archive*

Example: Restoring all files beginning with "oct":

```
# cpio -icvdmB 'oct*' < /dev/rmt/0m
```

Example: Listing files on a tape:

```
# cpio -icvtB < /dev/rmt/0m
```

General command line syntax for copying a directory tree:

cpio −p[*option...*] *directory* < *namelist*

Example: Copying a directory tree:

```
# cd Srcdir
# find . -print | cpio -pdumv Destdir
```

Using **labelit** and **volcopy**:

General command line syntax to create a media label:

labelit *special* [*fsname volume* [−n]]

Example: Labeling a fixed disk partition:

```
# labelit /dev/dsk/2s0 Dbase 2s0
```

Example: Labeling a tape:

```
# labelit /dev/mt/0m Dbase 101186 -n
```

General command line for using backing up or restoring:

volcopy [*options*] *fsname special1 volume1 special2 volume2*

Example: Backing up from one fixed disk partition to another:

```
# volcopy Dbase /dev/rdsk/2s0 2s0 /dev/rmt/0m 101186
```

Example: Backing up from a fixed disk partition to a tape:

```
# volcopy -bpi1600 -feet2400 Dbase /dev/rdsk/2s0 2s0 /dev/rmt/0m 101186
```

4

The UNIX File System

INTRODUCTION

All disk-based computer operating systems have file systems. File systems have two basic components: files and directories. A file is a collection of information kept on a disk or tape and is associated with a filename. A directory is a list of filenames.

Besides this basic architecture, file system designers have tacked on many additional features to their file systems. For instance, file access date, file ownership, file type, and invisible filenames have been added to the file and directory components.

You are privileged to be working with the UNIX file system. You can read any user's file or list their directories unless that user has seen fit to restrict these activities. And you have full control over your own portion of the file system. You can add new directories, change file permissions, and otherwise reorder your own directories and files. The file system lends itself to categorizing files into the appropriate directories. Directories can be created for each new topic of interest, and subdirectories created whenever a directory becomes overcrowded.

This power and flexibility comes with a price, of course. You can take advantage of the UNIX file system only after you have learned enough about the commands that manipulate it. The user who only logs in and uses their favorite word processor might as well be in a simpler environment. We are assuming that you are an advanced UNIX user, anxious to take full advantage of the power available to you, and that you will be willing to learn much more as a system administrator.

In this chapter we take a system administrator's point of view of the file system and investigate two distinct perspectives. One viewpoint is the structure of file systems. File systems are composed of parts that, although normally unnoticed, play important roles for system administration. The UNIX file system has one of the simplest and most elegant file systems architecture to learn about. You will know more about the basic structures that make up any file system once you have studied the UNIX file system. Learning the UNIX file system will also make your life as a system administrator much easier.

After learning about what a file system is made of, you will learn how to create one. The utility that creates file systems is simple to use and fast in operation. Here you will also gain an understanding of the physical organization of a file system and how it can affect your system's performance. Mounting file systems and maintaining optimal performance are also discussed.

The file system check program (**fsck**), our next topic, is like an on-line system programmer. **fsck** checks file systems and can repair most of the damage it finds. And like some programmers, the **fsck** program can perform "miracles" while making cryptic and unintelligible comments to you. These comments, although initially difficult to understand, are packed with information that can help you to recover files or directories that were affected by the restoration. You can also glean information about why the problems occurred and whether your hardware is faulty. A clear understanding of the **fsck** program's operation will also solidify your understanding of the file system and its parts.

The second point we explore is maintaining enough free space in your file systems for trouble free operations. Any file system that runs out of free space causes work to slam to a halt until more room is created. Paradoxically, systems with vast reserves of disk space can be harder to maintain, because you can procrastinate until the disk space problems are truly immense. We suggest methods for routine maintenance that will keep you out of trouble.

PARTS OF A FILE SYSTEM

The organization and layout of the file system's directories are visible, easily accessible, and probably familiar to most UNIX users. The hidden organization that transforms a disk into a file system is not nearly as accessible or familiar.

As a system administrator, most of your duties involve the file system in one way or another. And it is quite possible to perform much of this work without any knowledge of what you are doing. But our feeling is that you are reading this book

because you want to know what you are doing. And for ourselves, we have found
that the more we knew, the easier it was to get things done quickly and correctly.

   File systems need to be located on devices that can be read from and written
to at random locations. These devices are disks, and disks will be our starting
point. The UNIX system provides us with a simplified model of a disk that makes
things easier for the system administrator.

   How the UNIX operating system organizes the disk into files with the mysterious inodes is explained next. Not that inodes are truly mysterious; it's just that the
term *inode* doesn't summon up any concrete images. Well, relax, because we will.

   The supervisory organization of the file system is provided by the superblock.
The superblock holds global information about the rest of the file system, so it is
the master record keeper. After the superblock we will discuss the free block list.
The free block list organizes the available space in each file system.

   The filenames and directories make up the next part. The filenames and
directories provide organization for the people using the file system. File and directory names can be long enough (up to 14 characters in System V, longer in BSD)
to be truly descriptive. And directories provide a way for grouping similar files
(and subdirectories) together, keeping them separate from other files and directories.

   Finally, we will mention indirect blocks and special files. Indirect blocks
allow the UNIX system to handle large files. Special files make it possible to treat
physical devices, such as printers, terminals, and disks as if they were ordinary files.
Thus, all the facilities provided for files, for example, access permissions, apply to
hardware devices as well.

The Logical Disk, Partitions, and File Systems

Disks come in many shapes and sizes. The number of heads, sectors, tracks, and
total capacity vary from one model to another. The UNIX system handles the complex affair of controlling different types of disks through device drivers written by
system programmers.

   The system administrator doesn't need to know all the details for each type of
disk. The UNIX operating system provides a consistent model for any disk, which
we will call the *logical disk*. By a logical disk, we mean that a real, physical disk
has been converted by software into an ideal or model disk. This invention is nice
because it makes every disk "look" exactly like any other disk, except for its size.
Logically, all disks are similar, even though physically they may be very different.

   Okay. Now, I suppose you want to know what a logical disk "looks" like.
Imagine an ordinary-looking drawer. Wooden front, brass handle, maybe a kitchen
drawer, maybe a dresser drawer. Looking a little closer at the drawer, you notice a
label on the front of the drawer, **/dev/dsk/0s0**. Curiosity piqued, you reach out,
grab the handle, and pull open the drawer (see Figure 4.1).

Inside the drawer there are thousands of little compartments, each containing a block. Plastic overlays label each of the compartments. Squinting a little, you can see that the compartments are neatly numbered on the plastic overlays, starting with zero and running to some large number in the corner farthest from zero.

Intrigued, you reach in and pick up a block at random, from compartment 19. The block is crystalline in structure, very carefully broken into many smaller cells. You take this block, and by twisting it in the light, you can see that each cell contains a number from 0 to 255. In a different light, each of the little cells now holds a letter, number, or symbol. The next block you pull out is from compartment 0. It seems to be identical in structure, but appears to have numbers in almost every cell.

You try to close the drawer and walk away, but the drawer doesn't want to close. A bit of insight on your part, and you replace the two blocks into their compartments. Now you can close the drawer.

This is an analogy for the logical disk. The label on the drawer is one of the filenames in the **/dev** directory. It's the UNIX kernel that opens the drawer and gets any block from the logical disk.

Figure 4.1 A logical disk seen as a drawer containing blocks. Each block sits in a numbered compartment in the drawer.

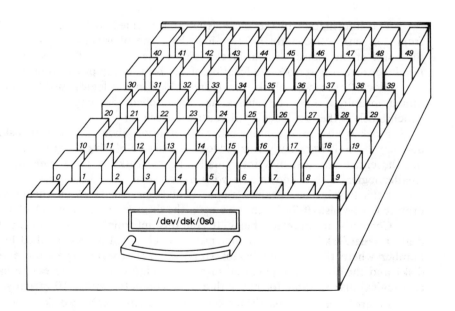

Figure 4.2 A logical disk with a partition "inserted." Partitions can be added anywhere in the logical disk. The location of partitions is described in block 0.

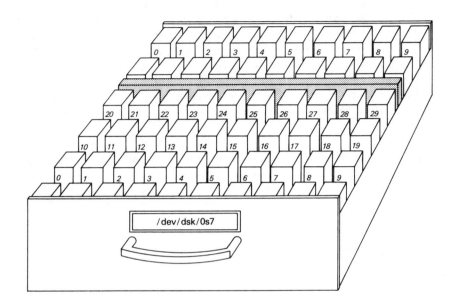

The information in the block from compartment 0 (which we'll call *block 0* from now on) will contain information about the physical disk. For example, the total size of the logical disk in blocks is given here. Block 0 is also called the *boot block* because it describes the location of the boot loader program on this disk.

Block 0, the boot block, is the only block in the logical disk with a predetermined meaning. (The last block has an implied meaning, but you don't know which block *is* the last block until you read block 0.)

Block 0 also may contain other information about the logical disk. A large disk can be split into many smaller logical disks. Splitting a logical disk representing the entire physical disk into smaller logical disks is called *partitioning*. Each smaller logical disk is known as a *partition* or *slice*.

Let's look at our drawer again. This time the label on the outside of the drawer is **/dev/dsk/0s7**. Then, let's open the drawer and pull out block 0.

Correctly interpreted, block 0 contains information for dividing the entire drawer (**/dev/dsk/0s7**) into smaller parts. Each partition is described by the block number where the partition begins (relative to the beginning of the entire logical disk) and the size of the partition in blocks. Figure 4.3 illustrates the partitioning of a logical disk suitable for use with a microcomputer with a 10-megabyte disk.

Figure 4.3a shows partitions possible on a 10-megabyte disk. The whole disk

Figure 4.3 An example of disk partitioning.

a. A sample partition table:

NAME	BEGINNING Block number	SIZE in blocks	PURPOSE
/dev/dsk/0s0	0	15928	File system, minus swap area
/dev/dsk/0s1	15928	4000	The swap area
/dev/dsk/0s2	0	19928	File system including swap area
/dev/dsk/0s3	0	9964	Half-sized file system
/dev/dsk/0s4	9964	9964	Other half-sized file system
/dev/dsk/0s5	19928	36	Boot loader area
/dev/dsk/0s6	19964	36	Alternate block area
/dev/dsk/0s7	0	20000	The entire disk

b. Diagram showing how the example partitions overlap:

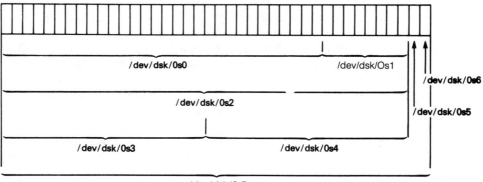

partition is 20,000 (512 byte) blocks long. You only would use the **/dev/dsk/0s7** partition while formatting or making copies of the entire logical disk.

The **/dev/dsk/0s0** partition can be used for making a file system. On systems with only one hard disk, partition **/dev/dsk/0s0** will be used for the **root** file system, leaving room for the swap area, the boot loader, and alternate blocks.

The swap area, partition **/dev/dsk/0s1**, is used as an extension to random access memory (RAM). When you reset your UNIX system, a copy of the operating system, the kernel, is loaded into your system's RAM. As more programs are started, they are also loaded into RAM while they are running. If the RAM becomes full, programs are loaded into the swap area instead. Then processes in RAM are exchanged with processes in the swap area so that each gets a chance to be run while in RAM.

Only one swap area is required, so if the swap area isn't on this disk, the combined areas of **/dev/dsk/0s0** and **/dev/dsk/0s1** can be used for one file system on **/dev/dsk/0s2**. Or this region can be split into two equal-sized file systems, **/dev/dsk/0s3** and **/dev/dsk/0s4**.

You may have noticed that the partitions in Figure 4.3 overlap. There's nothing wrong with this. What it does mean is that only certain combinations of partitions can be used. For example, if you have a file system on **/dev/dsk/0s0** and then create one on **/dev/dsk/0s4**, you will destroy part of the file system on **/dev/dsk/0s0**.

Returning to the drawer analogy, you can imagine that the logical partitions are real partitions that can be slipped in between sections of compartments. The partitions divide the one large logical disk, the drawer, into smaller compartments. For example, we could elect to use the partitions **/dev/dsk/0s0**, **/dev/dsk/0s1**, **/dev/dsk/0s5**, and **/dev/dsk/0s6**. This arrangement gives us a file system, a swap area, an alternate block area, and the boot loader area.

The plastic overlays that were used to label the compartments are changed to reflect the new partitions. The first compartment after each partition boundary has the label "0" (zero) added, and the last compartment is labeled with the number of blocks in the partition minus one. When you are working with one partition, it is as if the remainder of the disk doesn't exist.

Most UNIX systems have at least two partitions—one for the root file system and one for the swap area. The identity of these two partitions is built into the kernel, the operating system program. During system startup (in the **/etc/rc** script), other file systems may be added to the root file system by mounting. UNIX systems typically allow four, eight, or 16 partitions, and only a subset of the available partitions will be used.

The boot partition will probably be present on the same logical disk as the root file system. The boot partition contains a program that is used to load the kernel or diagnostic programs.

The alternate block partition may be present on every physical disk. The alternate blocks are just that—blocks used as alternate, or replacement, blocks. Occasionally, disk media develop defects resulting in errors when that portion of the medium is read. So the blocks corresponding to that region of the disk are assigned alternate blocks from the alternate block partition. (The program or procedure for assigning alternate blocks varies because the program is written for the requirements of the hardware used.) After an alternate block has been assigned, it becomes part of the partition and no different than any other block.

Older Partitioning Schemes.   We need to mention that not all UNIX systems use the partitioning scheme described here. Earlier versions of the UNIX system used different device names and device drivers for different types of physical disks. The partitioning information was part of the device driver for that type of disk, and block 0 was not used for partitioning information.

The numbers of disk types has increased enormously since 1980, and the old method of using a special device driver for each different disk configuration has become impractical. Using block 0 for partitioning information allows the disk-type configuration to be stored on the disk itself rather than being a part of the device driver. The device driver reads the partitioning information in block 0 when the driver first reads the disk.

A Partioning Example.   The partition table in block 0 is created when the disk is formatted. Special, vendor-supplied software may be used to modify the partition information after disks have been formatted. Changing partitions on a disk can result in damaged file systems. Never rearrange your system's partitions without performing a full backup first. If you are partitioning a disk, it's a good idea to keep the sizes of partitions smaller than the capacity of your backup media. Keeping the partition smaller than the backup media allows you to back up an entire partition on one medium (tape or archive cassette, for example).

One vendor delivers UNIX systems with built-in default partition sizes that are created during the installation process. The default partitions are appropriate for installing the UNIX distribution and adding one user file system. Figure 4.4 portrays this initial arrangement.

Figure 4.4 Example disk partitions; 1-kilobyte block sizes.

NAME	BEGINNING Block number	SIZE in blocks	PURPOSE
/dev/dsk/0s0	0	16002	Root file system
/dev/dsk/0s1	16002	16002	Swap area
/dev/dsk/0s2	32004	25002	/usr file system
/dev/dsk/0s3	57006	25002	First user file system
/dev/dsk/0s4	82008	64566	Remainder of disk

Figure 4.4 shows how a 150-megabyte hard disk is initially partitioned. In this system, the boot loader partition is in a reserved area, and not accessible when the UNIX kernel is running. The root partition is 16 megabytes, enough space for both the root file system and the temporary files in the **/tmp** directory. The swap area is also 16 megabytes, twice the maximum memory configuration for this system. Using a swap area that is twice as large as main memory seems to be a rule of thumb for UNIX systems.

The third partition (or slice) contains the **/usr** file system. This file system requires about 16 megabytes for its files (including on-line manual pages), leaving about 9 megabytes available for use in **/usr/spool** or **/usr/tmp**. Nine megabytes will be sufficient for the UUCP system unless this computer will be a feeder in the Usenet network.

The fourth and fifth partitions are not initially used. The persons installing this system could set up these last two partitions as user file systems. Or they could change the size of these two partitions. For example, the two partitions contain about 90 megabytes together. These could be split into two 45-megabyte file systems, or three 30-megabyte file systems, for users. The decision on how to split up the remaining space depends on the user population and the type of backup media. Commonly available archive tapes can store up to 45 megabytes, so even the larger partition size isn't necessarily an issue. If you have only two groups of users, you might want to have just two user file systems. For three distinct user groups, three file systems would be appropriate to use, for example, marketing, sales, and support.

Partition Naming Conventions.   We have chosen to use the partition naming convention adopted by System V, Release 2 throughout this book. This naming convention actually produces two similar forms for partition names. For example, both **c0d0s0** and **0s0** can stand for the same partition of the same disk. Here's how it works.

On smaller computer systems, there will only be one disk controller. There may, however, be more than one disk drive, so it is desirable to include the identifier for the disk drive in the partition name. The slice itself must also be identified. Both a drive number and a partition, or *slice*, identifier can be combined into a single name using an **s** (for slice) to separate the drive and the partition number. So partition zero on drive zero becomes **0s0** (read as: drive zero, slice zero), and partition two on drive one is **1s2** (drive one, slice two).

Larger computer systems may have more than one disk controller, each connected to several drives. To accommodate this additional hardware, the partition name is expanded to include identification of the controller number. A **c** is used to specify the controller number, and a **d** separates the controller number from the drive number. Thus, the zero partition on drive zero connected to controller zero becomes **c0d0s0**, which can be read as "controller zero, drive zero, and slice zero." Partition two on drive one of controller one is called **c1d1s2**, or "controller one, drive one, slice two".

BSD and XENIX use a different naming convention. Two characters, representing the name of the device driver, form the beginning of a partition name. A drive number comes after the two letters, followed by a single letter of the alphabet, signifying the partition. The first partition is **a**, the second is **b**, and so on. For example, if the device driver abbreviation is **hd** (for hard disk), the first partition on the zero drive is named **hd0a**. Partition two on drive one would be named **hd1b**.

By convention, the root partition gets named **0s0**, **c0d0s0**, or perhaps **hd0a**. The swap device will be the second partition on the first drive, **0s1**, **c0d0s1**, or **hd0b**. Beyond the first two partitions, root and swap, different manufacturers may use the other partitions for different purposes.

Blocks

So far, all we have said about the blocks themselves is that they contain a fixed "number of cells." The cells in our analogy each contain a unit of information, called a *byte*. Each byte contains 8 bits, which are arranged into patterns that can represent a number, a letter, or symbol. Exactly what a byte represents depends on the context in which it is used by a program. Bytes can be grouped together by programs to create larger numbers, or collected together to create text.

Each block contains the same number of bytes. The System V UNIX file system uses 1024 bytes in a block. Unfortunately, some UNIX utilities use the older 512-byte blocks (half of 1024) as their unit of measurement when reporting the sizes of files. The change to 1024-byte blocks is a recent one (starting with System V), and many UNIX commands predate this change. Many XENIX commands use 512-byte blocks, while BSD utilities use 1024-byte blocks. We'll expand on this discrepancy in block sizes when the time comes.

Blocks fit into the numbered compartments in the logical disk. The blocks themselves aren't labeled in any way. They are referred to by their compartment number, better known as the *block address*. Sometimes, the term *block number* is used instead of block address. We prefer block address, as the word "address" implies a location rather than a label.

Inodes—Collecting Blocks into Files

Logical disks provide us with thousands of uniquely numbered compartments containing blocks. Now, we need to talk about how these blocks are organized into files.

This time we will be using an analogy from real life. When systems programmers need to work with a new computer that doesn't have an operating system (yet), they sometimes use notebooks to organize files. A typical notebook entry for a file might identify the file's owner, the date that the file was created or modified, the purpose for the file, and the block addresses (locations of the compartments) that make up the file.

Figure 4.5 Neatly handwritten notebook entries.

```
toni, 4/19/84, memory test, blocks 24-56
jay, 3/25/84, downloader, blocks 10-22, 57, 58
jay, 4/22/84, keyboard echo, blocks 66-74
jack, 5/2/84, file system, blocks 1002-2111
```

On another page in the notebook is a list of the blocks that are currently unused, that is, the location of *free blocks* that are available for allocation to a file. The programmers would remove blocks from the free block list when they want to create a file, or add blocks to an existing file, and return blocks to the list when they delete a file. Thus, the notebook approach to organizing blocks into files is to maintain a list of entries describing the owner, a date, the purpose, the blocks used in each file, and another list of the free blocks.

Fortunately for us, the UNIX operating system handles the details of the notebook. In the UNIX system, each "notebook entry" describing a file is called an *information node*, or *inode* for short. The UNIX file system inode contains more useful information than the notebook entry. After all, we have a computer to handle the nitty-gritty details. Figure 4.6 illustrates the information stored in a typical inode, for the file **/bin/echo**.

Figure 4.6 Information contained in the inode for **/bin/echo**.

```
Type=ordinary Perm=rwxr-xr-x links=1 user-id=2 group-id=2 size=3624
a0:  726  a1:  725  a2:  724  a3:  723  a4:    0  a5:    0  a6:    0
a7:    0  a8:    0  a9:    0  a10:   0  a11:   0  a12:   0
Time of last access:          Fri May 17 17:41:03 1985
Time of last modification:    Sun Mar  3 13:40:49 1985
Time of last inode change:    Sun Mar  3 13:40:49 1985
```

The first line of the figure shows the file type, the access permissions, number of links, user (file owner) and group owner identification numbers, and the size of the file. This information is actually more familiar than it might seem at first. Let's look at the long directory listing for **/bin/echo** in Figure 4.7.

Figure 4.7 Long listing for the **/bin/echo** file.

```
$ ls -l /bin/echo
-rwxr-xr-x 1 bin    bin      3624 Mar  3 13:40 /bin/echo
^      ^   ^ ^      ^        ^               ^
¦      ¦   ¦ ¦      ¦        ¦               ¦
¦ perms ¦ owner ¦         size    date last modified
type       links      group
```

The leading dash in the long listing stands for an ordinary file. The next nine characters represent the access permissions. The number preceding the owner and group names is the number of links. The size (in bytes) precedes the time and date of last modification. A file is modified when it is written to.

An inode has space for storing 13 block addresses. In Figure 4.6, only the first four addresses represent actual locations; zero (0) is used to fill unused block address spaces in an inode. After the 13 spaces for block addresses appear three dates. The second date, time of last modification, is also reported in long listings (**ls −l**). The other two dates are available by using the **−u** or **−c** option with the **−l** option to the **ls** command. The **−u** option displays the last access time for the inode, as in the last time the file was **used**. The **−c** option displays the time that the inode itself was changed, for example, by changing the access permissions or adding another block. Other UNIX commands, like **find**, **cpio**, **make**, and **ff**, also make use of the dates kept in the inodes.

Notice that the name of the file is not included in the inode. The inode describes the collection of blocks used for a file. The name associated with a particular inode belongs in a directory, not the inode. Inodes are identified by their position in the file system, the inode number. Directory entries link inode numbers to filenames. Inode numbers are unique only within a file system.

Only two inodes have special, fixed meanings. The first inode, inode 1, was used for collecting bad blocks in a file system in earlier releases of the UNIX system. Although inode 1 is no longer used for collecting bad blocks, it retains its special meaning for compatibility with some backup utilities. The second inode, inode 2, describes the root directory for a file system. Programs such as **mount** and **fsck** rely on the predetermined meaning of inode 2. There is no inode 0. (Inode number 0 is used to mark a directory entry that has been removed.) The remaining inodes are used for creating any type of file. The inodes begin with the third block of the file system. Figure 4.8 shows the position of the inodes in relationship to the beginning of the file system and the data blocks.

Figure 4.8 Position of the inodes in the file system.

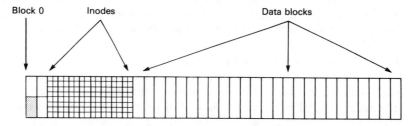

The file type, the link count, and the block addresses contained in each inode are featured when we discuss **fsck**. The time and date information are invaluable when picking files to backup or purge from a file system.

You may have wondered how files larger than 13 blocks can be described since there are only 13 block addresses in each inode. We will address the problem of describing files larger than 13 blocks (13K) shortly.

Keeping Track with the Superblock

The superblock maintains information about an entire file system. The block with logical address 1 contains the superblock for every partition that is used as a file system. Although the rest of the file system is described in terms of 1024-byte blocks, the boot block and superblock are each 512 bytes long. This is because "old" file systems are allowed, that is, a block size of 512 bytes. The boot and superblock fit the lowest common denominator of block size, 512 bytes. Thus, the boot block and the superblock both fit into the first 1-Kilobyte block. (Note that some versions of UNIX System V keep a duplicate copy of the superblock in the second 1-Kilobyte block. The BSD Fast File System keeps many copies of the superblock around.) Figure 4.9 illustrates the position of the superblock for System V file systems.

Figure 4.9 Position of the superblock in the file system.

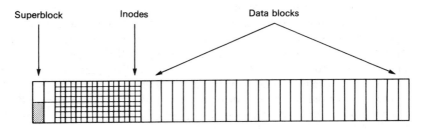

The size of the entire file system, the address of the first data block, the count and list of free blocks, and a count and list of free inodes are kept in the superblock. The date that the superblock was last updated (by the **sync** command or system call) is part of the superblock. The file system's name (displayed by the **mount** command) is stored here, as well as the volume name, the label used when the file system has been created on removable media. Appendix F contains an example superblock, with the various parts labeled.

As a system administrator, you do not manipulate the superblock as you would edit a file. Instead, various utilities and operating system functions use the information stored in the superblock. For example, your system's notion of the date after being rebooted comes from the update time written in the superblock of the root file system (unless your system has a hardware clock). The **fsck** command uses the sizes in the superblock for testing the validity of the superblock itself, and as a basis for further checks of the file system. The UNIX operating system uses the free inode list and free block list for creation of new files.

A copy of the superblock for the root file system and any mounted file systems is kept in memory to speed up disk operations. This memory copy gets changed immediately, for example, when blocks are removed from the free list and added to a file. However, the superblock copy on the logical disk gets updated later. So if the system is halted before the disk copy gets updated, the most recent changes to the superblock will be lost and the file system will have become inconsistent.

Other file system information is kept in memory, such as copies of the inodes that are in use and the most recently used data blocks. Shutting off a machine without copying this information to disk will create inconsistencies in the file systems.

The **sync** command writes every superblock and any other file system information that has been changed since being read to the logical disks. The file system check program, **fsck**, can fix the problems that occur when **sync** wasn't used before system shutdown.

Free Block List

The free block list in a UNIX file system is used in the same way as the free list in the notebook example. Files are created or enlarged by taking blocks from the free block list. Blocks are returned to the free block list when files are removed.

The superblock contains the addresses of up to 50 free blocks for that file system. The last of these 50 addresses specifies the block containing the addresses of the next 50 free blocks. The last of these 50 addresses specifies the block with the next 50 addresses, and so on. You can visualize the list of free blocks as a chain, where the last address in each block provides the link to the next block.

Figure 4.10 The free block list seen as a chain of linked sublists.

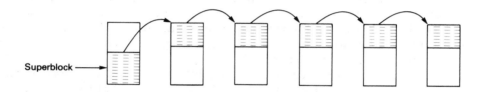

The UNIX operating system uses the free blocks from the superblock's list first. When the last of the 50 addresses has been reached, the next 50 addresses are read into the superblock. Conversely, block addresses are added to the superblock's list when files are removed until the superblock's list has 50 addresses in it. Then the next free block acquired is used to store the 50 addresses currently in the superblock.

Filenames and Directories

Something obvious seems to be missing from the inode: the file's name. This lack was not an oversight by the designers of the file system. Names are collected together in a special type of file called a *directory*. The advantage of this approach is that there can be many directories. And a name that appears in a directory may also be a directory, producing the familiar upside-down tree structure of the file system.

Let's start out by examining a well-known directory, /, the root directory. We will use the **ls** command with the **−i** option. The **−i** option displays the *inode number* associated with each name in a directory listing.

Figure 4.11 Directory entries consist of inode numbers and filenames.

```
# ls -i /
    60 bin
   177 dev
   237 etc
   346 lib
     3 lost+found
  1781 tmp
  1812 unix
   367 usr
# □
```

Each directory entry consists of an inode number and a filename. Inode numbers range from 2 (the root inode) to 65535. The name can be up to 14 characters long. There is (almost) no limit on the number of directory entries that can be in a directory. Like any other file, a directory can grow until it has occupied all the available space in the file system.

Each directory entry provides the relationship between one name and one inode. So when you specify the name of a file, the UNIX system uses the inode number associated with that name to access the correct file. This substitution happens transparently; that is, the user doesn't know, or need to know, that the name provides the connection to an inode.

The directory itself is a collection of data blocks containing filename-inode number pairs. The inode for this collection of data blocks is marked to indicate that this file is a directory, not an ordinary file.

The UNIX system uses system calls to change directory entries. You don't edit a directory as you can a text file. Only through UNIX commands, like **mv**, **mkdir**, **rm**, and **rmdir**, can you modify directories. This protection prevents accidental (or malicious) damage from occurring to a file system's directory hierarchy.

Every directory has two "special" entries named dot (.) and dot-dot (..). The dot entry contains the inode number of the directory itself, and the dot-dot entry holds the inode number of the parent directory. These dot entries provide UNIX users with the ability to specify the current or parent directory as command arguments without knowing their names.

Since the UNIX file system handles these details, why are we bothering you with them? Well, for two reasons. One is that directories, being a type of file, are subject to the same sorts of accidents that can befall other files—hardware problems or incorrect shutdown of the system.

The second reason involves *links*. Think of how the name in a directory is linked to an inode number. Now, suppose that two different names in a directory refer to the same inode number. Using either of these names as command arguments will access the same inode. These two names are thus linked to the same file.

Consequently, many different names in the same file system can be linked to the same inode. You can access a particular file without using a complete path-name from any directory where a link to it appears. This is useful, for instance, when a program requires that a particular file appear in the current directory before the program will function correctly. Instead of making copies of that file, a link to it can be made in the current directory. Using links conserves disk space.

Each time another link is made (by creating a directory entry with the same inode number), the link count in that inode increases by one. And each time a name is removed from a directory, the link count is decreased by one. When the link count in an inode becomes zero, there are no longer any names referring to that inode, so the inode itself is erased and all block addresses are returned to the free block list.

Special Files

Besides ordinary file and directory inodes, System V UNIX supports three more inode types: fifo, block special, and character special files. Fifos (from **first in, first out**) are named pipes that are created by processes as a means for communicating with other processes. Fifos act as temporary files with a maximum size of 5 kilobytes, and should disappear after the processes using them for communication terminate. A long directory listing for a fifo will begin with the character "p." The LP system scheduler, **lpsched**, uses **/usr/spool/lp/FIFO** for communicating with user-invoked **lp** commands.

Block- and character-type inodes connect the file system and physical devices (peripherals) via the device drivers. Device drivers are the part of the kernel that communicates with and controls devices such as disks, printers, terminals, modems, plotters, or whatever. Device drivers transform the many different varieties of hardware into logical devices. And names in the **/dev** directory make the connection to these inodes.

Inode entries for the special files do not contain the addresses of data blocks. Instead, the first block address contains the major and minor device numbers. Major device numbers select a group of driver routines that handle one particular type of device, for example, a tape streamer. Minor device numbers pass information to the selected driver routine, for example, which one of several disks of a given type to use. The other 12 block addresses in special files are unused.

Indirect Blocks

You may have wondered about the 13 block addresses in an inode entry. This translates into 13 X 1024 (block size) or only 13 kilobytes (13K) for the maximum number of bytes in a file. Since many files in the file system are greater than 13K, something else must be happening that allows longer files.

Obviously, the UNIX system must have more room for block addresses, so an inode can describe larger files. The solution to this problem is to use a data block for holding block addresses. When a data block is used to extend the list of block addresses in an inode, it is called an *indirect block*.

An indirect block has room for up to 256 additional block addresses. The eleventh block address in an inode entry is the address of an indirect block. Together with the first 10 blocks addressed, 266K bytes may be accessed (10K + 256K). Many files fall within the range where an indirect block is needed: 10K to 266K.

Let's examine the consequences of an indirect block a little. A copy of the inode for a file that is in use is kept in memory. And any request for a byte within the first 10K of a file can be satisfied by reading the appropriate block using one of the 10 block addresses contained in the inode.

But if a request is made for some byte past 10K, the kernel must first read the indirect block (block address 11 in the inode) to get the block address of the correct data block. Then the data block is read and the request can be satisfied. This means that the kernel must make an additional access before it can locate any portion of a file beyond 10K. The practical effect is that working with larger files takes longer. If you have the option, you are better off using small files (less than 10K) for greater speed and efficiency.

Figure 4.12 shows the inode for a small file, **/bin/echo**, requiring only four block addresses. The small rectangles represent the places for block addresses in the inode. The lines from the first four rectangles show how these block addresses point directly to four blocks. The second illustration, Figure 4.13, depicts what happens in a larger file, **/bin/cat**. The first 10 rectangles point directly to the first 10 data blocks. The eleventh rectangle, however, points to an indirect block, which points to the final four data blocks of this 13360-byte-long file.

Figure 4.12 The first four block addresses in the inode for **/bin/echo** directly reference all data for the file.

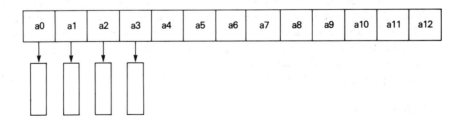

A doubly indirect block is required to describe larger files (greater than 266K). Doubly indirect blocks contain the addresses of 256 singly indirect blocks. With double indirection, up to 67,381,248 bytes (slightly more than 64 megabytes) can be stored in a file. But in order to read, say, the one millionth byte, first the doubly indirect block, then a singly indirect block must be read to find the address of the block containing the millionth byte. The twelfth block address in the inode provides the address of the doubly indirect block.

Figure 4.13 Although the first 10 block addresses for **/bin/cat** directly reference the first 10 blocks of the file, a singly indirect block is needed to point to the last four blocks.

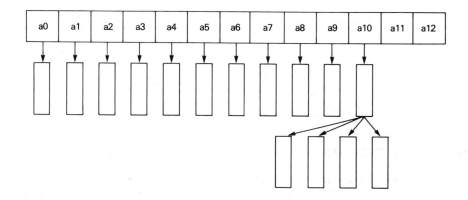

If this isn't enough, there are triply indirect blocks. Files that require triple redirection are so large (greater than 64 megabytes) they won't even fit on most disks. With triple redirection, you could (theoretically) have a file that is 16 giga-bytes, about the same size as the largest file system possible (because block addresses are 24-bit numbers). The thirteenth block address in the inode is used to address the triply indirect block.

Summary

The file system is both the organization of file and directory names that we are familiar with and the organization of blocks into different types of files.

The first block on a disk is the boot block, containing the boot loader's address and partition information. The second block on each partition of a disk that contains a file system is the superblock, with file-system-wide information.

The inodes (information nodes) follow the superblock and are like the note-book entries, with type, permission, ownership, links, dates, and space for 13 block addresses— but no name.

The free block list contains the addresses of the available data blocks in a file system.

Directories are files containing pairs of inode numbers and filenames.

Special files make the connection to devices (printers, disks, etc.).

Indirect blocks contain the addresses of other blocks used when files get large.

The arrows in Figure 4.14 point to the boundaries at the beginning and end of the data blocks, which will vary from one file system to another. The location of the boot, superblock and first block of inodes will always be the same. The block address of the first data block and the address of the first block past the end of the file system define the data block region.

Figure 4.14 Organization of file system parts.

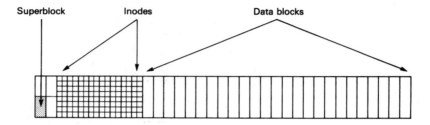

MAKING FILE SYSTEMS

The **mkfs** command builds new file systems on logical disks. To do this, **mkfs** first creates two parts of the file system, the superblock and the inodes. **mkfs** then organizes the data blocks by creating the free list. Finally, **mkfs** makes the root directory for this file system.

The superblock is created using arguments given in the **mkfs** command line and the current date. The superblock also contains the beginning of the free block list. In a new file system the entire data block area is included in the free block list, except for the data block allocated to the root directory inode.

The inodes (remember the notebook entries) are prepared by writing them full of zeros. Inodes containing all zeros are unallocated (free). Then **mkfs** creates the root inode (inode 2) for the root directory for this file system.

The recipe for using **mkfs** can be quite simple. All you need are the name of the logical disk and its size. There are also optional arguments that you can use that can increase the efficiency of the file system or vary the number of inodes created. Figure 4.15 depicts the general command line for using **mkfs**.

Figure 4.15 Simple command line for **mkfs**.

mkfs *diskname size*

The *diskname* is the name of the logical disk that will contain the file system. The **mkfs** command will write over anything that already exists on this logical disk, much the same as formatting erases everything on a disk. Creating a file system is a drastic step, so be certain of the logical disk name before preceding.

The *size* is the total number of 1K blocks available on the logical disk. The size is determined through the documentation provided with your system or with the disk system where the logical disk resides. If you have customized partitions on your disk, the sizes of logical disks should be written in your system's logbook, in the *Devices* section.

As an example, suppose that you have a logical disk named **/dev/dsk/1s2** that has 20,000 blocks available. To make a file system on it, you would enter the command shown in Figure 4.16.

Figure 4.16 Making a new file system using a simple command line.

```
# mkfs /dev/dsk/1s2 20000
bytes per logical block = 1024
total logical blocks = 20000
total inodes = 4992
gap (physical blocks) = 9
cylinder size (physical blocks) = 400
# □
```

Soft Interleave

This example shows the simplest way to make a file system, but ignores a potentially beneficial option to **mkfs**. **mkfs** can build the free list incorporating a *soft interleave*, using the arguments *gap* and *blocks-per-cylinder*. These arguments are stored in the new superblock. The **fsck** command will use the soft-interleave values when salvaging (rebuilding) the free block list. Using the correct soft-interleave will increase the speed with which the system can read from and write to file systems. Most of the time, files are read sequentially (as opposed to randomly), and organizing the blocks in files appropriately decreases the amount of time necessary to read them.

The way that the soft interleave works can best be understood by an analogy. Forget for the moment our logical disk as drawer analogy and visualize a slowly rotating disk (like a record turntable). Sitting on this rotating disk are 10 sequentially numbered blocks. Your task, as a pseudo-operating system, is to grab the blocks from the disk in the correct order and to place them in numbered holes as quickly as possible. As long as the disk is rotating slowly, you can easily reach each block as it comes around and drop it into the appropriate hole (more a test of manual dexterity than of intelligence) (see Figure 4.17).

But if we speed up the rotating disk, the next block has sped away from your outstretched hand before you can get to it, and you must wait until it comes around again (Figure 4.18). What you need is more space between sequentially numbered blocks so that you can reach them before they pass your hand.

Figure 4.17 As the blocks pass the arrow, they are removed and lined up in order.

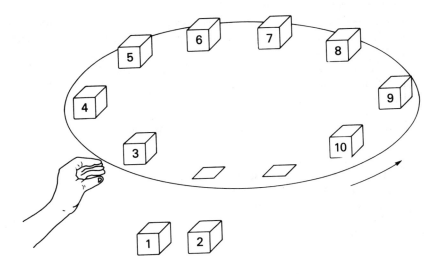

Figure 4.18 But if the disk rotates faster, the second block has moved away before it can be removed.

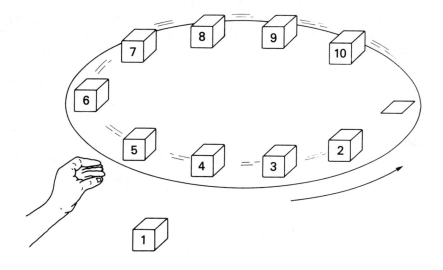

A solution to this problem is to arrange the blocks so that the next numbered block will be moving into position when you are ready for it, as in Figure 4.19. You arrange the blocks on the disk so that three block positions are skipped between the first and second blocks, the second and third blocks, and so on. When you get back to the first block and you still have more blocks to arrange, you fill in the positions between the previous blocks, using the same number of positions to skip, the *gap*, until you have positioned all the blocks. Now you can remove the blocks and place them in the holes correctly without missing a single one while the disk is rotating swiftly.

Soft interleave uses the same technique—leaving a gap between blocks to create the free list. Then, when files are created using the newly ordered free list, the next block in the file will be in the correct position when the operating system is ready to access it.

The gap used by **mkfs** is just like the one in our analogy—the number of block positions to skip. The number of blocks per cylinder is like the number of blocks sitting on the rotating disk. For your system's disks, the number of blocks per cylinder represents how many blocks will pass the disk's read/write heads without moving the heads (stepping). Both the gap and the number of blocks per cylinder should be provided by your system's manufacturer or distributor in their documentation. These values are best determined experimentally by systems programmers, and there can be as much as a 50% difference in disk performance between the best and the worst solutions.

Figure 4.19 The solution is to reorder the blocks on the disk so that the next block to be removed is coming into the correct position.

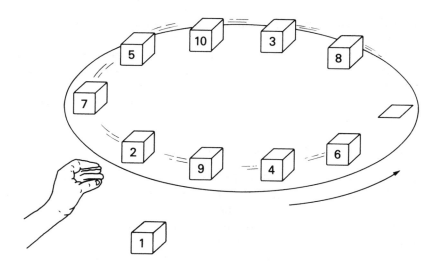

When no gap or blocks per cylinder is specified, **mkfs** uses the default values of 9 blocks to skip and 400 blocks per cylinder. **mkfs** also uses these values if you provide illegal or nonsensical arguments. Illegal arguments include:

- 0 for the gap (1 is the minimum);
- a gap larger than the number of blocks per cylinder;
- more than 500 blocks per cylinder.

Using **mkfs** without providing the gap and blocks to skip, as in the first example, is like typing

mkfs /dev/dsk/1s2 20000 9 400

because **mkfs** supplies these default values. (Note that the defaults used by your system may be different, and more appropriate.) Always use the values you get from your system's installation notes. And when you create new file systems, write down the values that you used in your system's logbook. For example, if the values are 8 blocks to skip and 36 blocks per cylinder, your command would be

mkfs /dev/dsk/1s2 20000 8 36

Number of Inodes

The **mkfs** command also allows you to select the number of inodes to create. The default for the number of inodes is one inode for every four blocks. These values allow you to fill your logical disk completely with 4K-long files without running out of inodes. Since the average file is longer than 4K, this approach usually provides enough inodes.

However, there are circumstances where more inodes are necessary. The Usenet news network typically creates many files shorter than 4K. In this case, you can run out of inodes before the file system is full. You can control the number of inodes created by placing a colon after the size argument and including the desired number of inodes.

mkfs /dev/dsk/1s2 20000:6400 8 36

creates 6400 inodes, instead of the default 4992, that is, 20,000 divided by 4.

If you don't believe that 20,000 divided by 4 equals 4992, you are quite correct. Sixteen inodes fit into one block, and **mkfs** can't create half a block of inodes, so it rounds the number of i-nodes down (modulo 16) from 5000 to 4992. And if you are curious, 4992 inodes use up 312 blocks, the superblock and boot block use two blocks, leaving 19,686 blocks for files and directories.

Creating a lost + found Directory

There is one more step that you should complete after making a new file system. The **fsck** command uses a special directory, named **lost+found**, for creating directory entries. The **lost+found** directory must exist and have room for directory entries before **fsck** is used on the new file system. **fsck** cannot allocate blocks from the free block list when it needs to add to the **lost+found** directory because the free block list is checked after **fsck** uses with the **lost+found** directory.

To create this directory, you must **mount** the new file system, change the directory to the root directory of the new file system, and make the new directory. Figure 4.20 illustrates creating the **lost+found** directory on a file system that exists on the logical disk **/dev/dsk/1s2**.

Figure 4.20 Creating the **lost+found** directory.

```
# mount /dev/dsk/1s2 /a
# cd /a
# mkdir lost+found
# chmod 777 lost+found
# □
```

At this point, you have created a **lost+found** directory with the appropriate permissions. This new directory has one data block allocated to it with two entries: dot (.) and dot-dot (..). There are room for 62 more directory entries, since 64 directory entries will fit in one 1024-byte block. Now, what you may want to do is play it safe by creating more empty directory slots, in case **fsck** needs more than 62 entries in **lost+found**. Figure 4.21 depicts a simple script that creates empty directory entries by creating enough files to allocate 10 data blocks.

Figure 4.21 Adding 9 blocks to a **lost+found** directory.

```
:
cd lost+found
for i in 1 2 3 4 5 6 7 8 9        # create nine blocks
do
    for j in 1 2 3 4 5 6 7 8      # with eight times
    do
        for k in 1 2 3 4 5 6 7 8 # eight names in each block
        do
            > i $ j $ k
        done
    done
done
rm * # remove the names, leaving empty blocks behind
```

This simple script creates empty files with numbers for names. The two inner loops, "for n in" and "for k in," together generate 64 directory entries each time they execute—enough to fill one data block. The first "for i in" loop repeats nine times, so that nine data blocks will be allocated. When the loop has completed, all the directory entries are removed, leaving room for 638 (64 times 10 minus dot (.) and dot-dot (..) entries) directory entries.

Allocating 10 data blocks to **lost+found** is a bit of overkill. If you suddenly had 600 files with numbers for names show up in **lost+found**, you most likely would have other serious damage to the file system as well. It would be easier to replace the file system from backups. Instead, we suggest that you add two additional blocks to your **lost+found** directory. The script in Figure 4.22 will add two blocks to **lost+found** directory, providing room for 190 directory entries.

Figure 4.22 Adding only two blocks to **lost+found**.

```
:
cd lost+found
for i in 1 2 3 4 5 6 7 8 9 10 11 12        # make twelve times
do
      for j in 1 2 3 4 5 6 7 8 9 10 11 12 # twelve
      do
      do > $ i $ j                          # files to fill two blocks
      done
done
rm *                                        # then, remove them
```

In Chapter 5 we explain how you can edit the appropriate scripts to **mount** the new file system routinely. You will also want to add the new file system to the **/etc/checklist** used by **fsck**, to check the new file system routinely.

Labeling New File Systems

The System V **mount** command will produce a warning message if the name of the file system being mounted does not match the mount point. The **/etc/labelit** command writes the file system name and a volume name into the superblock. These names will also appear during the initialization phase of the **fsck** program.

You must be logged in as the superuser to execute the **labelit** utility. The file system to be labeled must be unmounted. And you must know where in the file system hierarchy you intend to mount the file system being labeled. The name of the mount point can be up to six characters long. The volume name is usually a descriptive name for the file system and may also be up to six letters long. For example, to label the file system that we created earlier in this chapter, you would use the command line in Figure 4.23.

Figure 4.23 Using the **labelit** utility on a new file system.

```
# /etc/labelit /dev/dsk/1s2 usr1 1s2
Current fsname: , Current volname: , Blocks 20000, Inodes: 4992
FS Units: 1Kb, Date last mounted: Wed Jan 29 22:50:03 1986
NEW fsname = usr1, NEW volname = 1s2 -- DEL if wrong!!
# ☐
```

In the example, a nameless file system is given the file system name of **usr1**. This file system name implies that you will be mounting this file system as a directory named **/usr1**. The volname is **1s2** and is intended to identify the particular disk partition or removal media. The "DEL if wrong!!" warning means that you have 10 seconds to stop the program (by using your interrupt key) if you've made a mistake.

Mounting File Systems

The **/etc/mount** command adds file systems to the file system directory hierarchy. The **/etc/umount** command removes file systems from the hierarchy. Both commands write in the file **/etc/mnttab**, keeping a record of which file systems are currently mounted. The **/etc/mnttab** file (mount table) is a data file and not readable. The **mount** command without arguments lists the file systems currently mounted by reading the mount table and translating its contents (see Figure 4.24c).

Figure 4.24 The **mount** command.

a. Syntax of the **mount** command. The **−r** flags mount a file system as read-only:

mount [*partition-name directory*] [**−r**]

b. Mount the file system /**dev/dsk/c0d0s4**:

```
# mount /dev/dsk/c0d0s4 /u
mount: warning! <> mounted as </u>
# ☐
```

c. Display contents of mount table, /**etc/mnttab**:

```
# mount
/ on /dev/dsk/c0d0s0 read/write on Wed Oct  7 20:48:30 1987
/usr on /dev/dsk/c0d0s2 read/write on Wed Oct  7 20:48:43 1987
/tmp on /dev/dsk/c0d0s6 read/write on Wed Oct  7 20:48:44 1987
/u on /dev/dsk/c0d0s4 read/write on Wed Oct  7 21:18:25 1987
# ☐
```

d. Trying to mount an already mounted file system:

```
# mount /dev/dsk/c0d0s4 /b1
mount: /dev/dsk/c0d0s4 or /b1 busy
# □
```

The **mount** command does not check for file system integrity before adding a file system to the directory hierarchy. The designers of the UNIX system made the assumption that you know what you're doing and have already checked the file system using **fsck** before trying to mount it. (As of System V, Release 2, the system will prevent you from mounting a file system that needs checking. The **mount** and **fsstat** commands look at a flag in the superblock that shows whether the last file system operation was completed.) The **mount** command will produce a warning message if the mount point doesn't match the file system name (Figure 4.24b). The **/etc/labelit** utility can add a file system name and volume name to the superblock of the file system.

The **mount** command will display a message and fail to mount a file system if that file system or the *mount point* directory is busy. A file system is busy if its already mounted. A directory is busy when it is the current directory of a process or has been opened for reading (with **ls**, for example) or writing.

When a file system is mounted, it replaces the mount point directory with its own root directory. Thus, the contents of the mount point directory, if any, "disappear" when a file system is mounted there. The contents aren't gone, of course. Figure 4.25 illustrates how the **mount** command adds a file system to the directory hierarchy.

Figure 4.25 Adding a file system to the directory hierarchy.

a. Before mounting **/dev/dsk/c0d0s2** on **/usr**:

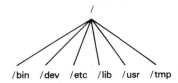

b. After mounting **/dev/dsk/c0d0s2** on **/usr**:

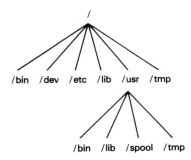

Although the name of the mount point directory doesn't change, it has been replaced by the root directory of the file system in **/dev/dsk/c0d0s2**. The UNIX kernel has marked the **/usr** directory as a mount point for the file system on **/dev/dsk/c0d0s2**. Now, instead of reading the contents of the mount point directory, the kernel reads the root directory of the mounted file system. When the **/dev/dsk/c0d0s2** file system is unmounted, the mark is removed from the mount point directory and the **/usr** directory's contents may be accessed again.

File systems may be mounted on any directory that is not already busy. Remember that the free space within a file system is shared by all processes requesting to enlarge files. Dividing the file system hierarchy into separate file systems serves to isolate the user and system regions.

Unmounting File Systems

The **umount** (not unmount) utility detaches a file system from the directory hierarchy. **umount** first issues a **sync** command, to copy any modified portions of its file system from memory back to the disk partition. (All mounted file systems are updated by the **sync** command.) Then the mark is removed from the kernel's copy of the mount point directory and the mount table, **/etc/mnttab**, is updated.

File systems can be unmounted only when they are not busy. A busy file system is one where a process has its current directory or has opened a file there (for reading or writing). Generally, file systems are unmounted as part of the shutdown process. The **/etc/shutdown** script kills all processes before unmounting file systems, unbusying all file systems except the root file system. Figure 4.26 provides an example of unmounting a file system.

Figure 4.26 A file system is busy when it contains the current directory of a process.

```
# cd /usr
# umount /dev/dsk/c0d0s2
umount: /dev/dsk/c0d0s2 busy
# cd /
# umount /dev/dsk/c0d0s2
# □
```

In Figure 4.26 we make the assumption that the only process using the **/dev/dsk/c0d0s2** file system is the root's shell. By changing the current directory to the root directory (/), we unbusied the **/usr** directory, permitting us to unmount the file system. The only time you can be sure that only the superuser's shell is keeping a file system busy is when the system is in single-user mode.

You may want to unmount a file system without changing to single-user mode. The **fuser** (find user) utility can either display the process id of the process keeping a file system busy, or kill the offending process. Simply killing the offending process strikes us as heavy handed. By obtaining the process id, you can use the **ps** command to determine what command is being executed by that process. Figure 4.27 shows how the **fuser** command is used.

Figure 4.27 Finding a user and process that is using a file system.

```
# umount /dev/dsk/c0d0s7
umount: /dev/dsk/c0d0s7 busy
# fuser -u /dev/dsk/c0d0s7
/dev/dsk/c0d0s7:          194(rik)

# ps -fp194
     UID  PID  PPID  C   STIME TTY      TIME COMMAND
     rik  194     1  0 20:34:39 tty01   0:04 -csh
# write rik
Please change directory to your HOME directory with cd.
<cntl-D>
# umount /dev/dsk/c0d0s7
# □
```

The **fuser** utility is slow, slower even than the **ps** command. It will do the detective work of discovering which processes are keeping a file system busy. In Figure 4.27, process number 194, owned by the user **rik**, is keeping **/dev/dsk/c0d0s7** busy. We notified the user by writing to his terminal, and asked that he change the directory. Of course, changing the directory works because we knew that his home directory was not in the file system that we wished to unmount. After the user has changed the directory, the file system was unmounted.

REORGANIZING FILE SYSTEMS

The **mkfs** command builds empty file systems with optimally ordered free block lists. This optimal order disappears, however, after the new file system gets mounted and used. Eventually, most files and directories are fragmented, that is, the blocks that comprise these files are scattered throughout the file system.

How does this happen? Let's examine what happens when you move a group of users to a new file system. After making the new file system, you use the **cpio** or **tar** command to copy the users' directory hierarchies to the new file system. Then you edit the **/etc/passwd** file, changing the users' home directories to the new file system. Now, the new file system, with its optimally ordered free block list and nonfragmented files and directories, is ready to use.

If only a single person were working in the new file system, things wouldn't get so scrambled. Instead, a small horde of people will be creating new files, enlarging existing ones, or removing files. This activity occurs in parallel, that is, while one user is creating a file, another user may be removing a file. The block addresses in the free block list get shuffled, rather like a deck of cards. And the files that are created, and the directories that are enlarged, are made from this shuffled free block list.

Fragmented files slow down your UNIX system. Most often, files are read sequentially, from beginning to end. When the block addresses making up the files are scattered, reading a file involves moving the disk's heads often, a time-consuming process. Thus, the longer a file system is used, the slower it is to use.

Not all file systems suffer equally from fragmentation. The directories and commands that are part of the UNIX distribution are generally not removed or replaced after the system is installed. So the root file system, and parts of the **/usr** file system, remain unfragmented. It's the user file systems, the file system containing **/tmp** and the spooling directories, that become terribly fragmented.

The BSD Fast File System handles this problem by using *cylinder groups* instead of free block lists. A cylinder is a collection of disk blocks that may be accessed without moving the disk heads. A cylinder group is a set of cylinders located in the same region of a disk. The Fast File System arranges files so that each file's block addresses are in the same cylinder group. If a file grows too large to fit in a cylinder group containing other files, the entire file is copied to another cylinder group with more room.

The Fast File System keeps files from becoming fragmented, speeding up sequential access of files. There is a penalty, however. The Fast File System is more complicated than a System V file system, and takes more of a computer's resources to operate.

Well, the Fast File System takes care of its own fragmentation problems. What do System V system administrators do about the problem? There are two commands that you can use remedy fragmentation—**dcopy** and **mkfs**.

The dcopy Command

The **dcopy** command copies a file system from one partition to another. While making this copy, **dcopy** also reorganizes the files, directories, and free block list for optimal performance during sequential access. The **dcopy** utility can also move all files not accessed in a selectable number of days to the end of the file system (after the free block list) and (by default) put entries for subdirectories first in their parent directories.

You use **dcopy** by first making a file system of equal or greater size on a spare partition. Then the old file system is copied to the new one, while **dcopy** performs its optimization.

Figure 4.28 Using **dcopy** to reorganize a fragmented file system.

```
# dcopy /dev/rdsk/c1d1s8 /dev/dsk/c1d1s10
From: /dev/rdsk/c1d1s8, to /dev/dsk/c1d1s10
(DELETE if wrong)
Available mem 3256320, got 112640 for inodes (that's 1760 inodes)
Pass 1:   Reorganizing file system
Pass 2:   Fixing inums in directories
Pass 3:   Remake freelist
Complete
# □
```

Figure 4.28 shows how **dcopy** is used to reorganize a file system. The old file system is read from the raw device, and the reorganized file system is copied to the block device. Both the old and new file systems must be unmounted. When **dcopy** completes, run **fsck** on the new copy, and copy the new copy over the old with **dd** once you are satisfied that the **dcopy** was successful.

For a 10-megabyte file system on an AT&T 3B2/310, **dcopy** took 31 minutes to complete. You can get progress reports from **dcopy** by sending an interrupt signal (often, the DELETE key), telling you where **dcopy** is in the inodes or directory hierarchy. If you want to kill **dcopy**, send two quit signals (the default is a control-\). If you have started **dcopy** in the background (not a bad idea), you can still see progress reports. **dcopy** modifies the copy of the command line that is kept by the process (in the u_area) and reports its current position in the inodes or directory hierarchy (a nice trick). You can see these reports by using the **ps** command with the −**f** option.

The administrators of large systems told us that a **dcopy** should be performed every several days on busy file systems. **dcopy** improves file system performance (speed of access) by an average of 15 to 20%, which is nothing to sneeze at. However, you might have noticed a couple of problems with this approach.

First, there's that "spare" partition. Not every system has spare partitions that are "equal to or greater than" the size of the old file system. Second, **dcopy** is slow. We had heard that it is slow, but were surprised to find how slow when we finally located a suitably sized "spare" partition with which to experiment. To test the difference in file access, we copied the entire file system to **/dev/null** both before and after the **dcopy**, using **cpio**. Using **cpio** simply to read the file system took less than one-sixth of the time that **dcopy** took to complete.

If you have the facilities and the time to perform routine **dcopy** operations, by all means do so. If not, you can still improve file system performance by using **mkfs**.

Using mkfs to Improve Performance

Lacking a "spare" partition, you can imitate **dcopy** by backing up and restoring an entire file system. You do this in four steps. First, back up the entire file system that you want to reorganize. Then, read back your backup to make sure that there are no errors in your archive media. In Chapter 3 we described how to do this. (If you're really paranoid, make two backup copies.) Once you are sure of your backup, rebuild the old file system using **mkfs**. Be sure to use the optimal soft interleave, since the point of this exercise is performance. Finally, restore the file system from the backups. Run **fsck** to check your reorganized file system, and remount it.

While not as elegant as **dcopy** perhaps, the backup-**mkfs**-restore operation will reorganize your file system similar to the way that **dcopy** does. You will also have acquired a complete, up-to-date backup of a file system. If you wish to emulate the manner in which **dcopy** reorganizes directory entries by moving subdirectories to the beginning of their parent directories, use two find commands to build your list of files to be backed up.

Figure 4.29 Backing up before reorganizing the **/mrkt** file system.

```
# find /mrkt -type d -print > /tmp/directories
# find /mrkt ! -type d -print > /tmp/files
# cat /tmp/directories /tmp/files ! cpio -ocvB > /dev/backup
./Sales
./Sales/East
...
# □
```

Figure 4.29 shows how two **find** commands make two lists. The first list contains only names of the directories in the hierarchy. The second list contains the names of all the files that aren't directories. Together, these two lists are concatenated to produce a backup that has all the directories first, followed by the other files. When this backup is restored to a newly made file system, the results will be almost identical to what **dcopy** can do.

CHECKING AND REPAIRING FILE SYSTEMS

The **fsck** program (file system check) can detect and repair most problems that can occur in file systems. These problems come about through improper shutdown or hardware failure. Improper shutdown means that the system was reset or powered down without using the **sync** command after returning to single-user mode. Failing to use **fsck** after an improper shutdown may result in spreading corruption throughout your file system. Since there is no sure way to know that your system has been shutdown correctly, you should run **fsck** when starting up your system and before mounting any file system.

With Release 2 of System V, a flag in the superblock is set when a modification to a file system is begun, and this flag is cleared when the operation is complete. The **/etc/fsstat** utility checks this flag to determine if the file system needs to be checked. In theory, the file system will only need to be checked if the flag is still set, indicating that a modification to the file system was not completed. While this check seems to work, it also means that the **fsck** command is rarely run. The system administrator should run **fsck** on all file systems routinely, whether the flag for each file system is set or not.

The **fsck** program may change the file system to repair inconsistencies. In so doing, **fsck** may clear inodes, remove directory entries, or make other changes to the file system. The changes wrought by **fsck** require that you, the system administrator, be knowledgeable of the UNIX file system and **fsck**'s operation. While **fsck** makes careful reports concerning what it finds and how it wishes to deal with the problem, the reports are cryptic and need explaining. Later in this section we interpret every report produced by **fsck** and show you how to deal with each.

fsck relies on consistent information that should always exist in a file system. This information involves the parts of the file system and how different parts either agree in a healthy file system or are inconsistent in a damaged one. For example, each inode stores the number of links (directory entries) that refer to it. The number of directory entries for each inode is determined independently of the inodes when **fsck** scans through the directory hierarchy. The number of links stored in the inode should agree with the number of directory entries counted, and **fsck** reports an error when the counts do not match.

Phases of Operation

The **fsck** program works in well-defined stages, called *phases*. You have probably seen the reports produced by **fsck** as it progresses through these phases. The synopsis that follows outlines the part of the file system being examined and how it is checked for consistency during each phase.

Initialization

Although initialization is a distinct phase, the only message output is the file system and volume name (as set by **/etc/labelit**). The command line options are interpreted and the special device file opened. Then the *superblock* is checked for validity by comparing the sizes of the inode list with the total size of the file system. If the inode list is larger than the entire file system, the superblock is corrupt.

** Phase 1 - Check Blocks and Sizes

The *inodes* are checked. Each inode must have valid file type, a nonzero link count, valid block addresses, and size. Information is collected about the block addresses, number of links, and state of each inode for use in later phases.

** Phase 2 - Check Pathnames

The *directory entries* are checked, starting with the root directory and descending through the entire hierarchy. Each directory entry must refer to a valid inode, determined from the inode state list created during phase 1. The number of directory entries referring to each inode is entered in the number of links list collected during phase 1.

** Phase 3 - Check Connectivity

If a directory type inode (from the inode state list) doesn't have a directory entry (discovered during phase 2), an entry may be created to connect it.

** Phase 4 - Check Reference Counts

Other types of inodes without directory entries may have entries created for them; the number of directory entries counted during phase 2 must agree with the link count in each inode; the total number of inodes allocated must agree with the count stored in the superblock.

** Phase 5 - Check Free List

The block addresses in the *free block list* are checked for valid addresses and that no block addresses also appear in inodes. Every block must either be allocated to an inode or be in the free block list.

*** BOOT UNIX (NO SYNC) ***

As **fsck** completes, it will make a report on the number of inodes used, blocks used, and blocks free. And if the root file system has been modified, you will be instructed to reboot the system. If you fail to reboot the system at this point, the changes made by **fsck** will be undone. The root file system is always mounted, and parts of it (including the superblock) are in memory. **fsck** repairs the *disk* copy of a file system, not the parts in memory. Not rebooting when you see the **BOOT UNIX** message will create more problems with your root file system.

fsck is not infallible. It uses the information it discovers while examining the file system and suggests remedies. Often, these remedies are as severe as amputation: the removal of a file. The philosophy used in **fsck**'s design is that files with corrupted inodes should be replaced from backup copies. This approach is certainly the best way to go and will make your life much easier if you follow this philosophy and don't neglect to back up your file systems consistently.

Active File Systems

Before we can talk about running **fsck**, we need to explain *active file systems*. Active file systems are file systems that are mounted. Therefore, they are capable of changing while being examined by **fsck**. Any changes that occur during **fsck**'s examination introduce inconsistencies in the information collected during the different phases. These apparent inconsistencies aren't true problems with the file system, but they will be reported as errors by **fsck** and "corrected."

Imagine, for example, that **fsck** has just completed the phase 1 check of the inodes. At this point, someone copies a 10-block-long file, creating a new inode using 10 blocks from this file system's free block list. **fsck** will report these 10 blocks missing from the free list during phase 5 and will request permission from the operator to reconstruct the free list including these 10 blocks. If this request is granted, these blocks will appear in both the new file's inode and the free list. Files created later may also use these blocks, writing over the blocks of the new file. (Blocks that are claimed by two or more inodes are called *duplicate blocks*.)

fsck refuses to work on mounted file systems (with one exception). This refusal helps prevent damage to mounted file systems, but you can subvert **fsck**'s safeguards in two ways.

First, the root file system is always mounted. You must ensure that the root file system is inactive by running the **fsck** program while in single-user mode. The **fsck** command is run by the **/etc/bcheckrc** shell script during the transition from single-user to multiuser operation. This approach guarantees that there is no other activity during the check of the root file system.

If you wish to run **fsck** on the root file system and aren't sure if you are running in single-user mode, you can discover the current run level by using the **who** −**r** command. Numeric run levels generally indicate multiuser operation, and **S** stands for single-user mode.

Figure 4.30 Determining the current run level.

```
# who -r
  .             run-level 2  May 20 01:25     2     0     S
                           |
                           Current run-level
# □
```

The correct way to change from multiuser to single-user operation is to run the **/etc/shutdown** script (see Chapter 5).

The second way of slipping past **fsck**'s safeguards happens because there are two interfaces to logical disks. The block device interface is used when mounting a file system. The character, or *raw* device, is a more efficient interface for copying or checking a logical device. Thus if you check a mounted file system using the raw device interface (because it's faster), **fsck** can't detect that the file system being checked is mounted.

The usual solution to this problem is to run **fsck** during the transition from single-user to multiuser operation. The shell scripts that handle the transition should check all file systems before mounting the file systems. And if you are mounting a file system at any other time, always use **fsck** on that file system before mounting it.

fsck Command Syntax

The **fsck** command line uses the syntax shown in Figure 4.31a. In part b we show a command that reorganizes the free block list (specified by the −**s** option). Part c shows a typical run after a reboot that follows a power failure. The "POSSIBLE FILE SIZE ERROR" is from **/usr/spool/lp/FIFO**, and the unreferenced files were probably removed immediately before the power went out, leaving inodes without names.

Figure 4.31 Syntax used by the **fsck** utility.

a. Syntax:

   # **/etc/fsck** [*−options*] [*devicename...*]

b. Checking the **/dev/rdsk/0s2** file system, using the **−s** option:

```
# fsck -s /dev/rdsk/0s2
/dev/rdsk/0s2
File system: usr   Volume name: 0s2

** Phase 1 - Check Blocks and Sizes
** Phase 2 - Check Pathnames
** Phase 3 - Check Connectivity
** Phase 4 - Check Reference Counts
** Phase 5 - Check Free List (Ignored)
** Phase 6 - Salvage Free List
962 files 17466 blocks 8422 free
***** FILE SYSTEM WAS MODIFIED *****
# □
```

c. Checking the same file system after rebooting the system after a power failure.

```
# fsck /dev/rdsk/0s2
/dev/rdsk/0s2
File System: usr   Volume: 0s2

** Phase 1 - Check Blocks and Sizes
POSSIBLE FILE SIZE ERROR I=1760
** Phase 2 - Check Pathnames
** Phase 3 - Check Connectivity
** Phase 4 - Check Reference Counts
UNREF FILE   I=1128   OWNER=root MODE=100444
SIZE=731 MTIME=Nov 30 19:02 1987   (NOT EMPTY)

RECONNECT? y

UNREF FILE   I=1307   OWNER=root MODE=100664
SIZE=1119 MTIME=Nov 30 19:02 1987   (NOT EMPTY)

RECONNECT? y

** Phase 5 - Check Free List
962 files 17466 blocks 8422 free
*** FILE SYSTEM WAS MODIFIED ***
# □
```

The *devicename* is the filename (which appears in the **/dev** directory) that makes the connection to the logical disk containing the file system.

    fsck obtains the names of the file systems to be checked from the file **/etc/checklist** if **fsck** is invoked without any device name arguments. This file consists of the device names for file systems to be checked routinely, one per line. The root file system name should appear first. Figure 4.32 shows a typical **/etc/checklist** file, with its ownership and permission modes.

Figure 4.32 A **/etc/checklist** file.

```
# cat /etc/checklist
/dev/dsk/0s0
/dev/rdsk/0s2
/dev/rdsk/0s3
# ls -l /etc/checklist
-rw-r--r-- 1 bin  sys          32 Mar  3 10:44 /etc/checklist
# □
```

Notice that in the **checklist** file, the second and third device names are from the **rdsk** (raw disk) directory. When **fsck** uses the raw disk, blocks are copied directly into **fsck**'s data area without buffering. Using the raw disk means that **fsck** finishes faster.

    The raw disk shouldn't be specified for checking the root file system. **fsck** can detect that it is checking the root file system when the block device interface is specified. After the root file system is modified by **fsck**, you must reboot the system without the **sync** command to ensure that the old in-memory superblock doesn't overwrite the corrected superblock on the disk. **fsck** will prompt you to reboot (**BOOT UNIX - NO SYNC**) when necessary unless you use the raw device interface for the root file system.

fsck Options

The **fsck** programs recognizes several options that modify its behavior. Here are the options, along with a little bit of commentary.

−y   Automatically inserts the answer "yes" to any queries from **fsck**. Not recommended, because you can miss seeing what files (such as those with bad or duplicate blocks) are being removed. Then you won't know what files to recover from backups.

−n   Don't write to the file system and always answer "no" to any queries from **fsck**. Useful for checking disks with possible hardware problems. You don't want to have **fsck** change a file system when the problem is actually due to hardware failure.

−s[X]   Unconditionally rebuild the free list. X stands for the optional soft interleave and blocks for cylinder, as in 8:36. If X is unspecified, the values used when the file system was created will be used. See the section on **mkfs** for a more detailed explanation of soft interleave.

−S[X]   Rebuild the free list only if no errors were discovered during phases 1-4. X is the optional soft interleave (see −s option).

−t*name*   Temporary file for tables. Needed only if **fsck** consistently complains of not having enough memory. For example, **fsck** reports "NEED SCRATCH FILE" and will also ask for a file name when it needs a temporary file. The −t option is explained in detail below.

−q   Quiet fsck. Cause **fsck** to act as if the −y option was specified for some queries, unreferenced fifos (named pipes) are silently removed, counts in the superblock are fixed, and the free list salvaged if necessary. File size diagnostics are also not printed. Using the −q option hides problems that may be getting out of hand, so it is not recommended.

−D   Perform additional checks on directories. The special directory entries, dot (.) and dot-dot (..), are checked to see if they refer to valid inodes, and directory entries are checked for the illegal filename character, "/". Useful after system crashes.

−f   Fast check, ignores phases 2, 3 and 4, checks only blocks and sizes (phases 1 and 5), and rebuilds the free list if necessary (phase 6).

Of these options, we can recommend using only four: −n, −s, −D, and −t. Use the −n (no write) option to check file systems that have suspected hardware problems. This approach prevents **fsck** from causing further damage to the file system while it reports what it finds. For example, an improperly functioning disk controller may scramble data read from or written to a disk. If **fsck** is allowed to operate on this misinformation, more problems will be introduced. On the other hand, using **fsck** with the −n option allows you to check a logical disk safely.

Usually, you will be warned of a hardware failure through console error messages referring to the logical disk containing the file system. If this is a mounted file system, you can unmount it and use **fsck** with the −n option as a diagnostic tool.

Sometimes, however, your first warning will come when **fsck** reports a large number of errors (or skips a file system) where previously everything was okay. Although incorrect shut down will introduce some errors, hardware failure will always manifest itself as a sudden, enormous increase in the numbers of errors detected. The cause of this condition might be changes in cables or physical configuration that occurred when the system was off. Halt **fsck** and shut down the system so that you can check your cable connections. Also, look in your logbook for recent entries referring to reconfiguration. If you don't discover bad connections, you will need to contact a service representative. You can aid in diagnosing the problem by providing information from your logbook.

The −s (or −S) option rebuilds the free list. During normal system activity, files are being created, growing larger, or being removed. Free blocks are taken from or returned to the free block list. Pretty soon, the free block list, initially organized with the soft interleave by **mkfs**, becomes shuffled. The block addresses in the free list are randomized, and new files built from the free block list will not be sequentially numbered blocks. The −s option tells **fsck** to throw away the current free block list and reorganize the list using the soft interleave. Now new files can be built with blocks organized correctly for fastest sequential access.

A good time to rebuild free lists is immediately after cleaning up a file system (by removing many files). The action of removing files adds many blocks to the free list, and rebuilding the free list at this point in time will make the most difference. If your **/tmp** directory is a separate file system, you may use the −s option every time you check the **/tmp** file system. However, don't add the −s option to the command line in the script (**/etc/bcheckrc**) that checks the root file system. Salvaging the free list modifies a file system, and checking the root file system would always be followed by the **BOOT UNIX** message. If you want to salvage the root file system's free list, you must do it interactively from single-user mode.

The −t option is necessary only if **fsck** consistently complains about not enough memory. This depends on two conditions: the amount of memory (RAM) available for running **fsck** and the size of the file system. These conditions are relatively constant, so once **fsck** has requested a scratch file, you might as well change the **fsck** command line (in **/etc/bcheckrc**) to include the −t option.

However, there is a catch here. The temporary file must be on a mounted file system that is not being checked. But you want to check all file systems before you mount them. A solution to this dilemma is to mount a file system on a floppy disk before running **fsck**, and use a temporary file on this file system. This approach requires only that you have a floppy drive, a floppy disk with a file system created on it, and that you mount this file system before **fsck** is run. Other solutions are similar—use a mounted file system that won't be checked at this time. Don't use a file in the root file system, such as in **/tmp**, because you will introduce activity (and very likely damage) to the root file system.

The −D option causes **fsck** to perform two additional checks on directories. Each directory entry name is checked for the slash character (/) and for filenames less than 14 characters long that don't end with nulls (the character that ends a string). The UNIX system won't allow creation of files that include a slash (try it), and always adds nulls to the ends of short filenames. Errors such as these can only be introduced by hardware failures, either memory or disk related. This is why we suggest using the −D option after hardware crashes.

The second check is made for the special directory entries dot (.) and dot-dot (..). Without the −D option, **fsck** treats these as ordinary entries. With −D, you will get an additional message if these entries do not contain inode numbers for valid inodes. However, no check is made to see if these entries refer to the correct inodes, that is, the dot (.) entry refers to the inode for the current directory, and the dot-dot (..) entry refers to the inode for the parent directory.

fsck Error Reports

When you finish reading this section, you will understand how **fsck** works and how to direct repairs of your file systems. You will understand why you don't want to take shortcuts, like using the −**y** or −**q** options. These options allow **fsck** a free hand to make changes without your consent. You, as the system administrator, must have control of **fsck** so that you can keep your file systems healthy. Take command!

We suggest that you keep a record in your logbook of the errors detected (and possibly repaired) by **fsck**. During phase 1 you should write down the numbers of the inodes containing bad or duplicate blocks. And if phase 1 detects problems with duplicate or bad blocks addresses, phase 2 will report these files by name and request permission from you to remove the directory entries for these inodes. Write down the filenames that are removed, so that you can avoid surprises later. Any error report by **fsck** is an indication of trouble, and a log can help you discover trends.

The diary section of your logbook is an appropriate place for these notes. Log keeping is even more important for systems where more than one person performs any system maintenance task.

The **fsck** command produces terse error reports, enigmatic at best. Although the *UNIX System V Administrator Guide* contains a section describing these error conditions, the explanations aren't much better than **fsck**'s own error messages. No guidance is given, except to suggest recompiling **fsck** with larger limits, which requires source code for **fsck**.

We have organized the error reports into 10 categories based upon what point during the execution of **fsck** they occur. We suggest what your best response should be and describe the effects of any response. And during the discussion of phase 1 reports, we mention the repercussions of certain error reports, since these reports will affect error reporting and your responses during later phases. The 10 categories are:

    Read, write, or seek errors
    Initialization
    Phase 1
    Phase 1B
    Phase 2
    Phase 3
    Phase 4
    Phase 5
    Phase 6
    Termination

Except for read, write, and seek errors, which can occur any time, other errors occur only during a distinct period of **fsck**'s execution. To use this section as a handy guide, note the phase or period when you received the error report, find the corresponding section in this book, and look for the error report printed in bold letters.

Besides terse reports, **fsck** consistently uses abbreviations in its reports. These abbreviations stand for parts of the file system. Table 4.1 explains these abbreviations, so we won't waste your time discussing them for every error report where they appear.

TABLE 4.1 ABBREVIATIONS USED IN **fsck** MESSAGES

Abbreviation	Description
BLK	A block address on the logical device being checked
I	An inode number in this file system
DUP	A duplicate block
BAD	An out of range block address
DIR	An inode of directory type, or a directory name
OWNER	The owner of this inode (from the **/etc/passwd** file)
MODE	The type of inode and the permissions (last three digits)
SIZE	The number of the last byte written in this inode's data blocks
MTIME	The time of last modification for this inode
NAME	The current pathname (displayed during phase 2)

Responding to fsck's Queries

fsck is easy on you. It only expects two responses from you: **y** for yes and **n** for no. Always follow your responses by typing a RETURN. **fsck** signals that it wants a response by printing a one word query followed by a question mark and waits for your response. For example, to respond affirmatively to a request to remove a filename, you would type **y** followed by RETURN, as in Figure 4.33.

Figure 4.33 Answering queries from **fsck**.

```
REMOVE?  y[RETURN]
```

There is no limit on the amount of time available for making decisions, so relax, be sure of yourself (or as sure as you can be), write down whatever you need before answering the query.

When to Say "NO" to fsck

Since **fsck** is an expert, you will most often respond to queries by answering "yes." However, there are several cases where you will always want to say "no" to **fsck**'s query. In each of these special cases, **fsck** will be requesting permission to

REMOVE a file (name) or **CLEAR** an inode. Although responding "yes" to this request is often appropriate, it's the wrong thing to do when you see:

SORRY: NO lost+found DIRECTORY or NO SPACE in lost+found DIRECTORY. fsck has failed to reconnect a file or directory because of a problem with the **lost+found** directory in this file system. After failing to reconnect the inode, **fsck** will request permission to **CLEAR** this inode. Answer **n**, and run **fsck** a second time after fixing **lost+found**.

DUP TABLE OVERFLOW. fsck's list of inodes with duplicate blocks has grown larger than the space allotted for it. Write down the inode numbers of inodes with duplicate blocks found after this point, and don't **REMOVE** any of the filenames connected to these inodes or **CLEAR** these inodes. Run **fsck** a second time.

Read, Write, or Seek Error Reports

The read, write, or seek error reports indicate that a hardware error has occurred while accessing the file system being checked. These errors may happen any time during a **fsck** session. These messages have the form

CAN NOT READ: BLK 56

CONTINUE?

where "READ" may be replaced with "WRITE" or "SEEK" and the "56" will be replaced with the actual block address. Read or write errors mean that a hardware error occurred while trying to read or write that block. A seek error means that the disk drive was unable to move into the correct position for a read or write. These messages may be preceded by messages produced by the kernel in response to the same error condition. The kernel error message provides you with additional information (see Chapter 10).

You should write down the block number with the error and answer "yes" to the first "CONTINUE?" prompt. However, if you see more errors of this type, you should respond "no," which terminates checking this file system. Hardware errors while checking a file system are cause for alarm because they mean that you have a hardware failure. Perhaps the failure is minor, for example, a single block that has developed a read error.

Or this may be the tip of the iceberg. Chances are that if you can run **fsck** on the root file system, both the disk controller and the logical disk with root file system are okay. But if you get several read, write, or seek error messages, or this problem increases over time (new errors each time you check this file system), you have a hardware problem with the disk or controller and should not run **fsck** on this file system until your hardware has been checked out. Remember, using **fsck** to repair a file system on ailing hardware will create more problems in the file system.

Answering "no" to the "CONTINUE?" prompt causes **fsck** to terminate.

Initialization Error Reports

Initialization errors are reported while **fsck** is preparing to check a file system. The first few errors result from trying to run **fsck** with illegal or conflicting options. These error messages are similar to those produced by other UNIX commands.

The legal options were listed previously. Conflicting options are −s and −n (you can't salvage the free list without writing to the file system) and −q and −n (−q means answer "yes" quietly to many error conditions, which contradicts −n, which means to answer "no.").

Can not fstat standard input

fsck has requested the file statistics for the standard input, for example, who owns it, what the permissions are, etc. **fsck** can't be run in the background, because the standard input has been cut off when the process is put in the background. **fsck** will stop after this error message, because there is no way for it to receive responses from the operator.

Can not get memory

fsck keeps large tables in memory as it runs. The error occurs when **fsck** can't get its minimum memory requirement. This error is not related to file system size, and should never occur (unless your system is missing memory because of hardware failure or you have reconfigured your kernel with larger tables and/or more buffers).

NEED SCRATCH FILE (10 BLKS)
ENTER FILENAME

fsck got its minimal memory requirements, but needs more, in this case, 10 blocks on a disk. This disk-based memory is used for the tables that **fsck** creates, and the table size will vary according to the size of the file system. Once this happens, add the −t option followed by a filename (follow the directions in **fsck** Options section) for the command line invocation for **fsck**.

Cannot stat root

fsck's request for the root directory's (/) statistics (inode information) failed. **fsck** uses this information to discover if it is working on the root file system.

Cannot open checklist file: /etc/checklist

The file containing the list of file systems to check couldn't be opened. This problem can happen when **fsck** is used by an ordinary user who does not have the proper access permissions. Check to see that **/etc/checklist** exists, is readable by all, and writable for the owner, **bin**, or a system account.

Cannot stat *devicename*

fsck can't get information (the statistics) about this file system (identified by the *devicename*)—means that this file system doesn't exist or can't be opened (because its of permission mode). **fsck** continues with the next file system argument (if there is one).

devicename **is a mounted file system, ignored**

fsck won't check mounted file systems, except for the root file system. **fsck** skips this file system and proceeds with the next, if there is one. *Solution*: Dismount the file system and try again.

devicename **is a pipedev, ignored**

filename **is not a block or character device**

Only block or character special files can contain file systems; **fsck** ignores other file types and proceeds with the next file system in the argument list if there is one.

Size check: fsize 12 isize 13714

The number of blocks of inodes (isize) is greater than or equal to the number of blocks in the file system (fsize). Since these values are impossible in any file system, **fsck** ignores this file system and proceeds with the next. Hopefully, you have used the wrong device name instead of a logical device containing a file system. You should also check to see if the correct disk pack (or other removal media) has been physically mounted.

If this logical device should have a file system on it, the superblock has been corrupted. The UNIX system does not provide tools for patching corrupted superblocks, and you will have to make a new file system and restore this file system from backups. (Note that **fsdb** may help. See Appendix F.)

Phase 1 - Check Blocks and Sizes

fsck scans every inode during phase 1, checking parts of the inodes and gathering information used during the other phases. Please recall that the inodes begin with the second block of the logical device, providing **fsck** with a consistent starting point.

fsck first checks each inode's mode word for the file type: ordinary, directory, fifo (named pipe), block special, or character special. The values for the five legal types of inodes (MODE) are given in Table 4.2.

TABLE 4.2 VALUES OF LEGAL INODE TYPES

Mode	Legal inode types and other information
10XXXX	ordinary files
6XXXX	block special files
4XXXX	directories
2XXXX	character special files
1XXXX	fifo's (named pipes)
X4XXX	file with set-user-id bit set
X2XXX	file with set-group-id bit set
X1XXX	file with sticky bit set

The type of inode is represented by the first one or two digits; the four X's represent access permissions and other information (set user, set group, and sticky bits) included in the mode word, but not checked by **fsck**. For example, a mode word for an ordinary file would appear as 100755, with "10" for the mode and "0755" for the access permissions and other information.

There are 11 other possible modes, all illegal. An attempt to read or write to a file whose inode has an illegal mode word fails without any error message from the operating system. Inodes with illegal modes cannot be accessed (unless the mode is changed with **fsdb**).

Next, **fsck** checks each block address stored in the inode and any indirect blocks belonging to the inode. Block addresses less than the first data block address or greater than the last block address are considered *bad* (**BAD**) blocks. It's not the blocks themselves that are bad—it's that the block address is out of range.

After checking each block address for valid range, **fsck** adds the correct block addresses to the allocated block table. However, if the block address is already in the block table, it is called a *duplicate* (**DUP**) block, a block address claimed by (appearing in) more than one inode. **fsck** keeps a list of inodes with bad or duplicate blocks for disposition during later phases.

fsck calculates the approximate size of each file by counting the blocks claimed by the inode during the block address checking. The approximate size is compared with the size written in the inode; a warning is given if there is a discrepancy. Directory-type inodes should have a size evenly divisible by 16 (the length of a directory entry).

fsck also collects the link count found in each inode. This count will be compared to the actual number of directory entries found for each inode during phase 2.

Error messages during phase 1 reflect the checks made on each inode. And file system errors discovered during phase 1 will result in related messages in later phases. For example, when an unallocated (that is, an illegal file type) inode is discovered during phase 1, **fsck** will request to remove directory entries linked to this inode during phase 2.

To test **fsck**, we created a file system on a small logical disk. This file system was 2052 blocks long, with 512 inodes contained within 32 blocks. After mounting the file system and creating a small directory tree with a selection of files and unmounting it, we operated on it with **fsdb**, creating inconsistencies. This approach allowed us to control what must go wrong in order to invoke a particular error report, and is a good way to learn how **fsdb** and **fsck** work.

UNKNOWN FILE TYPE I = 14

CLEAR?

and

PARTIALLY ALLOCATED INODE I = 15

CLEAR?

These messages mean the same thing: that the inode is not one of the five legal types. Some garbage value has insinuated itself here, making the file type unrecognizable. Partially allocated means that the inode has type 0 (an illegal type), but some information appears in the mode word. Also, if there's garbage in the mode word, there is likely to be garbage throughout the inode.

Your choices are to clear the inode, by answering affirmatively to the "CLEAR?" query, or ignore the problem. Clearing the inode involves writing zeros throughout the inode. The list of blocks and indirect blocks are never checked or added to the allocated block list if the inode is cleared, so the blocks will show up missing in phase 5.

We suggest that you clear these inodes. The unrecognizable file type ensures that the UNIX system won't be able to read these files. Write down the inode number, because you may need it during phase 2 to discover the filenames linked to this inode (if any). This error indicates either that the inode was corrupted, or that some random information was written into an unallocated inode.

LINK COUNT TABLE OVERFLOW,

CONTINUE?

fsck has discovered more inodes with a zero link count than there is room for in **fsck**'s internal tables. In fact, **fsck** will continue to complain about table overflow each time it finds another inode with a zero link count. You need to answer yes to continue until **fsck** is finished. Then run **fsck** on this file system again, until all zero link count inodes have been eliminated.

2583 BAD I = 3

or

52 DUP I = 4

A bad or a duplicate block address was discovered while checking the blocks claimed by an inode. 2583 is a bad block address in the example above and 52 is the address of a duplicate block. Recall that bad blocks are out-of-range block addresses, and duplicate blocks have been claimed by another inode. No operator response is required at this time, since **fsck** only marks this inode as bad. But write down the inode number, and the block address in the case of duplicate blocks, for use during later phases.

fsck will search for directory entries referencing inodes with bad or duplicate blocks during phase 2 and will request permission to remove these directory entries. During phase 4 **fsck** will request permission to clear these inodes.

EXCESSIVE BAD BLKS I = 13

or

EXCESSIVE DUP BLKS I = 12

CONTINUE?

Ten bad or 10 duplicate blocks have been detected while checking this inode's blocks. This evidence of wholesale corruption of the inode and/or one of its indirect blocks causes **fsck** to quit checking the blocks owned by this inode. **fsck** does not report whether the 10 bad or 10 duplicate addresses were addresses in the inode or in an indirect block. The one thing that you can be sure of is that something is seriously wrong with this inode.

You should respond "yes" to the "CONTINUE?" prompt, unless this message has appeared many times. Responding "yes" causes **fsck** to continue with the next inode.

If you see this message more than once, you may have a hardware problem. You can either respond "no" to the "CONTINUE?" prompt and **fsck** will quit checking this file system and continue with the next one (if any). Or you can continue with the check of this file system, letting **fsck** survey the damage, but respond no to any request to clear inodes, adjust counts or remove directory entries until you are sure that your hardware is not causing the error reports.

fsck will have already presented 10 bad or 10 duplicate block error reports before making the "EXCESSIVE" report. **fsck** has marked this inode as bad, with the same consequences as described for inodes with bad or duplicate blocks.

DUP TABLE OVERFLOW

CONTINUE?

The block addresses of duplicate blocks are kept in the duplicate block table. **fsck** uses the duplicate block table to find the first inode that claimed a block address. Picture this: **fsck** encounters a block address already claimed by an inode. Now it must save this block address so it can locate the other inode, the first inode claiming the duplicate block. When the duplicate block table is full, **fsck** can't find the first inode claiming a block during phase 1b, the second look at the inodes for duplicates.

By responding "yes" you tell **fsck** to complete the check of this file system. But **fsck** won't find all the inodes with duplicate blocks and you, the operator, will need to make some decisions during phase 2.

Your task is to write down the inode number of the duplicate block message that immediately precedes the table overflow message. (The overflow message will follow each DUP message after the table is full.) Then *don't* remove any of filenames associated with these inodes during phase 2 or clear any inodes during phase 4 that you wrote down after the table overflowed. Run **fsck** again to discover the rest of the inodes with duplicate blocks. If you clear an inode whose duplicate blocks don't fit into the duplicate block table, the other inode claiming the block will go undiscovered. Then you may have a corrupted file, undetectable by **fsck**, just waiting to cause trouble later. Dangerous waters.

If you respond negatively to the "CONTINUE?" prompt, **fsck** terminates or skips to the next file system. This approach won't solve your problem unless you are capable of recompiling **fsck** with a larger table size. The first route is simpler.

POSSIBLE FILE SIZE ERROR I = 14

Each data block claimed by an inode represents 1024 bytes of a file. **fsck** calculates the file size and compares this value with the file size value written in the inode. The "FILE SIZE" error message appears when the calculated size differs from the inode's size value and is only a warning.

The UNIX system allows files with "holes," and these files will produce the file size warning message. (A "holey" file is created by skipping at least 1024 bytes and than writing a byte.) The **lp** demon uses a fifo (a pipe named **/usr/spool/lp/FIFO**), and it will also produce file size warnings if it exists when the file system is checked.

But, you shouldn't be complacent about these warnings. Discover the file's name by using **ncheck** with the −i option and the inode number. For example, Figure 4.34 shows how to discover the name of inode 14 on the logical disk **/dev/dsk/0s2**.

Figure 4.34 Converting an inode number into a filename.

```
# ncheck -i 14 /dev/dsk/0s2
14      /Prog/dwrite.c
# □
```

Only fifos or data files can have file size errors and not be corrupt. Use the **ls** −l command to discover the type of file (after this file system has been mounted). You can use the **file** command to see what this file contains. A file containing data can have holes. Other files with file size errors should be replaced from a backup copy.

Or you can examine the file for errors (if the file contains text), make a copy of the file, remove the old file, and rename the copy. Copying the file removes the size discrepancy but won't fix the file if it has been corrupted.

DIRECTORY MISALIGNED I = 12

The size value stored in this inode can't be evenly divided by 16 (the size of a non-BSD directory entry). Write down the inode number, as you must replace or fix this directory. You can use **ncheck** to discover the directory name and check the listing with **ls**. You can use **cpio** to copy the directory, creating a new, aligned copy of the directory inode. Then you can remove the old one with **rmdir**.

Phase 1b - Rescan for More DUPS

If any duplicate blocks were found, **fsck** must make a second pass through the inodes, looking for the other inodes that claimed the duplicate blocks. **fsck** compares the block numbers in the duplicate block table with the blocks claimed by each inode until all inodes with duplicate blocks have been found.

52 DUP I = 4

This message reports the inode number for the other inode claiming a block. **fsck** marks this inode for action during phases 2 and 4. Check the notes that you made during phase 1 and match up the block number (52 in this example) with the other inode that claimed the same block address. You will need these matched pairs for later phases.

Phase 2 - Check Pathnames

Phase 2 collects information from the directories in the file system and compares it with the information collected during phase 1. When a directory entry is found that refers to an inode with a bad or duplicate block, **fsck** reports the filename (found in the directory entry) and requests permission to remove this entry. For each directory entry referring to a valid inode, **fsck** reduces the link count for that inode by one in **fsck**'s link count list.

If you add the −D option to your command line, **fsck** will make additional checks of directory entries during this phase.

Phase 2 always begins by examining inode number 2, the root directory inode for any file system. If this inode isn't of directory type or is unallocated, descending the directory hierarchy won't be possible.

ROOT INODE UNALLOCATED. TERMINATING

The root inode is the beginning of the directory hierarchy. If the root inode was marked as unallocated (not one of the five valid file types) during phase 1, **fsck** cannot continue with phase 2 and terminates. You may attempt to salvage this file system by using **fsdb** to change the mode of inode two to type directory, setting up a **lost+found** directory and running **fsck** again. See Appendix F for information about using **fsdb**.

ROOT INODE NOT DIRECTORY,

FIX?

The root inode is not directory type, but one of the four other valid types. **fsck** will change the mode to be directory type and attempt to continue if you answer "yes." Saying "no" doesn't gain you anything. If the rest of the inode is garbage, you will probably see the next message.

DUPS/BAD IN ROOT INODE,

CONTINUE?

The root inode was found to have bad or duplicate blocks during phase 1 (or 1b). Pretty ominous, this message suggests that your root inode is corrupt. Once again, if you abort here you don't gain anything. By continuing, you might discover that most of the root inode's blocks are okay and actually contain directory entries. If they don't, you will see the "I OUT OF RANGE" message many times, and you probably should give up on this file system and get out your backups for restoring this file system. If you decide to use your backups to replace the entire file system, first use **mkfs** to build an empty file system on this logical device. For those of you who are feeling either adventurous or desperate, you may try reading Appendix F on using **fsdb**.

I OUT OF RANGE I = 1000

NAME = /temp (NOT EMPTY)

REMOVE?

While checking directory entries, **fsck** uncovered a directory entry with the name "temp" and an invalid inode number in it, that is, an inode number greater than the last inode in this file system, an obvious impossibility. Responding "yes" causes **fsck** to remove the directory entry. Responding "no" leaves this entry around to cause trouble later. Since this entry refers to a nonexistent inode, it can never be useful, so remove it. The "(NOT EMPTY)" message appears to be a mistake on **fsck**'s part, since a nonexistent inode can't be empty or not empty.

UNALLOCATED I = 25 OWNER = root MODE = 0

SIZE = 0 MTIME = Dec 31 19:00 1969

NAME = /testfile (EMPTY) -- REMOVED

This time **fsck** has found a directory entry referencing an inode that was unallocated (or cleared) during phase 1. An unallocated inode is filled with zeros. So the information in the error message reflects this: OWNER = root (user id of 0), MODE = 0, SIZE = 0 and MTIME = Dec 31 19:00 1969 (the 0 date, reflecting the local time zone, Pacific Standard Time). **fsck** removes directory entries pointing to unallocated inodes without asking unless you invoked **fsck** with the **−n** option.

DUP/BAD I = 34 OWNER = rik MODE = 100755

SIZE = 121220 MTIME = May 20 17:41 1985

FILE = /important

REMOVE?

This time **fsck** has reached a directory entry referring to an inode marked as having bad or duplicate block addresses during phase 1. If you didn't write down (or still have on your screen) the information on inodes with a bad or duplicate block address, you won't know whether this inode has a bad or duplicate address, and **fsck** can't tell you. Your safest move is to remove this file by responding "yes." Write down its name and recover it from backups.

But suppose you don't have a good backup? If the inode has a bad block address, you can't make a copy of it (**cp** will balk and quit when it reaches the bad block number), and you are out of luck. If the inode has duplicate blocks and contains text, you can make a copy of the file, edit the copy, and perhaps recover most or all of the file after some work. Executable files cannot be checked for correctness by examination and must be replaced from backups (or recompilation of source files).

If you decide to try to make a copy of a file with a duplicate block, *don't* remove the file after making the copy. Removing the file puts the duplicate block address back into the free list, ready to destroy other files. Run **fsck** on this file system again, and let **fsck** remove the file with duplicate blocks and clean up.

DUP/BAD I = 14 OWNER = root MODE = 40755

SIZE = 96 MTIME = May 22 11:41 1985

DIR = /tmp/Backup

REMOVE?

Another inode with bad or duplicate block numbers, except this time the inode is directory type. This message will be displayed *before* **fsck** attempts to check the entries in this directory. Responding "yes" removes the directory entry. Answer "no" and **fsck** will attempt to search through this possibly corrupt directory. Many "I OUT OF RANGE" messages indicate that this directory inode is indeed corrupt.

We suggest that you respond affirmatively. It is true that removing this directory entry means that **fsck** will be unable to check this directory's directory entries. However, **fsck** will attempt to reconnect unreferenced inodes (those with entries in the vanquished directory) to the **lost+found** directory, so all is not lost. Phases 3 and 4 will reconnect unreferenced files and directories. If this directory happened to be **lost+found**, then **fsck** won't be able to connect unreferenced inodes. But there shouldn't be any entries in the **lost+found** directory if you have been doing a good job. That is, if you have followed the directions in the section "Recovering Files and Directories from **lost+found**" later in this chapter.

BAD DIR ENTRY I = 13

BLK 370 I=13 OWNER=root MODE=40777

SIZE=112 MTIME=May 20 21:40 1985

DIR=/etc

This message appears only when the −**D** option is used. It is a warning that means a directory entry in this inode (13) has an illegal name, like "bad/name," which contains a slash (/). The only way to get rid of this is with **fsdb**. See the Appendix F section that explains using **fsdb**.

NO VALID '.' in DIR I = 12

or

NO VALID '..' in DIR I = 12

or

MISSING '.' or '..' in DIR I = 12

(appended to all three messages)

BAD DIR ENTRY I = 12

BLK 292 I=12 OWNER=rik MODE=40755

SIZE=176 MTIME=May 19 10:22 1985

DIR=/Scripts

More warnings produced when the −**D** option is used. The first two entries in every directory are: a reference to self, dot (.), and a reference to the parent directory, dot-dot (..). The −**D** option causes **fsck** to check if the inodes for these two special directory entries are valid. **fsck** checks only to see that these are allocated inodes, not if these entries are truly correct, that is, "." references the same inode as the directory, and that ".." references the parent directory.

If either dot (.) or dot-dot (..) are invalid, the next report will be that the inode in the directory entry for one of these entries is unallocated (see "Unknown File Type" explanation above). You can respond "no" to the request to remove the dot (.) or dot-dot (..) entry if you plan to repair this file system with **fsdb**. Otherwise, answer "yes."

Phase 3 - Check Connectivity

In phase 3, **fsck** makes names for directory inodes that weren't found during phase 2's search through the directory hierarchy. These directory inodes aren't connected, that is, they aren't referenced by a directory entry that connects them with the directory hierarchy.

fsck attempts to make a directory entry for unreferenced directories in the **lost+found** directory of the file system being checked. The **lost+found** directory must not only exist, but must also have room for additional directory entries because **fsck** can't grab the next free block to make room for more directories. **fsck** has not checked the free list yet, so taking a block from the free list could be hazardous. We explained creating the **lost+found** directory earlier in this chapter.

Every time that **fsck** succeeds in connecting a directory, it makes a phase 2 search through this directory's entries, so you may see phase 2 messages during phase 3. Remember that phase 2 attempts to match directory entries to allocated inodes. This search prevents files whose only directory entries were in this directory from turning up unreferenced in phase 4.

UNREF DIR I = 12   OWNER = root   MODE = 40777

SIZE = 132   MTIME = May 23 17:41 1985 (NOT EMPTY) MUST reconnect

fsck found a directory inode that was missed during phase 2 pathname check. The "NOT EMPTY" message will always be followed by "MUST reconnect." **fsck** will look for the **lost+found** directory and add a directory entry for this inode if there is room. This directory entry will have its inode number for its name, padded with "0" to make six digits. If the reconnection was successful, **fsck** reports

DIR I = 12   CONNECTED.   PARENT WAS I = 2

for an orphaned inode 12 whose parent directory is the root inode (2). The name in **lost+found** will be **000012**.

> **SORRY. NO lost+found DIRECTORY**

or

> **SORRY. NO SPACE IN lost+found DIRECTORY**

These messages indicate problems with the **lost+found** directory. It may not exist, or it may be full, as indicated by the second message. **fsck** can't allocate more space to any file in a file system it is checking, including a directory file like **lost+found**. If **lost+found** isn't there or isn't right, look in the section "Making New File Systems" and learn how to create a large and empty **lost+found** directory.

Phase 4 - Check Reference Counts

In phase 4 **fsck** checks the link count information (that was gathered during phase 1) by comparing each count with the directory references to inodes found during phases 2 and 3. If **fsck** discovered an inode that was never referenced, that has a nonzero link count, and that is not empty, **fsck** will request to reconnect the inode to **lost+found**. If the link count in the inode varies from the actual number of directory entries referencing the inode, **fsck** will request permission to adjust the link count in the inode.

And any inodes that were found to have bad or duplicate blocks during phase 1 can be cleared. During phase 2 you were given the opportunity to remove files with bad or duplicate blocks; this procedure removed the directory entries for the inodes, not the inodes themselves. **fsck** will also request clearing inodes that are not connected by a directory entry.

This phase completes the checking and repairing of the inodes. After this, only the free list is left to check and repair.

> **LINK COUNT DIR I=13 OWNER=root MODE=40755**
>
> **SIZE=112 MTIME=May 20 21:40 1985**
>
> **COUNT 4 SHOULD BE 3**
>
> **ADJUST?**

fsck read the number of links stored in each inode during phase 1, and counted actual links (the references to each inode in the directory entries) during phases 2 and 3. Now **fsck** is reporting on a discrepancy: the link count stored in the inode disagrees with the number of links counted. You should respond "yes" and let **fsck** adjust the link count stored in the inode. Saying "no" will create problems later.

> **UNREF FILE I=15 OWNER=rik MODE=100644**

SIZE = 631   MTIME = May 21 00:30 1985 (NOT EMPTY)

RECONNECT?

This inode is not referenced by a directory entry anywhere in the known universe (this file system, for **fsck**). Saying "yes" allows **fsck** to attempt to connect this inode by creating a directory entry in **lost+found**. The name used will be the inode number padded with leading zeros to six places, like **000015**.

fsck will either say nothing and continue if successful, or complain about problems with the **lost+found** directory. Problems with **lost+found** will persist until you fix the directory yourself. The discussion of phase 3 talked about **fsck's** complaints dealing with **lost+found** (see above). Recovering files and directories from **lost+found** is discussed in a later section.

Phase 5 - Check Free List

The entire list of unused (free) blocks is checked for bad block addresses, presence of allocated blocks, and multiple appearances of a block in the free list. Phase 5 also detects missing blocks, that is, blocks that are in neither the allocated block list (collected during phase 1) nor the free list. If you cleared any inodes during phase 4, their blocks will be reported missing during phase 5. Any errors during phase 5 will cause **fsck** to suggest running phase 6 (Salvage Free List) unless the −**n** option was used.

1 BAD BLKS IN FREE LIST

Bad blocks, that is, out-of-range block addresses, were discovered while checking the free list. The free list must be salvaged because the operating system may discard the free list when it encounters the bad block address. Discarding the free block list means that there is no space left (no free blocks) in this file system until **fsck** is used to salvage the free list.

2 DUP BLK(S) IN FREE LIST

Duplicate blocks were discovered in the free list. Salvage the free list or you will corrupt your files.

58 BLK(S) MISSING

Some blocks weren't found in either the allocated block list or in the free list. These blocks are lost to the file system until the free list is salvaged. Clearing a nonempty inode (through **fsck** or **clri**) will always cause blocks to be missing.

FREE BLK COUNT WRONG IN SUPERBLK

FIX?

The free blocks counted by **fsck** differs from the count of free blocks stored in the superblock. Allow **fsck** to fix this count by responding "yes."

EXCESSIVE BAD BLKS IN FREE LIST

EXCESSIVE DUP BLKS IN FREE LIST

CONTINUE?

More than 10 bad or duplicate blocks have been discovered in the free list. **fsck** is requesting (with "CONTINUE?") to skip checking the remainder of the free list. Since even a single bad, duplicate, or missing block is cause for salvaging the free list, you should respond affirmatively and allow **fsck** to continue. Either of these messages will cause the "10 BAD or DUP BLKS IN FREE LIST" message to appear next, where "10" will be replaced by the actual number found.

BAD FREEBLK COUNT

The entire free block list is divided into a chain of smaller lists, each with 50 or fewer free blocks. The number of free blocks in each sublist is called the *freeblk count*, and refers to that part of the list only. If this count is bad, that is, greater than 50 or less than 0, this message will be displayed, and the entire free list is considered corrupted.

BAD FREE LIST

SALVAGE?

If anything is wrong with the free list (bad, duplicate, missing blocks, or bad freeblk count), **fsck** will report that the list is bad and request permission to salvage the list. Responding affirmatively actually results in **fsck** tossing out the old free list and rebuilding a new one based on the allocated block list. Any block that isn't allocated (claimed by an inode) belongs in the free block list. Responding negatively means that you will corrupt this file system.

Phase 6 - Salvage Free List

The free block list is rebuilt by including all the blocks not used, that is, those not found in the allocated block list collected during phase 1. **fsck** also organizes this list according to the blocks-to-skip and blocks-per-cylinder information taken from the superblock or from the −s or −S command line options. If these values aren't sensible, **fsck** uses default values instead.

Default free-block list spacing assumed

The blocks-to-skip or blocks-per-cylinder values specified on the command line or found in the superblock weren't reasonable, so the default values of 9 blocks-to-skip and 400 blocks-per-cylinder are used instead. Explanation of these values is given in the section "Making New File Systems."

Completion Reports

fsck always reports the number of files (allocated inodes), the number of blocks used, and the number of blocks free in the form

14 files 704 blocks 3332 free

Of course, these numbers will vary for each file system. This message gives you free space information (number of blocks free) without running the **df** command, so it pays to watch this report.

If **fsck** made *any* changes to the file system, you will get the report

**** FILE SYSTEM WAS MODIFIED ****

Changes include any modifications made, such as removing directory entries, clearing inodes, adjusting counts, connecting unreferenced files, or rebuilding the free list. This message does not require any action on your part.

If the file system is the root file system and the superblock was modified, you will get a different message:

**** BOOT UNIX (NO SYNC) ****

The superuser prompt will not reappear. This message means that you *must* reboot your system.

fsck has modified the superblock that is on the logical disk containing the root file system. However, the copy of the superblock in memory has *not* been corrected. If you perform a **sync** command, the incorrect memory copy of the superblock will be written over the corrected disk copy, undoing **fsck's** work, and setting yourself up for trouble.

fsck won't produce the "BOOT UNIX (NO SYNC)" message if you specify the raw device name for the root file system. Don't take chances. Eliminate the possibility of human error, and always check the non-raw-root device.

Recovering Files and Directories from lost + found

When **fsck** discovers inodes that aren't referenced by a directory entry, **fsck** attempts to create a directory entry for them in the **lost+found** directory. This directory entry will have a six-digit name based on the inode number. For example, inode 173 will have the name **000173**.

Directory entries provide a handle for accessing inodes. The problem facing the system administrator is that this "handle" doesn't give any clues as to a meaningful name for the file described by the inode. The system administrator must play sleuth and uncover clues as to the lost pathname for the file.

Two commands provide immediate assistance in this matter: **ls** and **file**. The **ls** command provides the account name of the inode's owner. The owner of an inode is in the best position to uncover the correct name for a file. The system administrator is responsible for discovering names for inodes owned by the **root** and other administrative accounts (like **bin**, **uucp**, **adm**, **lpr**, or **daemon**).

The **ls** command with the −l option uncovers the inode's owner and file type. For example,

```
# ls -l lost+found
drwxr-xr-x 2 root    root      48 May 20 17:33 1985    000173
# □
```

tells us that this inode is owned by the **root** account. If the inode is owned by an ordinary user, the system administrator can mail information about the directory entry to the user and move the directory entry to the home directory of the user.

The **ls** command also tells us that this inode is of directory type (the leading "d" in the file permissions). This means that the **ls** command can be used on this inode to list its contents, possibly revealing its place in the order of things.

If the file isn't a directory, perhaps it is some other special type, like block or character. This is indicated by a "b" or a "c" at the beginning of the permissions list. Special files belong in the **/dev** directory and can be identified by their major and minor device numbers. Major and minor device numbers should be part of the Device section of your system logbook.

Ordinary type files' permissions will begin with a dash (−). In this case you can get more information about the file with the **file** command. The **file** command reads the beginning of a file and attempts to classify its contents. There are three broad categories of files (from our point of view): executable programs, data, and text.

Executable programs will be classified "executable" by **file**. These files can't be examined with an editor for clues. But you can use the **strings** utility to look at the parts of the program that are in readable form. Most UNIX programs will contain some strings, at least for error reporting. The **strings** utility will pick out and send to the standard output all collections of characters that look like strings. (**strings** is a Berkeley enhancement not found in vanilla System V. A listing of our C-program version of **strings** appears in Appendix G.)

The **what** utility can also be of help sometimes. The **what** command will display the SCCS information about an executable file. SCCS is Source Code

Control System, and includes a scheme for identifying revisions made to a program. If SCCS has been used with a file, the revision number and the *name of the program* will be displayed. Unfortunately, this is too good to be true. Some systems don't have the **what** utility, and others didn't use SCCS. Still, it's one method for uncovering the name of an executable file, and worth a try.

Files containing text can be viewed with an editor to determine their true pathname. This is a task for the owner of the inode, unless the owner is an administrative log-in.

Ordinary, block, and character files can be moved to their correct pathname by ordinary users and the **mv** command. For example,

mv lost + found/000015 /usr/rik/Prog/strings.c

changes the pathname of **000015** to **strings.c** in a subdirectory belonging to the user **rik**. The **mv** command cannot create a link across file system boundaries. But **fsck** doesn't cross file system boundaries either, so the true pathname must be somewhere within the file system where the **lost + found** directory is.

If the inode is of directory type, the system administrator will need to perform the pathname change. The **/etc/mvdir** script is restricted to the superuser and can change the pathname to almost anywhere within the file system. (The exception is the logical impossibility of making a directory a subdirectory of itself.) The **mv** command will suffice for changing the pathname of a directory if the parent directory will be the same after the change.

Figure 4.35 Using **/etc/mvdir** to move a directory.

a. Renaming the directory **/usr1/lost + found/000147** to **/usr1/rose/letters**:

```
# /etc/mvdir /usr1/lost+found/000147 /usr1/rose/letters
# □
```

b. Moving a directory the "dangerous" way:

```
# /etc/link /usr1/lost+found/000147 /usr1/rose/letters
# /etc/unlink /usr1/lost+found/000147
# /etc/unlink /usr1/rose/letters/..
# /etc/link /usr1/rose /usr1/rose/letters/..
# □
```

If you try moving a directory outside of its current file system, the **/etc/mvdir** script issues the message "Cannot link to *name*." Although this report doesn't tell you exactly what's wrong, you at least have a clue. Figure 4.35 shows an example of moving a directory. The directory **/usr1/lost+found/000147** is moved to **/usr1/rose/letters**. Notice that both directories share part of the path in common, **/usr1**. **/usr1** is a mounted file system in this example.

In Figure 4.35b you can see the steps used to move the same directory without using **/etc/mvdir**. Using the **/etc/link** and the **/etc/unlink** commands directly removes any safeguards that prevent you from accidentally destroying the file system hierarchy. (The **mv** and **rm** commands use **link()** and **unlink()** system calls with safeguards.) The first **link** command adds a directory entry, **letters**, to the **/usr1/rose** directory for the directory inode 147. The first **unlink** command removes the directory entry in **/usr1/lost+found** for inode 147. So directory inode 147 is now connected only to **/usr1/rose**.

The second part of this process is to correct the dot-dot (..) entry. The ".." entry refers to the parent directory, and we have just changed the parent directory. The second **unlink** command in Figure 4.35b removes the old link to the **/usr1/lost+found** directory, the previous parent. The second **link** command creates a link from the new parent to the ".." entry. With this final **link** made, the **/usr1** file system is now consistent. What would happen if you reversed the two arguments in the second **link** command?

THE RACE FOR (DISK) SPACE

Although removing files from a UNIX file system is even easier than making them, this ability doesn't prevent file systems from becoming full. Naturally, your system's users, and the system itself, will create and enlarge files. And eventually, unless files are removed, even the largest disk will run out of free space.

All users share the same free block list for a file system. The UNIX system, except for Berkeley versions, does not impose quotas on disk usage. Thus, one user could consume all the available space in a file system. If your file system runs out of space, users cannot save their edited files, compilations will not complete, and any command that requires another disk block will fail. Essentially, operation of your UNIX system will come to a dead halt for users of that file system.

You, the system administrator, need strategies for maintaining free space. The three basic methods are: eternal vigilance against running dangerously low on free space (using the **df** command); watchfulness for conspicuous consumption (with the **du** command); and routine techniques for "garbage collection." Garbage collection means locating old and worthless files, like **core** files that were created by software that crashed months ago.

You must also watch out for files that grow. These files are log files. The **init, login, su, cron,** and several UUCP programs write in log files. The UNIX kernel also keeps log files when per process accounting is enabled. Table 4.3 lists these files and the programs that write in them. We cover files that grow when we discuss the programs that enlarge these files. System accounting handles most of these files.

TABLE 4.3 A LIST OF FILES THAT GROW

Pathname	Description
/etc/wtmp	Cumulative log of **/bin/login** and **/etc/init**
/usr/adm/sulog	Record use of the **su** command
/usr/adm/cronlog	Record **cron** activities
/usr/lib/cron/log	Release 2 **cron** log
/usr/adm/pacct?	Per-process accounting records kept by kernel

The UUCP systems also maintains log files and uses special cleanup scripts to take care of the log files.

Avoiding Trouble: Monitoring Free Space

Trouble may strike the blissfully unaware system administrator with astonishing swiftness: a quiet little message appearing on the console beginning with "no space." This kernel error message indicates that there are no free blocks remaining in the free block list for a file system. Immediate measures, like requesting all users to remove nonessential files, will provide short-term relief.

But you don't need to be surprised by running out of space. Instead, you can monitor your system's free space on a regular basis. The **df** (**d**isk **f**ree) utility reports on free space. We will explain how you can add a simple **awk** script that regularly monitors the free space for all your file systems and makes reports only when free space falls below an established safe threshold.

The **df** utility accepts the name of either the logical disk where a file system resides, or the directory name where the file system is mounted (the mount point). When no name is specified, the **df** program reads the mount table file, **/etc/mnttab**, to determine which file systems are mounted, and reports on all of them. Figure 4.36 shows a typical **df** report. Notice that any user may execute the **df** command.

Figure 4.36 User's invocation of **df** without options.

```
$ df
/u          (/dev/dsk/0s7):    76784 blocks    9838 i-nodes
/tmp        (/dev/dsk/0s8):     7860 blocks    1001 i-nodes
/usr        (/dev/dsk/0s2):     3170 blocks    1259 i-nodes
/           (/dev/dsk/0s0):     1738 blocks     825 i-nodes
$ □
```

The report starts with the pathname of the root directory, followed by the name of the logical disk (in parentheses) that contains this file system. The first value is the number of 512-byte blocks remaining in the free block list. This number is read from the superblock of the file system. The second value reported is the number of unused inodes remaining in this file system, also read from the superblock.

The **df** command makes its reports in terms of 512-byte blocks rather than in the System V standard of 1024-byte blocks. The **df** command uses the older block size for compatibility with older versions of the UNIX system. (Note that BSD and some other systems use 1024-byte blocks for this report.) You need to be aware of this inconsistency when you create your free space monitoring scripts, or otherwise use **df**.

The −t option instructs **df** to include the total number of blocks in the file system to the report. Thus, the −t option reveals the total size of a file system partition. The −f flag changes the way that the **df** command operates. Instead of reading the values from the superblock, **df** −f will traverse the free block list, counting free blocks. The −f option with **df** should produce the same values as the **df** command executed without options, and will take longer to do so. If the values reported were different, the superblock or free list has been damaged and the **fsck** program must be executed for this file system.

You need to run the **df** command on a regular basis. Exactly how often depends on the amount of free space that you normally have available and the volume of daily disk usage your system has. On a system with only one user, yourself, once daily might be sufficient. It's a good idea to add **df** to your shell startup file, like **.profile**, so you get a report as soon as you login. With more users, the **df** command can be run hourly by **cron** to avoid embarrassing disk space loss.

In their documentation Bell Labs recommends that the file system with the **/tmp** directory have 1000 free blocks for general system use and 1000 free blocks for *each* user. On some micro-based UNIX systems, this may seem extravagant (and on some, impossible), but these are reasonably liberal limits that will keep you, the system administrator, out of trouble. Generally speaking, any file system with less than 1 megabyte of free space (2000 512-byte blocks) needs close watching. The exception to this rule would be file systems containing commands and/or documentation only, that won't be increased in size by daily use.

Rather than simply adding the **df** command to a cron table file, we suggest that you use our **min_free_space** awk script. We wrote this script so that a report appears on the console only after free space has passed below a predetermined threshold. We still suggest that you run **df** daily to monitor disk use. And you will be warned by the script before an emergency situation develops at other times.

The **min_free_space** awk script gets its input through a pipe from the **df** command. The command line entry in the appropriate cron table file is shown in Figure 4.37.

Figure 4.37 Entry in cron table file for running **min_free_space**.

```
30 * * * * /bin/df | /bin/awk -f /etc/min_free_space > /dev/console
```

The cron table file entry runs the **df** command every hour on the half hour. Next, let's look at the script in Figure 4.38.

Figure 4.38 The **min_free_space** awk script.

```
/0s2/ && $(NF-3) < 5500 {
printf "/usr running out of free space, %5d K left.\n", $(NF-3)/2 }
/0s7/ && $(NF-3) < 3500 {
printf "/usr1 running out of free space, %5d K left.\n", $(NF-3)/2 }
```

Each pair of lines in the **min_free_space** **awk** script in Figure 4.38 works this way. The beginning of the line contains a regular expression, like **/0s2/**, that will match one line of output from the **df** command pipeline. The double ampersand means that if the regular expression matches, check the next condition. The next condition is a logical test—if the third-from-last argument, **$(NF-3)**, is less than, <, some value, for example, **5500**, the logical test is true.

The remaining portion of the line, surrounded by braces ({ }), is the statement executed when both conditions are true. We use a formatted print statement to display the sentence that follows in double quotes. The **%5d** is replaced by the amount of free space remaining divided by 2, **($(NF-3)/2)**. Don't divide by 2 if your **df** reports the number of 1024 byte blocks.

You don't need to understand how **awk** works to use the **min_free_space** script. To use the script, you simply replace the name of the logical disk, for example **0s2**, with the name of your logical disk. Then you replace the threshold value, for example, **5500**, with the value that you have selected. As an example, to add a file system on a logical disk named **/dev/dsk/1s0** with a minimum threshold of 3000 512-byte blocks, you add two lines to the script that look like Figure 4.39.

Figure 4.39 Line added for **/dev/dsk/1s0** with minimum of 3000.

```
/1s0/ && $(NF-3) < 3000 {
printf "/usr2 running out of free space, %5d K left.\n", $(NF-3)/2 }
```

It is important that you place the opening brace ({) on the same line as the test conditions. The **awk** program expects to find the condition and the beginning of the action to take all together on one line. If you put the action to take (the portion in braces) on a separate line, the printf statement will be executed every time the script is run. You should test this script to be certain that it works to your satisfaction. You want to be alerted by the script only when free space is running low.

The **/etc** directory, or perhaps **/usr/lbin**, is an appropriate place for the **min_free_space** script. Figure 4.40 illustrates the ownership and permissions for the script.

Figure 4.40 Ownership and permissions of **min_free_space**.

```
$ ls -l /etc/min_free_space
-rw-r--r-- 1 root  root        180 Jun  8 18:16 /etc/min_free_space
$ □
```

Once you have installed the script and the cron table file entry for executing it, you will be warned whenever free space falls below the established threshold. For example, if free space for the file system on logical disk **/dev/1s2** fell below the 3000 (512-byte) block limit, the message "/dev/1s2 running out of free space, 1495 K left." will appear on the console.

When free space becomes low on a file system, you can use the suggestions in the section "Removing Garbage Files." Another very effective technique is simply to edit the "Message of the Day" file, **/etc/motd**, and add a notice like that in Figure 4.41.

Figure 4.41 Using **/etc/motd** as a tactic in getting more free space.

```
$ cat /etc/motd
We are running out of disk space in the /usr1 file system.
Please clean out your directories and remove non-essential
files.
$ □
```

Although we were initially skeptical that users would clean up on their own, all the system administrators that we have interviewed said that this approach was helpful in creating free disk space. But if a message like this one doesn't succeed, you can use the approach outlined next.

Exposing Conspicuous Consumption

System V places no limits on the amount of disk space each user may utilize. What you need are strategies for uncovering those who are greedy, or perhaps simply unconscious, of their usage of a shared resource—disk space.

Your first step as a system administrator is to control what portions of the file systems are available to users, since any user may consume all the free space available in a file system. This approach makes the task of policing disk usage simpler. After all, users, including privileged users, don't need to create files scattered throughout the entire file systems. Leaving stray files around the directory hierarchy corrupts the very organization provided by the file system layout.

In Chapter 9, we detail how to arrange permissions on directories that limit the creation of files in that directory. Essentially, users should only be allowed to create files in their own directory tree, **/tmp**, **/usr/news**, **/usr/tmp**, a backup directory, and **/usr/spool/uucppublic**. Since users control their own directory's permissions, it is possible for a user to allow other users permission to create files in their directory trees; checking for other user's files in your directory area is also described in Chapter 9.

With users limited to creating files in their own directory tree, looking for space hogs becomes a matter of a simple script that runs **du** on a list of the home directories. Start out by creating a file containing a list of users' home directories.

The **awk** command illustrated in Figure 4.42 will pick out the home directory field of each entry in **/etc/passwd** and place these directory names in the file **/etc/homes**.

Figure 4.42 Creating a list of home directories.

```
# awk -F: '/usr1/ { print $6 }' /etc/passwd > /etc/homes
# □
```

The first argument given to **awk**, −**F:**, tells it to use a colon as the field separator. The argument in single quotes directs **awk** to select password file entries containing the string *usr1* and to print their home directory field, field six. If your system uses a different parent directory than *usr1* (which is not unlikely), substitute the name of that directory here. The reason for using this directory name is to select only user password entries, and to ignore administrative entries. You should examine the **/etc/homes** file, and remove nonuser directories, like the root (/) or **/bin**, if they occur.

Once you have a file containing a list of home directories, picking out the heaviest consumers is an easy matter. Figure 4.43 shows the command line and some sample output.

Figure 4.43 Picking out the big consumers.

```
# du -s `cat homes` | sort -rn
10149   /usr1/beccat
1259   /usr1/rik
1250   /usr1/pete
592   /usr1/guest
126   /usr1/canyon
32   /usr1/davidf
18   /usr1/rose
# □
```

Like the **df** command, the **du** command uses 512-byte blocks in its reports. In Figure 4.43 the biggest consumer is immediately obvious. The **sort** −**rn** command arranges the output of **du** with the largest numerical value first.

Before getting nasty with the top space consumers, you need to realize that these users are often the people getting the most out of the UNIX system. They may be programmers, writers, or administrators that keep copies of everything that they have ever created on-line. We suggest that you display for these heavy users the disk usage report. Then you can discuss strategies for selecting several-months-old files for archiving. Figure 4.44 shows how the **find** command can perform the selection of files. Be gentle, because you do not want to alienate your system's most prolific users.

Figure 4.44 Picking out files not modified in a half year.

```
# find /usr1 -mtime +180 -print ¦ tee half-year-olds
/usr1/rik/Prog/strings1.c
/usr1/rik/Book/Fsys/fsck1
...
# □
```

A list of files not modified in more than 180 days (half-year-olds) may also be helpful in convincing other users to remove unused or unnecessary files.

Removing Garbage Files

An easy way to free up space in your file systems is to remove garbage files. Garbage files are temporary files that lose their usefulness after several days. A prime example of a garbage file is a file named **core**. These **core** files are created when an executing program attempts to do something illegal, like accessing some other user's memory. The UNIX operating system detects the attempt and sends a signal to the program. The signal not only halts the offending program, but creates a copy of the program and its environment named **core** in the current directory.

core files can be used to determine what went wrong with the program with the aid of a debugging program like **adb**. However, if the user isn't interested in debugging the program, or doesn't know what a **core** file is, the file may languish forever in some branch of the directory hierarchy.

The key here is that all files created this way have the same name—**core**. Another file with a generic name is **a.out**, the default name for the output of the **ld** command (a part of the C compiler). In both cases, the true identity of these generically named files, **a.out** and **core**, gets lost in the mists of time within a week. The user that created these files could determine their identity and rename these files but has failed to do so.

The **find** command can be used to search throughout the directory hierarchy and remove such files. You, working as superuser, establish the criteria for the **find** command and let it do the cleansing of your file systems. Figure 4.45 exhibits a typical **find** command line.

Figure 4.45 Finding and removing garbage files.

```
# find / -name a.out -o -name core -atime +10 -exec rm { }\ \ ;
# □
```

The **find** command line in Figure 4.45 starts at the root (/) directory and selects files with the name **a.out** or **core**. The —**o** flag means "or." Next, the access time, **atime**, is checked. If the file selected has not been accessed within the last 10 days, the **rm** command will be executed. The empty braces (**{ }**) are replaced with the pathname of the file selected, and the remove command is executed. On our system, we created 1200 free (512-byte) blocks by executing this **find** command.

You may modify the command line in Figure 4.45 by changing the access time (**+10**). You may also elect to execute the remove command interactively by using **−ok** instead of **−exec**.

There are several other garbage files that you can search out with **find**. People often use names like **test**, **temp**, or **tmp** when creating temporary files, and then forget to erase these files. You can substitute these names for **core** and **a.out** and remove these temporary files also. Ordinary users can use either of these commands on their own directory trees and clean up after themselves if you make this suggestion. However, don't erase the "real" **test**, **/bin/test**.

QUICK REFERENCE GUIDE

Making new file systems — **/etc/mkfs**:

   # **mkfs** *device size*[*:inodes*] [*gap blks/cyl*]

Labeling new file systems — **/etc/labelit**:

   # **/etc/labelit** *device-name fsname volname*

Reorganizing file systems with **dcopy**:

   # **/etc/dcopy** *inputfs outputfs*

Checking file systems with **fsck**:

   # **fsck** [*−options*] [*device-names*]

Advice for using **fsck**:

- Always run on unmounted file systems
- Never use **−y** or **−q** options
- Write down the names of any files removed during Phase 2
- You can answer **y** to almost any query except when the **DUP TABLE** overflows or there are problems with the **lost +found** directory.

Matching an inode number to a filename with **ncheck**:

> # **ncheck** **−i** *inode-number device-name*

Checking for free space with **df**:

> # **df**

List of files that grow:

Pathname	Description
/etc/wtmp	Cumulative log used by **/bin/login** and **/etc/init**
/usr/adm/sulog	Record **su** command usage
/usr/adm/cronlog	Record **cron** activities
/usr/lib/cron/log	Release 2 **cron** log
/usr/adm/pacct?	Per-process accounting records kept by kernel

5

System Startup

and Shutdown

YOU CAN'T JUST TURN IT OFF

There is an important difference between your UNIX system and a television set (besides the price) — you can't just turn it off. You may be familiar with single-user computers that can be turned on or off as you would a stereo or household appliance. To start the personal computer up, you turn on the power. To turn it off, you simply complete what you are doing, and turn it off. The distinction that must be made between a microcomputer and a computer of any size running the UNIX system is that the UNIX system is a multiuser and multitasking operating system. Even if you are the only one using the system, it is quite likely that other activity is occurring and you need to be certain that this other activity finishes.

Because the UNIX operating system juggles many activities at once, it keeps as much information as possible in memory, as opposed to in disk storage. Changes are made to the information kept in memory first, then written out to a disk later, when more memory is needed or a specific command is given. Shutting off a UNIX system without using the shutdown procedure guarantees that the information in memory that should have been written to disk storage will be lost. At best, the last changes made to the file systems will be lost. At worst, the file systems will have become inconsistent, and even more damage to the file systems will result if the proper procedure isn't followed for starting up the next time.

The proper startup procedure requires testing the file systems before they are put into use. If an improper shutdown occurred, or inconsistencies developed because of hardware problems, the **fsck** program will discover the problem and attempt to fix it (see Chapter 4). The startup procedure also provides for the correct setting of the system clock, starting of background processes (daemons), and preparing terminal ports for multiuser operation. The shutdown procedure correctly reverses the startup, and in an orderly fashion brings your system back to single-user state either for backing up files, running **fsck**, or turning off the power.

Most likely, you are already using startup and shutdown procedures for your UNIX system. Besides explaining exactly what these procedures are doing, we will describe what you can do to modify these operations. These procedures are controlled by scripts and tables that can be changed, and modifying these files is often the most appropriate approach for solving some administration problems.

Also, this chapter describes one of the most important system programs, **init**. **init** does what its name implies—it initiates activities. The **init** program directs much of what happens during system startup and shutdown. The **/etc/inittab** (**init** table) configuration file guides the **init** program.

A related program, **getty**, works with **init**. **getty** stands for "get a tty," in other words, establish communication with a *tty* (from "teletype," the trade name of terminals used when UNIX was first designed). The **/etc/gettydefs** (**getty** definitions) configuration file sets the conditions used for establishing communications between your UNIX system's ports and each terminal. Terminal problems that show up during log-in can be corrected by editing the **/etc/gettydefs** file.

SYSTEM STARTUP PROCEDURES

By system startup procedures we mean the steps that you, and your system, take to bring your UNIX system up in a multiuser state. At the moment that you turn on your system, its memory is blank. The programs that allow it to perform complex processes are missing. Your computer is a vacant-headed idiot. The startup procedure gradually adds smarts until the familiar and friendly UNIX system replaces the empty idiot.

Figure 5.1 shows the messages that appear on a typical microcomputer UNIX system during system startup. The legends appearing to the right in italics are comments, and serve to break the startup into distinct phases. These phases are:

1. The hardware ROM routines
2. The boot loader
3. Kernel initialization
4. The **/etc/init** program

Figure 5.1 Four phases of UNIX system startup.

```
Morrow TRICEP System   (prom 2.4)        1. ROM instructions test
Testing Memory.                             memory, check floppy disk
Memory OK
1048576 bytes
Start from the floppy?  n                and reads the boot loader


:<RETURN>                                2. The loader waits
mw(0,0)unix                                 for a response, then
Loading at 0x400:  86268+8928+74072         loads unix.


(C) Copyright 1983 - UniSoft Corporation 3. The kernel takes over.
    68000 UNIX System V - June 1983


Created Tue Sep 10 07:24:06 PDT 1986



mem=802816                               initializes its memory tables
4 SIO4 ports                                and some hardware.


                                         4. /etc/inittab guides init.

Is the date Sep 10 10:02:16 1987 correct? (y or n) n<RETURN>
Enter the correct date:  09111125<RETURN>
Is the date Sep 11 11:25:16 1987 correct? (y or n) y<RETURN>
Do you wish to check the file systems? (y or n) y<RETURN>

    /dev/mw0a
    File System:  root  Volume:  fixed

    ** Phase 1 - Check Blocks and Sizes
    ** Phase 2 - Check Pathnames
    ** Phase 3 - Check Connectivity
    ** Phase 4 - Check Reference Count
    ** Phase 5 - Check Free List
    1953 files  31935 blocks  28950 free
Starting errdemon
cron started

The message of the day:  Thank Allah!  It's Friday.

process accounting started
LP scheduler started

amber system
log-in: □
```

The four phases of a UNIX startup can also be described through a diagram. Figure 5.2 presents each major phase of startup within a large box, and the files that control each phase within smaller boxes.

Figure 5.2 Diagram describing system startup and the files that control it.

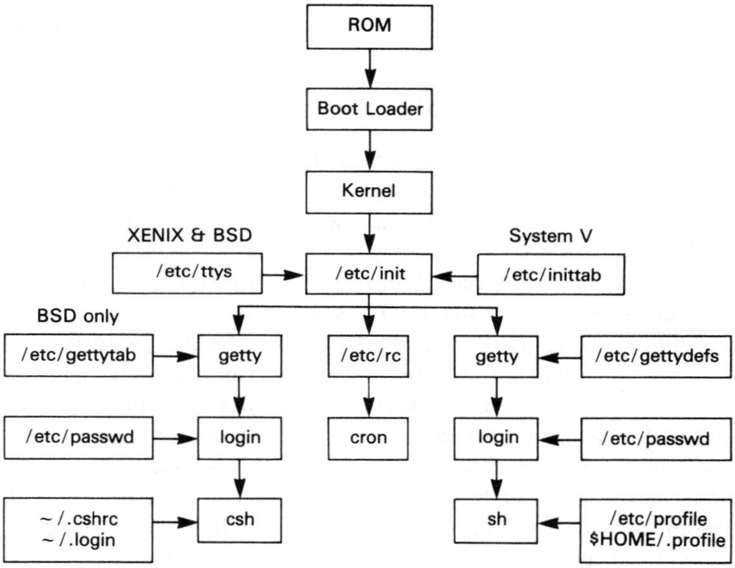

Phase One: Running in ROM

At the beginning of phase one, your computer's memory is empty, but not completely. A small section of memory, called ROM, for read-only memory, doesn't get wiped clean when your system is powered down. As the power in your system reaches operating levels, the CPU becomes active and starts executing the instructions stored in the ROM. These instructions start out by looking for more memory. This time, the memory is the ordinary, forget-everything-when-the-power-is-off, RAM, also known as random access memory. The purpose for checking RAM is to see if there is enough memory there to continue with the startup process. Present-day UNIX systems require a minimum of 512 kilobytes (one-half megabyte) for operation. (This minimum size seems likely to increase.) The total amount of memory, and other information about its configuration, is saved so that the kernel can use the information that has been gathered.

Besides checking for memory, the ROM instructions may test for the existence of other components, such as hard and floppy disks. The ROM instructions may also check, in a very cursory manner, that these components work. On some systems, the ROM will also copy instructions to intelligent controller hardware. The hardware tests performed by your system will vary.

If successful in the search for sufficient memory, the ROM instructions next cause a program to be copied from either the boot partition of a disk, a floppy disk, tape, or a cassette, into RAM. This program is called the *boot loader*, or *loader* for short. The ROM program may read the (first) *boot block* on the hard disk to locate the loader; then it copies the loader to RAM and passes control to it.

Phase Two: The Loader Takes Over

Phase two begins with the loader in RAM. The loader, a more complex program than the ROM instructions, can access file systems and work with alternative devices. And the loader does just what its name implies—it loads a program and transfers control to it. When you enter a response after the colon prompt, the loader looks for the specified program on the specified device, or the default program and device. Pressing RETURN by itself at the colon prompt usually causes the defaults to be used, loading the kernel, **/unix**. Note that most XENIX systems never present the colon prompt, and proceed immediately with loading the kernel.

In Figure 5.1, the defaults used are **mw(0,0)unix**. The letters **mw** stand for the name of a device driver built into the loader program. The numbers **(0,0)** are arguments used by the device driver to select which disk and partition to use. The default device specification is system specific, so your system will most likely have a different device driver name. And if you are using XENIX, the program to load will be **xenix**, not **unix**. Other vendors may use different names for the kernel program, **syst** or **syst5**, for example.

Figure 5.3 Arguments for loading the kernel program.

```
                        :mw(0,0)unix
        driver name /  /  \    \program to load
            drive number  offset into device
```

The loader copies the specified program into memory (RAM). You may get a progress report in the form of three numbers on the line in Figure 5.4. The first number is the size in bytes of the program's code (instructions), the second is the size of the initialized data area, and the third is the size of the uninitialized data area. These sizes are mainly for the use of systems programmers who are designing or configuring kernels.

Figure 5.4 The description of the program being loaded.

```
Loading at 0x400: 80800+9124+132000
```

Now we're getting somewhere. The loader usually loads the kernel, the heart of the UNIX operating system, into memory. Alternatively, you may have commanded the loader to start up a stand-alone diagnostic program. Stand alone diagnostic programs run without the UNIX operating system kernel. Thus, they "stand alone." Diagnostic programs are discussed in Chapter 10, *System Problems*.

The kernel is the operating system program. It interfaces between programs and the computer's hardware. A program can access memory in its own area, but makes requests to the kernel (via system calls) to communicate with the file system, disks, terminals, printers, or other memory. The kernel is always in memory after it has been loaded. It is never swapped out, since a part of the kernel performs the swapping.

Phase Three: Kernel Initialization

The kernel starts out by following an initialization sequence, which we have labeled phase three. Initialization means "preparing hardware and software for use." The kernel begins by initializing itself. To begin with, the memory information collected by the ROM is organized into an internal table by the kernel. The message "mem = 802816" (see Figure 5.1) tells us that there is about 800 kilobytes of memory available for executing programs after loading the kernel. The amount of memory available is system dependent. Then the device drivers, software that communicates with devices, initialize the different devices, such as serial ports and disks. In our example, the message "4 SIO4 ports" tells us that the serial port device driver found and initialized four serial ports. Other initialization routines, such as those for the hard or floppy disks, do not make reports on our example system.

Phase Four: init Gets Started

As phase three ends, your UNIX system is almost ready to work for you. The ROM has checked memory and copied in the boot loader. The boot loader has loaded the kernel. The kernel has organized available memory and initialized the device controllers.

What is lacking now are the programs that will start users' shells. Various other tasks, like starting the **cron** program, or mounting other file systems, must still be done. To accomplish these tasks, the last part of the kernel's initialization sequence creates two processes, **swapper** and **init**. Figure 5.5 shows the listing from the **ps** (process status) command that illustrates that **swapper** and **init** are indeed the two first processes.

Figure 5.5 Listing all processes.

```
$ ps -ef
    UID    PID   PPID   C   STIME  TTY   TIME  COMMAND
   root      0      0  31 22:58:48   ?   0:37  swapper
   root      1      0   0 22:58:48   ?   0:06  /etc/init
   root    814      1   0 12:00:02  co   0:00  [ sh ]
   root     39      1   0 09:24:34  co   0:00  [ errdemon ]
   root     57      1   0 09:24:46  co   0:22  /etc/cron
     lp     96      1   0 09:25:14   ?   0:01  [ lpsched ]
    rik    104      1   0 09:25:20  co   0:11  -csh
   root    105      1   0 09:25:20   ?   0:01  [ getty ]
 beccat    922      1   0 12:09:12   1   0:15  -csh
 beccat   1089    922   7 12:21:34   1   0:15  vi feb28a.86
    rik   1136    104   5 12:25:50  co   0:06  [ vi ]
    rik   1149   1148  73 12:26:30  co   0:03  [ ps ]
$ □
```

The **swapper** process is actually the part of the kernel that schedules all other processes. There is no program named **swapper** in the file system. The swapper has the process id (PID) of zero and is given its name by the **ps** command. (Newer **ps** programs may use **sched** for the name.) Process status (**ps**) reports from UNIX systems that use paging will show two "swappers" or perhaps use other names.

The **swapper** process, or scheduler, examines the kernel's process table every clock tick (usually, a sixtieth of a second), whenever a process completes, and whenever a process must wait for input or output. The process in the process table that isn't waiting for another event (like keyboard input) and has not been run recently will be scheduled to run next.

The scheduler's first action is to start the **init** process. The **init** process starts (is the parent of) all other processes. When **init**'s child processes complete, a signal gets sent to the **init** process. The signal causes **init** to examine the file **/etc/inittab** to see if the child that completed should be run again. The **init** process also receives other signals to look at the **/etc/inittab** file.

The order of what happens during phase four of the startup procedure is controlled by the **init** process and its configuration file, the init table, **/etc/inittab**. Since the way that **init** works is really a story all its own, **init** and **inittab** are covered later in this chapter.

Setting the Date.   Phase four of our example begins with a question: Is the date correct? Changing the system's date must be done before the system has started the **cron** background process. If you set the date or time ahead while **cron** is running, the **cron** program will attempt to start all the processes in its control table that weren't started since the old date. If you have ever changed the date, for example, by advancing the date by a day with **cron** running, you will certainly remember how activity suddenly increased, to the point where trying to run **ps** and discover what's happening was perhaps impossible.

Other programs rely on the orderly advance of time. When changing the date always work in single-user mode, or during startup. During startup, the **/etc/bcheckrc** file contains a shell script for displaying and changing the date. BSD and XENIX set the date in **/etc/rc**.

The **date** command expects you to enter the date in a numeric format. This format is easy to use once you have a grasp of exactly what the **date** command expects. The System V **date** command uses the following syntax for changing the time:

date *MMDDHHMM[YY]*

Each pair of letters in the argument to **date** represent two digits that stand for the month, the day, the hour (in 24-hour notation), the minute, and (optionally) the last two digits of the year. The **date** command is very particular about what it will convert to the time, and will fail if you have anything wrong. The important thing to remember is that the **date** command takes its data as *two numbers* at a time, and that four pairs of numbers are required.

The last two digits, the year, are optional. Notice that there is no way to enter A.M. or P.M., or the day of the week. You must provide the date in 24-hour format. That is, to convert say, 3:00 P.M., into 24-hour notation you add twelve to three, and get 1500. Ten o'clock in the evening becomes 2200 (10:00 + 12:00), and 11:30 P.M. becomes 2330.

Another bit of funniness can pop up while entering the date. The **date** command gets its notion of local time through the **TZ**, or time zone, variable in the environment. (BSD UNIX versions have the time zone built into the kernel.) If the date displayed at this point doesn't match your time zone, you need to add two shell commands to the **/etc/bcheckrc** script (**/etc/rc** for XENIX) before the **date** command is invoked, similar to the specific example that follows:

    TZ=PST8PDT; export TZ

The time zone variable (**TZ**) has three different parts packed together. The first three letters, PST in the example, provide the standard time identification letters. The last three letters are used during daylight savings time. If you don't include the last three letters, **date** assumes that your area doesn't use daylight savings time. The **date** command knows which Sunday to "spring ahead" to daylight savings time or "fall back" to standard time.

At the time this book was written, the U.S. Congress had changed these dates by two weeks. So, by an act of law, the **date** command no longer works correctly. And neither will **ls** −**l**, **touch**, or other commands that can display dates. As newer versions of these commands are created, they will be updated to reflect the legislated changes.

The question is: What do you do if you have the old version of **date**? Well, the UNIX system uses the number of seconds since December 31, 23:59, 1969 GMT (the "epoch") to represent dates internally. The number of seconds gets converted into a more humanly recognizable format when commands like **date** are used. If you don't do anything when the change between standard and daylight savings time is made, your UNIX system won't even notice. But your users might.

If you elect to change the date to correspond to the time showing after everyone has changed their watches, your system will experience either a missing hour (in the spring) or an extra hour (in the fall of the year). The missing or extra hour might affect your backup or accounting procedures. However, if you make the change at the appropriate time (2:00 A.M., Sunday morning), with **cron** not running, you probably won't hurt anything. Then, when the **date** command feels that it's time to make the change, you will have to undo your correction, this time, having an extra hour (spring) or losing an hour (fall). Our suggestion is that you leave the time alone, and use **/etc/motd** to inform your users that the date will appear off by one hour for two weeks. Otherwise, you are responsible for changing the date twice at 2 A.M. Sunday morning. (*Hint*: Use a shell script, but remember to stop **cron** first, and restart it afterward.)

The number sandwiched between the identifying letters, "8" in our example, stands for eight hours earlier than Greenwich Mean Time. The **date** command treats Greenwich Mean Time as zero, Eastern Standard Time as 5, Central Standard as 6, Rocky Mountain as 7, and Pacific as 8. On a map of the world, each time zone is counted, starting with zero in Greenwich, as you move west.

For countries east of Greenwich, you can count backward from zero. All of Europe (except Portugal, Greece, Rumania, Bulgaria, and Great Britain), is -1, Egypt and Greece are -2, Moscow and Baghdad are -3, Hanoi and Chungking are -8, and so on. Countries using fractional time zones, such as India, aren't supported, and neither is Saudi Arabia, which is on Solar Time, nor Mongolia, which has no legal time. (Note that some versions of UNIX, such as Apple's AUX, do support fractional time zones.) Figure 5.6 provides several examples of **TZ** variables.

Figure 5.6 Examples of time-zone variables from around the world.

```
TZ=GMT0           Greenwich Mean Time, Great Britain
TZ=AST4           Atlantic Standard Time/no daylight savings time
TZ=EST5EDT        Eastern Standard Time/Eastern Daylight Time
TZ=CST6CDT        Central Standard Time/Daylight Savings Time
TZ=MST7MDT        Mountain Standard Time/Mountain Daylight Time
TZ=PST8PDT        Pacific Standard Time/Pacific Daylight Time
TZ=YST9           Yukon Standard Time
TZ=HST10          Hawaiian/Alaska Standard Time
TZ=NST11          Nome Standard Time
TZ=AST-10         Australia Standard Time (Sydney/Melbourne)
TZ=TST-8          Thailand Standard Time
```

The **TZ** variable must be included in every user's environment for the **date** command to work correctly for that user. The **cron** program also uses the **TZ** variable.

So you should include the correct **TZ** variable in the **/etc/rc** file, **/etc/profile** file for Bourne shell users, and **.login** files for C-shell users. On some systems, the **TZ** variable must be set within the **/usr/lib/uucp/uushell** script, if this script exists, for UUCP system log-ins.

You can centralize changing the **TZ** variable by creating a very simple script, **TIMEZONE**. This two-line Bourne shell script gets run wherever you would set the **TZ** variable. Figure 5.7 lists this script.

Figure 5.7 The **TIMEZONE** script for the Pacific states.

```
:

TZ=PST8PDT; export TZ
```

The **TIMEZONE** script should be installed in the **/etc** directory, and made readable and executable by all.

Check Your File Systems. The **/etc/bcheckrc** script will next ask you if you wish to check your file systems. You should always respond "y" to this question. There are rare and unusual cases where you might not run **fsck**, but these are the exceptions. Several systems that we have seen run **fsck** as a stand-alone program on the root file system before loading the kernel. In this case you can skip checking the root file system a second time. Other systems rely on the **/etc/fsstat** program, which looks at the "needs checking" flag in the superblock to determine if a file system should be checked. Our inclination is to check these file systems weekly, regardless of what the **fsstat** reports. A stitch in time saves nine.

The **fsck** program checks the file systems listed in **/etc/checklist**. The **/etc/checklist** file contains a list of file systems, one file system partition name per line. You can use the "raw" device name for file systems other than the root. An example "checklist" file is shown in Figure 5.8.

Figure 5.8 An example **/etc/checklist** file.

```
$ cat /etc/checklist
/dev/dsk/c0d0s0
/dev/rdsk/c0d1s0
/dev/rdsk/c0d1s1
$ □
```

Your **checklist** file will contain the name of your file system devices that need to be checked at this point. If your system checks the root file system at an earlier time, it won't contain the name of the root file system (**/dev/dsk/c0d0s0** in Figure 5.8). A complete explanation of the **fsck** program, and "raw" devices, is given in Chapter 4. Note that Berkeley-based UNIX systems use the file **/etc/fstab** instead of **/etc/checklist**. The Berkeley version has a different format and functionality.

The Run Commands File

We have now reached the **/etc/rc** file. *rc* stands for "run commands." The run commands file was the only script executed by older releases of the **init** program, such as UNIX Version 7. The present-day version of **/etc/rc** still performs many of the same functions as those of the earlier **/etc/rc** files. On BSD systems, the script **/etc/rc.local** contains local additions to the run commands file, usually including initializing networking and remote file systems.

With Release 3 of System V, the **/etc/rc** script has been changed drastically. Instead of containing the shell commands, the script, now named **/etc/rc2**, contains a simple loop that executes the shell scripts found in the **/etc/rc.d** and perhaps the **/etc/rc2.d** directory as well. Each script in the "rc" directory deals with a different topic, like networking, the LP system, or **cron**. The division of the **/etc/rc** file into many shell scripts serves to better organize the material in the scripts. Note that the order in which these scripts will be executed depends on their names—scripts with names that begin with characters earlier in the ASCII collating sequence will be executed before ones that have names beginning with characters that occur later in this sequence.

Figure 5.9 An example **/etc/rc** file from System V Release 2.

```
if [ ! -f /etc/mnttab ]         # if no mount table exists,
then                            # make a mount table
   /etc/devnm / /tmp | /etc/setmnt
fi
set `who -r`                    # check the current run-level
if test $9 = S -a $7 != S       # if entering a numeric run-level
then                            # from single-user, start these commands
        mount /dev/dsk/c0d1s0 /a # mount file systems here
        mount /dev/dsk/c0d1s1 /b
        /usr/lib/expreserve     # preserve ex sessions, if any
                                # remove all files still in /tmp
                                # including those starting with "."
                                # but not "." and ".."
        rm -rf `ls -a /tmp | sed   '/^\.$/d;/^\.\.$/d'`
        rm -f /usr/spool/lp/SCHEDLOCK
        /usr/lib/lpsched        # remove lockfile and start scheduler
        /usr/lib/errdemon       # start error reporting daemon
                                # save yesterday's log files
        cp /usr/adm/cronlog /usr/adm/OLDcronlog
        cp /dev/null /usr/adm/cronlog
        cp /usr/adm/sulog /usr/adm/OLDsulog
        cp /dev/null /usr/adm/sulog
        /etc/cron               # start the cron daemon
                                # start per process accounting
```

```
        /bin/su - adm -c /usr/lib/acct/startacct
                                 # set system activity counters
        /bin/su adm -c "/usr/lib/sa/sadc /usr/adm/sa/sa`date +%d` &"
                                 # remove lockfiles from UUCP
        rm -f /usr/spool/uucp/LCK*
        chown lp /dev/tty2        # correct permissions
        chown uucp /dev/cu0
fi
```

Creating a Mount Table.   The first task in **/etc/rc** is to create a mount table, **/etc/mnttab**, if one doesn't already exist. (BSD uses the **/etc/mtab** file, which has a format similar to its **/etc/fstab** file. No special commands are used to set up this file.)   To create the mount table, two special-purpose commands are used. The **/etc/devnm** command takes each filename argument and outputs the file system device name (partition) where it is found, along with the filename argument. The **/etc/setmnt** command translates this information into mount table format. Figure 5.10a shows how these two commands are connected through a pipeline.

Figure 5.10 Creating the mount table.

a. The line in **/etc/rc** that creates the mount table:

```
        /etc/devnm / ¦ grep -v swap ¦ grep -v root ¦ /etc/setmnt
```

b. Adding additional mount points to the pipeline:

```
        /etc/devnm / /tmp ¦ grep -v swap ¦ grep -v root ¦ /etc/setmnt
```

The two **grep** commands in the middle of the pipeline remove lines containing the words "swap" or "root." The product of the pipeline is a new mount table with an entry for the root device, unless the root file system is located on **/dev/root**. If you have mounted other file systems before the run command file is executed, you can edit the pipeline in Figure 5.10a and add the mount points as arguments to the **/etc/devnm** command. Part b of Figure 5.10 adds the device name and mount point for a file system mounted as **/tmp** to the newly created mount table.

A new and empty **/etc/mnttab** is created each time the **/etc/setmnt** command is used. **/etc/mnttab** is not in human-readable format, but can be displayed using the **mount** command without any arguments.

The Run Level 2 Section of /etc/rc.   After creating a mount table, the **/etc/rc** script examines the *run level*. The run level is a concept introduced with the System III **init** program.   BSD and XENIX use the older **init** program and use two modes (instead of run levels), single-user mode and multiuser mode. The new **init** program expands these two modes into eight possible run levels. The **s** run level corresponds to single-user mode, while run levels 0 through 6 are all multiuser modes. How the numeric run levels are used is determined by the system administrator or system vender.

The **who** command with the −**r** (run level) option reports on the current and past run levels. The shell's **set** command captures the output of the **who** command and then breaks it into strings. The seventh string represents the current run level, and this string, **$7** in shell notation, is tested in the next shell command in the **rc** file. In Figure 5.11 we explore this little bit of madness.

Figure 5.11 How the **rc** file discovers the run level.

```
$ who -r
        .        run-level 2   Apr   2 21:34    2     0     S
>>$1            $2        $3   $4  $5  $6       $7    $8    $9   << Added for clarity
$ set `who -r`
$ echo $7
2
$ □
```

So you can see where the **$7** comes from in the test that follows the **who** command. When the current run level is identical to "2," the rest of the **rc** script gets executed. If you wish to have the **rc** script executed when you enter run levels other than 2, you can edit the **/etc/rc** file and change this test. For example, suppose that you wanted to execute the entire **rc** script every time you left the single-user run level. We can accomplish this feat by testing to see that the previous run level (**$9**) is "S" *and* that the current run level is not "S" (**$7**) with the test in Figure 5.12.

Figure 5.12 Changing the test in the **rc** file.

```
set `who -r`
if test $9 = S -a $7 != S
then
      the rest of the rc script
fi
```

The test for run level 2 in the **/etc/rc** file is the primary reason that this run level is considered the multiuser run level. Run level 2 is not sacred; it's just traditionally the multiuser run level, and you can change the **rc** file so that the entire script is executed whenever entering any run level after leaving single-user run level by using a test like that shown in Figure 5.12. You may also wish to use this test if you routinely change between run level 2 and some other run level. Otherwise, every time you reenter run level 2, the **/etc/rc** script will start another **cron** daemon and perform other tasks that you've already done.

The next part of the **rc** file mounts additional file systems. These file systems are the ones listed in the **/etc/checklist** file, and have previously been checked by **fsck**. Now is the time to mount these file systems, before any users can log in.

Each **mount** command requires two arguments: the block device name of the file system, and the mount point. The block device name is simply the name, in the **/dev** directory, for the partition corresponding to this file system. The mount point is the directory where this file system will be mounted. For example, to mount the file systems in the example **/etc/checklist** file, we would use the following two commands after the test in **/etc/rc**:

```
mount /dev/dsk/c0d1s0 /a
mount /dev/dsk/c0d1s1 /b
```

The **mount** command can mount only one file system at a time, so you cannot **mount** multiple file systems with the same command. (But, remember that the Berkeley **mount -a** will mount all the file systems in **/etc/fstab**.) The directory where you wish to mount a file system must already exist. The **mount** command also will refuse to mount the corresponding character (raw) device.

Clearing the /tmp Directory.   After mounting additional file systems, the **/etc/rc** script removes all files in the **/tmp** directory. The **/tmp** directory is used only for temporary files, so clearing it enforces this strategy. First, **rc** preserves any edit buffers left by the **ex** command after an accidental hang-up, or a system crash. The **/usr/lib/expreserve** command looks in the **/tmp** directory for files with the prefaces **Ex** or **Rx**. These files, for example **/tmp/Ex05548**, are the result of an incomplete editor session with **vi** or **ex**. The **expreserve** command sends mail to the owner of the file explaining how to reclaim the lost buffer. The edit buffer gets copied to the **/usr/preserve** directory, so it can be claimed by the user. If you are using another editor that uses a similar rescue mechanism, that is, a method for restoring edit buffers left in **/tmp**, add the command for saving lost edit buffers here.

The second phase in clearing **/tmp** is simply to remove all files with the command **rm −rf /tmp/***. This command assures you that the **/tmp** directory remains clear and empty, and is the repository for truly "temporary" files.

Starting Background Processes: Daemons.   Daemons are started by the **/etc/rc** shell script so that they are functioning before your system has allowed user log-ins. A good example of a daemon is the **cron** process. This process's task is to start programs at designated times. If the **cron** program were started by a user, it obviously wouldn't begin working until the user had logged in. Besides, **cron**'s duties aren't directly connected to any user's activities. It carries out routine administrative tasks on a regular basis. The **cron** program has superuser access privileges, so it can perform tasks that require this privilege.

A log kept by **cron** shows every program that **cron** has started and contains the output of these programs (if the output hasn't been redirected). The logfile, called **/usr/adm/cronlog**, (**/usr/lib/cron/log** after Release 2 of System V), grows every time the **cron** program starts another program. So something must be done to control the size of the logfile. The **/etc/rc** script uses a command that renames **/usr/adm/cronlog** as **/usr/adm/OLDcronlog**. Thus, there is at least a short term archive of the **cron** program's activities available, besides the most recent one.

Another program, **/bin/su**, also keeps a log, named **/usr/adm/sulog**, as it works. The **su** program (for substitute user) is used to become the superuser, or some other user, without logging out. Because the superuser is so powerful, the **su** program, for security reasons, keeps track of the users who invoke it. And like the **cron** log, the **/etc/rc** file uses a move command to keep an archive file around.

Both of these logs are security sensitive. You want them for administering your system and don't want just anybody to read them. You can improve the way the **/etc/rc** file handles the security of these files by replacing the moves with the lines shown in Figure 5.13.

Figure 5.13 Archiving logfiles in the **rc** script.

```
cp /usr/adm/cronlog /usr/adm/OLDcronlog
cp /dev/null /usr/adm/cronlog
cp /usr/adm/sulog /usr/adm/OLDsulog
cp /dev/null /usr/adm/sulog
```

Then, you need to correct the permissions on these files just once. Working as **root**, excute the commands given in Figure 5.14.

Figure 5.14 Establishing the correct permissions for logfiles.

```
# cd /usr/adm
# chmod 600 *log
# □
```

Now these important logs and their archives are readable and writable by their owner (**root**) only. Remember that System V Release 2 has changed the location of the **cron** log to **/usr/lib/cron/log**, so substitute this filename for **/usr/adm/cronlog** in Figures 5.13 and 5.14.

After preparing an empty **cron** log file, the **/etc/rc** script will start up the **/etc/cron** program. There are two other daemons that may be started at this point, **errdemon** and **lpsched**. The **errdemon** captures device error messages and stores then in the file **/usr/adm/errfile**. The **lpsched** process wakes up whenever anyone makes a request to print a file with **lp** and stays awake until all files are printed.

The **lpsched** program will kill itself immediately after it is invoked if it finds the lock file **/usr/spool/lp/SCHEDLOCK**. Lock files are often used to prevent two occurrences of the same program (or event) simultaneously. In this case, the **SCHEDLOCK** file prevents the existence of two **lp** schedulers. If two schedulers were allowed to coexist, they could both access the same printer at the same time, resulting in jumbled printouts. The **lpshut** command normally removes the **SCHEDLOCK** file during shutdown. By including a command to remove this file in the **/etc/rc** file, you cover yourself against an incorrect shutdown and guarantee that the scheduler will start.

Other programs besides the **lp** scheduler use lock files. Most notably, the UUCP **uucico** program (UNIX to UNIX copy-in copy-out) creates a lock file whenever it attempts to contact a remote system and erases the file when it completes the transaction with the system. The **cu** program and the **uucico** program also create lock files whenever they open a device file. The **uucico** program is the UUCP file transfer daemon, and uses the lock file to prevent simultaneous access to the same system or same port. However, if your system was shut down before the **uucico** program could exit gracefully and remove the lock file, the file is still around. And the lock file will prevent **uucico** program from contacting a remote system or accessing a port used for the lock. To avoid this dilemma, the **/etc/rc** file forcibly removes the lock files for **uucico** and **cu** programs, with the command in Figure 5.15.

Figure 5.15 Removing UUCP system lock files.

```
rm -f /usr/spool/uucp/LCK*
```

Other Tasks Performed by /etc/rc. Two other programs that are often started by **/etc/rc** are **startacct** and **sadc**. The **startacct** script writes an entry in the **/etc/wtmp** file indicating that process accounting has been turned on (see Figure 5.16). Then it signals the kernel to begin writing summaries after every process terminates.

Figure 5.16 Command to start process accounting.

```
/bin/su - adm -c /usr/lib/acct/startacct
```

The system activity package reads counters built into the kernel. These counters measure things like the total number of characters transferred or the number of processes swapped. Even more important, these activity counters measure kernel table overflow, an indication that the kernel may need to be changed. The **/usr/lib/sa/sadc** program writes an initial entry in the file where system activity data are collected. This initial entry is essential if you wish to use the sys-

tem activity package. The command in the run command file looks like the line in
Figure 5.17.

Figure 5.17 Creating the daily system activity file.

```
/bin/su adm -c "/usr/lib/sa/sadc /usr/adm/sa/sa`date +%d` &"
```

This command line creates a file named **/usr/adm/sa/sa***MM* (where *MM* is
the day of the month), containing the initial counter readings. The **/bin/su** command establishes the owner of these processes as the administrative account, **adm**.
Otherwise, processes started by the **/etc/rc** file have the identity of the **root**
account.

The **rc** script is also the appropriate place for archiving files other than logfiles
that grow. You may wish to refer to Chapter 7 for files that may grow with every
process completed, or through log-in activity. There, techniques for handling these
files are discussed.

Another task accomplished with the **rc** script is to correct the ownership of
some device files. The serial ports used by the UUCP programs to call out should be
owned by the **uucp** administrative account. Similarly, any serial port used by the **lp**
process must be owned by the **lp** administrative account. However, the ownership
of these device files is changed to the **root** account any time a **getty** process is run
for these ports. If you have configured your system so that the ports used by **uucp**
and **lp** are sometimes also used as log-in ports, you need to restore the proper ownerships in the **rc** script. In Figure 5.18 we show how to correct the ownership of
/dev/tty2 (used by **lp**) and **/dev/cu0** (used by **uucp** for calling out).

Figure 5.18 Correcting ownership of some device files.

```
chown lp /dev/tty2
chown uucp /dev/cu0
```

LOG-INS AND THE getty PROGRAM

Finally, we have reached the point where the system has been prepared for users to
log in. The **init** process, which has been in control of phase four, will start an
/etc/getty program for serial ports enabled for this run level. As mentioned earlier,
"getty" stands for "get a tty". The task of the **getty** program is to establish communication with a user's terminal. As soon as a **getty** process has collected a possible log-in name, it replaces itself with the **/bin/login** program. The **login** program
checks the log-in name against the **/etc/passwd** file, and prompts for a password if
necessary.

The **getty** program uses the arguments provided by its invocation command line in **inittab** to select a serial port and an entry in the **/etc/gettydefs** file. (BSD **getty** programs use the **/etc/gettytab** file instead of **/etc/gettydefs**.) When terminals are "permanently" connected to a system, **getty**'s task is simplified. The terminal can be expected to be configured at a particular baud (transmission) rate. However, when the port is attached to a modem or multiplexer, the baud rate may not be known in advance. The **getty** program adjusts to different baud rates by trying another entry line in the **gettydefs** file when **getty** detects an error. The **getty** program will also set the terminal device to be in upper-case-only mode if the log-in name received is composed of upper-case letters. Upper-case mode translates all upper-case letters not preceded by a backslash (\) into lower-case letters, and was for use with ancient upper-case-only terminals. And if the log-in name is followed by a carriage return, carriage returns will be translated into newlines on input. The reverse transformation, newlines into carriage returns, will be performed on output.

The /etc/gettydefs File

It's easy to see what the **getty** program does by examining example **/etc/gettydefs** (**getty** definitions) entries. Each entry in the **/etc/gettydefs** file is separated from the next entry by a blank line. Long entries can include newlines that aren't escaped (preceded by a backslash). Let's start with the entry in Figure 5.19.

Figure 5.19 A sample **gettydefs** entry.

```
co_9600 # B9600 # B9600 SANE TAB3 # \r\nConsole login: # co_4800
   |         |         |                       |                  |
 Label    Initial  Final Conditions      Initial Prompt      Next Label
```

There are five fields (parts) in a **gettydefs** entry. (See the section on XENIX V **gettydefs** for the differences between System V and XENIX V **/etc/gettydefs** files.) A pound sign (#) separates each field from its neighbor. The **getty** program stops interpreting the **/etc/gettydefs** file as soon as it encounters an error. If an error occurs on the first line, the entire **gettydefs** file is ignored and a default entry hard-coded in the **getty** program is used. The default entry sets the baud rate to 300 baud.

The first field, **co_9600** above, is the entry's label. Other entries in **gettydefs** and the arguments used when invoking **/etc/getty** refer to this label. The second field contains the initial conditions used while trying to make contact with a terminal. **B9600** stands for "9600 baud," or 9600 bits per second. The initial and final conditions can be gleaned by reading the TERMIO manual entry in section 7 of the *System V Administrator Reference Manual*. However, we have found the standard documentation heavy reading, so we have included a table containing the most commonly used baud rates, Table 5.1, and a second table containing commonly used conditions (Figure 5.20). (Note that the TTY(4) entry is used by BSD systems, and TTY(M) by XENIX, instead of TERMIO(7).)

TABLE 5.1 BAUD RATE SYMBOLS USED WITH **getty**

Symbol	Baud rate	Symbol	Baud rate
B50	50 baud	B1200	1200 baud
B75	75 baud	B1800	1800 baud
B110	110 baud	B2400	2400 baud
B134	134.5 baud	B4800	4800 baud
B150	150 baud	B9600	9600 baud
B300	300 baud	EXTA	System dependent
B600	600 baud	EXTB	System dependent

The next field consists of the final conditions, final from the viewpoint of **getty**. Once the **getty** program has gathered a possible log-in name, it sets the terminal to the final conditions and replaces itself with the **login** program. So these final conditions are eventually inherited by the user's log-in shell.

There's a nondocumented condition flag named **SANE** that's used in **gettydefs** files. By experimentation we've found that the **SANE** condition produces reasonable (sane?) terminal conditions as shown in Figure 5.20:

Figure 5.20 TERMIO(7) symbols represented by SANE condition.

Symbol from TERMIO(7)	Description
BRKINT	Signal interrupt on receiving BREAK
IGNPAR	Ignore characters with parity errors
ISTRIP	Strip off high (most-significant) bit
ICRNL	Convert carriage returns to newlines (on input)
IXON	Enable start/stop control of output (XON/XOFF)
OPOST	Enable output processing
ONLCR	Convert newlines to carriage return and newline
CS7	Use seven data bits
CREAD	Enable receiver
PARENB	Enable parity check, even parity
ISIG	Enable signal processing
ICANON	Process input for backspace and line kill
ECHO	Echo characters as they are received
ECHOK	Echo line kill with a newline

As you can see, the **SANE** condition covers a lot of ground. You could include all the symbols that are listed in Figure 5.20 in the final condition field and get the same effect as with the **SANE** condition.

The TAB3 flag shown in the example entry means "expand tabs into spaces." This condition prevents the terminal device driver from outputting tab characters. Instead, the appropriate number of spaces to move to the next tab position will be output. Tab positions are every eight spaces.

The fourth field in an entry is for the initial prompt presented by the **getty** program. Notice the **\r** and **\n** escape sequences, identical to the sequences used with the **echo** command, to include carriage returns and newlines in the output. You can use the initial prompt to identify your system. For example, the log-in prompt might be "XYZ Systems\r\n enter your name, please." Or, you can tailor the initial prompt to provide as little information as possible for entries used with modem lines. You don't want to tell potential system "crackers" the identity of your system.

System V's **getty** will display any message contained in the file **/etc/issue** before displaying the log-in prompt in the fourth field. This message will appear indiscriminately on all terminal lines with **getty** processes associated with them. So you can include part of the log-in message in **/etc/issue**. Or, you may not want to use it, since this message will also appear on remote terminals that are accessing your system via a modem.

The final field tells the **getty** program which entry in **/etc/gettydefs** to examine next. If the **getty** program receives a null character, indicating that there was either an error in transmission or that the user pressed the BREAK key, the **getty** program uses the initial conditions in the entry pointed to by this final field. Perhaps you are beginning to understand how several entries can be linked together in a cycle. The **getty** program starts with the initial conditions in the first entry, then tries initial conditions in the next entry, then the next, until finally the cycle begins again. Figure 5.21 depicts a short cycle that is used for ports connected to modems.

Figure 5.21 gettydefs entry cycle for modems.

```
mo_2400 # B2400 # B2400 SANE TAB3 HUPCL # \r\nlogin: # mo_1200

mo_1200 # B1200 # B1200 SANE TAB3 HUPCL # \r\nlogin: # mo_300

mo_300 # B300 # B300 SANE TAB3 HUPCL # \r\nlogin: # mo_2400
```

You can see how the **getty** program cycles from one entry, to the next, to the next, and back to the initial entry by following the next label fields. This scheme allows the system administrator to control the sequence of baud rates. Older versions of the **getty** program offered several cycles that started according to the index used in the **/etc/ttys** file. BSD versions of the **getty** program use the **/etc/gettytab** file for modifying these cycles. The **/etc/gettytab** file also allows the system administrator to establish terminal characteristics, as in **/etc/termcap**, to do such things as clearing the screen and printing a customized log-in prompt.

Figure 5.21 shows two essentials in the **gettydefs** for modems—an uninformative log-in prompt and the **HUPCL** flag. The initial prompt is now simply "login:," without any other identification. No sense in making things easier for system breakers. Some system administrators don't even use the word "login:" because it identifies the system as a UNIX system. The other thing to note is the use of the **HUPCL** final condition. The **HUPCL** condition means to send a hang-up signal to the controlling program if the carrier detect signal from a modem is lost. Without the **HUPCL** condition, a shell attached to a modem port continues to wait for input if the line is accidentally (or purposely) hung up. Thus, the next caller gets the previous caller's shell prompt instead of the initial prompt from the **getty** program. From a security point of view, failure to include the **HUPCL** condition presages disaster for **getty**'s running on modem ports.

XENIX V /etc/gettydefs. The XENIX V **getty** program requires a slightly different format for its **/etc/gettydefs** file. The label (and next label) strings must be a single character. When the XENIX V **init** program starts the **getty** program, it can pass only a single character as the label of an entry in the **/etc/gettydefs** file. The first entry in the **gettydefs** file is the default entry, and is used if a matching label is not found.

The XENIX **getty** recognizes an additional symbol in the log-in message field. If the character "@" appears in this field, the "at sign" is replaced with the first line of the file **/etc/systemid**. The **/etc/systemid** file contains system identification.

Finally, a sixth and optional field may be added to any entry. This field contains the name of a program or shell script to be run instead of **/etc/login**. The **getty** process still presents a log-in prompt, but passes the name, or anything that is entered, to the program in the sixth field. By using a **gettydefs** entry with a specially designed program in the sixth field, you could limit access to your system. A special log-in program could be written to provide more information on lines connected to modems. Or, the program could provide a bulletin board service, without exposing your file system to possible security risks.

Modifying the gettydefs File. You, working as a system administrator, may wish to change the **gettydefs** file in several places. First, you can change the initial prompt. Changing the initial prompt is primarily cosmetic and doesn't affect how the **getty** program works. It may, however, affect other UNIX systems that are attempting to contact your system with UUCP. If you expect another system to use UUCP access, you will either need to include the string "login:" in your initial prompt, or communicate the string you are using to the other system administrator. Changing the string expected during log-in is easy.

The second change is to alter the cycle that **getty** follows while attempting to make contact. For directly connected terminals, changing the baud rate will rarely be necessary. For dial-up ports, it is useful to have a short cycle consisting of the baud rates that your modem can handle. Figure 5.21 provides an example of a short cycle. If a directly connected terminal always has a garbled log-in prompt, which means the baud rate is mismatched initially, you need to change the label used in the **getty** invocation for this port in the **/etc/inittab** file.

Finally, you'll want to add the **HUPCL** condition to those lines used for ports connected to modems. We cannot overemphasize the importance of using **HUPCL** for modems.

Checking Changes to /etc/gettydefs

After editing your **/etc/gettydefs** file, you can use the **getty** program to check your edited version with the **−c** (for check) option. For example, imagine that you have just created a file, named **newdefs**, containing the three-entry cycle for modems, as shown in Figure 5.21. Before you add these entries to your existing **gettydefs** file, you need to check them. Figure 5.22 depicts what the output from the check looks like.

Figure 5.22 Check out new **gettydefs** with **getty** −c.

```
# /etc/getty -c newdefs

**** Next Entry ****
mo_2400 # B2400 # B2400 SANE TAB3 HUPCL # \r\nlogin: # mo_1200

id: mo_2400
initial flags:
iflag- 0 oflag- 0 cflag- 2273 lflag- 0
final flags:
iflag- 2446 oflag- 14005 cflag- 2653 lflag- 53
message:
login:
next id: mo_1200

**** Next Entry ****
mo_1200 # B1200 # B1200 SANE TAB3 HUPCL # \r\nlogin: #mo_300

id: mo_1200
initial flags:
iflag- 0 oflag- 0 cflag- 2271 lflag- 0
final flags:
iflag- 2446 oflag- 14005 cflag- 2651 lflag- 53
message:
login:
next id: mo_300

**** Next Entry ****
mo_300 # B300 # B300 SANE TAB3 HUPCL # \r\nlogin: #mo_2400

id: mo_300
initial flags:
iflag- 0 oflag- 0 cflag- 2267 lflag- 0
```

```
final flags:
iflag- 2446 oflag- 14005 cflag- 2647 lflag- 53
message:
login:
next id: mo_2400
# □
```

If **getty** uncovers a problem in your file it will stop processing the file, and indicate with an arrow at what point it failed. The four flags, in the initial and final conditions, correspond to **c_iflag** (input modes), **c_oflag** (output modes), **c_cflag** (control modes), and **c_lflag** (local modes) in the TERMIO(7) manual pages. The numbers after the flags are in octal and can be translated into descriptions by selecting the lines with numbers in the TERMIO(7) entry that will give the displayed sum. (This sounds more difficult than it really is.)

For example, each entry has an **lflag** of 53 in the final flags. (The corresponding flag in TERMIO(7) always begins with "c_".) Looking in the TERMIO(7) manual pages, for the **c_lflag** field (page 6 in our copy of the manual), you can decipher 53 as flags shown in Figure 5.23.

Figure 5.23 Deciphering the flags from **getty** −c.

```
ISIG          0000001 Enable signals
ICANON        0000002 Canonical input (Erase and kill processing)
ECHO          0000010 Enable echo
ECHOK         0000040 Echo NL after kill character
              0000053 Sum of four preceding line flags
```

getty's Command Line

As system administrator, you can use **getty** −c to check **gettydefs** files. Otherwise, the **getty** is run by the **init** program. The **getty** program will be invoked with at least two arguments, a device name (line) and a (**gettydefs** file) label.

Figure 5.24 Invocation of **getty** from the **/etc/inittab**.

a. General invocation command line:

/etc/getty *line label* [−t*DD*]

b. Specific example:

```
/etc/getty tty2 mo_1200
```

The *line* is the name of a character device file (serial port) in the **/dev** directory. The *label* argument is the label from an entry in the **/etc/gettydefs** file. An example invocation from the **/etc/inittab** file is shown in Figure 5.24.

The example invocation starts a **getty** process that watches **/dev/tty2** for input and uses the **/etc/gettydefs** entry labeled **mo_1200** for the initial conditions.

The **−t** flag (for timeout) causes **getty** to exit if no one enters anything within the number of seconds specified. The timeout flag is useful with modem lines, because it forces a response within a reasonable length of time. However, don't use this flag with terminals. The **getty** process will constantly exit when the timeout expires and then be restarted by the **init** process until someone finally logs in using the terminal. This exiting and restarting comprises a lot of unnecessary thrashing about. So, using the timeout flag for **getty** processes running on terminal lines slows down your system.

init, THE STARTER PROGRAM

The **init** program is the great initiator. It starts processes that users can't (or shouldn't have to) start. For example, the **init** process starts the **getty** processes that allow users to log in. It also starts the the various daemon processes through **/etc/rc**. If the system administrator had to log in each time the system entered the multiuser level to start the daemons, it would certainly be a nuisance.

The **init** process is also the ancestor of every other process with the exception of the "swapper" and the kernel (which is not a process). The **init** process's position as grandparent allows it to receive signals from its descendents whenever they complete. When the **init** process receives a completion signal, it checks its table to see what action to take next. The BSD and XENIX **init** programs don't use the same information as System V's **init**.

The **init** program reads its configuration file table (**/etc/inittab**) and starts (or restarts) programs when appropriate. The **init** program scans the table after three types of events: when the **init** program first begins to execute (boot state), when a process started by **init** completes, and when system administrators signal **init** by executing the **init** program as a command with a run-level argument. (XENIX and BSD system administrators *must not* use **init** as a command. These versions of the **init** program are based on an earlier design, and will halt your system if **init** is restarted.)

The concept of *run level* is a relatively recent one. XENIX and BSD systems, and Versions 6 and 7 UNIX systems, use a two-level scheme. When these systems are reset, they are in single-user mode, appropriate for file system checking or backups. The second level, multiuser, is entered when an exit or end-of-file (control-D) is typed at the console. Note that many BSD and XENIX systems automatically enter multiuser level after being reset, and must be shut down to enter single-user mode. The **/etc/ttys** files controls enabling and disabling ports for

log-ins and the **/etc/rc** script is run during the transition from single-user to multiuser level. The **/etc/shutdown** script is used to return to the single-user level.

The System III release of the **init** program introduced run levels and the
/etc/inittab file for controlling the **init** program. The way that the init table works
was changed slightly in System V. The XENIX and BSD systems' approach to
startup and shutdown is considerably simpler, but less flexible, and is discussed in
their own section.

System V's Run Levels

System V has a single-user run level, which is designated by the letters **s** or **S**.
Single-user run level is essential for checking the root file system and backing up.
However, System V can bypass single-user level during startup. A system administrator can also perform maintenance tasks from a remote terminal in single-user
level when necessary. In XENIX and BSD systems, a return to single-user level
requires that the system administrator be working at the console.

System V also differs from BSD and XENIX by having seven numeric run levels, numbered zero through six. The numeric run levels do not have any special
meaning to the **init** program. Rather, they are used to select entries in the init
table. The actions specified in table entries matching the run level are carried out
by **init**, and processes started by init table entries that don't match the run level are
killed.

One use for multiple run levels is to enable different groups of log-in ports.
For example, one run level may be used to enable all log-in ports that are attached
to terminals, while a second run level could be used to activate additional log-in
ports connected to modems. The system administrator can use the different run
levels to control remote access through these modem ports. Another example would
be to use a different run level to disable log-ins on terminals sitting on desks after
people have left work for the day. The system could still be accessible through
modems and terminals that are kept in secure places. AT&T's 3B series of computers uses run level 0 during system shutdown, and reserves run level 5 for
firmware operations.

The init Program

The System V **init** program can start any program that appears in the init table.
The earlier (and current BSD and XENIX) **init** programs will execute the **/etc/rc**
script and run **getty**'s on enabled ports. That's all. The System V **init** table can be
used to run other programs or scripts. For example, a graphics demonstration program could be run for a port instead of **getty**. People using the graphics device
would have their access to the file system completely controlled by the demonstration program. There would be no log-in and no shell. Thus, secure access to a system can be provided through the **init** table and a special program.

The **init** process can be in one of three internal states. When the **init** process
is loaded by the kernel during initialization, it enters the *boot* state. The **init** pro-

cess remains in the boot state until the run level is changed from single-user level to a numeric run level. After **init** leaves the boot state, it enters its *normal* state.

On systems capable of detecting power failure (through hardware), the **init** process will enter the *powerfail* state. The powerfail state allows **init** to execute emergency procedures, for example, a **sync** command, that will preserve the integrity of the file system.

Now, you have had a glimpse of three things that drive the **init** process: the current state, the event that signaled it to read the init table, and the current run level. Let's take a look at a typical entry from an **/etc/inittab** file (Figure 5.25).

Figure 5.25 Example init table entry.

```
        co:2:respawn:/etc/getty console co_9600
         :  :     :                  :
        label :   action       program to start
          run level
```

There are four parts to an entry, separated by colons. The first part, *co* in the example, is a label. The **init** program writes a record to the **/etc/wtmp** file each time it starts or stops the program in an entry. The label is used to identify which init table entry caused the record to be written in the **/etc/wtmp** file. (The **/etc/wtmp** file is used by system accounting.) A record of current activity is maintained in the **/etc/utmp** file. The **who** command displays the current information written in the **/etc/utmp** file by **init** and **login**.

The second part of the entry specifies the run-level. When the current run level matches the run-level part of an entry, the program associated with the entry may be started, or allowed to continue if the process already exists. An empty run level field matches all numeric run levels. For example, the run-level fields in the two entries in Figure 5.26 are equivalent.

Figure 5.26 Equivalent run-level fields.

```
        co::respawn:/etc/getty console co_9600
        co:0123456:respawn:/etc/getty console co_9600
```

Also, please notice that when there is more than one run level for a particular entry, they are combined without spaces, commas, or other separators, as in **:0123456:**. If the current run level doesn't match the run-level part of an entry, the process associated with the entry will be sent a hangup signal, given 20 seconds to complete, and then terminated.

The next part of an entry, **respawn** in our example, represents the action to take. The **respawn** action means "start the program if it isn't currently running." The last part of the entry is the name of the program to run. This part of the entry will be passed to a Bourne shell to execute if it is a script. Optionally, a comment may be placed at the end of a line, following the Bourne shell's comment delimiter, the "#."

The Action Field. There are 11 possible choices for the action part of an init table entry. The actions depend on the current state of the **init** process—boot, normal, or powerfail. The 11 actions are listed in Table 5.2.

TABLE 5.2 THE 11 POSSIBLE ACTIONS IN **/etc/inittab** ENTRIES

Boot State Actions

---

initdefault	Set the initial run level. This action will never have a program associated with it. The **initdefault** entry should be the first entry in the init table. The third colon that ends this entry is necessary or the entry will be ignored.
sysinit	Start the program part of entries with the **sysinit** action the first time that the **init** process scans the init table, and wait for it before continuing with the scan. Infrequently used, the **sysinit** entries perform *system initialization* that may be necessary before **init** can proceed.
boot	Execute the program part of this entry once the first time that the **init** process enters any numeric run level.
bootwait	Execute the program part of this entry once the first time that the **init** program enters any numeric run level, and wait until the process completes before examining the next entry.

Normal State Actions

---

off	If the program, or the descendant of a program, listed in the program part of this entry is alive, terminate it.
once	Start the program listed once, and don't restart it when it (or its descendent) completes.
wait	Start the program listed once, and wait for it to complete before examining the next entry.
respawn	Start the program listed, and restart it every time it completes. Used with **getty**.
ondemand	Like **respawn**, start the program; causes the **init** process to restart it when it completes. The **ondemand** entry is reserved (by convention) for run levels a, b, or c.

Powerfail State Actions

---

powerfail	Start the program listed once, and don't restart it when it completes.
powerwait	Start the program listed part once, and wait until it completes before examining the next entry in the init table.

The *initdefault* action should be the first entry in the init table. If this entry is missing, when it begins to execute, **init** will prompt for a run level:

```
ENTER RUN LEVEL (0-6, s or S):
```

We recommend that you use an initdefault entry and configure your system to come up in a multiuser (numeric) level. If your system is configured to start up in single-user level, or to request the run level, then anyone who can reset your system can become the superuser. Alternatively, you can configure the **root**'s **/.profile** so that a password is required before a single-user shell is available. Larger installations that are kept in secure areas can be configured to come up single-user without a password.

The boot state actions are performed the first time that the **init** program enters a numeric run level. If you specify a numeric run level in the **initdefault** entry, then the boot state is entered immediately. The run-level part of boot state entries must match the run level, or the program will not be run. When the **init** process reenters the single-user run level, the init table is not scanned for programs to start. Instead, the **/bin/su** program is executed, with **/dev/syscon** used for input and output.

The distinction between the **once** and the **wait** normal state actions is that the **init** program waits for the program with the **wait** action to signal completion before examining the next init table line. Earlier in this section we mentioned that the **init** process gets notified when a process that it started has completed (terminated). When the action is not a **wait** action, the **init** process examines the next entry as soon as the program in the current entry has been started without waiting for the completion signal. Checking the file systems (with the **/etc/bcheckrc** script) requires a **bootwait** action. You don't want to proceed until **fsck** has completed and the file systems are cleaned.

The **respawn** action is used with programs that you want restarted every time they signal completion. Usually, these programs are **getty** programs that are watching for log-in names. Here there is a little UNIX magic going on, because the **getty** program will usually not complete and signal the **init** program. Instead, the **getty** process replaces itself with a **login** process when **getty** succeeds in making contact with a user. If the log-in attempt is successful, the **login** process is replaced with a user's shell. Since the previous program was replaced with the succeeding program each time, the user's shell winds up a child process of the **init** program (see Figure 5.27). So, when a user logs out, the user's shell completes, sends a completion signal to its parent, the **init** process, and the **init** process respawns another **getty** process.

The **powerfail** actions were designed to work with computers that not only can detect failing power, but can also continue functioning long enough to do something about it. Generally, reasonable things to do are to execute the **sync** command, thereby writing out file system information to the disks, and to halt the processor.

Figure 5.27 A user's shell has the same process id as the **getty** and **login** processes that precede it.

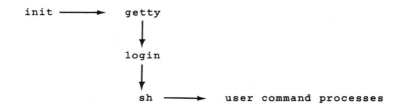

To carry out the **sync** operation successfully, the system must have a standby power supply that provides adequate power for several seconds of operation. In the "old" days, a motor-generator-flywheel combination would provide the emergency power for the short time necessary. Newer computers use much less power, and a battery-powered backup system or UPS (uninterruptible power supply) can provide power from several minutes to several hours.

The catch is that these battery systems will probably *not* signal the **init** process with a powerfail signal. The ability to generate a powerfail signal depends on the design of the computer, and not upon an external backup power supply.

TABLE 5.3 SUMMARY OF THE **init** PROGRAM

Characteristic	Description
states	Three states, boot, normal, and powerfail, affect which actions will be taken next by the **init** process.
labels	Part of init table entry written in **/etc/wtmp** records.
run levels	Single-user, denoted by *s* or *S*, or one of seven numeric values, control which entries in the init table are currently active. The second field in an init table entry specifies the run level(s) that the entry may be active. An empty run-level field indicates that the entry matches all numeric run levels.
actions	One of 11 keywords used in init table entries, the action controls what the **init** process does with the program in the entry and to which of the three states the entry applies.

An Example Init Table.   Now we are ready to take a look at a sample init table and talk about how it works. Our example system has four serial ports. Two ports are used for the console and a terminal, one for a modem or a direct connection to another UNIX system, and one for a serial printer.

Figure 5.28 An example init table (**/etc/inittab** file).

```
is:2:initdefault:
bl::bootwait:/etc/bcheckrc </dev/console >/dev/console 2>&1
bc::bootwait:/etc/brc 1>/dev/console 2>&1 # bootrun command
sl::wait:(rm -f /dev/syscon;ln /dev/systty /dev/syscon;)
                                        1>/dev/console 2>&1
rc::wait:/etc/rc 1>/dev/console 2>&1    # run commands
co::respawn:/etc/getty console co_19200
tty0:2:respawn:/etc/getty tty0 mo_1200  # modem - log-in
cu0:3:respawn:/etc/getty cu0 to_9600    # modem - direct connect
tty1::respawn:/etc/getty tty1 co_9600   # h19 - becca
tty2::off:/etc/getty tty2 po_1200       # printer line
```

Our example starts out by establishing run level 2 as the default (the **initdefault** action). Note that this entry ends with a colon. If the third colon were missing, the **init** process would ignore this entry and prompt for the run level to use, as if the entry did not exist. The **init** process ignores misformed entries and continues scanning the init table on the next line.

The next two entries have **bootwait** as the action to take. The program part of these entries will be executed the *first* time that the **init** process reads the init table, since we have instructed the **init** process to enter a numeric run level (2) immediately with the **initdefault** entry. The **/etc/bcheckrc** file contains the script for setting the date and checking file systems. The **/etc/brc** script removes the old mount table, if one exists because of an improper shutdown. The **init** process waits for these scripts to complete before examining the next entry.

What the next entry in Figure 5.28 does may not be immediately apparent. Although this entry appears all on one line in the **/etc/inittab** file, we have broken it into two lines so that we can print the entry in the allotted space (Figure 5.29).

Figure 5.29 Relinking the virtual console to the system console.

```
sl::wait:(rm -f /dev/syscon;ln /dev/systty /dev/syscon;)
                                        1>/dev/console 2>&1
```

The entry's action says to wait until the program part completes. The program part will be executed by a shell every time the **init** process changes between single-user and a numeric run level. So every time the system makes this transition, the file **/dev/syscon** is removed and the file **/dev/syscon** is linked to **/dev/systty**. **/dev/systty** stands for the *system teletype*, and on most computers, will be identical to the system console. The standard output and the error output of these commands get redirected to the console.

Now, what has happened is this. When the **init** program enters the single-user mode, it links the file named **/dev/syscon** to the terminal device from which it received the enter single-user mode command. (This command will normally come from the terminal from which the **/etc/shutdown** script was started.) Without this link, an administrator logging in remotely would be unable to work with the system in single-user mode. As soon as the system became single user, only the real console would have a shell running on it, and the terminal that the command was executed on would be inactive.

So the **init** process uses **/dev/syscon** for the standard input, output and error of the single-user shell. The remote superuser can administer to the system and return it eventually to multiuser operation without ever being on site. And when the system administrator returns the system to a numeric run level, the link to the terminal is removed, and the link to the real console, **/dev/systty**, is remade.

After restoring the virtual console link, the **/etc/rc** (run commands) script starts, and the **init** program waits until the script completes so that file systems are mounted and daemons are started without interference. One point that we need to make before continuing is that the run commands script contains a test for the current run level. So, even though the entry is active at all numeric run levels, the script itself won't do anything if its internal run-level test fails. This test prevents multiple copies of daemons from being started by the **/etc/rc** script.

The last five lines of the init table example all have **/etc/getty** for the program part. Each entry controls one of the four serial ports, except for the **cu0** and **tty0** entries—they both control the same port, but through different device files. The first four entries have **respawn** in the action field. So every time the **getty** process (or its descendant) completes, another instance will be started. The very last entry has **off** for the action. Our serial printer uses **/dev/tty2** and doesn't need to have a **getty** running on it. This entry serves mainly as a reminder that this port is used with the printer, not as a log-in port.

Since the entries labeled "co" and "tty1" have an empty run-level field, these entries are valid for all numeric run levels. As soon as the **init** program examines these entries, a **getty** process is started for the console and the **/dev/tty1** ports. The **respawn** action means that the **init** process does not wait for the process to complete before examining the next entry. If you used the **wait** action instead of **respawn**, once the **getty** program started, no other entries in the init table would be examined until the **getty** process (or its descendent) completed.

Because the "tty0" entry has "2" in the run-level field, the **getty** program will be started only if the current run level is 2. When the run level changes from 2, the **getty** for this entry, or possibly someone's log-in shell, will be terminated. The **init** program is somewhat polite about the termination and sends a *hangup* signal first to the **getty** or log-in shell. Then, 20 seconds later, the **init** program gets serious, and sends the no nonsense, cannot-be-caught-or-avoided *kill* signal if the process is still around. This kill signal is the same one that is generated by the command **kill −9** *process-number*.

The program in the "cu0" entry gets started when the run level is "3," but not at any other run level. The "cu0" and the "tty0" entries are mutually exclusive, that is, the program part of at most one entry can be running at any time.

When our system enters run level 2, the **init** program starts a **getty** on the port that is connected to a modem. However, we sometimes connect this port directly to another computer running the UNIX system. Then we change the run level to 3, which starts a **getty** for **/dev/cu0** and terminates the one for **/dev/tty0**. (These are both the same physical port. The reason for the two different names will become clear after reading Chapter 8.) When we reconnect the modem, we change the run level back to 2, terminating the direct connect **getty** and restarting the modem line **getty**.

Although our example system is quite small, you can perhaps begin to understand how you can get the **init** process to work for you. Older versions of the **init** program allowed the system administrator to enable or disable ports with **enable** or **disable** commands, which changed the **/etc/ttys** file. But changing the **/etc/ttys** file doesn't cause the old **init** process to terminate any process that may be active on that port. The system administrator would need to use the process status command (**ps**) and the **kill** command (twice) to accomplish the same thing that the new **init** program does when the run level is changed.

Talking to init

The system administrator signals the **init** process by using either **init** or **telinit** (tell init) followed by the new run level, or one of several letters. For example, to change the current run level to 3, the superuser would enter **telinit 3**. The **init** program examines the init table, **/etc/inittab**, and sends *hangup* signals to any process that is a descendant of an entry invalid at run level 3. Then the **init** process waits (actually sleeps) for 20 seconds before awakening, then sends a *kill* signal to any disallowed process that is still running. With disallowed entries' programs terminated, the **init** program examines the init table again and starts programs that are active when the run level is 3.

Although we haven't mentioned it yet, you may have guessed that having the run level changed, and possibly being logged out, may come as an unpleasant surprise to your users. We recommend that you use **write** or **wall** to warn any users that will be affected by a change in run level. For example, you could use the message shown in Figure 5.30 to warn users that you are shutting down terminals in nonsecure areas for the night. When you change to the single-user run level, you will be using the **shutdown** script, which uses **wall** to warn users.

Figure 5.30 Warning users before changing run levels.

```
# wall
Warning:  We will be suspending operation of terminals in
non-secure areas in five minutes.  Log out now.
<CONTROL-D>
# □
```

Pseudo-Run Levels.   Besides the seven numeric run levels that a system administrator can use to configure a system, there are also three pseudo-run levels, named **a**, **b**, and **c**. Changing to a pseudo-run level does not affect the current run level. In other words, if the system administrator entered **init a**, the current numeric run level remains the same. If your system was in run level 2 before you entered **init a**, it will still be in run level 2 afterward.

The **init** process will also be in pseudo-run level **a**. Any init table entry with an **a** in the run-level field matches the pseudo-run level, and the program part may be started, depending on the action field. Once a pseudo-run level has been entered, the **init** program remembers it. Leaving a pseudo-run level requires that you signal **init** to enter the single-user run level (through the **shutdown** script). For this reason, you should use the action **once** in init table entries with pseudo-run levels. The **init** process will constantly restart an entry with the action **respawn** once the matching pseudo-run level is entered. You can stop **init** from respawning these processes by editing **/etc/inittab**, removing the entry or changing the action to **off**, and signaling **init**.

Forcing init to Examine the Table.   The system administrator can force the **init** program to examine the init table by using **init** or **telinit** and a run-level argument (they're both links to the same program) to change the run level. Also, the system administrator can use the letters **q** or **Q** to make the **init** process reexamine the init table without changing the run level.

Although the system administrator can signal the **init** process to enter the single-user run level with **init s**, we recommend that you use the **/etc/shutdown** script instead. Simply sending the **init** process the message to change to the single user run level won't stop any of the background processes (the daemons). Thus the daemons will remain active in the background, possibly causing havoc during a backup or file system check procedure. And if the **shutdown** script wasn't used, returning to a numeric (multiuser) run level may result in two copies of some daemons running.

TABLE 5.4 SUMMARY OF MESSAGES TO init

Message	Description
s or **S**	Signals the **init** process to enter the single user run level with a shell attached to the terminal that the signal was sent from. Any program that the **init** process started will be terminated. Daemons won't be terminated as they are designed to continue after the death of their parent process.
0–6	Tells the **init** process to enter a numeric run level, generally used for multiuser operation. Different numeric run levels can be used to enable different groups of ports, or to change the way a port is being used.
q or **Q**	Forces the **init** process to examine the init table. Used after editing the init table to make the changes effective immediately without changing the current run level.
a, b, c	These pseudo-run levels do not affect the current run level. Once entered, these run levels remain in force until the **init** process enters single-user mode.

Problems with init

In our experience the **init** program has proven relatively trouble free. There are provisions built into the **init** program for reporting possible error conditions. For example, the **init** process starts the programs that are in the init table entries, and keeps an internal table containing the process numbers for these programs. If the **init** process has difficulty executing a program, or its internal table fills up, you will see error messages on the system console. For instance:

```
execlp of /bin/radish failed; errno = 2
```

execlp is a system call used to execute (start) a program. The problem with the program in this example, **/bin/radish**, is indicated by the error number (errno), 2. The list of error numbers appears in the INTRO(2) entry at the beginning of second section of the *System V Programmer Reference Manual*. Error number 2 means "No such file or directory." Maybe **/bin/beet** was meant ...

```
internal process table is full.
```

As mentioned, the **init** process keeps track of all the processes that it starts so that these processes can be terminated depending upon changes in the run level. You will see this error message if you have used the **init** process to start more processes than will fit in its internal process table. The **init** program's table should be the same size as the kernel's process table, so this problem should not occur.

```
Command is respawning too rapidly.  Check for possible errors.

id:tty5 "/etc/getty tty5 tu_9600"
```

In our system, if an entry in the init table was restarted (respawned) 10 times in less than 2 minutes, this warning appeared on the console. The number of respawns and the time limit may be different for your system, but the meaning is the same. The **init** process doesn't expect to be restarting a process time after time after time. Doing so places a tremendous load on your system's resources, and the programmers that wrote the **init** program know this. So they included a warning whenever rapid respawning begins.

Why would rapid respawning occur? Most often, rapid respawning indicates a problem with a terminal or port. For example, the DC Hayes Smartmodem will echo back any characters sent to it, depending upon how the modem's switches are set. So the **getty** sends out a log-in prompt that includes a carriage return, and the modem echos (sends back) the prompt *including the carriage return.* **getty** thinks this is just great (ha! I've got a live one) and passes the prompt as if it were a log-in name to the **login** program. The **login** program won't find the prompt in **/etc/passwd**, so it asks for a password, and waits. This time, the modem echoes back the password prompt, so the log-in attempt fails. The **init** process gets the signal that a child has died, and restarts the **getty**. And the procedure repeats, with the modem echoing back whatever it receives and the **getty** program being fooled. If this procedure happens fast enough, you will get the "respawning too rapidly" message. The *id* tells you which entry in the init table is causing the problem (as does the program in quotes), and you can halt the problem by editing **/etc/inittab** to turn the entry **off**. Then you should adjust, fix, or replace the hardware. Loose cable connections or problems with multiplexers can also cause this symptom.

The BSD and XENIX init Programs

The BSD and XENIX **init** programs are based on the Version 7 (pre-System III) AT&T UNIX version of the **init** program. These versions read the **/etc/ttys** file to discover which terminal lines should have a **getty** process started for them. Each line in the **/etc/ttys** file contains three fields, all combined in a single string without spaces. Figure 5.31 shows several lines from an **/etc/ttys** file taken from a XENIX system.

Figure 5.31 Several lines from a XENIX system **/etc/ttys** file.

```
1mconsole
1mtty02
0mtty03
0mtty04
02tty11
```

The first number specifies whether the line should be turned on, represented by a one (1), or off, represented by a zero (0). The second character is a key into a table containing line speeds and other line condition information. For XENIX systems, the **/etc/gettydefs** file contains the line information. The BSD version uses a different file, **/etc/gettytab**, with a format similar to that of the **/etc/termcap** file, for setting line conditions.

The last part of each line in the **/etc/ttys** file, from the third character to the end, contains the name of a file in the **/dev** directory to be used as an argument by the **/etc/getty** program. For example, the first line in Figure 5.31, *1mconsole*, will start an **/etc/getty** process on line **/dev/console** using the entry labeled "m" from the **/etc/gettydefs** file for line conditions. A **getty** process will also be started for **/dev/tty02**, but not for **/dev/tty04** or **/dev/tty11**.

The **/etc/ttys** file may be edited while the system is in single-user level to control which lines will have a **getty** process started for them when the system is changed to multiuser level. During multiuser operation, the XENIX **enable** and **disable** commands communicate with the **init** process to enable or disable particular terminal lines. If the **init** process enables or disables a terminal line, it will also update the first character of the **/etc/ttys** file. The **init** process will not disable a line after a user has logged in on it, but will display the message in Figure 5.32 on the console.

Figure 5.32 The **disable** command fails if a user is logged in.

```
# disable tty04
disable:  rik is on tty04
disable:  /etc/ttys not updated
# □
```

With BSD systems, you edit the **/etc/ttys** file and signal the **init** process with **kill −1 1** to force **init** to examine the **/etc/ttys** file.

SYSTEM SHUTDOWN, OR GOING SINGLE-USER

Just as getting your system going is not as simple as turning on the television, turning your computer off also requires some work. You must consider the remnants of the day's activity, relaxing in memory buffers before being frozen into place on a disk. Or, the busy daemons, working more like little elves to keep your system running smoothly. What if one of the "elves" decides to spring into action when you're ready to quit?

That's why there's a shutdown script which gracefully halts activity and prepares your system for slumber. Simply signaling the **init** process to enter a single-user run level won't hack it. The **init** process will faithfully halt all the processes that it has started. And offspring of these processes will be halted. However, the daemons have cleverly been made immune to the **init** process's signals to cease and desist. Otherwise, the daemons would have died after the **/etc/rc** script completed.

So you need to use the **/etc/shutdown** script. Perhaps the way this script doddles along annoys you. Well relax, because you can edit a copy of this script and speed things up if you like. The System V script has two one-minute-long sleeps that are designed to give users enough time to log off. If you are in a hurry, or the only user of a system, you don't need these delays. And, you don't have to have them. From the opposing perspective, you can modify the script to provide better ways of warning users before cutting them off. Table 5.5 outlines the **shutdown** script's activities. (Note that BSD systems use a compiled **/etc/shutdown** program instead of a script.)

TABLE 5.5. SHUTTING DOWN A SYSTEM GRACEFULLY WITH **shutdown**

1. Warns users
2. Halts daemons with the appropriate command
3. Kills all active processes
4. Unmounts all mounted file systems
5. Signals the **init** program to enter single user run level
6. Issues the **sync** command

With the advent of Release 3 of System V, the syntax of the **shutdown** script's arguments has changed. Figure 5.33a shows the pre-Release 3 syntax for invoking the script, and 5.33b depicts the newer version.

Figure 5.33 Command syntax — **/etc/shutdown**.

a. Pre-release 3 of System V (and XENIX) invocation:

/etc/shutdown [*grace*]

b. System V Release 3 version:

/etc/shutdown [−g*grace*] [−i*state*] [−y]

c. 4.x BSD version:

> \# **/etc/shutdown** [−h|−k|−b] +*grace-minutes*

All versions allow you to specify the *grace* period. The grace period is the number of seconds (System V) or minutes (BSD and XENIX) that the script pauses (sleeps) after warning users. Note that there are two **sleep** commands in the scripts, so the real grace period is twice the time specified on the command line.

The −i flag is used to communicate the run level which the **init** process will enter when the script completes. The default run level is zero (0). The **inittab** file for Release 3 versions contains entries that match run levels 0, 5, and 6, which kill all processes and either power down the system (run level 0), enter a firmware state (run level 5), or reboot the system (run level 6).

Without the final flag for Release 3 versions (−y), the script asks you if you wish to continue with shutdown after warning users. There is a similar question that is asked in older versions of the script ("Do you wish to continue?"). Frankly, you can cancel the script by pressing the interrupt key (DELETE) at any time up to this point. Still, it's a nice way to give the operator a last chance before killing any processes.

Checks and Warnings

Let's start with the beginning of a typical **shutdown** script. The output of the **pwd** command is stored in a variable and compared to the directories **/** and **/etc**. If the shell script wasn't started by a user in one of these directories, it quits immediately. This check must be done because you want to unmount file systems during shutdown. You can't unmount a file system while the current directory of your shell is located there. So the script "plays it safe" by requiring that the operator be in the root or **/etc** directory. You can't simply put the command **cd /** into the script because it would change the current directory for the shell that is running the script, but not for the user's shell that started the script.

Next, the **shutdown** script needs to ensure that users log out. A default "grace" period is established if one wasn't specified on the command line. The grace period is the number of seconds (minutes for XENIX and BSD systems) to wait (actually, sleep) if other users are logged on when the shutdown script is executed. For example, invoking the script with argument "0," as in **shutdown 0** provides no grace period. (Newer versions of the **shutdown** script accept multiple arguments. For example, the grace time is specified as −g*N*, where *N* is the number of seconds.) If the grace period (in seconds) isn't specified, the following shell command used in the script supplies a 60-second default grace:

```
grace=${1-60}
```

If you change the "60" to some other value in the **/etc/shutdown** script, you change the default grace period.

The shutdown script next tests for the number of logged-on users with the pipeline

```
who ^ wc -l
```

The circumflex (^), is an alternative (and older) method for representing the pipe character (¦) to the shell. If the value returned from this pipeline is greater than 1, the script's user gets asked if she wants to send her own message to the logged-on users. The message entered is given to the **wall** command (write all users), and must end with the end-of-file character (Control-d). After sending the **wall**, the script waits out the grace period. If you are working with a small system, with centrally located users, you probably know if your users are ready to quit *before* you start the shutdown script.

On larger systems, however, your users may be scattered to the four winds, not across the room from you. Rather than sending a single message and waiting the grace period, you may wish to be more elaborate and send a message every minute during the last 5 minutes of the grace period. To do this, you can replace the **sleep $grace** command with the lines given in Figure 5.34.

Figure 5.34 Providing warnings every minute until all users log off.

```
left=`expr "$grace" / 60`
while [ "$left" -gt 0 ]
    echo "Shutdown in $left minutes.  Log off now.\n" ¦ /etc/wall
    users=`who ¦ grep -v root`
    case $users in
    "")   echo "All users logged off now."; break ;;
    *)    echo "$users" ;;
    esac
    left=`expr "$left" - 1`
    sleep 60
done
```

These commands not only bug users every minute; the script also quits as soon as the only user remaining is **root**. If you aren't logged in as **root**, this "trick" won't work correctly, because the **grep** command will consider you another ordinary user.

After waiting for the grace period, the typical shutdown script sends another **wall** message,

```
SYSTEM BEING BROUGHT DOWN NOW ! ! !
```

and waits a minute unless you have specified zero seconds of grace. If everyone has logged off, you hardly need to wait another minute.

Finally, you get a message out of the mists of time. Back when hardware was incredibly big and expensive, modems were rack mounted. The operator needed to walk over to the rack of modems and physically disable (busy out) each modem before continuing with shutdown. System V UNIX and newer modems have made this step (pressing buttons on modems) obsolete. Instead, when the **init** process goes to a single-user level, a hardware signal is sent to modems (and terminals) telling them to hang up and not answer the phone. You may wish to remove the pair of **echo** commands used to display these outdated comments.

Then the shutdown script asks you if you are ready to continue. At any point you can halt shutdown by using your interrupt key (usually, the DELETE character). The query does give you a moment for reflection that you don't need, unless you're busying out modems (preventing the modems from responding to calls). You could replace this query with something like

```
echo "Last chance to halt shutdown (Press DELETE to quit).\n"
sleep 10
```

The message lets you know that you've reached a critical point, and the sleep gives you 10 seconds to do something about it. Note that this won't work if your shutdown traps interrupts and doesn't exit. The **trap** command used by the shutdown script that we're describing here is given in Figure 5.35.

Figure 5.35 Trapping signals in our example script.

```
trap "rm -f /tmp/$$; exit 0" 0 1 2 15
```

This **trap** command lets you exit from the shutdown script after removing a temporary file. Our example script doesn't create a temporary file, and we suspect that this file was created in older versions of the **shutdown** script. What do you think? The XENIX system **shutdown** script is written differently, and ignores the interrupt character while warning users of imminent shutdown. You can interrupt the XENIX shutdown script before or after the **while** loop that warns users.

Killing Processes and Unmounting File Systems

Now, the **shutdown** script has finished with its preparations (at last). This next part of the script halts process accounting and any daemons that have specific stop commands. If you have added software that provides specific shutdown programs, add them here. A few typical commands appear in Figure 5.36.

Figure 5.36 Stop commands appearing in the **shutdown** script.

```
/usr/lib/acct/shutacct     # halts per process accounting
/usr/lib/lpshut            # stop lp scheduler
/etc/errstop               # stop error logging
```

If you aren't using per process accounting (see Chapter 7), you don't need to shut it down. The same applies to the **lp** and **errlog** daemons.

The **cron** daemon doesn't have a special shutdown command. It, and everything else not associated with the user running the **shutdown** script, gets terminated next with the next command, **/etc/killall**. In XENIX, there isn't a **killall** program, and a section of the **shutdown** script is used to collect the process id's of running processes and kill them.

Once all active processes not associated with the shutdown procedure have been terminated, file systems may be unmounted. Remember that this script starts by ensuring that the user is in the root file system (which can't be unmounted). With all other processes with open files terminated, the **shutdown** script uses a command pipeline to select names from the **/etc/mnttab** (mount table) file, and unmount them (see Figure 5.37).

Figure 5.37 Unmounting any mounted file systems.

```
mount ¦ sed -n -e '/^\/ /d'
     -e 's/^.* on\(.*\) read.*/umount \1/p' ¦ sh -
```

The **mount** command without arguments displays the mount table. The **sed** command removes the line for the root file system ("/ mounted on ...") and extracts just the device name of other mounted file systems. The device names are combined with the **umount** command name and passed to a Bourne shell for execution. It's possible that a file system was not unmounted (because the **init** process has started some activity, for example), so this pipeline appears a second time. In some cases, both attempts to unmount a particular file system will fail, and an error message (like "umount: /dev/dsk/c0d1s0 busy) will appear on the console. You may be able to unmount this file system by entering the **umount** command from the console after the **shutdown** script completes.

With all processes terminated and file systems unmounted, the **init** process is sent the signal to enter single-user run level. The **init** process sends a *hangup* signal to all the processes it has started (in response to the **killall**), waits 20 seconds, then sends the *kill* signal. Short of recompiling the **init** program, you can't speed up this process.

The pipeline that unmounts file systems is repeated here, followed by many (six in my specimen) **sync** commands. A single **sync** command copies any in-memory parts of file systems out to disks. Using many repeats of the **sync** command will catch any stray activity that occurs in the closing moments of the shutdown process. Whether this is really a problem or not is not an issue: the **sync** command is very fast once all in memory information has been flushed out to disk.

The **shutdown** script will exit at this point and you will see your usual prompt. But don't turn off the machine yet. Just wait until you see the message

```
INIT:  SINGLE USER MODE
```

and the single-user shell prompt (usually **#**). Then enter a **sync** command before halting the system. Although AT&T documentation doesn't suggest this final **sync** command, it will do no harm. And it might be necessary. For example, if the **/.profile** file, which is run by the single-user Bourne shell, performs any file system activity, a final **sync** command is necessary. Otherwise, you will have recurring problems when checking the root file system with **fsck**.

If you do anything while in single-user mode, you must use the **sync** command before halting the system. Failure to use the **sync** command at this point means that some modifications to the file systems from your final commands weren't written to disk and will cause havoc to your file systems later.

Sometimes, the **shutdown** script fails due to some flakiness in the system. We keep a hard-copy printout of the script handy that we use as a guide in shutting down the system properly. We don't use the **sed** script for unmounting file systems—it's easier to list the mounted file systems and use the **umount** command. Of course, if you're in a hurry (and **shutdown** has failed), you can use the emergency shutdown procedure.

Emergency Shutdown Procedure

If you are ever faced by a situation that requires you to shut down quickly, enter the **sync** command immediately. Although microcomputer-based UNIX systems and most mini-based systems are relatively immune to slow-motion system crashes, larger minicomputers and mainframes are more liable to have a partial failure that is noticeable through either console error messages or lengthened response time. Any user can enter the **sync** command with exactly the same results as when it is entered by the superuser. So use **sync** command any time you feel a crash situation developing, whether or not you are the superuser.

With a little more time to work, you can execute the commands in Figure 5.38 (as superuser).

Figure 5.38 Commands for an emergency shutdown.

```
# sync
# /etc/killall
# /etc/init s
# sync
# □
```

Although you haven't warned any logged-in users, nor gracefully halted daemons, you will have halted activity on your system in less than a minute. XENIX users can invoke the **/etc/haltsys** command instead of **/etc/killall** and **init s** to stop their systems in a hurry. **haltsys** is called from within the XENIX shutdown script.

QUICK REFERENCE GUIDE

Setting the time with the **date** command; use at least four pairs of numbers (the year is optional):

```
# date 0423191188
Sat Apr 23 19:11:01 PDT 1988
# □
```

Format for a System V **/etc/gettydefs** entry:

```
co_9600 # B9600 # B9600 SANE TAB3 # \r\nConsole login: # co_4800
   ¦           ¦        ¦                      ¦                ¦
 Label    Initial   Final Conditions   Initial Prompt   Next Label
```

Format for an **/etc/inittab** entry:

```
      co:2:respawn:/etc/getty console co_9600
      ¦ ¦    ¦                   ¦
  label ¦  action        program to start
     run level
```

Enable a **/etc/getty** for a port by having **respawn** in the action field.

Disable a port by replacing **respawn** with **off.**

Format for an **/etc/ttys** file (BSD or XENIX):

```
  1mconsole
  ¦¦   +---> device name
  ¦+------> flag for baud rate
  +-------> one for enabled/zero for disabled getty
```

Use **enable tty02** or **disable tty02** to enable or disable a **getty** on XENIX systems.

Use **shutdown** to go single-user before powering down:

    # **shutdown** [*grace-seconds*] (System V)
    # **shutdown** [*grace-minutes*] (XENIX)

New command line arguments to **shutdown** after Release 2:

    # **/etc/shutdown** [−g*grace*] [−i*state*] [−**y**]

Arguments to the BSD **/etc/shutdown** program, −**h** to halt, −**k** to kill all processes (become single-user), or −**b** to reboot:

    # **/etc/shutdown** [−**h**|−**k**|−**b**] +*grace-minutes*

Use **wall** to warn all users before shutdown:

```
# wall
System coming down in five minutes.
<Control-D>
# □
```

Always use **sync** (at least twice) before powering down.

6

The UNIX LP System

INTRODUCTION

The LP system accepts printing requests from users and arranges for the files or data to be printed later. Any computer installation with more than a single user needs a similar system. Even single-user workstations that allow multiple simultaneous processes require a method for sharing printers among the processes that may simultaneously send jobs to the printer.

UNIX System V brings some welcome improvements to the AT&T line printer spooling system. In earlier versions of the LP system, there was no way to change the appearance of the header or banner page or add accounting to the LP system, short of rewriting the scheduler daemon. Also, a user's request could not be assigned to the first available printer. The System V LP system eliminates these shortcomings. The System V version uses new terminology:

request

Each time the **lp** command is used, the LP system creates a print job *request* and assigns a unique request-id for this job.

destination

Each printer has a logical name that is called a *destination*. When the term "destination" is used in this chapter, it refers to the logical name established for a particular printer when it was added to the LP system. For example,

252

laser might be used as the destination for a laser printer.

class

A *class* is a collection of printers. When a user makes a request, he or she can designate a particular destination printer or he or she can designate a class of printers. If a class is chosen, the first available printer in the class will receive the print request.

interface

The *interface* is a Bourne shell script or C program that outputs the information given in LP requests. In addition to simply printing a file, the interface can add a header or banner page, filter (transform) the output for a particular printer, and save accounting information.

Figure 6.1 LP Directory and File Layout

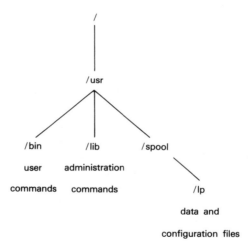

Perhaps you feel that the LP system is just another level of complexity that you don t require on your system. Let's suppose you don't want to use the LP system. You can redirect the contents of a file directly to the printer (device), putting the commands in the background so that you don't have to wait for the job to complete (see Figure 6.2a). And if you or someone else starts redirecting more output to the printer, the two files will intermingle freely (Figure 6.2b). Without the LP system, the UNIX system will not prevent two (or more) processes from writing to the same printer at the same time.

Figure 6.2 What can happen when you share printers without using the LP system.

a. You redirect the output of two processes to the printer; the printer is connected to port /**dev**/**tty2** in this example:

```
$ cat /etc/passwd > /dev/tty2 &
$ cat Declaration > /dev/tty2 &
$ □
```

b. The result is intermingled output on the printer:

```
root:H2H/hjRkEIqC2:0:0::/:/bin/sh
rootcsh:i2Q/4rCzyVjOM:0:0::/:/bin/csh
daemon:xxxxxxxxxxxx:1:1::/:
bin:xxxxxxxxxxxxx:2:2We, the People, in order to form a more
perfect union, do
::/bin:
sys:xxxxxxxxxxxxx:3:3::/bin:
```

Although you can still recognize the parts of the two files that appeared in Figure 6.2b, it doesn't do you much good to combine two different print jobs on the same page.

The LP system solves this problem by allowing users to queue up work for the printer. Many users can add files to the queue to be printed without ever intermingling files on the printout or waiting for the printer to become available. We'd like to mention that adding these requests for printing to a queue is called spooling, an acronym for simultaneous peripheral operations on line.

The System V LP system really contains four distinct parts. The last two of these parts, however, do not normally concern ordinary users, unless something goes wrong. But as a system administrator, you need to understand how all four parts work together.

lp—Create a printing request.

Users are most familiar with this command. The **lp** program arranges print requests by setting up the control file that accompanies each print job.

lpstat, **cancel**, **disable**, and **enable**

These commands are available to all users: **lpstat** monitors the status of the LP system, **cancel** cancels print requests, **disable** disables a printer (useful while changing the ribbon or paper), and **enable** reenables a printer.

lpsched—Starts each print job

> The **lp** scheduler gets notified each time the **lp** command sets up a printing job. The scheduler waits for the current print job (if any) for the requested printer to complete, and starts the interface shell script.

The Interface Script

> The **lpsched** program starts the interface shell script (or program) with a list of files to be printed and some other arguments. The output of the interface script is redirected to the appropriate printer device. Any special formatting or filtering can be performed by this script. Optionally, the interface script can use the arguments to create a header page, complete with the user's name in large letters, and collect accounting information.

The rest of the LP system consists of the administrative, control, and status commands that manipulate the system. The system itself is configured with files and directories in the **/usr/spool/lp** directory.

XENIX V uses a system practically identical to the AT&T System V. The Berkeley version of the LP system functions similarly to System V in that it supports multiple printing destinations. However, the configuration of the Berkeley LP system is very different. The administrator edits the **/etc/printcap** file to change the configuration, and two programs are used in place of the interface shell script used in System V. Our experience with the Berkeley version indicates that it deserves a chapter of its own, and we won't discuss it here.

Installing and Maintaining the LP System

The commands and utilities for using the LP system are part of the run-time UNIX system software and should be included even in unbundled systems. So, installing the LP system is a matter of editing two scripts (**/etc/rc** and **/etc/shutdown**) and using some administrative commands. You'll probably find this part of your system administration job easier than you thought.

The LP system requires that the scheduler daemon be running to service requests. The scheduler daemon, **/usr/lib/lpsched**, is started from an **/etc/rc** system startup script, and halted by **/usr/lib/lpshut** in the **/etc/shutdown** script.

Figure 6.3 Starting and stopping the LP scheduler.

a. These lines are added to the **/etc/rc** file:

```
rm -f /usr/spool/lp/SCHEDLOCK
/usr/lib/lpsched
```

b. This line is added to **/etc/shutdown**:

```
/usr/lib/lpshut
```

The **/usr/spool/lp/SCHEDLOCK** lock file prevents more than one scheduler from being started by an administrator. The **lpshut** program uses the information found in this file, the process id for **lpsched**, to halt the scheduler during shutdown. **lpshut** will remove the lock file after halting the scheduler. The lock file must be removed in the **/etc/rc** file in case the system was halted without running the shutdown script. When the lock file is present, you cannot start the scheduler.

The **lpshut** command also removes a named pipe, **/usr/spool/lp/FIFO**, that is used for communicating with the scheduler. The **fsck** program will produce a "POSSIBLE FILE SIZE ERROR" when this named pipe hasn't been removed before running **fsck** on the file system containing **/usr/spool/lp**. You may need to add the **/usr/lib/lpshut** command to your **/etc/shutdown** script if you get the file size error during file system checks.

The remainder of this chapter details the installation and maintenance of the LP system. We'll start off with a discussion of a "system essential" — the printer and its connection to the computer. A printer, after all, is pretty essential to a computer setup. A computer without a printer is like a slide rule — you have to write down any results. Unfortunately, connecting printers to computers ranks high on the list of none-too-clearly documented tasks. Most often, the printer will be manufactured by one company and the computer by another. And what each end of the connection expects in the interface will be different, too.

Once the printer and the computer are working correctly together, you can configure the LP system for them. Setting up the LP system is really simple if you know the answers to several questions. Configuring the LP system will create several files and directories. We will examine what these files are and how they are involved with the activities of the LP system.

During our installation, we will use a default interface program that will be available on all System V (or XENIX V) systems. This script, entitled **dumb**, is actually lengthy and somewhat complex. We will explore how the interface scripts work by creating a simple script (with no "bells or whistles"), and adding in the extras gradually. The extras include header pages, accounting information, and processing of the options collected by the **lp** command.

Next, we will discuss the commands that allow any user to cancel a print job or disable a printer. These control functions give everybody the means to halt a misfunctioning printer, or stop the printing of garbage. And the **lpstat** command reports on what the LP system is doing, what jobs remain to be printed, and the status of printers.

Finally, we will examine solutions to problems you may have with the LP system. For example, if the **lpsched** refuses to start, the reason will be hidden away in a logfile and not displayed on the console unless someone is logged in as **lp**. Also, the interface script redirects its standard error output to the printer, so errors from the interface script won't appear in the logfile or on any terminal.

THE HARDWARE CONNECTION

Connecting printers and computers is probably not anybody's favorite activity. By comparison, installing telephones is easy. There are many companies, and subdivisions of companies, all building computers, serial interface cards, and printers, and each one uses a slightly different interface. So instead of just connecting two ends of a standard cable together, you may also need to modify one (or both ends) before the cable will work correctly.

Two Worlds—Serial and Parallel

There are two common interfaces to printers—serial and parallel. By an "interface" we mean the method for transmitting characters to be printed and status information to be exchanged between computers and printers. In parallel interfaces, the seven or eight coded bits that make up each character are transmitted simultaneously. Serial interfaces send one bit of information at a time, one bit after another. Although parallel transmission has the potential to be much faster, the speed that the printer can correctly handle usually limits transmission rates.

Parallel interfaces, if they use the Centronics interface, can have a tremendous advantage over serial ones. The Centronics interface completely defines all the wires used in the connection between a computer and a printer. You can buy standard Centronics cables (with the correct connectors at each end) and expect them to work without modification. Even the status wires are firmly established, unlike the serial interface.

Serial transmission generally follows accepted standards too—the RS-232 standard. This standard was designed for use between Data Communication Equipment (DCE) and Data Terminal Equipment (DTE). A modem is DCE, and a terminal is DTE. Seems simple, but what will we call a printer, or a computer? As it turns out, most printers are considered DTEs, like terminals, and many smaller computers are considered to be DCEs, so they can easily be connected to terminals or printers. Many computers, however, are configured as DTEs, since they are really the end (terminal) of a data transmission, not the communication equipment (a modem) itself. So logical, and the beginning of the serial problem.

The Serial Interface Blues.   In a serial cable, one wire is used for transmitting data from the terminal, and another is used for receiving data. A third wire is used as the *common* or return line. These wires are connected to pins (or sockets) in connectors. Figure 6.4a depicts these basic connections. (Note that Chapter 8 goes into more detail about connecting modems, terminals, and computers together.) At the DCE or modem end, the transmitting and receiving wires are reversed, so that the transmitting wire from the terminal is connected to the receiving wire of the modem, and vice versa (Figure 6.4b).

Figure 6.4 A simple serial connection.

a. At the terminal end, three wires connected to pins 2, 3, and 7:

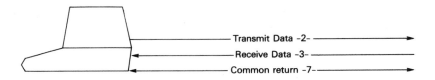

b. And at the modem end, the same three wires, except that the transmitting and receiving pins are reversed:

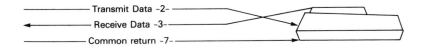

While this description is clear enough, what happens when you don't know whether the computer's serial port is configured as a DTE or DCE? The computer's or serial board's documentation should help, but often doesn't.

The second serial problem concerns *handshaking*. Handshaking is a method for communicating simple information between two devices. One device sends (outputs) the information, and the other receives (inputs) this information. In our case, the printer uses handshaking to signal the computer to stop transmitting data.

Computers can transmit characters faster than a printer can print them. The printer makes up for this deficiency by storing the characters in some local memory, called a *buffer*. When the printer's buffer fills up, it must be able to signal the computer, via handshaking, to stop transmitting for a while. When the printer has emptied most of its buffer, it will remove the signal that has been inhibiting transmission. Figure 6.5 shows how a fourth wire can be used for the handshaking signal.

Figure 6.5 Adding handshaking to a simple connection.

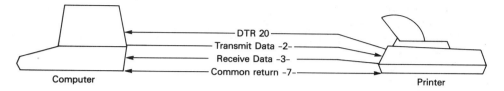

The RS-232 standard defines uses for 21 different wires. And it doesn't specify any wire for pausing transmission. After all, the RS-232 standard began as a terminal-modem interface, not a computer-printer connection. Once again, you must refer to the documentation for both the printer and the computer's serial port. Which wire does the printer manipulate to cause the computer to pause? And on which wire does the computer's port expect this signal to arrive? Table 6.1 lists several computers and printers and the pin number used for exchanging handshaking information.

TABLE 6.1 SEVERAL COMPUTERS AND PRINTERS AND THE PINS USED FOR HANDSHAKING*

Computer or Printer	Type	Transmit	Receive	Handshake
IBM PC, XT, AT	DTE	2	3	5
Dual Series 83	DCE	3	2	20
AT&T 3B2-300,400	DCE	3	2	20
ARIX 1200	DCE	3	2	20
Sun 3/50	DTE	2	3	
NEC Spinwriter	DTE	2	3	19
Okidata	DTE	2	3	11
Texas Instruments	DTE	2	3	11
DEC LA 100	DTE	2	3	5 + 6
DEC LN03	DTE	2	3	11

*The Transmit Data pin will be 2 if the computer is a DTE, or 3 if its a DCE. The ARIX system uses pin 20 for power-up handshaking, and uses XON and XOFF for (software) handshaking. Sun Microsystems 3/50 use XON and XOFF handshaking. Although the LN03 documentation specifies pin 11 as "Restraint," it is reserved for future use and not supported.

There's yet another issue. Some printers and serial ports require that certain handshaking be present before they will even start to communicate. This handshaking, called *power-up handshaking*, tells the printer or port that there is something connected and turned on at the other end. If the other device doesn't provide this signal, the printer or port must be fooled so that the handshaking appears to be there. This trickery is accomplished by looping the device's outputs right back to its inputs. Figure 6.6 shows how the IBM PC and NEC serial ports are "fooled" to enable them (pins 4 and 20 feeds 6 on the PC side and pin 4 feeds 5 and pin 20 feeds 6 and 8 on the NEC side), and how the handshaking signal from the example printer, an NEC Spinwriter, is sent to the computer's serial port (pin 19 to 5).

Figure 6.6 Interfacing a PC serial port to an NEC Spinwriter.

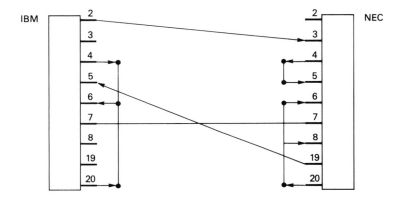

Entire books have been written about how to make the connection between a computer and a printer easily and correctly. One book, *The RS-232 Solution* by Joe Campbell (Sybex Inc., Berkeley, CA, 1984), describes how to make the connections without plowing through the computer's or printer's documentation. Rather than try to accomplish in a few words what takes entire books, we're referring you to this other source (see the Bibliography.)

Baud Rates and Start and Stop Bits.   Serial communication comes with its own somewhat mysterious nomenclature. Each character that is transmitted by a serial port is surrounded by a little "container" of start and stop bits. Additionally, a parity bit may be included in this container of information. The start bit signals to the receiving serial port that a character is beginning to arrive. Serial communication between computers and printers is asynchronous, meaning that characters can be sent one at a time, in bursts, or in a continuous stream. The start bit warns the receiving device that a character has arrived (see Figure 6.7).

Figure 6.7 The container for a character sent through a serial port.

a. An empty bit container:

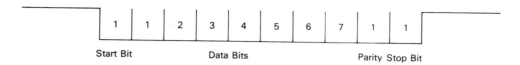

b. The letter "A" with even parity (1100101 in binary with parity bit of 0 in a bit container):

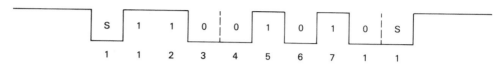

The start bit is discarded by the receiver, and the receiver then begins to assemble the data bits. There are 128 characters in the ASCII character set. You can look at the UNIX system file **/usr/pub/ascii** for two tables that describe this character set. At least seven data bits are needed to describe all 128 characters, because seven data bits are necessary to specify the numbers from 0 to 127. Most UNIX systems use seven data bits for serial communication with terminals (the UUCP system requires all eight bits). It is possible to use eight data bits, but the eighth bit is discarded by many terminals and printers. If only six data bits are used, you would use only the first half of the ASCII character set, and not even reach the letters of the alphabet. (There are methods for working with fewer than seven bits, like the obsolete Baudot code.)

The parity bit may follow the seven or eight data bits. Parity is a technique used for checking the accuracy of the character transmitted. To create the parity bit, the serial port hardware adds together each of the data bits for a character, producing a sum that is either even or odd. For even parity, the hardware sets the parity bit to zero when the sum of the data bits is even, and to 1 when the sum is odd. Odd parity works exactly the opposite, with the parity bit being zero when the sum of the data bits is odd, and 1 when the sum is even. In Figure 6.7b, there are four ones in the character, for a sum of four. Four is even, so the parity bit is zero.

Parity checking is not normally used for serial communication to printers and terminals (at less than 19,200 baud). Serial communication is robust, that is, it usually works, and when it doesn't, you can *see* that some characters are being received scrambled. If you are receiving scrambled (incorrect) characters, the solution is to use the next-lower baud rate. One bit of parity can't be used to correct errant data bits, and can only signal that something is wrong. The parity bit is just one extra bit that doesn't need to be transmitted, and serial transmission to printers and terminals will be faster and no less accurate without it.

The last bit in the character container is the stop bit. The stop bit simply signals the end of the character package. There can be one or two stop bits. Serial ports for computers, terminals, and printers will usually allow you to adjust, through switches or software, these four different parameters:

stop bits   The number of stop bits (one or two) to be sent after every character
data bits   The number of data bits to use (seven is the minimum for character transmission)
parity   Whether or not to include a parity bit
parity type   The type of parity to use, even or odd, if parity has been enabled

Now, after you have read about serial nomenclature, we have an announcement to make. In one experiment, we discovered that the number of stop bits, whether you use seven or eight data bits, and whether parity is used may not matter one whit. We purposely mal-adjusted a terminal and found that the wrong number of stop bits, wrong or no parity, even the wrong number of data bits (eight instead of seven), introduced no errors in our transmission. We want to tell you because we don't want you to be overly concerned with serial nomenclature. However, there's a critical aspect of serial communication that can't be ignored—the baud rate.

The baud rate stands for the *number of bits transmitted per second*. In the example character in Figure 6.7b, there are a total of 10 bits—one start, seven data, one parity, and one stop. If a stream of characters is being transmitted at 1200 baud using the bit container described in Figure 6.7a, then 120 characters, or 1200 divided by 10, can be transmitted each second. You can increase the transmission rate slightly by not using parity (1200 divided by 9 equals 133 characters per second). By using two stop bits, eight data bits, and parity you are using 12 bits per character and can transmit only 100 characters per second at 1200 baud.

Generally, you will want to use the fastest baud rate possible for the serial device you are using. The device, whether a printer, modem, or terminal, will be designed so that it can't be set to receive characters faster than it can handle. If you occasionally see errant characters, you need to adjust both the UNIX system and the device to the next-lower baud rate. When nothing, or only strange characters appear on the device, the baud rates at the UNIX system and the device don't match and must be corrected.

Testing Your Connection

Having explained the product-specific-area issues of connecting your printer to your serial port, and serial nomenclature, we come to the next step. Connecting two pieces of equipment is certainly related, although not in the realm of a book about administering an operating system. What is in our territory are the commands that you can use to test your connections.

You start out by discovering the device name for the port that you are using. Most serial ports will have names beginning with **/dev/tty**. You need to read your computer's documentation for the name of the port that you are using. On some computers, the names of ports will be silk-screened near the connector on the computer, making your task simple.

You may also have this serial port configured as a log-in port. You can check the **/etc/inittab** file (System V), or **/etc/ttys** (Berkeley and XENIX), and see if you have started a **getty** for this port. Chapter 5 explains enabling and disabling log-in ports. You must disable serial ports used as log-in ports while you are using them for printing.

There aren't any standard names for parallel ports under the UNIX system. You might find a device file named **/dev/centronics** or **/dev/parallel** if you're lucky. On XENIX systems, the parallel port is initially named **/dev/lp**. Once you have discovered the name of your port, write it in your log book, in the section describing your devices. And keep the port's name handy, because we'll be using it soon.

With the name of your printer port handy, you are almost ready for the first test. The first test is to make a short transmission to the printer. Log in as superuser while making this test. If you are using a Centronics interface, you can skip the next section. If you are using a serial interface, you must next set the transmission speed.

Setting the Baud Rate for Serial Ports. The UNIX system supports 13 standard baud rates, which we described earlier in Chapter 5, in the section on the **getty** program. Many printers use baud rates from the middle of this range: 300, 600, 1200, or 2400 bits per second.

In UNIX System V, the serial lines are set to a default baud rate (9600 baud, usually) whenever they are unused (closed). A serial line is in use (open) as long as a process that references that line exists. We need to change the baud rate for the serial port that you will be using with your printer. Simply using the **stty** command to change the baud rate doesn't work, because the serial port gets reset to the default baud rate as soon as the **stty** process completes (Figure 6.8a).

Figure 6.8 Setting a serial port's baud rate.

a. The baud rate gets reset to the default after the **stty** command completes:

```
# stty 1200 < /dev/tty2
# stty < /dev/tty2
speed 9600 baud; evenp hupcl
-inpck icrnl -ixany
echo echoe echok
# □
```

b. You keep the serial line open by using a sleep command; then the baud rate can be set, and stay set.

```
# chown lp /dev/tty2
# sleep 10000 < /dev/tty2 &
# stty 1200 onlcr tab3 < /dev/tty2
# stty < /dev/tty2
speed 1200 baud; evenp hupcl
-inpck icrnl -ixany onlcr tab3
echo echoe echok
# □
```

The key is to use a long-lasting command to keep the serial line busy. The **sleep** command shown in Figure 6.8b holds the serial line open while consuming a minimum of system resources. Then the **stty** command can effectively set the baud rate. The baud rate will remain at 1200 baud for 10,000 seconds, which is about 3 hours, long enough for you to test out your connection and debug your LP installation. You need to execute the commands shown in Figure 6.8b, substituting the correct baud rate for your printer. Later in this chapter, in the section "Maintaining the Baud Rate," we explain how to keep the baud rate from changing while using the LP system. We changed the ownership of port **/dev/tty2** to **lp** to avoid problems later.

You probably have noticed that we have also set two other terminal conditions, **onlcr** and **tab3**. The **onlcr** flag causes the kernel to convert newlines to carriage return—newline pairs during output. The **tab3** flag causes tab characters to be converted to the correct number of spaces, useful with printers that don't handle tabbing correctly. You can use any of the output processing conditions shown in TERMIO(7) with serial printers. Parallel ports are another story. The parallel port's device driver differs from the serial device driver; more than that, the parallel driver comes to you not from the standard UNIX kernel, but from the vendor of your UNIX system. Whether output processing works depends on how your vendor implemented the parallel driver for your system.

The baud rate that you use will depend on how fast your printer can accept and print characters. The speed at which the printer can receive characters can usually be selected by switches on the printer itself. The speed that you should use depends on how fast the printer can actually print characters. Printers are often rated in terms of CPS, or characters per second. A good letter-quality printer (like the NEC Spinwriter) can print 120 characters per second. A less expensive letter-quality printer might only handle 20 CPS. The rule of thumb for converting from CPS to a baud rate is to multiply the speed in CPS by 10:

speed in CPS × 10 = baud rate

For a 120-CPS printer, you would use 1200 baud. While this works out neatly (UNIX system supports 1200 baud), what about a printer that can print at 150 CPS? The UNIX system doesn't support 1500 baud. Try the next-highest baud rate available, 2400 baud in this case. When the computer gets ahead of the printer, the printer can use the handshaking line to pause the transmission of characters until the printer's buffer is ready to receive more characters.

Send a Short Text Message. For the first test we'll have the printer print a word or two. We'll simply redirect output to the printer device. This step checks some basics—baud rate, cable connections, printer setup—and it assures that the hardware works, so that we can configure the software confidently. We'll be using **/dev/tty2** for our example printer port. You will need to have the name of your printer port handy. If you are using a serial interface, you must also have set the baud rate correctly, by setting switches on the printer and following the instructions in the preceding section for setting the baud rate of the printer port.

We suggest that you turn the printer off, then on again, before starting the test. Turning a printer on resets the printer, clearing its buffer of any characters and forcing it to examine switch settings. Most printers will not check switch settings for baud rate unless they are reset first. Next, check to see that the printer is ready (switch settings for ONLINE or REMOTE), and that the paper, printwheel, and ribbon are ready.

The test is simplicity itself (Figure 6.9). By echoing the two famous words "Hello there" to the printer's port, we can immediately determine if you are using the correct port name and hardware connection. You can also determine if you are using the correct baud rate.

Figure 6.9 Sending a short test message.

```
# echo "Hello there" > /dev/tty2 &
762
# wait
# □
```

In Figure 6.9 we are using **/dev/tty2** as the printer port's pathname. You need to substitute the name of your printer port for **/dev/tty2**. We put the **echo** command in the background, just in case something goes wrong. Sometimes the device driver for the printer port will "hang," preventing the reappearance of the shell prompt. The **wait** command will complete after the last command put in the background finishes, so you can tell that process 762 (in Figure 6.9) is done without using the **ps** command. If the **wait** command doesn't return the shell prompt almost immediately, something is wrong. You can interrupt the **wait** command with the interrupt key (often DELETE or Control-C).

Did the message get printed? If so, you can go on to the next section. Otherwise, use the checklist that follows.

/dev/tty2: Permission denied

If you are working as **root**, permissions on the device file can't be the problem. What has occurred is that you are using the wrong port name. If you are working as the **lp** administrative account, you will need to become superuser and adjust the ownership and permissions for the port so that you can write to it as **lp**. The port must be owned by the **lp** account and writable by the owner.

echo command completes without printing anything

You may be using the wrong port name or an incorrectly designed interface cable. Check the port name first (this is simplest); then work on the cable, if necessary.

Wrong characters appeared

You are using the wrong baud rate. Check the switch settings of the printer, and use the **stty** command to check the baud rate of the UNIX system (see "Setting the Baud Rate").

echo command never completes

The **echo** process has failed in its attempt to communicate with the printer port. There are two possibilities here—either you are using the incorrect device name, or your interface cable isn't enabling the printer's (or computer's) port, thereby preventing transmission of the message (see Figure 6.4).

Before you continue with printer installation, you need to succeed in this simple test. So keep working at it. You may find more information about the solution in the documentation provided with your equipment. Your system's supplier will hopefully be able to provide you with the necessary information. As a last recourse, you may attempt to contact the manufacturer, although this course often proves to be more frustrating than useful.

Sending a Long Text Message: Testing Handshaking. Before assuming that you've mastered the fine art of computer–printer interfacing, your system should pass one more test. Because most printers use some local memory (their own buffer) to collect characters before printing them, you can often send quite a lot of text to the printer without filling the buffer. The use of the buffer can hide handshaking problems. When handshaking is working, the printer will stop the computer's transmission when the buffer fills up. However, if handshaking isn't working and the buffer is full, the printer will send characters into oblivion, ignoring any characters until it's ready to receive again. You test handshaking by sending a long text message, two pages (120 lines) or so, directly to the printer using redirection. Sections of the text will be missing if the handshaking is incorrect.

Figure 6.10 Testing handshaking with a long text message.

```
# man getty > /dev/tty2 &
# wait
# □
```

The manual entry for the **getty** command is about two pages long. If your system doesn't have on-line manual pages, choose some other lengthy text (5000 or more characters), with which you are familiar enough to recognize missing sections. Your system has passed this test if all the text is printed flawlessly. If some sections of the text are missing, you need to check the cable. We really don't expect that parallel interfaces will exhibit handshaking problems. However, it's better to check.

If your printer produced double-spaced text (blank lines between every line), your printer is converting carriage returns into carriage return–newline pairs. You can disable this conversion by changing a switch on the printer. Alternatively, you can prevent the serial port from performing the conversion by using the **stty** command with the **−onlcr** option.

ADDING A PRINTER TO THE LP SYSTEM

Once your computer–printer connection works correctly, you are ready to make this printer known to the LP system. You use the **lpadmin** command, which changes files and directories to configure the LP system.

Before you start, we want to discuss the concept of a logical printer name. A destination is a logical name in the LP system. You have taken your printer, connected it with a cable to a port on your computer, and accessed the printer through a UNIX file system pathname. What you will be doing next is to tie a name, the destination, to this printer. As we shall see, a single printer may have more than one destination name in the LP system.

The printer's LP system name is also the name of its queue, the list of requests for this printer. Each destination that you create with the **lpadmin** command has its own list of print requests.

The LP system has two commands, **accept** and **reject**, that either allow requests to enter the queue, or prevent a request from being accepted. Canceling a request removes a print request from a destination's queue—possibly halting printing if it has already begun.

Once a request has entered the destination's queue, the **lpsched** process may create another process to print the request, based on whether that particular destination has been enabled. The **enable** command allows the scheduler to start printing a request. The **disable** command prevents print requests from being started. Note that disabling a destination does not prevent requests for that destination from entering the queue. Figure 6.11 depicts the flow from a user's request to the beginning of the printing, showing where the **accept-reject**, **enable-disable**, and **cancel** commands come into play.

Figure 6.11 Tracing the flow of an **lp** request.

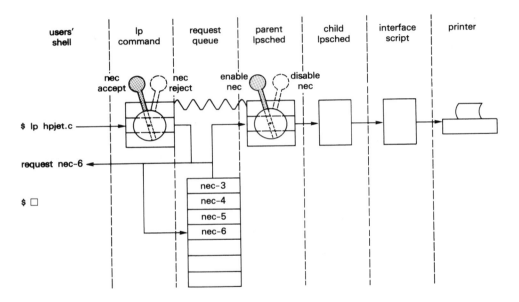

The flow in Figure 6.11 starts when a user invokes the **lp** command. The **lp** command checks to see if the destination is accepting or rejecting requests. A request-id is returned to the user and the request is added to the queue if the destination is accepting requests. Otherwise, a message is sent to the user saying that the request was not accepted. The **lp** command also notifies the scheduler that it has added a new request to the queue.

The LP scheduler, **lpsched**, checks the output queue and the printer status file to see if the request can be started immediately. If not, the scheduler goes back to sleep, awaiting the completion of printing the job currently in progress or another notification from the **lp** command. If the destination requested is available and the destination has been enabled, the scheduler starts an interface shell script or program to handle printing of the request.

Note that if the destination is a class of destinations, the request is added to the queue for the class, and printing begins as soon as any member of the class becomes available. This feature allows you to hook up two or more printers to be used on a first-available basis.

Sample Printer Installation

Most of the programs used to configure the LP system are in the **/usr/lib** directory. If you are using the **lp** system account, you should include this directory in your command search path. For those of you working as **root**, you can add this directory to your path with one of the commands shown in Figure 6.12. You must be working as either **root** or **lp** to use the LP configuration commands. (Working as **root** will probably be the most convenient method.)

Figure 6.12 Adding **/usr/lib** to your command search path.

a. When using the Bourne shell:

```
$ PATH=${PATH}:/usr/lib
```

b. When using the C shell:

```
% set path = ( $path /usr/lib )
```

To start out your installation, chose a descriptive name for the logical name for your printer, the destination. The destination's name will be used as a filename, so it must follow the rules for naming files (14 characters or less). We suggest that you select a short name and that you not be cryptic about it. For example, **nec** adequately describes an NEC Spinwriter, whereas **p** hardly implies a Printronix line printer. Instead, you might use **fast** for the Printronix, a high-speed line printer, and **laser** for an LN03 laser printer. Note that some application software may dictate the name of the printer device—so check its documentation.

You will also need the name of the printer port. We have been using **/dev/tty2** as our example port. Finally, you will need the name of an interface program. We suggest using the **dumb** interface program for now. We'll have more to say about the interface programs later.

If you are already using the LP system, the scheduler program, **lpsched**, will probably be running. The **lpadmin** command can't make changes to the LP system while the scheduler is running (with two exceptions). You halt the scheduler by using the **lpshut** command. Simply enter the **lpshut** command without options to halt the scheduler. Users will still be able to use the **lp** command to queue their requests while you are reconfiguring the system.

For our example installation, we will be using **nec** for our destination name
and **/dev/tty2** for the port to which it is connected. As mentioned, **dumb** is the
name of an interface program. Figure 6.13 shows the command lines to use.

Figure 6.13 Sample installation commands.

```
# chown lp /dev/tty2
# lpshut
# lpadmin -pnec -v/dev/tty2 -mdumb
# lpsched
# □
```

The installation shown in Figure 6.13 has created a new *queue* for the destination named **nec**. Requests directed to this destination will be processed by the
interface program **dumb**, and the output directed to the device **/dev/tty2**. Installation of the destination is *not* complete, however. You must use the **accept** command to permit requests to enter the queue for the new destination, and **enable**
command to allow the scheduler to start printing the requests (Figure 6.14).

Figure 6.14 Completing installation—allow requests to be accepted, and enabling the printer.

```
# accept nec
destination "nec" now accepting requests
# enable nec
printer "nec" now enabled
# lpstat -pnec
printer nec is idle. enabled since Oct 3 18:03
# □
```

Now you can test your newly installed printer (destination). Although many
LP system commands use the **−p** option to specify a particular printer, the **lp** command expects the option **−d**, for destination, instead (Figure 6.15).

Figure 6.15 Testing the new destination.

```
# lp -dnec declaration
request id is nec-001 (1 file)
# □
```

If everything has gone as planned, your test file should print. You'll notice
that the **lp** command takes some time getting the request set up. Then the
scheduler takes over and starts the interface script, and the actual printing begins.

What if something goes wrong? You entered the command in Figure 6.15 and you get an error message in response. Well, there are several things that can go wrong. If you try to print a file that the **lp** administrative account can't access, you'll get the message "Permission denied." The **lp** process must have access permission to the file you want to print. Even though you are executing the command, it is the interface script, which is started by the scheduler (**lpsched**), that will access the file to be printed. The **lp** command is owned by the **lp** administrative account and set-user-id. So the file to be printed must be accessible by the **lp** account, that is, readable by **lp** or the "other" category.

Suppose you get back a request id and the printer doesn't start. Have you remembered to restart the scheduler? You can check the status of the entire LP system by using the **lpstat** command with the −t (for total) option (Figure 6.16).

Figure 6.16 Checking everything about the LP system.

```
# lpstat -t
scheduler is not running
device for nec: /dev/tty2
nec accepting requests since Oct  3 18:02
printer nec is idle.  enabled since Oct  3 18:05
nec-001          root          1396    Oct  3 18:06
# □
```

Figure 6.16 shows that everything is correct except that the scheduler is not running. The request that we made, nec-001, is waiting patiently for the scheduler to start it up. If you can't get your scheduler to run, refer to the end of this chapter, where we discuss solving problems with the LP system.

Before completing this section, let's set up a second destination connected to the same port as our first destination. You might want to share one port with two destinations because both destinations refer to the same printer with a different type of paper (or forms or ribbon) in it. For example, if people occasionally need to print on wide paper, we could configure a new destination with the commands in Figure 6.17.

Figure 6.17 Setting up a second destination, and sharing the same printer.

```
# lpshut
# lpadmin -pwide -mdumb -v/dev/tty2
# lpsched
# accept wide
destination "wide" now accepting requests
# □
```

Notice that we did not **enable** the destination **wide**. If you enable two destinations that share the same port, as **wide** and **nec** do, print requests for the two destinations may be intermingled. The trick is to allow requests for jobs printed on wide paper to queue up. Then, when no request for **nec** is being printed, enter **disable nec** and change the paper in the printer. After changing to wide paper, you can enable **wide**, and requests for the **wide** destinations will begin printing. When the requests for **wide** have finished printing, you reverse the procedure, disabling **wide**, changing the paper, and enabling **nec**.

lpadmin Options

The **lpadmin** command recognizes 11 options with the fastidiousness for detail that's to be expected of UNIX commands. Some options must be used with other options, and two options must be used alone.

One of three options must be present whenever you use the **lpadmin** command. Options that are followed by a name, like **−pnec**, cannot have a space separating the option letter (**p**) and the name (**nec**). These options are:

−p Printer—used in conjunction with the remaining eight options. The −**p** option stands for "printer" name, the destination. You use this option when you set up a new destination or make changes to existing destinations.

−d Default—make the destination that follows this option the default destination. This option may not be combined with other options.

−x Excise—remove from the LP system the destination that follows this option. This option may not be combined with other options.

We've already given an example for using the −**p** option, in the example installation of the destination **nec**. Now, you may have noticed that when we sent a test file to the LP system we needed to specify the destination to the **lp** command. But your users want to say simply **lp filename**. So you can set one up as the default printer using **lpadmin −d**. Figure 6.18 depicts making the destination "nec" the default destination.

Figure 6.18 Establishing a default destination with the **lpadmin** command.

```
# lpadmin -dnec
# lp outline
request id is nec-002 (1 file)
# □
```

The **lp** command can be used without the −**d** option to queue up requests for the default destination. You can change the default destination at any time, even if the scheduler is running (one of the exceptions we mentioned earlier). After changing the default, subsequent requests will be printed by the new default destination. Users can establish their own default destination by setting the environment variable **LPDEST** in their **.login** or **.profile** file.

The —**x** option removes the files and directories created when you configure the LP system for a new destination. The —**x** option will also remove this destination from any classes of which it might be a member. Always use the —**x** option when removing destinations. Although you can remove some configuration files, you can't edit the status files to remove a destination properly. The LP system will not function correctly if you attempt to remove a destination without using the —**x** option. Symptoms of partially removed destinations include being unable to start the scheduler and "extra" schedulers that appear in **ps** listings. At the end of this chapter we discuss correcting these occurrences.

The eight remaining options are all used with the —**p** option. The —**p** option specifies which destination (the named printer) you wish to change or create. These options are:

—**c**_class_

Class—add this printer to the named _class_. If the class doesn't already exist, it will be created. If this is a new class, use **accept** _class_ to allow the class to accept requests.

—**r**_class_

Remove from class—remove the named printer from the named _class_. If this printer is the last member of this class, the class will also be removed.

—**h**

Hardwired—the named printer is "hardwired," that is, "permanently" connected to a particular port that is used only for printing. Hardwired is the default and need not be specified.

—**l**

Log-in line—the named printer is connected to a port that is normally connected to a log-in terminal. The LP system will automatically **disable** this printer when the scheduler starts running.

—**m**_name_

Model interface—copies the _name_ interface script in the **/usr/spool/lp/model** directory and makes it the interface script for the named printer.

−i*pathname*

> Interface—copies the file *pathname* to be the interface script for the named printer.

−e*printer*

> Existing script—makes a copy of the interface script for *printer* that has already been configured, and uses the copy as the interface script for the named printer.

−v*device*

> Device—(Well, device does have a "v" in it.) Establish the port named *device* as the output destination for the named printer.

The concept of a class of destinations is useful for large installations that have more than one printer. When a request is made with a class as a destination, the next available member of the class will receive the request. Thus, a user doesn't have to know which printer is currently idle, and may send the request to a class of printers. If a user wants to send the request to a particular destination, the **−d** option may still be used with the **lp** command. A class may be made the default destination by using the **−d** option with the **lpadmin** command.

Note that after creating a class, you must also use the **accept** command with the class as the argument before the class destination will accept requests.

The distinction between hardwired and log-in connections is simple. The LP system assumes that printers are hardwired, that is, always connected to a port, by default. If the printer is not always connected, and a terminal used for system access normally is connected, the LP system assumes that this port is used as a log-in port. The **−l** option configures the LP system to **disable** a destination connected to a log-in port each time the scheduler starts. This configuration prevents the LP system from sending print requests to someone's log-in terminal.

Suppose, for example, you are using a workstation that has a single port that you usually have connected to a modem. You want to share this port with the LP system. You would include the **−l** option when creating a destination with the **lpadmin** command, and the scheduler will **disable** this destination every time the scheduler is started. Now, you can still use the port with the modem and add requests to the destination's queue.

When you want to start up the printer, the **init** process must be signaled to disable the port for the modem. (Refer to our discussion of the **init** program in Chapter 5.) Then you can disconnect the modem, connect the printer, and use the **enable** command to allow the scheduler to start printing. To reconnect the modem, you **disable** the printer, change the connections, and signal the **init** process to start a **getty** process for this port.

There are three ways to associate an interface script with a printer. Each of the three methods is associated with a different option, and all three work essentially the same way—each causes the **lpadmin** command to copy a file. The difference between these options lies in where they expect to find the script that is to be copied. The **−m** option forces the **lpadmin** command to look in the **/usr/spool/lp/model** directory. The **−e** option directs the **lpadmin** command to look in the **/usr/spool/lp/interface** directory. The **−i** option is followed by a complete (or relative) pathname for the script.

Configuration Files and Directories

As we mentioned earlier, the LP system uses certain files and directories that are in the **/usr/spool/lp** branch of the file system. Some of these files and directories are created when you use the **lpadmin** command, while others are part of the LP system as it is delivered (unconfigured). Table 6.2 lists the files and directories that are part of an unconfigured LP system.

TABLE 6.2 FILES AND DIRECTORIES IN THE LP SYSTEM DIRECTORY TREE (**/usr/spool/lp** DIRECTORY)

File or Directory	Description
class	A directory containing files named for classes, where each file contains class members.
interface	A directory containing installed interface scripts, where each script is named for a destination.
log	A file containing a record of **lpsched** errors.
member	A directory containing files named for destinations, where each file holds the device name associated with that destination.
model	A directory of model (uninstalled) interface scripts.
oldlog	A file containing errors from the previous **lpsched** process.
outputq	A file containing status information about current requests.
pstatus	A file containing status information about destinations (enabled or disabled, busy or idle).
qstatus	A file containing status information about queues (accepting or rejecting requests).
request	A directory containing directories named after each destination; these subdirectories contain the actual printing requests.
seqfile	A file containing the next sequence number for the LP system.

The **class** directory will contain a file for each class that has been established. The file will have the same name as the class, and each member of the class will be listed, separated by newlines, in the file for the class.

The **interface** directory will have an interface script named after each destination that exists in your LP system. The **member** directory will have a file for each destination that holds the pathname of the device for the destination. The **model** directory contains the model interface scripts that are provided with your UNIX system. The **request** directory will have a subdirectory for each destination. The subdirectories are named after the destinations.

There are three status files, **outputq**, **pstatus**, and **qstatus**. These files are *not* human-readable, and are used by the **lpstat** and **lpsched** commands. The **log** file holds the standard error output of the **lpsched** process. You can discover why the scheduler is not running by looking in the logfile.

Table 6.2 shows what the LP system directory looks like before you have used the **lpadmin** command. In earlier examples we configured two printer destinations, **nec** and **wide**. In Table 6.3 we depict the new files and directories created by using the **lpadmin** command three times, and what the contents of these files are.

TABLE 6.3   CHANGES TO THE LP SYSTEM TREE CREATED BY
EARLIER EXAMPLES (FIGURE 6.13, FIGURE 6.17, FIGURE 6.18)

File or Directory	Description
default	file containing the default destination **nec**
interface/nec	interface script for destination **nec**
interface/wide	interface script for destination **wide**
member/nec	file containing the device name **/dev/tty2**
member/wide	file containing the device name **/dev/tty2**
request/nec	directory for requests for **nec**
request/wide	directory for requests for **wide**

Changes have also been made to the three status files, **outputq**, **pstatus**, and **qstatus**. Although you could create the files and directories used by the LP system yourself instead of using the **lpadmin** command, you can't modify the status files directly.

One thing that you can do is edit the interface script for a destination. Even though you may have used a model interface script, you can't edit the model script and have the changes affect an installed interface script. You can edit the installed interface script itself, and these changes will take hold next time the script is started.

INTERFACE SCRIPTS

The **lpsched** daemon starts an interface script to process each request. The LP system expects either a Bourne (not C) shell script or a program for the interface script. We will describe how to edit and modify Bourne shell interface scripts. A

C program interface script would work identically to the shell script, as it will receive the same arguments. We suggest that you develop your interface program as shell scripts first. If you later wish to convert your interface shell scripts to programs, the interface will start up faster and execute slightly more quickly.

Each time a user invokes the **lp** command, the request is accepted and a request id is returned to the user. A request consists not only of a list of files to be printed, but additional information that may be processed by the interface script. This additional information is:

1. Request id—the request id that was returned to the user when the **lp** command was invoked (like nec-001);
2. User—the log-in name of the user who invoked the **lp** command;
3. Title—an optional title for the request that is included if the user included the −**t** option when invoking the **lp** command;
4. Copies—the number of copies to be made of each file that is specified in this request; the default of one may be changed by specifying the option −**n***N* (for *N* copies) to the **lp** command;
5. Options—a list of options that may be interpreted by the interface script. You specify these options by arguments to the −**o** switch on the **lp** command line.

The scheduler passes this additional information (or an empty string for each unused option) to the interface script when the interface script is started. A list of the files to be printed is also passed as arguments to the interface script.

The standard and error output of the interface script is redirected to the output device for the printer that uses this script. The standard input is redirected from the null device (**/dev/null**). We'll have more to say about these redirections later, as they introduce some interesting side effects.

A Simple Interface Script

Figure 6.19 shows the information on which interface scripts operate. There are five arguments, followed by a list of files.

Figure 6.19 Arguments passed to an interface script.

```
request-id user title copies "options" file1 [file2 file3 ...]
```

The simplest interface script that we could write would print the files in the list, while ignoring all the additional information presented to the script. This script is depicted in Figure 6.20a.

Figure 6.20 A simple interface script and how it is invoked by a scheduler.

a. Listing of the **simple** script:

```
shift 5                     # throw away additional information
for name in "$*"            # for all files (remaining args)
do
        cat $name             # output file
        echo "\n \014"      # send a newline and a form feed
done
echo "\014"                 # send a form feed (optional)
exit 0                      # exit successfully
```

b. How the interface script would be invoked from a Bourne shell:

```
/usr/spool/lp/interface/nec request-id user title copies "options" \
file1 file2 file3  < /dev/null 2>&1 /dev/tty2
```

The **simple** interface script (Figure 6.20a) really is simplistic. Essentially, the task of the interface script is to handle the arguments and output the characters in the file(s). The simple script handles the arguments by throwing them away. Then the **for-do** loop **cats** the files one at a time. The **echo** command sends a newline to complete the last line output, which may or may not be necessary, and sends a form feed. The form feed (**\014**) commands the printer to advance the paper to the top of the next page after each file is printed. The final **echo** command sends a form feed to tell the printer to advance the paper to the top of the next page, making the print job easy to remove from the printer. Note that this last form feed is optional and will waste paper on many printers.

Redirecting the output to the printer port is handled by the **lpsched** process when it starts the interface script. In Figure 6.20b we show how the command line that invokes the interface script (for our example printer, **nec**) would look if it were entered for the Bourne shell. Both the standard output and the standard error (**2> &1**) are redirected to the device port. The standard input is redirected from the null device.

Having the standard output redirected to the printer port makes writing scripts easier. However, having the error output go to the printer also makes debugging scripts more difficult. The reason for redirecting the error output is that there isn't a terminal attached to the interface script when it starts. The scheduler is a daemon, a program that operates independent of a controlling terminal. The scheduler program was written so that it sends its error messages to the one device that it knows about—the printer.

Similarly, the standard input won't be coming from a terminal. The null device, **/dev/null**, sends an end-of-file as soon as it is read, guaranteeing that the script won't be waiting for nonexistent input.

A good trick to use while testing and developing interface shell scripts is to configure the destination to use the port that you are working from as the destination's device. Then, all the output, including the error messages from the script, will be displayed on your terminal. When you are satisfied with your script, you can use the **lpadmin** command to change the device to the real printer port. For example, if you are logged in on **/dev/tty09** while developing an interface script, you would test this script by installing the destination with **/dev/tty09** as the device.

```
lpadmin -ptest -i/u/rik/Prog/test -v/dev/tty09
```

You must allow the **lp** account write permission for your terminal (with **mesg y**, for example). And you must specify the full device name for your terminal and not use **/dev/tty**. **/dev/tty** is a special device that refers to the controlling terminal for a process. Since the scheduler doesn't have a controlling terminal, trying to use **/dev/tty** will fail and the interface script will never complete.

Since the **simple** script ignores all the arguments (except the files), invoking the **lp** command with options for a title or more than one copy prints only one copy, without a title. The way that the LP system handles the options and prints the files depends entirely on the interface script.

The **simple** interface script is appropriate for UNIX systems that don't use high-speed printers and have a low volume of print requests. The **dumb** script (which comes with System V) starts up 25 processes to print a single file, and prints both a banner page and two trailing pages. While the **dumb** script produces output appropriate for a large data processing shop, you would be wasting resources if you use it in an environment with fewer than several users.

The simple script starts three processes to print a single file, and doesn't produce a header or trailing page. If you are using a UNIX system in an office environment, people can walk over to the printer and pick out their own print jobs. A fancy header page isn't necessary. If you do want to use some of the additional information, the next section shows you how.

Processing Some Options

We are going to start out by saving the additional information passed to the script by the **lpsched** process. We used the **dumb** script as a model and created our own script, **fancier**, to process this information to produce a simple header page. You may wish to follow this example if you want to produce header or banner pages and print multiple copies of files.

Saving the additional information away is simplicity itself. Besides the five arguments we mentioned previously, we can also squirrel away the name of the printer for which the request is destined. Argument zero in Bourne shell scripts is the name of the shell script program being executed. In the LP system, the basename of the interface script will be identical to the printer name, so we can use the **basename** command to capture the printer name. In Figure 6.20b, the basename of the script **/usr/spool/lp/interface/nec** is **nec**. Figure 6.21 displays the enhanced interface script, **fancier**, that processes the additional information and produces a header page similar to the **dumb** script.

Figure 6.21 Interface script with header page that prints multiple copies (if desired).

```
printer=`basename $0`    # get printer (destination) name
request=$1               # save the five arguments
user=$2
title=$3
copies=$4
options=$5

echo "\n\n\n\n\n"
banner $user             # print login name in big letters

# then, get comment field from the /etc/passwd file
name=`grep "^${user}:" /etc/passwd | line | cut -d: -f5`

if [ -n "$name" ]        # if there's anything in the comment
then                     # field, print it out
    echo "\n\n\nUser:  $name\n"
else                     # else print blank lines
    echo "\n\n\n\n"
fi
echo "Request id: $request      Printer:  $printer\n"
date                     # print date
if [ -n "$title" ]       # if there's a title,
then                     # print it in big letters, too
    banner $title
fi
echo "\n\014"            # move to new page (form feed)

shift 5                  # shift past first five arguments
files=$*                 # get list of files
c=1                      # start a counter
while [ $c -le $copies ] # while the counter is less than
do                       # or equal to the number of copies
    for file in $files
    do                   # print all the files
        cat "$file"
        echo "\n\014"
```

```
     done
     c=`expr $c + 1`        # add one to the counter
done                        # go back to 'while' and try again
echo "\n\014"               # a final form feed
exit 0
```

As you can see, the **fancier** interface script is much longer than the **simple** script and does much more. After collecting the printer name and the first five arguments, we print the user name in big letters with the **banner** command. Then the **grep** pipeline finds the matching entry in the **/etc/passwd** file and **cut**s out the comment (fifth) field. If the comment field, now held in the variable **name**, is nonempty, the script prints it out. In a large installation, you can quickly understand how important a comment field containing the user's real name and phone number can be.

The **fancier** script then prints out the request id, printer name, and date. If the −**t** option was used with the **lp** command, the script will put the title in large letters on the header page. Finally, the header page is ejected with a form feed.

A modified version of the **simple** script follows. We shift past the five arguments (**shift 5**), collect the file list in the variable **files**, and start a counter, **c**. The counter is checked in the test part of the **while** loop. As long as the counter is less than or equal to the number of **copies** desired (one by default), the list of files will be printed.

The **fancier** script uses almost all the information passed to it by the scheduler. What we have ignored so far are the options, which are passed as argument five. We shall explore the options as soon as we have tackled a topic dear to the hearts of serial port users—the baud rate.

Maintaining the Correct Baud Rate

Serial port users may have already run into a problem. It has been many pages since we set the baud rate on the printer port. Possibly several days have elapsed since you started working with the LP system. And the **sleep** that we started to keep the port open and the baud rate set has expired. In this section we explain how to incorporate setting the baud rate within the interface script itself.

We found two tricks to setting the baud rate from the interface script. The most obvious way to set the baud rate is to include a **stty** command within the script. And it almost works. (That's where the second trick comes in.) First, redirect the input of **stty** to come from the printer port device. Since the scheduler redirects the output of the interface script to the printer port device file, you can instruct the Bourne shell that invokes **stty** to use the same device file for standard input to the **stty** command. (The **stty** command affects the device connected to its standard input, not the standard output.) Figure 6.22 shows the approach.

Figure 6.22 Setting the baud rate within the interface script.

```
      .  .  .
copies=$4
options=$5

stty 1200 onlcr tab3 <&1

echo "\n\n\n\n\n"
      .  .  .
```

Here the directive **< & 1** causes the Bourne shell to use the file associated with the file descriptor 1 (the standard output) as standard input for the **stty** process.

We set the baud rate *before* anything is sent to the printer. The reason for redirecting the input from the printer is twofold. In System V you must redirect the input (not output) to use the **stty** command. The second reason is that the **lpsched** process has connected the interface script's standard input to the null device (**/dev/null**). Thus, if you forget to redirect the input of the **stty** command, you are attempting to set the baud rate for the null device (which doesn't do anything).

Okay. Now there's a second trick to keeping the baud rate set. As is, the interface script **cat**s the files to the standard output, the printer device, then exits. Meanwhile, the kernel is sending the files to the printer, which is *much* slower than the script. When the interface script process is exited, the kernel closed the printer device port and *reset the baud rate to the default speed*. So the end of every LP request wouldn't be printed because the baud rate changed. The next request would start up with the correct baud rate again. The solution we found was to start up a **sleep** process that would keep the port open for a few seconds after the interface script process completes. The sleep subprocess is added at the end of the script, after the **while** loop (Figure 6.23).

Figure 6.23 Keeping the baud rate set after the interface script completes.

```
      .  .  .
done
(trap "" 1 15; sleep 10 <&1) &
exit 0
```

The parentheses around the **sleep** command cause the Bourne shell to start a subshell to execute the command. The **trap** command tells this subshell to ignore the exit and hang-up signals that are sent from the parent shell (the interface script) when it completes. The ampersand (**&**) puts the subshell in the background, so the LP system doesn't have to wait for the **sleep** to complete before starting on the next request. We used a **sleep** for 10 seconds, which was sufficient for our UNIX system to send the remainder of its buffer out at 1200 baud. You may need to increase argument to the **sleep** command if the baud rate continues to get reset before the end of the file is printed.

Using the Options

The **lp** program passes options to the interface script when the −o option is used. For example, in Figure 6.24a a request was made to print the file **Feb22.let** with the **s** option. Now, exactly what the **s** option will do depends on how you have written your interface script. Two scripts provided with System V in the **model** directory, **1640** and **hp**, each accept two options (see the entry for LPADMIN(1M)). In Figure 6.24b we show how to use the option letter **s** to suppress the printing of a header page.

Figure 6.24 Passing and handling options to the interface script.

a. Adding an option to a request:

```
$ lp -os Feb22.let
request id is nec-005 (1 file)
$ □
```

b. Using the option to suppress creating the header page:

```
    . . .
options=$5
if [ "$options" != s ]
then
    . . .         # process arguments and print header page
fi
shift 5
    . . .
```

The double quotes around the **$options** in the test are important. Without the double quotes, if there isn't an option, the **test** command (invoked by using the square brackets) will fail and the interface script will exit before printing any file. The error message from this failure will not be printed on anyone's terminal, but at the printer. Therefore, while you are debugging interface scripts, remember to look at your printer.

The **lp** command collects each instance of the −o key letter and the characters that follow the key letter into a single quoted string. For example, if you wanted to send two options to the interface script, you might use the command line in Figure 6.25a.

Figure 6.25 Processing multiple options.

a. One way of sending multiple options to the interface script:

```
$ lp -oh -opr Apr09.inv
request id is nec-011 (1 file)
$ □
```

b. An alternative way to send the same options:

```
$ lp -o"h pr" Apr09.inv
request id is nec-012 (1 file)
$ □
```

c. Processing multiple options in the interface script:

```
        . . .
options=$5
filter=cat
for o in $options
do
        case $o in
        pr) filter=pr;;
        h) header=yes;;
        *) ;;
        esac
done
if [ -n "$header" ]       # if h option used, then
then
     . . .                # print header page
fi
```

In Figure 6.25b we use an alternative method for passing options to the inter-face script. Instead of using the −o key letter twice, we use the key letter once and surround the options we want to pass with double quotes. Now, it doesn't matter to the **lp** command whether you use the key letter −o twice or only once with quoted arguments. The **lp** command will take all the options it collects and pass them to the interface script as one doubly quoted string.

Figure 6.25c exhibits a technique for processing multiple arguments in the quoted string. Argument five is stored in the variable **options**, the same as in the **fancier** script. Then we use a **for-in-do** loop to separate each of the options. Within the loop is a **case** statement that matches the options and either sets vari-ables or initiates some activity.

We are only checking for two variables, **pr** and **h**, in the script fragment in Figure 6.25c. If an **h** is included in the options, the variable **header** is set to **yes**. Later, if **header** is set to **yes**, the header page will be printed.

We have introduced another new variable for our interface script, **filter**. Currently, we are using the **cat** command to send the files to the standard output in the **fancier** script. Any command that writes to the standard output can be used in place of the **cat** command. We can use the **filter** variable to stand for the command that processes the files to be output. In Figure 6.25c we initially set **filter** to be **cat** and will change it to be **pr** if the **pr** option is used.

You may want to use the **troff** program as a filter if you are sending typesetting output to a printer. The output of a typesetting program is only marginally readable and much larger than the initial text. By using **troff** as a filter, you not only save file system space, you also batch up requests to use the **troff** program, a notorious CPU hog.

You can change the **case** statement to process as many different options as you like. Just pick a letter or word to use as a selector in the **case** statement, and add another selection.

Collecting Accounting Information

In the next chapter we explain how to charge fees for different services by using the **chargefee** script. For example, it may cost between 2 and 5 cents for toner to print a page with a laser printer. That cost doesn't include paper, electricity or purchase of and maintenance for the laser printer. You may wish to include a mechanism in your interface script for making users accountable for the pages that they print.

You need to do two things to leave accounting information for the accounting system—count the pages and produce a record. You can't use the **chargefee** script from within the interface script—the **chargefee** script writes in the **/usr/adm/fee** file, which is accessible only to the **adm** account. If other users could write in the **fee** file, they could erase fees for themselves or create phony fees for others. What you can do is to leave a record that the accounting scripts can read and process.

To estimate the number of pages, we can use **awk** to count the number of lines from the output and divide it by 56 (number of lines in a page) to come up with the estimated total number of pages. We will use the **awk** program as a filter; that is, we will insert the command in the output stream, so that the pages are counted on their way to the printer.

We connect our **awk** script by using a pipe symbol at the termination of the **while-do-done** loop. Figure 6.26 shows how the **awk** script appears after the terminating **done**.

Figure 6.26
Counting pages and collecting accounting information in the interface script **fancier**.

```
while [ $c -le $copies ] # while the counter is less than
do                       # or equal to the number of copies
  for file in $files
  do                     # print all the files
```

```
        cat "$file"
        echo "\n\014"
    done
    c=`expr $c + 1`         # add one to the counter
done |                      # pipe all the output through awk
awk '{print}
    END {print "'$user'", int((NR+55)/56) >> "/usr/spool/lp/fees"}'
```

The first **{print}** directive in the **awk** script sends every line of input directly to the standard output. The standard output is still the printer device. The **print** directive that follows the **END** statement is effective only when the end of file is reached (the end of the last file to be printed). The value of the shell script variable **$user** is printed first, followed by the number of pages, and appended to the file **/usr/spool/lp/fees**. There is nothing sacred about the file **/usr/spool/lp/fees** except that it is the one we will be using for our example in Chapter 7.

There are two things to note about the **awk** script. First, it is peppered with quote and double-quote marks. Every mark is essential to the correct working of the script. (This script won't work if you keep it in a file and call it with the −**f** **awk** option.) The second is the way that we are counting pages. **NR** is a built-in **awk** variable that stands for the number of records (lines). We are assuming that a page is 56 lines long, an assumption with which you may or may not agree. To create our page count, we add 55 to **NR** (to round up) and divide by 56. The **int** function forces the result to be an integer; otherwise, the answer would most likely have a fractional part.

While using **awk** certainly does the trick, the **awk** program is somewhat slow both to start up and run. For those of you who feel comfortable with C programs, we have included a short C program that does the same job as the **awk** script. A compiled C program will run faster than **awk**, something to remember when performance is an issue. Figure 6.27a shows how the C program, **pgaccount**, fits into the **fancier** script, and Figure 6.27b is a listing of the program itself.

Figure 6.27 Using a C program to count pages and write an accounting trace.

a. Attaching the **pgaccount** program to the output stream:

```
while [ $c -le $copies ] # while the counter is less than
do                       # or equal to the number of copies
    for file in $files
    do               # print all the files
        cat "$file"
        echo "\n\014"
    done
    c=`expr $c + 1` # add one to the counter
done | /usr/lbin/pgaccount $user # pipe output through pgaccount
```

b. Listing of the pgaccount C program:

```
1   /* pgaccount - counts the pages that pass through this filter
2    * and writes the user name and page count to the file
3    * /usr/spool/lp/fees - Rik
5    */
6
7   #include <stdio.h>
8   #define NL '\n'
9   #define FF '\014'
10
11  main(argc, argv)
12  int argc; char *argv[];
13  {
14          int c, pages, lines;
15          FILE *file;
16
17          while (c != EOF) {
18                  if ((c = getchar()) == NL) {
19                          lines++;
20                          if (lines == 56) {
21                                  pages++;
22                                  lines = 0;
23                          }
24                  }
25                  if (c == FF) {
26                          pages++;
27                          lines = 0;
28                  }
29                  putchar(c);
30          }
31          file = fopen ("/usr/spool/lp/fees", "a");
32          fprintf ( file, "%s %d\n", argv[1], pages);
33          fclose (file);
34
35  }
```

The **pgaccount** program writes the same two parameters to the **fees** file—the user name and the number of pages printed. The **pgaccount** program also checks for form feeds, so that one page is either 56 lines or one form feed. The **awk** script could also be rewritten to account for form feeds, instead of treating each form feed as one line (as it currently does). If you rewrite it, remember that the quotes used in the script are important.

MAINTAINING THE LP SYSTEM

We expect that you'll have more trouble setting up or changing the LP system than you will maintaining it, so perhaps this title is misleading. In our experience, the computer–printer connection and the printer itself (running out of ribbon, paper, malfunctions) are the main causes of problems. We'll discuss hardware problems first.

The second most common problem stems from file access. Users may complain of being unable to print a file that they have access to but the LP system doesn't. Infrequently, so much work will be queued up for the printer (or UUCP system, which shares this file system) that you will run out of space for more requests.

In the remainder of this chapter we explain how to monitor the LP system and how to uncover the reasons why the system may not be working properly. We also explain how anyone can cancel a troublesome print request, and enable or disable a printer. And the "mysterious multiple scheduler anomaly" will be demystified at the chapter's end.

Check the Printer Connection

If your LP system suddenly stops working, when it was working before, the computer–printer connection is a prime suspect. Check the simple things first—is the printer cable still connected to the port? Is the printer on, on-line, complete with paper and ribbon? Since printers are mechanical and quickly consume resources, you will be able to fix most printer problems simply by checking out the printer.

If the printer and its connection check out and the LP system still isn't working, try redirecting some output directly to the printer port (Figure 6.28a). If the output doesn't reach the printer, you may also want to check the ownership and permissions of the device file. The printer device must be owned by **lp** and writable by the owner (Figure 6.28b).

Figure 6.28 Checking ownership and permissions for the printer device port.

a. Testing the port connection:

```
# echo "Hello there" > /dev/tty2 &
# wait
# □
```

b. Desired ownership and permissions:

```
# ls -l /dev/tty2
crw-r--r--  1 lp     admin      0,  3 Dec  4 10:47 /dev/tty2
# □
```

c. Correcting ownership and permissions for /**dev/tty2**:

```
# chown lp /dev/tty2
# chmod 644 /dev/tty2
# □
```

The permissions and ownership of the printer will be changed if you use the same port as a log-in port. The /**etc/init** program changes the ownership of a log-in port to **root** any time a user logs out. Although this action is a good security precaution, it will make trouble for you when you share a port between a terminal and a printer. The superuser will need to change the ownership of the printer port after a user has logged off and before the LP system attempts to print using that port. Use the **chown** command in Figure 6.28c.

Baud Rate Changes

Baud rate is a problem only for printers with serial interfaces. We described earlier how to edit the interface script to set the baud rate correctly for each printer. However, sometimes we have found that our baud rate changed while the printer was banging out a request. The printer (a NEC Spinwriter) would beep sadly, an error light would turn on, and pressing RESET on the printer would produce more sad beeps.

What had happened was that someone tripped over the printer cable and disconnected it. The person reconnected the cable, expecting that everything would be okay. Unfortunately, the System V character device driver resets the baud rate to the default rate whenever a device is closed. In this case, disconnecting the printer "closed" the device, and the baud rate was changed to the default of 9600 baud. Note that turning off a printer while it is printing may have the same effect. The solution is to **disable** the printer, then **enable** it again (see "Enabling/Disabling Printers"). The print job will start over with the correct baud rate. You'll probably need to realign the paper to the top of the page before reenabling the printer.

File System Problems

There are, of course, other things that can happen. For example, the file system containing the spooling directory, probably /**usr**, might fill up. If you are following the suggestions we gave in Chapter 4 you shouldn't be surprised at running out of space. And you know what to do about it. When the file system is out of space, the LP system will refuse to accept requests. The console will be displaying "out of space" messages for the file system device.

Can't Access File Problem

Very commonly, users will complain to you that the **lp** command refuses to print a file. As we mentioned earlier, the **lp** administrative account must have access to any files that the interface script will be reading. This behavior differs from the way most commands will execute. Most commands will have the same access to files as the user who started the command. Some commands, like the **passwd** command, give special access abilities. However, the **lp** command accesses files as the **lp** administrative user, not as the user.

Figure 6.29a displays the error message produced when the LP system can't access a file. The solution is quite simple—have the user pipe the contents of the file into the **lp** command (Figure 6.29b).

Figure 6.29 Trouble accessing a file with the **lp** command.

a. Error message obtained when the **lp** account can't access a file:

```
$ lp secret
lp: can't access file "secret"
lp: request not accepted
$ □
```

b. The solution is to use a pipeline:

```
$ cat secret ¦ lp
request id is nec-675 (standard input)
$ □
```

Users can become confused by the fact that although they can access files through commands that they start, the **lp** command cannot access the same files. The reason is that the interface script started by the scheduler must access these files, and the owner of the interface script process is the **lp** account. You wouldn't want the interface script or the scheduler, **lpsched**, to have superuser privileges, or any file in the system could be printed out.

Monitoring the LP System

The LP system stores current status information in several files in the **/usr/spool/lp** directory. These files hold a record of unfulfilled requests, whether a printer is accepting requests or is enabled. The current state of the LP scheduler can also be ascertained by examining a file in this directory.

But these status files from the LP system are not designed to be humanly readable. Instead, you must use the **lpstat** command, which will select portions of these files for your perusal. Any user may use the **lpstat** command to obtain the same information.

When used without options the **lpstat** command reports on the status of any output request for the user that initiated the command. Jobs that are in the process of being printed will be followed by the word "on" and the name of the printer (Figure 6.30).

Figure 6.30 Using **lpstat** without options.

```
$ lpstat
nec-993              rik              42420     Oct 22 15:31 on nec
nec-994              rik              59686     Oct 22 15:32
$ □
```

In Figure 6.30 the request **nec-993** is currently being printed "on nec," and request **nec-994** is waiting in the queue. The third column shows the length of the file for this job, and the fourth column gives the date the request was submitted.

The **lpstat** command offers quite an array of options (10) that control its output. Some options select an aspect of the LP system to report on. Two options produced reports that are identical to a combination of other options. Table 6.4 summarizes these options and provides mnemonics for remembering what the option keys stand for.

TABLE 6.4 lpstat COMMAND OPTIONS

—**a**	accepting requests, a list of all printers and whether they are accepting or rejecting requests;
—**c**	class names, and a list of each class's members;
—**d**	default printer name;
—**o**	output requests, a list of all pending output requests, including those currently being printed; you can limit the list of requests to particular printers, class names, or request-ids by including the printer or class name or request-id after the key letter; —**onec** limits the output to requests for the destination *nec*;
—**p**	printer, a list of printers, whether they are idle or busy, and enabled or disabled; the report may be limited by including a list of printer names after the option.
—**r**	running, is the scheduler currently running or not;
—**s**	system default and device information, this option produces the same results as combining the —**d** and —**v** options;
—**t**	total report, print all **lp** status information; you can get the same report by using options —**r** —**d** —**v** —**a** —**p** —**o**;
—**u**	user requests, like the —**o** option for users only;
—**v**	device (remember the "v" in device), the name of the device file for each printer or just the printers that follow the option letter.

The **a, c, o, p, u**, and **v** options can be followed by a list. If you only have one item in the list, simply follow the keyletter immediately with the item. When you have several items in the list, follow the option letter by a doubly quoted list of names, separated by commas, for example, —**p**"**nec, draft**." Using any of these options without a list defaults to all the information relevant to the option.

The list of options for **lpstat** is long and overlapping. We personally recommend that you remember only two options. The −**o** option reports on the current list of output requests. You can use this option to determine what request is currently being printed if it needs to be canceled. (We'll talk about canceling jobs in the next section.)

The −**t** option shows you everything at once. When you are having problems with the LP system, you get a rundown on the entire system—whether the scheduler is running, the name of the default device, the acceptance and enable/disable status for printers, and the requests waiting in the queue. You get all the status information at once without having to remember the option letters— useful for debugging the system.

Canceling Print Requests

The LP system allows any user to cancel a print request. Any user who notices that the printer is outputting blank pages, or that the print head is stuck over at the right margin (no carriage returns), can stop that request from being printed. In order to cancel the offending print job, the user needs to get the request id from **lpstat**.

Figure 6.31 Canceling a print request.

a. Getting the request id:

```
$ lpstat -onec
nec-986          rik          1302   Oct 18 12:56 on nec
$ □
```

b. Use the command **cancel** and the request id to cancel the job:

```
$ cancel nec-986
request "nec-986" canceled
$ □
```

When a request is canceled by any user other than the user that made the request, the LP system sends mail to the user telling the user which request was canceled. The user canceling the request may also want to send mail to the user, explaining the reason for canceling the print job.

A print request may be removed from a printer's queue before printing begins. The syntax is exactly the same as in Figure 6.31.

Enabling/Disabling Printers

Any user may **enable** or **disable** a printer. You should disable a printer when a printer will not be functioning for some length of time. Don't disable a printer simply to change the paper or ribbon. To change the paper or ribbon, simply set the printer off-line (sometimes called local mode) while servicing the printer. Why not just disable and reenable the printer?

When a destination is reenabled, the LP scheduler will restart the request that it was printing from the beginning. If all you have done is load more paper, and the printing stopped at the end of the second-to-last page of a long print job, you don't want to start over from the beginning. You would be better off to set the printer off-line while adding paper. Most printers will use their buffer-full handshaking to stop the computer from sending data, so no information will be lost.

With that in mind, we will explain how to **disable** a printer. The **disable** command must be followed by the name of one (or more) printer destinations (Figure 6.32a). Optionally, you can supply a reason for disabling the printer, for example "Printer being repaired." The reason follows the −**r** option and appears in quotes before the destination(s) (Figure 6.32b).

Figure 6.32 Using the **disable** command.

a. The basic request:

```
$ disable nec
printer "nec" now disabled
$ □
```

b. Including a reason:

```
$ disable -r"Being repaired" nec
printer "nec" now disabled
$ lpstat -pnec
printer nec disabled since Dec  4 14:54 -
    Being repaired
$ □
```

c. Disabling and canceling with the same command:

```
$ disable -c -r"Being replaced" nec
printer "nec" now disabled
$ □
```

d. Enabling a printer:

```
$ enable nec
printer "nec" now enabled
$ □
```

The **disable** command will also cancel *all* pending request for a printer if the −**c** option is used. While this may seem handy, a better policy is to move the requests with **lpmove** rather than canceling them, which loses print jobs (see the next section).

The **enable** command was introduced when we discussed adding a new printer. The **enable** command when used without options (Figure 6.32d) simply allows the scheduler, **lpsched**, to start an interface script if there are any requests waiting in the queue.

A possibly undesirable effect of having commands like **disable** and **cancel** around is that someone can disable a printer or cancel a request as a prank, to be annoying, or simply out of ignorance. For these reasons, you may wish to limit access to these commands to system administrators. You can limit the use of these commands to an administrative group by changing the mode and group ownership of **cancel** and **disable** (Figure 6.33).

Figure 6.33 Limiting use of **cancel** and **disable** commands to an administrative group.

```
# chgrp admin /usr/bin/disable /usr/bin/cancel
# chmod 4710 /usr/bin/disable /usr/bin/cancel
# ls -l /usr/bin/disable /usr/bin/cancel
-rws--x---  1 lp      admin     24544 May 16  1985 /usr/bin/cancel
-rws--x---  1 lp      admin     24052 May 16  1985 /usr/bin/disable
# □
```

After changing group ownership and removing the set-group-id bit, both commands will still work as expected, for members of the **admin** group and the superuser. (The **s** in the permissions for owner column means that these programs are set-user-id. Since they are owned by **lp**, they have **lp**'s access privileges.)

Accepting and Rejecting Requests

Where **enable/disable** control the scheduler, the **accept/reject** commands work with the **lp** command. You allow a destination to accept printing requests when adding a printer. Normally, you'll never change the acceptance status. However, if you decide to remove a printer (destination), you may want to stop the **lp** command from adding new requests to this printer's queue with **reject**.

The **reject** command takes the name of a destination (printer) as an argument. Optionally, you can add a reason by preceding the destination with the keyletters −**r** and the reason in double quotes (Figure 6.34a).

Figure 6.34 Using the **reject** command.

a. Including the reason why the destination is not accepting requests:

```
# /usr/lib/reject -r"Please use laser" draft
# □
```

b. What a user sees when a destination is rejecting requests:

```
$ lp -ddraft let1112
lp: can't accept requests for destination "draft" -
    Please use laser
$ □
```

Instead of giving a reason in our example, we provide a helpful suggestion to users accustomed to using the printer draft—use the printer "laser" instead. Using the reason to explain the transition makes life easier for you and your users.

Moving Requests

When you are retiring an old or broken printer and bringing a new printer on-line, you may wish to transfer accumulated requests from the old printer to the new one. Another reason for moving requests is to distribute the work evenly between two equivalent printers. The **/usr/lib/lpmove** command changes the appropriate files in the LP system to move requests between queues.

Only the LP administrator or the superuser can use the **lpmove** command. The **lpsched** program must be halted (with **lpshut**) before you can move requests. The **lpmove** command works two ways—a list of requests can be moved to a different destination, or all requests can be moved from one destination to another. When all requests are moved, the **lpmove** command also sets the source destination to *reject* any new requests, carrying out two actions at once. Unfortunately, you don't have the opportunity to add the reason for rejecting requests unless you use the **reject** command before moving requests.

Figure 6.35 Moving requests from one destination to another.

a. Moving a list of requests:

```
# /usr/lib/lpshut
# /usr/lib/lpmove draft-1011 draft-1012 laser
total of 2 requests moved to laser
# /usr/lib/lpsched
# □
```

b. Moving all requests and setting the source to reject requests:

```
# /usr/lib/lpshut
# /usr/lib/lpmove draft laser
destination draft not accepting requests
move in progress ...
total of 3 requests moved from draft to laser
# /usr/lib/lpsched
# □
```

Checking the Logfile for Other Problems

The LP scheduler is a daemon program—it is designed to run unattended and not connected to any terminal. For this reason, the scheduler, **lpsched**, sends its error output to a file named **/usr/spool/lp/log** instead of to a terminal. Each time the scheduler is started, the current **log** file is moved (renamed) to **oldlog** in the same directory, so you have at least two logfiles around at any time.

You will seldom have need to examine the **log** file when the scheduler is working correctly. Only the date when the scheduler was started (and the date it was stopped if not running) appear in the logfile, if everything is okay.

We have found an occasional system where the scheduler program would start up, perform some activity, then exit silently after removing the lock file, **/usr/spool/lp/SCHEDLOCK**. The solution to this mystery lay in the **log** file. A system administrator, working directly with the LP system files instead of using **lpadmin** with the −**x** option, removed some files or directories. (Damage to the file system can also remove crucial files.) When the scheduler started up, it couldn't find a directory that it expected. So it wrote a message in the logfile (Figure 6.36b) and exited.

Figure 6.36 Messages in **/usr/spool/lp/log**.

a. Normal startup message:

```
$ cat /usr/spool/lp/log
***** LP LOG: Jan  3 11:04 *****
$ □
```

b. An indication of a missing directory:

```
$ cat /usr/spool/lp/log
/usr/lib/lpsched: can't open request directory request/pr1
$ □
```

For the example shown in Figure 6.36b, someone had removed the request directory for the destination "pr1" without removing the destination in the **member** directory and in the **pstatus** file. The **lpsched** program failed to find the directory and exited, preventing the LP system from working. The solution was to use the **lpadmin** command with the −**x** option to remove the "pr1" destination properly and completely.

The Mystery of the Multiple lpsched's

Sometimes a **ps** −**e** listing will reveal several **lpsched** processes. You might wonder if this is cause for alarm. The **lpsched** program creates a lock file to prevent multiple occurrences of itself from being initiated. And the **lpshut** command removes this lock file, **SCHEDLOCK** after terminating the scheduler. The **lpshut** program kills only one scheduler, the one that is started by the **/etc/rc** script or by an administrator. The process id of this scheduler is written in the **SCHEDLOCK** file (not in ASCII, unfortunately). The **lpshut** program reads this process id and kills the scheduler referred to by this id.

If you have used the **ps** command while a request is being printed, you may have noticed that there is more than one **lpsched** process. The other **lpsched** processes are all children of the original scheduler. For each printer in the process of printing a request, there is one separate scheduler process, and briefly two.

The reason for this strange behavior is fairly simple, and the technique is very ordinary in a UNIX system. The original scheduler forks a new copy of itself to handle one request for one printer. This copy, a child scheduler, will wait for the request to be printed. The copy then forks again (now there are three **lpsched** processes) and almost immediately exec's the interface script to handle the details for the request. So, while a request is being printed, there is the original **lpsched**, the child waiting, and the interface script—three different processes.

When the interface script finishes, it exits (Figure 6.37). The child scheduler gets the signal it has been waiting for, and cleans up by removing files that are no longer needed and writes to the status files. Then the child scheduler exits, and the original scheduler gets a message telling it to look for new requests to schedule. Unless other printers are currently active, there is once again only one **lpsched** process.

Figure 6.37 Multiple schedulers.

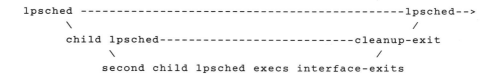

```
lpsched --------------------------------------------lpsched-->
     \                                                    /
      child lpsched--------------------------cleanup-exit
          \                                        /
            second child lpsched execs interface-exits
```

Normally, the additional **lpsched** processes will exit after the interface script completes. If an interface script is unable to complete (for example, because it can't write to the output device), both the interface script and the child **lpsched** processes will remain alive. Since these processes are waiting for an event that may never occur (writing to a nonexistent output device), you can't kill these processes (see Chapter 10—"Processes That Can't Be Killed").

Additional **lpsched** processes should be a problem only while configuring your LP system. If you find that after rebooting the same interface script has started up again, you need to correct the configuration of your LP system. Check the devices used as destinations (in the **member** directory). Each file in the **/usr/spool/lp/member** directory is named after a destination and contains the pathname of the port for that destination. You may find that someone has incorrectly configured a destination for the LP system. For example, using **/dev/tty** as the device while testing interface scripts will result in a child scheduler that can't be killed.

Some reasons for a troublesome LP system may be buried in the nonreadable status files. As a last resort, you may find it necessary to remove the files that configure your LP system, and reconfigure it from scratch. Remove the files in the **interface, member,** and **class** directories, the files in the request directories, and the destination directories that are subdirectories of **request.** Truncate the **default, outputq, pstatus,** and the **qstatus** files by copying **/dev/null** to them. Once these files and directories are removed, you have an unconfigured LP system and can start from scratch.

Summary

The LP system is well constructed and easy to configure. It can channel-print jobs among various printers. Requests for typeset-quality jobs can be satisfied by a laser printer, while accounting reports are being pounded out by a heavy-duty, wide-carriage, dot matrix printer. Users can apply emergency first aid to stop endless form feeds, they can monitor where their jobs are in the queue, and they can print multiple copies of a job.

The administrator can use the LP system to charge users for printing costs, and to add or remove printers with a minimum of fuss. Printers can be grouped in equivalent classes, allowing print requests to go to the first available printer. The LP systems works for installations of two users or 40 users. Quite a step up from sitting in front of a PC and wishing it could be printing your report while you're using the database.

QUICK REFERENCE GUIDE

Starting the scheduler—add to **/etc/rc** (run level 2 section):

```
rm -f /usr/spool/lp/SCHEDLOCK
/usr/lib/lpsched
```

Stopping the scheduler—add to **/etc/shutdown** (where other daemons are halted):

```
/usr/lib/lpshut
```

Creating a request with **lp** for the default destination:

```
$ lp filename
request id is nec-1109 (1 file)
$ □
```

Selecting a different destination and the option **p**:

```
$ lp -dlaser -op filename
request id is laser-1110 (1 file)
$ □
```

Setting a shell variable specifying the default device:

For Bourne shell:

```
$ LPDEST=laser; export LPDEST
$ □
```

For C shell:

```
% setenv LPDEST laser
% □
```

Setting up destination **new** on port **/dev/tty12** with interface **dumb**:

```
# /usr/lib/lpshut
# /usr/lib/lpadmin -pnew -v/dev/tty12 -mdumb
# /usr/lib/lpsched
# /usr/lib/accept new
# enable new
# lpstat -pnew
printer new is idle.  enabled since Oct  3 18:03
# □
```

Establishing a default destination (scheduler may be running):

```
# /usr/lib/lpadmin -dnew
# □
```

Adding the printer **new** to the class **fast**:

```
# /usr/lib/lpshut
# /usr/lib/lpadmin -pnew -cfast
# /usr/lib/lpsched
# □
```

Removing the destination **new** from the LP system:

```
# /usr/lib/lpshut
# /usr/lib/lpmove new laser
# /usr/lib/lpadmin -xnew
# /usr/lib/lpsched
# □
```

Checking status of all output requests:

```
$ lpstat -o
$ □
```

Checking status of the entire LP system:

```
$ lpstat -t
$ □
```

7

UNIX System Accounting

INTRODUCTION

Somewhere, deep inside your UNIX box, electrons dash blindly along strictly ordered pathways. Programs are executed, processes are swapped in or out, disk files are read or written, all in the blink of an eye. This activity, completely invisible except for what you see on your terminal, is summarized by system accounting. Who logged in, how much time they spent, and *what they did* can be recorded and converted into a humanly digestible form. In fact, your UNIX system may already be creating accounting reports without your even being aware of it.

Running the accounting system requires a significant share of system resources in terms of disk space and CPU usage. Most parts of the accounting system can be disabled if you desire to conserve these resources. It is important to check the configuration of your accounting system because an accounting system that is halfway activated will rapidly consume disk space with files that grow endlessly. In this chapter we describe the accounting records that your UNIX system keeps, how to activate or deactivate record keeping, and how to create and understand accounting reports. As an application of the accounting system, we will also explain how to create a billing script. You can use the billing script to charge your system's users, or you can use it to produce reports that summarize system use by department and justify expanding your data processing budget, staff, or equipment.

MOMENT-TO-MOMENT RECORDS

Since system accounting summarizes records, let's look at what these records are: the **/etc/wtmp** file, the inodes, and the **/usr/adm/pacct** file. (On Berkeley UNIX systems and pre-System V versions, the file **/usr/adm/wtmp** is used instead of **/etc/wtmp**.)

We like to call **/etc/wtmp** the "who temp" file. Although **/etc/wtmp** is not used by the **who** command (**/etc/utmp** is), the data contained can be translated into a readable form with **who**. Let's look at the last 10 lines from the "who temp" file, after processing it with **who** in Figure 7.1.

Figure 7.1 Records kept in the "who temp" file.

```
% who -a /etc/wtmp | tail
LOGIN      tty0        Dec 15 12:17   3:13      259   modem - log-in
uucpuw     tty0        Dec 15 13:02   3:13      259   modem - log-in
uucpuw     tty0        Dec 15 13:03   3:13      259   id=tty0 term=0    exit=0
getty      tty0        Dec 15 13:03   3:13      705   id=tty0
LOGIN      tty0        Dec 15 13:03   3:13      705   modem - log-in
rik        console     Dec 15 13:28    .        50   console - log-in
rik        console     Dec 15 13:50    .        50   id=  co term=0    exit=0
getty      console     Dec 15 13:50    .      1165   id=  co
LOGIN      console     Dec 15 13:50    .      1165   console - log-in
rik        console     Dec 15 16:11    .      1165   console - log-in
```

Both **/etc/wtmp** and **/etc/utmp** use the same internal format (**/usr/include/sys/acct.h**), but **/etc/utmp** contains only the current records, the information normally displayed by the **who** command. **/etc/wtmp** is the cumulative log of activities that are recorded by the **init**, **getty**, and **login** programs.

Figure 7.1 shows six columns of information. Let's focus on the last three lines, which we emboldened for emphasis, and digest the information in each line.

The third line from the bottom shows a **getty** process created by the **init** program. This **getty** is for the console (the second column), and started at 13:50 on December 15. The "lonely" dot indicates that there has been some terminal activity within the last minute. The number 1165 is the process identification number (PID) of the **getty**. Finally, there is a comment field, copied from information in the **/etc/inittab** file. In this case, the only information provided is the letters "id = co." The letters "co" are from the label for the entry in **/etc/inittab** for the console.

The second line from the bottom shows that a **login** process has replaced the **getty**, indicating that someone has entered a possible log-in name. The information in the other columns has remained pretty much the same, including the process identification number. The time difference between the second line from the bottom and the last line indicate that no one was logged in on the console for 2 ½ hours. Finally, in the last line, rik has successfully logged in at 16:11 the same afternoon. The **login** program wrote these last two lines. When rik logs out, **init** will make another entry in **/etc/wtmp** showing his name and log-out time (see Figure 7.2). Entries for a user's log-in session will always be paired, with one entry at log-in, and a second at log-out.

Figure 7.2 An entry showing the user rik logging out.

```
rik          console      Dec 15 18:11     .      1165   console - log-in
 |              |              |            |       |           |
NAME          PORT          DATE        ACTIVE    PID      COMMENTS
```

The reason for keeping the "who temp" record is twofold. All activity begun by **init** is recorded, so that the time that a user, for example, rik, is logged in can be readily determined. And by comparing the times for the last two entries for rik (last line of Figure 7.1 and line in Figure 7.2), you can see that rik was logged in for exactly 2 hours (16:11 to 18:11).

Earlier in the day, rik was logged in from 13:28 to 13:50 (the fourth and fifth lines from the end of Figure 7.1). You can perhaps begin to understand how a clever program or shell script could take the information in **/etc/wtmp** and calculate the time spent logged in by each user. And that is exactly what the **acctcon** (accounting-connections) programs do. (XENIX systems don't have the accounting summary programs, like **acctcon1**, and BSD systems use different programs.)

The file inodes provide the second type of accounting information. Please recall that the inode contains all the information about a file except the file's name and the data. The information in the inode is updated whenever the file is modified. Included in this information is the identity of the file's owner and the size of the file. The **acctdusg** program (accounting-disk usage, if you haven't already guessed) captures this information for later merging with other accounting records.

Lastly, there is process accounting information collected in **/usr/adm/pacct**. Instead of trying to pronounce "pacct," you can use the name "process accounting file." Let's look at process accounting by creating a process, **date**, then examine the record it leaves in Figure 7.3.

Figure 7.3 Completed process report from **acctcom**.

```
% date; acctcom -b | sed '8q'
Sun Dec 15 17:43:45 PST 1985
COMMAND                          START     END       REAL     CPU     MEAN
NAME         USER     TTYNAME    TIME      TIME     (SECS)  (SECS)  SIZE(K)
date         rik      console    17:43:44  17:43:44   0.55    0.53    36.31
sh           beccat   tty1       17:43:22  17:43:22   0.05    0.05    40.67
date         beccat   tty1       17:43:22  17:43:22   0.33    0.33    31.10
echo         beccat   tty1       17:42:21  17:42:21   0.33    0.32    23.47
% □
```

The **acctcom** program reveals information from the **/usr/adm/pacct** file about completed processes. On the command line in the figure, I actually created three processes, **date**, **acctcom**, and **sed**, but only the process that has completed, the **date** command, shows up in the output of **acctcom**. The —**b** option to the **acctcom** program tells it to display process accounting information started from the end of the file (backward). If you try these commands and you don't see your **date** process in the output, process accounting for your system may not be turned on. But we're getting ahead of ourselves, since we'll be discussing turning on or off process accounting later.

Information about a process collects in the **/usr/adm/pacct** file after that process has terminated. In our example, the name of the command, the log-in name of the user who executed the command, the controlling terminal, the beginning and ending time, real and CPU times, and average kilobytes of memory used are displayed. All this information, and more, collects in the process accounting file every time a process completes.

The **/usr/adm/pacct** files grow fast. Besides the records displayed by the **acctcom** command in Figure 7.3, seven additional items of information are collected about each process as it completes. The record for each process is 32 bytes long, so 32 records will use up 1024 bytes. If your UNIX system is very busy, processes are completing several times a second and the process accounting file will grow quite rapidly. The **ckpacct** script creates a new process accounting file if the old one gets very large, or halts process accounting entirely if the file system with the process accounting file runs low on space—if you have configured your system correctly.

CONFIGURING FOR SYSTEM ACCOUNTING

Now let's see how to set up the system accounting package that comes with your UNIX system.

Deciding What You Want

Now that you understand what records are kept, you are in a better position to decide whether you want all of system accounting enabled, or just parts of it. You can't turn off record keeping in the inodes. What you do have is three basic decisions to make—whether to collect records after every process terminates (in **/usr/adm/pacct**), whether to collect log-in records in **/etc/wtmp**, and whether to produce summary reports.

Keeping records of every process has its up and down sides. On the up side, you are keeping a complete record of all the activity that occurs on your system. You can track down system breakers, see what your employees (or supervisors) have been up to, or distribute the user load more evenly over several systems. With record keeping on, the **acctcom** command can display every program that has been executed by the system. And clever scripts and programs can provide summaries of the CPU time, the average amount of memory used, and the number of processes. This information, along with disk and connect time data, provides everything necessary for fair and accurate billing.

On the down side, you will be sharing your system's resources with the accounting system itself. Every time a process completes, your UNIX kernel writes a record to a disk file. Writing to a disk takes time and competes with other users for disk buffers. Then the files created by process record keeping grow quite fast, consuming possibly precious disk space. It's these consumer issues that you must balance against the possible benefits of record keeping.

Obviously, if you aren't interested in billing users, identifying major users or programs, or in using **acctcom** to track command history, you don't need to use process record keeping.

The second decision involves keeping the **/etc/wtmp** records created by the **init** and **login** processes. The "who temp" file grows continuously, although not as fast as the process accounting files, and must be processed or archived often. The "who temp" file can be used for summarizing (and billing for) the time spent logged in by different users. You can also uncover some system problems by examining this file with the **who** −**a** command. Many unsuccessful log-in attempts, the symptoms of which are many entries labeled "getty" and "LOGIN" on a particular line without any successful logins (Figure 7.4), show a badly connected modem or terminal. The same symptoms, many unsuccessful log-in attempts, may also indicate someone's attempt to break into your system by trying random user name−password combinations.

Figure 7.4 Evidence of a bad connection or a break-in attempt.

```
getty      tty0      Jul  1 19:16   .   2214   id=tty0
LOGIN      tty0      Jul  1 19:16   .   1672   modem
LOGIN      tty0      Jul  1 21:22   .   1672   id=tty0 term=14  exit=0
getty      tty0      Jul  1 21:22   .   2214   id=tty0
LOGIN      tty0      Jul  1 21:22   .   2214   modem
LOGIN      tty0      Jul  1 21:23   .   2214   id=tty0 term=14  exit=0
getty      tty0      Jul  1 21:23   .   2223   id=tty0
LOGIN      tty0      Jul  1 21:23   .   2223   modem
LOGIN      tty0      Jul  1 21:25   .   2223   id=tty0 term=14  exit=0
getty      tty0      Jul  1 21:25   .   2240   id=tty0
LOGIN      tty0      Jul  1 21:25   .   2240   modem
```

Notice how close together in time the failed log-in attempts are in Figure 7.4. Two "LOGIN" entries that appear back to back indicate that the first attempt at logging in has failed. On our system, the **login** program gives a user 1 minute to log in, then exits. (The 1-minute timeout may be longer or shorter on your system.) At the end of the minute, the System V **getty** program closes the line connection, hanging up the modem, before waiting for another possible user name. Just examining the output in Figure 7.4 doesn't tell you whether you have a potential system cracker or simply faulty equipment. You must determine that. However, if you don't keep the **/etc/wtmp** file, you won't have the record you need to spot these troubles.

The third decision concerns summarizing the accounting data that your system is generating. Remember that logging of connect time (in "who temp") and disk usage (in inodes) may occur whether or not you set up the kernel to write process records.

The reports produced by the accounting system have other uses besides billing users. You can discover faulty terminal or modem connections, accounts that aren't used, line-use "hogs," and disk-space "hogs." You can also analyze the total use of your system and answer the question: "Do we need to expand our memory, disk, or get another system?" In other words, this built-in set of programs can help you be a systems analyst. (The system activity programs, such as **sar**, which we don't discuss in this book, provide further information for system analysis.) If you elect not to summarize the data and produce reports, you must add or enable routines that archive the record files, **/etc/wtmp** and **/usr/adm/pacct**.

Keeping Log-in Records in /etc/wtmp

We recommend that you keep log-in records in the **/etc/wtmp** file. The overhead involved in using this file is minimal, and we will discuss a simple method for keeping a short archive in a later section.

If you don't want to keep log-in records in "who temp," simply remove the **/etc/wtmp** file. If the file doesn't exist, the **init** and **login** processes won't create the file, and won't complain about its absence either. (Removing the **/etc/wtmp** file works for XENIX systems also.) You should also check your **/etc/rc** file and the appropriate cron table file for entries that truncate or archive **/etc/wtmp**. If you remove **/etc/wtmp** and leave commands around that refer to it, it may be recreated. You can use the command **grep wtmp** *filename* to search for commands that may recreate the file. Figure 7.5 exhibits how this works. If you wish to prevent the recreation of **/etc/wtmp**, you must comment out any commands that refer to it.

Figure 7.5 Searching for commands that might recreate **/etc/wtmp**.

```
# grep wtmp /etc/rc /usr/lib/crontab
/etc/rc: cp /etc/wtmp /usr/adm/acct/nite/owtmp; > /etc/wtmp
# □
```

Turning Process Accounting On or Off.   The UNIX kernel collects information in the **/usr/adm/pacct** (process accounting) files. Each time a program is executed, the UNIX kernel records the information about the new program in its *process table* and within the process's memory. When the program completes, the kernel removes the entry from its process table and releases the memory allocated to the process. It's at this time that the kernel will write a process accounting record based on the information collected about the completed process.

The kernel does not write process accounting records unless given a command to do so. The **/usr/lib/acct/accton** program passes requests to start or stop writing process accounting records onto the kernel. Although you can invoke this program directly, you will normally be using scripts that execute the **accton** program.

Writing process records is often enabled after booting by the **/etc/rc** script, in the run level 2 section, when you make your system multiuser. To enable record keeping, you add the line in Figure 7.6a to the **/etc/rc** file (if it's not there already).

Figure 7.6 Starting or stopping process record keeping.

a. Command to start process record keeping in **/etc/rc**:

```
/bin/su - adm -c /usr/lib/acct/startup
```

b. Commenting out the command line:

```
# /bin/su - adm -c /usr/lib/acct/startup
```

c. Line to comment out in the **/usr/lib/acct/runacct** script:

```
# turnacct switch
```

The **startup** script adds a record to **/etc/wtmp** denoting that accounting has been started, executes **accton**, and cleans up files presumably left over from the previous day's accounting.

To keep process record keeping off, you must check that the **startup** script either doesn't appear, or is commented out, in the **/etc/rc** script. To comment out a line in a script, place a "#" before any commands on the line (as in Figure 7.6b).

If you use the **/usr/lib/acct/runacct** script (which we describe in detail later) to process your **/etc/wtmp** file, **runacct** will turn process accounting on as part of its duties. If you don't want process accounting on, and will be using **runacct**, you still need to comment out the line that appears at the beginning of the "SETUP" section of the **runacct** script (Figure 7.6c).

Enabling or Disabling Accounting Summary Scripts

The accounting summary shell scripts summarize the information collected in **/etc/wtmp** and **/usr/adm/pacct**. The accounting summary scripts are run by the **cron** daemon. So you will either be adding or "uncommenting" several lines in the cron table file to enable these scripts, or commenting these lines out to disable the creation of summary reports. There are three scripts that run the daily accounting reports: **ckpacct**, **dodisk**, and **runacct**. A fourth script, **monacct**, summarizes the daily reports, removes the daily reports, and leaves a monthly report in the **/usr/adm/acct/fiscal** directory.

The **/usr/lib/acct/ckpacct** script checks the size of the **/usr/adm/pacct** file and the amount of space available in the file system where the **/usr/adm** directory is. The **ckpacct** script renames the old process accounting file with a numeric

postfix (**/usr/adm/pacct1** for the first file, **/usr/adm/pacct2** for the next, and so on)
if the file gets larger than 500 blocks. This script also halts the writing of process
records if there are only 500 blocks left in the file system. If your kernel isn't writing process accounting records, you don't need to use the **ckpacct** script.
Otherwise, the **ckpacct** script should be run hourly, at 5 minutes after the hour
with the cron table entry:

Figure 7.7 Entries in the cron table file that run accounting scripts.

a. **ckpacct** checks the pacct file size, and for space on /**usr**:

```
5 * * * * /usr/lib/acct/ckpacct
```

b. The **dodisk** program processes file statistics before the runacct script starts:

```
0 2 * * 4 /usr/lib/acct/dodisk
```

c. **runacct** merges accounting records and creates reports:

```
0 4 * * 1-6 /usr/lib/acct/runacct 2> /usr/adm/acct/nite/fd2log
```

The **/usr/lib/acct/dodisk** script collects disk usage information from all
mounted file systems. This script must complete before the **runacct** script is begun,
so you can either time **dodisk** and arrange to have **cron** give it sufficient time to
complete before starting the **runacct** script, or can simply run **dodisk** a long time (2
hours) before **runacct**. The line in Figure 7.7b in the cron table file starts **dodisk**.
Notice that this script is being run only on Thursdays at 2:00 A.M. (We'll have
more to say about the early morning schedule shortly.) Running the **dodisk** script
once a week generally provides enough information for tallying up the (relatively)
static quantities of disk space utilized by each user.

Finally, the big guy. The **/usr/lib/acct/runacct** script takes all the information that has been collected and merges it into several different reports. (Understanding these reports is covered later.) While **runacct** runs, it archives the old
"who temp" file as **/usr/adm/acct/nite/owtmp** and removes the old process
accounting (**/usr/adm/pacct**) files after summarizing them. The **runacct** script is
run by the line in the cron table entry shown in Figure 7.7c.

This script is run Monday through Saturday at 4 A.M.. The standard error
output from the script is redirected into the file **fd2log** (cryptic for "file descriptor
2," the standard error, "log"). Other errors will be reported in a variety of files,
unfortunately. More on this later.

Of course, running accounting scripts at 2 and 4 A.M. works only if you run
your system during those hours. If not, select times when your system is generally
idle, since the summary scripts really hog your system's resources when they run.

Remember that **dodisk** must have time to complete *before* **runacct** starts. The **dodisk** script uses a **find** command to recursively descend all mounted file systems, starting with the root directory (/), to collect pathnames, and then to read the inodes to gather statistics. So **dodisk** will take even longer than a **find** command that just searches through all your mounted file systems.

Monthly reports are generated by the **monacct** (monthly accounting) script. The reports from **monacct** are the ones that we will use for billing purposes. The **monacct** script also consolidates all the daily reports generated by **runacct**, and removes the old reports. The **monacct** script is run monthly at 5:30 A.M. by the following cron table entry in Figure 7.8.

Figure 7.8 A cron table entry that runs the monthly summary script.

```
30 5 1 * * /usr/lib/acct/monacct
```

Disabling Report Summary Scripts. You disable the report summary scripts by commenting out the three cron table entries that invoke them. To comment out a cron table entry, add a "#" as the first character on the line. (You could alternatively erase these lines, but keeping them around makes it easier to reenable them if you ever decide to do so.) Besides commenting out these entries, you need to deal with the growing record keeping files that you won't be summarizing, **/etc/wtmp** and **/usr/adm/pacct**.

The **/etc/wtmp** file grows any time a user logs in or out. You can keep a 1-day archive of this file around by imitating the behavior of **runacct**. Each day, or every reboot, you need to rename the old "who temp" to be **/usr/adm/acct/nite/owtmp** and create a new **/etc/wtmp**. The commands in Figure 7.9a can be added to the run level 2 section of **/etc/rc** to do just this. If you don't reboot your system on a daily basis, you can use the same commands in a cron table file, and archive the file during the early morning hours.

Figure 7.9 Archiving accounting files.

a. Archiving and emptying **/etc/wtmp**:

```
cp /etc/wtmp /usr/adm/acct/nite/owtmp; > /etc/wtmp
```

b. Archiving and emptying the process accounting file:

```
cp /usr/adm/pacct /usr/adm/acct/nite/opacct; > /usr/adm/pacct
```

c. Archiving multiple pacct files (when **ckpacct** is used):

```
cat /usr/adm/pacct* > /usr/adm/acct/nite/opacct
rm -f /usr/adm/pacct*
/usr/lib/acct/nulladm /usr/adm/pacct
```

If you are keeping process records and not using **runacct**, you must follow a similar strategy with **/usr/adm/pacct**, that is, rename the file and create a new one (Figure 7.9b). The > notation tells the Bourne shell to copy "nothing" into **/usr/adm/pacct**, thereby truncating the file.

You may also wish to let **cron** run the **ckpacct** script to prevent your process accounting file from consuming all the free space on its file system. If you are using **ckpacct**, you will need a slightly different strategy, as **ckpacct** keeps **pacct** from growing too large by starting a new file when the old file gets large. You can use the commands in Figure 7.9c instead. Add these lines to the run level 2 section of **/etc/rc**. The **nulladm** script creates a new file with appropriate permissions (mode 664) that is owned by the accounting account, **adm**. You could simply create a new and empty file owned by **root**, but this will complicate matters later if you decide to start running the summary scripts.

Timing.   The **cron** daemon runs the accounting summary scripts, **dodisk**, **runacct**, and **monacct**, and the script that checks the size of the process accounting file, **ckpacct**. You want to check the size of the process accounting file every hour, so timing is less of an issue there. The summary scripts, however, must be run when your system is relatively inactive and operating in multiuser mode.

The suggested running times for the summary scripts are the early morning hours—2, 4 and 5 A.M.. These times work well if your system is up 24 hours a day and your system has light activity during the early morning hours. The **dodisk** and **runacct** scripts will noticeably slow system response.

However, if you don't run your system all night, accounting summaries won't be prepared. Instead, you must select a different time of day when your system will be running in multiuser mode and the usage will be light. The best alternate times are right before you shut down or immediately after startup. You'll thereby (we presume) avoid midnight, which is preferable because the **acctcon** program has problems processing the **/etc/wtmp** file when there has been a date change. We'll have more to say about the date-change problems in the next section. The other reason is that these are times when your system will be running with (presumably) light usage.

For example, on one of our UNIX systems that has two users and 34 megabytes of hard disk, we run **dodisk** at 9 P.M. and **runacct** at 9:30 P.M.. These times coincide with light usage while the system is reliably running in multiuser mode. And the system is conveniently located so that shut down and backup are accomplished later, without having to rush to go home. We are already home!

Your system probably has more users, and may have a much larger file system. You might also be rushing to leave the office late in the day, so an afternoon or evening time is not appropriate. You might find that startup time works best for you. You can even insert the **dodisk** and **runacct** commands into your **/etc/rc** script as part of your boot routines. For example, the commands in Figure 7.10 first check to see whether the accounting summary script has already run today, runs **dodisk** (only on Thursdays), then runs **runacct** after **dodisk** completes, placing both processes in the background.

Figure 7.10 Running summary scripts after reboot from **/etc/rc**.

```
if test "`date +%m%d`" = "`cat /usr/adm/acct/nite/lastdate`"
then
  echo "Accounting already run."
else
  if test `date +%w` = 4
  then
    (/usr/lib/acct/dodisk;/usr/lib/acct/runacct 2> /usr/adm/acct/nite/fd2log) &
  else
    /usr/lib/acct/runacct 2> /usr/adm/acct/nite/fd2log &
  fi
fi
```

FIXING ACCOUNTING PROBLEMS

You may encounter several different problems while using the accounting utilities. You may be immediately confronted with file ownership and permissions problems. Adjusting file ownership and permissions is straightforward.

Second, processing the **/etc/wtmp** file may produce some warnings mailed to **root**. The "who temp" file contains information collected by **/etc/init** and **/bin/login** and is used by accounting scripts primarily for calculating connect time (the length of time a user is logged in). Unfortunately, date changes confuse the program that processes the "who temp" file. The **runacct** script will send mail to **root** and **adm** complaining of "bad times" after any date change since the last time accounting was run. We haven't learned how to fix the "who temp" file, but we can tell you how to minimize the problem and how to stop **runacct** from sending mail.

Third, the **runacct** script sends its messages far and wide. The **runacct** script is perhaps the best-commented long Bourne shell script we have seen. Its main problem is that it will send error messages to different destinations, depending on where the error occurred. We'll show you how to uncover what went wrong with **runacct**. We will also describe how to restart **runacct**.

The fourth problem occurs when you remove account entries from the **/etc/passwd** file. The **/usr/adm/acct/sum/tacct***DD* files and the summary "total accounting" (tacct) files may contain lines labeled with the impossible user id of 65535. These lines refer to user accounts recently removed from the password file. The script that we provide for billing will ignore these entries. And if you follow our suggestions for deactivating accounts in Chapter 2, you won't have these problems.

Finally, mail may be sent to the **root** and **adm** accounts when the "holidays" file needs updating. The holidays file defines what part of each day is considered "prime time." It also defines what days are "prime" days, and what days are "nonprime." The idea is that you want to encourage use of your UNIX system when it is usually not busy, like Saturday night, by charging lower, non-prime-time fees.

Adjusting File Permissions

Like other UNIX utilities, the accounting utilities require that file ownership and permissions be correct. The **adm** administrative account owns the accounting programs and scripts, with the exception of the **/usr/lib/acct/accton** program. (The **accton** program must be owned by the **root** account and set-user-id.) The accounting programs and scripts reside in the **/usr/lib/acct** directory. You can check the ownership and permissions of these files with the command in Figure 7.11. If you don't find these commands, then either your system doesn't have the accounting utilities or you haven't installed them yet. System V.2 comes unbundled, and you may not have purchased the accounting utilities. XENIX System V does not have the programs and scripts necessary to summarize accounting reports.

Figure 7.11 Permissions for files in the **/usr/lib/acct** directory.

a. Command to check file permissions:

```
# ls -l /usr/lib/acct
```

b. Correct permissions and ownership for **accton**:

```
# ls -l /usr/lib/acct/accton
-rws--x--- 1 root     adm      14628 Mar 19 08:11 /usr/lib/acct/accton*
# □
```

The accounting programs and shell scripts should have the permissions 755, that is, all permissions for owner and read and execute permissions for all others. Be certain that the directory itself is write protected from others! You particularly want to deny write permissions for others on these files to prevent tampering by users trying to avoid charges. Allowing execute permission for all has little negative effect since only the **accton** program is set-user-id and all other accounting files are protected against writing by others. As for the **acctcon** program, we recommend that the group owner of the file be changed to **adm**, and the permissions for the file be 710, that is, no permissions for others. Processes owned by the **adm** account will be able to execute the **accton** program, and ordinary users will not. Correct permissions and ownership for **accton** are shown in Figure 7.11b.

The **/etc/wtmp** file must also be owned by **adm**. For example, if **/etc/wtmp** is owned by the **root** account, you will see the message (in Figure 7.12a) during startup.

Figure 7.12 Correct permissions for **/etc/wtmp**.

a. Error message is "who temp" not owned by **adm**:

```
/usr/lib/acct/startup: /etc/wtmp: Permission denied
```

b. Correcting ownership of /**etc**/**wtmp**:

```
# chown adm /etc/wtmp
```

Avoid this message by correcting the ownership (if necessary) of the "who temp" file (see Figure 7.12b). The accounting programs and scripts use other files during their execution. If you receive a "Permission denied" or "cannot create" message while running an accounting utility, change the ownership of the file mentioned in the error message to **adm**.

The remainder of the accounting files live in four different directories. The process accounting files (**pacct**) are in the **/usr/adm** directory. All process accounting files, and the directory itself, must be owned by **adm**. Temporary process accounting files may have been left in the **/usr/adm** directory by unsuccessful accounting summary runs. These temporary files will contain the name "pacct," for example, **Spacct1.0105**. The date that these files were created makes up the last part of the filenames. Restarting the **runacct** script may process these files. If these temporary files are older than one month, you may remove them.

The other three directories that hold accounting files are subdirectories of **/usr/adm/acct** and are named **nite**, **sum**, and **fiscal**. The **nite** directory contains the files used by **runacct** during its nightly (or daily) run. The **sum** directory contains the summary reports created by each day's **runacct**, and the **fiscal** directory contains the monthly summaries created by **monacct**. All the files in these three directories should be owned by the **adm** account, so you can use a "shotgun" approach, working as the superuser, as in Figure 7.13.

Figure 7.13 Clearing up permission problems.

```
# cd /usr/adm/acct
# chown adm sum/* nite/* fiscal/*
# □
```

Permissions on these files and directories should be 755, that is, writing denied for group and others.

Figure 7.14 Accounting directory hierarchy.

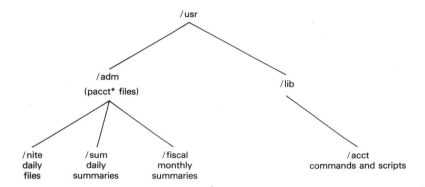

Problems with /etc/wtmp: bad times

The **acctcon1** program has an unfortunate sensitivity to date changes. If your system runs 24 hours a day, and you make only minor date changes, you will not encounter this problem. However, users of microcomputers often find running the system 24 hours a day to be impractical, since the only resources likely to be consumed during the wee hours are electricity and the lifespan of the hard disk.

What happens is that the **acctcon1** program stumbles after date changes and fails to collect connect times. Instead, the **acctcon1** program outputs error messages that are mailed to **adm** and **root** by the **runacct** script. An example of these errors received in **adm**'s mail appears in Figure 7.15.

Figure 7.15 Mail about bad times problem with **/etc/wtmp**.

```
Mon Jan  6 11:58:40 PST 1986
acctcon1: bad times: old: Tue Jan  7 00:57:14 1986
new: Mon Jan  6 11:57:59 1986
acctcon1: bad times: old: Tue Jan  7 00:57:14 1986
new: Mon Jan  6 11:57:59 1986
acctcon1: bad times: old: Tue Jan  7 00:57:14 1986
new: Mon Jan  6 11:57:59 1986
```

The **/usr/lib/acct/wtmpfix** program is supposed to adjust the "who temp" file and correct for date changes. However, date changes beyond some yet-to-be-determined limit, foil **wtmpfix**. A solution to this problem is to delete records that were written between the last time **runacct** was run and the date change. The side effects result in the loss of connect time information between the last accounting run and the date change that most likely occurred during the next day's startup. The script in Figure 7.16 depicts the scenario where the utility **fwtmp** is used to convert the "who temp" file to an editable format. Then lines are removed up until the "new date" entry.

Figure 7.16 Removing lines prior to date change in "who temp."

```
# cd /usr/adm/acct/nite
# fwtmp < /etc/wtmp ¦ sed '1,/new date/d' ¦ fwtmp -ic > xwtmp
# if test $? = 0
> then cp xwtmp /etc/wtmp; rm xwtmp
> fi
# □
```

On the successful completion of the pipeline, the "fixed" version of "who temp" replaces the old copy. Of course, you must use this script *before* using **runacct**. You could also include these lines in the "SETUP" section of the **runacct** script.

Another approach to the "bad times" problem is to run accounting right before shut down or immediately after startup. Using the **runacct** script at these times minimizes the number of entries with "bad times." The **root** and **adm** accounts will still get mail from the **runacct** script, however, until you edit the script, find the "WTMPFIX" section, and comment out the line where the file **log** gets mailed to the **root** and **adm** accounts.

RUNNING THE runacct SCRIPT

The **runacct** script processes files that are often very large. The procedure involves several passes through some files and consumes considerable system resources while it is taking place. That's why the **runacct** script is normally run early in the morning when it can take over the machine and not disturb anyone.

The **runacct** script is divided into different stages, or *states*. The states allow you to restart the **runacct** script where it stopped, without having to rerun the entire script. The **runacct** script won't halt itself after finishing the "WTMPFIX" state, but could be stopped by a system crash, or simply by an impatient superuser who killed the script. You can restart the **runacct** script by specifying the day's date in month/day format, as in Figure 7.17. The date that you use should be for the day that the **runacct** script failed.

Figure 7.17 Restarting the **runacct** script for October 27.

```
# runacct 1027
```

If the **runacct** script has completed the "SETUP" stage, the necessary data files have been renamed with the day's date in *MMDD* format appended. However, if the **runacct** script was aborted during "SETUP," you may need to perform the setup yourself and restart the **runacct** script in the next state, WTMPFIX, as in Figure 7.18.

Figure 7.18 Restarting the **runacct** script at state WTMPFIX.

```
# runacct 0514 WTMPFIX
```

The **runacct** script suggests that you not restart the script in the "SETUP" state, but perform the setup "manually." The setup procedure involves three steps. The example in Figure 7.19 assumes that today is May 14.

Figure 7.19 "Manual" setup for the **runacct** script.

a. Move all "pacct" files to temporary names, as in:

```
# cd /usr/adm
# mv pacct1 Spacct1.0514
# mv pacct2 Spacct2.0514
# □
```

b. Copy "who temp," make a runacct entry, and truncate "who temp":

```
# cd /usr/adm/acct/nite
# cp /etc/wtmp wtmp0514
# /usr/lib/acct/acctwtmp "runacct" >> wtmp0514
# /usr/lib/acct/nulladm /etc/wtmp
# □
```

c. Remove lock files (in case they exist):

```
# rm -f lock*
# □
```

When the **runacct** script encounters problems, it sends messages flying in several directions. The date and a message are sent to the console, and the same message is mailed to both the **root** and **adm** accounts. The message sent most often doesn't describe the error. Instead it says to look in the **active***MMDD* file, which is in the **/usr/adm/acct/nite** directory (bureaucracy in the UNIX system).

The **/usr/adm/acct/nite/active** file contains a running account of the **runacct** script's progress. Even on a successful run, warnings may appear here. When the **runacct** script aborts itself, it moves the **active** file to **active***MMDD*, and appends a message describing the problem. Sometimes, the **active***MMDD* file will direct you to another file. For example, problems with the "who temp" file detected by **wtmpfix** will appear in **wtmperror***MMDD*.

Figure 7.20 Contents of an **active** file for a normal **runacct** run.

```
# cat /usr/adm/acct/nite/active
Sat May 17 14:25:11 PDT 1986
-rw-rw-r--   1 adm        adm           972 May 17 14:25 /etc/wtmp
-rw-rw-r--   1 adm        adm             0 May 16 12:13 fee
-rw-rw-r--   1 adm        adm         10880 May 17 14:25 pacct
files setups complete
wtmp processing complete
connect acctg complete
process acctg complete for /usr/adm/Spacct1.0517
all process actg complete for 0517
tacct merge to create daytacct complete
no fees
no disk records
updated sum/tacct
command summaries complete
system accounting completed at Sat May 17 14:29:04 PDT 1986
updated sum/tacct
#  □
```

runacct Script States and Error Messages.　　Tables 7.1 and 7.2 list the possible states that the **runacct** script enters, and where it sends messages. The label "<pre>" used in Table 7.1 stands for pre-state, the section of the **runacct** script used for argument and other checks, before entering any of the 11 states depicted in Table 7.2. The label "<wrong>" also does not represent a state, but rather, that somehow something other than one of the correct states was written in the statefile, **/usr/adm/acct/nite/statefile**.

TABLE 7.1 PRELIMINARY STATE AND ERROR MESSAGES FROM THE **runacct** SCRIPT

STATE	PROGRAM	FATAL?	ERROR MESSAGE	DESTINATIONS
<pre>	runacct	yes	* 2 CRONS or ACCT PROBLEMS * ERROR: locks found, run aborted	console, mail, active
<pre>	runacct	yes	runacct: Insufficient space in /usr (nnn blks); Terminating procedure	console, mail, active
<pre>	runacct	yes	SE message; ERROR: acctg already run for `date`: check lastdate	console, mail, activeMMDD
<pre>	runacct	no	* SYSTEM ACCOUNTING STARTED *	console
<pre>	runacct	no	restarting acctg for `date` at STATE * SYSTEM ACCOUNTING RESTARTED *	active, console
<pre>	runacct	no	restarting acctg for `date` at state (argument $2) previous state was STATE	active
<pre>	runacct	yes	SE message; Error: runacct called with invalid arguments	console, mail, activeMMDD

TABLE 7.2 STATES AND ERROR MESSAGES FROM THE **runacct** SCRIPT

STATE	PROGRAM	FATAL?	ERROR MESSAGE	DESTINATIONS
SETUP	runacct	no	`ls -l fee pacct* /etc/wtmp`	active

SETUP	runacct	yes	SE message;
			`ERROR: turnacct switch`
			`  returned rc=error`
				console, mail,
				activeMMDD

SETUP	runacct	yes	SE message;
			`ERROR: SpacctMMDD already`
			`  exists`
			`file setups probably`
			`  already run`
				activeMMDD

SETUP	runacct	yes	SE message;
			`ERROR: wtmpMMDD already`
			`  exists:`
			`run setup manually`
				console, mail,
				activeMMDD

WTMPFIX	wtmpfix	yes	SE message;
			`ERROR: wtmpfix errors see`
			`  wtmperrorMMDD`
				activeMMDD,
				wtmperrorMMDD

WTMPFIX	wtmpfix	no	`wtmp processing complete`	active
CONNECT1	acctcon1	no	SE message; `(errors from acctcon1 log)`	console, mail, activeMMDD
CONNECT2	acctcon2	no	`connect acctg complete`	active
PROCESS	runacct	no	`WARNING: accounting already` `  run for pacctN`	active
PROCESS	acctprc1 acctprc2	no	`process acctg complete for` `SpacctNMMDD`	active
PROCESS	runacct	no	`all process actg complete` `  for date`	active
MERGE	acctmerg	no	`tacct merge to create` `  dayacct complete`	active
FEES	acctmerg	no	`merged fees OR no fees`	active
DISK	acctmerg	no	`merged disk records OR` `  no disk records`	active
MERGETACCT	acctmerg	no	`WARNING: recreating` `  sum/tacct`	active
MERGETACCT	acctmerg	no	`updated sum/tacct`	active
CMS	runacct	no	`WARNING: recreating sum/cms`	active
CMS	acctcms	no	`command summaries complete`	active
CLEANUP	runacct	no	`system accounting completed` `  at 'date'`	active
CLEANUP	runacct	no	`*SYSTEM ACCOUNTING COMPLETED*`	console

<wrong>	runacct	yes	SE message;
			`ERROR: invalid state,`
			`  check STATE`
				console, mail,
				activeMMDD

Table 7.3 provides a summary of the various message destinations used by
runacct.

TABLE 7.3 MESSAGE DESTINATIONS USED BY THE **runacct** SCRIPT

Destination	Description
console	The **/dev/console** device
mail	message mailed to **root** and **adm** accounts
active	the file **/usr/adm/acct/nite/active**
activeMMDD	the file **/usr/adm/acct/nite/active**_MMDD_
wtmperrorMMDD	the file **/usr/adm/acct/nite/wtmperror**_MMDD_
STATE	current state in **/usr/adm/acct/nite/statefile**
fd2log	any other error messages

The abbreviation _MMDD_ stands for the month and day, such as 0514 for May 14. For example, a fatal error during the SETUP process on May 14 would create the file **active0514** containing the error message. The abbreviation "SE message" stands for the standard error message, or

```
******** ACCT ERRORS : see  active0514 *********
```

Generally, if anything goes awry, the "standard error" message will be displayed on the console, and will also be mailed to the **root** and **adm** accounts. When you get such a message, your duty is to look in the **active**_MMDD_ file and puzzle out what has happened. You can use the information in Table 7.1 and 7.2 to discover during which state the problem occurred, or refer to the **runacct** script itself. If the problem is a corrupted file, you may be able to edit the file if it's **/etc/wtmp**. Use the commands that convert the "who temp" file into a readable format, as shown in the pipeline in Figure 7.16. Since the process accounting files and the disk usage files cannot be converted for editing, you will need to remove them if they have been corrupted.

Updating Your Holidays File

A program started from the **runacct** script, **acctcon1**, will send mail to the **root** and **adm** accounts when the **/usr/lib/acct/holidays** file gets out of date. The holidays file contains a list of holidays (not surprisingly) and provides the accounting system with the distinction between prime and nonprime time. Prime time is assumed to be the period when your system is most active, that is, workdays. Saturdays and Sundays are always nonprime times for the accounting system, as are any holidays that you list. The holidays file is out of date after the last holiday listed has passed or the year has changed.

The holidays files contains three types of entries: comments, the year and prime-time period, and a list of holidays. Figure 7.21 shows an example **/usr/lib/acct/holidays** file.

Figure 7.21 Example **/usr/lib/acct/holidays** file for 1988.

```
* Prime/Nonprime Table for UNIX Accounting System
*
* Curr           Prime              Non-Prime
* Year           Start              Start
  1988           0830               1700
*
* Day of         Calendar           Company
* Year           Date               Holiday
*
     1           Jan 1              New Year's
    20           Jan 20             Martin Luther King Day
    46           Feb 15             President's Day
   143           May 30             Memorial Day
   186           Jul 4              Indep. Day
   248           Sep 5              Labor Day
   329           Nov 24             Thanksgiving
   330           Nov 25             Friday after
   360           Dec 25             Christmas
   361           Dec 26             Day after Christmas
```

Any line in the holidays file that begins with an asterisk (*) is a comment. The first noncomment line must specify the current year (as four digits) and the beginning and end of prime time, also as four digits each. The concept of prime and nonprime times only affects the way that the accounting programs process the accounting records. Generally, you will use the "official" starting and ending workday at your installation.

Following your definition of prime—nonprime, you can list company holidays. The first number in each line is the day of year, or Julian date. Many desk calendars contain the day of the year on each page and are a great help in creating this list. The rest of the line contains comments that serve to make the file understandable to humans. If you list too many holidays, the **acctcon1** program will complain and you will need to shorten your list. The exact definition of "too many" will vary, so we can't be more explicit. You are probably safe with fewer than 10 or 15 holidays. If you want to add more holidays, just edit the holidays file each month.

ANALYZING ACCOUNTING REPORTS

Hopefully, by now, you have coaxed some activity out of your accounting package. Or perhaps you're still deciding if it's worth the bother. Your accounting reports are the fruits of accounting, and if you don't know what to do with them, or never use them, you should turn accounting off and leave it off.

We will describe three benefits of accounting—the **acctcom** program, the daily accounting report and a method for billing users using the monthly report.

Using the acctcom Program

Back at the beginning of this chapter, we showed you one way to use the process accounting records. The **acctcom** command produces reports based on information about all the processes that have completed since the **runacct** script last ran or your process accounting files were removed. For XENIX users, the **acctcom** program is the only way to report on process accounting files. The **runacct** script and its supporting programs are also not a part of the most recent Berkeley distribution.

Well, we mentioned that you could uncover incredible things about the doings of your co-users. It's true. For instance, you might want to know what your boss has been doing the last hour. The **acctcom** in Figure 7.22 displays all the processes that have completed for the user 'boss' after 3 o'clock.

Figure 7.22 An audit trail of your boss's activities.

```
$ acctcom -s 15:00 -u boss -h

END AFTER: Tue May 27 15:00:00 1986
COMMAND                          START     END         REAL      CPU       HOG
NAME            USER    TTYNAME  TIME      TIME        (SECS)    (SECS)    FACTOR
nroff           boss    tty1     14:58:19  15:04:57    398.27    356.83    0.90
vi              boss    tty1     15:05:25  15:10:52    327.07     43.93    0.13
pwd             boss    tty1     15:12:11  15:12:11      0.77      0.38    0.50
cat             boss    tty1     15:12:07  15:12:28     21.45      9.32    0.43
lp              boss    tty1     15:12:07  15:12:29     22.40      4.33    0.19
$ □
```

The −**s** option selects processes completing at or after 15:00. Please notice that the **acctcom** command expects the time in 24-hour notation (typical for UNIX commands), with a colon between the hour and the minutes. The −**u** option specifies the user in the **/etc/passwd** file to get the user id. The −**h** flag replaces the report on the mean memory sizes with the *hog factor*.

The hog factor measures how much of the CPU's time was consumed by this process. When you are running your system in single-user level, with no background processes, the hog factor is 1. You're getting it all. In a multiuser run level, users share the CPU. Programs that require a lot of user interaction, like the shell or an editor, have very low hog factors. The accounting commands and **nroff** have high hog factors. Games involving volumes of display output, like **aliens**, are the biggest hogs. When a running program has a high hog factor, it's literally hogging the system, and the time between entering a command and getting a response increases.

You can use the **acctcom** command to pick out the programs that have high hog factors with the command shown in Figure 7.23. Hog factors range from 0 to 1.0.

Figure 7.23 Picking out the hogs.

```
$ acctcom -H .5 -h

COMMAND                          START     END         REAL      CPU        HOG
NAME           USER    TTYNAME   TIME      TIME        (SECS)    (SECS)     FACTOR
rm             adm     console   14:40:44  14:40:44    0.22      0.22       1.00
echo           root    console   14:40:44  14:40:44    0.32      0.18       0.58
cron           root    console   14:41:00  14:41:00    0.05      0.05       1.00
stty           rik     console   14:41:15  14:41:15    0.97      0.58       0.60
tset           rik     console   14:41:21  14:41:23    2.05      1.33       0.65
touch          rik     console   14:41:26  14:41:27    1.07      0.63       0.59
cron           root    console   14:42:00  14:42:00    0.05      0.05       1.00
nroff          beccat  tty1      14:58:19  15:04:57    398.27    356.83     0.90
pwd            beccat  tty1      15:12:11  15:12:11    0.77      0.38       0.50
$ □
```

Notice that many of the programs shown in Figure 7.23 run for a very short time. The **rm** command, for example, completes very quickly, since all it does is make a system call. The hogs that concern you are the long-running ones, like the **nroff** process, which in Figure 7.23 ran for six minutes. As a system administrator, you can arrange for long-running programs with high hog factors to be run when the system is relatively idle. Converting your database files, running the accounting software, or doing mathematical simulations are jobs that can often wait until the evening or late at night. These jobs can be run by using the **at** command (available in System V.2), using **cron**, or simply by using **nice**.

The **nice** command allows users to decrease the priority of a process. For example, the command in Figure 7.24 runs **nroff** with the highest niceness possible, 19 (for the Bourne shell):

Figure 7.24 Being nice about **nroff**.

```
$ nice -19 nroff -ms head acct* > n.acct &
```

C shell users would enter **nice +19** followed by the program name instead of minus. Adding a lot of niceness to a hog-prone program assures that it will have a lower priority than other processes that are ready to be run. You can prove this to yourself by examining the hog factor after running **nroff** with a lot of niceness. The problem with using **nice** is that it depends on the cooperation of users. A process that runs with a lot of niceness takes longer to complete. Even if it does make everyone else happier, the user must decide to use **nice**, and not be nasty.

Daily Reports from runacct

Each time the **runacct** script runs, it leaves a report named **rprt**_MMDD_ in the **/usr/adm/acct/sum** directory. The information in the report is repeated in individual files in the **nite** directory, but these files are reused by each invocation of **runacct** script. The daily reports in **sum** are summarized by the **monacct** script and removed once a month.

TABLE 7.4 THE SIX SUBSECTIONS IN A DAILY REPORT

Subsection	Description
Changes	Each time the **init** program changes state, or a user logs in, an entry is made in the "who temp" file. Also, date changes and accounting activity (like the start of the **runacct** script) are recorded here. The changes section notes the period of time the **/etc/wtmp** file covers and the totals of each change.
Line Duration	Line duration measures the number of minutes any user logged in at each terminal line. This time is also presented as a percentage of the total time covered in the "who temp" file, the number of sessions, the number of successful log-ins, and the number of **getty** processes started.
Daily Usage	A one-line report for each user account in **/etc/passwd**. Each line summarizes information culled from the "who temp" file, disk usage reports, fees, and from the process accounting files.
Daily Commands	A report like the ones produced by the **acctcom** command for the 51 programs with the highest average memory use. (**/usr/adm/acct/nite/daycms**)
Month Commands	Similar to the daily commands report, this report provides a running total for the month. (**/usr/adm/acct/sum/cms**)
Last Login	A cumulative report giving the date of last log-in for all accounts in the **/etc/passwd** file. (**/usr/adm/acct/sum/loginlog**)

Before reading further, you should print out a daily report using **lp**, and follow along with us. (We didn't include a copy of a report because the reports are five pages or more long.) The daily report for April 3, for example, is named **/usr/adm/acct/sum/rprt0403**. Reports come preformatted by the **/usr/lib/acct/prdaily** command. We will provide excerpts from one of our system's reports.

Changes and Durations Reports. The changes section begins the daily report (see Figure 7.25). These changes are comments that have been written in the "who temp" file. Something you might find of interest here is the number of "system boots." (The first column in the changes report contains the number of entries for each category of change.) If you don't keep a log, and several people administer your system, you might be surprised to find that your system has been rebooted when you weren't around. (Reboots should always be written in your logbook.) Rebooting the system can mean that your system security has been broken. If your system comes up in single-user shell after being rebooted, anyone can have superuser privileges simply by rebooting.

Figure 7.25 The changes report.

```
from Tue Apr   1 05:52:51 1986
to   Thu Apr   3 07:07:12 1986
1       date change
1       acctg off
1       run-level S
1       system boot
1       run-level 2
1       acctg on
1       runacct
1       acctcon1
```

On the same page, the line duration report (see Figure 7.26) details the amount of time a user was logged in on each terminal line that had a **getty** running for it. This time is measured in minutes and is followed by a percentage calculated by dividing the time logged in by the total elasped time (TOTAL DURATION). The number of sessions (# SESS) are the number of times a user succeeded in logging in, and will be exactly the same as the number of times on (# ON). The last column, the number of times off (# OFF), stands for the times that the **getty** program timed out after collecting some characters (but not receiving a RETURN), **login** failed to match the name and password, or a user logged out. If the number of times off greatly exceeds the number of times on for a terminal line, this terminal line probably has noise problems or bad connections. It's not uncommon for the number of times off to times on ratio to be 3 or 4 to 1. A ratio of 10 to 1 is a sure indication of trouble. Check your terminal connections. A large ratio of times off to on can also indicate someone trying to break into your system by randomly trying name and password combinations.

Figure 7.26 Duration report from the **runacct** script.

```
TOTAL DURATION IS 2954 MINUTES
LINE      MINUTES PERCENT # SESS   # ON    # OFF
tty1      1418    48      3        3       9
tty0      8       0       4        4       11
console   1063    36      4        4       9
TOTALS    2489    --      11       11      29
```

Daily Usage Report.   The daily usage report (Figure 7.27) contains information from the "who temp" file about the total connect time and number of sessions for each user. The other information in this report comes from the disk usage accounting script (**dodisk**), the fees in **/usr/adm/fees**, and the per process accounting records (**pacct** files). The total number of processes started by each user, their CPU, and average memory usage are reported. The columns prime and nonprime are based on the holidays file and divide the per process totals so that users can be rewarded for their nonprime-time system use. The information in this report will be summarized by the **monacct** script and forms the basis for billing users.

Generally, you can ignore lines for administrative accounts and focus on the lines for users' accounts. Look for users with a lot of connect time and very few processes. These users are logging in and not doing very much. If you have a limited number of ports (who doesn't?), you would be better off restricting such users' access to the system so that more-active users can log in. Idle, logged-in terminals are also a security problem. Chapter 9 provides a script for logging-out inactive users.

On the other side of the coin, you may have users with an enormous number of processes compared to other users. These users might have cute little scripts that run once a minute and display a report on system use, the time, or whether they have mail. If your system is verging on being overloaded, examine these users' processes. You can use the **acctcom -u** *username* command to uncover what these busy souls are doing. You may wish to ask these users to limit themselves to "necessary" activities, and save their frills for off-peak time.

Commands Summaries.   The next two pages contain daily and the monthly (cumulative) command reports. This information is collected from the process accounting records, listed by command (instead of by user, as in the usage report), and ordered by the third column, KCOREMIN. A KCOREMIN is the average (mean) number of kilobytes of memory used times the number of minutes the program ran, the product of the total CPU time, and the mean size in kilobytes shown in this report. The KCOREMIN provides a rule of thumb for comparing

UID	LOGIN NAME	CPU (MINS) PRIME	NPRIME	KCORE-MINS PRIME	NPRIME	CONNECT (MINS) PRIME	NPRIME	DISK BLOCKS	# OF PROCS	# OF SESS	# DISK SAMPLES	FEE
0	TOTAL	74	83	3837	3895	957	1138	25868	20938	11	15	0
0	root	15	22	502	830	42	6	1	8049	2	1	0
2	bin	0	0	0	0	0	0	8619	0	0	1	0
4	adm	2	4	48	145	0	0	2016	585	0	1	0
5	uucp	2	3	149	142	0	0	353	245	0	1	0
5	uucpuw	0	2	2	132	6	1	1	50	4	1	0
7	lp	1	0	22	5	0	0	46	68	0	1	0
112	rik	3	3	373	264	301	320	1463	30	2	1	0
113	beccat	51	50	2741	2376	608	810	12059	11911	3	1	0

Figure 7.27 Daily Usage Report on users from the **runacct** script.

programs by the amount of central processor (CPU) and memory resources used. Programs that are executed often and are at the top of the monthly command summary are good candidates for having their sticky bits set.

A program with the sticky bit set remains in memory or in swap space after it is executed, until the system is rebooted. Programs without their sticky bits are released from memory and swap space as soon as they complete. Programs that are sticky hang around, usually in swap, so that they may be restarted faster. The advantage to using sticky bits on often used programs is faster response time for starting these programs. For example, the **vi** program starts up (on our system) in 4 seconds when the sticky bit is set and 11 seconds when it's not.

The disadvantage is that you can totally fill up your swap space if you have too many sticky programs. On some systems, an editor is sticky. You don't need to make shells sticky because there will almost always be a copy of a shell already in memory. On systems where programming is a priority, the several passes of the compiler may be sticky. If you get console error messages about running out of swap space, remove the sticky bits from some of your lesser-used programs. (In Chapter 10 we go into more detail about console messages.) You can uncover files with the sticky bit set with the command in Figure 7.28.

Figure 7.28 Uncovering files with the sticky bit set.

```
# find / -perm -1000 -print
/bin/vi
/bin/as
/bin/e
/bin/edit
/bin/ex
/bin/view
/usr/lib/c2
/usr/games/robots
# chmod -t /usr/games/robots
# □
```

The **chmod** command resets the sticky bit for the file **robots**. The fast startup of the game **robots** is certainly not a priority. To make a program sticky, you use the argument **+t** instead of **−t**. Only the superuser can set the sticky bit on an executable program.

The other fruit that you can pick out of the commands summary are the hogs. As we mentioned earlier, programs that hog the CPU are best run late at night or with a lot of niceness. Educating your users to be considerate when using these programs is one approach. A more direct approach is to use the **cron** program to prevent execution of hogs (by removing execute permission with **chmod**) during peak hours and restoring permission during more appropriate times. The same approach can be used to limit access to games during work hours. Figure 7.29 shows a pair of cron table entries that control when games in the **/usr/games** directory may be accessed.

Figure 7.29 Letting **cron** open and close the game room.

```
30   08   *   *   1-5   /bin/chmod   700 /usr/games # Prevent game playing
30   17   *   *   1-5   /bin/chmod   755 /usr/games # Allow access
```

Last Login Times.   The final report, Last Login, is sorted by the least recent log-in by an account to the most recent (see Figure 7.30). Candidates for archival and removal can be picked out readily by their lack of activity. You may also discover some surprises, such as activity in an account while the user is on vacation or after the user has supposedly quit. You can change the passwords if you discover surprises for an account.

Figure 7.30 The Last Log-in report.

```
00-00-00   bin          85-11-05   uucp         86-02-21   ssa
00-00-00   check        85-11-29   uucpwiz      86-03-09   buric
00-00-00   daemon       85-12-09   mail         86-03-21   david
00-00-00   lp           85-12-24   busho        86-03-26   canyon
00-00-00   rootcsh      86-01-17   who          86-04-03   beccat
00-00-00   rose         86-01-22   zilog        86-04-03   rik
00-00-00   sys          86-01-23   adm          86-04-03   root
85-11-05   guest        86-02-09   uucpj        86-04-03   uucpuw
```

BILLING USERS

Besides using the accounting reports as a way of analyzing system use, you can use the reports as a basis for billing your users. For systems that are used exclusively within a single organization, billing users (or departments) creates an audit showing which departments make most use of the computer. And audit reports can be used to justify the existence of the computer, its staff, and any plans for expansion. If you are sharing your system, either as a personal favor or because you are actually running a time-sharing service, you will want to bill your users for the resources they are using.

We have created a shell script that uses the information gathered by the **runacct** and **monacct** scripts. Essentially, our script strips out the information contained in the Usage Report for each user, and calculates the cost of services for several categories of use. We have focused on four categories:

CPU   The total number of minutes that the central processing unit (CPU) was working for a user accurately reflects the amount of processing time consumed.

Connect The length of time that a user was logged parallels their usage of a limited resource: log-in ports and possibly modems.

Disk   The total number of disk blocks utilized by a user. Disk space is always limited, so charging for each block used encourages conservation.

Fees   Fees can be charged for any special services, such as file restores or use of a laser printer.

The first three categories deal with your system's physical boundaries. Your central processing unit gets divided between system work and your users' programs. The more CPU time a user requires, the less time is available for other users. Connect time is limited by the number of ports available. By charging users for time logged in, you encourage them not to log in unless they have work to perform. On systems where all ports are hardwired to terminals on people's desks, connect time means less, since a terminal that is dedicated to one user consumes the same amount of resources whether a **getty** process runs on it or an idle shell sits waiting.

The third category is disk usage. You have only so much free file system space to go around. Through the use of this script, you can reward the careful and prod the careless.

The **/usr/lib/acct/chargefee** script charges fees. For example, if you have just restored a file that the user **john** inadvertently erased, you could bill john for your trouble with the command in Figure 7.31.

Figure 7.31 Charging the user **john** 10 units.

```
# /usr/lib/acct/chargefee john 10
# □
```

The **chargefee** script requires two arguments: the log-in name, as found in the **/etc/passwd** file, of the user to be charged, and the number of fee units to be charged. The **chargefee** script writes entries in the **/usr/adm/fee** file. You will define what a fee unit means when you write or use a billing script.

Your minimum price establishes the fee unit. For example, if your smallest fee will be 10 cents a page for printing, your fee unit will be 10 cents. And you have just charged "john" 1 dollar for the file restore.

If you wish to charge $0.50 a page for the use of your laser printer, it would be nice if you could invoke the **/usr/lib/acct/chargefee** script in your interface script, and charge 5 units of fee per each page. But only the superuser (or the **adm** user) can execute the **chargefee** script. Instead, you must design the interface script so that it maintains an **lp**-owned file containing a list of users and their fees. **lp** ownership prevents tampering. Then you edit the **runacct** script, find the FEE section, and add the two lines in Figure 7.32 to the beginning of the section.

Figure 7.32 Adding the fees charged by the **lp** interface script.

```
xargs -11 /usr/lib/acct/chargefee < /usr/spool/lp/fees
cp /dev/null /usr/spool/lp/fees
```

The **xargs** command takes each line from the file **/usr/spool/lp/fees** and executes the **chargefee** command with the line as an argument. After **chargefee** posts all the fees to the **/usr/adm/fee** file, the file is emptied and ready to be used again. Chapter 6 contains the rest of this example for charging printing fees. You can use a similar mechanism for automating other fees. For example, you could add a fee-charging command to a script used for file restoration.

A Simple Billing Script

Our billing script is designed to extract information from the consolidated monthly report, **/usr/adm/acct/fiscal/fiscrpt*MM***, where *MM* stands for two digits representing the month. The **fiscrpt*MM*** report begins with the Usage Report, then lists command summaries for every command executed since the last time the **monacct** script was run. To make the information in **fiscrpt*MM*** available, we must strip away the parts of the report that we aren't interested in. The **sed** command makes this easy.

Figure 7.33 Trimming the monthly report so that only entries for users remain.

```
sed -n '/0       TOTAL/,/^$/p' fiscrpt04 | sed '/^$/d' > fs04
```

The first **sed** command shown in Figure 7.33 prints only the lines between the beginning of the Usage report and the first blank line following the report. The first line of the Usage report contains totals and begins with **0** *<tab>***TOTAL**. The second **sed** command strips out the blank line that remains. As we develop these scripts, we will be using intermediate files, such as **fs04**, instead of showing you the final result. We suggest that you follow our example and test each part of the billing script separately. Your UNIX system may be different than our example system, or you may make mistakes in entering commands. Either way, complete one step at a time, check it, and you will have a working billing script sooner.

The second part of our simple billing script involves processing each line and producing values for each of our four categories and a total. We have deliberately ignored the distinction between prime and nonprime time. You can edit our example and use different rates for prime and nonprime use. We have used the **awk** command for doing the processing, and the file **feescript** contains the **awk** script (Figure 7.34).

Figure 7.34 Using **awk** for totaling fees.

a. The **awk** command that uses the script **feescript**:

```
awk -f feescript fs04 > bill04
```

b. The **awk** program that computes totals using the fields in each entry:

```
BEGIN {
OFMT = "%6.2f"
OFS = "          "
cpurate = .18
conrate = .0018
diskrate = .005
fee = .1
}
{ cpu = ($3 + $4) * cpurate
  con = ($7 + $8) * conrate
  if ($12 == 0)
      disk = 0
  else
      disk = ($9 / $12) * diskrate
  fees = $13 * fee
  total = cpu + con + disk + fees
  print $2, cpu, con, disk, fees, total
}
```

c. The correspondence between the labels used by **feescript** and the fields in the Usage Report entries:

```
UID     NAME    CPU     CPU     KCORE-MINS    CONNECT (MINS) <- Report Label
                PRIME  N-PRIME  PRIME N-PRIME PRIME N-PRIME
 0      root    15      22      502   830     42    6        <- Value
$1      $2      $3      $4      $5    $6      $7    $8       <- Field no

DISK    # of    # of    DISK    FEES
BLOCKS  PROCS SESSIONS SAMPLES
 1      8049    2       1        0
$9      $10     $11     $12      $13
```

awk scripts may appear to you to be distressingly like computer programs. However, by keeping things simple, you can modify our basic **awk** script so that it suits
you better. The script begins by setting the output format (**OFMT**) to be %**6.2f**,

```
$ cat fiscrpt04
Apr 1 23:16 1986    Page 1
```

UID	LOGIN NAME	CPU (MINS)		KCORE-MINS		CONNECT (MINS)		DISK	# OF	# OF	# DISK	FEE
		PRIME	NPRIME	PRIME	NPRIME	PRIME	NPRIME	BLOCKS	PROCS	SESS	SAMPLES	
0	TOTAL	2133	2968	112244	155383	28572	84033	2008849	646323	492	1138	0
0	root	648	698	26806	28239	14351	30584	83	220988	74	83	0
2	bin	0	0	0	0	0	0	715377	0	0	83	0

```
 ... and so on, for five pages.
```

```
$ sed -n '/0    TOTAL/,/^$/p' fiscrpt04 | sed '/^$/d' > fs04
$ cat fs04
```

UID	LOGIN NAME	CPU (MINS)		KCORE-MINS		CONNECT (MINS)		DISK	# OF	# OF	# DISK	FEE
		PRIME	NPRIME	PRIME	NPRIME	PRIME	NPRIME	BLOCKS	PROCS	SESS	SAMPLES	
0	TOTAL	2133	2968	112244	155383	28572	84033	2008849	646323	492	1138	0
0	root	648	698	26806	28239	14351	30584	83	220988	74	83	0
2	bin	0	0	0	0	0	0	715377	0	0	83	0
4	adm	64	163	2073	6421	81	72	180979	16775	10	83	0
5	uucp	55	77	3429	4943	0	0	29256	6709	0	83	0
5	uucpuw	0	42	4	3001	90	63	640	1401	184	83	0
7	lp	9	9	310	322	0	0	3802	1395	0	83	0
112	rik	141	154	13669	13336	8551	23328	112155	2884	93	83	40
113	beccat	1200	1736	65305	94736	5424	29789	857944	395531	95	83	120

Figure 7.35 Files and individual commands used to create the final billing script.

meaning six digits long with two decimal places. The output field separator, **OFS**, contains a tab character and a space, so the output will appear in regular columns. The four lines that follow contain the four rates that we decided to use. We'll talk more about rates later.

The first pair of curly braces ({ }) set apart the beginning of the **awk** script. We use the part inside the first pair of curly braces to define the constants. In the second pair of curly braces, the commands process every line of the input, which will be account entries from the Usage Report (see Figure 7.34c). Essentially, we are using **awk** to perform an addition of the prime and nonprime values, then to multiply that sum by our rate. (The asterisk * stands for "multiply.")

The disk blocks represent a special case. We noticed that each user's value for the number of disk blocks was cumulative and increased each time the disk was sampled (the **dodisk** script run). So we divided the value for disk blocks (contained in column 9) by the number of disk samples (from column 12) and came up with the mean or average number of blocks used. However, if the number of samples is zero, the **awk** program would quit, because division by zero is illegal. The line beginning with *if* tests for this special case.

After calculating our four categories of fees, we add them together for a total and print the user's name followed by the results. Figure 7.35 contains an illustration showing the commands and intermediate files that we created for the purpose of the example.

```
$ awk -f feescript fs04 > bill04
$ cat bill04

TOTAL    918.18   202.69     8.83    0        1129.70
root     242.28    80.88     0.00    0         323.17
bin        0        0        43.09   0          43.09
adm       40.86     0.28     10.90   0          52.04
uucp      23.76     0         1.76   0          25.52
uucpuw     7.56     0.28      0.04   0           7.87
lp         3.24     0         0.23   0           3.47
rik       53.10    57.38      6.76   4.00       17.24
beccat   528.48    63.38     51.68  12.00      643.55
$ □
```

In Figure 7.35 we show how we have reduced five pages of the **fiscrpt04** monthly summary report to six columns of information, one line for each account. Before going any further with our discussion, we need to emphasize that although the examples worked on two different computers running different variants of System V, they may not work exactly as shown for you. Remember to take a step-at-a-time approach rather than entering the final version of our billing script and expecting it to work the first time.

Relating Addresses to Log-in Names

Now that we have usable results, what will we do with them? If you are simply creating a report for an in-house audit, you can stop here. Just take the output and add some commentary to it. However, if you wish to send bills to your users, you need to go at least one step further. We created a directory containing files with the addresses of each user and a billing template; each file is named for the user. For example, the file named "rik" follows in Figure 7.36.

Figure 7.36 An example billing template containing an address and the billing template.

```
$ cat /usr/adm/acct/address/rik
                        Rik Farrow
                        1531 Fulton
                        San Francisco, CA 94117


Our records show that your computer account has accrued the charges
that follow.  Please remit your payment within 30 days to

   Sirius Computing Services
   1 Market Plaza, Suite 1401
   San Francisco, CA 94103

logname   CPU    Connect   Disk   Fees   TOTAL <- PAY THIS AMOUNT
$ □
```

Each file contains the appropriate address, cleverly arranged so that the address will show up in the window of the envelopes that you will be using. Finally, bringing everything together, we show the final version of the billing script, without the intermediate files, that will produce individually addressed bills. The **billscript** and **feescript** files are kept in the **/usr/lib/acct** directory with other accounting commands.

Figure 7.37 Simple billing script that processes **fiscrpt**.

```
PATH=bin:/usr/bin:/usr/lib/acct
case $1 in
   [0-1][0-9]) ;;
   *) echo "Usage: billscript·MM - where MM is two digits for month"
      exit 1 ;;
esac
cd /usr/adm/acct
sed -n '/0    TOTAL/,/^$/p' fiscal/fiscrpt$1 |
sed '/^$/d' |
awk -f feescript > /tmp/bill$$
trap 'rm /tmp/bill$$; exit 0' 0 1 2 3 15
_date=`date`
```

```
cd address
for n in *
do
  echo Now processing $n
  echo $_date > $n-bill
  cat $n >> $n-bill
  grep $n /tmp/bill$$ >> $n-bill
  lp $n-bill
  mail $n < $n-bill
  rm $n-bill
done
```

Running the billing script requires that the **awk** script appears in the **/usr/lib/acct** directory and that the addresses appear in the **/usr/adm/acct/address** directory. You may, of course, change the script as well as where these directories and files will exist.

The **echo** command that sends "Now processing $n" to the standard output is helpful while debugging this script. We are assuming that you have previously tested the portions of the script that pick out the lines to process from the **fiscrpt***MM* file and the **awk** script **feescript**. It is always wise to develop shell scripts in stages and to test each section as it is completed.

Selecting Appropriate Rates.   The rates that we used in the **feescript** file are derived from the rates used by the U.C. Berkeley Computing Services for a nonstudent account on a VAX 11/780 during 1986. We actually chose their "twilight" rates, rather than prime time, because they were lower and produced more reasonable results. We suggest that you adjust the rates that you use according to the goals that you wish to accomplish through billing.

If a fair return on your investment in your UNIX system is your goal, you need to begin with a clear notion of what your total investment is. You must also decide how fast you can depreciate your hardware and software. Suppose you calculate that your total cost for your system comes to $24,000 a year. For an annual $24,000 expense, you must take in at least $2000 a month to cover your expenses.

Using a similar philosophy to set rates, you can set up an in-house accounting system. You can justify your total yearly budget by showing that the services your division offers accurately reflect what other divisions of your company require. You can also use this information to justify a larger budget or staff by showing how much UNIX services your department has provided.

Whether billing outside users, or measuring costs of inside users, some juggling of rates is necessary. We can't give you hard and fast rates good for all UNIX systems. Some UNIX systems cost less than $10,000; others start at well over $1 million. The rule of thumb that we propose is that your monthly total billing cover your monthly cost of operation and depreciation. When you adjust your rates, keep in mind the relative scarcity of resources. The central processing unit (CPU) time is the most precious commodity your system possesses, followed by disk space. You may not even use fees or charge for connect time. The decision is yours.

QUICK REFERENCE GUIDE

Files that grow:

/etc/wtmp

Log-in and log-out times, billing, connect time, and security.

/usr/adm/pacct?

Process summary records, billing, CPU and commands summary.

These files are truncated by running the accounting script **runacct**, or by using commands in **/etc/rc** or in the cron table files.

Display the record containing log-ins and log-outs:

```
# who -a /etc/wtmp
```

Display information in the process accounting records, starting at the most recent record:

```
# acctcom -b
```

Display information in the process accounting records, starting at the most recent record, for the user bob:

```
# acctcom -b -u bob
```

Line in **/etc/rc** that starts process record keeping:

```
/bin/su - adm -c /usr/lib/acct/startup
```

Entries in the **cron** table for starting the accounting scripts:

```
5 * * * * /usr/lib/acct/ckpacct
0 2 * * 4 /usr/lib/acct/dodisk
0 4 * * 1-6 /usr/lib/acct runacct 2> /usr/adm/acct/nite/fd2log
30 5 * * 30 /usr/lib/acct/monacct
```

Places to look for error messages from the **runacct** script:

> mail to **root** and **adm**;
> **/usr/adm/acct/nite/active**;
> **/usr/adm/acct/nite/activeMMDD**;
> **/usr/adm/acct/nite/wtmperrorMMDD**

Daily accounting summary reports are in **/usr/adm/sum/rprtMMDD**.

Monthly accounting summary reports are in **/usr/adm/acct/fiscal/fiscrptMM**.

The fee-charging script adds *units* of fee for a *user*. Fees are processed by the **runacct** script.

```
# /usr/lib/acct/chargefee user units
```

8

UUCP Communications

INTRODUCING THE UUCP SYSTEM

Communication is a major feature of the UNIX system. After all, this operating system was developed at Bell Laboratories, the research and development arm of what was (before divestiture) the world's largest phone company—AT&T. Most commonly this communication involves the UUCP system linking two UNIX-based computers.

The major UNIX communication program is **uucp**, which stands for UNIX-to-UNIX copy program, since it's used to copy files from one system to another. However, UNIX communications involves several more programs and many files and directories. So we'll be referring to the entire communication system as (all capitals) UUCP, to stand for "UNIX-to-UNIX communication package."

Here's a brief look at the history behind the UUCP system: In 1976 Mike Lesk at Bell Labs wrote the original UUCP system. A second improved version, known as Version 2 UUCP, was distributed with the Version 7 UNIX system. Many problems and shortcomings of the Version 2 UUCP system became apparent over the years. Finally, beginning in 1983, Peter Honeyman, David A. Nowitz, and Brian E. Redman rewrote UUCP to yield a new version popularly named after them (Honey-DanBer). However, the AT&T documentation refers to this new version as the "Basic Networking Utilities."

We'll discuss both the pre-HoneyDanBer Version 2 release of UUCP, as well as the new HoneyDanBer version throughout this chapter. But how do you determine which one you have? That's easy. Just look in your **/usr/lib/uucp** directory: if you have a file named **L.sys**, you're running the older Version 2 system, but if you have a file named **Systems**, you've got HoneyDanBer UUCP.

Now let's get down to particulars. Figure 8.1 illustrates the part of the UNIX file system hierarchy concerned with the UUCP system.

Figure 8.1 Directory and file layout for the UUCP system.

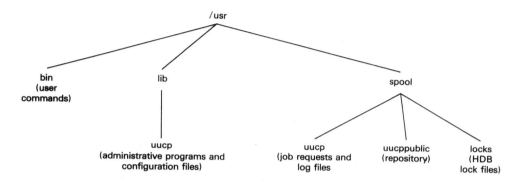

Although the UUCP system may at first glance appear formidable because there are so many components, it's really logically organized and comprehensible. Referring to Figure 8.1: Briefly, the **/usr/bin** directory houses the commands a user employs for making communication requests and checking their status; **/usr/lib/uucp** contains the UUCP administrative programs and configuration files used for setting up, running, and maintaining the communication system; the communication requests become files stored in the **/usr/spool/uucp** directory (or in subdirectories of this directory in the HoneyDanBer version) along with various logging files; **/usr/spool/uucppublic** is a common holding area for files transferred between systems; and HoneyDanBer versions generally create locks files in **/usr/spool/locks**.

In this chapter you'll first learn what the UUCP system can do for you and why it's a cost-effective approach for moderate-speed data transmission. Then we'll help orient you by describing the major UUCP programs, files, and directories and how they work together in a typical application—sending electronic mail to a neighboring site. And you'll learn a nine-step method for setting up your site to communicate with other UNIX-based systems. Finally, you'll learn about securing your UNIX system from unauthorized access through a UUCP communication link.

Although the UUCP system appears large and complex, it's really not as bad as it looks. Take heart. You can learn to set it up, operate, and maintain it. We'll provide step-by-step guidelines, examples, tips, and techniques that will make you a UUCP "guru" in short order.

Now for our disclaimer. For this discussion we assume that your UNIX system is licensed to use a binary copy of all the programs. Also, the requisite directories and data files should be installed. We're not covering UUCP source code and its installation. Those proprietary details are best left to the AT&T installation documentation. Okay, here we go ...

What Does the UUCP System Do?

The UUCP system allows remote system access, file transfer, and remote command execution over a network of UNIX systems. Table 8.1 shows a summary chart of these facilities.

TABLE 8.1 WHAT'S THE UUCP SYSTEM GOOD FOR?

- Log into a remote UNIX system with **cu**.
- Transfer files between UNIX systems with **uucp**.
- Execute commands on a remote UNIX system with **uux**.
- Support electronic mail file transfer.
- Support the Usenet network news file transfer.

Now let's examine each of these features in more detail.

Log into a Remote UNIX (or Non-UNIX) System. Use the **cu** (call UNIX) program to log in directly to a remote UNIX or even a non-UNIX system. Then you can interact with that system just as you would had you logged into one of its local terminals.

The **cu** program is closely allied with the UUCP system—it uses some of the same configuration files. If you can get **cu** working, then you know these files are configured correctly—and you're well on your way to getting the UUCP subsystem working.

And having **cu** as a tool will aid you further in bringing up UUCP. In particular, the steps for manually logging into a remote system with **cu** will provide information for instructing the UUCP system how to log into that system automatically.

Transfer Files Between Sites. You use the **uucp** command to request file transfers from your system to a remote site, from a remote system to your local site, or between two remote sites that are linked together. Furthermore, you can have the UNIX mail system notify you whether the transfer succeeded or not. Each transfer request is also known as a UUCP job request.

You can even transmit binary data with **uucp** since 8-bit data transfer is supported. Forwarding of files through machines is often difficult since each site in the chain of machines needs to use the same forwarding mechanism. It's best to use electronic mail when forwarding text files. And if you need to forward binary files, you can use specialized utilities (discussed later) to transform them into a text file for mailing, then convert them back to binary form at the destination system.

Execute Commands Remotely. You use the **uux** (UNIX to UNIX execute) command to request execution of commands on a remote system. Generally, for security reasons, the commands allowed are limited. The restricted mail command, **rmail**, is generally permitted so that remote users can receive UNIX system mail. Sometimes, a remote site might allow you to use a scarce or expensive resource, such as a laser printer.

Support Electronic Mail.   The UUCP system provides communication support for UNIX system electronic mail. The UNIX **mail** command invokes **uux** to request that **rmail** be run on the remote machine to deliver the message to the recipient's "mailbox" file.

Generally, file transfers using the UNIX mail facilities are easier to specify and offer fewer permission restrictions than do transfers with the **uucp** command. However, only text files can be handled by the UNIX mail system. Binary files (8-bit data) must be sent with **uucp**.

UUCP communication links connect thousands of UNIX system installations all over the world. Collectively, these installations are known as the UUCP network. You can send mail messages to any user on this network if you know a routing path to the user's machine and their log-in name on that machine.

Support the Usenet Network.   Usenet (short for "user's network") is the collection of UNIX installations that run the **netnews** software. Most sites in Usenet communicate via UUCP, but other networks may be involved as well.

The Usenet is a public network for the exchange of information and ideas in the form of news articles. Articles are posted to the "net" with the **netnews** software and are broadcast to subscribing sites. The restricted **rnews** command (at a receiving site) delivers the articles. While the **netnews** software is not distributed with the standard UNIX operating system release, it is public-domain software that can be obtained from a cooperative site on this network.

Why Use the UUCP System?

Widely Available.   The UUCP system is the most widely used networking facility for UNIX systems because the software comes standard with every major version of the UNIX operating system. Although the UUCP software is generally different in detail from version to version, any one version of the UUCP system can communicate with all other versions, including Version 2 and HoneyDanBer releases.

Inexpensive Networking.   UUCP communications is relatively inexpensive to implement. The software comes bundled with most UNIX systems—there's no extra charge for it.

If you wish to link two UNIX machines directly, all you need is the cabling between their RS-232 serial ports. If you wish to contact remote machines, all you need is cabling to an autodial modem that connects to the telephone network. And if you wish to be contacted, you need the cabling, an autoanswer modem, and a telephone connection.

The cabling costs about $20 to 50 depending on length, number of wires, and noise shielding. Modems cost only a few hundred dollars at today's prices—and advances in circuit miniaturization are bringing the price down all the time. After installation, your biggest expense will be your telephone bill, but the phone calls are typically short, and you can instruct the UUCP system to call when the phone rates are least expensive.

Reliable Transport.   After you've set up the UUCP system correctly, it reliably transfers files again and again. The major problems involve the communication link, not the UUCP software itself. Files are transferred in discrete units called packets. If a packet isn't received correctly (a checksum is used to ascertain that), the packet will be retransmitted until it is received intact. Noisy communication lines slow down the overall transmission, but generally don't prevent arrival of valid data unless the link is lost completely.

A Common Denominator.   The UUCP system may be used to link machines of different vintages from different vendors running different versions of the UNIX operating system. It's also available for MS-DOS. Thus, it provides a common denominator for file transfer. For instance, you might use a UUCP network within an office building to back up files among different systems or send files from several different machines to a "hub" system attached to a relatively expensive resource, such as a tape drive or laser printer.

Access a Worldwide Community of UNIX Users.   Your UUCP system provides a gateway to a worldwide network of UNIX system users. Electronic mail and network news are exchanged around the globe on a daily basis. Set up your UUCP system, find a willing neighbor to link with, and you can talk to UNIX systems all over the globe.

Road Map to the UUCP System

This section is a "road map"—a guide to the programs, files, and directories that make up the UUCP system. You need to know about the pieces of the UUCP puzzle before we can discuss how they fit together.

The UUCP system has a reputation for a dismaying overwhelming complexity. Most of this reputation stems from the numerous components that make up this system. A systematic discussion of these components and how they are interrelated will go a long way to dispelling your concerns about the complex UUCP subsystem. First let's discuss the most important programs in the UUCP system.

Some Important Programs

The UUCP system provides programs for accessing remote systems, transferring files, and executing commands remotely. Table 8.2 lists the more important programs by several categories. We'll list the directories where these programs are located in another table.

TABLE 8.2 UUCP SYSTEM PROGRAMS

Specify job requests:

cu	Call up a remote system, log in, and transfer files
uucp	Request file copy between systems
uux	Request command execution on remote systems
uuto	Easier file copy request between systems
uupick	Retrieve files copied with **uuto**

Status checks and job control:

uulog	Examine UUCP logging information
uustat	Control jobs and check status of previous commands and accessibility of remote systems
uucheck	HoneyDanBer program that interprets the **Permissions** security file

Utility functions:

uuencode	Convert binary to ASCII file for mailing
uudecode	Convert from ASCII to binary form

System access:

uugetty	A HoneyDanBer **getty** variation that supports dial-in and dial-out access to the same port
Uutry	A HoneyDanBer shell script that invokes **uucico** for debugging.

Maintenance:

uuclean	Remove unwanted files from UUCP directories
uucleanup	Improved HoneyDanBer version of **uuclean**
uudemon	Shell scripts for UUCP system maintenance

Daemons:

uucico	Contact remote machine and transfer files
uuxqt	Execute commands requested by a remote system
uusched	HoneyDanBer file transfer daemon scheduler, which starts up **uucico**

Now, let's learn more about the programs you'd run to contact remote systems, transfer files, or execute remote commands.

cu. **cu**, the "call UNIX" (or perhaps "call up") program, allows you to connect and log in to a remote UNIX (or even a non-UNIX) computer. You can then work interactively on the remote system while still logged on to your local UNIX system. Local keyboard input will be sent to the remote system and any output from that system is displayed on your local terminal screen. So it's just as if you had access to a terminal connected directly to the remote system.

The **cu** program also supports the transfer of text files between a remote UNIX system and your local system. However, no error checking (such as checksumming) is performed, so line noise could introduce spurious characters into the file that was received.

Commands can be executed on your local system while retaining the communication link. The output from a local command is generally displayed on your local terminal, but you can instruct **cu** to divert the output to the remote system. This feature lets you send a text file to a remote non-UNIX system if that system has software that can store the received character stream into a file.

uucp. **uucp**, the UNIX-to-UNIX copy program, transfers one or more files between UNIX systems. The command syntax mimics the UNIX copy command, **cp**. You could use **uucp** for copying files locally, but **cp** would be much quicker.

The **uucp** program first creates a "work" or "command" file, which contains instructions for transferring the data. Depending on the version and options selected, the **uucp** command may copy the source data to a data file in the spooling directory or transfer it to the other system directly without this intermediate copy step. After a request has been made, **uucp** invokes a "daemon" program, **uucico**, which connects to or calls up the remote system and transfers the files.

uux. **uux**, the UNIX-to-UNIX execution program, is used to request execution of a command on a remote UNIX-based system. It creates work and any necessary data files on the local system, then invokes **uucico** to transfer them to the remote site. On the remote system an "execute" file is created, which contains directions for command execution. The **uucico** program on the remote site calls another daemon program, **uuxqt**, to service the command execution request. In the section "How the UUCP System Works," we present these steps diagrammatically.

uuto. **uuto** is a shell script program that invokes **uucp** to transfer files to a particular subdirectory of the public directory (**/usr/spool/uucppublic**) on the remote system. This command is simpler to use than **uucp** since you don't have to specify the pathname of the destination file on the remote system. So as an administrator, you may wish to instruct novice users on its usage. Also, if you're a novice or casual user, you may want to use **uuto** first since its invocation syntax is very similar to that of the UNIX mail command. Another advantage for using **uuto** is that a file will more likely get to its destination—since most systems allow access to their public directory.

uupick. **uupick** is a shell script designed to retrieve files placed in the public directory area by **uuto**. After invocation it enters an interactive command mode where further directions are specified as one-letter commands.

uulog. **uulog** is used to monitor the progress of UUCP transactions. Since the UUCP system does its work silently in the background, you need a way to inquire into the progress of communication with a remote site.

The Version 2 **uulog** command displays information from the Version 2 **LOG-FILE** logging file, which is located in the spool directory, **/usr/spool/uucp**. The UUCP system writes several status messages to this log file for each transaction. To help you make sense out of all these data, **uulog** lets you select subsets of this information for display.

The HoneyDanBer **uulog** command is actually a shell script. It also helps you examine the log files, which are named after the process that writes to them, and are located in subdirectories of **/usr/spool/uucp/.Log**.

uustat. **uustat** obtains status information about UUCP job requests. You can also use this command to determine the accessibility of remote systems connected to your site.

Ordinary users, who don't have the superuser privilege to remove job request files, need a way to cancel their own UUCP job requests. They'd use **uustat** to remove (or "kill") jobs before they're sent to the remote system.

If you don't specify any options, **uustat** reports the status of your UUCP job requests. Generally, you'd tailor the report by using command line options. The workings of this command depend on the version you're using. Consult your own system documentation to see what options your version of **uustat** recognize.

uuencode and uudecode. The **uuencode** and **uudecode** utilities convert binary files to an ASCII representation and back again. Although binary files can be sent using the **uucp** command, they aren't compatible with the UNIX **mail** command. Electronic mail is the method of choice for transfer of files through more than one machine since these so-called "multiple-hop" **uucp** transfers entail too many restrictions. For instance, all sites along the route need a common setup that controls forwarding.

So if you need to send a binary file to an adjacent site, **uucp** would work fine. But if you need to send it through another machine, first encode it to an ASCII form using **uuencode**, and then transmit it using UNIX **mail**. The recipient will use **uudecode** to reconvert the file to its original binary form.

Changing from binary to ASCII form is not without a price. Since every three bytes in the binary file becomes four ASCII bytes, the encoded file is larger by some 35 percent. Also, some control information is added, which includes the original permission modes for the file and the destination pathname. Thus, it will take somewhat longer to transmit an ASCII-encoded file than to its binary equivalent.

Note that the **uuencode** and **uudecode** utilities come standard on Berkeley UNIX systems but not on AT&T systems. However, they are generally available in the public domain—contact someone on the Usenet and ask for a copy. You'll find that people on the Usenet are often willing to help with such requests.

Figure 8.2 provides a couple of simple C programs that encode binary files to ASCII and back again. Part a lists the program that converts binary data to an ASCII hexadecimal representation. Part b lists the complementary program that converts the ASCII representation back to binary. Parts c and d shows a sample usage for both programs.

Figure 8.2 Binary-to-ASCII conversion programs.

a. Listing of the binary-to-ASCII program:

```
 1   /*
 2    * enhex.c -- convert (possibly) binary files to hex
 3    * Author: Bill Tuthill
 4    */
 5
 6   #include <stdio.h>
 7
 8   main()
 9   {
10       register int c, i = 0;
11
12       while ((c = getchar()) != EOF) {
13           printf("%02x", c);
14           if (++i == 30) {
15               printf(" \n");
16               i = 0;
17           }
18       }
19       printf(" \n");
20       exit(0);
21   }
```

b. Listing of the ASCII-to-binary conversion program:

```
 1   /*
 2    * dehex.c -- convert hex to (possibly) binary file
 3    * Author: Bill Tuthill
 4    */
 5
```

```
 6   #include <stdio.h>
 7
 8   main()
 9   {
10       int c;
11
12       while (scanf("%2x", &c) != EOF) {
13           putchar(c);
14       }
15       exit(0);
16   }
```

c. Using **enhex** to encode and mail a program:

```
$ enhex < program | mail rik
$ □
```

d. Using **dehex** to decode a program:

```
$ /bin/mail
>From beccat Fri Mar 20 16:58 PST 1987
To: rik
54010300bcfcc51e00000000000000000028000f010b0100001423000094040
00dc550100dc540100ec000000cc000000e003010054760002e746578740
[Interrupt]
? w program.rcv
? q
$ [edit program.rcv to remove mail header and trailing lines]
 . . .
$ dehex < program.rcv > program
$ □
```

These programs use a hexadecimal ASCII representation as the intermediate language. The **enhex** program inserts a space and a newline every 60 characters, because **mail** and editor programs don't work with long lines. The **dehex** program just ignores the space and newline when recreating the binary file.

uugetty. The standard **getty** program has been enhanced on HoneyDanBer systems so that it allows outgoing calls on a dial-in line. It recognizes the standard UUCP lock files to prevent port conflicts.

Uutry. This handy shell script is supplied with HoneyDanBer systems. It invokes **uucico** with debugging, saving its output in a temporary file. Then a **tail −f** command is run on the file to monitor any characters added to it. This shell script is useful for following the handshaking between two systems as they call out and log in.

The uudemon Shell Scripts. These shell scripts are designed to perform periodic maintenance of your UUCP system. There are three separate Version 2 shell scripts, all named with the **uudemon** prefix and having a suffix that indicates how often they should be executed−**.hr** for hourly, **.day** for daily, and **.wk** for weekly. The hourly script tries to deliver all pending UUCP system requests, and the daily and weekly scripts are concerned primarily with managing disk space used by the UUCP system.

The HoneyDanBer system has added another script to support polling of remote sites. Also, the other three scripts have been renamed and rewritten. The **uudemon.hour** script invokes **uusched** to process UUCP requests. The new **uudemon.poll** script will create a connect request file for any site that's scheduled to be polled (determined by the **/usr/lib/uucp/Poll** file). The **uudemon.admin** script sends UUCP status information to the UUCP administrator, and **uudemon.cleanu** cleans up the UUCP directories and archives the logfiles.

Both Version 2 and HoneyDanBer **uudemon** scripts are invoked by **cron**, and entries generally come in the system cron table files for executing these shell scripts (either in the **uucp** or **root** cron table file in the **/usr/spool/cron/crontabs** directory; in **/usr/lib/crontab** for older UNIX system versions).

uuclean. The Version 2 **uuclean** command is provided for managing disk space used by the UUCP system. It is invoked by the **uudemon.day** and **uudemon.wk** shell scripts for this purpose. Options select which files to remove and how old they must be. A record is kept of files that are removed−log entries are made in **/usr/spool/uucp/LOGDEL**. The improved HoneyDanBer version, **uucleanup**, invoked by **uudemon.cleanu**, maintains a log in **/usr/spool/uucp/.Admin/uucleanup**. **uuclean** or **uucleanup** can invoke **mail** to inform the owner whose file it removed.

uucico. **uucico**, the UNIX-to-UNIX copy-in copy-out program, is generally invoked automatically by the UUCP system in the background (which is why it's called a "daemon" program) to transport files that have been queued by the **uucp**, **uux**, or electronic mail programs. You may invoke it manually to start a file transfer immediately or for debugging the UUCP system. A debug option lets you select different debugging levels from terse to voluminous output.

The **uucico** program on the calling system is started up in MASTER role so that it will initiate a connection with the remote computer. The program or user who invokes **uucico** specifies the **−r1** option to use role 1 (MASTER role).

Another **uucico** program is started up in SLAVE role on the remote system. It's specified as the log-in program for the UUCP access account on that system. Since no **−r1** option is used when invoked as a log-in program, it's started up in SLAVE role.

The two **uucico** daemons converse with each other in dialogue fashion, sending control information and data back and forth between the two systems. We'll discuss these steps in more detail later.

uuxqt. **uuxqt**, the UNIX-to-UNIX execute daemon program, is invoked by the **uucico** program on the remote system to service a command request entered by the **uux** program on the local system. It searches a spool directory for files containing the request. Then it checks to see that all required data files are available and accessible and verifies that it has permission to execute the requested command.

Figure 8.3 shows the "chain of command" from **uux** to MASTER **uucico** on the calling system to SLAVE **uucico** and **uuxqt** on the called system.

Figure 8.3 The chain of command from **uux** to **uuxqt**.

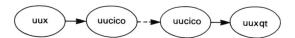

As with **uucico**, you can specify a debug option when invoking **uuxqt** that lets you select different debugging levels from terse to volumes of terse information.

Directories Used by the UUCP System

The UUCP system uses several directories. Table 8.3 lists these directories with a brief description.

TABLE 8.3 UUCP SYSTEM DIRECTORIES

Directory	Description
/usr/bin	Command directory—user commands
/usr/spool/uucp	Spool directory—request and logging files
/usr/spool/locks	Location for lock files on Honey-DanBer systems
/usr/lib/uucp	Library directory—maintenance programs and configuration files
/usr/spool/uucppublic	Public directory—a repository for files

Now let's discuss each in turn.

/usr/bin. This "command directory" contains UUCP commands that could be invoked by any system user. You'll commonly find the UUCP programs that specify requests (**uucp**, **uux**, **uuto**, and **uupick**), report status information (**uulog** and **uustat**), and perform utility functions (**uuencode** and **uudecode**) in this directory.

/usr/lib/uucp. This "library" directory is generally the home directory for the UUCP administrative account. Commands used for administering the UUCP system are located here. This directory also contains the configuration files used to tailor the UUCP system to your requirements.

/usr/spool/locks. This "lock file" directory is where lock files are created on HoneyDanBer systems.

/usr/spool/uucp. This "spool" directory for Version 2 UUCP is where the job request files are placed before the request is serviced. Temporary files used during the UUCP transaction, such as files for the incoming data, lock files to coordinate access to system resources, and status files that record transmission problems, are created here. Transaction and error logging files are stored permanently in this directory, too. Note that HoneyDanBer systems use subdirectories of **/usr/spool/uucp** for the purposes described here (except for lock files). The subdirectory structure helps ensure that no single directory gets too large.

/usr/spool/uucppublic. This "public" directory is a general repository for files sent to a system. In fact, many sites are set up so that remote computers can *only* send files to this directory. Generally, you'll enable all permissions on this directory so that any user can add, change, and remove files at will. The **uuto** and **uupick** commands send and retrieve files only from this directory. If you don't want other users to read your outgoing or incoming information, encrypt your files before storing them in this "public" area.

Some Important Files Used by UUCP System

We briefly discuss several of the more important files used by the UUCP system in this section—first for Version 2, then files unique to the HoneyDanBer UUCP version. Table 8.4 lists the important files for the Version 2 UUCP system with a brief description. Files in the "spool" directory, then files in the "library" directory are listed. Note that the text in parentheses indicates a prefix used for the filename. Thus a data file has a name starting with **D.**, a work or command filename starts with **C.**, and so forth.

TABLE 8.4 SOME IMPORTANT FILES USED BY THE VERSION 2 UUCP SYSTEM

File	Description
/usr/spool/uucp	directory:
data (**D.**)	Data for transfer
work (**C.**)	Instructions for **uucico**
execute (**X.**)	Instructions for **uuxqt**
status (**STST.**)	Transaction status with a given site
lock (**LCK..**)	Prevent access to a resource in use
temporary (**TM.**)	Incoming data before renaming
LOGFILE	General log information
SYSLOG	Transfer statistics
ERRLOG	System error log
/usr/lib/uucp	directory:
L-devices	Configuration file for communication lines
L.sys	Configuration file for contacting systems
L-dialcodes	Telephone prefix abbreviation definitions
USERFILE	Allowed file system hierarchy access
L.cmds	Allowed commands for remote execution

Now let's examine each in turn.

Data Files. When a file transfer request is made, either the file is sent directly from its original location in the UNIX file system (no copy is made) or an intermediate copy is created first in the spool directory. This copy is known as a *data file* and is named with a **D.** (for "data") prefix.

Some UUCP system versions make the copy to the spool directory by default; others require that the user use a particular command line option to request a copy. If a copy is made, the user can change the original file without the changes affecting the copy to be transmitted.

Work or Command Files. Work or command files are created in the spool directory by the **uucp** and **uux** programs. These files contain the instructions needed by **uucico** for processing the UUCP job request. You can always spot a work file by the **C.** (for "command") prefix to their filename. Although you could refer to them as "command" files because of this prefix, the AT&T UUCP documentation uses the term "work" files.

Execute Files. Execute files contain instructions needed by the **uuxqt** daemon to service the execution request on the remote system. They are created in the spool directory on the remote machine by the **uucico** process handling the file transfers on that machine. Their filename begins with an **X.** (for "execute") prefix.

Note that other files besides the execute file may be needed for the execution request, such as the data file containing the text to be printed by a remote **lp** execution request. The **uuxqt** process will wait until all the necessary files are available before it attempts to carry out the request.

Status Files.   Status files are created in the spool directory by **uucico**. These files have a filename with a **STST.** prefix and a suffix that's the node name of the system being conversed with. For instance, if you're contacting site **northpol**, the status file would be named **STST.northpol**.

The status file is updated by **uucico** several times during the conversation with the remote machine to reflect the current status. If the transaction is successful, the status file is removed at the end of the conversation.

If there was a problem with the transaction, such as a log-in failure, the error condition is noted in the file and **uucico** exits without deleting the file. The presence of the file prevents further attempts to contact the remote system until the "retry" time limit has expired—generally 55 minutes (the default value—which can be customized for each remote site).

Lock Files.   Lock files are created in the spool directory to prevent more than one **uucico** process from using the same communication port, attempting to contact the same remote system, or use the same UUCP status or logging file. All these lock files have the same filename prefix, **LCK..**, and the suffix that indicates the type of lock—device, system, or file. For instance, **LCK..tty2** would be used to lock port **/dev/tty2**, **LCK..northpol** to block access to remote site named **northpol**, and **LCK..LOG** to prevent access to the logging file, **LOGFILE**.

These lock files may stay in the spool directory if the daemon program is killed or the transaction is aborted. The presence of the lock files prevents a daemon from using the device or contacting the site that was locked. The locks "expire" after a certain time (generally 90 minutes), but you'll need to remove them manually if you wish to contact another site before that time.

Note that during a transaction that takes longer than the lock file expiration time, it's possible that another **uucico** process could be invoked, erase the old lock file, create its own lock file, and attempt to use the same resource at the same time. Of course, this situation is undesirable, but a possibility with the Version 2 UUCP system.

Temporary Files.   When a data file is received during a UUCP transaction it is first written as a temporary file in the spool directory. Such files have a filename that begins with a **TM.** prefix. If the UUCP transaction completed successfully, the temporary file is moved (by renaming) to its final destination.

The temporary file would remain in the spool directory if the transmission were interrupted. However, such a file causes no problem except perhaps to take up disk space—it doesn't affect future UUCP transactions. One of the maintenance shell scripts will eventually remove any leftover temporary files.

LOGFILE.   This file is a general logging file located in the spool directory. The UUCP system records information about job requests, file transfers, and system status in this file. If transmission problems occur, they are noted here as well. Ordinary users can use the **uulog** command to display selected data from this file, such as the progress of transactions they've requested.

Entries are appended directly to **LOGFILE** by newer versions of the UUCP system. On some older systems, and when it's not possible for some reason, entries are first written to a temporary log file, whose name begins with **LTMP.** (for **LOGFILE** temporary). When possible the **uulog** command appends this temporary file to **LOGFILE.**

SYSLOG.   The UUCP system makes a record of file transfers between sites in the **SYSLOG** logging file. Among other things, the entries in this file note the time required and the number of characters sent or received for each file that's transmitted.

ERRLOG.   System errors that occur during a UUCP transaction are recorded in the **ERRLOG** file. These errors are known as "assert errors" and result from system problems that should be looked into immediately. Some examples include problems from improperly set up, corrupted, or missing configuration files, a shortage of disk space, or low-level transmission errors resulting from poor connections or overloaded systems.

If your attempts to send or receive files fail, check the **ERRLOG** file for an indication of trouble. When you use the debugging option with **uucico** or **uuxqt**, "assert errors" are displayed on your terminal screen instead of being written to **ERRLOG.**

L-devices.   This configuration file contains information about the communication ports used by the UUCP system. In particular, this file maps the device type and line speed specifications in the **L.sys** file (discussed next) to an actual communication line. Entries in this file must be set up properly before either **cu** or **uucico** will work with a given device at a particular line speed.

L.sys.   Entries in this configuration file describe how to contact remote systems. The description includes the time of day and days of the week that contact will be permitted, the device and line speed to be used, the telephone number (for automatic call units), and the sequence of character strings to expect and to send in reply in order to log into the remote system.

L-dialcodes.   This optional configuration file defines strings that can by used to substitute for prefixes (or all) of the phone number specified in the **L.sys** file. The strings could either be abbreviations or more mnemonic sequences for the digits in the phone number.

USERFILE.   This configuration file helps provide security for your file system during UUCP transactions. This file tells **uucico** the directories that remote (and local) users of the UUCP system are allowed to access. (Of course, your local file and directory permissions are still in effect as well.) Generally only access to the public directory is allowed. Some systems may not even allow this—so you couldn't send them files via **uucp**—you'd have to use UNIX system electronic mail facility instead. Note that the electronic mail system bypasses **USERFILE** restrictions.

Caution—As delivered on many systems the **USERFILE** is not set up to restrict file system access adequately. Be sure to reconfigure your **USERFILE** as described later in this chapter before connecting up to remote sites.

L.cmds.   This configuration file tells **uuxqt** the commands that may be executed on your local machine by a remote user. Generally, only the restricted **rmail** command is specified—so the mail will go through, but other commands will fail.

Table 8.5 lists the HoneyDanBer files in the "library" directory, **/usr/lib/uucp**, that aren't in the Version 2 release. Both Version 2 and Honey-DanBer use many of the same files in the "spool" directory, except for the log files, as was mentioned in the "Directories" section above.

The following files are from Table 8.5:

Devices.   This configuration file serves the same function as the Version 2 **L-devices** file, namely it maps device type and line speed specifications in the HoneyDanBer "systems" file (**Systems**) to actual communication lines. However, the HoneyDanBer version has one additional field to map the communication line to the actual dialer device entry in the HoneyDanBer **Dialers** file.

Dialcodes.   Functions the same and has the same syntax as the Version 2 **L-dialcodes** file discussed above.

Dialers.   This file was added to the HoneyDanBer release to provide for general support of dialers and modems. Specifically, it describes commands used for coaxing the device to dial.

TABLE 8.5 SOME IMPORTANT HoneyDanBer FILES IN THE
/usr/lib/uucp DIRECTORY

File	Description
Configuration files:	
Devices	Configuration file for communication devices
Dialcodes	Telephone prefix abbreviation definition file
Dialers	File describing supported dialers and modems
Maxuuscheds	Contains maximum number of **uusched** processes
Maxuuxqts	Contains maximum number of **uuxqt** processes
Permissions	File specifies permissions given remote sites
Poll	File lists hours to poll named systems
Systems	Configuration file for contacting systems
Uutry	Shell script for debugging contact with remote
Shell scripts:	
remote.unknown	Logs information about unknown site
uudemon.admin	Sends UUCP status information to administrator
uudemon.cleanu	Clean up UUCP directories and archive logs
uudemon.hour	Starts up daemon programs
uudemon.poll	Creates dummy work file for polling

Maxuuscheds. Contains maximum number of **uusched** processes, which is two, by default.

Maxuuxqts. Contains maximum number of **uuxqt** processes, which is two, by default.

Permissions. The HoneyDanBer security configuration file. It specifies permission for remote systems to access (log in) the local system, to access files on the local system, and to run commands on the local system.

Poll. A HoneyDanBer-specific file that lists the hours to poll named systems. It's used as a database by the **uudemon.poll** script, which creates a "work" file for a system that's scheduled to be polled in a given hour.

Systems. This configuration file serves the same purpose as the Version 2 **L.sys** file (discussed above), that is, it describes how to contact remote systems. Furthermore, the internal structure of this file is identical to **L.sys**.

Uutry.   A shell script useful for contacting a remote system with debugging. It invokes **uucico** in MASTER role with a default debugging level of five. In particular, this script is handy for checking the dialer- and log-in chat scripts in the **Dialers** and **Systems** files, respectively.

remote.unknown.   A shell script that logs system access attempts by an unknown system (one not listed in the **Systems** file).

uudemon.admin.   A maintenance shell script scheduled to run by **cron** that performs several UUCP system checks and mails the results to the UUCP system administrator.   In particular, it lists active lock files and the processes using them, lists failed calls, and lists requests to copy files named **passwd**.

uudemon.cleanu.   A maintenance shell script scheduled to run by **cron** that cleans up UUCP directories and archives log files.

uudemon.hour.   A maintenance shell script scheduled to run by **cron** that runs **uusched**, which invokes **uucico** to contact all systems with pending jobs or poll requests; it also runs **uuxqt** to deliver incomplete mail transactions.

uudemon.poll.   A maintenance shell script scheduled to run by **cron** that sets up for polling of systems specified in the **Poll** file.

How the UUCP System Works

Now that you know about the components of the UUCP system, let's see how they work together in a common application—sending electronic mail to a remote site. For simplicity, assume that the transaction is a "one-hop" transfer to an adjacent site.   The long chain of events starting with the UNIX **mail** program and ending with the message being delivered to the recipient's mailbox file will be discussed. Note that a file transfer request initiated with **uucp** is much the same in that it involves steps 4 through 17 discussed below.

Figure 8.4 is a schematic diagram depicting the components and their interrelationships for sending electronic mail to a neighboring site.   We've indicated 20 steps for the entire process.   The actual number is arbitrary—it just depends on the level of detail you wish to consider.

Now let's examine the steps one by one.   As shorthand we'll use a generic name for some of the Version 2 and HoneyDanBer configuration files.   Thus the "systems" file refers to either the Version 2 **L.sys** or HoneyDanBer **Systems** file; "devices" file refers to either the Version 2 **L-devices** or HoneyDanBer **Devices** file; "dialcodes" file refers to either the Version 2 **L-dialcodes** or HoneyDanBer **Dialcodes** file.

Also note that Version 2 UUCP writes log messages to **/usr/spool/uucp/LOGFILE**, whereas HoneyDanBer UUCP writes them to a subdirectory of **/usr/spool/uucp/.Log**.   The file in this subdirectory is named after the program writing the message—either **uucico**, **uuxqt**, **uucp**, or **uux**.

Figure 8.4 Twenty steps for sending electronic mail.
The files specific to the HoneyDanBer release are named in parentheses

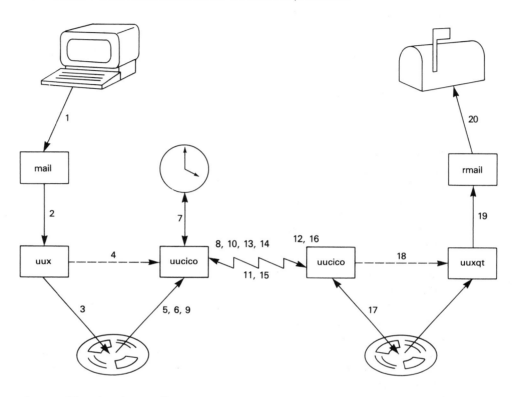

1.   User invokes **mail**
2.   Local **mail** invokes **uux**
3.   Local **uux** spools request
4.   Local **uux** starts up **uucico** as MASTER
5.   Local **uucico** scans for work file, then
6.   Creates lock file for remote site
7.   Checks **L.sys (Systems)** for time to contact
8.   Consults **L-devices (Devices)** to find port
9.   Creates lock file for communication port
10.   Connects to or dials remote system
11.   Log-in sequence between systems
12.   Remote **uucico** started up as SLAVE
13.   Handshaking sequence between **uucico**s
14.   Protocol negotiation between **uucico**s
15.   MASTER **uucico** sends request files
16.   MASTER and SLAVE switch roles
17.   Pending requests on remote site sent to local site

18.   Remote **uucico** starts up **uuxqt**
19.   Remote **rmail** invoked to deliver message
20.   Message delivered to recipient's mailbox

Step 1. The user on the local system invokes the UNIX **mail** command to deliver a message to a user on a remote system. For example, say that a user on local system **hometown** types the command shown in Figure 8.5.

Figure 8.5 Making an electronic mail request.

```
$ mail northpol!santa < wishlist
$ □
```

The **mail** command is instructed to send the file **wishlist** to user **santa** on the remote machine **northpol**. This command represents the only step that the local user performs—the **mail** program and the UUCP system does the rest.

Step 2. When the **mail** program realizes that the destination is a remote machine (because of the ! notation), it invokes **uux**. The **uux** program will request execution of the restricted **rmail** program to deliver the message (sent to the standard input) to account **santa** on **hometown**.

Step 3. The **uux** process creates three files in the spool directory on the local machine to specify the request: (1) a *work file* or *command file* named with a **C.** prefix followed by the remote or destination node name (as in **C.northpol**) that contains instructions for sending the other two files; (2) a *data file* named with a **D.** prefix followed by the remote or destination node name (as in **D.northpol**) that contains the mail message itself; and (3) a *receive-execute file* named with a **D.** prefix followed by the local or source node name (as in **D.hometown**) that will become an *execute* file named with a **X.** prefix followed by the source node name (as in **X.hometown**) on the remote system. It contains instructions for executing the **rmail** command to deliver the message in the *data file*.

Step 4. Just before **uux** exits, it invokes a **uucico** daemon program to contact the remote system. The daemon is started up in MASTER role, which means that it can initiate contact with the remote site.

Step 5. The **uucico** daemon scans the spool directory for *work files*. When it finds one, the daemon determines the remote system node name from the filename suffix.

Step 6. Then **uucico** tries to create a lock file to prevent duplicate conversations to that remote site. The lock file is named **LCK..northpol** when trying to contact system **northpol**.

The Version 2 **uucico** program can't create a lock if one is already present that's less than 90 minutes old. In this case, the daemon logs a "LOCKED (call to **northpol**)" message and exits.

The HoneyDanBer version manages lock files in a more sensible manner. The process that creates the lock file stores its process-id number in the lock file. So instead of relying on the modification time of the file, **uucico** opens the lock file and reads the PID number that's stored within. This mechanism allows **uucico** to determine unequivocally if the lock file is still in use. It does a **kill**(*pid*, **0**) system call, which determines if a process with PID of *pid* exists. If the process that created the lock doesn't exist, **uucico** will erase the lock file without delay and create its own lock file.

Step 7. The daemon scans through the "systems" file until it finds an entry corresponding to the destination system, **northpol** in our example. If located, **uucico** checks a field that specifies the times that the site can be contacted. If the current date and time falls within the allowed range, it will try to contact the remote system. If not, the daemon writes a "WRONG TIME TO CALL" message to the appropriate log file and exits.

Step 8. Next, **uucico** reads the "devices" file to locate a communication line with the correct speed (baud rate). (The device and line speed to use for a given remote site were specified in the "systems" file entry for that site.)

Step 9. The **uucico** process tries to create a lock file for the communication port. This file will prevent another **uucico** or **cu** program from using the same port at the same time. The lock file is named with the **LCK..** prefix followed by the basename of the communication port—such as **LCK..tty3** for port **/dev/tty3**. If the lock file can't be created, Version 2 writes "NO (DEVICE)" and HoneyDanBer **uucico** writes "DEVICE LOCKED" to the appropriate log file and the daemon exits.

Step 10. If the connection is direct (**DIR** in Version 2 **L-devices** or node name keyword in HoneyDanBer **Devices** file), the daemon attempts to open the communication line device file. If the open fails, Version 2 **uucico** will log a "DIRECT LINE OPEN FAILED" message and HoneyDanBer a "CAN'T ACCESS DEVICE" message before quitting.

If the "systems" and "devices" configuration files have been set up correctly, an open failed message may mean that the device file can't be accessed by the **uucico** process. Check the file access permissions for this file. This situation can happen, say, if the port had been previously used as a dial-in port (running a **getty** process) without restoring ownership to **uucp** or read and write permission for others if not owned by **uucp**. In this case log-in as superuser, change the ownership to **uucp** or permissions to 666, and try again.

If the connection is to be made using an automatic calling unit (ACU), the daemon first tries to open the dialing device. The Version 2 **uucico** will log a "NO DEVICE" message and HoneyDanBer a "CAN'T ACCESS DEVICE" message if the open fails. If so, check the ownership and permissions of the dialer device file.

If the open succeeds, the dialer device receives the phone number. The phone number used is obtained from a field in the "systems" file entry for the remote site. If any alphabetic string was used in the phone number, it is expanded to its numerical equivalent using information from the "dialcodes" file. The dialing must occur within a certain time limit, else a "TIMEOUT" message is logged.

For an automatic call unit, which has separate dialing and data port, after the dialing is complete, **uucico** attempts to open the data line. The Version 2 daemon logs an "OK (DIAL)" if all goes well, otherwise a "FAILED (DIALUP LINE open)" message is written to the log file. The HoneyDanBer daemon reports "CAN'T ACCESS DEVICE" under these circumstances.

Step 11. If the connection can be made to the remote system, the "systems" file is consulted for information on how to log into the site. The information is a series of strings to expect and strings to send in response—as in expect the "login:" prompt and send your UUCP access account name in response. If the log-in to the destination system succeeds, "SUCCEEDED (call to northpol)" is written to the appropriate log file on the **hometown** system; otherwise, a Version 2 "FAILED (call to northpol)" or HoneyDanBer "FAILED (LOGIN FAILED)" message is logged.

Step 12. The UUCP access account password file entry on the remote system (**northpol**) for the local system (**hometown**) specifies **uucico** as the log-in program. This program starts up in SLAVE role when the site **hometown** logs in.

Step 13. Next comes a handshake sequence initiated by the remote SLAVE daemon—it sends the string "Shere = northpol," which tells the calling system (**hometown**) that the system it contacted has the name **northpol**. If this expected message isn't received, the Version 2 **uucico** writes a "BAD LOGIN/PASSWORD (call to northpol)" and the HoneyDanBer daemon writes "WRONG MACHINE NAME" to the appropriate log file before aborting the connection attempt.

The **uucico** daemon on system **hometown** responds to the "Shere = northpol" message by sending a string of the form "Shometown-Q" followed by an optional number. This number, if present, is a conversation count. If both **hometown** and **northpol** are set up to count their conversations, the count is sent to identify this particular conversation. If conversation counts aren't used, no number is sent after the string. The conversation count is a security feature that helps prevent one system from masquerading as another system.

If conversation counts are being used, and the number sent to **northpol** by **hometown** isn't the one expected, **northpol** will send back a string meaning bad conversation count sequence number. After receiving this reply, the Version 2 **hometown uucico** daemon would then log "HANDSHAKE FAILED (BAD SEQ)" and the HoneyDanBer daemon would write "HANDSHAKE FAILED (BAD SEQUENCE CHECK)" to the log file and then abort the conversation.

Alternatively, if **northpol** replies with the string that indicates that a call-back is required, then the Version 2 **uucico** on **hometown** would log "HANDSHAKE FAILED (CB)" and a HoneyDanBer daemon would log "HANDSHAKE FAILED (CALLBACK REQUIRED) in the log file and hang up. Then the remote system (**northpol**) will attempt to contact the local **hometown** system to complete the receipt of the mail message. The call-back feature is the best way to assure the identity of a system. But in this case, it means that **northpol** would be charged for the return phone call. The UUCP system doesn't handle collect calls at all.

If **northpol** replied with a go-ahead message string, the conversation can proceed. Thus, the sequence check (if used) was successful, and no call-back is required. Now protocol negotiation begins in the next step.

Step 14. The remote system sends a "P" (for protocol) followed by one or more characters, each representing a possible line protocol. The calling **uucico** program checks these protocols against the available ones. If one is found, it returns a "U" (for use) followed by a character representing the chosen protocol (usually "g" named for its creator, Greg Chesson). If there's no acceptable protocol, the daemon returns the string "UN" (for unknown). If protocol negotiation was successful, the calling **uucico** daemon, whether Version 2 or HoneyDanBer, writes "OK (startup)" in the log file on **hometown**, else it writes "FAILED (startup)" and aborts the conversation.

Step 15. Now the MASTER and SLAVE **uucico** daemons proceed with the actual transmission, sending 64-byte packets of data containing control messages and the files that have been queued for transmission. Packets are retransmitted if they aren't received intact (determined by a checksum).

There are five control messages used during work processing: "S" for send a file, "R" for receive a file, "C" for copy complete, "X" for execute a command, and "H" for hang-up. The MASTER **uucico** daemon will send "S," "R," or "X" messages to indicate the type of work. The SLAVE daemon will reply by returning the same capital letter followed by "Y" or "N" to signify yes or no for each request.

The replies to the work requests depend on permission to access files and run commands. These permissions are determined by entries in the security files (**USERFILE** and **L.cmds** on Version 2 and **Permissions** on HoneyDanBer systems), as well as the actual permission modes for directories on the destination system.

As each file is received, the SLAVE daemon on **northpol** writes it into the spool directory of that system as a temporary file (name begins with **TM.**). After the file is received it will be moved to its final destination (by renaming). Then a copy-complete message is returned to the sending system, **hometown**. "CY" is the message for success and "CN" for failure. If there was a failure the temporary file is retained in the spool directory—it will eventually be erased by the maintenance shell scripts if no one deals with it manually.

The work requests and transaction results are logged to the appropriate log files in the spool directory on both systems. Each file that is transferred is noted in both the Version 2 **LOGFILE** and **SYSLOG** file. File transfer statistics, which include the transfer time and number of characters sent, are written to **SYSLOG**. Any system-related errors are written to the Version 2 **ERRLOG** file.

On HoneyDanBer systems routine status messages are posted to a file named after the host being contacted in the **.Status** subdirectory, transfer statistics are noted in **.Admin/xferstats**, and serious system-related errors are logged in **.Admin/errors**, all in the spool directory, **/usr/spool/uucp**.

Step 16. After the MASTER daemon on the local **hometown** system has processed all job requests, the daemons reverse roles—the SLAVE becomes the MASTER and the MASTER the SLAVE for the rest of the transaction. The remote **northpol** SLAVE then scans the spool directory on that system for any jobs destined for the system that called it (**hometown**).

Step 17. The new MASTER daemon processes all job requests on **northpol**. After the transfers from **northpol** to **hometown** are complete, the MASTER sends the SLAVE a hang-up request message.

Step 18. After the hang-up request has been granted, the connection breaks,

and the lock files and any temporary files that were used are erased, and both daemon processes exit. If the communication link was interrupted, the lock and temporary files remain as testament to the aborted conversation. As its last act, the
uucico daemon on the remote **northpol** site starts up the **uuxqt** daemon to scan the
spool directory for work.

Step 19. The **uuxqt** daemon checks the spool directory and finds the execute
file and associated data file (the mail message received from **hometown**). Then the
uuxqt process checks the appropriate security file (**L.cmds** on Version 2 and **Permissions** on HoneyDanBer systems) to see if it's allowed to execute the **rmail** command.

Step 20. If allowed to do so, **uuxqt** invokes **rmail** (restricted mail), which
delivers the mail message into the mailbox file of the recipient (**/usr/mail/santa**).
The **rmail** program is restricted because it can only deliver mail, not read incoming
mail (and there is no "shell escape"). Note that **rmail** is often a link to the UNIX
mail program—it knows to act restricted if it's called by the name **rmail**.

USING THE UUCP SYSTEM

You need to know how to operate the UUCP programs so that you can set up and
maintain the UUCP system. This section will give you enough background to use
the programs for administering the system. Also, as an administrator you may
have to answer questions from the users on your system about using these programs.

We'll cover sending electronic mail, sending files with **uuto** and retrieving
them on the destination end with **uupick**, requesting file transfers with **uucp**, making
remote execution requests with **uux**, and accessing a remote system with **cu**.

Sending Electronic Mail

In this section you'll see how to send mail to users on your local system as well as
on remote systems. System V provides two different electronic mail programs, the
original **mail** program and the new entry, **mailx**, which is derived from the Berkeley
Mail program. We'll use mail (not boldfaced) to refer to any of these programs in
a generic sense.

Composing Your Message.   There are two ways to compose your mail
message: (1) create your message by typing it while running the mail program, or
(2) use an editor to create your message, save it as a disk file, then use shell
redirection to input it to the mail program. The first method is generally used for
shorter messages that don't need revision. The second one is preferred for either
longer messages or if you need to make changes.

Sending Your Message.   Figure 8.6 shows two ways to send a mail message using **mail**. In part a, you invoke the **mail** program naming the recipient on
the command line. Then, whatever you type will be entered into a buffer. You end

the session, send the contents of the buffer, and exit **mail** by either typing either a control-D or a dot (.) as the first character on a line.

In the part b the message was already created with an editor and stored as a disk file, named **wishlist**. Since the **mail** program takes the message from its standard input, you can instruct the shell to redirect the standard input of **mail** to come from the **wishlist** file.

Note that if you're using the C shell, you must precede the so-called "bang" symbol, the exclamation point (!), with a backslash (\) so it won't be interpreted by this shell as signifying a command event from the shell history list. Part c shows an example.

Figure 8.6 Sending a message using **mail**.

a. Composing within the **mail** program:

```
$ mail northpol!santa
Dear Santa,
Please send me a new PostScript
laser printer for Christmas.
Thank you,
Robin
.
$ □
```

b. Sending an existing message file:

```
$ mail northpol!santa <wishlist
$ □
```

c. Sending an existing file from the C shell:

```
% mail northpol\!santa <wishlist
% □
```

You have many more options for sending mail with **mailx**. Besides the techniques discussed above for **mail**, you can invoke an editor for adding to or changing your message buffer. When you've finished composing your message, exit the editor, then exit **mailx** to send your message. Also, the operation of **mailx** can be customized by defining variables; and this program recognizes several useful commands while in composition mode. See the **mailx** documentation for more detail.

Forwarding Your Mail.   The examples above assumed that the recipient was on an adjacent system. The UNIX electronic mail facility can easily handle forwarding of mail through more than one site. Figure 8.7 shows an example. Here the mail to **northpol** is first forwarded through two systems, **seattle** and then **alaska**. Part a shows the syntax for the Bourne or Korn shells and part b for the C shell.

Figure 8.7 Sending mail through more than one system.

a. Forwarding when invoking **mail** with the Bourne or Korn shell:

```
$ mail seattle!alaska!northpol!santa <wishlist
$ □
```

b. Forwarding when using the C shell:

```
% mail seattle\!alaska\!northpol\!santa <wishlist
% □
```

Routing Your Mail.   The primary difficulty with forwarding your mail is determining the best sequence of machines to use as your routing path. The Usenet community maintains databases that describe the paths between machines that have registered as a Usenet site. But you may wish to reach machines that aren't in this database.

One reliable method we've found is to determine the path to a major *backbone* machine (or node). Then ask the desired recipient on the final destination machine to give you the path from their machine to the same backbone node. The overall path is then uniquely determined. In other words, local sites feed into backbone sites, and backbone sites connect to other backbone sites, so this arrangement means that mail can travel from any two sites on the worldwide UUCP network.

For instance, let's say the path from my machine, **uworld**, to the backbone site, **decwrl**, is **uworld!sun!decwrl**. Now I wish to send mail to someone at **microsoft**. I find out that **microsoft** is already connected to **decwrl**, so the path of machines is **uworld!sun!decwrl!microsoft**.

Using the uuto Program

Using the **uuto** shell script to send files to an adjacent system is generally easier and more reliable than using **uucp**. Also you can send binary files since **uuto** actually invokes **uucp**, which can handle binary files using 8-bit character transfers. It's easier because you don't have to specify a destination pathname—as with sending mail you only give the remote system name and the user on that system who should receive the file. It may be more reliable than using a **uucp** command line because the files are always sent to the public directory (**/usr/spool/uucppublic**) on the remote system. Most systems allow writing to their public directory, even if they restrict access to other portions of their file system hierarchy.

Example for Using uuto.   Figure 8.8 shows how easy it is to use **uuto** to send a file to a remote site. Part a shows the syntax for the Bourne or Korn shell, and part b for the C shell.

The local user first changes to their home directory, where the source file is located, and then instructs **uuto** to send the file named **wishlist** to user **santa** on the remote system **northpol**. The sender will be informed by mail when the file has been transferred to the destination system because the −**m** option of **uuto** was specified. The recipient, *user*, on the remote system will always be informed by mail that a file has arrived since **uuto** will invoke **uucp** with the -n*user* option.

Figure 8.8 Sending a file from the home directory with **uuto**.

a. Using the Bourne or Korn shell:

```
$ cd
$ uuto -m wishlist northpol!santa
$ □
```

b. Using the C shell:

```
% cd
% uuto -m wishlist northpol\!santa
% □
```

In this example, **wishlist** is located in the sender's home directory. Of course, the sender needs read permission for the file being sent. But what's not so obvious is that the Version 2 **USERFILE** (or HoneyDanBer **Permissions** file) on the local system must allow access to the home directory of the sender. If access to this directory isn't allowed, which is often the case, the user would need to copy the file to the local public directory, since access to that directory is generally granted to all users. Then the sender can invoke **uuto** to queue the file for transmission to the remote site. Figure 8.9 shows an example where the file is first copied to the public directory before transmission.

Figure 8.9 Sending a file from the public directory with **uuto**.

```
$ cd
$ cp wishlist /usr/spool/uucppublic
$ cd /usr/spool/uucppublic
$ uuto -m wishlist northpol!santa
$ □
```

Even if file system access is granted to a local directory by Version 2 **USERFILE** or HoneyDanBer **Permissions**, the **uucp** program (invoked by **uuto**) may be restricted by local file permissions. The **uucp** program runs as the user **uucp** (since it's a set-user-id program file owned by the UUCP administrative account, **uucp**), so read access is determined by permissions for the "other" user category.

General Syntax for Using uuto.   Figure 8.10 shows the general **uuto** command line syntax for sending files.

Figure 8.10 General command line for **uuto**.

uuto [−m −p] *sourcefile... remote!user*

Here *remote* is the site name of the destination system and *user* the account name of the person on that system who's to receive the file. You can specify one or more ordinary files to be sent. If *sourcefile* named a directory, then all files in that directory (and any subdirectories) will be sent. Unlike the UNIX electronic mail programs, **uuto** only allows transfers to an adjacent site—it's not set up to support forwarding.

Specify the −**m** option if you wish to be notified by mail when the copy is complete. The user on the remote system is always notified by mail after the file arrives.

Normally, the source files are sent (read) directly from their directory. However, you could specify the −**p** option with **uuto**, which causes them to be copied to the spool directory when making the transfer request. This copy step would be necessary if you wished to change, move, or delete the source file before it was transmitted to the remote system.

Your version of **uuto** may act differently from what we describe here. Since **uuto** is a shell script, it's easy to modify and your vendor may have changed it. However, you can read the shell program with any UNIX utility that examines text files (such as **cat**, **more**, **pg**, or **vi**) to see how your version operates. Generally, the **uuto** shell program lives in the **/usr/bin** command directory and is made accessible to ordinary system users.

How uuto Works.   First, it processes command line options and arguments, then makes sure that each of the designated source files or directories exist. If all checks show no problems, **uuto** invokes **uucp** to copy each source file individually to the remote site. If a directory tree is to be transferred, **uuto** calls itself recursively to copy each file in the tree.

Using the uupick Program

The **uupick** command retrieves files sent using **uuto**. The recipient on the remote system will be notified by mail when files sent by **uuto** arrive. Since **uupick** is a shell script, you can examine it to see how your local version works.

Example for Using uupick.   Figure 8.11 shows an example, where user **santa** just logged in to **northpol** and found that he had mail.

Figure 8.11 Notification that a file has arrived.

```
login: santa
Password:
you have mail
$ mail
From uucp Thu May 21 20:01 PDT 1987
/usr/spool/uucppublic/receive/santa/hometown/wishlist from hometown!robin
has arrived.

? □
```

You might wonder, "Why the long pathname shown in Figure 8.11?" Well, **uuto** actually specifies that the file be delivered to a particular subdirectory of the public directory on the destination system. In general terms the pathname is

/usr/spool/uucppublic/receive/_user_**/**_site_**/**_file_,

where _user_ is the recipient's account name, _site_ is the source system site name, and _file_ is the basename of the file before it was sent. Thus the actual pathname for the file sent to **santa** in the example above is

/usr/spool/uucppublic/receive/santa/hometown/wishlist

Figure 8.12 shows an example where user **santa** invokes **uupick** to retrieve the file mentioned in the mail message. The **uupick** command displays the filename and the system from which it came. Then it runs interactively, expecting a command from the user.

Figure 8.12 Invoking **uupick** to retrieve the file mentioned in Figure 8.11.

```
$ uupick
from system hometown: file wishlist
?
*
usage: [d][m dir][a dir][p][q][cntl-d][!cmd][*][new-line]
?
p
Sun 4 Workstation
AST Postscript Laser Printer
Wizard/PS software
?
m Lists
?
q
$ □
```

First, as a reminder, **santa** types an asterisk (∗) to print a usage message. Then he decides to print the contents of the file with the **p** command. Finally, he saves the message by moving it to the **Lists** directory.

Interactive uupick Commands. Table 8.6 lists the interactive commands that **uupick** understands with a brief explanation for each one.

TABLE 8.6 INTERACTIVE **uupick** COMMANDS

Command	Action
RETURN	Skip current file, exit if no others.
d	Delete the file.
m[*dir*]	Move the file to directory *dir* (or current directory is *dir* not used).
a[*dir*]	Same as **m**, only move *all* files received from *site*.
p	Display file contents on the screen.
q	Exit **uupick**.
Control-D	Same as **q**.
!command	Run the shell *command* and return to interactive mode of **uupick**.
*	Print a usage message.

General Syntax for Using uupick.   Figure 8.13 shows the general command line for invoking the **uupick** command.

Figure 8.13 General **uupick** invocation command line.

uupick [−s*site*] [*file*]

If no command line arguments are used when invoking **uupick**, any file sent by **uuto** to the user invoking the command can be retrieved. The user can limit the files retrieved to those sent from a particular system, *site*, by using the −s*site* option. If the recipient knows the name of the file (given in the mail message notifying the user that the file has arrived), he or she can select that particular file by specifying its name on the command line when invoking **uupick**.

Figure 8.14 shows how **uupick** could have been invoked to retrieve the file **wishlist** from **hometown**.

Figure 8.14 Retrieving a particular file from a particular system.

```
$ uupick -shometown wishlist
...
```

Using the uucp Program

You can use the **uucp** program to copy one or more ordinary files to a remote system. The syntax is similar to the **cp** command—you first specify the source file(s), then the destination file or directory. The difference is that **uucp** let's you copy files to another system, so special syntax for naming remote systems is used.

Example for Using uucp. Figure 8.15 shows a specific example. Here part a shows the syntax when using the Bourne or Korn shell, and part b the C shell. Note that instead of specifying a user on the destination machine (as you do with **uuto** or a mail command), you specify a destination pathname, as in the directory **/usr/santa/Lists**.

Figure 8.15 Sending a file to a remote system.

a. Using the Bourne or Korn shells:

```
$ uucp wishlist northpol!/usr/santa/Lists
$ □
```

b. Using the C shell:

```
% uucp wishlist northpol\!/usr/santa/Lists
% □
```

General Syntax for Using uucp. Figure 8.16 shows a generalized format for the **uucp** command line. As with **cp**, you have possible options, then one or more source files followed by a destination that can be an ordinary file or a directory. We'll discuss the command line options in a moment, but first let's find out about the special naming conventions recognized by **uucp** for the source and destination files.

Figure 8.16 General **uucp** command line syntax.

$ **uucp** [*option...*] *source-file... destination-file*

Either *source-file, destination-file,* or both can have the form shown in Figure 8.17 to signify their location on a remote system. In our examples, the remote site will be **northpol** and the local one **hometown**. As in the other examples above, if you're using the C shell, you must precede the so-called "bang" symbol, !, with a backslash (\).

Note that most systems don't support forwarding of files using **uucp**. If you must forward files, use UNIX electronic mail instead.

Figure 8.17 Syntax for specifying a remote site.

system-name!path-name

File Naming Conventions Used by uucp.   Figure 8.18 shows several different ways to write file names understood by **uucp**.

Figure 8.18 Various ways to name files and directories from the system **hometown**.

a. Using a full or absolute pathname:

hometown:
      /usr/robin
      /usr/robin/wishlist

northpol:
      northpol!/usr/santa
      northpol!/usr/santa/Lists

b. Using the shorthand for home directory:

hometown:
      ˜robin/wishlist

northpol:
      northpol!˜santa/Lists/wishlist

c. Using shorthand for the "public" directory:

hometown:
      ˜/
      ˜/wishlist

northpol:
      northpol!˜/
      northpol!˜/wishlist

A conventional full (or absolute) UNIX system pathname can always be used to reference a file or directory. Part a shows some examples for naming files on both the local and a remote system.

For convenience, **uucp** recognizes a tilde (˜) prefixed to an account name to stand for the home directory of the account. (This usage may seem familiar to you because the Berkeley C shell and AT&T Korn shell interpret this abbreviation in the same way.) And for this reason, you must escape the tilde (with a backslash) if it occurs at the beginning of an argument —for instance, \˜**santa**, when using the C or Korn shells.

Part b of Figure 8.18 shows two references to the file **wishlist**—one is in the home directory of account **robin** on the local system; the other is in the **Lists** sub-directory of the **santa** account home directory on **northpol**.

An important special case is a special shorthand for **PUBDIR**, a variable that stands for the current notion of the public directory. Version 2 UUCP **PUBDIR** always refers to the conventional public directory, which has pathname **/usr/spool/uucppublic**. However, HoneyDanBer UUCP allows you change the directory associated with **PUBDIR**. Why do this? One reason would be to segregate files from different systems.

Most UUCP implementations recognize the tilde (˜) as a shorthand for **PUBDIR**. And to emphasize that we are referring to a directory, we recommend using the notation tilde-slash (˜/) to represent the **PUBDIR** directory. When using the C shell you must precede the tilde by a backslash to prevent it from being interpreted as your home directory—as in \˜/.

Part c shows several naming examples using the tilde shorthand for the public directory. The first example refers to the directory itself on the local system and the second to the file **wishlist** in this same directory. The last two cases refer to the corresponding directory on the remote system.

If you don't use a full pathname or one of the abbreviations mentioned above for the destination file, the pathname of the source file will be used. For instance, if **uucp wishlist northpol** is entered from the **/usr/robin** directory on **hometown**, the UUCP system will attempt to send **wishlist** to **/usr/robin** on **northpol**, which is probably not what you intended.

It's important to tell your system users to be patient when making requests of the UUCP system. Explain that the **uucp** command only spools the request—it may not be acted upon immediately. Also, if there's a problem servicing their request they may not find out for awhile. Some errors are reported immediately, such as a syntax error when entering the **uucp** command line. Other problems won't show up until later, such as no write permission in a directory on a remote system. Warn your users—if nothing seems to happen, don't repeat the request—all that does is queue up another (perhaps erroneous) request. Instead have your users use one of the UUCP system status utilities, such as **uustat** or **uulog**, to find out the reason for the failure of their request. These utilities are well documented in the UNIX manual pages.

Command Line Options Recognized by uucp.   The **uucp** command recognizes several command line options for changing its default behavior. Table 8.7 divides the options for the **uucp** command distributed with the first release of System V into two groups—operational and status. The two additional options introduced in Release 2 are listed separately. Because of differences in various Version 2 UUCP implementations, your **uucp** command may not recognize the options or act upon them as described here. HoneyDanBer systems generally recognize and act on the options as described below.

TABLE 8.7 INVOCATION OPTIONS FOR THE SYSTEM V **uucp** COMMAND

Operational Options:

−**f**	Do not make directories on the destination system for the copied files.
−**C**	When sending a file, first copy it to the spool directory, **/usr/spool/uucp**.

Notification Options:

−**m**	Send mail to the user making the request when the copy is complete.
−**n***username*	Notify *username* on the remote system when the file has arrived.

Additional Options with Release 2:

−**r**	Submit the request, but don't start the file transfer.
−**j**	Display the job number on the standard output.

If necessary, **uucp** creates a directory to store the destination file. You can prevent this default behavior by using the −**f** command line option. You might wish to prevent a file copy if, say, the destination directory doesn't exist. This option would be passed to the **uucico** daemon on the remote system. Note that some versions of **uucico** may not recognize this option.

After you request a file transfer, the file is referenced by a full pathname in the control (or work) file for that job request. When the remote system is contacted, UUCP will then access the source file. But what if the source file had been changed, or worse, erased before contact was made? Perhaps you or one of the system users had assumed that the file transfer had been completed and erased the source file. Of course, if the UUCP system can't find the file, the request fails. You can use the −**C** option and the source file will be copied to the spool directory (**/usr/spool/uucp**) instead of storing a pathname for the file.

The two notification options are useful for determining when the **uucp** request was completed. Specify the −**m** option when making the request, and **uucp** will send you mail so that you'll know when the file has been transferred.

You can ask **uucp** to mail a notice to a particular account on a remote system when your requested file transfer is complete. You may wish to do so especially if the recipient isn't expecting your file. Use the −**n** option with the recipient's account name as its argument. Note that these notification requests are ignored if the transmission is local to your machine. When you use **uuto** the recipient is notified automatically because **uucp** is invoked with the −n option using the account name you specified on the command line as the argument to this option. Thus, **uuto wishlist northpol!santa** is translated to

uucp −nsanta wishlist northpol!˜/receive/santa/hometown/wishlist.

The **uucp** command distributed with Release 2 of System V has two more options for controlling and monitoring your file-transfer request. Normally, immediately after setting up the necessary work and data files, **uucp** starts up **uucico** to contact the remote system and start the file transfer. Specify the −r option to prevent invocation of **uucico**.

 You might use the −r option to queue several jobs at different times for transmission all at once. This approach would be more economical on dial-up lines since only one call would be made compared to several. This option is also useful for debugging. You'd use −r to queue a job but suppress its transmission. Then you invoke **uucico** with a debugging option to monitor the job transmission.

 Every **uucp** transaction has a unique *job number* associated with it. Specify the −j option when you invoke **uucp** to display this number on your terminal screen. With Version 2 (but not HoneyDanBer) UUCP you can have the job number displayed automatically; define the shell variable **JOBNO** equal to **ON**, and mark it for export to the environment. Now the job number display would be the default case. However, it can be suppressed if the −j option is specified—sort of a "toggle" effect.

 Further uucp Examples.   Figure 8.19 shows some more examples of sending files. You need to know two things to send a file with **uucp**: (1) the name of the remote site, and (2) the destination directory.

 You can use the **uuname** command to list all adjacent sites that your UUCP talks to. Most adjacent sites don't support so-called *forwarding* to a more remote site. You'll have to talk to the UUCP administrator on the adjacent site to see if they do.

 Most sites restrict access to most directories in their file systems. However, the public directory, **/usr/spool/uucppublic**, is generally made accessible for both reading and writing for all users (mode 777).

Figure 8.19 Sending and fetching files via the public directories.

a. Sending a file:

```
$ cp wishlist /usr/spool/uucppublic
$ uucp ˜/wishlist northpol!˜/
$ □
```

b. Using wildcards to send more than one file:

```
$ cp wishlist[1-3] /usr/spool/uucppublic
$ cd /usr/spool/uucppublic
$ uucp ~/wishlist? northpol!~/
$ □
```

c. Fetching a file:

```
$ uucp northpol!~/wishlist ~/
$ □
```

d. Using wildcards to fetch more than one file:

```
$ uucp northpol!~/wishlist? ~/
$ □
```

Part a of Figure 8.19 shows the source file in the local public directory being sent
to the corresponding directory on the remote site. You have the greatest chance for
success when transferring files between systems if you use the public directories.

Part b shows that you may use a single **uucp** command line to transfer more
than one file. The filename generation wildcards are expanded by the local shell
before **uucp** is invoked. This is why (in this example) you change to the directory
containing the files to be sent before entering the **uucp** command line.

You can also use **uucp** to fetch files from a remote system. You need to know
their location and have permission to access them on that system. In part c a single
file is requested.

Part d shows an example where multiple files are requested using wildcards.
You should quote the wildcard to prevent expansion by the local shell before it's
passed onto **uucp** for interpretation. If there's no match to a local file the Bourne
shell won't complain, but the C shell will give a "No such file or directory" message and abort the command.

The remote system must allow you to execute the **uucp** command to request
files using wildcards. Generally, permission to run a command like **uucp**, which can
read files, is restricted for security reasons. So generally, fetching files using wildcards is not allowed. Ask the UUCP administrator on the adjacent system if they
allow you to run **uucp** remotely. If not, you'll need to request each file with a
different **uucp** command invocation.

Forwarding Files through More Than One Site.   Forwarding files with
uucp is generally difficult for two reasons:

One, each major version (Version 2, Berkeley, and HoneyDanBer UUCP)
implements forwarding differently. So all sites in the *forwarding chain* would have
to be using the same version of UUCP.

Two, Administrators need to restrict forwarding since it creates a security hole—especially on HoneyDanBer implementations because each site in the chain has to allow execution of **uucp**, which is a security hazard.

Thus, it's generally better to use electronic mail to send files through more than one site. *One caution.* Good network etiquette requires that you limit the size of the file you're mailing—you're using resources paid by someone else. Generally speaking, keep your files to less than 64 kilobytes. Some sites limit the size automatically, and perhaps to an even smaller value—you may need to experiment. If you need to consistently send large files, you should set up a direct phone link to the destination so that you can foot the phone bill.

Transferring Multiple Files. If you need to send several files or an entire directory tree, you should first combine the file into an *archive file* using a backup utility, such as **cpio** −**c** or **tar**. Then you can transfer this archive using **uucp** or electronic mail if all the files are text.

Figure 8.20 shows a typical scenario. Here, you first change to the starting directory—generally the current directory for the files if they're all in one directory, or the top of the directory hierarchy if the files form a tree structure. Then use **find** to locate all the files and pipe the names into **cpio** running in copy-out mode, redirecting the output to a file in the public directory. Finally, queue up the file for transmission with **uucp**. *Caution:* Don't exceed the file size limit (**ulimit**) on the source or destination machine. The files can be recovered on the destination machine by extracting the archive file into the final directory location.

Figure 8.20 Transferring user **robin**'s directory hierarchy.

```
$ cd /usr/robin
$ find . -print ¦ cpio -ocav >/usr/spool/uucppublic/arch
$ uucp ~/arch northpol!~/
$ □
```

Using the uux Command

You can use the **uux** command to request execution of UNIX commands on a remote system. You need to supply the remote system name and the command to be executed. You can also specify files to be sent for command operation, and the destination for the command output, if any. The **uux** command stores your request as files in the *spool* directory, **/usr/spool/uucp**. After the request has been serviced, you'll be notified by mail if it succeeded or failed.

One common use for **uux** is to request printing on a remote machine that has a printer. The file to be printed could reside on the remote site or locally on your system. Of course, the command to spool a file for printing, **lp**, must be listed as an allowed command for the remote system (more on this in a moment).

Thus, **uux** is not a general-purpose remote execution command, but rather a limited-use facility. For one thing, it can't run commands interactively. In practice, it's often used to access a remote resource, such as a laser printer, if the remote administrator allows execution of **lp**. Instead, you'd use **cu** to access a remote system and run commands interactively.

Specifying Allowed Commands. For security, most installations severely limit the commands you may execute on their site. Generally only restricted mail, **rmail**, is allowed. This command is necessary so that users can receive UNIX electronic mail. Recall that the **mail** program invokes **uux** to run **rmail** on the remote system for you.

For Version 2 UUCP the commands you allow a remote user to run on your system are listed in the configuration file, **/usr/lib/uucp/L.cmds**, which must be present. As of Release 2 of System V you can specify allowed commands on a remote system basis. For instance, you can allow all systems to run **rmail**, but only systems connected to you in a local network to run **lp**.

For HoneyDanBer UUCP the allowed commands are listed in the **Permissions** file. And you can specify commands on a remote system basis. Generally, only the **rmail** command is allowed for remote systems by default. You have to add any other commands on a list for each particular remote system.

Examples for Using uux. As an example, the commands shown in part a of Figure 8.21 request the remote printing of the **wishlist** file that's located on the local system. Part b shows that you can omit **hometown** when specifying the file pathname on the local machine, but we recommend using the prefix for clarity. Note that when a local file is to printed, it is first sent to the remote machine, where it's stored temporarily in the remote execution directory, **/usr/spool/uucp/.XQTDIR** on Version 2 and **/usr/spool/uucp/.Xqtdir** on Honey-DanBer systems.

Figure 8.21 Remote printing of a local file.

a. Printing a local file on a remote system:

```
$ uux northpol!lp hometown!wishlist
$ □
```

b. Another way to specify the local file to be printed:

```
$ uux northpol!lp !wishlist
$ □
```

Figure 8.22 shows examples for printing a remote file on a remote system. *Caution:* If you use the command shown in part a of the figure, the UUCP system will expect to find **wishlist** in the remote execution directory. If it's not there, the request will fail.

In part b of this figure **wishlist** was previously copied to the **/usr/santa/Lists** directory on **northpol** (shown in Figure 8.15).

Figure 8.22 Remote printing of a remote file.

a. One way to specify the remote file:

```
$ uux northpol!lp wishlist
$ □
```

b. Specifying the correct remote path for the file to be printed:

```
$ uux northpol!lp /usr/santa/Lists/wishlist
$ □
```

General uux Command Line Syntax. The general **uux** command syntax is depicted in Figure 8.23.

Figure 8.23 General **uux** command line syntax.

$ **uux** [*option...*] *command-string*

The *command-string* consists of one or more arguments that appear like an ordinary shell command line except that command and file names may be prefixed by *system-name!*. This prefix tells **uux** that the command or file is located on the remote site, *system-name*. The file argument naming conventions for the **uux** command are the same as those for the **uucp** command discussed previously.

Using Shell Metacharacters in Command Lines. If you use shell metacharacters, such as those that specify input redirection (<), output redirection (>), the multiple commands (;), or a pipeline (¦) in the **uux** command line, you must either quote the entire *command-string* or quote the special characters as individual arguments. You can use single, double quotes, or backslashes as appropriate.

Figure 8.24 illustrates running the **who** command on remote system **northpol** and sending the output to your local system, **hometown**. In part a the output is redirected, and in part b it's mailed to your local system.

Figure 8.24 Running **who** remotely and returning the result.

a. Redirecting the result to a file on the local system:

```
$ uux "northpol!who > hometown!~/who.northpol"
```

b. Mailing the result to a user on the local system:

```
$ uux "northpol!who | rmail (hometown!robin)"
```

In both cases you need to enclose the **uux** *command-string* argument in quotes to prevent the local shell from interpreting the redirection and pipe directives before they're passed to **uux**. In part b the parentheses are necessary around the argument to **rmail**; without them, **uux** would interpret **hometown!robin** as an *input file* to **rmail**.

Options Recognized by uux. Table 8.8 lists some of the options recognized by the System V Release 2 **uux** command. The −**m**, −**r**, and −**j** options work in the same way as they do for **uucp** (discussed previously).

TABLE 8.8 SOME INVOCATION OPTIONS FOR THE SYSTEM V
RELEASE 2 **uux** COMMAND

−**m**	Send mail to the user making the request.
−**r**	Submit the request but don't execute it.
−**j**	Control display of the job number on the standard output.

General Guidelines for Using uux. Table 8.9 lists some guidelines for using **uux**.

TABLE 8.9 SOME GUIDELINES FOR USING **uux**

- Remote commands are run as a process with effective owner **uucp**. Files created by this user would thus be owned by the **uucp** administrative account.

- Only commands that can normally be run in the background can be executed on a remote system—interactive commands don't work.

- You need to redirect or pipe the standard output from a command, else it will be lost.

Using the cu Program

In this section you'll see how to use the **cu** remote terminal program to log into a remote UNIX system. We'll also describe how to transfer text files between a remote and your local system.

You'll need an account on the remote system to gain access. If the account allows access to a general-purpose shell, you can interact with the remote system just as if you were a local user on that system. You can run commands, edit files, and so forth. Whatever you type on your keyboard is sent to the remote system, and standard output from remote commands is sent to your local terminal screen.

Berkeley UNIX systems also supply a similar program named **tip**. In addition to the capabilities that **cu** has, **tip** recognizes a set of variables that control its operation. This facility is similar to the use of variables by the **vi** and **mailx** programs.

Besides acting as a remote terminal program, **cu** lets you send or receive text files from a remote system. You could use this facility to transfer, say, shell scripts or text-based databases between systems. (Binary programs and nontext data must be transferred with **uucp** itself.)

You can use either a dial-up or hardwired connection to connect to the remote system—a UUCP link is not necessary. The Version 2 **L-devices** or HoneyDanBer **Devices** file and perhaps the Version 2 **L.sys** or HoneyDanBer **Systems** file used by the UUCP system are also used by **cu**. Many newer versions of **cu** also contain the same dialing and file locking code present in UUCP for compatibility.

After you connect to the remote system, **cu** issues a "Connected" message and you should see a "login" prompt from the remote UNIX system. You log-in just as you would on your local system—entering an account name and password.

Anything you type will be sent through the communication link to the remote system. Any response from the remote system will be sent back through the link to your terminal screen. Commands to the **cu** program itself begin with a tilde (˜). The tilde is trapped by **cu**, so the characters that follow (up to a newline) can be interpreted as a command. If you really wish to send a tilde character to the remote system, you type a pair of tildes (˜˜).

Example of System Access with cu. Figure 8.25 shows a sample communication session using **cu**. Here we invoked **cu** with the name of a remote system, **northpol**. Newer versions of **cu** recognize this command line format and consult the appropriate configuration files to get the necessary information for contacting the remote system.

Figure 8.25 Using **cu** to access a remote system.

```
hometown $ cu northpol
Connected

login: robin
Password:

northpol $ who
santa        console      May 14 08:36
robin        tty0         May 14 11:45
<^D>
login: ˜[hometown].
Disconnected

hometown $ ▯
```

In our example user **robin** on local system, **hometown**, is calling the remote system, **northpol**. After **cu** makes contact it issues the "Connected" message. Then user **robin** logs into **northpol**. In this example, the connection was good—no spurious characters were seen. If you get a noisy line and have trouble accessing a remote system, disconnect and try again later.

Next, the **who** command is run and **robin** logs out with a control-D (indicated by ^D, which isn't printed). Then **cu** is exited by first typing a tilde (~) followed by a dot (.). After the dot is typed, **cu** prints "[hometown]" after the tilde and before the dot, to identify the local system and shows that it recognized the command.

You can use **cu** to help set up the UUCP system because it uses some of the same configuration files. Thus, if you get **cu** working, you are well on your way to getting UUCP to work as well.

Invoking the cu Program.   Now let's learn about the several different possible **cu** command lines for contacting a remote system. The appropriate one to use depends on your version of **cu**, the setup of your UUCP configuration files, and the communication device you're using.

First, let's discuss the simplest usage—contacting a remote system by name. Figure 8.25 showed an example for contacting a particular site, **northpol**. The remote system must be accessible by your UUCP system for this approach to work. You can use the **uuname** command to list all systems that UUCP can contact by name.

Several conditions must be satisfied to contact a system by name: (1) You'll need a version of **cu** that recognizes a remote system name argument. (2) The Version 2 **L.sys** or HoneyDanBer **Systems** file must have an entry for contacting **northpol**. That entry would designate the type of communication device (ACU or Automatic Call Unit with either Version 2 or HoneyDanBer UUCP, or DIR for Version 2 UUCP or the system node name for HoneyDanBer UUCP when using a direct connection) and the line speed to use. (3) The Version 2 **L-devices** or HoneyDanBer **Devices** file would need an entry to translate the information from the Version 2 **L.sys** or HoneyDanBer **Systems** file into a particular communication line. Then the **cu** program would either dial the phone number for **northpol** for an ACU or make a direct connection to **northpol** for a DIR-type device.

Alternatively, if the system isn't on your UUCP network, you may be able to specify the telephone number as an argument. Figure 8.26 shows an example of the syntax.

In this case the Version 2 **L-devices** or HoneyDanBer **Devices** file needs to have an entry for an ACU. Note that your dialing device doesn't need to be an actual 801C ACU, but your version of **cu** must have the code to dial your communication device. HoneyDanBer UUCP systems support many different dialing devices with a **Dialers** file, discussed later. Most Version 2 UUCP systems require separate dialing programs for devices other than the 801C ACU.

Figure 8.26 Calling a system by specifying the phone number.

```
$ cu 9=1-8005551212
Connected
...
```

When specifying the phone number, you can designate that the dialer wait for a secondary dial tone by using the equal sign (=). A pause is specified by a dash (−). In our example, the telephone number **9=1−8005551212** would be interpreted to mean send a 9 (to get an outside line), wait for a dial tone, dial the 1 digit, pause, then dial the rest of the number.

You may need to indicate a −l*line* argument to **cu** if there's more than one ACU communication line. The **cu** command scans the Version 2 **L-devices** or HoneyDanBer **Devices** file from beginning to end using the first ACU entry found. If the first ACU entry is not appropriate, you'll need to specify a particular communication line. Figure 8.27 shows an example.

Figure 8.27 Specifying a particular ACU line.

```
$ cu -1/dev/tty2 9=1-8005551212
Connected
...
```

Imagine for this last example that the first ACU line was for **/dev/tty1**, but that device was not operational. You chose the next one by specifying the device name for the communication line, **/dev/tty2**, after the −l option to **cu**. Note that the **/dev** directory designation is optional—so −l**tty2** would work as well.

You may need to specify the −s*speed* argument if there's a possible ambiguity to the line speed. Let's say there were two entries for **/dev/tty2**. The first one was for 300 and the second for 1200 baud. Since you wish to use your faster 1200-baud modem you'll specify a *speed* argument, too. Figure 8.28 shows the example.

Figure 8.28 Specifying a particular ACU line and line speed.

```
$ cu -1tty2 -s1200 9=1-8005551212
Connected
...
```

The *speed* argument is generally one of 300, 600, 1200, 4800, or 9600 baud. Direct connect lines can operate at the higher baud rates; dial-up lines using modern modems generally operate at 300, 1200, or sometimes 2400 baud. There are a few 9600-baud modems becoming available that operate over ordinary phone lines. If the line speed option is not specified, **cu** uses the baud rate specified in the "devices" file for the line.

With Version 2 UUCP, if you need to ensure that a direct connection (DIR specified in the first field of the **L-devices** file entry for the line) is used, you can specify the **dir** argument when you invoke **cu**. Figure 8.29 shows an example.

Figure 8.29 Specify a particular DIR line and line speed.

```
$ cu -1tty2 -s9600 dir
Connected
...
```

Transferring Files with cu.   You can use **cu** to transfer files between systems. Since no error checking or spooling is performed, you're generally limited to small text files. You'll need a good noise-free connection, else garbage characters will be introduced in the received file.

You can either instruct **cu** to send (known as a "put") or accept (or "take") a single file. Think of the put or take relative to your local system, not the remote system. That is, you either *put* a file from the local to the remote system, or *take* a file from the remote to the local system.

The actual commands begin with a tilde-percent sign (˜%) followed by either **put** or **take**. Only the source file name is required, and it can either be a full pathname or a name relative to your current directory. The destination file will have the same pathname as the source file unless you specify a different one as the second file argument to the command. Table 8.10 shows several sample command lines and their interpretation.

TABLE 8.10 SAMPLE FILE TRANSFERS WITH **cu**

`~%put /etc/motd`	Transmit **/etc/motd** to remote, where it will have the same absolute or full pathname.
`~%take /etc/motd msgofday`	Request **/etc/motd** from remote, where it will be stored in the current directory with name **msgofday**.
`cd /etc ; ~%put motd /tmp`	Transmit **/etc/motd** to remote, where it will be stored in **/tmp** with the name **motd**.
`~%take /etc/motd /tmp/motd`	Request **/etc/motd** from remote, where it will be stored as **/tmp/motd** on the local system.

When sending or receiving files with **cu**, it's a good idea to compare the character count (use **wc**) and perhaps the checksum (use **sum**) of the source and destination files so that you can tell if characters are missing or were garbled. *Note:* For counting purposes, if the source file contains tab characters, make sure that neither the source nor destination system expands tabs to spaces by running the **stty tabs** command before the file transfer.

Of course, you need to consider the permissions for the files and directories you send and receive. Remember that **cu** is probably running as the **uucp** account since the **cu** program is generally set up to be set-user-id owned by **uucp**. For instance, if **cu**, acting as an "other" class of user, can't write into a destination directory, then you can't put a file there.

Multihop Connections with cu. Occasionally, when accessing a remote system with **cu**, you'll need to contact a third system. You can do so by invoking **cu** from the remote system, while still connected to it from the local system. As an example, let's say that a user on the local system **hometown** is accessing the remote system **northpol** using **cu**. While logged into **northpol**, this user wishes to connect to **workshop**, which is linked to **northpol**. Figure 8.30 shows a typical session. For easier interpretation, the nodename of the each system is displayed as part of the shell prompt.

Figure 8.30 Connecting through a remote system.

```
hometown $ cu northpol
Connected
login: robin
Password:
Welcome to the North Pole
northpol $ cu workshop
Connected
login: robin
Password:
Welcome to Santa's Workshop
workshop $ mail elves < wishlist
workshop $ <^D>
login: ~~[northpol].
northpol $ <^D>
login: ~[hometown].
hometown $ □
```

The problem comes in when **robin** wishes to sever the connection between the second and third systems, **northpol** and **workshop**, without breaking the link between **hometown** and **northpol**. If **robin** enters the usual tilde-dot (˜.) sequence, the connection from the local system, **hometown**, and the second system, **northpol**, will be broken, since the local **cu** will interpret the disconnect sequence. Instead, the tilde-dot sequence needs to be transmitted to **northpol**.

A sequence of two catenated tildes (˜˜) will cause a single tilde to be transmitted to the remote system. Thus, the correct way to disconnect from **workshop** is to type tilde-tilde-dot (˜˜.), which will be sent to **northpol** as tilde-dot for interpretation by the **cu** program running on that system.

The same considerations apply to other commands that begin with a tilde, such as ˜%**put** and ˜%**take**. For instance, while interacting with **workshop** through **northpol**, use ˜˜%**put wishlist** to send a copy of **wishlist** from the current directory (on **northpol**) one-hop to the current directory on **workshop**. Note that you can't do multihop file transfers with the "put" and "take" commands.

And there's no reason you can't invoke **cu** to connect through even another machine. You just have to keep your count of all the tildes correct. Happy connections!

SETTING UP UUCP COMMUNICATIONS

In this section we explain how to set up both the hardware and software for UUCP communications. We assume that all necessary UNIX communication binary programs and shell scripts and associated data files are present on your system (with the correct ownership and permissions). The basic steps for establishing a UUCP link between systems are summarized in Table 8.11.

TABLE 8.11 BASIC STEPS FOR ESTABLISHING A UUCP CONNECTION BETWEEN SYSTEMS

- Make the hardware connection between computer systems—either directly between two serial ports or between each system's serial port and a modem for access by telephone.
- Determine and perhaps change your system or node name. The UUCP system identifies your computer system using this name.
- Create UUCP access accounts for other systems to log-in to your system.
- Add an entry to the Version 2 **L.sys** or HoneyDanBer **Systems** file for each remote system you wish to contact. Also, you may need "dummy" entries for sites that contact you.
- Add an entry to the Version 2 **L-devices** or HoneyDanBer **Devices** file for each serial port that connects to a remote system.
- For dial-out lines, make sure that your system supports your dialing device or modem.
- Configure **/etc/inittab** entry for your communication port. Generally, you'd enable **getty** for a dial-in line and disable it for a dial-out port. You can use **uugetty** with HoneyDanBer UUCP for a bidirectional port that supports both dial-in and dial-out functions.
- Secure your UUCP communications—establish the file system and command access given to remote systems. We cover UUCP security in the next section of this chapter.
- Optionally, set up to poll any sites that can't call you. As delivered, Version 2 systems don't provide polling, whereas HoneyDanBer systems do. We'll show you how to set up polling for both Version 2 and HoneyDanBer UUCP.

STEP ONE: Making the Hardware Connection.

In this section we discuss the types of connections between computer systems.

Types of Connections.   There are three common types of communication links—direct, modem, and local area network (LAN). We'll discuss how to set up the direct connections and modem links in this chapter. LAN configuration is a specialized topic that's beyond the scope of this book, but we'll describe the UUCP interface to an existing LAN.

Direct and dial-out links use at least one serial port with an RS-232-C interface to communicate with another system. If the other system is located nearby, you can link to it directly with a cable. If the other system is more distant, you'll need to communicate using a modem.

A direct link is convenient when you communicate with another computer on a regular basis. The link is always ready to be used and the time to access the other computer is minimal. Also, a high transfer rate—typically up to 9600 baud—can be used. But the length of the direct link is limited—the RS-232-C standard guarantees no more than 50 feet. However, greater distances can generally be used in practice—depending on the actual data rate, shielding from noise, cable capacitance, and the type of line drivers employed. Short-haul modems costing less than $100 on each end can extend the distance from hundreds of feet to miles.

If you wish to communicate with a distant site, you'll probably use the telephone—a method with its own advantages and disadvantages. An advantage to this approach is that one communication port can be used to connect to more than one remote computer. One disadvantage is that the port is more likely to be busy (already in use). Also, the dial-up connection requires more hardware than a direct connection. You'll need an RS-232-C connection from your local computer to a modem, which converts the digital data pulses to audio tones so that the information can be transmitted over the telephone network. And a modem is required on the receiving end to convert the tones back to digital signals.

UUCP is not generally used for file transfers within a LAN, since LANs often have their own file transmission facilities. However, UUCP may still be used in the environment to communicate with remote sites over a modem connection. Two common configurations are described here.

A particular UNIX system is designated as the *gateway* to the external telephone system. In this case other machines on the LAN send messages to the gateway machine, which uses a conventional modem connection to the telephone.

Another common arrangement is to have the LAN address the modem directly through a *network switch*. The switch gives users on the LAN transparent access to the modem. In this case the UUCP system must first access the switch, then dial the modem.

ACUs, Modems, and Dialers. Modern modems have the data transmission and dialer functions combined in one unit. They are relatively inexpensive—about $200 for a 300/1200-baud DC Hayes-compatible modem (the current standard for low-cost intelligent modems).

ACUs (automatic call units) were developed in the early 1970s to handle the dialing functions since at that time the all-in-one modem and dialer were difficult to design and thus expensive. Back then a simple counter circuit using discrete transistors might require an entire circuit board!

Today, ACUs are used only on some larger computer systems—generally in rack-mounted computer equipment. This setup has separate ports for dialing (the ACU) and for transferring data (the modem). For more information on setting up ACUs, see the *UNIX System V Administrator Guide* available from AT&T. Practically all UUCP systems provide direct support for an AT&T 801-type ACU, but very few actually use this device. Other ACUs and modems can be used, but may require "work arounds"—see the section on Version 2 device support for specific directions.

HoneyDanBer UUCP provides good uniform support for many popular modern modems, dialers, and data switches by using a new configuration file, **Dialers.** Some of the more recent revisions of Version 2 UUCP provide for some of these communication devices, too. However, different implementations use different approaches, and the range of devices supported is generally limited in scope.

Now let's see how to connect the communication devices to the computer. These connections are almost always made through a serial port. And the port uses a standard interface called RS-232-C. So the next step is to discuss this interface standard.

RS-232-C Interfacing

In 1969, the Electronic Industries Association (EIA), Bell Laboratories, and communication equipment manufacturers formulated a much needed standard for connecting equipment that communicates serially. This standard, known as RS-232-C, describes how to connect (or interface) data terminal equipment (DTE) to data communication equipment (DCE).

Generally, data terminals are wired as DTE and modems as DCE. However, to set up UUCP communications you need to connect one UNIX computer to another or to a modem—not the same thing. The RS-232-C standard provides some guidelines, but it doesn't furnish all the answers. As a result, microcomputer manufacturers, especially, have used the RS-232-C standard in nonstandard ways.

The physical connector used for RS-232-C interfacing is typically a 25-pin connector known as the DB-25. However, since in practice only three to eight pins of this connector are actually used, other connectors with fewer pins are coming into vogue, such as the DB-9 and eight-pin modular connectors.

Connecting a Terminal to a Computer. We'll discuss the terminal-to-computer interface first, because in many cases it's a simple interface—requiring only three wires. Figure 8.31 shows the lines (or signals) for connecting these devices together.

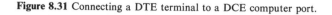

Figure 8.31 Connecting a DTE terminal to a DCE computer port.

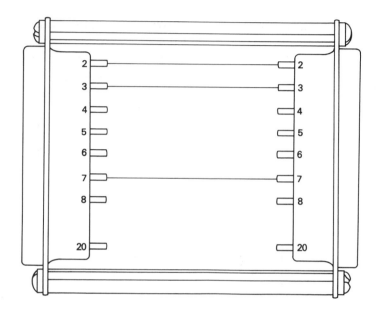

Pin 7 always serves as a common voltage reference point for *all* other signals on the interface. Pins 2 and 3 pass the data. Data are always sent from the DTE device on pin 2, thus it's labeled "TRANSMITTED DATA," "TD," or "TxD." However, pin 2 of the DCE device, where the data are received, is labeled the same (TRANSMITTED DATA). Similarly, pin 3 of both the DTE and DCE devices is called "RECEIVED DATA," "RD," or "RxD," even though data are only received by the DTE device on this pin. Thus, you need to think of these names relative to the DTE device.

The example in Figure 8.31 is straightforward since the terminal is a DTE and the computer serial port a DCE device. So pin 2 on the terminal (an output) is connected to pin 2 on the computer (an input). Similarly, pin 3 on the computer (an output) is connected to pin 3 on the terminal (an input). And pin 7 is always connected directly across.

A Null Modem Connection.   What happens if the computer port is wired as a DTE device and we're trying to "talk to" a DTE terminal?   In this case both the computer and the terminal would be trying to send data out pin 2 and receive data in pin 3—so connecting these pins together would accomplish nothing—no data would be transferred.   Since an output needs to be connected to an input, the answer is to connect pin 2 of one device to pin 3 of the other.   Figure 8.32 shows this interface, which is commonly referred to as a *null modem.*

Figure 8.32 Connecting a DTE computer to a DTE terminal via null modem cabling.

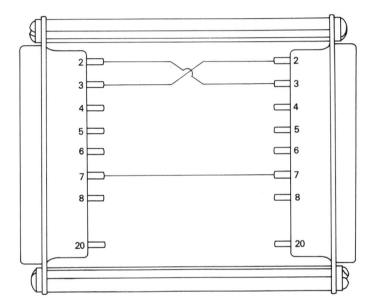

Power-up Handshaking.   In our previous two examples we discussed the *data signals*, describing how data are transferred across an RS-232-C interface. But most equipment also needs *control signals* to regulate the data movement.   For our discussion, data signals are on the pins that actually transmit and receive characters (2, 3, and 7), whereas the control signals are on everything else on the RS-232-C interface.

Now for some definition of terms.   We'll refer to control inputs as either being *enabled* (turned on) or *disabled* (turned off) and control outputs as being *asserted* (activated) or *inhibited* (deactivated).   Thus, an asserted output will enable the input to which it's connected, and an inhibited output will disable its input.

Some DTE devices assert a signal on pin 20 (Data Terminal Ready, or DTR) to indicate they are powered up and ready. They may also expect an enable signal back on pin 6 (Data Set Ready, or DSR) to indicate that the device it's connected to is ready. Conversely, the DCE device may expect an enable signal on pin 20 before it will communicate and will assert a signal on pin 6 when it's powered up. This so-called "power-up handshaking" happens to be the same as described in the RS-232-C interface standard. However, in practice, the equipment manufacturers may use this handshaking, no handshaking, or even invent their own scheme.

Connecting a Computer to a Modem. As the next step, let's see how you could connect a computer port (wired as a DTE) to a modem (wired as a DCE). Figure 8.33 shows the most commonly used lines (or signals) for connecting these devices together. Although still only a small subset of the full-blown RS-232-C interface, which specifies use of 21 pins, it is sufficient for the majority of practical interfaces between today's computers and modems.

Figure 8.33 Connecting a DTE computer port to a DCE modem.

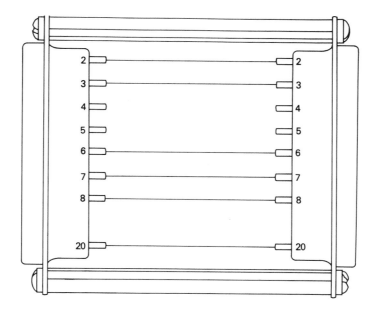

Table 8.12 lists the pin numbers we'll be discussing, their names, a common abbreviation, and brief description for the connection described relative to the DTE end.

TABLE 8.12 RS-232-C SIGNALS USED FOR A COMPUTER-TO-MODEM INTERFACE

Pin	Signal name	Abbreviation	Usage (relative to DTE)
1	Frame ground	---	Shield grounding (often optional)
2	Transmitted data	TxD,TD	Transmit data to modem
3	Received data	RxD,RD	Receive data from modem
6	Data Set Ready	DSR	Input to computer saying that modem is ready
7	Signal ground	---	Common ground for all signals
8	Data Carrier Detect	DCD	Used to control data reception
20	Data Terminal Ready	DTR	An output used to enable the modem

Now we need to discuss the function of the control lines used between the computer and the modem, which brings us to the subject of UNIX-style modem control.

UNIX-style Modem Control.   The computer and modem may use power-up handshaking. If so, the DTE computer port will assert its Data Terminal Ready (DTR) output line (pin 20), which enables the modem's DTR input line. This signal tells the modem that the computer is powered up and ready to transmit data. And in turn, the modem may assert its Data Set Ready (DSR) output line (pin 6),

Figure 8.34 Diagram of two computers connected via modems.

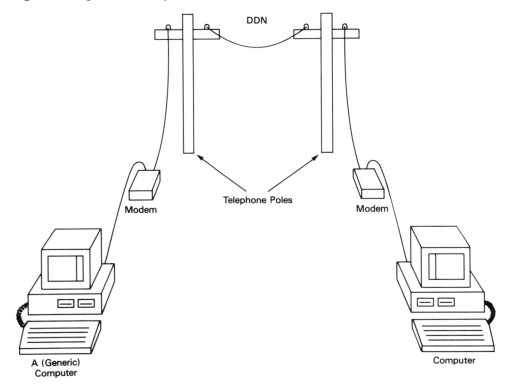

which enables the computer's DSR input line. This signal tells the computer that the modem is powered up and ready. The term *data set* is a synonym for modem. Most computers and modems use DTR for power-up handshaking, but they might not use DSR for this purpose.

The modem regulates data transfer between the local and remote computers by using its Data Carrier Detect (DCD) line. Figure 8.34 diagrams the two computers with their associated modems. DDN stands for the Direct Dial Network (telephone system).

When the local modem makes a connection to another remote modem, it will assert its Data Carrier Detect (DCD) output (pin 8), which is monitored by DCD input of the local computer. When the computer's DCD input is enabled, it will complete the connection with the remote system and begin data transfer. When carrier is lost, the modem's DCD output line is inhibited, which disables the computer's DCD input, causing the computer to stop sending data out the modem. As an example of this so-called *modem control* for the UNIX operating system, consider the events that occur when a remote user logs in and out of your local UNIX system.

Table 8.13 tabulates the events for logging in and Table 8.14 the events for logging out of a UNIX system.

TABLE 8.13 THE EVENTS FOR SUPPORTING A LOG-IN REQUEST USING A DIAL-UP LINE

(1) The **init** process spawns a **getty** process for the dial-in modem line.

(2) The **getty** process attempts to open the modem line, and the open routine in the device driver asserts the computer's DTR output.

(3) The modem can now receive a call since its DTR input has been enabled.

(4) The **getty** process sleeps in the open routine, waiting on the event that carrier is detected.

(5) When the local modem detects a ring, it answers the phone (goes off hook) and when it recognizes the "idle" transmitter tone of the remote modem, the local modem asserts its data carrier detect (DCD) output.

(6) The device driver on the UNIX system wakes up when the modem line DCD is asserted, and in turn, wakes up the waiting **getty** process to complete the open of the serial port line connected to the modem.

(7) The **getty** process will display the log-in prompt and can begin the usual log-in sequence.

TABLE 8.14 THE EVENTS THAT ENSUE WHEN A USER LOGS OFF A DIAL-UP PORT

(1) When the user logs-off the system, their log-in shell terminates.

(2) The modem line was held open by the shell, and after it terminates, the line is closed.

(3) When the modem line is closed, the device driver causes the computer's DTR output to become inhibited (System V specific action).

(4) Since the modem's DTR input is disabled, it hangs up the phone.

(5) Meanwhile, after the log-in shell terminates, the **init** process receives the death-of-child signal, and it wakes up.

(6) After waking, **init** finds out that the child process has been a log-in shell and thus spawns another **getty** to open the modem line in place of the shell that died.

(7) The attempted open of the modem line causes the device driver to assert the computer's DTR output, which enables the modem's DTR input and readies the system for another log-in request.

Broken Communication Link. What happens if the communication link is broken before the called party logs out? A *hangup* signal should be sent to the log-in shell to terminate it. When the connection is severed, the DCD output of the local modem is inhibited so that the local computer's DCD input becomes disabled. The device driver for the modem line monitors the DCD input, and if the HUPCL flag (hang up on close) is set for the terminal line connected to the modem, the driver generates a hangup signal, which is sent to the log-in shell, terminating it. (HUPCL is enabled by specifying it in the *final-flags* field for the appropriate entry in the **/etc/gettydefs** file.)

A serious security loophole exists on systems that don't terminate the log-in shell if the line to the remote system is disconnected. If the user hangs up the phone without logging off, the next caller can begin interacting with the previous user's shell (with that user's access privileges) without going through the usual password-protected log-in sequence. Thus, you should always be sure that the log-in shell terminates whenever the phone is hung-up. Use HUPCL for the dial-in line and make sure the modem-computer interface supports UNIX modem control.

As an example, the log-in shell won't be terminated if the DCD output of the modem isn't connected to the computer's DCD input or if the device driver doesn't monitor this input. Sometimes the computer's serial port doesn't support DCD, although this is not common with today's hardware. Occasionally, you may run across a modem that doesn't handle DCD properly—luckily, this is rare.

Connecting Two Computers Together. A direct connection between the serial ports of two computers can be a complicated interface because (1) the ports will probably be wired the same—both DCE or DTE devices—so you have to use null modem cabling for both the data and control lines, (2) modem control handshaking using the Data Carrier Detect line (discussed above) may be used even through there's no modem involved, and (3) additional handshaking using Request to Send and Clear to Send (discussed below) may be needed.

Of course, none of these complications may be applicable. For instance, we've connected two computers together with only four wires (pins 2, 3, 7, and 20) going straight across the interface since one computer was a DTE, the other a DCE, and only Data Terminal Ready power-up handshaking was used. However, we'll present the complicated case as an example. Please note that the requirements for your actual situation may be different and later we'll provide a reference for helping you further.

Figure 8.35 shows the wiring diagram for the interface under consideration. For this example assume that both computer serials ports are DTE and that control signal handshaking is used by both computers.

Here we've crossed over Transmitted Data (pin 2) and Received Data (pin 3), so the data output of one computer would be connected to the data input of the other one. And, of course, the signal ground line goes straight across the interface as always.

Figure 8.35 Interfacing two DTE computer ports.

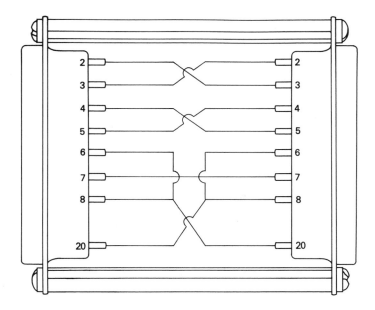

Recall that a DTE device asserts a Data Terminal Ready signal (pin 20) and may expect both a Data Set Ready (pin 6) and Data Carrier Detect (pin 8) to be enabled before transmitting any data. In our example, the DTR output of one computer serial port is connected to both the DSR and DCD inputs of the other computer—to provide the required handshaking signals.

And two other handshaking lines are used as well in this example. Each computer asserts its Request to Send output (pin 4) when it's ready to send data and expects back an enabled signal on its Clear to Send input (pin 5) to indicate that it's okay to transmit characters. These lines are crossed over so that the RTS output of one computer is connected to the CTS input of the other. Of course, these signals might also be used for a computer-to-modem interface; in fact, RTS and CTS signals are a holdover from half-duplex modems, which could pass data in only one direction at a time.

Other RS-232-C Interfacing Problems.   If your equipment works as we've described in our examples, then you can use our wiring diagrams. However, computer, modem, and terminal manufacturers may use RS-232-C lines in nonstandard ways. We don't have space here to delve into all the permutations. However, *The RS-232 Solution* by Joe Campbell (Sybex, Inc., Berkeley, CA., 1984), outlines a practical and virtually foolproof method for connecting two RS-232-C-compatible devices. The author describes a general approach for determining the connections across the interface based on a simple series of electrical tests. The approach used even obviates the need for manufacturer's documentation, which is often confusing and sometimes incorrect.

STEP TWO: The Node Name

After you've got your computer interfaced to your modem and UNIX-style modem control operating correctly, the next step in setting up UUCP communications is to determine your node name (also called site name). Your node name is the name by which your system is known on a UUCP communication network.

The node name is located in the UNIX kernel. On standard System V implementations it occurs in a special structure called **utsname**, which is defined by the file **/usr/include/sys/utsname.h**. Table 8.15 lists the elements of this structure with a brief description. Each element on our System V Release 2 implementation can contain up to eight bytes plus a null character terminator. We show those values in the third field of each table entry.

TABLE 8.15 A SAMPLE **utsname** STRUCTURE

Structure member	Description	Value
sysname	The system name	Opus5
nodename	The node name	sirius
release	The operating system release number	2.0v2
version	The operating system version	C2.1
machine	The machine hardware name	Opus32

Most Version 2 UUCP implementations limit the node name to seven characters, and some truncate (only consider the node name to be six characters). In this case the first six characters of your node name must be unique (not duplicated in the node name of another system that communicates with you). HoneyDanBer UUCP allows up to 14 characters without truncation. But for compatibility with all pre-HoneyDanBer systems, you will have to limit the name to six characters.

Determining your Node Name. Most UNIX System V implementations include two different utilities for determining your node name, **uname** and **uuname**. The **uname** utility displays the contents of the **utsname** structure. Without options (or with the −s option) it displays only your system name; the −n option displays your node name. The −a options displays all other parameters as well, including the UNIX system release and version and your machine hardware name. Figure 8.36 shows the **uname** output obtained on one of our systems.

Figure 8.36 Display system identifying information with **uname**.

```
$ uname
Opus5
$ uname -n
sirius
$ uname -a
Opus5 sirius 2.0v2 C2.1 Opus32
$ □
```

The **uuname** command, which comes with the UUCP software, displays information about sites known to the UUCP communication system. Without options it displays all known systems (those listed in Version 2 **L.sys** or in the HoneyDanBer **Systems** file). The −l option causes **uuname** to run **uname** −n to display your node name. Version 2 UUCP **uuname** recognizes a −v option to print any additional information contained in the **/usr/lib/uucp/ADMIN** file for those sites listed in **L.sys**. Figure 8.37 shows the results obtained on our system when we ran **uuname**.

Figure 8.37 Display system identifying information with Version 2 **uuname**.

```
$ uuname
uworld
opusys
$ uuname -l
sirius
$ uuname -v
uworld Unix/World magazine
opusys Opus Systems
$ □
```

Changing your Node Name.   The location of the local node name and methods for changing it vary widely from one UNIX system implementation to the next.   Most systems have the node name built into the kernel (in the **utsname** structure), some systems store it in an ordinary file, and we have seen systems that put it in the boot block of the root file system.

The methods for changing the node name vary depending on where it's located.   Of course, if the node name is in an ordinary file, you could change it with an editor.   However, if it's stored in the kernel or in the boot block, you need a special utility to change it, which should be provided by your UNIX system vendor.

Figure 8.38 shows a general technique for changing the node name that should work on most System V UNIX implementations that have a debugger, such as **adb**. In this example we operate on a copy of the disk-based kernel, as well as the in-core (memory) copy. We show use of the **adb** program to make the changes since this debugger is generally available on most UNIX systems. Of course, our approach should work with other common debuggers, such as **sdb**. You will have to use the particular commands understood by your particular debugger.

Figure 8.38 Changing the node name of a disk-based and in-core copy of the kernel.

```
# uname -n                                  display node name of kernel (in memory)
honeydew
# cp /unix /unix2                           safer to work on a copy
# adb -w /unix2 /dev/kmem                    invoke for writing on disk and in-core copies
bad core magic number                        can ignore this warning
utsname+9?s                                  display node name on disk (as string)
_utsname+9:        honeydew
!echo "banana\c" | od -x
0000000 6162 616e 616e
0000006
!
utsname+9?w 0x6162 0x616e 0x616e 0x00 update disk copy
f26981:        6f68      =      6162
f26983:        656e      =      616e
f26985:        6479      =      616e
f26987:        7765      =      0
utsname+9?s                                  display new node name on disk
_utsname+9:        banana
utsname+9/s                                  display node name in core
_utsname+9:        honeydew
utsname+9/w 0x6162 0x616e 0x616e 0x00 update core copy
_utsname+9:        6f68      =      6162
_utsname+b:        656e      =      616e
_utsname+d:        6479      =      616e
_utsname+f:        7765      =      0
utsname+9/s                                  display new node name in core
_utsname+9:        banana
$q                                           exit adb
# uname -n                                  display node name of kernel (in memory)
banana
# cp /unix2 /unix                           overwrite with updated kernel
# □
```

Here's a brief description of the commands in Figure 8.38:

```
    # uname -n
```

Displays the node name of the kernel running in memory.

```
# cp /unix /unix2
```

Make a copy of the kernel; it's safer to use a debugger on a copy than on the "real" kernel. Also, to be safe make a backup copy of the kernel, as in **cp /unix /unix.bak**.

```
# adb -w /unix2 /dev/kmem
```

Invoke **adb** for writing on the **/unix2** object file and the **/dev/kmem** "core" file, which is actually the in-core copy of kernel memory. You can ignore the warning "bad core magic number " since **/dev/kmem** doesn't have or need a "magic number."

Use a dash (−) in place of **/dev/kmem** if you only wish to change a disk-based copy of the kernel, as in **adb −w /unix2 −**. However, you can't just specify the memory copy using a dash instead of an object file argument, as in **adb −w − /dev/kmem**, because you need to have the symbol table for the kernel loaded.

```
utsname+9?s
```

The **s** suffix means to display the variable as a string of characters. The starting address for the display is given by **utsname +9**, which means to skip the first nine characters of the **utsname** variable. The first element (the system name) of **utsname** structure is nine bytes in length, so you will be pointing at the start of the second element, which is the node name. The question mark (**?**) means to access the object file, which is **/unix2** in this example.

```
!echo "banana\c" | od -x
```

Escape to the shell to run **od −x** to display the hexadecimal values of the string "banana" without a newline (**\c**). The output has the correct byte ordering for your machine architecture.

```
utsname+9?w 0x6162 0x616e 0x616e 0x00
```

Write (**w**) the (hexadecimal) bytes shown to the node name element (**utsname +9**) of the object file (**?**). The final zero (**0x00**) is necessary else the result will be **bananaew**, because **banana** only overwrites the first six characters of **honeydew**.

```
utsname+9/s
```

Display the node name of the in-core kernel as a string. The slash (**/**) represents addressing the "core" file, **/dev/kmem** in this case.

```
utsname+9/w 0x6162 0x616e 0x616e 0x00
```

Write (**w**) the (hexadecimal) bytes shown to node name element
(**utsname +9**) of the core file (**/**).

```
# cp /unix2 /unix
```

Overwrite the old disk-based kernel, which used **honeydew** as the node name,
by the new **banana** node name version.

Determine If Your New Node Name Is Unique.   If you're going to connect your system to the UUCP network, you should make sure that the name you
choose is not already used for another machine on the network. Ask someone who
is already on the network to examine a database that lists the node names of all the
machines on the network. If your node name is already in use, you'll have to
choose one that isn't.

What happens if your node name isn't unique? If you're connected directly
to a machine with the same name, the UUCP system won't allow communication
with that machine. If you're on the same UUCP network but not directly connected,
it's possible that electronic mail destined for your machine will be sent to the other
machine with the same name, and vice versa.

STEP THREE: Establish UUCP accounts

After wiring your connections and setting your system's node name, you'll need to
configure the communication software. As a first step, make sure your UUCP system has an *administrative account*.

The Administrative Account.   This account, named **uucp**, is used for file
and process ownership. Most systems don't allow system access via this account—it
will have an impossible password in the **/etc/passwd** encrypted password field. Of
course, the superuser can always use **su** to assume this account identity for UUCP
system administration.

The **uucp** account will own many of the UUCP programs, directories, and files.
You should either switch (using **su**) to this account from **root** when creating UUCP
files or remember to change their ownership to **uucp**. Writing to existing files will
retain the previous ownership.

The **uucp** account will receive mail about various activities. For instance, as
delivered, both the HoneyDanBer **uudemon.admin** and **uudemon.cleanu** maintenance
shell scripts send status information to the **uucp** account mailbox.

UUCP programs that need to access files readable only by the **uucp** account
will be set-user-id and owned by this account so that they can be run by ordinary
system users. Also, the **uudemon** scripts run by **cron** will execute as if invoked from
this account even though the **root** cron table entry is used, because of the **/bin/su**
uucp entry in the command line field of the cron table entry.

Figure 8.39 shows a typical password file entry for a UUCP administrative account. The log-in program (the startup program that is invoked by the **login** process as the last step of the log-in sequence) is a general-purpose shell, so you can log into this account and use it for administering your communication system. We suggest that you install an impossible password as shown; then, when logged in as superuser, use the **su uucp** command to switch to the **uucp** account.

Figure 8.39 Sample password file entry containing an impossible password for the UUCP administrative account.

```
uucp:**NO-LOGIN**:5:5:UUCP Administration:/usr/lib/uucp:/bin/sh
```

The user-id (or UID) and group-id (or GID) are both 5 in this example. Some older versions of UUCP required them to be 4.

The Access Account.   You'll need to establish a UUCP *access account* to allow a remote system to log-in to your local machine. We recommend establishing a distinct account for *each* different site that calls in. Why? Primarily for security—for controlling access to your system or its files. You can require that a given remote system must use a particular access account. Also tracing the activity (say with the system accounting package) of each remote system would be easier when debugging problems. Figure 8.40 shows two typical remote-access account entries.

Figure 8.40 Sample password file entries for UUCP access accounts.

```
nuucp:kPabRrowAt1Po:50:50::/usr/spool/uucppublic:/usr/lib/uucp/uucico
uunorth:wRgVdYGw0zgII:51:50::/usr/spool/uucppublic:/usr/lib/uucp/uucico
```

The first, **nuucp**, is a generic entry generally provided by your UNIX system vendor. The other entry is for remote system **northpol** to gain access. We suggest using an account name that suggests the remote node name. Thus, you could use a prefix like **uu** or **u** to indicate a UUCP account. For instance, I'd use **uusirius** for the site **sirius**—a six-character node name plus a two-character prefix adds up to the eight-character maximum used for UNIX account names.

Of course, you should install a password. You can't use **su** to switch to these accounts since they'll run **uucico** instead of a shell. Use **passwd** *accountname* when logged in as superuser.

Some UNIX systems allow sharing of the same user-id and group-id with other UUCP accounts; others don't. System V versions seem permissive—the actual user- and group-ids are arbitrary as long as they don't conflict with other non-UUCP accounts.

We chose user- and group-ids distinct from those for the UUCP administrative account on purpose. This approach is more secure—if the remote system was able to coax a shell out of **uucico**, they still couldn't read the sensitive UUCP configuration files owned by **uucp**. Furthermore, we use different user-ids for each UUCP account so that system accounting can keep track of each account individually.

The home directory field for all access accounts generally contains the UUCP public directory, **/usr/spool/uucppublic**. However, some security-conscious sites don't use this "public" directory as their home directory. HoneyDanBer UUCP systems allow you to specify different public directories (the directory corresponding to the ~/ abbreviation) in the **Permissions** file.

The UUCP copy-in-copy-out daemon program, **/usr/lib/uucp/uucico**, *must* be used as the log-in program instead of a general-purpose shell. We've seen AT&T System III and V UUCP implementations that specify a shell script as the log-in program so that they can pass the correct time-zone environment to the **uucico** daemon. This environment information is necessary for talking to a BSD system.

Figure 8.41 shows the contents of such a script, named **uushell**. The **fgrep** command "extracts" the value for the **TZ** variable from the systemwide Bourne shell startup file, **/etc/profile**, and the **env** command merges this value into the execution environment for **uucico**.

Figure 8.41 Contents of the **uushell** log-in shell script.

```
$ cat /usr/lib/uucp/uushell
exec env `/usr/bin/fgrep TZ= /etc/profile` /usr/lib/uucp/uucico
$ □
```

STEP FOUR: Configuring the L.sys and Systems Files

Now you're ready for the next step, configuring the file that specifies how to call a particular system. Version 2 UUCP calls this file **L.sys**, whereas HoneyDanBer designates it **Systems**.

L.sys and **Systems** are almost identical—the number and functions for the fields in each file are the same. However, the field contents may differ between the two files. We'll discuss both files in this section, pointing out differences.

Entries in Version 2 **L.sys** or HoneyDanBer **Systems** files describe how to access remote systems. Figure 8.42 shows an actual example of an entry line that could be found in either file for contacting the site named **northpol**. Below this line are the names we'll use to reference the fields.

Figure 8.42 An entry for contacting remote site **northpol**.

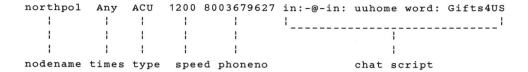

The first field (the node name) identifies the remote system to contact. The next four fields provide information for dialing and establishing the connection with the remote site. The last (and most complicated) field provides information necessary for logging into the UUCP access account on the remote machine. Contact the system administrator of the remote site to get the information you'll need to create the entry to contact that site.

The Node Name Field.   The node name of the remote system must be unique in the first seven characters. That is, you couldn't have entries named **newyork1** and **newyork2** in the same file.

The Times Field.   The days of the week and times of day when the remote system can be called. You can make a UUCP system request at any time, but the remote system won't be called unless the current time falls within the interval specified by this field. If you wish to call during a time when contact isn't allowed, you'll need to change the contents of this field.

This field consists of up to three parts catenated together in the order: *days-of-week*, *times-of-day*, and then a *retry-time* subfield. The *days-of-week* subfield is required, but the other two are optional.

The *days-of-week* subfield can name one or more days of the week—**Su Mo Tu We Th Fr Sa** or **Su**. If two or more are specified, they must be catenated together, as in **SaSu** for the weekend days. Use the abbreviation **Wk** for all days of the workweek (Monday through Friday, inclusive) and **Any** for all days of the week and weekend. You would specify **Never** in this subfield if your local site never calls the remote site. You might use such an entry to queue up mail or files for a remote site that will contact your site.

The *times-of-day* subfield should be a range of times of the form *time1—time2*, where *time1* and *time2* use the 24-hour format—that is, 9 P.M. would be 2100. Unlike the time range of some early versions, the more recent Version 2 and HoneyDanBer time range can span midnight (0000), as in 2300-0800 for all times between 11 P.M. and 8 A.M. the next morning.

Most Version 2 implementations don't allow multiple time specifications. Thus, you can't prescribe, say, one set of times for weekdays and another for weekends. However, some UUCP implementations allow multiple **L.sys** file entry lines for the same remote site. So you could add additional times by adding multiple file entries. Part a of Figure 8.43 illustrates this approach.

HoneyDanBer implementations do let you associate different time ranges with different days of the week, by separating the subfields with commas. Part b of Figure 8.43 shows the HoneyDanBer equivalent of the Version 2 example shown in part a. Note that we break the single (long) logical entry line into two physical lines using the backslash.

Figure 8.43 Using day-of-week and times-of-day combinations.

a. Using Version 2 **L.sys** file:

```
northpol Wk2100-0800 ACU 1200 8003679627 in: uuhome word: Gifts4US
northpol Sa          ACU 1200 8003679627 in: uuhome word: Gifts4US
northpol Su0800-1700 ACU 1200 8003679627 in: uuhome word: Gifts4US
```

b. Using HoneyDanBer **Systems** file allows calling at the same times as part a:

```
northpol Wk2100-0800,Sa,Su0800-1700 ACU 1200 8003679627 \
in: uuhome word: Gifts4US
```

The *retry* time is the minimum period (in minutes) UUCP waits before contacting a system after a previous unsuccessful attempt. The Version 2 default retry period is 55 minutes, whereas HoneyDanBer systems start with 5 minutes and double the time after each failed attempt.

You can change the default values by appending the *retry-time* subfield to your *times* field specification. Version 2 systems use a comma and HoneyDanBer uses a semicolon as a separator. Note that if you reset the HoneyDanBer retry time, the retry period stays the same—it doesn't double after each failed attempt.

Figure 8.44 shows some examples using retry times. Part a depicts an example for Version 2 UUCP. The first entry in part a allows calls between 11 P.M. and 8 A.M. with 30 minutes between retries. The second entry allows calling any time on the weekend with only 10 minutes between retries. Part b shows how these specifications can be combined into a single entry for HoneyDanBer systems.

Figure 8.44 Comparing retry time specifications.

a. Version 2 entries:

```
Wk2300-0800,30
SaSu,10
```

b. Equivalent HoneyDanBer entry:

```
Wk2300-0800;30,SaSu;10
```

After an unsuccessful attempt to contact a remote system, a "status" file remains behind to enforce the retry-time restriction. You can erase the status file to enable another call attempt immediately. The Version 2 status file has pathname **/usr/spool/uucp/STST**.*nodename*, and HoneyDanBer **/usr/spool/uucp/.Status**/*nodename*, where *nodename* is the node name of the remote system.

The Type Field. Version 2 and HoneyDanBer UUCP systems use this device-type field somewhat differently. In Version 2 it would contain ACU (for "automatic call unit") to denote a ACU or modem connection. Or this field would contain the basename portion of the special device file corresponding to the communication line for a direct connection, such as **tty1** for device **/dev/tty1**. Both ACU and direct-connect device names must index into an entry in **L-devices**, as we'll see later. This field may contain a special keyword, such as NET, for connection to a local area network, such as Ethernet (with TCP/IP protocol).

The HoneyDanBer *type* field can contain any keyword, such as ACU, a device basename, even a system name, as long as it points to a corresponding entry in **Devices**. We'll show some examples when we discuss the **Devices** file.

The Speed Field. The baud rate for the communication device, generally 300 or 1200 for a modem, or 9600 for a direct connection. If a network connection is used, this field would have a 0 or perhaps a dash (−) as a placeholder.

The Phoneno Field. The phone number to be dialed by the ACU. Two special characters are recognized in the phone number—a dash (−) causes the dialer to pause for a few seconds, where the exact time depends on the dialer hardware. An equals sign (=) tells the dialer to wait for a secondary dial tone. If the dialer can't detect a dial tone, the delay function could be used instead.

For instance, 9=1−8005551212, instructs the dialer to dial a 9 (to get an outside line), then wait for a secondary dial tone. When the dial tone is recognized, dial a 1, pause for a few seconds, then dial 8005551212.

An optional alphabetic prefix may be used with the phone number. For instance, you might use **outlong** as a mnemonic for the **9=1−** sequence, to mean access an outside line for a long-distance call. Then the *phoneno* field would contain **outlong8005551212** to correspond to our previous example. You'll need to define the alphabetic prefix in either the Version 2 **L-dialcodes** or HoneyDanBer **Dialcodes** file. We'll discuss these files and give more dialing prefix examples later.

If a direct connection is used, *phoneno* field is ignored, but a placeholder must be used to maintain the correct field count. Version 2 systems repeat the contents of the *type* field here, whereas HoneyDanBer systems use a dash (−) instead.

The Log-in Chat Field. This field comprises the remainder of the entry line after the phone number. Information in this field is used to log in to the UUCP access account of the remote site. Specifically, the local **uucico** process is talking to the **getty** process on the remote system, replying to prompts issued by the remote **getty** program to log in. With some Version 2 implementations you might also put device dialer or network switch connect information in this field. We'll discuss this approach later. HoneyDanBer systems keep all device dialing and connection sequences in the **Dialers** file.

The *log-in chat* field consists of pairs of *expect* and *send* strings separated by spaces. The *expect* string is a sequence of characters expected to be read from the remote system, such as the log-in prompt. The *send* string is transmitted to the remote site in response to the previous *expect* string, which would be the UUCP access account name in response to the log-in prompt.

Figure 8.45 shows a simple example that might be appropriate for either a direct connection between two systems or for an ACU that uses a high-quality (leased) telephone line with minimal noise and interference. The "e" and "s" above the entry designate the expect and send strings, respectively.

Figure 8.45 A simple expect-send sequence.

```
   e    s    e    s      e        s
   "" \r\c login: myuucp Password: mypasswd
```

This string example would be interpreted as by the **uucico** process as follows: expect nothing "" (an empty string) from the remote system, but send \r (a carriage return or control-M) and \c says to suppress the newline that's normally sent. Expect **login:** from the remote **getty**, send **myuucp** in reply, expect **Password:**, and send **mypasswd** in response to finish logging in.

In practice, the leading letters in the *expect* strings **login:** and **Password:** are omitted because these prompts might be capitalized on some systems but not on others. For instance, **login:** might be abbreviated as **ogin:**, or even **in:**. Such partial strings are allowed because **uucico** scans the *expect* string from left to right until a match is found.

What happens if the expected set of characters isn't received? In our previous example **uucico** would "give up" after a certain time period. But you can adjust the *expect* field for this contingency by adding *send-expect* subfields. Figure 8.46 shows a simple example based on the previous one.

Figure 8.46 A simple expect-send sequence with send-expect subfield.

```
   e    s     e   se    s      e        s
   "" \r\c in:-@-in: myuucp word: mypasswd
```

Here the local system expects **in:**, and if that's not received during a certain period of time (about 15 seconds), it sends an @, which is the default line-kill character. This character would cause the remote **getty** to discard all characters received so far—useful for noisy lines. Then the local system expects **in:** again. If that's not received within a certain time, the connection attempt is aborted.

Figure 8.47 shows an even more complicated (and realistic) example.

Figure 8.47 A more realistic expect-send sequence with send-expect subfield.

```
   e   s    e s e s   e    s   e    s    e     s
   "" \r\c in:--in:-@-in:-EOT-in:-BREAK-in: myuucp word: mypasswd
```

The subfield string always expects **in:**, and if not received, first sends a NULL (depicted by the extra dash), then a @ (the line kill character) in case "garbage" characters were received, then two EOTs (Control-Ds) in case upper-case mode was entered by mistake, and before "giving up," finally sends a BREAK in case the line speed isn't correct. The break character is simulated by using null characters and baud rate changes—so it may not work on all systems. Note that a newline is sent after each character sequence specified in the subfield since no \c directive is used.

Generally, the most difficult part of constructing an **L.sys** or **Systems** file entry is writing the *log-in chat* field. As a shortcut you could start with the expect-send string shown in the last example and change it as necessary for your site requirements. Writing the expect-send string, however, is generally trial-and-error for each remote system you call. There are just too many variables and timing possibilities to give a pat recipe that works for any generic site.

You can use the **cu** program to log in to a remote site and develop your *log-in chat* sequence. Once you've been able to log in successfully with **cu**, add that same sequence of characters that you typed and the responses (that you got in return) to your *log-in chat* field.

Table 8.16 defines all the special character sequences used in the *chat* field. Sequences recognized only by HoneyDanBer systems are indicated as HDB only.

TABLE 8.16 SPECIAL CHARACTER SEQUENCES USED IN *log-in chat* FIELD

""	Empty string
\N	Null character
\b	Backspace character
\c	Suppress newline that's sent by default
\d	Delay 2 seconds
\p	Pause for 1/4 to 1/2 second (HDB only)
\E	Turn on echo check (HDB only)
\e	Turn off echo check (HDB only)
\K	Send break (HDB only)
\n	Newline character
\r	Carriage return
\s	Space character
\t	Tab character
\\	A literal backslash (\) character
EOT	Control-D newline control-D newline
BREAK	Send break (simulated)
\ddd	Send character, where *ddd* is octal value

Connection Types. Figure 8.48 shows examples of ACU and direct connections for both the Version 2 **L.sys** and HoneyDanBer **Systems** file. The entries for the ACU connections are similar, but direct connection entries differ between Version 2 and HoneyDanBer systems.

Figure 8.48 Examples of **L.sys** and **Systems** file entries for both ACU and direct connections.

a. **L.sys** ACU connection:

```
northpol Any ACU 1200 8003679627 in:-@-in: uuhome word: Gifts4US
```

b. **L.sys** direct connection:

```
northpol Any tty02 9600 tty02 in:-@-in: uuhome word: Gifts4US
```

c. **Systems** ACU connection:

```
northpol Any ACU 1200 8003679627 in:-@-in: uuhome word: Gifts4US
```

d. **Systems** direct connection:

```
northpol Any northpol 9600 - in:-@-in: uuhome word: Gifts4US
```

As you can see, the ACU connections are the same for both files. However, the direct connections are significantly different.

STEP FIVE: Setting Up L-dialcodes or Dialcodes Files (Optional)

The Version 2 **L-dialcodes** or HoneyDanBer **Dialcodes** file defines the alphabetical character prefixes used in the phone numbers specified in the **L.sys** or **Systems** files. These prefixes are commonly used as either mnemonic aids or abbreviations. Figure 8.49 shows some sample entries.

Figure 8.49 Examples of **L-dialcode** or **Dialcodes** file entries.

```
sf                      415
sprint                  1-800-345-0008=0-
boonville               9=1-707-895-
```

The first example is the area code for San Francisco telephone numbers. The next example is the Sprint access number, useful when you wish to charge your UUCP call to this service. The wait for dial tone (=) is required by the Sprint system.

The sequence in the third example would be interpreted as dial 9 (for an outside line), wait for dial tone, then dial 1, the area code, and central office prefix (895) for any number in Boonville, California. The dashes in the examples are optional, but make the number more legible.

STEP SIX: Configuring the L-devices and Devices Files

The entries in these files describe the devices available for use by **cu** and the UUCP system. Each serial port used for communication by these programs must have an entry in the Version 2 **L-devices** or HoneyDanBer **Devices** file. The device name of each port must also appear in the **/dev** directory.

Earlier, you saw that the contents of the third (the *type*) field of the Version 2 **L.sys** or HoneyDanBer **Systems** file names the type of device used for contacting a remote system. Version 2 ACUs and all HoneyDanBer device types are mapped into a specific communication line by an entry in the Version 2 **L-devices** or HoneyDanBer **Devices** file. So let's discuss each of these files in turn since they are somewhat different from each other.

The Version 2 L-devices File

This file maps the device type and line speed, if any, specified in the **L.sys** file to a particular communication line. ACU and DIR connections are supported. This file is owned by the UUCP administrative account (**uucp**) and is readable, but not writable, by all users.

Version 2 devices are classified generally as either being direct connect (denoted as DIR) or as automatic call units (denoted as ACU). Hardwired connections between UNIX machines are always DIR connections.

As delivered from AT&T, the Version 2 UUCP system supports only the Western Electric 801-type automatic call unit. This device is a throwback to the days when an integral modem and dialer was difficult and thus expensive to make, so a separate dialer was used to service one or more modem data units.

The Version 2 **uucico** daemon knows about the 801 device and only needs to be told the phone number to dial. Thus a complete functioning unit consists of the dialer (the ACU), which requires one port (corresponding to the **/dev/cua0** autodialer device), and a modem data unit, which requires another port (corresponding to the **/dev/cul0** line device).

However, modern modems have the dialer and modem data unit in one unit. So to use these all-in-one modems with the UUCP system, you have to get the system to use only one port. One way to do this is to designate these modems as "directly connected" (DIR). In this case the commands for dialing and the data are sent to the same port. This is feasible since all the necessary commands can be specified in the **L.sys** *log-in chat* field.

Another approach is to use an ACU line but employ an appropriately written dialer program instead of the **/dev/cua0** device. The XENIX system, for instance, uses this approach. Figure 8.50 shows an entry for a Hayes Smartmodem.

Figure 8.50 A possible entry for a Hayes Smartmodem that uses a dialer program on a XENIX
system.

```
ACU   tty01   /bin/hayes   1200
 ┊      ┊        ┊           ┊
 ┊      ┊        ┊           ┊
type  device   dialer      speed
```

Now, also refer to Figure 8.51 as we discuss the fields one by one.

The Type Field.   Generally specifies either ACU (automatic calling unit) or
DIR (direct connection). Some implementations support other types, say for a network switch. More than one entry for a given type is used to specify more than one
communication link.

The Device Field.   The special device basename (found in **/dev**). Names
prefixed with **tty** refer to direct connect lines, as in **/dev/tty01**, or perhaps the communication line used with a dialer program, as is the case with Figure 8.50. The
/dev/cul0 entry shown in the last example in Figure 8.51 refers to the data line of
an 801 ACU connection.

The Dialer Field.   If an 801 ACU line this field contains the device name of
the auxiliary dialer, generally **/dev/cua0**. The pathname for a dialer program
might be used with some implementations. DIR lines would either repeat the
device name in this field or use an arbitrary number, such as zero or a dash, as a
placeholder.

The Speed Field.   The baud rate of the communication line for the modem
or direct link. The *speed* field of the **L.sys** file indexes into this field.

Figure 8.51 shows three examples of a direct entry and one of an ACU. The
first entry is for a "hardwired" connection using port **/dev/tty02**. The second and
third are for using a modern integral modem. Note that these two entries for **tty03**
allow you to use this line at *either* 300 or 1200 baud. The last entry is for an 801-
type ACU. Your particular Version 2 UUCP **L-devices** file may be set up somewhat
differently than the examples shown here, so consult your particular system documentation if there's a discrepancy.

Figure 8.51 Example of L-devices file entries.

```
DIR    tty02    0    9600
DIR    tty03    0     300
DIR    tty03    0    1200
ACU    cul0    cua0  1200
```

Relationship Between Version 2 L.sys and L-devices Files

Note that the *type* and *speed* combination used in a **L.sys** file entry match a pair of strings in the **L-devices** file. Figure 8.52 shows the relationship diagrammatically for an ACU device type that uses a dialer program.

Figure 8.52 Correspondence between the *type* and *speed* fields between the **L.sys** and **L-devices** file.

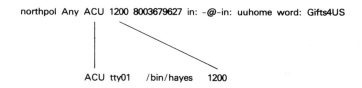

If you wish to use a modem with a different line speed or a direct connection to **northpol**, you'll need an additional **L.sys** entry for each case. Each **L.sys** entry will index into a different **L-devices** entry.

The HoneyDanBer Devices File

This file maps the device type and line speed, if any, specified in the **Systems** file to a particular communication line. ACU, direct, and network connections are supported. This file is owned by the UUCP administrative account (**uucp**) and is readable, but not writable, by all users. Figure 8.53 shows a sample entry.

Figure 8.53 A sample entry for a HoneyDanBer **Devices** file.

```
ACU       tty01    -        1200      hayes
 ¦         ¦       ¦         ¦         ¦
 ¦         ¦       ¦         ¦         ¦
type      device  acu       speed     dialer
```

The first four fields are analogous to those used in the Version 2 **L-devices** file. HoneyDanBer UUCP introduced a fifth field for supporting different dialing devices. Here's a recap of the first four fields from a HoneyDanBer perspective and a description of the new one.

The Type Field.   May contain several different keywords, including ACU, Direct (instead of DIR), a remote system node name, and a local area network switch name. The entry in this field corresponds to the *device* (third) field entry in the **Systems** file.

ACU type is used for modem communications. The modem may be connected directly to a computer serial port or indirectly through a network switch.

The **Direct** keyword indicates a line only used by **cu**. This enables you to invoke **cu** as in **cu −ltty01**. Recall that with Version 2 **cu**, you'd have to specify **cu −ltty01 dir** to use a direct line. Figure 8.54 shows an example of an ACU and Direct line.

Figure 8.54 An ACU and direct entry for the same communication line.

```
ACU       tty01    -          1200      hayes
Direct    tty01    -          1200      hayes
```

Direct links to a particular system can be specified using the node name of that machine as the device type. Figure 8.55 shows an example where two different direct connect lines connect to the same remote system.

Figure 8.55 Two direct connect entries to **northpol**.

```
northpol         tty01    -      9600      direct
northpol         tty02    -      9600      direct
```

The corresponding **Systems** file entry is shown in Figure 8.56.

Figure 8.56 A **Systems** file entry for a direct connection to **northpol**.

```
northpol Any northpol 9600 - in:-@-in: uuhome word: Gifts4US
```

The contents of the third and fourth fields of the **Systems** file entry in Figure 8.56 index into the first and fourth fields of either **Devices** file entry in Figure 8.55. This arrangement makes it possible to select more than one device to contact a given remote system while using only one **Systems** file entry.

The Device Field. The special device basename (found in **/dev**). Names prefixed with **tty** refer to direct connect lines or perhaps lines used with a dialer program. The **cul** prefix refers to an 801 ACU connection.

The ACU Field. If the device is an 801 ACU, this field contains the device name of the auxiliary dialer, generally with the prefix **cua** followed by a number. This field is ignored for other devices but should contain a dash (−) as a place-holder.

The Speed Field. The baud rate of the communication line for the modem or direct link. The *speed* field of the **Systems** file indexes into this field. Use the **Any** keyword in this field to match any speed specified in the **Systems** file that is supported by the device type.

The Dialers Field. This last field contains names of dialers or network switches and arguments, if any, to pass to them. AT&T documentation calls the arguments "tokens." Some dialers are known to **uucico**, for instance the 801 ACU, others are supported by the **Dialers** file (discussed later). Figure 8.57 shows a dialer-token pair example.

Figure 8.57 A dialer-token pair entry.

```
ACU    -    0    Any    DK    dial.    \T
```

The DK (Datakit) device will be passed the token "dial." followed by the desired telephone number (specified in the **Systems** file). The \T entry means to expand any string prefix of the phone number using the **Dialcodes** file before passing it to the DK device. A \D entry means to use the number exactly as it appears in the *phoneno* field of the **Systems** file (without **Dialcodes** file translation).

STEP SEVEN: Software Dialer Support

Version 2 UUCP had very limited dialer support—it only supported the AT&T 801 ACU. As a result, many vendors added support for other dialers, but in nonstandard ways. The HoneyDanBer system provides a general yet powerful facility for supporting a number of existing dialers as well as ones that haven't been invented yet.

The HoneyDanBer Dialers File

Each entry in this file contains information about dialing devices used on the local system. Entries have three fields: the *dialer* name, a *translate-string*, and a *handshake-string*, sometimes called a *dialer chat* string in analogy with the *log-in chat* field of the **Systems** file. Figure 8.58 shows an entry line for a DC Hayes Smartmodem.

Figure 8.58 Dialers file entry for a Hayes Smartmodem.

```
hayes   =,-,      " " \dATZ\r\c OK\r \EATDT\T\r\c CONNECT
```

The Dialer Name. The *dialer* name is referenced by the contents of the fifth and any additional odd-numbered fields of the **Devices** file. Sequences of dialers are supported, such as a network switch accessing a modem, by the cascaded dialer references. Figure 8.59 shows such an example.

Figure 8.59 Example of a cascaded dialer reference.

```
ACU culd0 - 1200 develcon vent ventel
```

Here a ventel modem (named the seventh field) is connected to a develcon data switch (named in the fifth field). The sixth field contains the token given to the data switch to reach the ventel modem.

The *dialer* name **hayes** is shown in the example above. It would be the only item in the fifth field of the corresponding entry in the **Devices** file, such as shown in Figure 8.53.

The Translate-String Field.   The translation used for the equal sign (=) and minus sign (−), which are used in the telephone number, into whatever the dialer uses for "wait for dial tone" and "pause," respectively. Where did these characters come from? The 801 ACU dialer used them first for the functions mentioned, but other dialers could use other codes.

In our example above the *translate-string* =,−, means to translate both the equal and minus sign into a comma (,), which the Hayes modem interprets as a 2-second pause (default value; can be programmed anywhere from 0 to 255 seconds). *Note:* The Hayes doesn't have "wait for dial tone" capability, so it's simulated with a pause.

The Handshake-String Field.   This "dialer chat" script specifies a sequence of expect-send strings for coaxing the device to dial. Table 8.17 interprets the *handshake-string* shown in Figure 8.58.

TABLE 8.17 INTERPRETING THE HAYES EXPECT-SEND DIALING STRINGS

""	Expect nothing
\dATZ\r\c	Two-second delay, then send "ATZ"
	(attention software-reset sequence)
	followed by carriage return (no newline)
OK\r	Expect "OK," then carriage return
\EATDT	Turn on echo checking, then send "ATDT"
	(attention dial with tones)
\T\r\c	followed by phone number ending in
	a carriage return without newline
CONNECT	Expect "CONNECT"

Echo checking is used for slowing down command sequences when necessary for certain devices. The next character in a command isn't sent to the device until the previous one is returned (echoed back) from the device.

The \T sequence means to substitute the telephone number found in the *phoneno* field of the **Systems** file, expanding any strings using the definition found in the **Dialcodes** file. The \D sequence would serve the same function, except that no strings are expanded.

Most, but not all, of the escape sequences used in the *log-in chat* field of the **Systems** file can also be used in *handshake-string* field of the **Devices** file. Table 8.18 lists the recognized sequences in ASCII sequence order.

TABLE 8.18: SPECIAL CHARACTER SEQUENCES USED IN Dialers *handshake-string* FIELD

`" "`	Empty string
`\D`	Dial phone number (no string translation)
`\E`	Turn on echo check
`\K`	Send break
`\N`	Null character
`\T`	Dial phone number (with string translation)
`\b`	Backspace character
`\c`	Suppress newline that's sent by default
`\d`	Delay 2 seconds
`\e`	Turn off echo check
`\n`	Newline character
`\p`	Pause for ¼ to ½ second
`\r`	Carriage return
`\s`	Space character
`\ddd`	Send character, where *ddd* is octal value

Version 2 Dialer Support

Version 2 UUCP always supports the 801 automatic call unit. Other devices may or may not be accommodated. Some implementations provide device-specific dialer programs, others supply termcap-like databases for modems. However, here is one approach that works for most devices and doesn't require any additional software.

To do it, you tell UUCP that you're using a direct (DIR) connection and place the dialing sequences in the *log-in chat* field of the **L.sys** file. Figure 8.60 shows an example.

Figure 8.60 Version 2 Hayes modem device support.

a. A **L.sys** file entry:

```
northpol Any tty02 1200 tty02 " " ATDT5551212\r \
in:-@-in: uuhome word: Gifts4US
```

b. Corresponding **L-devices** file entry:

```
DIR  tty02  -  1200
```

The Hayes Smartmodem modem interprets **ATDT5551212\r**, as attention (**AT**), dial (**D**), using tones (**T**), the number **5551212**, followed by a carriage return (**\r**) and NEWLINE (sent by default). The backslash (****) after the space character ends the current line, and the *log-in chat* field continues on the next line. Because we used a DIR line and not an ACU in this example, we can specify the dialing sequence in the *log-in chat* field.

Relationship Between HoneyDanBer Systems, Devices, and Dialers Files

Figure 8.61 shows an example of how the **Systems**, **Devices**, and **Dialers** files are interrelated. The contents of the **Systems** file *type* and *speed* fields index into the corresponding fields of the **Devices** file to select the **/dev/tty0** communication line and the **hayes** dialer. The *dialer* field of **Devices** indexes into the corresponding field in the **Dialers** file.

Figure 8.61 Interrelated HoneyDanBer configuration files.

Systems file entry:

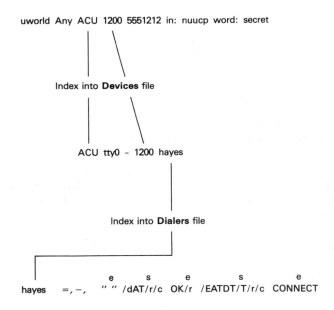

```
uworld Any ACU 1200 5551212 in: nuucp word: secret

                 │       \
                 │        \
                 │         \
           Index into Devices file

                 │         \
                 │          \
           ACU tty0 - 1200 hayes
                              │
                              │
                    Index into Dialers file

   ┌──────────────────────────┘
   │            e    s    e    s      e
hayes   =,-,   " " /dAT/r/c OK/r /EATDT/T/r/c CONNECT
```

STEP EIGHT: Testing the Communication Link

Now that you have all the configuration files set up for a remote site, you can do the final testing. First, let's test the call-in and call-out functions with **cu**. You can use **cu** to develop the necessary "chat" scripts. Then you can use **uucico** with debugging to walk through the "chat" scripts to test them. If that works, send a file using electronic mail and finally **uucp**. At that point your communication link should be fully functional.

Testing the Call-out Functions with cu. Now we'll describe some tests that check the physical connections, exercise the UUCP dialing functions, and test Version 2 **L-devices** or HoneyDanBer **Devices** files and the Version 2 **L.sys** or HoneyDanBer **Systems** file.

Also, login-chat strings can be developed using **cu** to access the UUCP access account of the remote system. You should note all characters you have to type to log in correctly. Ideally, you should make these tests several times over an extended period to catch transient problems, such as occasional line noise.

Before testing a call-out line, you'll need to disable any **getty** process for that line. Some HoneyDanBer systems may use **uugetty**, a new version of **getty** that allows call-out on a call-in line. So, in this case, you don't need to disable **uugetty** on your call-out test line.

Figure 8.62 shows a sample log-in session using **cu**. Here we invoked **cu** with the node name of the remote system, which is **northpol** in this example. This way you exercise the Version 2 **L.sys** or HoneyDanBer **Systems** file as well as the Version 2 **L-devices** or HoneyDanBer **Devices** file. Some **cu** releases distributed with Version 2 UUCP may not recognize a node name argument. In this case use a DIR-type connection and the alternative command line shown in Figure 8.64.

Figure 8.62 Using **cu** to access a remote UUCP account.

```
hometown $ cu northpol
Connected

<RETURN>
login: uuhome
Password:

Shere=northpol
[Wait about a minute for time out]
login: ~[hometown].
Disconnected

hometown $ □
```

After the call was made, **cu** issued "Connected" to say that the connection to the remote system was established.

In our example, the RETURN key had to be pressed before **northpol** would issue a "login" prompt. Then the UUCP access account name, **uuhome**, and corresponding password (not echoed) were entered. The remote **uucico** daemon issued the "Shere=northpol" message, indicating that log in was successful. After waiting about a minute, the remote daemon exited and another "login" prompt was issued from the newly spawned **getty** process. The user broke the link with the **cu** tilde-dot command.

The example session in Figure 8.62 showed that there were no surprises except for the RETURN, which is required before the remote system would issue a "login" prompt. Figure 8.63 shows the first attempt login-chat script that the user wrote based on the **cu** session above. We'll show you how to debug such login-chat scripts with **uucico** below.

The empty quotes mean to expect nothing. The \r\c sends a carriage return suppressing the newline terminator. Then "in:" is expected and "uuhome" is sent in response; finally, "word:" is expected and the password "Gifts4US" is sent in reply.

Figure 8.63 A preliminary login-chat script.

```
"" \r\c in: uuhome word: Gifts4US
```

If your Version 2 **cu** program doesn't recognize a node name argument, invoke **cu** to use one of your direct communication links (DIR). Part a of Figure 8.64 shows a sample command line for connecting to port **/dev/tty3**, a direct connection at 1200 baud. Part b shows the corresponding **L-devices** entry for this port. And part c shows what the analogous entry in the HoneyDanBer **Devices** file would look like.

Figure 8.64 Connecting to the remote system with a DIR connection.

a. Invoking **cu**:

```
# cu -l /dev/tty03 -s1200 dir
```

b. A **L-devices** DIR connection entry:

```
DIR   tty03   0   1200
```

c. A **Devices** direct connection entry:

```
Direct tty03   -   1200   direct
```

The details of dialing and establishing the connection need to be filled in by you. For instance, if you're connected to a DC Hayes-compatible modem after you get the message "Connected," type **ATDT** to begin the Hayes dialing function, followed by the desired phone number, and end the modem command sequence with a RETURN. Sometimes the modem may be in an indeterminate state and not accept your commands. You can do a software reset of the modem by typing **ATZ**; if that doesn't work, turn it off and then back on.

It will help you to have the volume control on the rear panel of the Hayes-style modems turned up so that you can hear it dial and establish the communication link with the answering modem. If you're not using an autodial modem, invoke **cu**, manually dial the number after you see the "Connected" message, and when you hear the other modem answer with a high-pitched tone, hang up the handset and begin the log-in sequence. Note that "Connected" means that the **cu** program has connected (opened) the communication port, but you still need to establish the link from your local modem to the remote site. Now, if all went well, you can log into the remote system, just as shown in Figure 8.62.

If you're having difficulty getting the "Connected" message, refer to Table 8.19 for some common **cu** error messages and their interpretation.

TABLE 8.19 SOME COMMON **cu** ERROR MESSAGES AND THEIR INTERPRETATION

Connect failed: CAN'T ACCESS DEVICE
  Can't open the calling device port. Check ownership and permission modes of the port.

Connect failed: DEVICE LOCKED
  Couldn't create a lock file for the calling device port. A valid lock file already exists.

Connect failed: NO DEVICES AVAILABLE
  The "devices" file doesn't contain a vaild entry for the calling device port.

Testing the Call-In Function. Choose a serial-line device file that supports modem control. You'll need to run a **getty** (or **uugetty**) process on this line to support log-in access. If using a System V UNIX system, check your system's **/etc/inittab** file for an entry corresponding to the desired line type. If using a Berkeley or XENIX system, check the **/etc/ttys** file instead.

Now you're ready to begin testing. Have a remote user log into your local site with **cu**. If you're experiencing difficulties, make sure that one of the baud rates you've chosen for the dial-in line matches the baud rate used to dial in. Are you using the correct dial-in port? And make sure that there's an appropriate account setup for the test. If everything works okay so far, you're well on your way to getting two-way UUCP communications up and running.

Using uucico with Debugging. You may have used **cu** to write a preliminary login-chat script; now let's really test it with **uucico**. You can invoke the **uucico** daemon with a debugging option to test the connection step by step. The **L.sys** or **Systems** file must permit the connection attempt. If necessary, you can change the *times* field in these files to contain **Any** so that you can call at any time.

Invoke the **uucico** program directly with the debugging option, −x*level*, where *level* is a decimal integer from one to nine, representing the *debugging level*. The debugging option causes **uucico** to display diagnostic information during the transaction. The greater the debugging level, the more information that is displayed.

You'll need source code for the UUCP system to interpret all the information completely—especially at levels greater than 4 or 5—but you can still glean valuable insight without source code.

We suggest starting at debugging level 4 for Version 2 and level 5 for Honey-DanBer Systems. These intermediate levels allow you to diagnose problems with the configuration file "chat" scripts, without being overwhelmed with superfluous information from the packet transfer code. We'll discuss debugging Version 2 and HoneyDanBer login-chat scripts separately.

Debugging the Version 2 login-chat Script.   Part a of Figure 8.65 shows a sample login-chat sequence and part b shows a test of **uucico**. The −**r1** option invokes **uucico** in MASTER role so that it can initiate the call. The −**x4** option provides an intermediate level of debugging output, useful for following the login-chat sequence. The −**snorthpol** argument tells **uucico** the system to call. We place **uucico** in the background since it may take a couple of minutes to finish and you can't terminate it with a keyboard-generated interrupt or quit signal.

Figure 8.65 A test of a simple Version 2 login-chat script.

a. The login-chat script for **northpol**:

```
""  ATDT5551212\r in: uuhome word: Gifts4US
```

b. Testing the connection:

```
# /usr/lib/uucp/uucico -r1 -x4 -snorthpol &
finds called
getto called
call: no. tty128 for sys uworld fixline - speed= 9
login called
wanted "" got that
wanted in: _got ?
exit code 0
# □
```

The first four lines name some of the routines used to make the connection. Pay attention to the "wanted" and "got" messages. First, **wanted "" got that** means **uucico** was looking for nothing and got that—this always works. But the next message, **wanted in: _got ?**, indicates a problem—**uucico** wanted the prompt "in:" from the remote system but never received it.

Debugging output from **uucico** is difficult to read since it appears all jumbled up—you have to look closely for the "wanted" and "got" strings. We "cleaned up" the output somewhat for the example above. Also note that nonprinting characters are displayed as underscores (_) during debugging. And to keep the display simple, we don't show any strings sent by **uucico**.

   Previous experience with **cu** revealed that the line to site **northpol** could be noisy. So an expect-send subfield was added to send the default line kill character (@) if the log-in prompt, "in:" wasn't received from the remote **getty**. The line kill character will cause all garbage characters due to line noise to be thrown away by the remote **getty** process. The new **L.sys** entry is shown in part a of Figure 8.66. Part b shows the **uucico** debugging output.

Figure 8.66 Another test of a Version 2 login-chat script.

a. The login-chat script for **northpol**:

```
"" ATDT5551212\r in:-@-in: uuhome word: Gifts4US
```

b. Testing the connection:

```
# /usr/lib/uucp/uucico -r1 -x4 -snorthpol
finds called
getto called
call: no. tty128 for sys uworld fixline - speed= 9
login called
wanted "" got that
wanted in: _got ?
wanted in: _____ogin: got that
wanted word: _rem_ote_wo___got that
valid sys Shere=northpol
...
# □
```

Figure 8.67 lists a useful "bare bones" Bourne shell script for diagnosing Version 2 login-chat problems. It was inspired by the HoneyDanBer **Uutry** shell script (discussed later), hence the name **uutry**.

Figure 8.67 A Version 2 login-chat diagnostic Bourne shell script.

```
:
# @(#) uutry
STATUS=/usr/spool/uucp/STST.$1
DEBUGLOG=/tmp/$1
# If status file exists, remove it
if [ -f $STATUS ]; then
    rm $STATUS
fi
echo "Saving debug output in $DEBUGLOG"
echo "Type your interrupt character to return to shell"
/usr/lib/uucp/uucico -r1 -x4 -s$1 >$DEBUGLOG 2>&1 &
```

```
# In case DEBUGLOG can't be created immediately:
if [ ! -f $DEBUGLOG ]; then
    sleep 5
fi
tail -f $DEBUGLOG
```

Debugging the HoneyDanBer dialer- and login-chat Scripts.   Both the chat scripts found in the **Dialers** and **Systems** file can be debugged conveniently using **uucico** with a debug option. HoneyDanBer systems provide a Bourne shell script, named **Uutry**, designed for this purpose. Figure 8.68 shows a general command for running this script.

Figure 8.68 Uutry general command line syntax.

/usr/lib/uucp/Uutry [−x*level*] [−r] *nodename*

Only the *nodename* argument is required—it's the nodename of the system you're contacting. A default debugging level of 5 is used. You can specify a different level with the −x*level* option. The debugging output is stored in **/tmp/***nodename*. A **tail −f** of the debugging output file is run to display any characters added to this file. Type your interrupt character to terminate the **tail** command and return control to your shell. You can specify the −r option when you invoke **Uutry** to remove any status file for the remote site. Removing this file eliminates any retry-time restriction.

Part a of Figure 8.69 shows a Hayes modem dialers-chat script, part b a simple login-chat sequence, and part c shows a diagnostic session using the **Uutry** shell script.

Figure 8.69 A test of a simple HoneyDanBer dialer- and login-chat script.

a. The dialer-chat script for the Hayes modem:

```
""   \dATZ\r\c   OK\r   \EATDT\T\r\c   CONNECT
```

b. The login-chat script for **northpol**:

```
in:-@-in: uuhome word: Gifts4US
```

c. Testing the connection:

```
# /usr/lib/uucp/Uutry northpol
/usr/lib/uucp/uucico -r1 -snorthpol  -x5 >/tmp/northpol 2>&1&
tmp=/tmp/northpol
```

```
mchFind called (northpol)
conn(northpol)
Device Type ACU wanted
mlock tty0 succeeded
processdev: calling setdevcfg(uucico, ACU)
gdial(hayes) called
expect: ("")
got it
sendthem (DELAY
<NO CR>ATZ^M)
expect: (OK^M)
^JOK^Mgot it
sendthem (ECHO CHECK ON
<NO CR>A^JATTDDTT55555511221122^M^M)
expect: (CONNECT)
^M^JCONNECTgot it
getto ret 5
expect: ("")
got it
sendthem (<NO CR>^M)
expect: (in:)
^M^J^M^M^Jlogin:got it
sendthem (uuhome^M)
expect: (word:)
 ^M^M^M^Jlogin: usirius^M^M^JPassword:got it
sendthem (Gifts4US^M)
Login Successful: System=northpol
...
send OO 0,exit code 0
Conversation Complete: Status SUCCEEDED
```

The first two lines shown above are issued by the **Uutry** shell script. The remaining lines are from the local **uucico** daemon. Look for lines that start with the keywords "expect" and "sendthem." The actual *expect* and *send* strings are recorded in parentheses after these keywords. Execution of the dialer-chat string sequences (from **Dialers**) is displayed first. If executed successfully, you'll see a message like "getto ret 5," which means that the connection was made to the remote system. Next you see the login-chat strings (from **Systems**). If the log-in attempt was successful, you'll see a "Login Successful" message. *Note:* If you're not logged in as superuser when you run **Uutry**, **uucico** won't reveal sensitive information. For instance, it will display a series of question marks instead of the password sent to the remote system.

If there's a problem with either chat script, the system will pause waiting for an *expect* string that never comes. After a timeout interval, usually 15 seconds, **uucico** will "give up." It will either continue with the send-expect substrings, if any remain to be used, or print an error message before exiting. Take note of where the problem occurred, and after the "Conversation Complete" message, interrupt the **tail** −**f** process (started by **Uutry**) to return control to your shell, and fix the chat script sequence. You may wish to test it with either **cu** or again with **Uutry**.

A good way to get familiar with debugging the communication link is to use the debugging option when initiating UUCP requests. You'll note that the transactions go through several phases—named a connection phase, a handshaking phase, the data transfer phase, and a shutdown phase. If you have access to source code for the UUCP system, use the higher levels of debugging output for interpreting these phases and the details of the transactions more closely.

Testing with File Transfers. By this point you've established that you can connect to the remote site and they can connect to you. Now for the "acid test": Can you transfer files? First, send yourself mail through the remote site. This exercises the outgoing and incoming connections, but also the ability to send a file (the mail message) and execute a command remotely (**rmail**). Figure 8.70 shows a sample command line where user **robin** sends a message file from **hometown** to **northpol** and back.

Figure 8.70 Testing a communication link using "boomerang" mail.

```
# mail northpol!hometown!robin < message
# □
```

If there's a problem delivering mail, contact the the administrator on the remote system. Have them check their Version 2 **L.cmds** or HoneyDanBer **Permissions** security files for permission to log-in and run **rmail**. Of course, check these files on your system if the "boomerang" message isn't returned to your system. Enabling access to the system for running **rmail** should be sufficient to get the mail through. See our discussion of UUCP security for more information on these security files.

If mail can go through, try to send a file using the −**m** option with **uucp** so you'll be notified when the transaction is successful. This approach tests the outgoing and incoming link again, but also checks to see if a file transfer request can be serviced by the remote system. If not, have the administrator on that system check the setup of their security files. Figure 8.71 shows a sample command line.

Figure 8.71 Testing a communication link using a file transfer request.

```
# uucp -m ~/testfile northpol!~/
# □
```

Good Luck!

STEP NINE: Setting Up to Poll Remote Sites

Sometimes you need to contact a remote site because it's a *passive site*, that is, it can't call you even if it has files destined for your site. So you need to force contact, or *poll*, that site. Version 2 systems don't have any built-in facilities to poll passive sites. However, it's easy enough to implement, as shown here.

Polling with Version 2 UUCP.   Use the command line shown in Figure 8.72 to force contact with the site, *nodename*. The **-s***nodename* argument forces a call to the remote site with the node name *nodename*, even if there is no work (i.e., a work or command file) destined for that site.

Figure 8.72 Invoking **uucico** to poll *sitename*.

```
$ /usr/lib/uucp/uucico -r1 -snodename &
```

Of course, either the presence of a status file, **STST.***nodename*, where the *retry time* hasn't expired, or a **L.sys** file entry that disallows a call at the current time, will prevent you from calling. So for polling, I keep an alternate file named **L.sys.Any** around, in which the *times* field for all sites that I would normally wish to poll specify **Any**. I rename the regular **L.sys** file to something else, such as **L.sys.Reg** (for regular), then rename **L.sys.Any** to **L.sys** when contacting the other site. This approach avoids an editing step, but means that you must remember to restore the files to their original names.

You may automate polling by using **cron** to drive a shell script. Figure 8.73 lists a shell script I've used for polling. It has the advantage that each transaction is logged in a file, which may be useful later for diagnostic purposes. Also any status files are removed, and time restrictions are obviated by use of the special **L.sys** files mentioned above. In the tenth line insert the actual names for the sites you wish to contact. The entries for these sites in the **L.sys.Any** file should contain **Any** in the *times* field.

Figure 8.73 A sample polling script.

```
1   trap "" 1 2 3 15
2   LIBDIR=/usr/lib/uucp
3   SPOOLDIR=/usr/spool/uucp
4   PATH=/usr/lib/uucp:$PATH; export PATH
5   TZ=PST8PDT; export TZ
6   cd $LIBDIR
7   mv L.sys L.sys.Reg
8   mv L.sys.Any L.sys
9   cd $SPOOLDIR
```

```
10   for site in remote1 remote2 remote3 ...
11   do
12        rm -f STST.$site
13        touch C.${site}AnPOLL
14   done
15   echo `date`" Polling started" >>POLLLOG
16   uucico -r1 >&2 >>POLLLOG &
17   echo `date`" Polling completed" >>POLLLOG
18   cd $LIBDIR
19   mv L.sys L.sys.Any
20   mv L.sys.Reg L.sys
```

The **trap** on line 1 prevents hangup, interrupt, quit, and software termination signals from terminating the script. If the script was stopped before the **L.sys** files were moved back to their original names, it's possible to overwrite the "real" **L.sys** file with the contents of **L.sys.Any** the next time the script was run.

Next, a few environment variables are defined in lines 2–5, **LIB** and **SPOOL** make the script more readable, **PATH** is for convenience to avoid entering the full pathname for **uucico**, and the **date** command called from lines 15 and 17 needs the correct value of **TZ**.

Then the shell running the script changes to the "library" directory, **/usr/lib/uucp**. The "L.sys" files described above are renamed so that **L.sys** won't restrict polling.

Next, the directory is changed to the "spool" directory, **/usr/spool/uucp**. The two lines in the **for-do-done** loop erase any status files and create a "dummy" work file for each site to be polled. A starting-time entry is made in the **POLLLOG** file, and **uucico** is started up in MASTER mode. It will attempt to contact each site that has a work file, including those with the "dummy" work files created on line 13. An ending time entry is made by line 17.

Finally, the shell changes back to the "library" directory and lines 19 and 20 rename the "L.sys" files back to their original designations.

Polling with HoneyDanBer UUCP.   The HoneyDanBer release provides for automatic polling of remote systems. You just have to add entries for the sites and times you wish to poll to a file named **Poll** located in **/usr/lib/uucp**. Then the **uudemon.poll** shell script, which is generally run once or twice an hour by **cron**, will create the "dummy" work files for all sites scheduled to be polled that hour. Finally, the **uudemon.hour** script, which is generally scheduled to run shortly after **uudemon.poll**, will invoke **uusched**, which will then in turn invoke **uucico** in MASTER role to contact each site that has a "dummy" poll work file.

Figure 8.74 illustrates the HoneyDanBer **Poll** file. Part a shows the general entry format, and part b a few sample entries. In this example we poll remote site **northpol** five times a day, 6 and 7 A.M., noon, 5 and 9 P.M., but poll **sun** only once a day at 1 A.M.. Note that the tab between the remote node name and the hour entries is necessary—else the entry line will be skipped.

Figure 8.74 The HoneyDanBer **Poll** file.

a. General entry format:

site <tab> *hour1 hour2 hour3 ...*

b. A sample **Poll** file:

```
northpol  6 7 12 17 21
sun       1
```

SECURING THE UUCP SYSTEM

UUCP system security is important—you need to control how much access a remote system can have to your local system. There are several types of access to consider, including:

- Log-in access to a UUCP account.
- Read and write access to your files and directories.
- Permission to run commands on your system.
- Ability to forward files through your system.

The UNIX system provides the means to secure the UUCP system. However, it's vitally important that as system administrator you understand the security features of your UUCP system and how to implement them. All too often, a system is delivered in an unsecure condition and is operated that way for years, due to ignorance of the UUCP security features and how to set them up.

The **uucico** program handles security for file transfers either to or from your system. And **uuxqt** manages the security for remote command execution requests. Both these programs consult configuration files to see what level of access remote systems or local users are allowed. You, as administrator, maintain your UUCP system security through entries in these configuration files.

In this section we first compare the default security (as delivered) of Version 2 and HoneyDanBer systems. Charts of recommended ownerships and permissions modes for UUCP files are presented next. Then we discuss the Version 2 **USER-FILE** and **L.cmds** security configuration files, which define file system and command access, respectively. The **SQFILE** file, useful for preventing system masquerades, will also be covered. For HoneyDanBer systems we look at the **Permissions** security configuration file, which gives excellent control over file and command access on a remote system basis. We also discuss the **remote.unknown** shell script, which can be executed when an unknown remote machine (not listed in the **Systems** file) logs into your system.

We won't be covering file forwarding in this chapter for several reasons: (1) Most Version 2 implementations don't support it. (2) It's a security hazard in HoneyDanBer systems, as you must allow remote execution of **uucp**. (3) Every system in the forwarding chain will have to run the same version of UUCP. (4) You can always forward files using electronic mail—an approach that's secure. And if you need to mail a binary file, convert it to ASCII text first, using the **enhex** program that we list in this chapter. Have the recipient on the destination system convert it back to a binary file using the complementary **dehex** program.

Default Security

We'll use the term "default security" to mean the security of the UUCP system as delivered from a typical vendor. The Version 2 and HoneyDanBer system default security are diametrically opposite—Version 2 is permissive and HoneyDanBer is very strict.

Version 2 Default Security.   Typically, Version 2 UUCP system default security has been lax. Often, as delivered, this system allows a remote user to transfer out or in any file that has appropriate read or write permissions. To illustrate, here's a quote from Daniel Nowitz in his seminal paper on UUCP implementation: [*]

> The UUCP system, left unrestricted, will let any outside user execute any command and copy out/in any file that is readable/writable by a UUCP login user. It is up to the individual sites to be aware of this and apply the protections that they feel are necessary.

You can secure file transfer and remote command execution through the proper setup of two Version 2 configuration files, **USERFILE** and **L.cmds**. And if you wish to help prevent another system from masquerading as a known site, you can set up the **SQFILE** to keep a count of your conversations with other sites. We'll discuss how to setup these files later in this section. Now let's look at the improved default security provided in the HoneyDanBer environment.

HoneyDanBer Default Security.   When delivered, the HoneyDanBer security is maximal. You have to add entries to the **Permissions** file to make it permissive. This file contains one entry, **LOGNAME = nuucp**, which **uucico** interprets as—when a system logs in (as **nuucp**): (1) The local system doesn't allow them to

---

[*] D. A. Nowitz, "UUCP Implementation Description," *The Unix Programmer's Manual, Volume II*, AT&T Bell Laboratories.

request files from your system; (2) the local machine won't send files queued for them on this call; (3) they can only send files to the public directory, **/usr/spool/uucppublic**; and (4) only **rmail** (and perhaps **rnews**) can be executed on behalf of the remote system.

One possible security hole, even with a HoneyDanBer system, might be the UUCP accounts. Make sure they have passwords! Also, as discussed earlier, it's more secure if the access accounts have different user-ids than those used for the administrative account (generally, UID 5).

Ownership and Permission Modes of Files and Directories

Several files and directories necessary for a UUCP conversation are readable and writable only by their owner, **uucp**. Thus programs, such as **uucp**, **uux**, **uustat**, and **uuname**, that are designed to be run by ordinary system users must be set-user-id and owned by the UUCP administrative account, **uucp**. Also, you should allow only execute permission for ordinary users, so use mode 4711 for these program files. The **ls −l** command would show the symbolic pattern **r w s − − x − − x** for this octal mode.

Ordinary users shouldn't be allowed to write in any of the UUCP system files or directories except for the public directory, **/usr/spool/uucppublic**. Otherwise, a user could install a custom program or data file that would subvert the UUCP system into doing his or her bidding.

Because several files contain sensitive information, they shouldn't be readable by ordinary users. The most important of these is Version 2 **L.sys** or HoneyDanBer **Systems**, because it contains phone numbers, log-in names, and *unencrypted* passwords for contacting other systems. You may wish to restrict read access of the security configuration files so that users can't tell how secure (or insecure) your system is. And the **uudemon** scripts should not be readable—otherwise, users can learn details about how your system is maintained by **cron**. Also, the **SQFILE**, if used, should not be readable. And you may not wish users to read the logging files, Version 2 **LOGFILE**, **SYSLOG**, and **ERRLOG**, or any of the files in the **/usr/spool/uucp** subdirectories on HoneyDanBer systems. After all, the system provides the **uulog** and **uustat** commands so that ordinary users can get status information and control jobs they submit. There is one exception: Since HoneyDanBer **uulog** is a shell script, not a set-user-id program, the files in **/usr/spool/uucp/.Log** must be readable by others.

Table 8.20 tabulates the Version 2 files and directories used by the UUCP system along with some recommendations for their owners and permissions. Table 8.21 lists the HoneyDanBer files and directories. Within a given directory the files are listed alphabetically. You may wish to be more or less restrictive than these recommendations depending on the specific needs of your site.

TABLE 8.20 RECOMMENDED OWNERSHIP AND PERMISSIONS OF
VERSION 2 UUCP SYSTEM FILES

Directory	File	Owner	Mode
User commands (/usr/bin)		bin	555
	uucp	uucp	4111
	uudecode	bin	555
	uuencode	bin	555
	uulog	uucp	4111
	uuname	uucp	4111
	uupick	bin	555
	uustat	uucp	4111
	uuto	bin	555
	uux	uucp	4111
Library (/usr/lib/uucp)		uucp	755
	L-devices	uucp	644
	L-dialcodes	uucp	644
	L.cmds	uucp	600
	L.sys	uucp	600
	L_stat	uucp	600
	L_sub	uucp	600
	R_stat	uucp	600
	R_sub	uucp	600
	SQFILE	uucp	600
	USERFILE	uucp	400
	uucico	uucp	4111
	uudemon.day	uucp	400
	uudemon.hr	uucp	400
	uudemon.wk	uucp	400
	uusched	uucp	4111
	uuxqt	uucp	4111
	.XQTDIR (dir)	uucp	555
Spool (/usr/spool)		bin	555
	uucp	uucp	755
	uucppublic	uucp	777

Version 2 Security Configuration Files

All Version 2 UUCP systems use two security files, **USERFILE** and **L.cmds**. The
uucico daemon process on your local system consults **USERFILE** to see if a remote
system is allowed to send or receive a particular file. Your local **uuxqt** process
refers to the **L.cmds** file to see if a command request by a remote system is allowed.
The command program resides on your local system and the corresponding process
runs with the effective user-id of the UUCP administrative account, **uucp**.

The USERFILE Format

The **USERFILE** provides security for your local system since it controls the access
remote systems have to your system and to its files. Of course, the **/etc/passwd** file

also controls system access, but the **USERFILE** can specify that a given remote machine must log in to a certain account. For instance, it could insist that the machine with node name **northpol** must log in as **uunorth**.

You can have **USERFILE** grant remote users access to your entire file system tree (not recommended) or to only a subset (generally, the public directory, **/usr/spool/uucppublic**). The access comes bundled on a system basis (granted to

TABLE 8.21 RECOMMENDED OWNERSHIP AND PERMISSIONS OF HoneyDanBer UUCP SYSTEM FILES

Directory	File	Owner	Mode
User commands (/usr/bin)		bin	555
	ct	root	4111
	cu	uucp	4111
	uucp	uucp	4111
	uudecode	bin	555
	uuencode	bin	555
	uulog	uucp	555
	uuname	uucp	4111
	uupick	bin	555
	uustat	uucp	4111
	uuto	bin	555
	uux	uucp	4111
Library (/usr/lib/uucp)		uucp	755
	Devices	uucp	444
	Dialcodes	uucp	444
	Dialers	uucp	444
	Maxuuscheds	uucp	444
	Maxuuxqts	uucp	444
	Permissions	uucp	400
	Poll	uucp	444
	SetUp	uucp	555
	Systems	uucp	400
	Uutry	uucp	555
	remote.unknown	uucp	550
	uucheck	uucp	4110
	uucico	uucp	4111
	uucleanup	uucp	4110
	uudemon.admin	uucp	555
	uudemon.cleanu	uucp	555
	uudemon.hour	uucp	555
	uudemon.poll	uucp	555
	uugetty	uucp	111
	uusched	uucp	4111
	uuxqt	uucp	4111
Spool (/usr/spool)		bin	555
	uucp	uucp	755
	uucppublic	uucp	777

all users at once on a remote system). So if you granted a remote host access to your entire file system, say, any user on that host could request a copy of your password file, group file, or any other sensitive file that's readable by the "other" user category. Not good.

Of course, local UNIX file permissions can control access to files. If a file isn't readable by the **uucp** account (generally an "other" user), the file can't be copied, even if **USERFILE** allowed access to the directory containing the file.

You want to prevent remote users from copying out your password file. Since it must be readable by all users (mode 444), local UNIX file permissions will allow the copy. However, you can prevent the copy by not providing access to the **/etc** directory with the **USERFILE**.

USERFILE also specifies the access that local users have *through* the UUCP system. For instance, **USERFILE** might not allow a user to request a copy of **/etc/passwd** to another system because it allows only access to the **/usr/spool/uucppublic** directory. Of course, a local user can get around this limitation—they simply use **cp** to copy **/etc/passwd** to **/usr/spool/uucppublic**, then use **uucp** to request a copy of ˜**/passwd** to another system. You have to limit activities of your local users with local UNIX file permissions.

The best way to ensure the identity of a remote system is to call it yourself. So if you're worried about remote systems masquerading as other systems, use the **USERFILE** call-back feature. How does it work? Let's say that the **USERFILE** specifies call-back for **northpol**. Then, whenever **northpol** calls (no matter what account they log in to), the local **uucico** daemon hangs up, then calls **northpol** before transferring any files.

Now, you may ask: What about UNIX mail? How can it get written to the **/usr/mail** directory if you only allow access to **/usr/spool/uucppublic**? **USERFILE** controls file access for **uucico**, not **uuxqt**. Recall that electronic mail is an execution request to run **rmail** on a remote system to deliver the message that was the standard input for the UNIX mail program. And on our system, **rmail** is set-group-id to the group **mail**, which is also the group owner of the **/usr/mail** directory, thus **rmail** can write to this directory.

Part a of Figure 8.75 shows the general format for an entry in **USERFILE**. Part b illustrates a specific example for remote system **northpol**. This **USERFILE** entry specifies that **northpol** *must* log in as **uunorth**, and we'll call **northpol** back before transferring any files, and then only to or from the public directory, **/usr/spool/uucppublic**.

Figure 8.75 The **USERFILE** security configuration file.

a. General entry line format:

[*username*],[*systemname*] [**c**] *pathname* [*pathname*]...

b. A specific entry line example:

```
uunorth,northpol c /usr/spool/uucppublic
```

Now let's describe the four fields of **USERFILE**.

The Username Field. The user (account or log-in) name used by a remote system for logging in to your local system via a UUCP access account (occurs in your local **/etc/passwd** file). It can also be the account name of a local user. This field may be blank.

The Systemname Field. The node name for a remote system. This field may also be blank.

The Call-back Field. If present, the remote system requesting access must be called back before and UUCP file transfers can proceed. A lowercase "c" must be used in this field position—no character can substitute.

The Pathname Field. Names the directory or directories in the local file system where UUCP software permits file access. (No metacharacters are allowed.) Note that local file permissions could still prevent file access.

Scanning the USERFILE

First a disclaimer. Not all Version 2 UUCP releases will scan the **USERFILE** as we describe here. Different releases have applied different fixes so they work somewhat differently. We've tried to present a description of the scanning behavior for a typical System V Release 2 **USERFILE**. However, understanding the **USERFILE** is probably one of the most difficult parts about the UUCP system. Let us recommend that you consult the fifth edition of *Managing UUCP and Usenet* (see bibliography) for a more comprehensive description of the **USERFILE**.

The **USERFILE** is scanned from beginning to end. The matching performed to select an entry depends on whether **uucico** is running in MASTER or SLAVE role. **uucico** runs in MASTER role when its operating under direction of a work file on the local system, and in SLAVE role when its getting directions from the remote system. For instance, when your local system initiates a call, the **uucico** you invoke is initially in MASTER role, and when a remote system logs into a UUCP access account on your local system, the **uucico** program started up will initially run in SLAVE role. We say *initially* because the two conversing **uucico**s (one on the local system and the other on the remote system) will change roles sometime during a conversation.

Scanning USERFILE during Log-in. Consider what happens after a remote system logs in to one or your UUCP access accounts. First, log-in authentication is performed. The **uucico** process that is started up as the log-in program for that account scans **USERFILE** looking for a "successful" entry, that is, an appropriate match between the contents of the *systemname* and *username* fields and the node name and log-in name used by the remote system, respectively.

There are two successful entry cases to consider: (1) An exact match between *both* the remote node name and the contents of the *systemname* field *and* the log-in name and the contents of the *username* field, and (2) a log-in name matching the contents of the *username* field, but an empty *systemname* field, as long as the log-in name doesn't match another *systemname* field.

If, however, a matching node name and *systemname* field with nonmatching log-in name and *username* field occurs *before* an entry with the blank *systemname* field, the **USERFILE** entry with the empty field won't be used, so the entry will be considered unsuccessful. Part a of Figure 8.76 shows an example of the first case, part b the second case, and part c an example of the unsuccessful case mentioned last.

In part a we specify the call-back flag so that the local **uucico** will hang up and call back the remote system, **northpol**. Note that we give this site access to the **/usr/northpol** directory in addition to the usual "public" directory, **/usr/spool/uucppublic**, since we are virtually assured of their identity because we called them back.

Now what if the node name of the calling system doesn't match any entry, and furthermore, there isn't an entry with a blank *systemname* field, such as shown in part b. In this case **uucico** will terminate the connection without any file transfers. The entry shown in part b is commonly used for the "generic" access account, **nuucp**. This usage is less secure than the one in part a since any site could potentially log-in as **nuucp**, but the presence of a good password known only by the desired site(s) would help.

Now let's look at part c of Figure 8.76. Assume for the sake of example that **northpol** calls and logs-in as **nuucp**. Now there's a *systemname* field match, but the *username* field doesn't match (it's **xuucp**, not **nuucp**). In this case **uucico** will terminate the connection.

Figure 8.76 Some **USERFILE** entries used during log-in. The remote machine **northpol** logs into the **nuucp** account.

a. A successful match between both log-in and node name:

```
nuucp,northpol   c   /usr/spool/uucppublic /usr/northpol
```

b. A successful match with log-in name and empty node name:

```
nuucp,           /usr/spool/uucppublic
```

c. An unsuccessful matching case:

```
xuucp,northpol        /usr/spool/uucppublic
nuucp,                /usr/spool/uucppublic
```

If you're not that concerned about another site masquerading as the intended site, you could omit the call-back flag and save on phone charges for calling back. Note that two sites can't both use the call-back flag for contacting each other, else they'll be caught in an endless loop—always trying to contact each other and never transferring any files.

Scanning USERFILE During Callout. Now consider what happens when the local system has work and initiates contact with a remote system. The **uucico** process, which is running in MASTER role, will scan **USERFILE** looking for an entry with a match between the contents of the *username* field and the user who initiated the file transfer request. In many cases this will be **uucp** (for example, when mail is forwarded through this system) or even **root** (mail sent by daemons started from **cron** or **/etc/rc**). If **uucico** can't determine the user who made the request (which can happen) it uses the name of the user who invoked **uucico**. If no match is found, but a blank entry is available, that null entry will be used. Figure 8.77 shows two sample entries.

Figure 8.77 Some **USERFILE** entries used when calling out.

```
beccat,      /usr/spool/uucppublic /usr2/beccat
,            /usr/spool/uucppublic
```

In this example, UUCP would honor a file transfer request for **beccat** from either the public directory, or her home directory tree, starting with **/usr2/beccat**, since an exact match to the first entry was found. However, for any other user, which would only match the blank entry, file transfer requests only to or from the public directory would be honored.

Note that restrictions offered by **USERFILE** for local users are essentially useless since a local user could always copy a file for which they have read permission (such as **/etc/passwd**) to a remote system by first copying it to the public directory and then invoking **uucp**. Thus, you might as well give local users complete access to their file system by using the root (**/**) directory as the entry in the *pathname* field. Figure 8.78 shows an example.

Figure 8.78 More sample **USERFILE** entries.

```
nuucp,    /usr/spool/uucppublic
,         /
```

Here, machines that log in as **nuucp** can only access the public directory. Local users can send files from anywhere on the local system.

Dealing With Null Entries. When **uucico** is invoked, it scans the entire **USERFILE**, looking for entries with blank *username* or *systemname* fields. The first time it finds a line with a blank *username* field, it marks that line as the "unknown username" case. Similarly, the first time it finds a line with a blank *systemname* field, it marks that line as the "unknown systemname" case. Note that a line such as the last entry in Figure 8.77 *does not* define both cases; it sets only one—whichever case has not yet been defined. If neither case has been defined, then only the "unknown username" case is set. And when the "unknown systemname" case is left undefined, no remote site can request file transfers, and **uuxqt** will not run on their behalf.

Figure 8.79 shows you can example of how you can get into trouble with a null entry. Assume that **xuucp** is a highly secure, protected access account—so we give it complete access to our file system. Then say an unknown site manages to log in (the account name they use is irrelevant). Since the site is unknown then the "unknown systemname" case (line 2 in part a of Figure 8.79 will be used to determine file access permission, so this unknown site will have complete access!

Instead place null entries that restrict file system access first in the file as shown in Figure 8.79b. In this case the unknown site would match the first line and only have access to the public directory. The second line would be used for the "unknown username" and restricts access to the public directory. If you do want to let your local users transfer files from any directory you could use the alternative shown in Figure 8.79c and be safe.

There's still one more wrinkle with this example. If a site does log in as **xuucp** they won't have complete access to the file system, because **uucico** will be in SLAVE role and only look for a system name match (and thus select the first line with a null *systemname* field). This example should emphasize the point—*specify both the remote system name and account name to define access for a particular remote site*. The **uunorth,northpol** entry would be one such example.

Figure 8.79 Scanning **USERFILE** with null entries.

a. An example of incorrect placement of a specific entry:

```
uunorth,northpol          /
xuucp,                    /
,                         /usr/spool/uucppublic
```

b. Placing the restricted access "null" entries first:

```
nuucp,               /usr/spool/uucppublic
,                    /usr/spool/uucppublic
uunorth,northpol     /
xuucp,               /
```

c. Letting remote users transfer files from any directory:

```
nuucp,               /usr/spool/uucppublic
,                    /
uunorth,northpol     /
xuucp,               /
```

The L.cmds File

The **L.cmds** file lists the commands that your local **uuxqt** daemon may execute on your local machine for a remote user. If a command isn't listed, it can't be executed. Part a of Figure 8.80 illustrates the general syntax for entries in this file, and part b shows a specific example.

Figure 8.80 The System V **L.cmds** file.

a. General entry format:

PATH = *pathname*[*:pathname*]...
 command ...

b. A typical **L.cmds** file:

```
PATH=/bin:/usr/bin
rmail
rnews
```

In this example the command search path is limited to the two conventional directories containing executable programs, **/bin** and **/usr/bin**. Only the **rmail** (restricted mail) and **rnews** (restricted network news) commands are allowed. You can specify the full pathname for commands, if desired.

As of Release 2 of System V, the UUCP system supports restriction of particular commands to execution by particular remote systems. Part a of Figure 8.81 defines the general format for the System V.2 **L.cmds** file and part b presents an example.

Figure 8.81 The System V Release 2 **L.cmds** file.

a. General entry format:

PATH = *pathname*[*:pathname*]...
command[*,sitename*]...   ...

b. A typical System V.2 **L.cmds** file:

```
PATH=/bin:/usr/bin
rmail
rnews
lp,northpol
```

Unlike the last example, here *only* the remote site **northpol** may also execute **lp** on your local system.

As a minimum you should allow **rmail** to be executed on your system so that local users can receive UNIX mail from remote systems and because users will need notification (by mail) whether or not a UUCP request they made to a remote site was successful.

You should *never* allow programs that copy files to their standard output, such as **cat**, else a remote user could use the command to copy out sensitive information to his or her system. For instance, say that a remote user entered a request like the ones shown in Figure 8.82. You may ask: "Why would this work if the remote system was allowed access only to the public directory by **USERFILE**?" The **uuxqt** daemon doesn't consult the **USERFILE**, only **L.cmds**, and if allowed in **L.cmds**, **cat** runs as if a local **uucp** user invoked it, and any local user can read the password file, so the copy request succeeds.

Figure 8.82 Requests from **northpol** to copy out the password file on **hometown** using **cat**.

a. Using redirection:

```
$ uux "hometown!cat hometown!/etc/passwd > northpol!~/passwd"
```

b. Piping the output to **rmail**:

```
$ uux "hometown!cat hometown!/etc/passwd ! rmail (northpol!santa)"
```

Using the SQFILE

The **/usr/lib/uucp/SQFILE** helps prevent a remote system from masquerading as a known site. Both the remote host and your local one must agree on the number of times they've talked to each other. This number is known as the *conversation count*. A *conversation* is a UUCP system-mediated interchange between two systems that at least completes the "handshaking" phase. Both systems will need to use **SQFILE**, each of which contains an entry for the other system.

If the conversation count value, which is received from the remote system during the connection attempt (actually the handshaking phase) from a remote system, isn't what is stored in the **SQFILE** entry for that site, the conversation with that system is aborted and an error message is logged. Version 2 UUCP writes "HANDSHAKE FAILED (BAD SEQ)" to **LOGFILE**, and HoneyDanBer writes "HANDSHAKE FAILED (BAD SEQUENCE CHECK)" to the **uucico** Log file.

Setting up a **SQFILE** file is simple. Create an empty **/usr/lib/uucp/SQFILE**, change ownership to the UUCP administrative account (**uucp**), and make the permission mode 600 (other users shouldn't be able to read it). Then write on a line by itself the node name of any system with which you wish to maintain a conversation count. Ideally, you should do this with all systems you converse with, but those hosts will also need to set up an **SQFILE** and add an entry for your site.

The UUCP software initializes the **SQFILE** the first time you converse with any site listed in the file. The **uucico** daemon adds a count, a date, and the time of day to the entry. These fields are updated each time another UUCP conversation takes place with that host. Figure 8.83 shows examples of two **SQFILE** files for hosts that converse with each other.

Figure 8.83 Contents of sample **SQFILE** files.

a. **SQFILE** on host **sirius**:

```
# cat /usr/lib/uucp/SQFILE
uworld 46 8/10-15:36
# □
```

b. **SQFILE** on host **uworld**:

```
# cat /usr/lib/uucp/SQFILE
sirius 46 8/10-15:35
# □
```

There have been 46 conversations between hosts **sirius** and **uworld** since these files were installed. The last one occurred on August 10th. Note that the time of day is slightly different between the two systems. One system clock is slightly ahead of the other (both are in the same time zone).

The HoneyDanBer Security Configuration File

HoneyDanBer UUCP systems use one security configuration file,
/usr/lib/uucp/Permissions. The **uucico** daemon process on your local system consults **Permissions** to see if a remote system is allowed to send or receive a particular
file. Your local **uuxqt** process refers to this file to see if a command request by a
remote system is allowed. The command program resides on your local system and
runs as if the **uucp** user invoked it.

This file has two types of rules—LOGNAME and MACHINE rules. LOG-
NAME rule entries specify permissions for a remote site when they log in to your
local computer. MACHINE rule entries specify permissions for remote sites that
your local computer calls. Note that in the default-compiled configuration, if a site
calls you that doesn't have a LOGNAME entry, the connection attempt will be
rejected.

These rules can contain options, which specify the specific permissions
relevant to the rule. Each option consists of the option name, an equal sign (=),
followed by one or more values for the option.

Figure 8.84 shows an actual example of **Permissions** file LOGNAME entry.
This example illustrates several points about writing **Permissions** file entries. The
first line is a comment, which is ignored. Comments always begin with the nano-
gram (#) and end with a newline. The blank line that follows, which provides a
visual break between the comment line and the subsequent entry, is also ignored by
the UUCP software. You can use blank lines anywhere—even within the entry—and
they will be ignored.

The single logical LOGNAME entry is continued over several physical lines
by using a backslash (\) before the newlines. The LOGNAME rule entry consists
of several option-value pairs separated from each other by white space, with no
white space around the equal sign (=). Multiple values for an option are
separated by a colon (:).

Figure 8.84 A sample LOGNAME **Permissions** file entry.

```
# A sample entry for a "trusted" site:

LOGNAME=uufriend \
    REQUEST=yes SENDFILES=yes \
    READ=/  NOREAD=/etc:/usr \
    WRITE=/usr/spool/uucppublic:/usr/news
```

Now what do these options mean? Table 8.22 tabulates all the options for the
LOGNAME and MACHINE rules with a brief description.

TABLE 8.22 Permissions FILE OPTIONS

Options	LOGNAME action	MACHINE action
	(remote calls local)	(local calls remote)
REQUEST = yes/no	Can remote host request files *from* your local machine (default is no).	Same interpretation.
SENDFILES = yes/call	Can local system send files queued for the remote host (default is call—only send when local site calls remote).	Doesn't apply.
CALLBACK = yes/no	Local site must call back remote (default is no).	Doesn't apply.
READ = *pathnames*	Directories **uucico** may read from (default is PUBDIR).	Same interpretation.
WRITE = *pathnames*	Directories **uucico** may write to (default is PUBDIR).	Same interpretation.
NOREAD = *pathnames*	Exceptions to READ (or default path).	Same interpretation.
NOWRITE = *pathnames*	Exceptions to WRITE (or default path).	Same interpretation.
COMMANDS = *commands*	Doesn't apply because only used with MACHINE rule.	Commands **uuxqt** will execute for remote host (default **rmail**).
PUBDIR = *path*	Change notion of "public" directory (default **/usr/spool/uucppublic**).	Same interpretation.
MYNAME = *nodename*	Local system assumes *nodename* when remote calls.	Local system assumes *nodename* when it calls remote.
VALIDATE = *systems*	Remote systems that must use account specified by LOGNAME rule.	Doesn't apply.

Interpreting Permissions File Entries. HoneyDanBer UUCP provides a useful program for interpreting **Permissions** file entries—**uucheck** when used with the **−v** option. Part a of Figure 8.85 lists the "simplest" LOGNAME entry and part b shows how **uucheck** would interpret it.

Figure 8.85 Using **uucheck** to interpret a simple LOGNAME entry.

a. Entry in **Permissions** file:

```
LOGNAME=nuucp
```

b. Interpretation by **uucheck**:

```
# uucheck -v
*** uucheck:   Check Required Files and Directories
*** uucheck:   Directories Check Complete

*** uucheck:   Check /usr/lib/uucp/Permissions file

** LOGNAME PHASE (when they call us)

When a system logs in as: (nuucp)
        We DO NOT allow them to request files.
        We WILL NOT send files queued for them on this call.
        They can send files to
            /usr/spool/uucppublic (DEFAULT)
        Myname for the conversation will be sirius.
        PUBDIR for the conversation will be /usr/spool/uucppublic.

** MACHINE PHASE (when we call or execute their uux requests)
# □
```

First **uucheck** reports that all required files and directories for proper functioning of the UUCP system are present and accounted for. This check is always made first. Then the permissions file itself is read and interpreted. There's no output after the "MACHINE PHASE" line since no MACHINE rule entries are present. The explanation of the LOGNAME rule entry should be self-explanatory. Note that this example represents the default security of many HoneyDanBer systems, since they are shipped with **LOGNAME = nuucp** as the only entry in the **Permissions** file.

Figure 8.86 shows how **uucheck** would interpret the LOGNAME entry used as an example in Figure 8.84. We repeat the entry in part a and show the **uucheck** −v output in part b.

Figure 8.86 Using **uucheck** to interpret a simple LOGNAME entry.

a. Entry in **Permissions** file:

```
LOGNAME=uufriend \
    REQUEST=yes SENDFILES=yes \
    READ=/  NOREAD=/etc:/usr/lib \
    WRITE=/usr/spool/uucppublic:/usr/news
```

b. Interpretation by **uucheck**:

```
# uucheck -v
*** uucheck:  Check Required Files and Directories
*** uucheck:  Directories Check Complete

*** uucheck:  Check /usr/lib/uucp/Permissions file
** LOGNAME PHASE (when they call us)

When a system logs in as: (uufriend)
        We DO allow them to request files.
        We WILL send files queued for them on this call.
        They can send files to
            /usr/spool/uucppublic
            /usr/news
        They can request files from
            /
        Except
            /etc
            /usr/lib
        Myname for the conversation will be sirius.
        PUBDIR for the conversation will be /usr/spool/uucppublic.


** MACHINE PHASE (when we call or execute their uux requests)


*** uucheck:  /usr/lib/uucp/Permissions Check Complete

#  □
```

The LOGNAME entry in this last example is appropriate for a trusted host. You are giving them the liberty to read any file on the local file system except those in **/etc**, which contains the sensitive password file, and **/usr**, which contains many other system configuration files. Of course, they can only read files that have their permissions for "others" enabled, since **uucico** will be running as the **uucp** account.

For more security you can mandate that a particular remote host must log in as **uufriend**. This way you'll be assured of the identity of the machine using this **Permissions** file entry. To do this, add a VALIDATE option, as shown in Figure 8.87.

Figure 8.87 Adding a VALIDATE option for more security.

```
        LOGNAME=uufriend VALIDATE=northpol \
            REQUEST=yes SENDFILES=yes \
            READ=/  NOREAD=/etc:/usr/lib \
            WRITE=/usr/spool/uucppublic:/usr/news
```

The VALIDATE option in this example means that remote host with node name **northpol** must log into the **uufriend** account. If the password to this account is only known by **northpol**, you have secure access.

Figure 8.88 shows an example where we combine LOGNAME and MACHINE rules. We also use the VALIDATE option for added security because we're allowing **northpol** to run three commands, **who**, **lp**, and **uucp**. The last command is especially dangerous, but we can trust **northpol**. They wanted to run this command to use forwarding of file transfer requests through our machine and to request copy of more than one file from our machine to theirs using wildcard filename generation characters.

We also let **northpol** have complete access to our local file system. And we changed the notion of the public directory, PUBDIR. This way we can keep files destined for the **northpol**'s "public" directory, **/usr/spool/uucppublic/northpol**, separate from the files in general "public" directory, **/usr/spool/uucppublic**.

Figure 8.88 Combining LOGNAME and MACHINE rule entries.

```
LOGNAME=uufriend MACHINE=northpol VALIDATE=northpol \
    REQUEST=yes SENDFILES=yes \
    READ=/  WRITE=/ \
    PUBDIR=/usr/spool/uucppublic/northpol \
    COMMANDS=who:lp:uucp
```

The remote.unknown Shell Script

The **remote.unknown** program is a simple shell script that, when executable, logs system access attempts by an unknown system (one not listed in the **Systems** file) into the **/usr/spool/uucp/.Admin/Foreign** file. Any transactions with the remote system are disallowed and **uucico** severs the connection. If **remote.unknown** exists but isn't executable, the unknown system can transfer files (subject to the restrictions set up by the **Permissions** file).

Part a of Figure 8.89 lists a typical **remote.unknown** shell script. Part b shows the warning messages an unknown remote system will get when they try to make contact using **Uutry**. Part c shows the log entry in **/usr/spool/uucp/.Admin/Foreign** for this conversation attempt. Note that **uudemon.cleanu** will send you notification of connection attempts by unknown systems.

Figure 8.89 The **remote.unknown** shell script.

a. Listing of a typical **remote.unknown** shell script:

```
FOREIGN=/usr/spool/uucp/.Admin/Foreign
echo "`date`: call from system $1" >> $FOREIGN
```

b. Warning messages an unknown system receives using **Uutry**:

```
  . . .
Login Successful: System=uworld
msg-RYou are unknown to me
HANDSHAKE FAILED: REMOTE DOES NOT KNOW ME
exit code 101
Conversation Complete: Status FAILED
```

c. The log entry in **/usr/spool/uucp/.Admin/Foreign**:

```
Sun Sep  6 18:32:31 PDT 1987: call from system sirius
```

Since you know the node name of the system attempting contact, perhaps you can send the administrator (**root**) on that system e-mail asking what they want to contact you for.

9

System Security

INTRODUCTION

Security. A word that may conjure up visions of armed guards, barbed wire, watchtowers, and fierce dogs; or, the impressive vault door at an old-fashioned bank. Your UNIX system, although only truly secure within a vault, can be made relatively secure when it is well managed.

What is system security? System security is an administrative policy that you establish to protect the files and resources of your UNIX system. This policy consists of controlling access to your system with passwords and using appropriate file permissions. Your security policy protects you from well-intentioned but misguided attempts at system administration by your users, and also from the assaults of those with more devious motives. By providing security for your UNIX system, you give yourself the confidence that your secrets, and the integrity of your UNIX system, are secure from all except the experienced system cracker.

There is another benefit to keeping your system secure. A secure file system has permissions correctly established. The permissions limit where each user can write to particular parts of the file system, thereby making backing up files and maintaining free space much easier. If permissions aren't set up correctly, users can create files anywhere in the file system, or change or remove configuration files.

You can secure your UNIX system with a few hours of your time and the information presented in this chapter. And you can help keep your system secure by implementing a few simple scripts that will serve as watchdogs. What you will be doing is like locking the front door of your home and putting away your valu-

444

ables. You probably don't leave your front door unlocked or stacks of money lying on the kitchen table. Similarly, you need to use the locks on your system and share the key only with trusted friends or co-workers.

The UNIX system has developed a reputation for being a very difficult system to secure. Multics, the predecessor of UNIX, was designed with security in mind. What happened is that the UNIX system was gradually changed to make it more convenient to work with. While these changes made life easier for users, the same changes opened up avenues for abuse. To make matters worse, the UNIX community is not a secretive one, in that known security problems are a topic for public discussion and publication.

You must decide to protect your system against the known security problems. The UNIX file system allows access to all unprotected portions of the file system. If parts of the file system are not protected, they are not secure.

Also, the same tools available to the system administrator for testing security are available to the potential system breaker. If a system administrator does not take the time to secure his or her system, the system won't be secure. That is why UNIX system security is a matter of administrative policy—either you take the time to establish and maintain system security, or your system will not be secure.

The first step in securing your system is shutting and locking the front door. Before an intruder can endanger your system, he or she must have access to it. This access is provided through logged-in terminals, logging in with knowledge of a password, using the reset switch to become the superuser, perusing your backups, or through the UUCP system.

The second step is securing your valuables. Your valuables are the files and directories in your file system, and you protect them by adjusting their access permissions. Once adjusted, you need only to keep watch over the most sensitive files and directories to maintain a secure system.

Last is patrolling and arranging watchdogs that look for burglary tools and for evidence of system breaking. You patrol your system by using commands like **ps** and **who**. The watchdog scripts make the task of maintaining security almost automatic. The scripts work to uncover discrepancies that indicate a problem. Solving the problem, and possibly discovering the intruder, will still be up to you.

LOCKING THE DOOR

Most of the information contained in this section is common sense. The reason we bother to point it out to you is that you may not be aware of all the access points to your system— terminals, modems, reset switch, UUCP, and backups. And you probably haven't developed a policy that protects these access points. At the end of this section we have included a checklist that you can use to secure your "front door." Although legitimate users pose some security problems, keeping out unauthorized users reduces your system's exposure to these hazards.

Unattended Terminals

Terminals on which a user is logged in are excellent points of access for intruders. And in fact, most system breakers typically get in via a terminal. An unattended terminal provides password free access to any resource available to the user who was logged in. A particularly wonderful occurrence for an intruder is finding an unattended terminal with the superuser prompt on the screen. An intruder (or prankster) can arrange to have "permanent" root privileges by executing just one command as the superuser. (The illicit root privileges won't be permanent if you maintain your system's security, as we'll describe later.)

The solution is obvious—if you are logged in, don't leave your terminal. Of course, if you work in a secure environment, that is, everyone who is allowed in the rooms with terminals shares access to files, you might be able to walk away from a logged-in terminal. But even organizations with adequate security allow some visitors inside, and a logged-in terminal can be irresistible to some people.

Never, never, never (and so on) abandon a terminal that is logged into the **root** account. The potential for disaster is so immense that you should always log out before your get up from the console or a terminal. Unless you are a hermit living in a salt mine, don't leave the superuser prompt (#) unattended on any terminal, ever.

There is a way that you can protect logged-in terminals while you are away for a few minutes. You can add a **lock** command to your system that "locks" your keyboard and ignores keyboard-generated signals until you enter your system access password. You can even lock your terminal from within an editor by using a shell escape. The source code to the **lock** C program appears in Appendix I.

Another way to guard against unattended terminals is to log out any user who has been inactive for a while. The 4.2BSD C shell can be compiled so that it automatically logs itself out if nothing is entered from the keyboard for 30 minutes. The Korn shell provides a **TMOUT** environment variable that you can initialize to the desired idle time (in seconds). If there's been no activity for that time, the Korn shell will prompt you to strike a key, and if no key is pressed within a minute, you'll be logged out. You can add an entry in a cron table file that works in a similar fashion for any user, no matter what shell they are using. The commands shown in Figure 9.1a logs out anyone who hasn't had any terminal activity in 15 minutes.

Figure 9.1 Setup to log out inactive users.

a. Simple script that logs out inactive users:

```
# cat /etc/timeout
:
# A simple autologout script
kill -1 `who -u | sed -e 's/./0/' -e 's/://' |
awk '$6 > 15 {print $7}'`
# □
```

b. Entry in cron table file to invoke the **/etc/timeout** script:

```
5,20,35,50 * * * * /etc/timeout
```

These commands must be executed by the superuser. By placing these commands in a file, **/etc/timeout**, for instance, you can have the **cron** daemon execute these commands every 15 minutes with the cron table entry in Figure 9.1b.

The **/etc/timeout** script shown in Figure 9.1 is very simple. Much more elaborate versions of autologout scripts have been published in the "Wizard's Grabbag" column of UnixWorld magazine.

Modems

Modems allow you to use telephone lines for accessing a system from remote sites. Dial-up access greatly increases the chances of system penetration. You no longer can control physical access to terminals—anyone who discovers the phone number can try to log in. A generous user might even establish for friends a games menu accessible through a dial-up line.

The computer underground shares the phone numbers for modems by posting them on computer bulletin boards. They even have special software that turns low-cost microcomputers into automatic calling devices that search for modems. The tireless microcomputer can try every number in an exchange, and keeps a list of all numbers where a modem answered.

If you require absolute security, don't use modems. A system with a single modem is no longer secure. You will be unable to guard against a very proficient UNIX user. The modem also provides the means to copy information to remote systems. So without ever entering the building where your computer sits, the breaker can spirit away your files to his or her own system.

If you are willing to take some risks, several techniques can ensure additional security—outgoing-only modems, callback systems, encrypting modems, and requiring additional passwords. An outgoing only modem won't answer the phone, allowing any outsider to log-in. Systems with outgoing-only modems can still call out to other systems. Danger may come from within, from a malicious user or from a poorly secured UUCP system.

Callback systems don't allow the caller to log in; instead, they accept requests to call back a particular number. The callback system guarantees that connections will be granted to none but numbers the system already knows, and requires only software and an autodialer at the system end. The callback system has two drawbacks—the calling system pays the phone bill, and only previously listed numbers can be called.

The third strategy involves having a pair (at minimum) of modems that encrypt the data that pass between them. Only modems using the same key and encryption scheme can communicate. This scheme carries the added advantage of some defense against wiretapping, works without software changes, but necessitates expensive hardware for each end.

Additional Passwords for Modems. We know of two ways to add an additional layer of password protection for dial-up access. One system uses both hardware and software. A piece of hardware connects the computer to the modem and acts as a guard that requires the additional password. The guardian device sends a number to a user who is attempting to log-in. The user enters this number into a personal encoding device which generates a unique password. The user then types in this password, and the device at the system end checks the password before allowing access to the system. This combination system uses both the user's name and hardware to produce a key that is different for every log-in attempt— all this before the user actually gets a log-in prompt from the system itself.

The second method is built into the System V **login** program. There's only an allusion to this method in the AT&T documentation for the **login** program. We learned about it in more detail through the UNIX grapevine. There are two files that are used by **login** for this purpose—a file listing the devices to watch, **/etc/dialups**, and a file with passwords, **/etc/d_passwd**. You add these files to your system. Then every time a user begins to log-in, the **login** process looks in the **/etc/dialups** file, if it exists, to determine if the device being used is listed. When a device is listed, the **login** process next checks in the **/etc/d_passwd** (dialup password) file. Figure 9.2a shows an example **/etc/dialups** file with only one line, the port **/dev/tty128**, listed. Additional ports would be listed one per line, and must be full pathnames.

The **/etc/d_passwd** file contains log-in program and password combinations. An entry in the dialup password file has the format shown in Figure 9.2b. The log-in program comes from the last field in the **/etc/passwd** entry for the user. Typically, the log-in program is a shell like **/bin/sh** or **/ucb/bin/csh**. When you are setting up the **/etc/d_passwd** file, the password can be copied from an **/etc/passwd** entry in the same way that a password is added to an **/etc/group** entry. Or you can use the **/usr/lib/makekey** utility to generate a password (as shown in Figure 9.2e).

Figure 9.2 Using the **/etc/dialups** and **/etc/d_passwd** files.

a. A dialups file for a system with one modem port, **/dev/tty128**:

```
# cat /etc/dialups
/dev/tty128
#
```

b. Format for **/etc/d_passwd** entries:

log-in_program:encrypted_password

c. A single-line dialup password file requires a dialup password for anyone using the port(s) listed in /etc/**dialups**:

```
# cat /etc/d_passwd
/bin/sh:f3okSwjTrpJOQ:
# □
```

d. A multiple-entry /etc/**d_passwd** file specifies the passwords to be used with different log-in programs. The last entry, for /**usr**/**lib**/**uucp**/**uucico**, instructs the **login** process not to request a dialup password for **uucico**.

```
# cat /etc/d_passwd
/bin/ksh:H4dFsW0JodW2D:
/bin/sh:f3okSwjTrpJOQ:
/usr/lib/uucp/uucico::
# □
```

e. The /**usr**/**lib**/**makekey** utility generates encrypted passwords. You enter eight characters for the password and two characters for the "salt." If the password is less than eight characters, enter a carriage return after the password and before the salt.

```
# /usr/lib/makekey > password1
LetMeIN!a6# cat password1
a6pIRQGaJnhQg
# □
```

If the /**etc/d_passwd** file contains only one line, the password given on this line is required of anyone attempting to log-in using any port listed in the /**etc/dialups** file. In other words, there is a default password required regardless of the log-in program listed in the /**etc/passwd** file (see Figure 9.2c). The **login** process requests the additional password by displaying the prompt "Dialup password:" after a user has successfully entered a user name and a password. If the user fails to enter the correct dialup password, the user must restart by reentering their user name at the **login:** prompt.

The /**etc/d_passwd** file works a little differently when it contains more than one line. There is no default entry, and every log-in program must match a line in the /**etc/d_passwd** file before a user can execute that log-in program. The system administrator can use different passwords for each type of shell. In other words, every user of the Bourne shell would have the same dialup password, and every user of the Korn shell could have a different dialup password.

If you don't want to force a program, for example, /**usr/lib/uucp/uucico**, to use a dialup password, you create an entry in the dialups file with an empty password field. Also, you prevent any program that you don't want to be run remotely as a log-in program by ensuring that the program doesn't appear in the dialup passwords file. For example, suppose that a user attempted to log-in as "who," an account that does not have a password in its **/etc/passwd** entry. Someone using a port not listed in the **/etc/dialups** file can run the **who** command from the **login:** prompt. However, if there is no entry for **/bin/who** in the **/etc/d_passwd** file, a dialup password would be requested, no password would match, and the use of the **who** account entry would be prevented.

You can see that the dialup password can reinforce your system with an extra layer of protection. By using a single-line entry in the **/etc/d_passwd** file, you can install a password for the modem port and distribute that password only to the group that is permitted to use the modem. Or you can add a dialup password for the different shells or log-in programs. In either case you have made breaking into your system via modem more difficult. A cracker program that uses common log-in name and password combinations may take at least twice as long to break in. And if a good dialup password is used, you have protected against bad individual passwords. We will describe good passwords later.

Incorrectly Installed Modems. Another security problem arises from incorrectly installed modems. Poorly installed modems can cause the system to fail to notice that the phone connection has been lost. The system simply waits for the next command, which will come from whoever happens to call up next. Instead of seeing the log-in prompt, the next caller gets the previous caller's shell prompt and the previous user's file access privileges. If the previous user was working as the **root**, a serious disaster has occurred.

The UNIX system can detect when a modem has lost its connection if the correct interface cable (and sometimes device name) is used. The interface cable must monitor the carrier detect line from the modem (pin 8 of the DB-25 connector at the modem end). The carrier detect line changes when the signal from the remote modem is received and changes back when the remote signal is lost. (Details on interfacing modems and computers were discussed in Chapter 8.)

The changes in the carrier detect line are monitored by the part of the UNIX kernel that handles terminal communication (the terminal device driver). Since terminals that are connected directly to your system don't need carrier detect lines, there may be two names for each terminal device, one for a modem connection and one for a terminal connection. For example, the terminal device name might be **/dev/tty1** and the modem device name **/dev/tty129**. The naming convention is system dependent, so you need to look up *modems* in the documentation for your installation.

When the phone is answered and communication is established with the remote modem, the local modem asserts carrier detect. The device driver sees the change and wakes up the **getty** process for logging the user on. If the connection is broken, carrier detect changes back to its unasserted state, signaling the device driver. The device driver will send a hangup signal to the shell if you have included the **HUPCL** flag in the **/etc/gettydefs** entry for this port. The hangup signal causes the shell to close all open files and exit. Then **/etc/init** will start up another **getty** process that waits for carrier detect to be asserted, and the cycle can repeat. If the device driver doesn't monitor carrier detect, or the interface cable doesn't pass the signal from the modem to the system, or the **HUPCL** flag isn't used, the hangup won't be noticed, and the shell will wait until the next user to access the port gives a command.

You can tell test your system by calling in on a modem, logging in, and then hanging up. Your system should respond by hanging up the modem, logging out of the shell, and starting another **getty** process. You should get a log-in prompt the next time you try to call in. You can also look at indicator lights on your modem to determine whether it is "on hook" or not and listen for a dial tone if you have a telephone connected to the same line. And you can use the **ps** command to see if caller's shell disappeared and a **getty** process has taken its place (Figure 9.3).

Figure 9.3 Looking for the modem's **getty** process.

```
# ps -e
PID TTY TIME COMMAND
  0  ?   0:58 swapper
  1  ?   0:06 init
 57 co   0:13 csh
 35 co   0:00 errdemon
 58  ?   0:01 getty
 46 co   0:21 cron
 53  ?   0:01 lpsched
 59  1   0:25 csh
882 co   0:02 ps
# □
```

Note that this **getty** process won't have a terminal associated with it, but will have a question mark (?) in the TTY field of **ps** listing. The question mark indicates that **getty**'s request to open the terminal line hasn't succeeded yet because carrier detect is not asserted. If you don't see the question mark, you are either using the wrong terminal device name or a cable that doesn't pass carrier detect to your system.

Passwords

Passwords are the keys to your system. Without a password, an intruder is effectively locked out. The use of passwords is simple, straightforward, and comes built into your UNIX system. That's the good news.

The bad news is that some problems are inherent in using passwords. First, and worst, is that some administrators allow password-free accounts on their system. For example, many systems offer a "guest" account without a password. Even if the shell used for the "guest" account is a restricted shell, a clever intruder can quickly acquire superuser privileges in a system with a loose security policy. (See Appendix H for a good example of how to create a truly restricted environment for guests.)

You can quickly check your password file for missing passwords with the simple command **grep '^[^:]*::' /etc/passwd**. The funny-looking regular expression translates as: Starting at the beginning of the line (^), match any number of characters that aren't colons ([^:]*), followed by two colons together (::). You will include this **grep** command in your watchdog scripts.

Your system may include several password-free accounts that don't use general-purpose shells as the log-in program. These restricted accounts run commands such as **tty**, **who**, and **sync**, and don't provide an intruder with access to the file system. If these commands are interrupted, the command exits and the log-in prompt is presented again. However, the **who** command can provide a potential system breaker with log-in names. Additionally, all of these commands are probably unique to UNIX systems and grant the breaker a clue about the nature of the system attached to the modem. We advise you to add passwords to these accounts if you haven't already done so.

Several other special account entries in your **/etc/passwd** file must have passwords. These are the administrative accounts — **bin**, **daemon**, **sys**, **uucp**, **lp**, and **adm**. You may have other administrative accounts: for example, an account that is the owner of your disks and memory. The primary reason for the existence of these accounts is the secure ownership of commands, scripts, files, and devices. And some administrators install passwords for these accounts and actually use them. If you intend to use these accounts, install passwords for them. If not, place an impossible password in the password field, for example, ***NO*LOGIN*** (see Figure 9.4). The asterisk is not a legal character for a password. A password-free **bin** account is extremely useful to a system breaker. Use passwords!

Figure 9.4 Protecting administrative accounts.

```
# cat /etc/passwd
root:H2HShjRkEIqC2:0:0::/:/bin/sh
daemon:*NO*LOGIN*:1:1::/:
bin:*NO*LOGIN*:2:2::/bin:
sys:*NO*LOGIN*:3:3::/bin:
adm:1BYmXEWnWqKdg:4:4:administration account:/usr/adm:/bin/csh
uucp:NJ/v5Kki6rmug:5:5::/usr/lib/uucp:/bin/csh
check:*NO*LOGIN*:6:6::/:
lp:*NO*LOGIN*:7:7:lp:/usr/spool/lp:
...
# □
```

Choose Good Passwords.   Next to missing passwords, poor choice of passwords ranks next as bad news. One study (Grampp and Morris) of over 100

/etc/passwd files found that between 8 and 30% of the passwords were either identical to the account's log-in name or a simple variant of the name. Other poor choices for passwords are the user's last name, their mate's or other relatives name, license or phone number, or even their pet's name. Anything susceptible to guessing begs to be guessed.

Good choices for passwords aren't found in any dictionary. Good passwords contain a mixture of upper- and lowercase letters, numbers, and punctuation. You can also use spaces and nonprinting characters, except for your backspace and line kill characters, and the default backspace and line kill characters, # and @. Make passwords easy to remember by creating a nonsense phrase that is mnemonic. Examples of such passwords are: z804Me2, I.love.U, 3DogNite, b_Dazld, rAgtAg3, hot.Fat, etc. Just imagine that you are creating a clever personalized license plate. Unfortunately, only you will ever be able to appreciate your own cleverness.

As an administrator, you must educate your users about good passwords. Make a game of it, encourage creativity. Also, you can log in as an ordinary user and try the obvious passwords, such as the user's first or last name. If you are a C programmer, you can modify the **lock.c** program that appears in Appendix I so that the program checks the **/etc/passwd** file for simple passwords by using the log-in name and information in the comments field of a password entry. This type of program can also be used against you by anyone who gets a copy of your **/etc/passwd** file. The **/usr/lib/makekey** utility can also be used to test passwords. So, educate your users!

Change Passwords Often. Finally, passwords get stale fast. The superuser password in particular is a status item that quickly spreads from those with a need to know, to those with know how, to those who know they want power but don't know how to use it. After all, if you can't do something as an ordinary user, you can become SUPERUSER and do anything! Person of steel—destroys entire file systems with one command!

Given the importance of the superuser password, and the ease of use of the **passwd** command, one would think that this password would be changed often. We once convinced a client to change their root password, and found that a year later they were still using the password that we suggested. Their problem was that several people all needed the root password, and changing the password required coordination and communication within this group. And they never bothered to spend the time to do it.

We suggest that you change the root password every two weeks or every month. And the experienced administrators at large UNIX installations whom we have asked agree with us. We don't think that this strains anyone's creativity or ability to communicate the new password to those who must know it. Don't write the password down, *don't* mail it, but verbally communicate the password to the administrator group just before you change it. Communicating this way guarantees that you don't forget the password and don't destroy its usefulness before the password is installed.

For ordinary users, and other administrative log-ins, we suggest a time period between 2 and 6 months. The time span that you choose depends on how much security you need for your system. You can select a day and place a message in **/etc/motd** such as:

Old passwords expire today. Please install a new password with the passwd command.

Make a copy of the **/etc/passwd** file the day before, and use the **diff** command the day after to uncover anyone who choose to ignore your request. You can, of course, give people several days to choose a new password. Speak with the recalcitrant ones, and get violent (change their passwords yourself) if necessary.

The System V **passwd** command will prevent a user from reencrypting their previous password. However, a crafty user could change their password to something temporary, then change back to their original password. The original password will have been encrypted differently, so it will look as if it's been changed. You can utilize the password aging mechanism to defeat this ploy.

Password Aging.   The UNIX system password aging mechanism forces users to change their passwords after a particular time period. This mechanism is part of the existing **passwd** and **login** programs and takes only a few minutes to implement. You, logged in as superuser or the administrative owner of **/etc/passwd**, append two or three characters to each user's password (or to the empty password field of a new user). The next time the person logs in and presents their old password (if any), they will be told that their password has expired and to enter a new password (see Figure 9.5). (Note that XENIX systems have the **pwadmin** command for administering to password aging.)

Figure 9.5 What happens when a password expires.

```
log-in: rik
Your password has expired.  Choose a new one
Old password:
New password:
Re-enter new password:

log-in: □
```

If the old password is entered again, **passwd** replies "Password unchanged" and unceremoniously logs the user out. If the user attempts to change their password again after changing it successfully and logging in, **passwd** will report "Sorry: < 1 weeks since the last change."

Before we explain password aging, we want to point out a major flaw. Suppose that it's Monday morning at 8:30, and a user logs in only to discover that her password has expired. How creative in choosing a new password will the user be when surprised this way? What if the user chooses to use the password that expired two months ago? Either way, you may wind up with passwords that are worse than if you simply announce that users have all day to select new passwords, and enforce the change pleasantly. There are ways to use password aging constructively.

Okay, you have been warned. Password aging uses a simple but unusual code based on the characters . (period), / (slash), 0–9 and A–z. The existing password, or empty password field, has a comma appended to it followed by the code representing the number of weeks until the password expires. You may optionally append a second character that represents the minimum number of weeks before the password can be changed again. Table 9.1 shows the relationship between the characters and the number of weeks.

TABLE 9.1 VALUES USED IN PASSWORD AGING

value	.	/	0	1	2	3	4	5	6	7	8	9	A	B	C	D
week	0	1	2	3	4	5	6	7	8	9	10	11	12	13	14	15

value	E	F	G	H	I	J	K	L	M	N	O	P	Q	R	S	T
week	16	17	18	19	20	21	22	23	24	25	26	27	28	29	30	31

value	U	V	W	X	Y	Z	a	b	c	d	e	f	g	h	i	j
week	32	33	34	35	36	37	38	39	40	41	42	43	44	45	46	47

value	k	l	m	n	o	p	q	r	s	t	u	v	w	x	y	z
week	48	49	50	51	52	53	54	55	56	57	58	59	60	61	62	63

To use password aging, you would first choose the character corresponding to the number of weeks until the password expires. For example, "6" corresponds to eight weeks, and "0" to two weeks. You may also select the minimum number of weeks before the password can be changed, although the default minimum, one week, usually suffices. Only one character may be used for each time period; the second character, the minimum, will be filled in by **passwd** if you don't specify it. After figuring the code you want, you edit the **/etc/passwd** file. In Figure 9.6 we have added **,6** to the password field for the user **sandy**.

Figure 9.6 Adding password aging to an account in **/etc/passwd**.

a. Format for adding password aging:

encrypted password,maximum[minimum]

b. To add a maximum time of eight weeks before user sandy must change the password:

```
sandy:orivb9p23/sHx:101:100:Sandy Smith:/user/sandy:
```

becomes

```
sandy:orivb9p23/sHx,6:101:100:Sandy Smith:/user/sandy:
```

c. For a password-less entry, add the comma and the date code to the password field:

```
tony:,6:114:100:Tony Willow:/user/tony:
```

After you make these changes, the user has to choose a new password before the system will allow him or her to log in again. The **passwd** command will add a period, ".", representing one week before the password may be changed, if you didn't provide a minimum. A week code, that represents the number of weeks since January 1, 1970 expressed as two characters using the date code, will be appended to the password field after the user has changed the password. This week code will be checked each time the user logs in and not modified until the next time the password is changed.

Anytime the password has expired, based on the week code and the maximum number of weeks, the account user will be forced to change their password. The week code is updated at this time. If you include a minimum number of weeks before the password can be changed, it must be less than the maximum number of weeks before the password must be changed. For example, if you added **,23** to a password field, the user would have been prevented from changing their password for five weeks (the minimum), but forced to change the password after four weeks, which are contradictory conditions. The user wouldn't be allowed to change the password if you selected these values, so the **passwd** command and **login** program will ignore password aging if you make this mistake.

You can use the password aging mechanism to force a user to change their password just once by selecting 0 (zero) weeks for the maximum time period. Simply append "," to the end of the password (or add to an empty password field), and the user will be asked for a new password during the next log-in. After changing the password, the **passwd** command erases the ",.", disabling further password aging.

For new accounts, rather than leaving the password field empty, the administrator can install a password and add the ",.". Then, you tell the new user the current password, and that he or she must choose a password before logging in. After the new user logs in, the administrator no longer knows the password for that account. As administrator, you don't want to know another user's password. You want that user to be accountable for using that log-in name.

What's a good, usable regimen? Warning your users in advance, then adding the characters **,z2** to their passwords in **/etc/passwd**. Your users will be forced to change their password the next time they log in, and not be able to change back to the previous password after entering a temporary password. Your users won't be forced to change their passwords again for 64 weeks. You can arrange to have passwords changed again by erasing the 2 character date code.

Reset Switch or Key

Certainly one of the easiest ways to become superuser is by resetting the system. Many systems are configured to come up in single-user mode after reset. And UNIX systems prior to Bell System V were designed so that they always came up single-user, without requiring a password. (XENIX does require a password under these circumstances, if one has been installed for the root account.) Although resetting a system is difficult to conceal while people are logged in, a reset during the early morning hours or late at night might very well go unnoticed.

For System V, you can change the configuration file, **/etc/inittab**, so that the system comes up in multiuser mode, requiring passwords from all. The line in **/etc/inittab** that determines the run state after rebooting shows **initdefault** in the action (third) field. If your system normally comes up in single-user mode, you can edit **/etc/inittab**, and change the "s" in the run level (second) field to a "2", the traditional multiuser run level, as the line from **/etc/inittab** shown in Figure 9.7.

Figure 9.7 Coming up multiuser with initdefault of 2.

```
is:2:initdefault:
```

Coming up multiuser, instead of single-user, is important if your system and console are accessible, and not kept in a locked room. The disadvantage to coming up multiuser is that it is occasionally very handy to be able to boot your system in single-user mode when you have system problems.

Another approach is to add password protection to single-user mode through a simple script. This script counts the number of processes using **ps** and **wc**, and if the number of processes is less than the number of processes during multiuser operation, requests a password. There will be considerably fewer processes running during single-user operation. The minimum number of processes during multiuser operation can be determined by using the same two commands while logged in as superuser immediately after entering multiuser mode (Figure 9.8a).

Figure 9.8 Adding password protection to single-user mode.

a. Discovering the minimum number of processes immediately after entering a multiuser run level:

```
# ps -e ¦ wc -l
8
# □
```

b. Script to test for single-user state and require a password:

```
trap "" 1 2 3 15   # Trap interrupts, prevent exit from .profile
min=8              # This value determined experimentally
set `ps -e | wc -l`
if [ $1 -lt $min ]
then
    /bin/lock      # lock must be in /bin; /usr unmounted
fi
trap 1 2 3 15      # Turn off trap
```

The **ps** and **wc** pipeline produces the number of processes. During single-user mode, no daemons or user processes will be alive. The shell script in Figure 9.8b uses this information to decide whether you are in single- or multiuser state.

If you add this script to the beginning of the **/.profile** file, it will run every time a superuser shell starts. If the number of processes is less than the minimum, the lock program is invoked, requiring the superuser password before the shell can be used. The **trap** command at the beginning of the script prevents escape from the **/.profile** shell script, and the second **trap** command turns off trapping. The **lock** program was described earlier. A listing of this short program appears in Appendix I.

Limit the ability to reset your system-to-system administrators. After all, you don't want users resetting the system as a means of regaining control of their terminal after making some mistake. For users of small microcomputers, resetting the computer is the natural and often the only way to regain control if a program causes the keyboard to lockup. For UNIX users, logging in on another terminal and killing the offending process is the appropriate approach.

If your system requires that a key be used for resetting it, we suggest that you keep the key itself locked away in the same place that you keep backups. For systems without keys, you can keep the cabinet with the reset switch in a locked room or in a cabinet or desk with good ventilation. You also need to protect the power supply. Many systems can be reset by turning the power off and back on. In any case, educate your users in how to kill runaway processes from another terminal, so that they won't be tempted to reset the system to solve their problems. And configure your system so that it requires a password for a root account-owned shell after reset.

Protect Your Backups

Standards for media have been developed so that tapes or disks written on one system can be read by another. This media compatibility is necessary for exchanging data and distributing software. However, if your backups can be read by another system, a person who gets the backups, and has superuser privileges on a compatible system, can peruse your information. Or the person could modify the information on your backups, return the backups, and create a situation where you would be forced to restore using the modified backups. (We have met students who had used this ploy to become superusers on one of their university's UNIX systems.)

We suggest that you keep your backup media in a secure location. A locking cabinet may be secure enough for some systems, and a fireproof vault more appropriate for the security conscious.

The same precautions go for off-site backups. The federal government requires some organizations to have disaster recovery plans that detail how off-site storage of media will be handled. Off-site backups are important to all who truly value their information and want to prevent damage by acts of nature, fire, or theft. Wherever you keep your backup media, keep them secure.

The UUCP System

The UUCP family of commands make information transfer between systems easy. This very ease of operation can conceal a threat to your system's security: an invader, working through a "friendly" system, can get information through the UUCP system even though she can't log in directly.

Up until System V, the UUCP system was delivered in a very permissive configuration. The permissive configuration reflects the friendly, sharing environment that exists around programmers cooperating on a project, but may be unsuitable for the outside world. You can adjust UUCP permissions easily, just by editing two files.

The file **/usr/lib/uucp/USERFILE** controls access to parts of the file system on a per user and per system basis. On HoneyDanBer, the file that arranges security is named **/usr/lib/uucp/Permissions**. Use the information in this book to configure correctly the file for your UUCP system.

The other configuration file to edit (for older UUCP systems) is the **/usr/lib/uucp/L.cmds** file. This file contains the list of programs that can be executed by **uuxqt**, the remote command execution portion of the UUCP system. Normally, only the programs required by **mail** are included in the **L.cmds** file. You may also wish to include **lp**, for printing files that have been copied to your system from a remote system, or **who**, a relatively benign command that does, however, give away log-in names. There is an example **L.cmds** file in Figure 9.9.

Figure 9.9 A sample of a secure **L.cmds** file.

```
# cat /usr/lib/uucp/L.cmds
PATH=/bin:/usr/bin
lp
rmail
rnews
#  □
```

Our example **L.cmds** file is fairly liberal, allowing access to the local line printer system. A much more conservative file would only list **rmail**.

CHECKLIST FOR SECURING ACCESS

Before we move on to organizing file and directory permissions, stop and look at the easy things that you can do to keep the unauthorized out of your system.

TABLE 9.2 CHECKLIST FOR SECURING ACCESS

---

1. Never leave a logged in terminal unattended. Either log out, or use the **lock** program that is listed in Appendix I.
2. Modems make a system less secure. If you must have modems on your system, consider ways to make them more secure. Use the **HUPCL** flag in the **/etc/gettydefs** entry for modem ports.
3. Install passwords for all accounts in the **/etc/passwd** file that use a shell as the log-in program. Encourage the use of good passwords.
4. Change your passwords often. Change the superuser password at least once a month.
5. Control physical access to your system's reset switch and power supply. Configure your system so that the superuser shell always requires a password.
6. Keep your backups secure. You certainly need them yourself, and probably don't want to share them with others.
7. Check the configuration of your UUCP system. In particular, make certain that **/usr/lib/uucp/USERFILE** and **/usr/lib/uucp/L.cmds** (or **/usr/lib/uucp/Permissions**) fence out intruders.

FILE AND DIRECTORY PERMISSIONS

You may succeed in controlling access to your system, or you might not entirely. And there are legitimate users of your system who are not privy to all your secrets nor capable as system administrators. The UNIX system provides you with a file permission scheme that allows you to control access to individual files and directories. Where controlling access to your system is like locking the front door, adjusting permissions is like adding locks to rooms or corridors as necessary. It's the second line of defense.

The UNIX file permission scheme is flexible, providing three types of access to three categories of users. The way that the permissions work for files and directories varies, but the categories of users are the same in both cases. The three categories are: the owner of the file (or directory), the group owner, and all others. The UNIX operating system obeys the flow outlined in Figure 9.10 for granting file or directory access to the three categories of requesters:

Something unexpected is going on here. Notice that if the user requesting access is the owner, the owner permission gets checked. If the owner has permission, he or she is granted access. If the owner doesn't, the request is denied, even if permissions are granted for group and others!

Figure 9.10 Granting access to a file or directory.

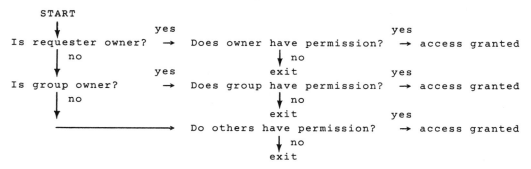

Not shown in Figure 9.10 is really a fourth category—the superuser. If the requester of a file enjoys superuser privilege, that user is automatically granted access to the file. Without superuser access, backing up files and making changes to file systems would be much more difficult. Not impossible, but a lot more complex. Thus, the superuser account, and superuser privileges simultaneously pose one of the UNIX system's most helpful aids and its worst security threat.

File Permissions

The three file permissions are read, write, and execute. These three types of access are straightforward, and apply to ordinary files, block or character special files, and named pipes (FIFOs). Directory files are treated a bit differently, and we discuss them later.

Read permission means that the user granted access may read a file but not change or execute it. Read permission also implies copy permission, since any file that can be read can also be duplicated. And once a person copies a file, he owns the copy and can alter its permissions any way he wishes.

Write permission allows changing a file. If a file is writable but unreadable, a user, lacking read permission, can't load the file with an editor to change it. But she can copy whatever she wishes *into* the file, completely changing its contents.

Execute permission enables a file to be executed as a command. To run a binary program, all that's necessary is execute permission. To run a shell script, however, you need read permission, for the shell must read the commands before it can execute them.

All files owned by administrative accounts, such as **root, bin, adm, lp, check** and **uucp**, should not be writable by others. Allowing write permissions for others on these files allows any user to change their contents. A user could, for example, replace **/bin/su** with a program of his own design. Even allowing write permissions for group is questionable—a person acting as a group member could make changes without leaving any record of her activities behind.

Files That Must Be Write-Protected. We promote the philosophy that all system-owned files not be writable by others. Of course, there can be the occasional exception; for example, the logfiles used by games, such as **aliens** and **robots**, must be writable by all if they are to keep a running tally of high scores. But game logs are minor exceptions. Files that log system activities are all owned by the administrative account that writes in the file, or are written in by programs that have **root** access privileges. No one needs to modify these files.

You may wish to differ with us and have a "permissive" system. But there are certain files that you *must* write-protect if you are going to have a minimal amount of system security. These files are listed in Table 9.3.

TABLE 9.3 FILE PERMISSION AND OWNERSHIP

Permissions	Owner	Group	Pathname [*]
-rw-------	root	root	/.profile
-rw-------	root	root	/.login
-rw-------	root	root	/.logout
-rw-------	root	root	/.cshrc
-rw-------	root	root	/.exrc
-rw-------	root	root	/.mailrc
-r--r--r--	root	sys	/etc/passwd
-rw-r--r--	root	sys	/etc/group
-rw-r--r--	root	sys	/etc/inittab (System V)
-rw-r--r--	root	sys	/etc/gettydefs (System V, XENIX)
-rw-r--r--	root	sys	/etc/gettytab (BSD)
-rw-r--r--	root	sys	/etc/ttys (BSD, XENIX)
-rwxr-----	root	sys	/etc/rc
-rwxr-----	root	sys	/etc/brc (System V, XENIX)
-rwxr-----	root	sys	/etc/bcheckrc (System V, XENIX)
-rwxr-----	root	sys	/etc/rc0 (System V, Release 3)
-rwxr-----	root	sys	/etc/rc2 (System V, Release 3)
-rwxr-----	root	sys	/etc/rc.d/MOUNT.rc (System V, Release 2)
-rwxr-----	root	sys	/etc/rc.d/cron.rc (System V, Release 2)
-rwxr-----	root	sys	/etc/rc.d/lp.rc (System V, Release 2)
-rwxr-----	root	sys	/etc/rc.d/uucp.rc (System V, Release 2)
-rwxr-----	root	sys	/etc/shutdown
-rwx------	root	sys	/etc/mvdir (System V)
-r--------	root	sys	/usr/lib/crontab
-r--------	root	sys	/usr/adm/cronlog
-r--------	root	sys	/usr/spool/cron/crontabs/root (System V, Release 2)
-r--------	root	sys	/usr/spool/cron/crontabs/sys (System V, Release 2)
-r--------	root	sys	/usr/spool/cron/crontabs/uucp (System V, Release 2)
-r--------	root	root	/usr/adm/sulog
-rw-------	uucp	bin	/usr/lib/uucp/L.sys
-rw-------	uucp	bin	/usr/lib/uucp/L.cmds
-rw-r--r--	uucp	bin	/usr/lib/uucp/L-devices
-rw-------	uucp	bin	/usr/lib/uucp/USERFILE
-rw-------	uucp	bin	/usr/lib/uucp/Systems (HoneyDanBer)
-rw-r--r--	uucp	bin	/usr/lib/uucp/Devices (HoneyDanBer)
-rw-------	uucp	bin	/usr/lib/uucp/Permissions (HoneyDanBer)

[*] Files that are unique to a particular version of the UNIX system are identified in parentheses.

Leaving some of these files writable guarantees that an experienced UNIX user can become the superuser in short order. Other files provide assistance in picking targets for trojan horses (programs that use unwitting accomplices to become superuser) or merely in creating havoc in your system (or other systems, via UUCP).

Also check the ownership of these files. User and group ownership are also shown in Table 9.3. Note that **sys** represents the system group, and may have a different designation on your system. You can use **chown** and **chgrp** to correct the ownership of these files.

Files That Must Be Read-Protected. The UNIX system relies on users being capable of reading some of the files in the write-protected list. For example, the **/etc/passwd** file must be readable by all if programs that map user-ids to user names are to work correctly. But some configuration and logfiles are better kept private. Table 9.3 also shows those files that must be readable by the owner only.

The configuration files for the UUCP system contain information that is sensitive for other systems, such as passwords. The cron table file(s) can alert intruders to what watchdog scripts are run and when they are run. The cron logfile provides the same information, that is, what security checks are being made. The **sulog** provides a potential breaker with information about who knows the root password.

The **root**'s configuration files (**/.profile**, **/.login**, **/.exrc**, **/.cshrc**, **/.logout**, and **/.mailrc**) contain information about the superuser's command path and the names of files and other scripts that are used regularly. This information can assist system crackers in setting up trojan horses.

Device Files. Device files make the connection to disk drives, terminals, printers, and tape drives. Execute permission makes no sense for device files, but access permissions work the same way for these files as for ordinary files. Device files' names are kept in the **/dev** (device) directory and in several subdirectories of **/dev** after Release 2.

Although access to devices through the file system is convenient, it also poses several real dangers to your system. The first danger is the possibility of accidental or malicious damage to file systems. Device files referring to file systems must not be writable by anyone except the file's owner. In Figure 9.11, you can see a listing of device files that are owned by **check**. The group owner is also **check**. Note that your system may use a different administrative account. Read and write permissions are granted for the owner only, with one exception. The **/dev/tty** file is owned by the **root** account and readable and writable by all. **/dev/tty** is a "magic" file that is always synonymous with the name of the terminal device for each user. The **passwd** command uses this file to read the invisible password from the user's terminal.

Your system may use a different name for the device owner, such as **system** or **daemon**. You need to check the ownership and permissions of all the device files. The only device files that ordinary users own are the **tty**NN devices, for example, **/dev/tty01**. The **tty** devices are owned by the user who is logged in through that port. The user may allow writing (with the **write** command) to that port. When

Figure 9.11 Correct ownership and permissions for device files referring to file systems, swap, or memory.

```
# ls -l /dev/rdsk/0s* /dev/dsk/0s* /dev/swap /dev/mem /dev/kmem /dev/tty
crw-rw-rw-  1 root    sys    2,   0 Oct 15 13:47 /dev/tty
crw-------  1 check   sys    2,   1 May 17 09:22 /dev/kmem
crw-------  1 check   sys    2,   0 Aug  3  1986 /dev/mem
crw-------  1 check   sys    4,   1 Jun  1  1986 /dev/swap
brw-------  1 check   sys    0,   0 Jul 17 22:07 /dev/dsk/0s0
brw-------  1 check   sys    0,   1 Aug  3  1986 /dev/dsk/0s1
brw-------  1 check   sys    0,   2 Oct 15 09:47 /dev/dsk/0s2
brw-------  2 check   sys    0,   5 Oct 15 09:47 /dev/dsk/0s5
brw-------  1 check   sys    0,   7 Oct 15 09:47 /dev/dsk/0s7
crw-------  1 check   sys    4,   0 May 26 17:13 /dev/rdsk/0s0
crw-------  1 check   sys    4,   1 Jun  1  1986 /dev/rdsk/0s1
crw-------  1 check   sys    4,   5 May 16  1986 /dev/rdsk/0s5
crw-------  1 check   sys    4,   7 Aug  3  1986 /dev/rdsk/0s7
# ▢
```

the user logs out, the **init** process changes the ownership of the port to the **root** account.

When any user can write to a file system, he can overwrite the file system structure, thereby damaging mounted file systems and destroying unmounted file systems. (Some parts of mounted file systems are in memory and won't be overwritten.) When any user can both read from and write to a file system, a knowledgeable user can access normally restricted parts of file systems, and copy or modify information. The character, or "raw", device file for file systems must also be protected. The character versions of file system devices are prefixed with an "r."

The device files for memory, **/dev/mem** and **/dev/kmem**, and the swap device (**/dev/rdsk/0s1** in our example) must also be protected against reading and writing by others. (Many systems use the second disk partition, labeled **0b**, for swap devices.) A user with access to these devices and a special program could modify the identity of a currently running process, granting illegitimate superuser privilege to that process. Although not as "easy" as modifying the file system, some people have successfully used this approach. By removing permissions for others, you thwart these attacks.

Directory Permissions

The UNIX system treats directories differently from other files. Only a limited set of system calls that are used by commands such as **mv** and **rm** modify directories. Otherwise, users could create their own versions of the file system, by accident or design, that would not be accessible to system maintenance programs for backup or repair. These "unofficial" user modifications to directories are also hiding places for burglary tools.

Access permissions for directories work differently than for other files. For example, the owner of a directory cannot edit the directory, but can change the names of files in that directory with the **mv** command.

Users read directories with the commands **ls** and **find**. (It is possible to read a directory with **cat**, but remember that directories have nontext parts, the inode numbers.) If a user doesn't have *read permission* for that directory, he or she will not be able to list the contents of that directory. A user without read permission cannot use wildcards (like using * to reference all files in a directory).

Write permission for a directory is the ability to change the filenames in that directory. As mentioned, commands such as **mv**, **rm**, and **ln** write in directories. While giving others read permission in a directory is relatively benign, providing write permission is potentially disastrous. If a user has write permission on a directory, that user can delete any file within that directory, without regard to the permissions on the file itself. Files can also be added to writable directories, including trojan horses.

For example, let's imagine that the root directory (/) is writable by all system users. Sounds reasonable, but allowing anyone to write in the root directory makes becoming the superuser easy. In one scenario, the system breaker simply renames (**mv**'s) **/.profile** and copies a specially designed **.profile** file in its place. The trojan horse **.profile** grants the breaker superuser permissions by creating a burglary tool the next time someone logs in as *root*. The bogus script then replaces the old **.profile**, thus covering the breaker's tracks (see Figure 9.12). And all this requires is write permission in the root directory.

Figure 9.12 Perverting root's profile.

```
$ ls -ld /
drwxrwxrwx 16 root     sys        304 Mar  3 21:14 /
$ mv /.profile /.tmp
$ mv bogus /.profile
$ □
```

Execute permission allows access to files in a directory. If a user has read permission but lacks execute permission, that user may list the directory but not access the contents of any file in that directory, or **cd** to that directory. Thus, removing execute permission prevents access to files in a directory. This access protection extends to all the subdirectories of the directory without execute permissions. Removing execute permission also stops someone from writing in the directory, changing filenames, removing files or copying in new ones, even if they have write permission there.

One more point about execute permissions on directories. A person can access a file in a directory where she has execute permission, even if she lacks read and write permission for the directory. The user with execute permission must know the exact pathname (no wildcards) of the file they wish to access. Users can protect their directory trees by removing read and write permissions for others, but leaving execute permission. Leaving execute permission on the directories will allow programs like **lp** to access specified files if the files themselves have read permissions for others. Or, a user can communicate the pathname of a file he wishes to share, and other users can access that file, as long as the file is readable, and the directories leading to it have execute permission for others.

Adjusting Your Permissions

We have created a procedure that will assist you in correcting the permissions on your system's files and directories. Since one script in this procedure keeps track of the filenames where permissions are changed, you can go back and totally, or partially, reverse the changes if adjusting permissions "breaks" programs on your system. During the development of this script, we "broke" **nroff** by removing read permission on a data file. The version of the procedure presented here was successfully tested on several different machines running variants of XENIX, System V, and V.2 UNIX operating system.

There are eight steps in the adjustment procedure, including one optional step. The steps are:

1. Create a directory for saving the lists of files and directories.
2. Use **find** to make a list of system-owned directories.
3. Edit the list of directories to remove publicly writable directories.
4. Remove write permission for others from the directories in the list.
5. Create lists of files to be adjusted with the shell script **holes**.
6. (Optional) Edit the lists of files to remove publicly writable logfiles.
7. Adjust permissions with the script we wrote named **adjust**.
8. Create a list of file system and memory devices, and correct ownership and permissions.

As a first step, you create a directory for saving the lists of files and directories that are adjusted. We suggest keeping copies of these lists around for at least one month in case someone discovers that some previously functioning command has failed.

We called this directory **perms**, and made it a subdirectory of **/etc**. To create this directory, you execute the command shown in Figure 9.13 as superuser.

Figure 9.13 Make directory for lists.

```
# mkdir /etc/perms
# chmod 700 /etc/perms
# □
```

The second step is to create a list of directories owned by administrative accounts. You do this by using one of the **find** commands shown in Figure 9.14.

Figure 9.14 Create list of directories.

a. List all directories in mounted file systems:

```
# find / -type d -print > /etc/perms/sys_dirs
# □
```

b. List only those directories owned by system accounts:

```
#  find / -type d \( -user root -o -user adm -o -user bin \
-o -user check -o -user lp -o -user uucp \) -print > /etc/perms/sys_dirs
# □
```

The first **find** command creates a file containing all the directories in your file system, including any mounted file systems. The second **find** command, much more restrictive, selects only those directories owned by one of the administrative accounts. Our list of administrative accounts probably differs from your list, so you need to modify this command line by changing the account names, or adding more names using the syntax **-o -user** *name* for each additional administrative account name.

Now, you are ready for the third step. Use your favorite editor on **/etc/perms/sys_dirs** and remove the directories that shouldn't be protected or changed. All user-owned directories should be removed from this list (if you used the first **find** command example). Also, the directories in the list shown in Figure 9.15 *must* be publicly writable.

Figure 9.15 Remove these directory names from the list of system directories.

```
/lost+found
/tmp
/usr/tmp
/usr/news
/usr/spool/uucppublic
/usr/mail (System V.2 only)
```

Remove the directory names in Figure 9.15 from your list of directories in **/etc/perms/sys_dirs**. You can use a **sed** script to remove these directory names, but examine your list of directories closely before proceeding. For example, **ex** and **vi** quit working if **/tmp** becomes unwritable. There may be other directories used by locally installed software that will be "broken" if you remove write permission.

The fourth step removes write permission for others from the directories in your list. As superuser, enter the command pipeline shown in Figure 9.16.

Figure 9.16 Remove write permission for others from selected directories.

a. Pipeline that removes write for others without keeping a record of which directories were changed:

```
# cat /etc/perms/sys_dirs ¦ xargs chmod o-w
# □
```

b. The **fixdirs** script records those directories that previously had write permission for others before removing write permission:

```
:
# fixdirs - Remove write permission for others from directories
# on the given list of (system) directories.
PATH=/bin:/usr/bin
case $# in
1)  ;;
*)  echo 'Usage: fixdirs sys_dirs' 1>&2; exit 2
    # As in "fixdirs /etc/perms/sys_dirs"
esac
DIRLIST=$1
if [ ! -r "$DIRLIST" ]
then
    echo "fixdirs: Can't read $DIRLIST." ; exit 3
fi
# Change the dir variable if you use a different directory.
dir="/etc/perms"
for i in `cat $DIRLIST`
do
    # Test for write permission for others with grep
    if ls -ld $i | grep '^d.......w' > /dev/null
    then
        echo $i >> $dir/directories
        echo Removing write for others from $i.
        chmod o-w $i
    fi
done
```

The **chmod o—w** command removes write permission for others without changing any other permissions that may be present. (By using the **xargs** command, we avoid the possibility of overflowing the command line buffer.) The **fixdirs** script, rather than blindly removing write permissions, tests for the presence of write for others, and records the name of the directory. If you have made a mistake, you can look in the file **/etc/perms/directories** for the names of directories that were changed.

Removing write permission for others is essential if you want even a minimal level of security for your system. If you have any problems after completing this step, you still have a complete list of all the directories that you have just removed write permission for others.

The script for the fifth step works on each directory in **/etc/perms/sys_dirs**, and collects the names of files with write permission for others and, for executable files only, read permission for others (binary programs, but not shell scripts). The script that collects the filenames is called **holes**. **holes** leaves rosters of files to be changed in the directory we created earlier, named **/etc/perms**.

Figure 9.17 Enter and run the holes script.

a. Listing of the **holes** script:

```
:
# holes - shell script to collect the names of files whose
# permissions need adjusting for security reasons
#
trap "rm -f /tmp/super$$ /tmp/lista$$; exit 0" 0 1 2 3 15  # cleanup
case $# in
1)  ;;
*)  echo 'Usage: holes directory_list' 1>&2; exit 2
    # As in "holes /etc/perms/sys_dirs"
esac
DIRLIST=$1
if [ ! -r "$DIRLIST" ]; then
    echo "holes: Can't read $DIRLIST." ; exit 3
fi
# Change the dir variable if you use a different directory.
dir="/etc/perms"
for i in `cat $DIRLIST`
do
    echo Checking $i ...
    # Next line collects names of files writable by others
    ls -l $i | sed -n '/^-.......w./s/^.*:.. //p' > /tmp/lista$$
    if [ ! -s /tmp/lista$$ ]; then
        echo NO files with write for others in $i.
    else
        # Add back directory to create full pathname
        sed "s@^@$i/@" /tmp/lista$$ >> $dir/writable
        echo '*** Writable files found.'
        > /tmp/lista$$
    fi
    # Collect names of files that are both readable and executable
    ls -l $i | awk '/^-.*r.x / { print $NF }' > /tmp/super$$
    if [ -s /tmp/super$$ ]; then
        cd $i
        cat /tmp/super$$ | xargs file |
        # select binary program files
        sed -n '/executable/s/\(.*\):.*$/1/p' > /tmp/lista$$
    fi
    if [ ! -s /tmp/lista$$ ]; then
        echo NO executable files in $i with read for others.
    else
        # Add back directory to create full pathname
        sed "s@^@$i/@" /tmp/lista$$ >> $dir/readable
        echo '*** Readable and executable files found.'
        > /tmp/lista$$
    fi
done
```

b. Run this script with the command line:

```
# holes /etc/perms/sys_dirs
Checking /bin ...
NO files with write for others in /bin.
...
```

The **holes** script creates files that contain the list of files needing adjustment for each directory examined. The two **ls −l** commands select files with the permissions we are searching for. (We can't use the **find** command because **find** travels down through directory hierarchies.) The file **/etc/perms/writable** contains the list of files that have write permission for others. The **/etc/perms/readable** file has the list of programs that can be read by others.

The sixth step is to check the files created by the **holes** script for the filenames that need to be writable (executable files never need to be readable except for administrative tasks). There aren't many files owned by the system that need to be writable by others. The game log files and the spelling history file, **/usr/lib/spell/spellhist**, are the only files known to us at this time. Use an editor to remove these filenames.

The seventh step is to run the shell script we call **adjust**. The adjust script uses the lists created in step 5 to adjust permissions on the files that were selected. The text for the script is given in Figure 9.18.

Figure 9.18 Enter and run the adjust script.

a. Listing of the **adjust** script:

```
:
# adjust - shell script that adjusts the permissions of files
# gathered by the holes script
PATH=/bin:/usr/bin
dir=/etc/perms
if [ -f $dir/readable ]; then
    echo Adjusting read permissions for others.
    cat $dir/readable | xargs chmod o-r # change o-r to o+r to unadjust
fi

if [ -f $dir/writable ]; then
    echo Adjusting write permissions for others.
    cat $dir/writable | xargs chmod o-w # change o-w to o+w to unadjust
fi
```

b. Run this script with the command line:

```
# adjust
Adjusting read permissions for others.
Adjusting write permissions for others.
# □
```

Step 8 neatly divides into two phases. First, collect a list of device files that refer to file systems, swap, or memory. Start out by creating a list of all your device files, using the **find** command shown in Figure 9.19. Then, examine this list with an editor. You want to remove the names of all ports (the **tty** files). You also want to check for device files that exist outside of the **/dev** directory tree. Don't remove these names from your list, but be aware that these files represent possible points of penetration.

Figure 9.19 Collect and edit a list of device files.

```
# find / -type b -o -type c -print > devicefiles
[ edit devicefiles ]
# □
```

The second phase of step 8 is to adjust the ownerships and permissions of your device files. The three commands in Figure 9.20 perform the adjustment. Notice that you must use your system's name for the user and group owner of the device files. We used **check** in our example. Any files that aren't in the **/dev** directory will also be adjusted. You may wish to examine the permission and ownership for these stray device files (if any), before adjusting anything.

Figure 9.20 Change ownership and permissions.

```
# cat devicefiles ¦ xargs chown check
# cat devicefiles ¦ xargs chgrp check
# cat devicefiles ¦ xargs chmod go-rw
# □
```

Steps 4, 7, and 8 change permissions on system-owned files and directories. These steps may cause some of your previously functioning software to quit operating. The software will (hopefully) provide reasonable error reporting that will clue you into what went wrong. For example, if a program named "aardvark" presents the error message

```
aardvark: can't open /usr/games/aardlog: Permission denied
```

you must readjust the permissions on the file **/usr/games/aardlog**. If all you get for an error message is "Permission denied," you will need to search for the file or directory related to the command that failed and adjust the permissions. You can, for example, search the files in the **/etc/perms** directory for pathnames that are similar to the failed command. If "aardvark" fails, use the command

```
grep aardvark /etc/perms/*
```

to uncover the pathnames containing the characters "aardvark." Then readjust the permissions for these files or directories.

If the result of adjusting your permissions is truly disastrous, you can unadjust everything. Simply edit the **adjust** script, replacing "o−r" with "o+r" and "o−w" with "o+w." Then, run **adjust** again, and your file permissions will be unadjusted. You can undo step 4 in the same manner: change the "o−w" to "o+w" when you execute the **chmod** command. Use the names in the **/etc/perms/directories** file to pick the directories to add write for others back to. We don't expect problems to occur, but we want you to be confident of your ability to correct any situation that may arise.

Once you have completed these eight steps, you will have tightened the permissions on your file system and increased your system's security. But you haven't finished adjusting permissions until every user has adjusted permissions in his own part of the file system. In particular, users who know the superuser password must protect their home directory from writing and protect their shell startup files from being read or written by others. Persons who know the superuser password are often targets for trojan horses and must follow the same precautions as the **root** account. Read and write permissions for others can be removed from all directories unless you desire to have a public directory. Remember that if you leave execute permission on your directories, specific files can be accessed by utilities like **lp**.

Permissions on New Files or Directories

You may have noticed that newly created files or directories have some permissions enabled and others disabled. For example, on one system, when we typed the commands in Figure 9.21, we found write permissions to be missing for group and others. The UNIX system sets up permissions on newly created files and directories depending on two things: the program that was executed and the **umask**. Editor programs try to create files that are readable and writable by all. Copy programs attempt to maintain the same permissions on the new file as existed on the original. The loader portion of a compiler tries to enable all permissions for everyone. So does the **mkdir** command. But some permissions are missing. What modifies the resulting permissions? The current **umask** value.

Figure 9.21 Permissions on a newly created directory.

```
$ mkdir Test
$ ls -ld Test
drwxr-xr-x    2 rik        users        32 Aug  3 15:37 Test
$ rmdir Test
$ □
```

The **umask**, or file creation mask, determines which permissions will be *missing* from newly created files and directories. The **umask** exists to protect, at least minimally, new files and directories. You can display your current **umask** by entering **umask** as a shell command.

Figure 9.22 The **umask** value.

a. Displaying your current **umask**:

```
$ umask
0022
$ ▢
```

b. Interpreting digits in the **umask**:

```
                22
               /  \
  no write for group   no write for others
```

Figure 9.22a tells you that the **umask** value is 22, which stands for "don't grant write permission for group or others when creating new files or directories." The **umask** value is expressed as an octal (base 8) number representing the permissions to be removed. Octal numbers may be familiar to some programmers, but not much help to most people. So Table 9.4 shows what the eight different octal digits mean when used as the **umask** value.

TABLE 9.4 MEANING OF THE OCTAL DIGITS IN **umask**

Octal Value	Interpretation
0	all permissions granted
1	no execute permission
2	no write permission
3	no write or execute permission
4	no read permission
5	no read or execute permission
6	no read or write permission
7	no permissions at all

The rightmost digit of the **umask** value stands for others, the left-hand digit for group (Figure 9.22b). If there were a third digit, it would represent the owner of the file or directory, but you wouldn't want to deprive the owner of permissions automatically.

The **umask** value built into the kernel becomes part of the environment of every process. However, the **umask** system call or the shell command can change the **umask** value. You can establish a **umask** for every Bourne log-in shell started by including the **umask** command in the file **/etc/profile**, umask **27**. A **umask** of 27 removes write permission for group and all permissions for others on new files or directories. This is more restrictive than the **umask** built into most kernels. The users who inherit this **umask** may also change it. Setting a restrictive **umask** helps users create files that are protected. If a user wants to unprotect a particular file, he or she can use **chmod**.

Superuser Access

The superuser, anyone with the effective user id of zero, may access any file or directory. This privileged access is necessary for performing system administrator functions, such as backing up and maintaining file systems. However, superuser access also violates the UNIX system's file access strategy.

Figure 9.23 Where the superuser fits into the access permission flowchart.

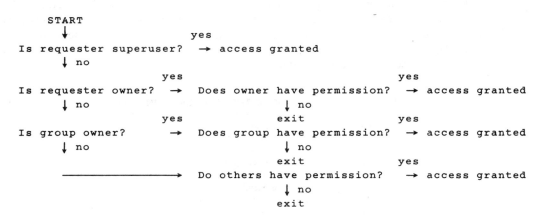

In the first flow diagram of how permissions are granted (Figure 9.10), we left out the first decision point. The first decision point checks to see if the requester is the superuser. If the requester is superuser, she is immediately granted access, regardless of the actual file permissions set. While unlimited access is necessary for certain activities, this unrestricted access exposes the user and the system to danger.

Use the **root** account only when you must perform specific tasks that require superuser privilege. Superuser access appears to be the easy way to get things to work, but this form of access is the brute-force approach. If you and the other system administrators remember to use superuser access sparingly, you will save yourself hours of repair work cleaning up mistakes made while superuser. Use it as you would a powerful drug or chemical— only when needed, on specific targets, with care—and resume your normal status as quickly as possibly.

Encrypting Files

Since the superuser may access any file, most system breakers hanker after gaining superuser permissions. But, what about those system administrators on your system who legitimately know the superuser password? These privileged users can peruse any file, regardless of the permissions that have been set.

How do you protect your sensitive files from prying eyes (superuser or not)? Use data encryption. Data encryption changes each character of a file in a reversible way, so that you can uncode the file later. Simple encoding schemes rely on a table of substitutions. For example, if the character to be encoded is an "A," the scheme changes it to "~". You may have seen versions of this encoding system that consisted of two disks, one larger than the other and both connected at their centers. Around the rim of each disk are all the characters, and by rotating one of the disks, you can change the encoding table. Then you find the character you wish to encode on one disk, and read the encoded character from the second disk.

Your UNIX system is based on the substitution method, but with an interesting twist. As each character is encoded, the table is rotated to a new position, based on the character encoded and the key. The table of substitutions is created using the password you provide, and the rotation used is calculated from a part of the password (the last two characters) called the *seed*. This method guarantees that each character will be represented differently, rather than substituting the same character over and over again. There are 4096 possible seeds, so you can create 4096 different cryptographic machines, each with a substitution table based on a unique key.

The **crypt** command performs encryption on those UNIX systems that have it. (Nondomestic versions of the UNIX system may not have this command.) Before describing how to use encryption on your UNIX system, we need to point out the three drawbacks in using encryption, all involving passwords. First, if you use an obvious password, such as your name or birthdate, all your encryption has done is to attract attention to a file that can easily be decoded. Use good passwords.

Second, the password that you use with **crypt** can appear briefly in the output of **ps** command if you enter the password on the command line. And although it's difficult, someone could then pick your password out by watching the output of **ps** with the −ef options.

Third, if you forget or mistype your password when asked for a key, you could be unable to recover the contents of the file you are trying to protect. You can get around the mistyped password problem by using a little script that asks for your password twice, and invokes **crypt** only after you have entered the same password twice. This simple script is presented later in this section.

The UNIX system encrypts files by two methods: with the **crypt** command, and with the **ed, ex-vi**, and **emacs** editors. Files encrypted with one command can be decoded by using another command. The **ed** and **ex** family of editors has a −x option that enables encryption mode. For example, to encrypt a text file with **vi**, you use the option on the command line, as shown in Figure 9.24.

Figure 9.24 Using **vi** to encrypt a file.

```
$ vi -x exempt/salaries
Key:
```

You will be prompted for a key. The key is actually a password that you will use any time you edit this file. If you mistype while entering this password the first time, you may be unable to decrypt this file later, so be careful. You won't be able to see the password as it's typed, just as when using the **passwd** command. You can use your line kill character and start over if you think you made a mistake while entering the password.

Now you will have to wait a bit because the process of creating the key takes several seconds. The pause while the key is created also occurs whenever you enter a password to log in because the same key creation routine is used. After the key has been created, the editor will take somewhat longer than usual to read in the file. Saving the file will also take longer than usual.

If you start with a plain text (not encrypted) file, **vi** will encrypt the file using the key that you provided. This file remains encrypted. If you wish to print out an unencrypted copy of your file, you must use **crypt** as a filter.

The **crypt** command is a filter program, that is, **crypt** processes what it reads from its standard input, and writes to the standard output. Although **crypt** accepts the key as part of the command line, putting the key on the command line makes it possible to read the key from a full **ps** listing. So don't include the key on the command line for **crypt**. Instead, use **crypt** without an argument, forcing **crypt** to ask you for the key.

If you wanted to print a copy of **exempt/salaries** that was encrypted with **vi**, you must first pass the file through **crypt**.

Figure 9.25 Using **crypt** to decrypt a file encrypted with **vi**.

```
$ crypt < exempt/salaries | lp
Key:
request id is nec-790 (standard input)
$ □
```

The **crypt** command will first request a key. You must provide the same key that you used when you encrypted the file. Then, **crypt** reads its standard input (the file **exempt/salaries**), unencrypts the file, and writes it to the standard output, which is connected to **lp** through a pipe. An unencrypted copy of **salaries** resides in **lp**'s spool directory until the printing completes.

Our **xcrypt** script adds a little front-end packaging to the **crypt** command. To use the script, type **xcrypt** and the name of the file you want encrypted. The **xcrypt** script requests the password twice and compares the passwords entered before continuing.

Figure 9.26 The **xcrypt** script.

```
:
# xcrypt - a simple front end that forces the user to enter the same
# password twice before encrypting a file
PATH=/bin:/usr/bin
if [ $# -ne 2 ]
then
    echo "Usage: xcrypt infile outfile"; exit
fi
trap "stty echo; exit" 0 1 2 3 15
stty -echo
yes="no"
# Continue until passwords match ( $yes no longer equals "no")
while [ $yes = "no" ]
do
    echo "Enter password:\c"
    read first
    echo "\nAgain:\c"
    read second
    if [ "$first" = "$second" ]
    then
        crypt $first < $1 > $2
        yes="correct"
    else
        echo "\nPasswords don't match; try again."
    fi
done
```

On the down side, using this script lets the encrypted password appear briefly on a long **ps** command listing. On the up side, you are more likely to have entered the password correctly.

UNDERSTANDING THE SYSTEM BREAKER'S TACTICS

Now, let's put on a different hat for a moment. Let's pretend that you are on the other side of the fence. You're the system breaker. What are your goals, and how will you set about accomplishing them? As for goals, a system breaker is interested in accessing or modifying a file, which we will call the target. The target might be sensitive information, such as financial or personnel records. Or the target could be the source code to some software. Sometimes, the target is simply to write in a file to prove conclusively that the system has been broken into. For this exercise, we'll assume that you are logged into a nonadministrative account.

If the target containing sensitive information has not been protected from reading or writing by others, your task is easy. You can do as you please with the target file, just like any other system user. But this is making your life too easy.

Let's assume that the file that you want to mess with has been carefully protected—its permissions are read and write for owner only. So you next look in the password file and see if the owner of the file is using a password.

You can use **su** to acquire the permissions of any user that hasn't installed a password. While the owner of the target might have a password, perhaps a member of the owner's group has a password free account. You may be able to get the group permissions to work for you where permissions for others are restricted.

There are still some other simple things to check. For example, what are the permissions on the **/etc/passwd** file itself? If the password file is writable by others (it's always readable), you can give yourself a superuser account and do anything you want. However, most systems guard against writable password files. System V's **passwd** command changes the permissions on this file to read only for all every time it is executed. So finding a writable password file is unlikely.

Much more likely are writable root (/) and **/etc** directories. It is not uncommon for the less security conscious to allow writing here, since they have protected all the important files. So they believe. But you know better. When the **/etc** is writable by others, it is a simple matter to become superuser. You create a copy of the **/etc/passwd** file, and add a superuser account without a password to it. Then you rename your edited copy as **/etc/passwd**. You can now log in as superuser (see Figure 9.27).

Figure 9.27 After discovering that the **/etc** directory is writable, the breaker adds a special entry to a copy of the password file, and becomes superuser.

```
$ ls -ld / /etc
drwxr-xr-x   12 root        root         336 Jul  7 18:11 /
drwxrwxrwx    4 root        root        1296 Jul 16 09:26 /etc
$ cd /etc
$ cp passwd temp
$ ed temp
a
bob::0:0:Superuser!:/:
.
w
q
$ mv temp passwd
$ su bob
# □
```

A similar strategy will work when the root directory is writable by others. There are other imaginative approaches along these same lines that will work if system directories are writable by others (like yourself).

Failing to find any writable directories, you may next go looking for a burglary tool left by a past system breaker. You don't really care whether the tool was left by a legitimate user with (mostly) good intentions, or by some other villain. This tool is a set-user-id (SUID) shell owned by the **root**. The command in Figure 9.28 searches for such tools.

Figure 9.28 Search for a **root**-owned SUID shell.

```
$ find / -user root -perm -4001 -print
/bin/mkdir
/bin/su
/bin/mail
/bin/newgrp
/bin/passwd
/bin/rcp
/bin/rmail
/bin/rmdir
/bin/lpr
/bin/remsh
find: cannot chdir to /etc/perms
find: cannot chdir to /usr/spool/at
find: cannot chdir to /usr/src
/usr/lib/ex3.7preserve
/usr/lib/ex3.7recover
/usr/lib/lpadmin
/usr/lib/lpmove
/usr/lib/lpsched
find: cannot chdir to /users/beccat/Mail
find: cannot chdir to /users/rik/Book
$ □
```

The search for useful (to a breaker) SUID shells doesn't look very promising. In other words, all the set-user-id programs shown in Figure 9.28 look legitimate. (We'll have more to say about set-user-id programs later.) From the breaker's point of view, success would be finding a set-user-id file owned by the **root** account in someone's branch of the file system. There might be such a file hidden in a directory that is protected from the search, for example **/users/rik/Book** or **/users/beccat/Mail**. The directories that the **find** command failed to search did not allow execute permission for others.

Up to now, you have been trying the direct approaches. By finding a usable SUID shell, or being able to change the **/etc/passwd** file, you could become the superuser immediately. So it's time to get a little bit more devious. If you can't become the superuser yourself, perhaps you can get the superuser to do your work for you. First, you need to decide exactly what you want to do. Next, you must write a script (or program) that will do the work. Finally, you must convince someone to execute your script while working as superuser.

The last step is the real trick. Any commands executed by the superuser will have the force of the superuser's access privileges. And tricking a system administrator into doing the dirty work may not be that hard. One approach is to send some mail, possibly masquerading as some other user, with a request to run the script. The justification might be that "the script used to work just fine, but someone must have changed permissions on me."

Of course, a wary system administrator might detect this ploy. It's much less obvious to slip the malicious script into another innocuous script that the superuser will execute. The **/.profile** is an obvious place, and only one of many scripts that will be executed with **root** privileges. The startup script, shutdown script, backup script, and any script run by the **cron** daemon (for **root**) will all work equally well.

If you have found that all the places where you might leave your nasty script have been protected, you can try something else. If you can find write permission on an appropriate directory, you can create a script that mimics a commonly used command and also carries out your bidding. A command directory, such as **/bin**, is a great place to leave your script. This type of script is known as a *trojan horse* because it looks like one thing but performs quite differently. The directories where the superuser might invoke the trojan horse are also good places if the system administrator has placed the current directory first in their **PATH** variable.

Even if the system administrator has protected the file system adequately, you might find a user that hasn't done as well. You could create a more complicated type of trojan horse, a *virus*. The virus script uses the permission of its host, the user executing it, to replicate itself throughout the file system. Eventually, the virus script may succeed in being executed by a superuser. And your will be done.

Exhausted your possibilities without success? Perhaps technology will lend you a hand in the form of an intelligent terminal. Some terminals have a really nifty feature that allows the terminal to store up some data that are sent to it, then send the data out later without ever displaying them on the screen. As a system breaker, your task is to research the correct set of commands to make the terminal behave "properly." Then you send these commands, along with the script that you want to execute, to the terminal while the superuser is working with it. The system can't tell that the superuser didn't send your commands. After all, the commands came from the superuser's terminal.

There are some problems with this approach, however. First, you must know what type of terminal a system administrator will be using. And not all terminals possess this diabolical cleverness. Then you must do your work while the system administrator is working as superuser (which isn't really that difficult to do). Finally, the system administrator must not have disabled writing for others with the command **mesg n**.

Still no luck? Let's check the permissions on file system device files. If you can read and write to a device that contains a file system, you can "operate" on an inode and change its permissions. If you can't access the file system with your target file, you can perhaps create a file with SUID permission and owned by the **root** account on some other file system by altering an inode. Alternatively, you can create a SUID file on a system where you have superuser access, and convince a system administrator to mount your file system (without checking it first).

There are still more nefarious strategies that can be tried. An entire class of tactics are known as *back door code*. Back doors are created by "trusted" programmers to show their cleverness and to access superuser permissions. For a back door to be effective, it must be part of a program that normally has SUID permissions and is owned by the **root** account. The **login** program is a notorious place for creating back door code. The back door code allows anyone who uses a particular log-in name to become the superuser. However, replacing a program like **login** usually requires access to the source code for the program. It will also require that someone with superuser privileges install the new version of **login**. That is why using back door code is usually an inside job.

Well, believe it or not, we haven't been trying to scare you. We have presented what is actually a collection of tactics that has been used successfully to break into UNIX systems. And there are known methods for protecting your system against all of these approaches. Otherwise, we wouldn't be talking about them.

Defeating the System Breaker

We have already described some of what you can do to protect your system. We have explained how to defend access to your system through

- Controlling physical access to your terminals, backups, and reset switch
- Protecting modem lines
- Using good passwords
- Adjusting the permissions on directories and files

The preceding section gives you a compendium of tactics, and indirectly, some clues as to how to defeat these tactics. Foremost in your line of defense are access permissions, especially on directories. Being able to write in a directory is almost as good as permission to write the file itself. Write permission on certain sensitive files is nearly as important. We listed these files in Table 9.3.

As a system administrator, there are several things that you must do (or not do, as the case may be). These are listed in Table 9.5.

TABLE 9.5 SECURITY RULES FOR SYSTEM ADMINISTRATORS

---

1. Protect your working directories against writing by others.
2. Keep the current directory out of, or at the end of, your command search path, **PATH**.
3. Never execute programs while working in a directory writable by others.
4. Don't execute an unknown or "gift" script or program as superuser.
5. Don't mount file systems without checking them with **ncheck** first.

Let's discuss the information presented in Table 9.5. If you took away write permission for others (and possibly also group) in your branch of the file system, you probably wouldn't even notice. If someone wants to give you a file, they can **mail** it to you. You should use group permissions to share files when you are involved in a group project. If you need to have a publicly writable directory, make one right off your home directory and call it **tmp**. Use it as a temporary directory, and don't keep files that you want to keep secure there.

The **PATH** variable determines the order in which directories are searched by a shell for commands that are entered without full pathnames. The **login** process puts the **PATH** variable in the environment and all users start out with the same **PATH**. Unfortunately, this default **PATH** starts out with the current directory (see Figure 9.29a). Having your current directory first in your search path means that a trojan horse would be found before the real command. Always list your current directory after the regular command directories if you include it in your **PATH** (Figure 9.29b).

Figure 9.29 How the **PATH** environment variable is set.

a. The *wrong* way to set your **PATH**:

```
PATH=:/bin:/usr/bin
set path=(. /bin /usr/bin)
```

b. Correctly setting your **PATH** in a **.profile** (or **.cshrc** for C shell users):

```
PATH=/bin:/usr/bin:
set path=(/bin /usr/bin .)
```

Point 3 in Table 9.5 refers to another way that a breaker could trick a superuser into unwittingly executing commands. Some programs, for example, **ex**, use startup files found in the current directory. A system breaker could create a startup file named **.exrc** and include commands that would create a SUID shell. Since only a few of your system's directories must be writable by others, you simply must be conscious enough not to execute commands while your current directory is writable by others or while you are working in someone else's directory.

The fourth point also involves executing commands unwittingly. We've already mentioned how a system breaker can be successful by adding commands to scripts run with superuser privileges. The breaker might also try the direct approach and ask the system administrator to execute the script or program as the **root**. Any such request should sound highly suspicious. Why does the user need the superuser privilege except to access some part of the file system that is normally off limits? When you receive requests to execute scripts or programs as superuser, *don't do it!* Sit down with the user and have him execute the script. If he has valid problems, the error messages will show you where you need to adjust access permissions.

Unfortunately, the same may be true of installation scripts. New software often comes with either a **makefile** or an installation script. Although we would like to believe that no one would include a trojan horse, we suggest that you execute installation scripts from an administrative account, such as **bin**, if at all possible. Otherwise, examine these scripts or **makefiles** for dubious commands. We'll cover the nature of these dubious commands later.

Finally, you may be requested to **mount** a file system for a user. As we mentioned earlier, a user could create a burglar tool on another system where the user has superuser access, and then trick you into mounting the file system on your system. The way clear of this tactic is to use the **ncheck** command with the −s option. This command will report the name and inode number of any SUID or device file. You should refuse to **mount** any file system that contains these files. If you must **mount** such a file system, you can do so in a way that the file system is not accessible to anyone else while you check out the suspicious files. You do this by mounting the file system on a subdirectory of a protected directory and examining the permissions and ownership of the file (see Figure 9.30).

Figure 9.30 Checking out a "foreign" file system before mounting it.

```
# ncheck -s /dev/dsk/2s2
123    /b/shell
# mkdir x
# chmod 700 x
# cd x
# mkdir y
# mount /dev/dsk/2s2 /x/y
mount: warning! <> mounted as </x/y>
# ls -l y/b/shell
-rws--x--x   1 root      root        32068 May 17 14:11 y/b/shell
# chmod u-s y/b/shell
# □
```

Basically, there isn't any reason for a device file to be on someone else's file system, unless they are attempting to break into your system. If you need to add a device file, you can use the **mknod** command—you can't make a copy of it. Similarly, a SUID file is very suspicious, especially if it is owned by the **root** account. SUID files owned by other accounts may possibly be justified. So, give the owner of the mountable file system a chance to explain any suspicious files before you give any access to the mounted file system.

Set User Identity—The Good, the Bad, and the Ugly

What is the only patented item of UNIX system software? The set user identity (SUID) principle was patented by Dennis Ritchie and bears this honor. The SUID principal is what makes it possible for you, working as an ordinary user, to change your password and write in the **/etc/passwd** file. The SUID principle also provides access to file system devices through the **df** command, allows users to send mail to each other, and make new directories. And the SUID principal creates a security loophole that a battleship could slip through.

Before describing how to defend your system against the threat of illegitimate SUID files, let's learn how they work. Every process is labeled (in a secure area) with two separate identities: the real user identity and the effective user identity.

(There are also real and effective group identities, and everything that we are saying about user identities is true for group identities.) When a user starts a process, such as the **date** command, both the user and the effective identities are the same as the user identity given for that user in the **/etc/passwd** file. The effective user and group identities are used when a user requests access to a file (see Figure 9.10).

When a user starts a process from a file that has the SUID permission, something different happens—the effective user identity for that process changes to the user identity for the owner of that file. In other words, if the process started from the file **/bin/passwd**, a file owned by the **root** account and with SUID permission, the effective user identity of the process is changed to be the **root**. Any requests made by this process to access a file will succeed, since the process now has the effective user identity of the **root**. This superuser access ends when the process completes. Figure 9.31 diagrams how this works for ordinary processes and ones started from files with SUID permissions.

Figure 9.31 Real and effective user identities and the SUID principle.

a. Processes normally inherit the identities of their parent processes. A user's log-in program process is set up by the **login** process according to the /**etc/passwd** entry for that user. Commands, such as **date**, inherit the same user identity.

Process	login	sh	date
Effective User ID	root	rik	rik
Real User ID	root	rik	rik

b. When a user shell starts up a command from a file with SUID permission, such as **passwd**, the process's effective user identity is changed to that of the owner of the command file, **root**, in this example.

Process	login	sh	passwd
Effective User ID	root	rik	root
Real User ID	root	rik	rik

Your system may have as many as 50 SUID files, although only a handful will be owned by the **root** account. What makes SUID files that come with UNIX systems safe when other SUID files are hazardous? The answer is in the design of the programs given this special access. UNIX system programs that are written to use SUID permission control the user's access to the file system. For example, the **passwd** command, a system SUID program, permits changing of only one field, in a single entry, in the **/etc/passwd** file. Another SUID program, the **df** command, reports on free resources in file systems but won't alter any file.

The problem with SUID permission arises when someone, working temporarily with superuser privileges, sets SUID permissions on a file containing a program of her own choosing. Many commands, such as the Bourne shell or an editor, do not provide the carefully controlled access to the file system that a program like **passwd** does. And with SUID permission, any user that can execute this program has superuser privileges.

To secure your system against unrestricted SUID programs, you must first create a list of all the SUID programs that currently exist in your file systems (see Figure 9.32a). Unfortunately, the next part is a little bit more difficult. You must examine this list and prove that each file in this list is a legitimate SUID program, not a cleverly hidden burglary tool. Figure 9.32b contains a list of the legitimate SUID programs that we have collected. However, this list won't be identical to your list. Some SUID files will be missing, and others added by your vendor or with applications software.

Figure 9.32 Listing SUID files.

a. Creating a list of all SUID files:

```
# find / -perm -4000 -print > /etc/perms/SUIDfiles
# □
```

b. An example listing of SUID files:

```
# cat /etc/perms/SUIDfiles
/bin/mkdir
/bin/cu
/bin/su
/bin/at
/bin/df
/bin/mail
/bin/newgrp
/bin/passwd
/bin/ps
/bin/pstat
/bin/rcp
/bin/rmail
/bin/rmdir
/bin/lpr
/bin/uustat
/bin/uucp
/bin/uulog
/bin/uuname
/bin/uux
/bin/uusub
```

```
/bin/remsh
/etc/ncheck
/usr/lib/ex3.7preserve
/usr/lib/ex3.7recover
/usr/lib/lpd
/usr/lib/accept
/usr/lib/lpadmin
/usr/lib/lpmove
/usr/lib/lpsched
/usr/lib/lpshut
/usr/lib/reject
/usr/lib/acct/accton
/usr/bin/cancel
/usr/bin/disable
/usr/bin/enable
/usr/bin/lav
/usr/bin/lp
/usr/bin/lpstat
/usr/bin/rlogin
# ▯
```

You can determine whether a file is legitimate by using your manuals and common sense. SUID files found in a user's directory are obviously illegitimate unless that file is owned by that user. If you find a SUID file owned by **root** in some user's directory, just change the ownership of the file to that of the user. And keep an eye on this user in the future. If you find a SUID file in a system directory and can't find a manual entry that justifies it, examine the file. You can use the **ls —l** command to discover the length of the file, and compare this length with that of your system's shells and editors. When the lengths match, you've found a hidden burglar tool. You might use the **strings** program to determine what the file is supposed to do. If you are even a little bit uncertain, remove the SUID permission with **chmod u—s** *filename*. Record what you have done in your logbook, so that if some application quits working, you know where to find the file and how to correct the problem.

When you have identified all legitimate SUID files, edit your list of files (**/etc/perms/SUIDfiles**). In the next section we describe how you will use this list to create an unmounted master list that you use to audit your system's security.

Checking Scripts for Trojan Horse Commands

The next step in checking your system's security may seem a bit of a nuisance. You must examine every script that will be executed by the superuser. Actually, you will be aiding yourself immensely by doing this because you will have a lot better idea what these scripts do.

Table 9.3 contains many of these scripts. Some of these scripts will reference other files that aren't on our list. Check these files also, and add them to your list.

You are looking for several things when you examine each script. Basically, you are searching for commands that may have been added by a system breaker. These will be commands like:

chmod   The **chmod** command can be used to grant SUID permission on a file, or otherwise alter permissions on a file or directory that make it more accessible.

chown   The **chown** command can also be used to grant access to a file by giving it away. The **chgrp** command can be used in a similar fashion to make a file more accessible.

cp   The **cp** command may be used to create a new version of a file with less restricted access permissions. The **cp** command could also be used to replace a legitimate SUID program with a less restrictive program. The **cp** program doesn't change the permissions or ownership when it copies to a previously existing file. (BSD versions remove SUID permissions whenever writing to a SUID file.)

cat   Similar strategies as those used with **cp** can be performed using redirection.

We want to make one point perfectly clear—not every use of these commands constitutes evidence of a system breaker's activities. There will be many appropriate occurrences of these commands. Also, other commands could be used to modify an existing file using redirection. There really is no other way to do this than to sit down and spend several hours deciphering your shell scripts. As soon as you declare a file "clean," make a copy of the file in a safe place. The safe place we are suggesting is a mountable file system that you will be using for your regular security audits.

CREATING YOUR SECURITY WATCHDOGS

Everything you have done while reading this chapter leads up to this point. By now, every unrestricted account should have a password, all your file and directory permissions should be corrected, and every script executed by the **root** should be checked. You should also have verified that every SUID file in your file systems is legitimate. Now, with your system "purified," you are ready to set up routine security auditing procedures, which we have nicknamed your watchdogs. Your watchdogs will make routine security checks simple and quick to complete.

Your security watchdogs are files and scripts that you will be keeping on a mountable file system. We suggest that you normally keep this file system unmounted, physically removed, and locked in a safe place when you are not using it. Keeping your security watchdogs in a secure place in a normally mounted file system is asking for trouble. Someone who successfully breeches your security could modify your data files to hide what they have done if you have left your security data accessible.

We suggest that you follow the seven steps that we devised for your routine security audits.

1. Check the **/etc/passwd** file for entries without passwords and for bogus superuser entries (script **passwdck**).
2. Check that no system directories have write permissions for others (script **dirck**).
3. Compare permissions, sizes, and the last time the inode was changed for all SUID files and other sensitive files (script **permchk**).
4. Compare the contents of files that were discovered to have been changed in step 3 with known good copies.
5. Compare the existing SUID files with a list of known good SUID files (script **suidck**).
6. Examine the **/usr/adm/sulog** for suspicious entries (script **sulogck**).
7. Check permission and ownership of file system, swap and memory device files (script **deviceck**).

Preparing a File System

Your security watchdogs need a relatively small file system. The scripts, data files, and backup copies of all scripts executed with **root** privileges required only 64K on our example system. Making reference copies of all SUID files on our system used another 858K. With sizes this small, you probably don't want to waste a disk pack for your security watchdogs. We suggest that you follow our example, if possible, and create a file system on a floppy diskette. Although slow, the floppy file system has ample capacity for the watchdogs, the data files, and backup copies of scripts. More system time will be spent examining the files and directories in the rest of your file systems than in reading the floppy file system.

Another approach would be to keep your security watchdogs on a backup tape. You restore the watchdogs to a secure directory before using the scripts, and make a new backup whenever you change the data files that work with the watchdog scripts. Remove the watchdog scripts and data files from the system when you are not using them. A clever intruder could survey your scripts and data and discover strategies that your audits miss.

The commands shown in Figure 9.33 create your watchdog file system. First, make a file system with the appropriate size for the partition or disk that you are using. Next, **mount** the file system and change permissions for its root directory to read, write, and execute for the owner only. Then create the two working directories that we will be using, **Files** and **Scripts**.

Figure 9.33 Making the watchdog file system.

```
# mkfs /dev/flp0    800:64
# mount /dev/flp0 /a
mount: warning! mounting <> as </a>
# chmod 700 /a
# cd /a
# mkdir Files Scripts
# cd Scripts
# □
```

The **Scripts** directory will hold the watchdog scripts. The **Files** directory will contain the supporting files and backup copies of **root**-executed scripts. We used a separate backup system for our SUID files, since our floppy file system doesn't have the space for them. If you have enough room in your watchdog file system, we suggest that you create a separate directory for copies of your SUID files.

As we explain how to create the scripts for each of the six steps, we will also tell you how to set up the supporting files.

Step 1: Checking /etc/passwd

Since **/etc/passwd** provides easy prey for the nefarious breaker, it should be scrutinized thoroughly. The **passwdck** script makes checks on the password file for passwordless accounts, for bogus superuser accounts, illegal user and group id numbers, and for write permission. A bogus superuser account is an account added by a system breaker that provides **root** privileges. The command that we are using will pick out all accounts with the **root** user identity of zero (0).

For simplicity, we have named each script after the step that it helps to carry out. Figure 9.34 shows the command lines for the first step, from script **passwdck**.

Figure 9.34 Commands to check the password file.

```
:
# passwdck - Examine passwd file for passwordless entries,
# permissions, accounts with root privileges, and format.
PATH=/bin:/usr/bin
export PATH
DIR=/a/Files
cd $DIR
echo "Collecting account entries without passwords.\n"
if grep '^[^:]*::' /etc/passwd
then
    echo "\nOnly restricted accounts can be without passwords.\n"
else
```

```
     echo "All accounts have passwords.\n"
fi
echo "Displaying accounts with superuser privileges.\n"
grep '^[^:]*:[^:]*:0' /etc/passwd
echo "\nOnly root and rootcsh should appear in the preceding list."
set - `ls -lc /etc/passwd`
case $1 in
    -r--r--r--) echo "Permissions okay for /etc/passwd." ;;
    *) echo "Permissions for /etc/passwd incorrect, currently \n
    $* \n
    Now changing permissions to read only for all.";
    chmod 444 /etc/passwd ;;
esac
echo "Running pwck to check entries for valid user and group id's"
if /etc/pwck
then
    echo "Fields and entries look okay to pwck."
else
    echo "Check these entries in the password file."
fi
```

The first **grep** command culls out accounts in the **/etc/passwd** file that have an empty second field, that is, no password. The second **grep** command displays all accounts with a user identity of zero. There should only be one or two of these accounts. You will want to edit the **echo** command in the script **passwdck**, which includes the account names that should have a user identity of zero.

The next test checks for correct permissions on the **/etc/passwd** file. Correct permissions are read only for all. If permissions are correct, the script reports that things are okay. If not, the script reports the current (incorrect) permissions, then adjusts the permissions to be read only for all. If your password file permissions were incorrect, the date displayed by the script will give you a clue as to when the permissions were changed. If write permission for others were in effect, your security has been compromised.

The last part of this script runs the **/etc/pwck** command. XENIX systems use a different name for this program, **pwcheck**. The **pwck** program examines the fields that make up a password entry and applies some validation to each field (except the comment field). The validation is somewhat simple. The log-in name is checked for capital letters (because capital letters used to fool the **getty** program). The user and group identity numbers must be positive numbers. On some XENIX systems, using an "O" (letter oh" instead of a zero in the user id field gave the account superuser privileges because the conversion of a letter to a number failed, and returned a zero). Another thing to watch for on XENIX systems is the size of the user identity number. Values above 30000 give the account superuser privileges. The **pwck** program also checks the home directory and log-in shell for existence. If **pwck** turns up any problems, you should edit **/etc/passwd** and mend the offending entries.

Step 2: Check for Writable Directories

Earlier in this chapter you made a list of all system directories. You edited this list to delete the five directories that must be writable by others, **/tmp**, **/usr/tmp**, **/usr/spool/uucppublic**, **/usr/news**, and **/usr/mail** (Release 2 and later of System V, only). Now you get to use this list of system directories again. The script we have named **dirck** checks the directories in this list to see if someone has restored write permission for others. If this check uncovers any system directories that have write permission for others, you need to check this directory for trojan horses and other surprises, and remove the write permission.

Before you use the **dirck** script the first time, copy the list of system directories that you created earlier in "Adjusting your permissions" to your security file system. You may wish to add to this list if you add new system directories, for example, when installing a software package.

Figure 9.35 Checking for writable directories.

a. Setting up the script by copying the list of system directories:

```
# cp /etc/perms/sys_dirs /a/Files
# □
```

b. The commands for checking for write permission for others:

```
:
# dirck - Check system directories for write for others.
PATH=/bin:/usr/bin
export PATH
DIR=/a/Files
cd $DIR
echo "Checking for system directories writable by others."
if cat sys_dirs | xargs ls -ld | sed -n '/^d.......w/p'
then
     echo "All system directories protected against writing by others."
else
     echo "Correct the permissions on the above with chmod o-w dir."
fi
```

c. Remove write permissions for others on /**usr/bin**:

```
# chmod o-w /usr/bin
# □
```

Note that the script in Figure 9.35 doesn't adjust any permissions for you. You are expected to investigate any directories that suddenly appear to have write permission for others for trojan horses and other surprises. You will also need to use the **chmod** command (shown in Figure 9.35c) to remove write permission for others.

Step 3: Watching Critical Files

Critical files are the ones that can be used to breech your system's security. Configuration files, cron table files, and scripts that are executed by **root** are all critical files. We also include any SUID files in this list. If a SUID file is writable by others, a user could temporarily replace the file with one of their own choosing (not possible in BSD versions). Or a clever programmer could add some "special features" to an existing SUID file, in the form of a trapdoor. Now that your SUID files are currently "clean," this step will allow you to monitor your SUID files' permissions, checksums, and sizes.

You will need to create the list of files to be watched, or **watchfiles**, for this step. Our **watchfiles** list includes all the files that we listed earlier as files that must be unwritable or unreadable by others in Table 9.3. You will be better off including more files than necessary than not enough. The list of set-user-identity files, **SUIDfiles**, should be the list of legitimate SUID files that you checked earlier in this chapter (Figure 9.32a). Figure 9.36 contains the script that creates a database from these lists of files.

Figure 9.36 Watching permissions, ownership, and sizes.

a. The script that sets up the permission checklist file:

```
:
# permsetup - script that creates a permission, ownership and checksum
# database for the files listed in watchfiles and SUIDfiles.
PATH=/bin:/usr/bin
export PATH
DIR=/a/Files
cd $DIR
echo "#Permissions\tOwner\tGroup\tSize\tCheck\tFile" | tee checklist
for file in `cat watchfiles SUIDfiles`
do
    if [ ! -r $file ]
    # If you can't read this file,
    then
        echo "# Can't read $file."
        # Put comment in database, and skip it.
        continue
    fi
    # Put parts of the file's long listing into shell variables
    set - `ls -lc $file`
    perms=$1
    owner=$3
    group=$4
    size=$5
```

```
    # Get a checksum
    set `sum $file`
    sum=$1
    # List everything, separated by tabs
    echo "$perms\t$owner\t$group\t$size\t$sum\t$file"
done ¦ tee -a checklist
```

b. Beginning of the **checklist** database:

```
#Permissions  Owner     Group     Size Check     File
-rw-------    root      sys 198   15473     /.profile
-rw-------    root      sys 244   20922     /.login
#Can't read /.logout.
-rw-r--r--    root      sys 901   9102 /.cshrc
-r--r--r--    root      sys 731   54437     /etc/passwd
-rw-r--r--    root      sys 167   14538     /etc/group
   ...
```

The **permsetup** script writes in the file **checklist**, the beginning of which is shown in
9.36b. This database consists of information taken from long **ls** listings of the files
in the two lists. Since it is possible to change the contents of a file without changing its size, a checksum is calculated and included with the entry for each file. A
checksum is a method for proving that the contents of a file haven't changed. Each
byte in a file is treated as a number, and a total of all the bytes in a file is calculated. The total will be a number between zero and 65535 because of the design of
the checksum calculating routine. Although checksums can be fooled, doing so is
tedious. Thus, the combination of the size of a file and its checksum provide
increased security beyond just looking at the size of a file.

Once you have set up the **checklist** database file, you can perform audits by
running the **permck** script.

Figure 9.37 Script to audit permissions, ownership, checksums, and sizes.

```
:
# permck - Compare the permissions of current files with the
# permissions, ownership, size and checksum found in the checklist
# database.
PATH=/bin:/usr/bin
export PATH
DIR=/a/Files
cd $DIR
PERMS=checklist
cat $PERMS ¦
while nextline=`line`
do
```

```
# Check for comments in checklist file.
  if expr "$nextline" : '#' > /dev/null
  then
    continue # If line begins with #, skip to next line.
  fi
# Save values from this entry in the checklist database.
  set - $nextline
  perms=$1
  owner=$2
  group=$3
  size=$4
  sum=$5
  file=$6
# Get current values
  set - `ls -lc $file`
  permck=$1
  ownerck=$3
  groupck=$4
  sizeck=$5
  dateck="$6 $7 $8"
  set `sum $file`
  sumck=$1
  if [ $perms$owner$group$size$sum != $permck$ownerck$groupck$sizeck$sumck ]
  then
    echo "              Permissions\tOwner\tGroup\tSize\tCheck\tFile/Date Changed"
    echo "Recorded: $perms\t$owner\t$group\t$size\t$sum\t$file"
    echo "Current: $permck\t$ownerck\t$groupck\t$sizeck\t$sumck\t$dateck"
    # Print notice if file is a log file.
    if echo $file | grep log > /dev/null
    then
      echo Change in the size and checksum of log files is normal.
    fi
  fi
done
```

The script, **permck**, compares permissions, ownership, size, and checksums with the listings contained in the database file **checklist**. The **line** program reads a line at a time from the input file (**checklist**). If the line starts with a pound sign (#), the line is ignored. So comments can appear in the **checklist** file. The line is then split into arguments, taking advantage of the Bourne shell's builtin **set** command, and stored as shell variables. Then essentially the same process that took place in **permsetup** is repeated to gather the current information about permissions, ownership, size, and checksums. If the current variables agree with the values taken from the **checklist**, the next entry in the database is checked. Otherwise, the inconsistent entry is reported, along with the time that this file was last changed (the inode change time).

Some files, like the log files **/usr/adm/sulog** and **/usr/adm/cronlog**, will be changing in size constantly. These files are included so that their permissions are monitored. When permissions, ownership, size, or checksum changes for scripts or configuration files, you'll need to investigate the differences between them. We describe a simple way to do this in step 4.

Step 4: Investigating Changes

When step 3 displays listings of files that have been changed, you must use your head and interpret what is different. Do the permissions match exactly? How about the size or file ownership? If permissions are incorrect, you can correct them with the **chmod** command. If the checksum or sizes have changed, someone has modified this file. Remember that the log files will change constantly, and that this is normal. The **/etc/passwd** file will also change often, and gets thoroughly checked during step 1.

How do you check scripts and configuration files that have changed? Use the **diff** command. The **diff** command will quickly pick out the minimum set of changes in lines between two files. Of course, you must set up your reference files if **diff** is expected to work correctly. You can perform the setup by copying all the files listed in **watchfiles** to your **Files** subdirectory with the command shown in Figure 9.38a.

Figure 9.38 Checking for changes in critical files.

a. Setting up the reference files:

```
# cp `cat watchfiles` /a/Files
# □
```

b. Using **diff** to discover how the **/etc/shutdown** script was modified:

```
# diff /a/Files/etc/shutdown /etc/shutdown
83a84
> /usr/lib/lpshut
# ls -l /etc/shutdown
-rwxr--r--   1 root      sys           1421 Jun 24  1986 /etc/shutdown
# sum /etc/shutdown
41810 3 /etc/shutdown
# □
```

Figure 9.38b shows how **diff** is used to pick out differences between two files. One line was added to the second file, the current **/etc/shutdown**. The added line, **/usr/lib/lpshut**, is not a trojan horse but a legitimate command. To prevent **/etc/shutdown** from showing up in future audits, you edit the **checklist** file and replace the size and checksum with the current values, 1421 and 41810. Note that the **sum** utility reports both the checksum and the number of blocks in the file. Use the checksum, the first number reported.

We suggested earlier that you survey any script that is executed with **root** access privileges. These are scripts executed through the **/etc/inittab** file, through the cron table files, through **/etc/shutdown**, and as setup files for the **root** account. As you examine these scripts, you may discover that they reference other scripts. Be sure to include these scripts in your **watchfiles** and check them too. Study these scripts carefully. You are looking for commands that change permissions or the contents of other files. As a side effect, you will have a complete copy of every configuration file and script as a backup, in addition to your regular backups.

If the file that has changed is a SUID file, you can't use **diff** to establish what has changed. If the permission has changed, you can readjust it. However, think about the consequences the altered permissions had. If the file had allowed reading and writing by others, a system breaker could have copied the contents of the file to a temporary location, copied their own command into this file, and used the SUID permission to carry out her misdeeds. Then she could have restored the file's previous contents from the temporary file. By leaving the permissions altered, she is ready to do the same thing again. (BSD prevents this ploy by resetting SUID permissions when the file is modified.)

If the size or checksum of the SUID file is incorrect, you must replace it from a backup copy. The SUID file may have been replaced completely with a burglar's tool, or altered more subtly by a programmer. Either way, you need to replace the file from a known good backup. An altered version of the SUID program, including a trapdoor, may have replaced the original version.

In any of these cases, you will want to look in your logbook, which will show all the changes to configuration files and scripts. When someone makes a legitimate change to a file, the change will be recorded in the logbook. So when you discover a change during step 3, you can verify its authenticity by checking it against the logbook. If the change doesn't appear in the logbook, add an entry explaining the change in the logbook after you have looked it over to see that the change is legitimate.

Step 5: Check for New SUID Files

Steps 3 and 4 check the authenticity only of the SUID files that you knew about when you set up your watchdogs. Now you're keeping a weather eye out for new SUID files. In step 5, you compare the list of known authentic SUID files with the currently existing SUID files using **find** and **diff**. Since you have already copied the list of files to the **Files** directory, your setup is complete. The commands in Figure 9.39 uncover new (or missing) SUID files.

Figure 9.39 Uncovering new SUID files.

```
:
# suidck - compare current SUID files with previously created
# list.
PATH=/bin:/usr/bin
export PATH
DIR=/a/Files
cd $DIR
echo "Checking for new SUID files."
if find / -perm -4000 -print | diff SUIDfiles -
then
    echo "SUID files unchanged since last check."
else
    echo "These are recently added SUID files. Check for legitimacy."
fi
```

New SUID files will be preceded by the "greater than" sign (>). Some files may have been added with the installation of new software. Verify these files carefully, as they may cleverly disguise system-breaking tools. When you aren't sure about a SUID file's authenticity, you can change the ownership of the file to be the same as the owner of the directory where the file appears, or remove the SUID permission with **chmod u−s** *file*. Add new SUID files that are legitimate to your master list, **SUIDfiles**. You will also have to edit the **checklist** database to include the new file.

Step 6: Check the sulog

Checking the "switch-user" log, **/usr/adm/sulog**, is an important security task that is easy to overlook. We have added a filter that you can use to screen out the entries that are normally legitimate, and display only the extraordinary ones.

The **sulog** contains a one-line entry for each time the **su** command was executed. The log-in name of the user executing the command, the name of the account that they switched to, and the date are included in each entry. When a user switches successfully, a plus sign appears after the date. Unsuccessful attempts are marked by a minus sign. Figure 9.40a shows a few lines from a **sulog**.

There are at least two users that may legitimately use the **su** command—the **root** and yourself, the system administrator. You can set up a file named **su-allow** that contains the list of users and the accounts to which they are allowed to switch. Figure 9.40b shows an example **su-allow** file. The **root** account is allowed to change to any user (**root-**). The user **rik** is allowed to become either the **root**, or **adm** (**rik-root, rik-adm**), and the user beccat can become **uucp** (**beccat-uucp**). These lines filter out corresponding entries in the **sulog**. Figure 9.40c shows the script that uses **su-allow**.

Figure 9.40 Checking the **sulog**.

a. Some entries from the **/usr/adm/sulog**. A minus sign indicates that the attempt to switch user failed, and a plus sign indicates success.

```
# cat /usr/adm/sulog
SU 10/18 20:53 - tty22 joec-root
SU 10/26 14:34 + console root-adm
SU 10/27 13:37 + tty02 rik-root
...
# □
```

b. A file containing users allowed to use **su**:

```
# cat /a/Files/su-allow
root-
rik-root
rik-adm
beccat-uucp
# □
```

c. The script that picks out other entries:

```
:
# sulogck - filter sulog for surprise entries.
PATH=/bin:/usr/bin
export PATH
echo "Scanning /usr/adm/sulog for entries not listed in su-allow."
DIR=/a/Files
cd $DIR
if fgrep -v -f su-allow /usr/adm/sulog
then
    echo "The preceding log entry(s) don't appear in the su-allow list."
else
    echo "SU log looks okay."
fi
```

Unexpected entries in the **sulog** may signal an attempt to guess the **root** password. Successful attempts by users that shouldn't know the **root** password mean that it's time to change the superuser password.

Step 7: Check Device Files

Tampering with file systems or memory requires an in-depth knowledge of the UNIX operating system and some special tools. However, these tools already exist, so you need to watch the permissions and ownership of device files that refer to file systems, memory, and swap space. You (should) have previously corrected the permissions and ownership of these device files during step 8 of "Adjusting your permissions." We shall use the list of devices that you created in that section as part of the **deviceck** script.

There are two commands needed to set up the **deviceck** script. The first is simply to copy your list of file system, swap, and memory devices to the **/a/Files** directory. The second command searches all your (mounted) file systems for device files, and stores this list in the file **/a/Files/devices** (see Figure 9.41a). Examine this list carefully. All your device files should be a part of the **/dev** directory.

Figure 9.41 Checking device files.

a. Setting up your lists of devices:

```
# cd /a/Files
# cp /etc/perms/devicefiles .
# find / -type b -o -type c -print > devices
# ex devices
[ Look for and remove device files not in /dev ]
# □
```

b. The script for step 7:

```
:
# deviceck - Check permissions on file system, memory and swap
# devices, and search for new device files.
PATH=/bin:/usr/bin
DIR=/a/Files
cd $DIR
echo "Checking permission and ownership of file system, memory,
and swap devices."
if cat devicefiles | xargs ls -l | grep -v '^.rw-r------.*check.*check'
then
    echo "Adjust the permissions and ownership of these files."
else
    echo "Permissions and ownerships okay."
fi
echo "Checking for new device files."
if find / -type b -o -type c -print | diff devices -
then
    echo "No new device files."
else
    echo "The preceding device file(s) aren't in the list of devices.
    Check their ownership and permissions with ls -l, and correct
    or remove them."
fi
```

Figure 9.41b depicts the **deviceck** script. The first part compares permission and ownership against the pattern used in the **grep** command. You will need to substitute the owner of your device files with the owner, **check**, used in the script. File system, swap, and memory device files that don't match this pattern will be listed. Remember that only those files contained in your list file **(devicefiles)** are checked at this point. These files must not be readable or writable by others.

The second part of the script checks for newly added device files, of either type, character, or block, anywhere in your file systems. If new device files show up, check their ownership and permissions immediately with **ls −l**.

Running Your Watchdogs

Once you have created your watchdog scripts and their support files, you can perform routine security audits of your system. It takes between 10 and 15 minutes to complete the audit on our test systems. Generally, the audit turns up changes in the critical files due to changes in configuration. Once we have verified the changes, we edit the file **/a/Files/checklist** (Figure 9.37) and make a copy of the corrected version of the script of file that changed in the **Files** directory. By using this system, you keep an up-to-date backup of every configuration file on your system, separate from your regular backup procedures.

The best time to run these scripts is while you are in single-user mode, with all file systems mounted. If all file systems aren't mounted, you may miss a newly created SUID or device file. And if others are using the system, the possibility exists that someone with illicit **root** privileges will edit your lists while you are performing your audit.

Figure 9.42 shows the procedure for running the audit after your system is running single-user with all file systems mounted.

Figure 9.42 Running your watchdogs.

```
# mount /dev/dsk/fd0 /a
# cd /a/Scripts
# ./passwdck
Collecting account entries without passwords.

canyon::107:150:Canyon Moon:/u/canyon:/bin/csh

Only restricted accounts can be without passwords.

Displaying accounts with superuser privileges.

root:XnMvQohRYB81A:0:3:0000-Admin(0000):/:
rootcsh:ooDhcBls1Xrw.:0:3:0000-Admin(0000):/:/bin/csh
```

```
Only root and rootcsh should appear in the preceding list.
Permissions okay for /etc/passwd.
Running pwck to check entries for valid user and group id's
Fields and entries look okay to pwck.
# ./dirck
Checking for system directories writable by others.
All system directories protected against writing by others.
# ./permck
        Permissions     Owner    Group    Size Check    File/Date Changed
Recorded: -rw-------     root     root     65   4548     /usr/adm/sulog
Current:  -rw-------     root     root     97   6750     Oct 27 13:37
Change in the size and checksum of log files is normal.
        Permissions     Owner    Group    Size Check    File/Date Changed
Recorded: -rwx------     rik      amber    416  23156    /u/rik/.cshrc
Current:  -rwx------     rik      amber    453  24327    Oct 25 10:32
# vi /a/Files/checklist
```
Edit checklist, and add in new size and checksum for .cshrc
```
# ./suidck
Checking for new SUID files.
43a44
> /u/rik/Prog/sh
These are recently added SUID files. Check for legitimacy.
# ./sulogck
Scanning /usr/adm/sulog for entries not listed in su-allow.
SU log looks okay.
# ./deviceck
Checking permission and ownership of file system, memory,
and swap devices.
Permissions and ownerships okay.
Checking for new device files.
No new device files.
# ☐
```

We suggest that you run your watchdogs weekly. The time you spend will be repaid manyfold because you will have avoided damage to your system through poor security. And the peace of mind you will gain, at the expense of system breakers, is well worth it.

Automating Watchdog Scripts

The watchdog scripts presented here can be run automatically by the **cron** daemon. You could also rewrite these scripts so that the scripts report only when there is a problem. The philosophy that we have espoused is that security requires the active participation of alert system administrators. If the watchdogs are run, and the results mailed to the administrator, the administrator is now isolated from the system whose security he or she is supposed to defend.

Automating security audits also makes things easier for the clever breaker. Much of the motivation for system cracking is to be as clever as possible. And the clever user who breaks root will look for evidence of security maintenance activities, such as the watchdog scripts. With the scripts being run by **cron**, the cracker has only to examine the cron table files, pick out the watchdog scripts, and modify the scripts so that his or her activity won't be reported.

What you can do is to automate *part* of the security audits. Use **cron** to make routine checks for new SUID files, unusual entries in the **sulog**, and watch permissions on critical files and directories. Design your scripts so that they mail reports to the **root** account only when a problem has been uncovered. You still need to mount your security watchdog file system and run the scripts regularly. Then your automated audits give you a first line of defense without luring you into a false sense of security. Even if someone gets past the automated watchdogs, you'll find the cracker when you run the scripts personally.

Catching the Cracker

Evidence of system-breaking activities may be subtle or glaring: a small change to a configuration file, a new SUID file, or a newspaper account detailing your company's finances. In each of these cases, you must become the detective and uncover clues as to the identity of the culprit.

The first thing that we encourage you to do is to remain vigilant. Security-conscious system administrators run the **ps** command routinely and watch for unusual activity. Watching **ps** listings, especially long ones, takes a practiced eye. But you will soon be able to divide your users into two categories—the stoic and the adventurous. The stoic user will be found running a word processor or database. This user seldom ventures outside his or her home directory, and may already be well known to you by the questions that he or she asks. Stoic users seldom prove to be system breakers, except by accident.

As you might have guessed, the adventurers know their way about the file system. They are likely to be programmers and may have added some useful utilities to your **/usr/local/bin** directory. It's these users that you want to watch for in **ps** listings. Remember that you can run the command **ps −ef** as an ordinary user, anytime. Try it the next time someone puts you on hold.

Another strategy is to run the **who** command to see who is logged in. **who** gives you a simpler-to-digest report than **ps**. And if your installation operates around the clock, **who** can provide very interesting information. For example, **who** shows you that someone who normally works 9 to 5 is logged in at 2 in the morning. The person using this account might be (probably is) an imposter. Even if the person is using a modem, you can **write** to him or her, engage in "conversation," and try to determine if this is the actual user or an imposter.

Suppose that you didn't catch the system breaker during the attempt. Instead, you discover a new SUID file while running your watchdog scripts. Now what do you do?

What you can do is determine which users were logged in when the file was created. You may be able to narrow the search down further if you have process accounting records for that day. The first step is to use **ls** **—lc** to determine the inode change time for the offending file. Figure 9.43a shows that the file **/usr/lib/libcsh.a** was last changed October 27, at 18:43.

Figure 9.43 Uncovering the perpetrator of an unruly deed.

a. Determine time the new SUID file was last changed, using the inode change time:

```
# ls -lc
-r-s--x--x   1 root      sys      85020 Oct 27 18:43 /usr/lib/libcsh.a
# □
```

b. Pick out entries from **/etc/wtmp** for the afternoon of October 27:

```
# who -a /etc/wtmp ¦ grep 'Oct 27 1'
jan         tty01        Oct 27 10:03  0:02      83
joe         tty02        Oct 27 10:12  3:42      84
jan         tty01        Oct 27 16:48  0:02      83  id=  c1 term=0   exit=0
getty       tty01        Oct 27 16:48  0:02    1071  id=  c1
# □
```

In Figure 9.43b we use the **who** command with the **—a** option file to display the contents of **/etc/wtmp**. The **grep** command passes through only those entries that match *Oct 27 1*, limiting the display to the time period of 10 in the morning to 7 in the evening on October 27. Since we miss anything that happens before 10 or after 7 (1900), we could have limited the output to entries for October 27, and seen more.

By examining Figure 9.43b, we can see that user *jan* has logged off, but *joe* is still logged in. *jan* logged in at 10:03 and logged out at 16:48. The log-out record is followed immediately by the **getty** process started by the **init** process to wait for the next log-in. *joe*, on the other hand, has no log-out record, and we know that the new SUID file was last modified at 18:43, while *joe* is still logged in. Circumstantial evidence points definitively to the user logged in as *joe*.

This example of using **/etc/wtmp** was deliberately simplified. Except on very small systems, the **wtmp** record for a single day will be much larger. Entries for the log-in and log-out of each user will be interspersed with perhaps hundreds of other entries. You can make the task of interpreting the list easier by using **sort** to organize the list by log-in names. Then each pair of entries indicate the time period that the user was logged in during that day.

If you have enabled process record keeping, you can use the **acctcom** command to pick out those commands executed during a selected time period. If many people were logged in when the incident occurred, the commands that users executed may help you decide who the culprit is.

Using the **/etc/wtmp** file for security reasons works only if you keep old **wtmp** records around. The process accounting script, **/usr/lib/acct/runacct**, moves the current **/etc/wtmp** file to **/usr/adm/acct/nite/owtmp** when it is run. So you have log-in records for the current day and the day before if you are using the accounting script. Or you may have set up other methods for truncating the **wtmp** file, as we suggested in the Chapter 7.

What we do is keep the **/etc/wtmp** records around for a long time (six months) on any system that has modems or that we consider a security hazard. An entry in the cron table file for **root** saves each day's **wtmp** file at midnight using a script that appends the date to the end of the file (Figure 9.44). The script uses a new directory, **/usr/adm/acct/wtmp**, which you must create. Set the permissions for this directory to read, write, and execute for the owner only, and make the owner the **root** account. If you use **runacct**, you can move the **owtmp** file to this directory by adding a command at the end of the **runacct** script.

Figure 9.44 Archiving the day's **/etc/wtmp** file as **/usr/adm/acct/wtmp/wtmpMMDD**.

a. Using **cron** (when **runacct** isn't used):

```
:
# savewtmp - save the day's wtmp file as wtmpMMDD; should be
# run by cron, with the entry (for the root account)
# 01 0 * * * /etc/savewtmp
# or, from /etc/rc in systems that are rebooted daily.
cp /etc/wtmp /usr/adm/acct/wtmp/wtmp`date '+%m%d'`
cp /dev/null /etc/wtmp
# □
```

b. Command line to add to the end of **/usr/lib/acct/runacct**:

```
mv /usr/adm/acct/nite/owtmp /usr/adm/acct/wtmp/wtmp`date '+%m%d'`
```

The process accounting records (**/usr/adm/pacct***) are much larger than the **/etc/wtmp** file. The previous day's records are kept in **/usr/adm/acct/nite/opacct**. If you want to keep records going back further than the previous day, you should keep the old **pacct** files off-line, on backups.

Dealing with the Law

What do you do when you uncover evidence of system breaking? As with any other misdeed, the response must be relative to the damage done. For mischief by legitimate users, a stern talking to, or perhaps an official reprimand, may be in order. For serious damage or financial loss, you may find yourself dealing with the law. And the law wants *paper*.

When you talk to the police about a possible computer crime, they will want to see documentation. The documentation that you bring are printouts of the files, reports, or directory listings that provided you with the evidence of the crime. Even though you might be the only one around who can interpret your listings, you must have them. If the case goes to court, other experts may be called in to interpret your evidence. Also, before a judge (or the police) will enlist the assistance of the phone company to trace calls to your modem, they will want to see evidence. The evidence can be the reports shown in Figure 9.43, showing when the system breaker logged in, or attempted to log in. Backup the source files, such as **/etc/wtmp** and the **pacct** files, so that other experts can examine these records in detail, in case you left something out.

SUMMARY OF SECURITY

Well, believe it or not, we didn't want to scare anybody. With all the publicity that computer security has had, we felt that you might be concerned. We certainly were. We practice the advice we give here on our own systems and on the other systems where we work as system administrators. Besides feeling a bit more secure, we also have better administered systems, because we cleaned up the permissions.

And nothing really terrible has happened. Perhaps our security has been tight enough to keep out the teenage computer wizards. More likely, we just don't work with attractive-enough targets. However, we did have a couple of scares.

One time, someone changed the password for the **root** account on a system with a modem. First, we had to break the system ourselves in order to restore the **root**'s password. (Remember that this is easy when you have a standalone file system and access to the computer.) Then we carefully searched the **wtmp** reports for log-ins using the modem, but found nothing unusual. The other system administrators were either out of town or had not changed the password. Finally, we ran the **sulogck** script (which hadn't been installed on this system) and got a surprise. Almost every single user at this site, some 22 people, had the superuser password! We had the system administrator change **root**'s password and asked her not to pass it out to anyone except the other administrator.

Another scare came when a user who had previously been a system administrator for this site offered to sell the company a security package. As a promotion for the security package, he submitted a report with suspicious SUID files highlighted. One of the suspicious SUID files was a **root**-account-owned C shell, executable by all, hidden in a discrete location in the file system. By examining the inode change time and the **wtmp** file, we discovered that the only user logged in when the file was created was the user trying to sell the security package! (He didn't make the sale.) The file dated to a time when he had the superuser password and left a "back door" for himself.

Somehow, we expect that most of your security surprises will be more like the ones we describe here than the ones you read about in the newspapers. At any rate, good luck. Security is a game of sorts and can be pleasurable if you enjoy deductive reasoning. You may even wish to enlist the assistance of your trusted associates by having them try to break your security. They get rewarded for the cleverness they show in finding ways to break into your system, and you get a more secure system when you plug up the hole that they found.

QUICK REFERENCE GUIDE

Make certain that all accounts have passwords; use this command to find password-less accounts:

```
# grep '^[^:]*::' /etc/passwd
```

Change the superuser password at least monthly. Have all users change their passwords twice yearly.

Check for bogus superuser accounts; only the **root** and possibly system administration menu shells should appear in the output:

```
# grep '^[^:]*:[^:]*:00*:' /etc/passwd
```

Search for system directories writable by others; it is okay for temporary directories and directories owned by nonadministrators to appear in this list:

```
# find / -type d -perm -2 -print
```

Check for new set-user-id files, using the list of trusted set-user-id files for comparison:

```
# find / -perm -4000 -print | diff - /etc/perms/SUIDfiles
```

Use **ncheck** to search for device files of set-user-id files before mounting a file system from another system:

```
# ncheck -s /dev/dsk/flp00
```

Run the **who** command often, and **write** to users logged in at inappropriate times.

Use the **ps −ef** command to watch what your users are doing.

Use file and directory access permissions correctly.

Permission	Meaning for File	Meaning for Directory
Read	File's contents can be read	Directory entries may be listed
Write	File's contents can be modified	Directory entries can be changed or removed
Execute	File may be executed	Files or subdirectories can be accessed

Remember to deny write access to system directories, and that removing execute permission on directories will deny access to the contents of that directory and prevent writing in that directory.

10

System Problems

INTRODUCTION

It may seem to you that almost anything in this book—backing up, running **fsck**, configuring UUCP—could generate UNIX system problems. While mishandling these tasks can indeed yield distress, sometimes other problems arise out of the blue—terminals lock up, processes take over terminals (and won't die), or odd messages, such as "no proc on q," appear on the console. This chapter goes beyond the topics already discussed to address a melange of troubles that may come your way. We look first at common sources of user miscontent—terminal mishaps and runaway programs. Then we will explain how to interpret error messages, from any source, and isolate those that come from the kernel.

Interpreting kernel error messages is somewhat sticky. While some messages broadcast an unequivocal meaning, others bewilder even the experienced UNIX user. Since many kernel error messages depend on the system's hardware, they cannot be treated in a general way. We will do our best to provide you with guidelines in understanding your system's error messages.

Finally, we talk about alternate root file systems. In many ways, this concept is appropriate for ending this book, because it ties together much of what has been said earlier. It also touches upon material that is usually reserved for those of "guru" status, those with intimate knowledge of UNIX source code. Using an alternate root file system can save you much time and trouble. Many tasks that would otherwise be impossible, or involve reinstalling the root file system, can be performed using an alternate root file system.

TERMINAL PROBLEMS

> **interface** (noun): the surface or plane that connects two different spaces (adapted from *Webster's New World Dictionary.* College Edition. Cleveland, Ohio: The World Publishing Co., 1964.)

Terminals present the interface between computers running the UNIX system and users. Therefore, reasonably enough, most users' problems will manifest themselves on their terminal screens. Often, the terminal's display appears incorrect while using a screen-oriented program, such as an editor or data entry program. You may also encounter user complaints that the terminal is not responding at all to keyboard input.

Trouble with Terminal Displays

The **terminfo** or **termcap** terminal capability databases contain terminal control information used by screen-oriented programs such as **vi**. The problems related to **terminfo** or **termcap** can be outrageously apparent, such as the entire display squeezed into a single line, or less obvious, for example, the cursor not following commands to move about the display.

AT&T and BSD versions of UNIX systems differ in where they keep terminal control information. BSD versions (and pre-System V AT&T and XENIX versions) use the **/etc/termcap** file as the database for terminal capabilities. Each entry in this database consists of several lines that define the terminal type and the control character sequences that manipulate the display. The **/etc/termcap** file is an ASCII file that can be read and edited.

System V and later releases use files in the **/usr/lib/terminfo/*** directories for terminal control. Because the **terminfo** files are not readable ASCII text, they can't be changed. Instead, the precursor source files, which can be changed, are edited, and the **tic** tool (terminfo compiler) used to compile the resulting **terminfo** description. **tic** also moves the compiled descriptions to the appropriate directories.

Getting the Terminal Type into the Environment. The versions of the UNIX system also differ in the way that a process associates with a terminal type. The BSD versions use the **/etc/ttytype** file to map a terminal device to a terminal type. The **tset** command (for terminal **set**) reads the **/etc/ttytype** file at log-in time to get the type of terminal and extract an entry from **/etc/termcap**. The information from the **tset** command can be added to the environment using commands in the Bourne shell (**.profile**) or C shell (**.login**) startup files located in the user's home directory.

Figure 10.1 Using **tset** to export terminal capabilities from **/etc/termcap**.

a. Sample entries in the Bourne shell's **.profile**:

```
export TERM TERMCAP
eval `tset -s -e -k -d\?wy50`
```

b. Equivalent lines in C shell's **.login** script:

```
set noglob
set term = (`tset -e -k -S -d?wy50`)
setenv TERM "$term[1]"
setenv TERMCAP "$term[2]"
unset term noglob
```

Figure 10.1a depicts using the **tset** command to get the terminal type and capabilities into the environment of a Bourne shell. The **tset** command gets the terminal type from the **/etc/ttytype** file. The **−d?wy50** argument instructs **tset** to ask for the terminal type if the line is a dial-up, while offering **wy50** as a default type.

The **−S** option used in Figure 10.1b tells the **tset** command to output two strings to the C shell containing the terminal type and capabilities. These strings are assigned to the variables **TERM** and **TERMCAP**, which become part of the environment and are automatically exported to child processes.

System V and newer releases of the AT&T UNIX system use a slightly different mechanism. These releases separate the **/etc/termcap** file into entries for each terminal, translated into a slightly different coding scheme, compiled using **tic**, and stored in the appropriate **/usr/lib/terminfo/*** directory. Each directory begins with the first letter of a terminal type name, so that **terminfo** files beginning with the same letter make up the subdirectory. For example, the **terminfo** file for the Microterm Act IV terminal, named **act4**, inhabits the **/usr/lib/terminfo/a** directory, and the file has the full pathname **/usr/lib/terminfo/a/act4**.

The standard System V distribution doesn't include a **tset** command. Essentially, the **tset** command copies the **termcap** entry into the user's environment, so that time-consuming searches of the **/etc/termcap** file can be avoided each time an editor is started up. System V avoids the search by separating each terminal capability entry into a separate file. In addition, breaking the files into subdirectories according to the first character in the terminal name speeds the search for the capabilities file.

System V also lacks the **/etc/ttytype** file used by BSD. Each user's **.profile** must explicitly set the variable named **TERM**. Not setting the **TERM** variable results in the **vi** program using "open" mode and refusing to use a full screen-oriented display. Other software will complain, perhaps more clearly, that the terminal type is unknown (or **dumb**, often the default type). Figure 10.2 depicts setting the **TERM** variable for both C and Bourne shells.

Figure 10.2 Setting the **TERM** variable for System V versions.

a. Bourne shell (in **$HOME/.profile**):

```
TERM=act4
export TERM
```

b. C shell (in **$HOME/.login**):

```
setenv TERM act4
```

Setting **TERM** in a user's shell startup file works only when a user always logs in on the same type of terminal. A system administrator can add her own version of **/etc/ttytype** by writing a script that extracts the terminal type from this file. Figure 10.3 shows an example script.

Figure 10.3 Extracting the terminal type from the **/etc/ttytype** file.

a. The **newtset** script:

```
$ cat /usr/lbin/newtset
:
# newtset - get terminal type from /etc/ttytype
TTY=`tty | sed 's./dev/..'`
set - `grep $TTY /etc/ttytype`
echo $1
$ □
```

b. Using **newtset** with the Bourne shell (in **.profile**):

```
TERM=`newtset`
export TERM
```

c. And with the C shell (in **.login**):

```
setenv TERM `newtset`
```

The **newtset** script executes more slowly than its antecedent **tset** and doesn't copy the terminal capabilities into the **TERMCAP** variable. It does, however, get the terminal type into the environment independent of the port on which a user logs in. An enhancement one might add to **newtset** would be a method that queries the user for the actual terminal type instead of a default (**dialup** or **dumb**).

The **/etc/ttytype** file must be readable by all, and writable only by the system administrator (**root**). Each line in this file consists of the terminal type and the filename in the **/dev** directory to which the terminal is hardwired (Figure 10.4).

Figure 10.4 The **/etc/ttytype** file.

a. Format for **/etc/ttytype** file; a space separates the *type* and the filename for the port. Notice that the **/dev** prefix is not included.

> *type* **console**
> *type* **tty***NN*

b. Example **/etc/ttytype** file:

```
$ cat /etc/ttytype
ansi console
wy50 tty0
h19 tty1
dialup tty2
$ □
```

For dial-ups or multiplexers (hardware allowing many terminals to share the same port), some other way of assigning terminal types must be developed. Instead of **newtset**, the administrator could write a script that presents the user with a list of choices and a "case statement" that converts the choice into the correct terminal type string.

The terminal type can also be set in the **/etc/profile** file for Bourne shell users, since this shell script will execute during log-in before the **.profile** in the user's home directory.

Discovering the Terminal Name. To work with the terminal, you have to know the terminal name to access the appropriate **/etc/termcap** or **terminfo** entry. For example, assigning the name "Televideo" to the variable **TERM** won't work to select the appropriate terminal capability entry. The UNIX system won't complain, but the **vi** editor will start up with a message "[Using open mode]" and not use the full screen (visual mode). Without a valid terminal type (name) specified, some programs will refuse to run. Here we are presented with the classic problem of a child told to look up his misspelled words in the dictionary. If you don't know what the word (terminal name) is, how do you look for it?

If you are working with **/etc/termcap**, it's easy—use the **grep** command. Figure 10.5a shows the search for Televideo terminals. The second name abbreviation on the line for the correct terminal should be added into the **/etc/ttytype** file for the terminal port. For instance, the line beginning with "v5" tells us to use **tvi950** for the Televideo 950 (with no screen memory). Abbreviations for terminals always start at the left margin (terminal capability definitions begin with a tab) and are separated from one another by a vertical bar (pipe symbol).

Figure 10.5 Looking for terminal capability descriptions.

a. Getting a terminal abbreviation from the **/etc/termcap** file. Use all lowercase letters in the search. The abbreviation to use with **TERM** for a Televideo 925 is tvi925.

```
$ grep televideo /etc/termcap
v0¦912b¦912c¦920b¦920c¦tvi¦new televideo 912/920:\
v1¦tvi912¦912¦920¦tvi920¦old televideo:if=/usr/lib/tabset/stdcrt:\
v2¦tvi9122p¦tvi9202p¦9122p¦9202p¦tvi2p¦televideo w/2 pages:\
v3¦tvi9502p¦9502p¦televideo950 w/2 pages:\
v4¦tvi9504p¦9504p¦televideo950 w/4 pages:\
v5¦tvi950¦950¦televideo950:if=/usr/lib/tabset/stdcrt:\
v6¦tvi950rv2p¦950rv2p¦televideo950 rev video w/2 pages:\
v7¦tvi925¦925¦televideo 925:\
$ □
```

b. Probing for an entry for a VT200 **terminfo** file:

```
$ ls /usr/lib/terminfo/v
. . .
/usr/lib/terminfo/v/vt100
/usr/lib/terminfo/v/vt200
. . .
$ □
```

Discovering the correct abbreviation to use with systems utilizing **terminfo** databases is a little different. The **terminfo** files aren't readable ASCII files, and are scattered across a directory hierarchy. Full names don't appear as names of **terminfo** files; **terminfo** uses abbreviations, all upper- and lowercase letters or digits.

Suppose that you want to see if there's an entry for a VT200 terminal. The **terminfo** file should be in the **v** subdirectory since the first letter of the terminal abbreviation is **v**. You can use the **ls** command to probe for this file (see Figure 10.5b).

The abbreviation likely to be used for a VT200, **vt200**, is obvious. Less obvious are terminal names that don't include numbers or abbreviations. One solution is to look for the **/etc/termcap** file. Even though System V.2 uses **terminfo**, there is often a **/etc/termcap** file supplied. You can search through the **/etc/termcap** file using the approach outlined in Figure 10.5a in hope that your terminal name will be listed there, along with the abbreviation also to name the **terminfo** entry.

Other Problems with Screen Appearance. You might still have a problem even after you have set the **TERM** variable correctly and exported it. Some capability descriptions are incorrect. Although there is a ANSI standard for terminal control, terminal manufacturers are either unaware of it or for the most part choose to ignore it. The wide assortment of terminals doesn't make the job of building the correct capabilities files any easier, either.

You have problems with the capabilities description when the cursor can't be directed to the correct position on the screen, the screen is drawn incorrectly, inserting characters doesn't work, lines overwrite one another, or you aren't getting the reverse video you know the terminal can generate. We're referring you to the bibliography for other resources that deal with creating and correcting **termcap** and **terminfo** descriptions. (Otherwise, we'd never finish this book.)

There are programs that can convert between **termcap** and **terminfo** description source files. The AT&T Software Toolchest offers them, and we found one named **captoinfo** available on the Usenet that worked well.

Terminal or Keyboard Not Responding

Once a system has been configured correctly, problems with terminal capabilities will largely go away. Instead, your users may come to you with descriptions of terminals that are "no longer working" or even "the computer's broken." These problems are always solvable, although the solutions range from easily entering a control character to the hassle of killing a group of processes.

The simplest problem that a naive user can create involves the output start and stop keys, control-Q and control-S. Pressing control-S will suspend output to the terminal, and pressing control-Q will restart output. Entering a control-Q at an unresponsive keyboard is a good place to start.

Some windowing systems have a mechanism that works like **pg** (or Berkeley's **more**). Once the window fills up with output, the sending process is blocked until the user allows the window to scroll. On SUN workstations, this is called "page mode," and if you forget that it's on in a particular window, it will prevent you from working in that window. When using a windowing system check to see if such a special mode has been enabled when you can't get output in a window.

Since most terminals obey control sequences, some terminals will recognize a *keyboard lock* sequence, which compels the terminal to ignore keyboard input. Often, the keyboard lock sequence occurs when a user uses **cat** in an attempt to display a non-ASCII file (an executable one, or some binary data). The clue will usually be a display of gibberish, often clustered at the top of the screen.

Terminals may enter other unusual modes that are triggered by a command sequence. For instance, the Teletype 513 enters a graphic character mode that causes all letters to be displayed as graphics characters. Having all alphabetic output appear on your screen as hieroglyphics is amusing only momentarily. As another example, an IBM PC/XT running System V.2 on a co-processor board emulates an ANSI terminal and sometimes crashes while working with **vi** through **cu** on a remote system. In this case, the **termcap** entry on the remote system was faulty, although the **terminfo** entry on the local system worked correctly. Thus, an unexpected failure occurred when working on the remote system.

Sending the terminal unlock keyboard sequence will undo the keyboard lock command. Although it would be handy if you could pick this sequence out of a terminal capabilities file, it's not there. Instead, you have two choices—look up the sequence in a manual and send it to the terminal from another terminal, or reset the terminal. The same is true for the sequence that enters graphics mode—use the sequence that exits graphics mode.

Terminal documentation generally includes a section detailing the control sequences. You can glean this information from the manual, and use the **echo** command to redirect the appropriate sequence to the locked-up terminal (Figure 10.6). If you like to plan ahead, you can research all the terminals connected to your system, and add their unlock sequences to a script, keyed by the device name. Then, unlocking a terminal means running this shell script with the port name as an argument. (You will have to be **root**, unless this user allows writing to the terminal.)

Figure 10.6 Unlocking a Wyse 50 terminal connected to port **/dev/tty02**; the control sequence is escape followed by double quote; the ASCII escape character is depicted as **<esc>** in the example and stands for the escape key. This sequence also works for Link 125, Televideo 925 and 910, and ADM3A terminals.

```
# echo '<esc>"' > /dev/tty02 &
# □
```

Resetting the terminal is what most people actually do. Some terminals have a key labeled "SETUP" or something similar that puts the terminal into a mode where the configuration can be changed. You may be able to unlock the keyboard while in this mode, or reset the terminal.

The other way of resetting a terminal is to turn it off, then on again. The terminal initializes itself when powered on, unlocking the keyboard and putting itself in a default state. Some UNIX systems are configured so that powering off a terminal sends a hangup signal to the shell. So the user not only resets his terminal, but also logs off. If resetting the terminal doesn't work, don't forget to check the cable that connects the keyboard to the terminal, it may be loose.

On systems where turning off the terminal doesn't log you off, your terminal may still be in a strange state after being reset. A program may have changed the line disciplines of the kernel terminal driver with the equivalent of **stty** commands. (Line disciplines are such conditions as character echoing and your line kill character, as set by the **stty** command.) You can, of course, log off at this point and let **getty** reestablish the correct line settings, but you might lose the work that you have accomplished. Or you can use the **stty** command to reset the line disciplines.

Terminal Settings. The **/etc/getty** program sets up terminal devices, such as **/dev/tty01**, so that users can work with the shell. Programs such as **vi** change line (device) conditions so that special things can be done, such as getting each character as it is typed without waiting for a carriage return. These programs may also turn off echoing, so that the characters entered to move the cursor don't appear on the screen.

A terminal device can be left in a strange state when a program, such as **vi** exits abnormally. Properly written programs catch signals, such as a hangup or interrupt, and reset the terminal conditions when they exit. However, if you signal a program with the "sure kill" (signal number **9** or SIGKILL), or the program · isn't written correctly, no cleaning up is done on exit.

The **stty** command both reports on and sets terminal conditions from the shell. Figure 10.7a shows all terminal settings when the terminal conditions are appropriately set for using a shell. Other combinations of conditions may be in force for your system; try **stty** **−a** to see what your terminal settings are (use **stty everything** on BSD systems).

Figure 10.7 Using the **stty** command.

a. Displaying all settable parameters with **stty** **−a**:

```
$ stty -a
speed 9600 baud; line = 0; intr = DEL; quit = ^\; erase = ^h;
kill = ^x; eof = ^d; eol = ^`
parenb -parodd cs7 -cstopb -hupcl cread -clocal
-ignbrk brkint ignpar -parmrk -inpck istrip -inlcr -igncr icrnl
-iuclc ixon -ixany -ixoff
isig icanon -xcase echo echoe echok -echonl -noflsh
opost -olcuc onlcr -ocrnl -onocr -onlret -ofill -ofdel tab3
$ □
```

b. Entering **stty echo** restores character echo:

```
$ $ $ $ stty echo $
$ □
```

c. The **sane** flag to the **stty** command resets line conditions:

```
$ stty sane
$ □
```

Commonly, a program or shell script may neglect to restore character echo. No echo manifests as a line of prompts without line feeds when you enter

RETURN several times. Commands don't appear (get echoed) when they are entered, although the output of the commands is visible. Entering **stty echo** restores character echoing (Figure 10.7b).

The **sane** flag used with **stty** will put the terminal conditions in a "sane" state. Using the **sane** flag will also restore character echo (Figure 10.7c). The section on **/etc/gettydefs** in Chapter 5 explores more fully exactly what is done by the **sane** flag. The STTY(1) and TERMIO(7) manual entries explain the others flags that are shown in Figure 10.7a.

C programs can use a system call (**fcntl()**) to make further changes in terminal conditions. In some cases, the terminal conditions may be such that it is impossible to enter any commands. For example, the **NO DELAY** flag may be set, so the shell returns immediately with the end-of-file character from an attempt to read a command. In the Bourne shell this flag will log you out. In the C shell it will generate a stream of prompts and the message "Use 'exit' to log out." If the terminal won't accept any commands, you must kill the log-in shell process. More on this soon.

Interrupt and Quit Keys. Terminal line disciplines, such as **stty echo** can do more than echo characters. From her keyboard, a user can send two signals to all processes connected to the controlling terminal. The interrupt signal (SIGINT) and the quit signal (SIGQUIT) can often terminate a runaway process. On many systems, pressing the DELETE key sends the interrupt signal and forces the process running in the foreground to exit.

Figure 10.7a lists all parameters configurable by the **stty** command. The flag **intr** precedes the key pressed to send an interrupt signal, here the DELETE key. Similarly, the **quit** flag specifies a Control-\, shown as ^\. Control-C is often used as the interrupt character by programmers familiar with CP/M or DOS.

The interrupt signal forces a process to terminate immediately (unless this signal is caught or ignored). The quit signal also causes a process to terminate immediately (unless caught or ignored), and also directs the kernel to write the process image as a file named **core** in the current directory. Programmers can use **core** files to determine what went wrong with the program that was terminated.

Some programs catch or ignore the interrupt and quit signals. The Bourne, Korn, and C shell programs all ignore these signals. Otherwise, using these signals to halt a runaway process would also kill the shell. Any program, even Bourne or Korn shell scripts (using the **trap** command) can arrange to catch or ignore these signals. So even if you know the interrupt and quit keys for your terminal, you can't always terminate a process.

The interrupt or quit signals cannot kill background processes. These processes have been disassociated from the controlling terminal, so aren't affected by the signals generated by these keys. To terminate background processes, you must use the **kill** command.

RUNAWAY PROGRAMS

Sometimes a process starts that can't be halted from the terminal that started it. Perhaps the terminal conditions have been set to a strange state (see the preceding section). Or the process has arranged to trap signals, such as the interrupt signal, that would normally halt a program. And the process goes into an infinite loop which prevents it from ever ending.

Bad program logic can cause infinite loops, which usually surface during testing of the program—but not always. Unless the program is a very simple one, it is almost impossible to test every combination of responses and conditions with which a program can be presented.

Sometimes a user can naively make a mistake that results in an infinite loop. The command in Figure 10.8, presented to the C shell, starts an infinite loop. The Bourne shell ignores arguments after processing redirection, so we can't use the Bourne shell for this example.

Figure 10.8
A command that can't be halted from the controlling terminal. *Don't try this example.*

```
% pr -d file1 > file2   lp file2
pr: can't open lp
□
```

The −**d** option causes the **pr** command to double space its output. The user wished to execute two commands on the same command line, **pr** and **lp**, but left out the semicolon between commands. So the C shell passed three arguments to the **pr** command—**file1**, **lp**, and **file2**. Since **file2** is the standard output of the **pr** command, and also the last file input in the command, the command never completes. **file2** grows until there is no more space left in the file system, or the **ulimit** (file size limit) is reached. The command cannot be interrupted when it stops because there is no more room on the file system. Erasing **file2** has no effect either, because the **pr** command prevents the file from being unlinked until it completes. The only way to solve this problem is to kill the offending process, **pr** in this example.

Killing a Runaway Process

Any user can kill a process. The only requirement is that she owns the process that she wants to kill. Only the superuser can kill any process (with several exceptions that we'll mention later).

To kill a process that has control of her terminal, the user must log in on another terminal. (You can kill a background process from your log-in terminal because it won't have control of your terminal.) The user can also use the **su** command and briefly "switch user" to himself by working on the terminal of someone else who is already logged in. For example, entering **su rik** and the correct password would allow **rik** to start a shell with his access privileges on another user's terminal. (After killing the offending process, you would exit the shell and the other user's shell reappears.)

Once the user has a shell going, she must discover the PID (process identification number or process id) of the process locking up the terminal. The PID is a number used in the kernel to identify processes. The **ps** command displays the list of processes currently in the kernel's process table. Without any options, **ps** displays processes that were started from the terminal where the **ps** command is entered (Figure 10.9). Table 10.1 summarizes the information in the columns that appears for each process.

Figure 10.9 A **ps** command executed on **/dev/console**.

```
$ ps
    PID TTY TIME COMMAND
     24 co  0:00 errdemon
     35 co  0:15 cron
    525 co  0:04 csh
    526 co  0:02 ps
$ □
```

TABLE 10.1 INFORMATION DISPLAYED BY **ps** WITHOUT OPTIONS

Heading	Description
PID	The process identification number
TTY	An abbreviation for the controlling terminal
TIME	The amount of CPU time spent on this process
COMMAND	The name of the file that became this process

The **ps** command in Figure 10.9 displays all the commands started from the console. The console is abbreviated in the display to **co** (in column headed **TTY**). If the command were entered from **/dev/tty12** instead, the abbreviation would be the digits **12**. In some systems that don't use abbreviations for the **TTY**, the basename, **tty12**, appears in this column.

Seeing the processes associated with the console doesn't help you kill a process connected to another terminal. Of course, you can't view the processes from the terminal that's locked up since you can't enter the **ps** command. You can either specify the other terminal device name with the −t option to **ps**, or specify the user name with the −u option, and get all the processes associated with either the terminal or the user. (To discover a user's terminal's name, you can use the **who** command.)

Figure 10.10 Getting processes associated with another terminal listed.

a. Using **who** to discover the name of the other terminal **peggy** is logged into:

```
$ who
peggy          tty01          Mar 14 09:12
peggy          console        Mar 14 12:57
$ □
```

b. Using **ps** to list the processes connected to **/dev/tty01**:

```
$ ps -t tty01
   PID TTY TIME COMMAND
   124 01  0:11 csh
   518 01  0:56 pr
$ □
```

c. Or, use the **−u** option to display all the processes owned by the user **peggy**:

```
$ ps -u peggy
   PID TTY TIME COMMAND
   124 01  0:11 csh
   518 01  0:56 pr
   525 co  0:04 csh
   526 co  0:02 ps
$ □
```

d. Killing the errant **pr** process from the console:

```
$ kill 518
$ □
```

You can see in Figure 10.10b or 10.10c that there are two processes connected to **/dev/tty01**, abbreviated by **ps** in the **TTY** column as **01**. The process **pr** (from the example in Figure 10.8) has taken control of **/dev/tty01** and attempting to interrupt it from the terminal hasn't succeeded. We now know the process id, **518**, and can send it a signal from a different terminal. In Figure 10.10d, we send process **518** the default signal, termination. If the terminate signal fails, you can always use **kill −9**, the sure kill.

The ps Command

The **ps** (process status) command reads the process table in the kernel. The kernel's process table keeps track of all processes, including those that are sleeping, waiting, swapped, or running. Even a dead process, a *zombie*, may show up in the process table.

The kernel's process table contains all the information that the kernel must know about processes at any moment. The kernel uses this information to keep track of where each process is, what it is waiting for, who owns the process, what process group this process belongs to, and how much CPU time the process has used recently. The kernel uses the recent CPU usage and the priority to determine which process to schedule next. (Programmers can look at the include file **/usr/include/sys/proc.h** to interpret each entry of the process table.)

The **ps** command must look beyond the process table for two names that appear in its output. The name of the command or program that appears in **ps** listings is not contained in the process table. The kernel doesn't use the program name internally, except when it is looking up the inode to load the program. The name of the command is stored in the **u_area**, or user area, for each process. The user area is part of the memory assigned to a process for storing its data. Although the user area is part of the process, only the kernel can read or write to the user area, and it is here that the name of the command is kept. (*An exception:* A subset of the information in the user area can be modified under a user's control when a process is being traced during debugging.)

The device number for the terminal also resides in the user area. So the **ps** command must access the user area for every process in the process table to determine which processes to display. Remember that the **ps** command may use the controlling terminal from which the command was issued to select processes to list. Accessing all user areas can happen quickly if all processes are in memory. However, if a process is swapped out, the user area must be read from disk.

Terminals are identified by a device number, not a name, in the user area. The **ps** command must also search the **/dev** directory to discover the filename associated with the device number in the user area (the major-minor device number) for each process entry displayed. The search for the user area (in swap space) and examination of the device directory are two reasons that the **ps** command is often aggravatingly slow in performing its task. Also, it's not uncommon for things to change before the **ps** command completes. Short-lived processes can be started and complete before **ps** prints its display.

The **ps_data** file is used on some systems to store some of the more static information, such as the correspondence between device name and device number, user name and user-id number. Then an up-to-date **ps_data** file can help speed up **ps** command operation. If necessary, the **ps_data** file is updated when a superuser runs **ps**.

ps Options. The options to **ps** are split into two categories—those that select which entries to list and those that add more columns to the display. As already seen, the **ps** command without options displays the process id, the terminal, the time running, and the name of the program for all processes associated with the controlling terminal. The —t option lists the processes connected to other terminals, and the —u option lists those processes owned by a specified user.

The —e option displays every process in the process table. Think of **e** for everything and it's easy to remember. Using the —e option is the opposite of using the selection options —**u** or —**t**, because every process is listed, rather than a selection of processes.

The —**e** option gives you a look at all the processes that exist. The drawback to using —**e** is that the listing can be several screenfuls long, and you can easily miss what you are looking for. You may wish to pipe the output of **ps** —**e** through the **pg** command to paginate it. On the other hand, if you are using a small system or a workstation, where you are the only user, the —**e** option is all you need to remember. Note that BSD versions of **ps** use some different option letters. The BSD —**a** option corresponds to —**e** in System V and XENIX. The —**u** and —**t** options work similarly in all three versions of the UNIX system.

The **ps** command offers two expanded listing formats, which can be combined into an even wider format. An example of the —**f** (for "friendly," or officially, full) format is shown in Figure 10.11. Table 10.2 summarizes the additional information obtained by using the —**f** option.

We call the —**f** option friendly because it displays the process owner as the log-in name, and it attempts to display the calling arguments to the command. The —**f** option surrounds the command name in square brackets when **ps** can't find the calling arguments. The minus sign in front of a shell indicates that it is a log-in shell. Also, processes that aren't connected to a controlling terminal, such as **init**, show a question mark in the **TTY** column.

Figure 10.11 Using the options —**ef** to display everything in a friendly way:

```
$ ps -ef
    UID   PID  PPID  C    STIME TTY   TIME COMMAND
   root     0     0 21 18:26:06   ?   0:29 swapper
   root     1     0  0 18:26:06   ?   0:06 /etc/init
    rik   124     1  0 10:54:45  co   0:11 -csh
   root    52     1  0 10:34:08   ?   0:01 /etc/getty tty0 mo_1200
   root    24     1  0 10:33:46  co   0:00 /usr/lib/errdemon
   root    35     1  0 10:33:57  co   0:54 /etc/cron
     lp    47     1  0 10:34:04   ?   0:01 /usr/lib/lpsched
   root    53     1  0 10:34:08   1   0:01 /etc/getty tty1 co_9600
    rik   258   124 54 10:55:06  co   2:19 /bin/vi chapter
    rik   518   124 48 13:00:06  co   0:09 [ ps ]
$ □
```

TABLE 10.2 ADDITIONAL INFORMATION DISPLAYED BY **ps**
WITH THE — f OPTION

Heading	Description
UID	The effective user-id translated into a log-in name
PPID	The parent's process id
C	Amount of CPU time recently used
STIME	Starting time for the process, taken from user area

The **UID** column displays the effective owner of the process. The **ps** command uses the **/etc/passwd** file to match the user id number to a log-in name.

The parent process id, **PPID**, refers to the process that started this child process. In Figure 10.11, the **init** process is the parent process for every entry except the **ps** and **vi** commands started from the **csh**, process id **124**.

The **C** column reflects the amount of time that a process has been using the CPU recently. The kernel uses the CPU value to decide which process will be scheduled to run next. The process currently utilizing the CPU gets its value incremented by one every clock tick (generally, one-sixtieth of a second). The kernel divides by 2 the CPU usage for the processes not running once a second. To users, the CPU usage value is only marginally useful, but does indicate which processes have been most active recently. High CPU values indicate recently active processes.

The **STIME** comes from the user area. When the process was forked, the starting time was written in the user area. You can examine this value to see how long a process has existed. Sometimes you can spot an unusual process because its start time is old. Usually, only system processes (for example, **swapper**, **init**, and **cron**) have old start times.

The −l (for long) listing option to **ps** isn't so friendly. Long listings introduce more information about the current state of a process, its priority, size, and address. Most of the additional information provided by long listings is not generally helpful for system administration. Figure 10.12 shows an example long listing and Table 10.3 explains the new columns of information.

Figure 10.12 A long listing of processes connected to the console:

```
$ ps -lt console
    F S   UID   PID  PPID  C PRI NI    ADDR  SZ  WCHAN TTY  TIME COMD
    1 S   112    54     1  0  30 20      8d  68  1be7e  co  0:12 csh
    1 S     0    31     1  0  26 20      90  44  1976c  co  0:00 errdemon
    1 S     0    42     1  0  39 20      a7  40  eef800 co  0:06 cron
    1 S   112    69    54  2  20 20      8e  72  1fb18  co  0:22 vi
    1 R   112   213   211 50  85 20      8f  96         co  0:02 ps
    1 S   112   211    69  9  30 20      c7  56  1c32e  co  0:03 csh
$ □
```

TABLE 10.3 ADDITIONAL INFORMATION DISPLAYED BY **ps**
WITH THE −l OPTION

Heading	Description
F	Flag codes—octal numbers representing bits in status word
S	State—the current process state
PRI	Priority—used in scheduling; high numbers mean lower priority
NI	Nice-ness; the higher the nice, the lower the priority
ADDR	The address in memory or swap area for this process
SZ	The size of this process (in *clicks*, each generally 1K)
WCHAN	Wait channel—an address representing what this process is waiting for

Table 10.4 describes the abbreviations that appear in the state (**S**) column when the **−l** option to **ps** is used.

TABLE 10.4 DESCRIPTION OF STATE ABBREVIATIONS

State Abbrev	Description
S	Sleeping, process is waiting for an event
R	Running; only one process will be running at a time
I	Intermediate; process is on the verge of starting the first time
T	Process is being traced; for example, by **adb**
X	Process is growing larger (requested more memory)
Z	Zombie, process that has completed and parent hasn't waited for it

We aren't going to talk about the flag values. You can examine the **proc.h** include file or PS(1) manual page if you are interested. The states are a little bit more interesting for system administration. At any one moment, most processes will be sleeping. A sleeping process is waiting for an event. This event might be that a disk block has been read into memory, that a user has typed a key, or that some amount of time has elapsed. A process can also sleep waiting for a signal.

At most one process can be running at any time. In *multitasking* systems, only a single process, one task, will be running at a time. The UNIX kernel frequently switches between processes, creating the illusion that many processes are running simultaneously. A running process has the full attention of the CPU until another event occurs that takes over the CPU (an interrupt), or the process must sleep waiting for an event.

The three states Intermediate, Growing (X), and Traced are rarer, and you won't see them as often. The Zombie state is somewhat more common and is associated with processes labeled as "defunct" by **ps**. We discuss defunct processes in detail later.

The only aspect of priority that can be controlled by users is the *nice* value. The term nice comes from being nice by letting other processes go first. Any user can increase the nice value when a process is started. The higher the nice value, the higher the calculated priority for a process. The higher the calculated priority, the less likely a process will be scheduled to run next. In Figure 10.12, all processes have the nice value of 20, the default. A considerate user could start **nroff** (which hogs the CPU) with a higher nice value, say an increment of 10, so that the **nroff** process will tend to run when the system would otherwise be idle.

Only the superuser can decrease the nice value. A nice value lower than 20 results in a process that is more likely to be run than other processes. You may want to run **ps** with a lower nice value if you are in a hurry to discover what's happening. Figure 10.13 shows how to run **ps** with a lower nice value (a decrement of 19 is maximal).

Figure 10.13 Using a lower nice value when running **ps**.

a. Using **nice** from the Bourne and Korn shells:

```
# nice --19 ps -ef
```

b. Using **nice** from the C shell:

```
% nice -19 ps -ef
```

The syntax for using the **nice** command is different for the C shell because **nice** is built into this shell.

A rogue superuser (someone making inappropriate use of root's privileges) could start up processes with low nice values, decreasing the system response time for their own processes, while stealing response time from all other users. The long listing allows you to scan the nice values for all processes and pick out any lower than the default, 20. We once discovered a user's program that was set-user-id to **root**, and that set all other users' nice value higher when the program was run. Not very nice.

The address and size of processes is not normally of interest to system administrators. Size may become an issue if your system's response becomes very slow suddenly. A very large process (one with a size value many times larger than other processes) may be hogging resources. Also if the sum of all the process sizes exceeds available RAM then process swapping will start so performance will degrade.

The wait channel is really an address in memory that represents a resource or an event. You can examine the **WCHAN** values and may notice that the values for **getty**'s are close. These processes are waiting for similar events, a character being received and entering a queue of characters. The values for **init** and **cron** may be identical. Since both processes are waiting for a signal before proceeding; **cron** is waiting for an alarm (clock) to go off, and **init** is waiting for the death of child signal.

Tracing Process Genealogies. Every process has a parent process. Both the long and friendly listings show a column of information giving the parent process id, or **PPID**. You can trace process "genealogy" by finding the process id that corresponds to the parent process id. Tracing processes back to their parents isn't an idle exercise. It provides information about what has happened and solutions to some problems.

Figure 10.14 Examining process genealogy.

```
!!ps -fu rik
    UID    PID   PPID   C   STIME  TTY   TIME  COMMAND
    rik    54      1    0  10:32:35 co  0:12  -csh
    rik    69     54    0  10:34:45 co  2:01  [ vi ]
    rik   1644    69    0                     0:00  <defunct>
    rik   1645    69    9  19:06:21 co  0:03  [ csh ]
    rik   1646   1645  61  19:06:25 co  0:02  [ ps ]
```

The **init** process is the parent of all log-in shells. So if the **PPID** field of a shell program is one, then this shell is a log-in shell. Now, each shell will fork off other processes as commands are started by this shell. These processes will have the **PID** of the shell as their **PPID**. Occasionally, a command will fork off another process and become the parent of the new process. Figure 10.14 shows a friendly **ps** listing of several processes owned by the user **rik**. The listing was created by using a shell escape from within the **vi** editor.

Process 54 is a log-in shell because the **PPID** is one. As mentioned previously, the friendly option to **ps** causes a minus sign to be displayed ahead of the command name of the log-in shell. Process 54 is the parent to process 69, which is running **vi**. The shell escape from within **vi** starts up two processes, 1644 and 1645. Process 1644 exits immediately and becomes a zombie process. We'll talk about zombies later. Process 1645 is a C shell that examines the command given in the shell escape, and forks off the **ps** process, 1646. So process 1645 is the parent of 1646.

Tracing process genealogies helps you pick the right process to kill. For example, if a terminal is still in a strange state after killing a runaway process, you may need to kill the log-in shell that started it.

Log-in shells are also called process group leaders. Although it is possible for a process that is not a log-in shell to become a process group leader, this usually isn't done. If you kill a process group leader, the kernel sends a hangup signal (**kill −1**) to all the descendents of this process. When you log-out, this mechanism terminates any other processes that are connected to your terminal.

Defunct Processes. Defunct processes are given that name by the **ps** command. A process labeled as "<defunct>" has terminated before the parent process terminated, and the parent process is neither waiting for nor ignoring death of child signals. The old name for a defunct process is "zombie" because the process is dead and the only part remaining (alive) is the entry in the process table.

When a process terminates, the kernel copies some information about the completed process into the process table entry for that process. The intent behind this mechanism is to pass this information along to the parent process. The parent process receives this information by waiting (the **wait()** system call and corresponding shell command). The process that executes a **wait** command suspends operations until the signal *death of child* is received. The **wait** ends immediately if there aren't any children alive when **wait** is executed.

Zombie processes occur when a child process completes before the parent process has completed and the parent process is not waiting for a death of child signal. The parent process might still execute a **wait** command to receive the exit code from the child process. So the kernel leaves the entry in the process table until a parent process can handle the death of child signal.

The Bourne, Korn, and C shells all ignore or catch death of child signals, so zombie processes aren't normally observed. However, it is easy to create a zombie process with a simple C shell command line (Figure 10.15). (The Bourne shell treats the ampersand as a line terminator, so this example works only with the C shell.)

Figure 10.15 Creating a zombie process. The **date** command completes before the subshell because the sleep delays the subshell's termination.

```
% ( date & ; sleep 60 ) &
2209
% 2210
Fri Apr  1 21:47:34 PST 1988
% ps -fu rik
     UID    PID   PPID  C   STIME TTY   TIME COMMAND
     rik   2205      1  0 21:46:59 co   0:04 -csh
     rik   2209   2205  0 21:47:32 co   0:01 [ sleep ]
     rik   2210   2209  0                0:01 <defunct>
     rik   2211   2205 73 21:47:49 co   0:02 [ ps ]
%  □
```

The parentheses in Figure 10.15 tell the C shell to create a subprocess, and the ampersand (**&**) at the end of the line puts this subprocess in the background so that we can examine it. 2209 is the process id of this subshell. Then the **date** command is started in the background within the subshell, and PID 2210 is displayed on the terminal. The **sleep** command keeps the subshell alive for 60 seconds.

The **ps −fu rik** displays all the process table entries describing processes owned by **rik** with the friendly listing option. Process 2209, the subshell, is still running, and a child of the shell, PID 2205. Process 2210, the **date** command, is labeled **<defunct>**. It has completed, and its parent process, 2209, is still alive and might **wait** for its exit status. A minute later, the **sleep** has completed, and the shell for process 2209 exits without waiting. The kernel arranges for **init** to inherit the defunct process (the parent of PID 2210 becomes 1, the **init** process). **init** is always waiting for death of child, and the kernel removes the entry for the defunct process.

You need to trace process genealogies whenever you find defunct processes in your **ps** listings. Each defunct process has a living parent process, other than **init**.

The defunct process will remain until its parent either executes a **wait** or exits and lets **init** wait for the defunct process. You can't kill a defunct process—it's already dead. You can, however, kill the parent of a defunct process. Killing the parent, or terminating the process by quitting the program, are the only ways to get rid of defunct processes, short of rebooting. Rebooting your system wipes the process table clean of all entries.

Signaling Processes with kill

The **kill** command signals processes. Unless otherwise directed, a signaled process will terminate. Processes can arrange to catch or ignore signals before receiving any signals. A process must specify which signals it wants to catch and which it wants to ignore. A process may be in a state where it can't be interrupted by receipt of a signal.

There are 19 signals (System V) that can be sent by the **kill** command. You need to know about five of these signals, and of these, only three, software termination (15), hangup (1), and kill (9), will find regular use. The five signals are listed in Table 10.5.

TABLE 10.5 FIVE SIGNALS THAT CAN BE USED TO TERMINATE PROCESSES

Signal number	Description
1	hangup; usually means that controlling terminal has been disconnected
2	interrupt; user can also generate this by pressing the interrupt (often DELETE) key from the controlling terminal
3	quit and leave a **core** file upon exit; can also be sent from controlling terminal
9	the "sure" kill; cannot be caught or ignored
15	terminate; a gentle kill, which gives processes a chance to clean up

Signals 2 and 3 can be generated from the controlling terminal. The controlling terminal is the terminal associated with the log-in shell. All foreground processes started from a log-in shell have the same controlling terminal. Background processes are cut off from the controlling terminal and aren't affected by the keyboard generated interrupt and quit signals. You can send signals 2 and 3 to background processes using the **kill** command, but background processes are set to ignore these signals.

You can send keyboard-generated interrupt and quit signals only to processes started from the controlling terminal. You can also send these signals from another terminal using the **kill** command. A programmer might want to send signal 3, quit, so that a **core** file is left behind for analysis by a debugger.

Signals 1 and 15 are "gentle kills." Euthanasia, as it were. The process may catch these signals and perform cleanup work before terminating. It may clean up by removing temporary files and by writing out any information that must be saved before the process terminates. Signal 1, hangup, gets sent when the modem loses the carrier signal or, in some cases, the terminal is turned off. Signal 15 is the software termination signal and gets sent by default when no signal argument is used with **kill**. You can use the shell's **trap** command to catch these signals and clean up before exiting shell scripts.

Signal 9 is called the "sure kill" because it cannot be caught or ignored. You can't include signal 9 in a **trap** command. It cannot be caught. That is why it is called a sure kill. However, there are some processes that no signal, even 9, can effect. Zombie processes, for example, are already dead and can't be killed again.

The **kill** command expects a process id, and optionally a signal number, as arguments. You can list as many process id's as you wish on the **kill** command line. Actually, there are tricks you can use with **kill** for signaling groups of processes, so you will rarely need to list many processes. The syntax and some examples for using **kill** are shown in Figure 10.16.

Figure 10.16 The **kill** command and some examples.

a. Command line syntax:

kill [*−signal*] *PID* [*PID2 PID3 ...*]

b. Examples using **kill** to send different signals to processes:

```
$ sleep 60
<press DELETE or interrupt key>
$ sleep 60 &
1487
$ kill -2 1487
$ kill -3 1487
$ kill 1487
1487 Terminated
$ sleep 60 &
1489
$ kill -1 1489
1489 Hangup
$ sleep 60 &
1491
$ kill -9 1491
1491 Killed
$ kill 1491
kill: 1491: no such process
$ □
```

The series of **kill** commands in Figure 10.16b exercises the different signals **kill** sends to processes. In the first example, the **sleep** begins in the foreground, but pressing the interrupt key (often DELETE) halts it. The interrupt key sends signal 2 to all processes connected to the controlling terminal. Shells ignore signals 2 and 3 to prevent the shells from being terminated when a user generates these signals through keypresses. Using the interrupt key is the normal method of killing a process from the controlling terminal.

The **sleep** command is invoked again, although this time in the background. Pressing the interrupt key will have no effect on the background **sleep**. Even sending the signals interrupt (2) and quit (3) via the **kill** command has no effect. The **kill** command without a signal number argument sends the software termination signal (15) to the **sleep** process. The **kill** command responds with "1487 Terminated" to indicate that the process has received the signal and terminated. The **sleep** is then restarted, and killed again twice, using signal 1 (hangup) and signal 9, the sure kill. Attempting to kill either a nonexistent process, or a process you do not own, results in an error message from the **kill** command unless you are working as superuser. The superuser can kill other users' processes.

The three most important signal numbers that you should remember are 1 and 15, for sending a signal that can be caught and allow the process to cleanup, and 9, for the sure kill.

Signaling Groups of Processes. The **kill** command (and the system call by the same name) can signal groups of processes. **kill 0** will terminate all processes started from your log-in shell. Your log-in shell, and any processes started by your log-in shell, are members of the same process group. **kill −1 −1** sends a hangup signal (−1) to all the processes that you own. Table 10.6 describes the different classes of process id arguments for the **kill** command.

TABLE 10.6 HOW **kill** INTERPRETS PROCESS ID ARGUMENTS

Argument	Interpretation
PID	Signal is sent to the process identified by the process id, *PID*, when the value is positive
0	Signal is sent to all processes *in the sender's process group* when PID is zero.
−1	Signal is sent to all processes *owned by the sender* when the PID is minus one.
−*PID*	Signal is sent to all processes in the process group identified by *PID*.

The **kill** command sends a signal to all the processes listed by process id. Using a negative number, or zero, changes which processes get sent a signal. Using zero in place of a process id sends a signal to all the processes in the sender's process group. The process group leader is a log-in shell, and all the descendent processes are members of the process group. You can quickly terminate all processes except your log-in shell by executing the command **kill 0**. If you used the hangup signal (1) instead of the default software termination signal (15), you might also get logged out (if the **HUPCL** flag was set by **getty**).

Figure 10.17 Using zero or −1 let's you terminate processes without knowing their process id's.

```
$ sleep 60 &
2096
$ kill 0
2096 Terminated
Terminated
$ kill -1 0

login: □
```

You can kill all processes owned by you, even if you are logged in twice, by using −1 for the process id. **kill -1** sends a software termination signal to all processes that have your user id in the process table entry. For example, if you logged in at a second terminal to kill a process that has control of your first terminal, you can simply enter **kill −1**. You don't want to do this if you are working as root.

The process id argument of −1 has a special meaning when you are working as superuser. The signal is sent to every process, except processes 0 and 1, when root enters the command **kill −1**. This can have the effect of killing all daemon processes and any other process that doesn't catch the software termination signal (as the shell does). You really don't want to do this, as there is a cleaner way to halt daemon processes, the **/etc/shutdown** script.

You can signal a process group by preceding the process id of the group leader with a minus sign. First, you must determine the process id of the process group leader. You can use the **ps** command with the −el or −ef options to list all processes and their parent processes. Log-in shells will always be process group leaders, and will always have process 1, **init**, as their parent process. You send a signal to all children of the process group leader by preceding the process leader's process id with a minus sign. For example, if 3944 is the process id for the log-in shell, the process group leader, that you wish to signal, you'd use the command **kill −3944** to send the software termination signal to every process started by the log-in shell.

Note that it is possible for a process to make a system call and become a process group leader. In this case, although the log-in shell may be the parent of this process, it would no longer be its process group leader. Daemon processes become process group leaders, protecting themselves from termination when their parent process dies.

Processes That Can't Be Killed

Three classes of processes can't be signaled and terminated by using the **kill** command—system processes, zombie processes, and processes sleeping at an uninterruptible priority. System processes have process ids of 0 and 1 and sometimes other low numbers. The **init** process started by the kernel at system bootstrap has the process id of 1. The kernel prevents this **init** process from being terminated by any signal.

Several processes may appear in the **ps** listings with process id of zero. Entries in the process table with PID of zero are kernel processes. These are not processes in the ordinary sense, in that they are not programs that were read in from disk and started. Kernel processes are part of the kernel, just like the **export** and **wait** commands are built into the Bourne shell. The kernel and kernel processes are never swapped.

However, System V Release 2 and earlier **ps** commands identify any process with a PID of zero as **swapper** in the command field. There isn't a **swapper** command (to be loaded from disk). By contrast, the **init** process gets loaded from a file named **/etc/init**.

Kernel processes are included in the process table so that they will be subject to the same scheduling paradigms as other processes. The processes that work as the **swapper** gets scheduled to execute so that it can swap processes between memory and disk when the processes in memory are blocked (waiting for I/O), or the processes that are on disk are ready to run. The **swapper** rearranges processes in memory and disk.

AT&T UNIX systems that support *demand paging* use a second "**swapper**," for a total of two processes with PID zero. The second "**swapper**," another kernel process, handles *page stealing*. UNIX systems that use only swapping copy entire processes—all of the memory associated with the program and its data—between memory and the swap space on disk. Demand paging systems have the ability to copy portions of processes between disk and memory. The page stealer copies pages, often 4096-byte-sized portions of memory, to the swap device when more memory is needed. The **swapper** copies a page back from the swap space when a process tries to use a page that has been swapped.

The second class of unkillable processes are the zombies. Since the zombie processes have already exited, they're already "dead" and can't be terminated. Zombie processes appear in the process table because their parent process still exists and hasn't waited for them or has chosen to ignore death of child signals. You get rid of zombie processes by terminating their parents. Then the zombie processes will be waited for by the **init** process after the parent process terminates.

The third class of processes that can't be killed are processes that are sleeping at an *uninterruptible* priority. A process that makes a **sleep()** system call, like the **sleep** command, sleeps at an *interruptible* priority and can be awakened by a signal.

Thus, you can terminate a **sleep** command that you have started in the background (see Figure 10.16).

Internally the kernel also uses something like the **sleep()** system call. For example, a process will go to sleep when it tries to read from a terminal and no input is available. The process will be awakened after someone enters something at the terminal keyboard. Similarly, the kernel puts a process to sleep while waiting for a data block of a file to be copied from disk into memory. Thus, another process can be scheduled to execute while the sleeping process waits for its I/O operation to complete.

Sometimes, the kernel needs to guarantee that a task can be completed without being interrupted. The kernel can arrange for a process to enter an uninterruptible sleep if catching a signal would have a deleterious effect. For example, a process enters an uninterruptible sleep while waiting for a block from a disk to become available in memory. If the process could be signaled, and the process caught the signal, the process would continue after handling the signal without completing the disk read. Every process that caught signals would have to include a mechanism for restarting interrupted system calls, such as the disk read. BSD versions of the UNIX system allow automatic restarting of interrupted system calls.

A process sleeping at an uninterruptible priority may look like any other process in a **ps** listing. You won't see any special flag or state that marks this process as special. Instead, your first sign of trouble will come when you try terminating this process. Even the "sure kill" signal (-9) will be fruitless. The kernel prevents you from interrupting this process's sleep.

Although you can't kill this type of process, short of rebooting, you can sometimes uncover what resource the unkillable process is waiting for. Once the process gets the resource, a disk block, for instance, its sleep ends and the process can be terminated.

An interesting example of an unkillable process developed on a system where turning off the terminal disabled output to that terminal line. Because this site was having a hardware problem with the console terminal, the system administrator turned it off. Various processes, largely started by the **cron** daemon, would write to the console periodically. Eventually, the buffers for the console reached the "highwater mark," the point at which the kernel stops adding characters to the buffer. Any process that tries to write to the console gets put to sleep at an uninterruptible priority, awaiting the event that there is space in the buffer.

The system administrator discovered that she had a problem when a user got a "No more processes" message from a C shell. She ran **ps** with the friendly option, noticed many old processes and tried killing these processes without any success. I suggested that she turn on her ailing console (and leave it on), allowing the hung processes to finish writing to the console. Turning on the console enabled the port. So no processes needed to be killed—once the resource was made available, the processes could complete and their entries were removed from the process table.

INTERPRETING ERROR MESSAGES

While the UNIX system's reputation for cryptic error messages does have a basis in fact, don't give up. The messages can be interpreted. And like everything else about using the UNIX system, the more experience you have with error messages, the easier they are to comprehend.

Just two sources of error messages exist — programs and the kernel. Unfortunately, of the thousands of programs that execute on UNIX systems, few use the same error messages. There are some patterns that you can learn to recognize, and even a function, **perror()**, that can be used for generating standard messages. Also, many of the errors that you will be dealing with will stem from the same issues over and over again — lack of access permission, nonexistence of files, and specifying command line options and arguments incorrectly.

How do you separate kernel error messages from the error messages sent by programs? All kernel error messages go to the console. You cannot change the port used, for instance, by linking **/dev/console** to a different port. Following a tradition established in the earlier versions of the UNIX system, a simple error printing routine copies information from the kernel directly to the console port, bypassing the device driver, inode, buffering, and access permissions. We are told that this section suggests that programmers "not be chatty" in their messages, because of the use of this low level routine. At times, this dictum seems to have been taken to extremes.

In the sections that follow, we present a guide to interpreting error messages. We discuss program error messages first, and provide some guidelines. Then we explain some of the kernel's error messages in detail and the steps to take to correct the problems.

Program Error Messages

Some program error messages are clear and easy to understand, such as the "No such file or directory" message displayed by **vi** when you start editing a new file. This message clearly comes from **vi** as a result of a failed system call, the attempt to open a file that hasn't been created.

The **vi** message comes from a list of error messages shown in the INTRO(2) manual page in the *System V Programmer Reference Manual* (which contains sections two through six), right at the very beginning of section two. A library function (listed in section three) called **perror()** (for **print error**) will print out the appropriate error message when a system call returns, indicating that an error has occurred. The index into this table of errors is contained in the variable **errno** and is valid only immediately after the system call.

perror() can be called with a string as an argument. It is suggested that the program that invoked the system call include its own name as the string argument to **perror()**. Some commands do this, and some don't. For example, **vi** uses the error message but doesn't identify the name of the calling program (itself). Since you are working within **vi**, you know where the error came from.

But not all programs use the **perror**() routine. **perror**() allows you to display all the error message strings for system errors. For many commands this is over-kill, because only a few errors are likely or possible. Let's look at two common commands and compare how they respond to the same error condition.

Figure 10.18 Two common programs and the error messages displayed for the identical error, "No such file or directory."

```
$ ls dog
dog not found
$ cp dog cat
cp: cannot access dog
$ □
```

The **ls** command neither uses the message from **perror**(), nor precedes the message with a self-identifier. **cp** doesn't use **perror**() either; however, it does identify the source of the error message by preceding the message with "cp: ". This labeling helps especially if the error message emerges from a command that is within a shell script. Without the identifier, you must guess which command failed.

Other error messages derive from the program itself. For example, the **cp** command will display a "usage message" when it is invoked with only one argument as shown in Figure 10.19.

Figure 10.19 A usage message from the **cp** command.

```
$ cp dog
Usage: cp f1 f2
       cp f1 ... fn d1
$ □
```

An invalid response to a prompt might produce a message. Some programs that require the existence of data files will produce messages complaining when these files aren't present: for example, when **troff** can't find a font file that it needs. The C compiler, **cc**, contains a host of messages which are displayed depending on the phase of the C compiler and the type of error discovered.

The most common of error messages obtained will come from lack of appropriate access permissions on files or directories. In Chapter 9 we discuss how the permission mode bits work and how directories can regulate search permission. You would be wise to master permissions thoroughly, because you will often have to deal with users who are frustrated by error messages involving permissions. To learn more, create a directory and some files and experiment by changing the permissions on these files with **chmod**. Try displaying them with **cat**, overwriting them with shell redirection (>), and executing them. Change permissions on the parent directory, and see what happens when you try to change directory (**cd**) or when you try to access these files using such metacharacters as * or ?.

Kernel Error Messages

Kernel error messages will always appear on the console. Even if the **/dev/syscon** has been linked to another terminal, the messages still are sent to the console. The kernel uses the console because it is the only device for which the kernel is guaranteed access. A primitive device driver built into the kernel sends the messages to the console.

When the UNIX system was first developed, and for several years afterward, the only terminal commonly available was Teletype model 33, a large, slow, and very noisy hard-copy terminal. You can consider yourself fortunate if you have seen one and never had to use it. The paper came from a big spool and slowly piled up on the floor beyond the Teletype. Since this hard copy could be saved, any error messages sent to the console would become part of a permanent archive.

Today, it is very unusual to have a hard-copy terminal for the console. Some systems use a modern display terminal as the console and send a copy of the output to a printer that creates a hard-copy record of the messages sent to the console. For the rest of us, old-fashioned technology must suffice; we must manually copy error messages into the system log. *It is vitally important to maintaining your system to keep a record of kernel error messages and the time they occurred.* You can't keep this record on the system itself, since the system might be inoperable when you need the records. Kernel error messages yield clues that explain what went wrong and how to remedy the problem quickly.

It would be nice to be able to provide a complete list of all kernel error messages and a clear explanation of them. Unfortunately, the error messages vary from one version of UNIX kernel to the next. And, until recently, information on error messages wasn't documented! AT&T System V documentation is the first place that we have seen any information on kernel error messages. For the 3B series of computers, a section entitled *Error Messages* in Appendix C of the *System Administration Utilities Guide* tabulates all system error messages. A separate volume entitled *Error Messages* is provided for Digital Equipment Corporation ports of System V.

Rather than reproduce what is contained elsewhere, we focus on explaining types of error messages and what to do about them. The error messages that we discuss are common to many different versions of the UNIX kernel. These errors are based on the older versions of the kernel, and are also some of the most terse.

We like to organize the kernel error messages into five categories:

- kernel table overflows
- file system problems

- swapping errors
- traps, interrupts, and other surprises
- device-dependent errors

The AT&T *Error Messages* appendix uses different categories, more specific to several particular computers. Your system documentation will (with luck) include a complete and thorough explanation of all kernel error messages, particularly those related to the hardware for your system. If you want to examine your kernel's error messages directly, you can use the **strings** program (listed in Appendix G) on the kernel file. Error messages are strings, and you can use the **strings** utility to print out the error message strings from the kernel, or any program that you want. The output of the **strings** program does take some deciphering, but many of our students consider **strings** an irreplaceable tool.

Severity of Errors and Panics. The AT&T *Error Messages* appendix also lists three "severity" classes—Notice, Warning, and Panic. Even though many System V implementations still do not comply with this classification scheme, it's a good place to start our discussion.

A Notice is an error message that you need to log and be aware of. Sometimes further action will be required, for instance, if there's a file system problem, running **fsck** or the program that will map out a bad disk block. Warnings are more severe. Your system is on the brink of disaster and action must be taken soon.

A panic message means that your kernel has panicked. This doesn't mean that you should feel panicked, too. A *panic* in UNIX jargon means that the kernel has encountered an error so severe that it cannot recover from it. However, rebooting the system will often resolve the problem. So the *panic* routine is called. The *panic* routine prints a *panic* message, tries to perform a **sync**, and halts the system. The **sync** command will write out any in-memory disk buffers to disk, hopefully minimizing file system damage.

A *panic* may also write the contents of memory to the *dump device*. The dump device is often identical to the swap device on smaller systems. And some systems don't do this at all. The memory image on the dump device, called a **core** file, can be examined with the **crash** command. Such post-panic examinations are best left to system programmers who have a knowledge of UNIX system internals.

Most often, you will be able to restart your system after the panic. You definitely need to run **fsck** on all file systems that were mounted when the panic occurred. And you may need to repair the damage that caused the panic before continuing.

Occasional panics are acceptable, frequent panics should cause alarm. Get help from your system's support group, whether local experts or the vendor.

Kernel Table Overflows

The UNIX kernel, as an organizer and manager, maintains lists, or tables, about the current state of affairs. The process table listed by the **ps** command is one of these tables. Table 10.7 lists some kernel tables.

TABLE 10.7 KERNEL TABLES *

Table name	Description
Process	The kernel's database for processes; read by the **ps** command (NPROC).
File	The open file table; each time a process opens a file, another entry appears in this table; more than one open file entry may reference a single file (inode): for example, if two users use the **who** command simultaneously (the **/etc/utmp** file is opened twice for reading using two file table entries) (NFILE).
Inode	The in-memory inode table; the most up-to-date version of the inode for an open file; there will be only one inode entry for each open file; even though more than one process has a file open, such as **/etc/utmp**, only one inode table entry is used for **/etc/utmp** (NINODE).
Text	The pure text table; programs that have their instructions (known as *text*) and data sections separated on a boundary corresponding to the memory protection permit the sharing of the instructions with more than one process; the text table keeps track of the text portion of processes (NTEXT).
Mount	The mounted file system table; generally the shortest of tables, with entries for 5 to 25 mounted file systems (NMOUNT).
Callout	The timeout table; device drivers in the kernel use callouts for pausing a short period of time, for example, the form feed delay that can be requested on a terminal line by the command **stty ff1** (NCALL).

* The capitalized names come from the kernel configuration file and set the number of entries in each table at system configuration time.

The sizes of these tables are set when the kernel was generated. (Some systems allow the dynamic sizing of these tables during the boot processes. For example, BSD versions, and some System V vendor-supplied kernels, can be changed "on the fly" while the kernel is being initialized.) As a system comes under heavier use, one or more of these tables can fill up. When a table is full, the kernel can't allocate the resource the table represents. With the exception of the process table, the kernel sends an error message to the console when a request for a table entry is made that can't be serviced because that table is full. Table 10.8 documents overflow error messages for several kernel tables.

TABLE 10.8 KERNEL TABLE OVERFLOW ERROR MESSAGES

Warning: Inode table overflow

> The inode table is full, and no files may be opened or processes started unless the command or program is already loaded.

Warning: mfree map overflow *XXX* / Lost *YYY* items at *ZZZ*

> The core memory map has overflowed, and as a result a fork, exec, or a request for more memory has failed; this message can also occur if the swap memory map overflows; *XXX* represents the address of the map as given in the kernel's symbol table list.

Warning: out of text

> The text table is full, and no new processes can be started; processes that allow shared text and are already loaded, such as the shell, can be started.

Notice: no file

> The file table is full; no file can be opened.

Panic: Timeout table overflow

> The callout table has overflowed, and a device driver cannot continue without an entry in the callout table.

Except for the timeout panic, most of these error states will go away on their own as system use declines. The filled tables will empty as processes complete and files are closed. You can also terminate some processes using **kill**, freeing up table space.

If you get any of these error messages often, you need to reconfigure your kernel to expand the tables or reduce the number of users. Sometimes the sizes of these tables were set for a minimum memory configuration. The original configuration kept the table size (and the kernel) as small as possible to keep usable memory as large as possible. If the activity on your system has increased and you've added more memory to accommodate the increase, you may want to increase the size of the tables, too.

The names of the corresponding table sizes are listed after each table description in Table 10.7. For example, **NCALL** is the number of timeout table entries. The process for generating a new kernel, the **/unix** file, varies from one UNIX system implementation to the next, so you must rely on your system's documentation. The description given in AT&T's *System Administration Utilities Guide* for 3B2's is one of the best we've seen. The process is fairly simple and the necessary precautions are clearly spelled out.

When the Process Table Becomes Full.   Although the process table is also a kernel resource, the kernel does not send an error message to the console when the table becomes full. The process table fills up as result of the process creation system call, **fork()**. **fork()** normally produces a child process that duplicates the parent process. When the process table is full, the **fork()** system call will return with the error "EAGAIN: No more processes." The Bourne shell program will wait a period of time and try to **fork()** again before reporting "No more processes." So out-of-process error messages don't come from the kernel, but from the shell or a command.

As a system administrator, you can choose from several options when the process table fills up. You can wait for more process table entries to become open, or you can terminate some processes (see below). You can also increase the size of the process table (**NPROC**) or decrease the number of users on the system.

It is possible for malicious users to tie up purposely almost all process table entries, in order to prevent others from using the system. This practice, called denial of service, constitutes a security problem. The UNIX kernel's configured limit, **MAXUP** (MAXimum number of User Processes), limits the number of processes that can be owned by each user id. **MAXUP** is generally between 15 and 25. The system reserves the last process table entry for the superuser, to allow the superuser to take action when the system "freezes," (process table fills up) whether by mistake or intentionally.

The best thing to do when your system has run out of processes is to log in as **root**. If you use **su** to become superuser, you use up the last available process slot with the new superuser shell created by the **su** command. So if you aren't already logged in as **root**, find an unattended terminal and log in. Logging in doesn't create a new process because the log-in shell replaces the **getty** process that waits for user input.

After logging in, use the **ps −ef** command to uncover the cause of the problem. Users with a large number of processes may be the cause if denial of service is involved. You can terminate all the user's processes by killing the user's log-in shell process and putting a minus sign in front of the process id so that the entire process group is included. And talk with the user. (You might want to try this first.) He or she may be innocent of malicious intent. If you have evidence that he or she is intending to disrupt your operations, you should bar the user by disabling the log-in account, and possibly report him or her to authorities. Remember to write down the evidence from the **ps** listing in your system logbook, and save a copy of the listing using redirection to a file.

File System Related Errors

The file systems are vitally important resources in the UNIX system. As file systems are used, the kernel can check parts of them and send error messages to the console when it detects values that are out of range. Table 10.9 lists these errors messages.

Chapter 4 has more information on the structure of file systems and how to use **fsck** to check and repair them.

The kernel often uses the major and minor device number pair when referring to file systems in error messages. Device errors also use the major and minor device numbers in their messages. The major and minor device numbers can be used to identify a file in the device directory that refers to this device. You can use the file name for the device and the **mount** command to determine where this file system is mounted.

TABLE 10.9 ERROR MESSAGES RELATED TO MOUNTED FILE SYSTEMS *

Notice: bad block on dev *M/m*

> A block address in the inode region or past the end of the file system was found in the free block list; the kernel will skip over this address and use the next one if possible; if not, a "no space on device" message will occur next; run **fsck** to repair.

Notice: bad count on dev *M/m*

> The superblock pointer or count identifies that the next free block is greater than 49; a "no space on dev" message will invariably follow; run **fsck**.

Notice: Bad free count on dev *M/m*

> A number greater than 50 was found at the beginning of the block containing the next group of free block addresses; a "no space on dev" message will invariably follow; run **fsck**.

Notice: iaddress > 2^24

> A block address in an in-memory copy of an inode is greater than the maximum block address, 2 raised to the 24th power; since we couldn't replicate this error condition (with **fsdb**), we are uncertain if this error is described accurately; suggest running **fsck**.

Notice: no space on dev *M/m*

> There are no free blocks left available in this file system; the free list could be corrupt (see above); or the file system could have became full during normal use—run **fsck** when the free list or count (see above) is bad or remove some files.

Notice: Out of inodes on dev *M/m*

> There are no free inodes remaining in this file system; remove some files.

---

* The *M/m* stands for a system dependent method for identifying the device where the file system is mounted, for example, the major/minor device number.

The kernel can detect some file system problems, such as out-of-range block addresses ("bad" block numbers) or an incorrect count of free blocks. Detecting and reporting these problems is not the same as fixing them. The kernel will simply ignore a bad block address in the free list and use the next free block. Later, as blocks are freed (when files are removed), the bad block address is overwritten. Although ignoring a bad block address works most of the time, it won't work when the bad address should point to the next block in the chain of free block lists, a 2% (1:50) probability. Then the remainder of the free block list is lost, and the file system is out of space until **fsck** can be run on this file system.

The kernel uses a pointer, called the *count*, to keep track of the next free block in a superblock's free block list. If the count is bad, for instance, a value greater than or equal to 50 (the number of free blocks kept within the superblock), the kernel can't determine which free blocks have already been used, and which are really free. So the kernel reports the error, throws away the free block list, and reports that the file system is out of space. The free list is untrustworthy. If the kernel simply picked an arbitrary count, it could allocate the same free block twice, a duplicate block. If you see a bad count message, run **fsck** on the file system after it has been unmounted.

The kernel is more capable of handling problems with free inode lists. The kernel can simply ignore and pass over a bad inode address, much as it does with bad free block addresses. And if the pointer (count) to the next free inode is incorrect, the kernel can throw away the current list, scan the sequential blocks containing the inodes, and create a new list containing free inodes. The kernel maintains a list of no more than 100 free inodes, since it can always search for more. The inodes are in an established location in a file system and are marked when allocated. Free blocks, by comparison, cannot be distinguished from already allocated data or directory blocks.

If you are running out of free space or free inodes, remove some files. Suggestions given in Chapter 4 will help you maintain adequate free space, and be aware of tactics for picking files to archive and/or remove. Even still, you can run out of free space in a file system by surprise. Sometimes, operations that create large files as a by-product, such as the **lp** print spooling or UUCP file copy systems, will use up all the remaining space in the **/usr** partition. Creating a backup file as an intermediate step before copying to tape, or using a temporary file for copying a floppy disk, can also cause a sudden depletion in free space. The file created by the operation that failed because free space ran out should be removed, as this file will be incomplete.

A user can also exhaust all free space by accident or design. Each user cannot create a file greater than the **ulimit**, or user limit, which is associated with every process. However, a malicious user can create many files below the **ulimit**, and quickly deplete free space. This problem constitutes another denial of service security issue. If the user has acted maliciously, document your evidence, disable the log-in, and turn the issue over to authorities if appropriate.

A user who has accidentally started a command that uses up all free space may need to terminate that command before free space becomes available. In an example earlier in this chapter, we showed how an improperly formatted command using redirection both took over control of a terminal and consumed all free space in a file system. Removing the file (**file2** in Figure 10.8) does not solve the problem, because the kernel maintains an in-memory copy of the inode until the command completes. Thus, the command that caused the problem must be terminated before the file can successfully be removed.

The command in Figure 10.20 will list out the large files that have been created or changed recently. This command should be used on the file system identified by the major and minor device number pair given in the error message (M/m). It will pick out files larger than 10 blocks and modified within one day. Substitute **/usr** with the mount point for the file system that is out of space.

Figure 10.20 Finding recently modified large files.

```
# find /usr -mtime -1 -size +10 -print
./spool/uucp/TM.0235
# □
```

Swapping Errors

The swap space extends memory. The kernel treats problems with the swap space with tremendous respect, normally panicking when something goes wrong. Most often, the problem will be one of running out of swap space. Your system can run out of swap space when the amount of memory has been increased, or when more processes than usual start up. Using a larger disk partition for the swap area will expand swap space. Note that if you want to use a different device for swap, the kernel must be reconfigured (relinked or patched) to recognize the major and minor device number pair for the new swap device and size. (Note that some systems have a **swapon** command that permits adding a second swap device without reconfiguring the kernel.)

Other swap error messages signal that what has been read from the swap area back into memory is unreliable. Input/output errors and changes in the recorded sizes indicate that things have gone awry. Table 10.10 lists the swapping errors.

TABLE 10.10 ERROR MESSAGES FROM SWAPPING

Warning: No swap space for exec args

> The kernel couldn't get enough swap space to copy arguments for an **exec()** (execute new program) system call; the **exec()** fails.

Warning: Not enough space to fork

> A **fork()** (to create a new process) system call has failed because there wasn't enough room to create the new child process.

Notice: swap space running out
needed: N blocks

> The kernel couldn't find a section of the swap area that was large enough; the kernel takes time out to shuffle things about in an attempt to make enough room.

WARNING: swap space running out
needed: N blocks

> The kernel failed in its attempt to clean up the swap area; a panic is imminent.

Panic: cannot expand TEXT with swap

> A request for text (program instructions) growth failed because the swap space is full; may follow soon on the heels of a "swap space running out" message.

Panic: text (data) size error in swapin

> The size of a swapped-in text (or data) section is not the same as was swapped out.

Panic: swapin lost text

> The text portion of a process in the swap area can't be found; text listed in the text table isn't in memory or in the swap area.

Panic: IO error in swap

> A hardware failure occurred while trying to read a process from swap into memory; this message will be accompanied by a device error message; note the block number and device and use bad block mapping to replace the block.

The swap area is not a file system. The kernel uses contiguous pieces of the swap area to copy entire text (program instructions) or data regions from memory. In paging systems, swap is still used, although a group of pages will be written to swap instead of the entire text and data portions of a process.

The swap area tends to fragment because the kernel simply maintains a list of "holes," that is, unused areas, in the swap area, and uses the first hole that is large enough. After a while, the swap area may become filled with "holes" too small to be of any use. The "Notice: swap space running out, N blocks needed" message precedes the kernel's attempt to reorganize the swap space. The attempt can be visualized as similar to what happens in a movie theater as it fills up. If one or two empty seats are scattered here and there in an otherwise full row, an usher urges people to move over and fill the empty seats, in order to make more room on the aisle. The kernel moves areas in the swap space to fill in the "holes" and leaves a large unfragmented area at the end of the swap space. If this still falls short, the kernel prints its "Warning:" message, and attempts to continue.

A panic will occur at this point if the kernel gets stuck. That is, a process must be swapped in to continue, but there's no room in memory unless a process can be swapped out. A deadlock develops since the kernel can't proceed. So the kernel panics and stops everything.

When memory is full with ready-to-run processes, new processes are started using the swap area. The **fork()** system call creates these new processes. This system call fails, that is, returns an error, when there is no room for the child process in either memory or swap ("Not enough space to fork").

The **exec()** system call replaces the current program in a process with another. Sometimes, because the new program is larger than the program to be replaced, more memory is required. If there isn't enough room in memory, the newly exec'ed program is copied into swap. And the **exec()** can fail when there isn't enough room left in the swap area.

Bad blocks in the swap area, denoted by a device error message and a panic ("IO error in swap"), must be replaced. Until this block is replaced, the system will panic every time swap fills up enough to reach this block. Bad block handling techniques vary widely, so you must refer to your system's documentation or support group for information.

Traps, Interrupts, and Other Surprises

These messages come about from occurrences that the kernel isn't expecting. Table 10.11 presents some of these messages.

Traps are software instructions that force the processor (CPU) to "change lanes" and initiate a special sequence of activity. The UNIX system call mechanism uses a trap instruction to make the transition between operating in user mode and in kernel mode. Traps may also be used for other functions: for example, halting a program before it can attempt a divide by zero.

A trap instruction forces the CPU to read the data stored at a particular address. These data will be the address of a routine that handles the trap. When a trap instruction isn't used by the kernel, the address of a default trap handler is put

TABLE 10.11 TRAPS, INTERRUPTS, AND OTHER SURPRISE ERROR MESSAGES

Notice: exec error: u_error *xx* u_dent.d_name *string*

>   This message appears when a program cannot be loaded because of a device error. The *string* is replaced with the name of the program that couldn't be executed. You will need to replace this program from backups if it has become unreadable.

Notice: proc on q

>   This garrulous message means that the kernel attempted to add a process to a queue (q, get it?) of processes that are waiting to run, and the process was already in the queue. Simply a low-level warning, and a cause for alarm only if it happens often.

Notice: unexpected kernel trap

>   A hardware instruction, the trap, has been executed for which the kernel is not prepared. Flaky software does this.

Notice: stray interrupt at *xxx*

>   A hardware signal, the interrupt, has occurred that the kernel is not configured for. Can denote hardware problems, poorly configured hardware, or missing device driver and interrupt handler. Usually shows up immediately after installing or changing hardware or with a reconfigured kernel.

Panic: no file system

>   The kernel was unable to find the in-memory copy of a superblock. Shouldn't happen.

Panic: no imt

>   The kernel's mount table does not contain an entry that corresponds to the indirect mount point field in an inode table entry. Shouldn't happen.

Panic: no procs

>   A process table entry wasn't found during a fork when an entry is available. Shouldn't happen.

---

into the address examined by that trap instruction. This default handler prints out an error message, "unexpected kernel trap," that is simply a notice that something isn't quite right. The address area used by trap instructions is in a region owned and protected by the kernel.

In contrast to traps, interrupts come from hardware. A unit of hardware, like a disk controller or serial port multiplexer, asserts a signal on a wire connected to the CPU board. This signal demands attention from the CPU, and usually denotes that the particular unit of hardware has completed some activity. For example, a disk controller may interrupt the CPU when it completes copying a block between disk and memory. More than one wire carries interrupt signals, and an interrupt signal generally denotes a particular unit of hardware.

Like trap instructions, interrupts tell the processor to look at a location in memory. This location in memory contains the address of the interrupt handler routine, which, in turn, determines the cause of the interrupt, awakens any processes that may have been waiting for the operation to complete, and sets up the next task for the unit of hardware.

A stray interrupt occurs because hardware has been incorrectly configured or some hardware has malfunctioned. It can also occur because the software, the device driver, and interrupt handler have been incorrectly installed in the kernel. Most likely, these errors will show up immediately after installing or changing hardware, or running a reconfigured kernel, in your system.

The panic messages refer to incidents that shouldn't happen. Essentially, a pointer or list has gone awry, and the kernel takes this as an indication that something is seriously wrong. And it is, or this wouldn't have happened.

Device Error Messages

Device error messages come from device drivers in the kernel. What you'll see depends on your particular system implementation (device driver code). Since device drivers are tailored specifically to match one type of hardware, they won't work at all for other types of hardware. For example, a device driver written for a particular disk controller board will work in any system that uses the particular disk controller board; however, it won't work if a different disk controller is substituted. Sometimes, even a different version of the same disk controller will require a different device driver. Since the drivers vary, we can't predict exactly what errors your driver will produce, but we can give you some general guidelines.

Device errors can happen both during initialization and during operation. Usually, some diagnostic checking will precede system initialization. Then, during the kernel's initialization, devices are probed to see which are present and responding. After initialization is complete, operation errors will appear whenever a malfunction is detected. Table 10.12 gives some examples of device errors.

Prominent in the examples in Table 10.12 are timeouts. Either the kernel or the firmware on an intelligent controller may set up a timer. (Recall the callout table from the section on kernel tables.) The software expects a task to be completed before the timer times out. When the device fails to complete some activity in the expected amount of time, an error message results. The device is "hung," that is, it stopped working sometime before the completion of its last operation, and it no longer will respond to a request from the kernel. Using timeouts prevents the kernel from waiting "forever" for a device to respond.

TABLE 10.12 SOME TYPICAL DEVICE ERROR MESSAGES

Warning: PORTS: timeout on drain board (x), port (y)

> A 3B2 error message referring to the serial I/O controller; the board failed during initialization, and the system must be rebooted.

Warning: floppy disk timeout: request flushed

> Another 3B2 device error message; an attempt to read or write to a floppy disk failed, probably because no diskette was inserted or the drive door wasn't closed.

Warning: disk read error
dk(16) blk(4928) rc(1100) intword(0)

> A hard disk error message taken from an ARIX system; 16 represents the minor device number and 4928 tells you the block number.

Warning: unreadable CRC hard disk
error: maj/min = 17/0 block = 2467

> A hard disk read error report from a 3B2 identifying the device by the major/minor number pair (17/0).

mw0a: error bn = 12392 sr = 0x7

> A disk controller error from a different BSD-style UNIX port; the device (partition) name begins the message, followed by the block number (**bn**) and the status register (**sr**). Seven in the status register denotes a CRC (cyclical redundancy check) error.

A CRC error means that the data written on a portion of a disk some time ago don't agree with what was just read. The CRC itself is a number that is calculated using the data written to a portion of the disk, usually a sector. It is unlikely that the data can change and still agree with the CRC that was calculated when the data were written. Typical CRC's are 16 bits long, so the odds of the data changing and matching the CRC value are low — 1 in 65,536.

In many systems, the major and minor device number pair identifies the device and partition where an error occurred. These systems will also use the major and minor numbers, along with the block number, to map out the portion of a disk with a problem. Although using the major and minor device numbers will work with the system software, it can leave humans "out in the cold." Use the table that you created for your logbook to match a major/minor device number pair to the filename for the device in the **/dev** directory.

You should write down in your logbook every kernel error message that you get. This suggestion is even more important when the message stems from a device error. The log can help the service representative or field engineer isolate the problem quickly. If all you can say is that "there was an error message and the thing stopped," you aren't helping much.

A field engineer will use your logbook to look for a pattern of errors. If errors are isolated to one physical disk and one region on the disk, a media failure may be indicated. If errors occurred only on a single physical disk, and in many regions at once, a drive failure is possible. Or a controller may be failing when all drives attached to this controller start acting up at about the same time.

Mapping out a Bad Block.   When the error message involves a hard disk, there is a second action to take. Some systems support bad block mapping, that is, replacing a sector that has a CRC error with a good sector somewhere else on the physical disk. (This is sometimes called sparing a block.) Each physical disk contains a table, the bad block map, that lists unusable sectors and their replacement sectors (spares). The device driver checks this list before using a physical block. If the block requested by the kernel is in the map, the replacement block is used instead. Although using a replacement block reduces system performance somewhat (because it takes time to check the map and access a block in the replacement region of the disk), it's much better than having to replace a disk because it has a few flaws.

Another approach to bad block mapping involves skipping tracks. A track consist of the group of sectors that can be accessed by a single disk head without seeking. Reading or writing from a disk is faster when a track that is bad is skipped entirely instead of requiring the disk to seek to the replacement block on some other track.

We can't tell you the name of the utility used to map out a bad block or skip a track because it is related to the device driver and is system dependent. We have seen such names as **badblk, mwbad, dsetup**, and **disktest** used. Research your system's documentation for the name of this utility and how to use it.

Regardless of the approach used to map out a bad block, you must find and replace the file that contained the bad block. Sometimes, the disk error message will be followed by the kernel error message "exec error: u_error 14 u_dent.d_name *filename*." The kernel failed to execute the file named *filename* because it encountered a hard-disk error while reading the file. So the kernel error message tells you the name of the file to replace from backups. However, don't remove the file with the error until you have spared out the bad block. You can move this file to a name such as **badblock.2134** until you can conveniently use the bad block mapping utility.

The execute error message appears only when a program can't be executed. When the disk error occurs in a block containing data or text, you can use a backup utility such as **cpio** to read files. Working at the console (so you can watch error messages), you would use the command

```
find /usr -print ! cpio -ov > /dev/null
```

to reveal the name of a file with a bad block in the **/usr** file system. Once again, don't remove this file until you have mapped out the bad block. You can **mv** it to another filename in the same file system. If you remove the file before mapping out the block, the bad block will be put in the free list and cause problems later.

Sometimes, the block that has become unreadable is critical, for example, the block contains the first 16 inodes of the file system. Or the utility that your system uses for handling bad block works by formatting the partition where the error occurred. In these cases, you will need to rebuild the file system with **mkfs** and restore all files from your backups.

USING ALTERNATE ROOT FILE SYSTEMS

Sometimes, you might find it impossible to reboot your system. Or you might lose the root password. Under these circumstances it is helpful to have an alternate root file system.

Although you are probably accustomed to using only a single root and swap partition, it is possible to have a second root and/or swap partition. The alternate root partition may nearly duplicate your ordinary root partition. Or it may contain only the files necessary to bring the system up and perform some repairs.

On some computers, an alternate file system resides in a different partition of a hard disk from the one occupied by the root file system. Any mountable file system can be used for this purpose. For example, one vendor's minicomputer uses the **/usr** file system for its alternate root file system.

Many microcomputers come with an alternate root file system on a floppy disk. This file system is often "disguised" as an installation disk. Sometimes the disguise is extreme. 3B2 systems have a "core" floppy disk file system that, when booted, establishes an environment restricted to installing the UNIX system. However, this diskette can be copied and modified to be a full-fledged alternate root file system. Some systems' boot diskettes come up running the Bourne shell, allowing full access to any of the commands in the floppy's file system. Stand-alone file systems are an awful security hazard; that's why vendors (for example, AT&T) hide them. You'll see why they're so dangerous soon.

Building a kernel that will work on an alternate root file system is a more complex task than we can expect to explain in detail. We will, however, explain what is necessary so that existing floppy root file systems can be modified and larger systems can reconfigure their kernels as appropriate. We also outline the files that are mandatory and files that are useful for an alternate root file system.

Finally, we discuss using the alternate root for solving some problems unsolvable from the real root file system without reinstalling it from backups.

Kernels for Alternate File Systems

The kernel from the normal root file system won't work if placed on a different file system. Built into the kernel are the major and minor device numbers for the root file system and the swap device. So the kernel knows which file system is the root without looking in the **/dev** directory. (It would be impossible to do so, since there isn't a device directory until after the root file system is mounted.)

If you simply copied your normal kernel to another file system and tried to boot it, this kernel would use the original file system and swap device. The major and minor device numbers for the root file system and swap can be changed by remaking the kernel or by patching a copy of your current kernel. These tasks are best left to system programmers. Table 10.13 describes the relevant kernel variable names and their general uses within the UNIX kernel. With this information, the company that designed your UNIX system's kernel should be able to provide an alternate root file system.

TABLE 10.13 KERNEL VARIABLES USED TO ASSIGN MAJOR/MINOR DEVICE NUMBERS AND SWAP DEVICE LIMITS

rootdev

   The major and minor device number for the root file system.

pipedev

   The major and minor device number used for temporary buffers for pipes, usually the same as the root file system.

swapdev

   The major and minor device number of the swap device.

dumpdev

   The major and minor device number of the dump device, often the same number as for the swap device. The dump device may be used as a place to write a core image during a panic.

swplo

   The first available block in the swap device, used when the root and swap devices share the same partition.

nswap

   The number of 512-byte blocks in the swap area.

The major and minor device numbers are packed into a single 16-bit word, with each number being an 8-bit value. The order of the major and minor device numbers is determined from a macro that is defined in the **/usr/include/sys/sysmacros.h** file. Typically, the major device number makes up the high-order 8 bits, and the minor the lower 8 bits. So a device with a major device number of two and a minor device number of one would have the value (in hexadecimal) of 0201.

Both the root file system and the swap device can share the same partition. If your immediate reaction is "that's impossible!", good for you. It seems that the root file system would be overwritten as soon as the first process was swapped. However, the kernel's design does allow this sharing. The root file system can be built by **mkfs** starting at the beginning of the partition and ending before the end of the partition. Then the value of **swplo** is set to the size of the root file system. The **swplo** value tells the kernel which is the lowest block available in the swap partition. The **nswap** value defines the number of blocks to be used in the swap area. So with the file system ending before the swap area begins, swap and the root file system can share the same partition.

(*Author's note*: Although I hesitated to include this section, I was so excited about discovering these values that I immediately "hacked" up a copy of my kernel with **adb** and changed the swap device to my second hard disk. I was pleased by the ease of this operation, which had the side effect of letting me listen to my noisy drive, and hear whenever my system swapped. Even though not everyone will feel this way, I wanted to make this information available to others who might feel as excited as I.)

Alternate kernels are installed in the root directory of the alternate root file system, never in the root directory. You must also install several other files, at a minimum, before you can use an alternate root file system successfully.

Minimum Root File System

In Chapter 5, we discussed the the files necessary for booting the UNIX system and running in single-user mode. These are listed in Table 10.14.

The boot loader, or system bootstrap, is designed for loading the kernel or another stand-alone program on a particular set of hardware. The loader will vary according to the system, and procedures for adding a loader to a hard disk also vary. Use your system's *Installation Guide* as the best reference for adding the boot loader to your hard disk. A boot loader will also be part of a stand-alone floppy disk alternate root file system, or the tape or cassette used when installing UNIX on a system.

The boot loader presents a colon prompt (:) when it is ready for your instructions. Generally, pressing RETURN instructs the loader to load the default stand-alone program, the UNIX system kernel, from the default device. However, you can enter the name of another stand-alone program, or the identification for a different

TABLE 10.14 FILES NEEDED FOR SINGLE-USER OPERATION OF UNIX SYSTEMS

loader

> The loader, or bootstrap program, is not a part of any file system. The bootstrap loader will be located in a special partition (or sometimes a reserved area) of a disk, on a tape, or on a floppy disk. The boot loader's task is to load and begin execution of stand-alone programs in UNIX file systems. The kernel is the usual stand-alone program, although diagnostic and installation-oriented programs are often created as stand-alone versions.

kernel

> The kernel is the UNIX operating system program. It organizes the system's hardware and provides basic operating system services, such as creating files, checking access privileges, and starting new processes.

/etc/init

> The **init** program is the grandparent of all nonkernel processes. In single-user mode, the **init** program starts a Bourne shell.

/bin/sh

> The Bourne shell that will be started by **init** in single-user mode. Some systems will require both the **/etc/passwd** file and **/bin/su** to run a single-user shell.

/dev/syscon

> The console device, usually linked to **/dev/console**, used by **init** for the standard input, output, and error during single-user mode.

---

file system, to change the default activity of the boot loader. Once again, this behavior is highly idiosyncratic and closely coupled to your system's hardware. Examples of loading a kernel named **unix** from partition zero of the second hard disk (drive 1) are shown in Figure 10.21 for two different versions of boot loader programs.

Figure 10.21 Different ways that boot loaders receive loading instructions for loading **unix** from the first partition, 0, of the second drive.

a. Minicomputer version for a System V, release 1.03, boot loader:

```
:c0d1s0unix
```

b. A version that boots **unix** on a microcomputer running a version of System V:

```
:hd(1,0)unix
```

Along with the files mention in Table 10.14, you must also have the associated directories. And you will want to have many other files present so that you can perform useful work. The main purpose for having alternate root file systems is to repair problems with the root file system. So you will want to have handy any program that you might want as part of the alternate root file system.

On larger systems with an abundance of disk space, the easiest approach is to make a copy of the root file system and replace the kernel with the version of the kernel modified to work in this partition. For many UNIX systems, devoting eight or nine megabytes to a file system that will be used only in an emergency is an extravagance. Instead, you can create a smaller, 1- to 2-megabyte partition and copy only the programs and files that you might conceivably need. Table 10.15 provides a list of essential and useful programs and files for a scaled-down alternate root file system.

TABLE 10.15 FILES USEFUL IN ALTERNATE ROOT FILE SYSTEMS, LISTED IN ORDER OF IMPORTANCE

fsck	for checking and repairing file systems;
mkfs	for making new file systems;
fsdb	a tool for careful modifications to file systems;
mount	the **mount** and **umount** commands, so file systems can be mounted and worked with;
ls	for listing directory contents;
mv*	for changing file names;
cat	for viewing, creating and overwriting existing files using redirection;
rm	for removing files;
cp*	for copying the kernel or other files between the alternate and mounted file systems;
cpio	or **tar**, for restoring files from backups;
dd	for copying the boot partition (although **cp** may suffice)
/dev	the entire **/dev** directory tree, for recreating device files that may have been destroyed, and for mounting file systems and performing file restoration;
/mnt	for mounting the regular root file system, and
/tmp	for temporary files and using the **ex** editor;
mkdir	for making new directories and
rmdir	for removing directories;
mknod	for creating new device files (**MAKEDEV** scripts use **mknod**)
ln*	and other useful small tools;
ex	an editor, for editing files; you must also have a **/tmp** directory to use **ex**;
adb	or a program for patching the kernel;
diskformat	a disk formatting program, in case the drive containing the real root partition has lost some sector headers due to hardware (controller) malfunction;
disktest	a disk testing program, for checking new formatted disks for bad spots; often, disk formatting and testing will be combined in a single program;
setup	disk partitioning program, to repartition a disk after reformatting it.

* Note that **mv**, **cp**, and **ln** are all links to the same program on most System V implementations.

A **MAKEDEV** shell script is often contained in the **/dev** directory on Berkeley UNIX systems. This script contains the instructions for using the **mknod** command to create device files.

Alternate root file systems provided by system designers often include scripts for installing all or part of a root file system. Other utility scripts may be provided for installing upgrades.

Although Table 10.15 doesn't list every file or command that could make up an alternate root file system, it does give you a good idea of what you want to include. An up-to-date copy of all configuration files, such as **/etc/passwd**, **/etc/group**, the UUCP configuration files, and so forth, would also be handy here. Make certain that any version of the **/etc/inittab** file configures the system to come up in single-user mode by using an **initdefault** entry of **s**.

Uses for Alternate Root File Systems

Before continuing, we want to warn you that alternate root file systems make dandy system-cracking tools. They are security hazards. Keep alternate root file systems that are on removable media (floppies, disk packs, and tapes) under lock and key. For alternate root file systems that are partitions on hard disks, you must prevent your system from being rebooted. Here's one more reason to prevent access to the console and reset switch.

Why do alternate root file systems threaten security? The UNIX operating system starts a Bourne shell with root's privileges when in single-user mode. You could say that it is operating in privileged mode. An alternate root file system is designed to start up in single-user mode, thereby giving root privileges to the user at the console.

This special access is not a bad thing when you really need it. The sections that follow describe techniques that can easily be accomplished from the alternate root file system that are difficult, if not possible, from the regular root file system.

Replacing a Lost Root Password. Earlier in this book, we suggested configuring your system so that it comes up at run level 2, multiuser mode. Multiuser mode forces users to log in, rather than granting superuser privileges automatically to the console user on reboot. A nasty problem can occur, however. You, or one of your esteemed associates, could change the root account password and forget what it is.

Don't laugh. People forget their mate's birthday all the time. And the root password might be changed by a successful system breaker or vengeful ex-employee. Although you can still start up your system, you won't be able to shut down correctly or perform backups without the root account password.

To clear up this problem, boot up the alternate root file system. Then mount the real root file system and edit the **/etc/inittab** file so that the system will come up in single-user mode when it is rebooted. If your alternate root file system doesn't contain an editor, you can rename **/etc/inittab** in the real root file system as shown in Figure 10.22. Then you can reboot the system and bring it up to single-user mode since **init** won't locate **/etc/inittab**, so it will request a run level to use. You simply specify **s** and you're in single-user mode. Once in single-user mode, use the **passwd** command to install a new root account password.

Figure 10.22 Renaming **/etc/inittab** in the real root file system.

```
[  boot from alternate file system  ]
# mount /dev/dsk/c0d0s0 /mnt
Warning: Mounting <> as <mnt>!
# mv /mnt/etc/inittab /mnt/etc/oinittab
# sync
# umount /dev/dsk/c0d0s0
# sync; sync
[  reboot from "real" root file system  ]
```

Replacing Boot Loader.   The boot loader is a program on a partition or reserved area of the first hard disk. The boot loader gets read in from disk after routine system power-up diagnostics complete. Sometimes the boot loader loads automatically. On other systems, a simple command loads the loader explicitly, like the letter **b** followed by a RETURN. In either case, once the boot loader has successfully been copied from disk to memory and started up, it presents a colon prompt at the console.

If your system finishes its diagnostics but never presents the colon prompt without displaying a disk error message, the boot loader program may have been corrupted. Although the boot loader is not contained within a file system, it is, rather, like a file system composed of a single long file. If someone inadvertently copied over this file, say with **cp**, **dd**, or file redirection, all or part of its contents could be replaced, and the program would no longer work. The PROM diagnostics that start the loader are not as sophisticated as the UNIX kernel, and can't determine if the loader is really an executable file. So the colon prompt never appears.

The boot loader can be replaced from the installation disk or tape. Follow the instructions given in the installation notes for your system. The boot loader can also be replaced from a file copy kept on the alternate root file system. Figure 10.23 presents several examples of the different methods for adding a boot loader to a device.

Figure 10.23 Different methods for copying a boot loader to a device.

a. Using a stand-alone program to copy boot loader from distribution tape to a disk in a minicomputer. First, the boot loader is copied from a tape to memory and started. Then **ldsa** was used to copy the boot loader to a reserved area (designated by **r** of the device name) of a disk:

```
>bt <RETURN>
Boot
Loading HSDT code
:ldsa
Standalone ldsa
Source device defaults to TAPE <RETURN>
Disk device c0d0r <RETURN>
Copying BOOTIMAGE to c0d0r:
14238 bytes transferred
: □
```

b. The 3B2 series script invokes **dd** to copy the boot loader to a special partition that is recognized by the diagnostic monitor:

```
# mkboot mboot lboot /dev/dsk/c0d0s7
```

c. Another microcomputer system simply uses **cp** to copy the boot loader from a floppy disk partition to a hard-disk boot partition:

```
# cp /dev/flpboot /dev/hdboot
```

Emerging most clearly from these examples is the diversity of methods for replacing the boot loader. Example 10.23a uses a special stand-alone program, **ldsa**, and a reserved area, not an ordinary partition, of a hard disk. The 3B2 example shows the use of a script that invokes **dd** to copy two files to a partition, **/dev/dsk/c0d0s7**, of a hard disk. The third example simply depicts copying a boot loader partition on a floppy disk to one on a hard disk. You must study the relevant portions of your system's documentation to discover how it is done for your computer.

Replacing Critical Files. Previously, we discussed the files that must be present to run the UNIX system in single-user mode. Accidental loss of the files can prevent your ordinary root file system from being able to run in either single-user or multiuser mode. If the kernel file is missing, you will notice that immediately after pressing RETURN to the boot loader's colon prompt. If the kernel file is present but has been corrupted, the loader will present a diagnostic message to the effect that the magic number that distinguishes stand-alone programs, like the kernel, is incorrect.

Once the kernel has been loaded, it proceeds to initialize itself. Initialization manifests itself as a series of messages sent to the console. These messages may tell you the date that this kernel was generated, the amount of memory available, and possibly, information about other devices discovered during initialization. You know the the kernel has started successfully when you see these familiar messages.

The **init** process controls the next phase of startup. If your system halts after the kernel's initialization messages, the **/etc/init** program is missing or corrupt.

Finally, the **init** process will use the Bourne shell to interpret and begin execution of the program entries in the **inittab** file. If the Bourne shell is unavailable, the **init** program will send a message to the console.

Replacing any of these files can be accomplished by booting on an alternate file system and mounting the ordinary root file system. The files indicated can then be copied, and in the case of the kernel, patched, the file system unmounted, and the system rebooted. Figure 10.24 provides an example of replacing the **/etc/init** file.

Figure 10.24 Replacing the **/etc/init** file after booting from an alternate file system.

```
# mount /dev/dsk/c0d0s0 /mnt
warning:  Mounting <root> as </mnt>!
# cp /etc/init /mnt/etc/init
# sync
# umount /dev/dsk/c0d0s0
# sync; sync
# □ <reboot>
```

Notice how simple this operation is. You can compare this to reinstallation of the root partition that would be necessary if the alternate root file system were unavailable. You must also either replace the kernel with one created especially for the normal root partition, or patch the kernel after copying it across from an alternate root file system.

One further step is advisable when you have mysteriously lost an important file and been unable to reboot—running **fsck** from the alternate root file system on the root file system.

Running fsck on the Root File System.   Some things can happen to the root file system that can't be repaired while working within this file system. This problem occurs because the root file system is always mounted, and some files in it are always open. The files **/dev/syscon**, **/etc/init**, and **/bin/sh** will be in use even in single-user mode. So will the **fsck** program itself. A problem with any of these can be unrepairable because these files are in use, and the kernel has kept an in-core copy of the inodes for these files. But by using the alternate root file system, you can repair files in use on the normal root partition.

You can tell that a critical file has an unrepairable problem when every time you run the **fsck** program on the root file system, the same problem gets reported. Even though you prompt **fsck** to repair the problem, it still occurs, time after time. (Here is where using your logbook really helps, because you know what error messages reoccur.)

The solution is to run the **fsck** program from the alternate file system. Now the files that were in use in the regular root file system will be inactive, and the **fsck** program will repair their inodes.

QUICK REFERENCE GUIDE

Terminal Problems:

Try **Control-Q** first when keyboard appears locked up.

Reset the terminal if gibberish appears on the screen after the user has displayed a non-ASCII file and locked up the keyboard.

Use **stty sane** followed by a **Control-J** (System V) to reset the terminal line to a sane condition if there is no character echo and carriage returns don't work.

If **sane** isn't recognized try this **stty** command (also followed by **Control-J**) to restore some line conditions:

```
$ stty echo echoe echok icrnl ixon opost onlcr isig icanon <Control-J>
```

As a last recourse, log out, and log back in to restore a terminal line with wrong baud rate or line conditions confused by abnormal exit from a program.

Problems with Processes:

Use the **ps** command without options to display the processes attached to the terminal from which the **ps** command is entered.

Use this **ps** command to display the processes attached to terminal **/dev/tty02**:

```
$ ps -ft02
```

Use **ps −ef** (**ps −al** for BSD) to display all processes.

The **−u** option (doesn't work on BSD) displays the processes owned by a user.

```
$ ps -fubeccat
```

The **kill** command signals processes.

$ **kill** [−*signal*] *PID* [*PID2 PID3 ...*]

The three signal numbers that you should remember are 1 and 15, for sending a signal that can be caught and allowing the process to clean up, and 9, for the sure kill.

Use the following **kill** command to terminate all processes, except shells, that are owned by you. (*Never execute this command as root.*)

```
$ kill -1
```

A

Environment Variables

This appendix is for reference purposes. It's not a tutorial on the UNIX shell—you should consult other documentation for learning about the shells. This appendix does discuss some of the more important environment variables for the Bourne and Korn shells (and to some extent) the C shell. If you're using the C shell, also read Appendix B.

Table A.1 lists several of the shell environment variables that are initialized after logging in to the UNIX system. The ones shown with a single asterisk (*) are set by the Bourne and Korn shells, and those with a double asterisk (**) are set by the Korn shell only.

Depending on your **login** program version, it will set one or more of the **HOME, LOGNAME, MAIL, PATH,** and **SHELL** environment variables. The other variables tabulated here are given initial values by the shell itself. For instance, the Bourne shell sets **IFS, MAILCHECK, PS1,** and **PS2,** whereas the Korn shell sets those and **EDITOR, FCEDIT, PPID, PS3, PWD, RANDOM, SECONDS,** and **TMOUT.** Now let's discuss these and other environment variables in more detail. We'll present them in alphabetical order.

CDPATH. The Bourne and Korn shells refer to this environment variable to locate the directory specified as an argument to the **cd** command. This variable contains a list of directories, which is searched if the argument to **cd** is given as a relative pathname, but not a full pathname (begins with a slash, /). The system doesn't set **CDPATH**—you have to define it.

TABLE A.1 SOME PRESET SHELL ENVIRONMENT VARIABLES

Variable name	Description
EDITOR **	Command history editor
FCEDIT **	Editor for **fc** command
HOME	The home directory
IFS *	Internal field separators
LOGNAME	The account name
MAIL	The mailfile pathname
MAILCHECK *	Mailfile check frequency
PATH	Command search path
PPID **	The parent process of the shell
PS1 *	Primary prompt string
PS2 *	Secondary prompt string
PS3 **	Tertiary prompt string
PWD **	The current working directory
RANDOM **	A random number
SECONDS **	Seconds since shell was started
SHELL	Startup program pathname
TMOUT **	Time until automatic logoff

A colon (:) separates each directory in the list. A single colon at the beginning of the list, an empty pair of colons (::) or a pair containing a dot (:.:) in the middle of the list, or a dot at the end of the list (:.) all denote the current directory.

You'll probably find the directory search feature convenient for getting around your file system without a lot of typing—especially if the directories have long pathnames. Generally, you'll want to list your current directory first, then your home directory, and finally any other directories you use frequently. Figure A.1 shows an example.

Figure A.1 An example for setting, displaying, and using **CDPATH**.

```
$ CDPATH=:/usr2/beccat:/usr2/beccat/Book
$ export CDPATH
$ echo $CDPATH
:/usr2/beccat:/usr2/beccat/Book
$ cd Chapter1
$ pwd
/usr2/beccat/Book/Chapter1
$ ▢
```

In this example the shell looks for the directory **Chapter1** first in the current directory (denoted by a single colon at the beginning of the directory list), then in **/usr2/beccat**, which is the home directory for the **beccat** account, and finally in the **Book** subdirectory of the home directory. The result of the **pwd** command verifies that the desired directory was located in **/usr2/beccat/Book**. The shell will issue a "bad directory" error message if the desired directory wasn't located by searching directories in this list.

COLUMNS. A Korn shell environment variable that sets the width of the edit window for the shell edit modes and printing **select** lists.

EDITOR. A Korn shell environment variable that specifies the editor used for editing the history list. It's used interchangeably with the **VISUAL** variable. Currently, **ed**, **vi**, and **emacs** modes are generally available. This variable may be set and exported in the **.profile** or ENV file. The default value is **/bin/ed**—the original UNIX line editor.

ENV. The Korn shell environment variable that specifies the pathname of the Korn shell-specific startup file, which we'll call the **ENV** file. Generally, it's given the value **$HOME/.kshrc** in the **.profile** startup file, which is executed by the Korn shell right after log-in. Then, commands in the **ENV** file would be executed after log-in and whenever another instance of the Korn shell is invoked.

FCEDIT. The editor used by the Korn shell **fc** history-list editing command. It's **/bin/ed** by default.

HISTFILE. Alternate file to store the Korn shell history list. If not set, the Korn shell uses **$HOME/.sh_history**.

HISTSIZE. The number of commands that will be stored in **HISTFILE**.

HOME. The **login** process initializes the **HOME** environment variable to be the contents of the home directory field of the password file for the account. The predefined C shell variable **home** gets its value from the **HOME** environment variable.

Certain programs read this variable to get your home directory. You've no doubt used **cd** by itself to go "home" to your home directory. In this case **cd** actually finds its destination from the value assigned to **HOME**. Because programs in the system count on **HOME** being a user's home directory, it's better not to change it, except perhaps for a special purpose—but watch out for undesirable side effects if you reset it.

IFS. The **IFS** or internal field separator variable has a particular meaning to the Bourne or Korn shell. It contains the characters that this shell uses for separating elements of the command line. The shell uses these characters for other purposes as well, but they're beyond the scope of this book. The default values are the ASCII space, tab, and newline characters—the so-called "whitespace" characters. You might change these values for special purposes in a shell script, but generally you shouldn't change these values when interacting with the shell directly.

LOGNAME or USER. This variable contains the name of the account. It would be initialized by the **login** process, which obtains its value from the account name field of the password file entry for the account. Some systems use **LOGNAME** and others use **USER** to stand for the same thing. Other systems may not use a variable to store the account name. It's useful for specifying your account name in a portable way in commands and shell scripts.

Some programs, such as **lp** and **uucp**, use this variable to determine which account is making a request. Here again is one variable you should rarely, if ever, change.

MAIL.   The System V **login** process initializes this variable by appending the account name to the **/usr/mail** directory and stores the result in **MAIL**. On XENIX and Berkeley systems, the account name is appended to the **/usr/spool/mail** directory, instead.

The Bourne and Korn shells access this variable to determine the pathname of your "mailbox" file. Instead, the C shell examines the analogous **mail** variable, which is discussed in Appendix B.

The Bourne and Korn shells will check the "mailbox" file as you log in and periodically thereafter (see also **MAILCHECK** below for how often this check is made). These shells will also notify you in case new mail arrives. In all cases the Bourne and Korn shells print "You have mail." These messages occur after you exit the command you're running and return control to the shell.

MAILCHECK.   This variable specifies how often (in seconds) the Bourne or Korn shell will check for the arrival of mail. The default value is 600 seconds (or every 10 minutes). If you set the value of **MAILCHECK** to zero, the shell will check for mail each time before displaying the command prompt. Of course, this check delays the display of the prompt (slows response time) since a disk file must be read. Generally, the 10-minute default value is suitable for most purposes.

MAILPATH.   You'd initialize this variable to contain a list of files that can be checked by the Bourne or Korn shell for the arrival of text, which is generally a mail message. The files are separated from one another by colons, and a "custom" notification message can be specified by supplying it after a percent sign (%) for the Bourne shell or question mark (?) for the Korn shell.

Note that if you stay logged on the system for an extended period, you may wish to check for new text in certain files, such as **/etc/motd**, the message-of-the-day file. Figure A.2 shows an example for setting **MAILPATH** to the standard mailfile and **/etc/motd**.

Figure A.2 Specifying a new "mail path."

```
$ MAILPATH=/usr/mail/$LOGNAME:/etc/motd
$ □
```

PATH.   Whenever you specify a command using a relative pathname, either the Bourne, Korn, or C shell searches a list of directories to locate the command.

This list is specified using the **PATH** environment variable for the Bourne or Korn shells. The C shell also maintains the **path** variable for this purpose (discussed in Appendix B.

The colon (:) separates the directories in the **PATH** variable. The dot (.) specifies the current directory. You may use some shorthand for the current directory, as it's also specified by an empty pair of colons (::), or a single colon at the beginning (but not the end) of the path list.

Many **login** programs assign the initial value of **PATH** to be **:/bin:/usr/bin**. Thus, first the current directory, then the **/bin** directory, and finally the **/usr/bin** directory would be searched.

You're setting yourself up for a trojan horse attack by having your current directory searched before the system command directories, **/bin**, **/usr/bin**, and **/usr/lbin** (if used). Thus, you should *always* change your **PATH** to place the current directory after these directories. And if you're not doing any programming or shell script writing, you probably won't need to include the current directory anyway—just leave it out entirely. You could always invoke a command in your current directory using a relative pathname of the form *./commandname*.

PPID. The process-ID number of the parent process of the shell.

PS1. This variable contains the character string used by the Bourne or Korn shell when prompting for command input. The default value is a dollar sign (**$**) followed by one space character. This variable is customized sometimes.

If you are using a version of the Bourne shell that recognizes shell functions (System V Release 2 and later), you could customize the **PS1** variable to include the current value of your working directory as part of the prompt. Part a of Figure A.3 shows how to do this by defining a function for changing directories, named **go**. Part b shows how to include the current working directory in the Korn shell prompt.

Figure A.3 Customizing the shell prompt.

a. Including current directory in System V Release 2 (and later) Bourne shell prompt:

```
$ go() { cd $1; PS1="[`pwd`] "; }
$ go /usr/games
[/usr/games] □
```

b. Including current directory in Korn shell prompt:

```
$ PS1='$PWD ) '
/usr2/beccat ) □
```

Every time **go** is invoked, the **pwd** command is executed and its standard output is used to reinitialize the prompt. Since **pwd** is built-into the Bourne shell as of Release 2 of System V, its invocation doesn't slow the display of the shell prompt significantly. You do have to remember to change directories using **go** instead of **cd** so that the **PS1** variable will be changed to the new working directory. This example first appeared on page 77 in the May 1986 issue of UNIXWORLD magazine.

The present (current) working directory is stored in the Korn shell **PWD** environment variable. You simply display the contents of this variable to include the current working directory in your Korn shell prompt. Note that single quotes, not double quotes, should be used to enclose the definition.

PS2. The secondary prompt string for the Bourne or Korn shell is contained in the **PS2** variable. It's displayed whenever the shell is expecting further input to complete a command: that is, after you type a newline and you haven't completed the expected command expression. Generally, this prompt is not customized. Its default value is a greater-than sign (>) followed by one space character. Figure A.4 shows an example of where you'll see this prompt.

Figure A.4 An example showing the secondary prompt.

```
$ for i in 1 2 3
> do
> echo $i
> done
1
2
3
$ □
```

PS3. The tertiary prompt string for the Korn shell. It's the selection prompt used with a **select** loop, by default a **#?**.

SECONDS. Contains the number of seconds since the Korn shell was invoked. You can assign a value to this variable, after which it will contain that value plus the number of seconds since the shell was invoked.

SHELL. The **login** process sets this variable to be pathname of your startup program. Programs use this variable in different ways. For instance, the Bourne shell startup program reads the variable to see if it should run in a restricted mode, and does so when the letter "r" appears in the name, as in **/bin/rsh**.

Other programs, such as **vi** and **pg**, examine the **SHELL** variable to see what shell should be invoked when a "shell escape" or command is specified. Thus, you can change the value of **SHELL** to change the shell invoked by these programs. In fact, you can prevent a shell escape if you set **SHELL** to a NULL value. For instance, Figure A.5 depicts a short shell script that prevents a shell escape for the **pg** command. This shell script first appeared in UNIXWORLD magazine on page 92 in the April 1987 issue.

Figure A.5 Changing the **SHELL** variable to prevent a "shell escape."

```
:
# @(#) pgg   A secure pg program
# Author: Andy Levinson
SHELL='' pg -ecnsp\
'Page %d: Press <RET> to continue or <q> to quit: ' $*
```

TERM. You place the name of your terminal in this environment variable. The name is used by screen-oriented programs, such as **vi** and **more**, to determine the terminal type being used. The terminal name should be one that can be used to locate the appropriate entry for the terminal in the **terminfo** or **termcap** terminal capability database files.

The Berkeley **login** program can get the terminal name for a given port from the **/etc/ttytype** file and set the **TERM** variable for you. Of course, this requires that the ports be hardwired to certain terminals. For dial-up ports the Berkeley **tset** command can be used to map a port to a particular terminal. Figure A.6 shows how you could use this command to initialize the **TERM** environment variable either for the Bourne, Korn, or the C shell. See your Berkeley system documentation for more information on this flexible command.

Figure A.6 Using **tset** to set the **TERM** variable.

a. Using the Bourne and Korn shell:

```
$ export TERM; TERM=`tset - -m 'dialup:adm3a'`
```

b. Using the C shell:

```
% setenv TERM `tset - -m 'dialup:adm3a'`
```

The —**m** option says to map the **dialup** port to a ADM 3a terminal; otherwise, if not a **dialup** type port, use the mapping determined in **/etc/ttytype**. The dash (—) argument causes the terminal name to be sent to the standard output so that it can set the **TERM** variable.

TMOUT. If set to a nonzero value, the Korn shell will exit if there's no terminal activity for **TMOUT** seconds. First the message "shell time out in 60 seconds" is displayed, and if a RETURN isn't pressed within 60 seconds, the shell exits.

TZ. A string representing the time zone for the local system is placed in this variable. For instance, the Pacific time zone sets **TZ** to the value PST8PDT, which means Pacific Standard Time, eight time zones west of Greenwich Mean Time, Pacific Daylight Time.

Commands such as **date** and **mail** use **TZ** when converting the time determined by a system call (which gives the time as the number of seconds since January 1, 1970 GMT) to a more readable format for the local time (month, day of month, hour, minute, and seconds).

VISUAL. A Korn shell environment variable that specifies the editor used for editing the history list. It's used interchangeably with the **EDITOR** variable. Currently, **vi** and **emacs** modes are generally available. This variable may be set and exported in the **.profile** or the **ENV** file.

Other Environment Variables. You may wish to define other variables and place them in the shell environment for specific purposes. Some variables are recognized by certain UNIX programs, such as **EXINIT** by **ex** and **vi**. Other variables might be useful shorthands, say for abbreviating long pathnames, like **PUBDIR** for **/usr/spool/uucppublic**.

You can display all your environment variables by executing the **env** command. Note that the related **set** command displays local as well as environmental variables known to the Bourne shell, however, only local variables are displayed by the C shell **set** command. Figure A.7 shows the result of executing **env** on a typical system using the Bourne shell startup program.

Figure A.7 Sample **env** command output.

```
$ env
HOME=/usr2/beccat
PATH=/bin:/usr/bin:/usr/ucb:/usr/lbin
LOGNAME=beccat
SHELL=/usr/ucb/csh
MAIL=/usr/mail/beccat
JOBNO=ON
LIB=/usr/lib/uucp
PUBDIR=/usr/spool/uucppublic
SPOOL=/usr/spool/uucp
TERM=ansi
TZ=PST8PDT
$ □
```

Here the **LIB**, **PUBDIR**, and **SPOOL** variables were created as abbreviations for pathnames frequently used when changing directories or invoking UUCP maintenance programs. But they don't have any significance to the UUCP software itself. However, the **JOBNO** variable is recognized by the Version 2 UUCP software, and the value **ON** causes display of the job number after a request is queued. The other variables were discussed earlier in this appendix.

B

Predetermined C Shell Variables

This appendix is for reference purposes; it's not a tutorial on the C shell—you should consult other documentation for learning about the C shell.

We'll discuss some of the more important C shell variables that have predefined meanings. We're listing the variables in alphabetical order. You can display the variables that have been set along with their values, if any, using the **set** command without arguments.

cdpath. The C shell uses **cdpath** like the Bourne or Korn shell uses **CDPATH** (discussed in Appendix A). You should put the definition for **cdpath** in **.cshrc** so that it's defined for all instances of the C shell. And besides **cd**, both the C shell **pushd** and **popd** commands recognize **cdpath**.

Figure B.1 shows an example for setting, displaying, and using **cdpath**. Here, the current directory, then the home directory (denoted by a tilde), and a subdirectory of the home directory, named **Book**, would be scanned in that order to locate the desired directory argument. The **pwd** reveals the current directory before and after running **cd Chapter2**.

Figure B.1 An example for setting, displaying, and using the **cdpath** variable.

```
% set cdpath = ( . ~ ~/Book )
% echo $cdpath
% . /users/beccat /users/beccat/Book
% pwd
/usr2/beccat
% cd Chapter2
```

```
% pwd
/usr2/beccat/Book/Chapter2
% □
```

cwd.   Current BSD versions and other recent implementations of the C shell will store the current working directory in the **cwd** variable. You wouldn't customize this variable, but you could read it to determine the current working directory without invoking the **pwd** program. Figure B.2 shows an alias definition of **cd** that reads the **cwd** variable to display the current working directory in the shell prompt.

Figure B.2 Using the **cwd** variable.

```
% alias cd    'cd \!*;set prompt="`echo $cwd`) "'
/usr2/beccat) □
```

histchars.   The **histchars** variable lets you redefine the default characters used to issue history commands, namely the exclamation point (!) and the circumflex (^). You should put any new definition for **histchars** in **.cshrc** if you define aliases in this startup file.

You may wish to reassign the history editing characters if you use one or both frequently for purposes other than for manipulating the C shell history list. For instance, if you use the UUCP commands often, you might like to reassign the ! to another less frequently used character so you don't have to quote the ! in each command line, as in \!. Figure B.3 shows how to reassign the ! to a # and yet retain the ^ as a history correction character.

Figure B.3 Reassigning the ! history character.

```
% set histchars = "#^"
% □
```

Note: If you reassign the ! to another character, make sure that all C shell aliases that depend on the ! are rewritten to depend on the new character.

history.   The C shell can "remember" commands using the so-called history mechanism. The remembered commands are stored in the history list. You initialize the **history** variable in **.cshrc** to a number, which represents the size of the history list. If this variable is not set, the history list has a size of one—only the last command is "remembered."

Generally, you'd keep only a screenful (less than 24) commands in the history list so that you can display the entire list without the beginning scrolling off the screen. You may want a shorter list if you work with a slow terminal using a dial-up line. Alternatively, you may choose to keep a larger list and use the **history** *number* command to limit the display to the last *number* commands.

home. This variable contains the full pathname of the home directory for the account. It's used by **cd** when no argument is specified. Also, its value replaces the tilde (˜) in pathname specifications. Normally, you wouldn't change the value of **home.**

ignoreeof. Set the **ignoreeof** variable in **.login** and the startup C shell program will ignore control-D as an end-of-file for the shell to prevent you from logging out of your system accidentally. When **ignoreeof** is set, you log off using the **logout** command. Set **ignoreeof** in **.cshrc** if you wish subshells to ignore end-of-file. Then you have to type "exit," instead of simply control-D, to leave a subshell.

mail. The **mail** variable specifies one or more pathnames for files that the C shell checks for arrival of new text. It has the same functionality as the **MAIL**, **MAILCHECK**, and **MAILPATH** environment variables combined, which are used by the Bourne and Korn shells.

By default, the files you specify are checked every 10 minutes. You can change this frequency as you specify the pathnames used to define the **mail** variable. Figure B.4 shows four examples. In part a we simply define the "mailbox" file for the **beccat** account, **/usr/mail/beccat**, but don't change how often it's checked for mail. In part b we check the same "mailbox" file every minute (by specifying 60 seconds). In part c we define the "mailbox" file, but use the default checking frequency, and we add a definition to check the message-of-the-day file, **/etc/motd**, checked once an hour (every 3600 seconds) for newly added text, which is useful if you're logged in for extended periods of time. Finally, in part d we check **/usr/mail/beccat** once a minute and **/etc/motd** once an hour.

Figure B.4 Examples for defining **mail**.

a. Defining a "mailbox" file:

```
% set mail = (/usr/mail/beccat)
% □
```

b. Checking the "mailbox" file once a minute:

```
% set mail = (60 /usr/mail/beccat)
% □
```

c. Checking the "mailbox" using the default interval and **/etc/motd** once an hour:

```
% set mail = (/usr/mail/beccat 3600 /etc/motd)
% □
```

d. Checking the "mailbox" file once a minute and the **/etc/motd** file once an hour:

```
% set mail = (60 /usr/mail/beccat 3600 /etc/motd)
% □
```

If the **mail** variable is set, the C shell will let you know that you have mail as you log in by displaying "You have mail." Also, it will inform you if new mail arrives after you're logged on by displaying "You have new mail" after you exit the command you're running and return to the shell.

noclobber.   Set the **noclobber** variable in **.cshrc** to prevent the C shell from overwriting an existing file using output redirection. *Note:* This variable also prevents creation of new files using output append ($>>$). You can override this protection by appending the ! character to the output redirection symbol. Figure B.5 provides an example.

Figure B.5 Setting and using the **noclobber** variable.

```
% set noclobber               set variable
% echo "hello" >>testfile     try to create using append
testfile: No such file or directory
% echo "hello" >testfile      can create this way
% echo "goodbye" >testfile    attempt to overwrite
testfile: File exists
% echo "goodbye" >! testfile   force it
% □
```

path.   The **path** variable lists the command search path analogous to the **PATH** environment variable. However, the information is formatted differently. The C shell will automatically update the **PATH** variable to be the same as **path**. This way you only have to set **path** (say in **.login**) and all other programs that the C shell invokes can use the value of **PATH**.

Figure B.6 shows an example of setting **path** and how it changes **PATH**. First the default value of **PATH** is displayed. Then **path** is set, and finally the values contained in both **path** and **PATH** are shown.

Figure B.6 An example for setting **path**.

```
% echo $PATH
:/bin:/usr/bin
% set path = ( /bin /usr/bin /usr/lbin ~/Bin . )
% echo $path
/bin /usr/bin /usr/lbin /users/beccat/Bin .
% echo $PATH
/bin:/usr/bin:/usr/lbin:/users/beccat/Bin:.
% □
```

prompt.   The default C shell prompt is a percent sign (%) followed by one space. You can reassign the prompt to something more useful by defining the **prompt** variable. Figure B.7 shows two examples. In part a we have the prompt include the C shell history event number. In part b we reset the prompt each time a **cd** command is given, so the prompt will always contain the current working directory (output by running **pwd**).

Figure B.7 Defining a new C shell prompt.

a. Redefining the prompt to include the event number and showing how the event number increments when you run a command (here **pwd**):

```
% set prompt = "\\!) "
13) pwd
/usr2/beccat
14) □
```

b. Using an alias for **cd** to define a prompt that displays the current working directory:

```
alias cd  'cd \!*;set prompt="`pwd`) "'
/usr2/beccat) □
```

savehist.   Set the value of **savehist** in **.cshrc** to be the number of commands in the history list that you wish the C shell to save on disk. Normally, the history list is saved in memory but not on disk, and thus is lost when you log out. The history list will be stored in a file named **.history** in the home directory and be used to initialize the history list when you begin a new session.

shell.   The C shell initializes the value of **shell** to the pathname for the C shell program file. This value is used to create a subshell or execute a shell script. Normally, you wouldn't change the value assigned to **shell**.

term.   The terminal type name. Generally set by the C shell from the value contained in the **TERM** environment variable, which would be set in **.login**.

time.   You would set the **time** variable in **.cshrc** to cause the C shell to display timing statistics for a command. The numerical value you assign to **time** provides the display threshold. That is, only if the command consumed more than the threshold value of CPU time (both user and system time) would the statistics be displayed. Below this threshold nothing is displayed.

Figure B.8 shows an example of setting **time** and running a command to view its time statistics.

Figure B.8 Setting and using the **time** variable.

```
% set time = 5
% sort largelist -o sortedlist
8.6r 7.2u 1.0s
% □
```

The result shows that the sort took 8.6 seconds of real time, 7.2 seconds of user time, and 1.0 seconds of system time. Note that UNIX timing statistics may vary from run to run.

C

Utilities for Account Management

We list two utilities you should find helpful for account management.

finger Shell Script

The **finger** shell script makes it easy to find a person's account name when all you know is some part of their personal name. For example, suppose that you want to send mail to Fred, but the mailer tells you that "Fred is unknown," and you don't know his last name, nor his initials, nor even if his name is Fred at all.

Berkeley systems provide a utility called **finger** that provides this function. The shell script shown below doesn't have all the "bells and whistles" of the Berkeley version, but it does the basic job. For **finger** to work best, you must have placed the full name of each account user in the comment (fifth) field of the **/etc/passwd** file entry for each system user.

If your system doesn't have the **cut** command, replace `cut -f1,5 -d:` by `awk -F: '{print $1, $5}'`. Also note that in AT&T versions of **grep** before Release 2 of System V, −y instead of the −i option was used to ignore case distinction.

Figure C.1 Listing of the **finger** shell script.

```
1   :
2   # @(#) finger  Get name information for user-ID
3   # Author: Lee Sailer
4   #
5   case $# in
```

```
 6        0) echo "Usage: $0 id [id...]" ;;
 7        *) for i in $*; do
 8               cut -f1,5 -d: /etc/passwd | grep -i ".*$i.*"
 9           done ;;
10  esac
```

Note: This shell script first appeared in the November 1986 issue of UNIXWORLD magazine on page 67.

newuser Shell Script

Here's a shell script for installing a user account on your system. If you specify only an account name, it will choose default values for a shell, group-ID number, and parent directory of the home directory. You can override these defaults with command line arguments.

If you specify two arguments on the command line, the second would be the pathname of the shell program; if three arguments, the third must be the group-ID number; if four arguments, the fourth must be the parent of the home directory. This last option would be useful, for instance, if you had a large installation and you wished to place different users on different mounted file systems.

Figure C.2 shows some sample command lines for using **newuser** and the script is listed in Figure C.3.

Figure C.2 Using the **newuser** shell script.

a. Using all the default values:

```
# newuser billp
```

b. Specifying a C shell:

```
# newuser billp /bin/csh
```

c. Changing all possible default values:

```
# newuser billp /bin/csh 200 /usr3
```

Figure C.3 Listing of the **newuser** shell script.

```
 1  :
 2  # @(#) newuser   Add a new user account
 3  # Author: Tom Barrett
 4  SHL=/bin/sh          # Default login shell - sh, csh, ksh
 5  GID=100              # Default group ID for user accts.
 6  USER_PARENT=/usr2    # Parent directory for user accts.
```

```
 7  MINUID=100            # Starting UID for user accts.
 8
 9  # check for valid usage - account name is required
10  #
11  if [ $# -lt 1 -o $# -gt 4 ]; then
12      echo "Usage: $0 accountname [ shellpath [ GID [ homeparent ] ] ]"
13      exit 101
14  fi
15  # Check to see if account already exists:
16  #
17  USER=$1
18  nm=`awk -F: ' $1 == '\"$USER\" /etc/passwd`
19  if [ -n "$nm" ]; then
20      echo User $USER already in passwd file
21      exit 102
22  fi
23  # Determine login shell and do simple validity check:
24  #
25  if [ $# -gt 1 ]; then
26      SHL=$2
27      if [ ! -x $SHL ]; then
28          echo "$SHL is not an executable file"
29          exit 103
30      fi
31  fi
32  # Determine group and check validity:
33  #
34  if [ $# -gt 2 ]; then
35      GID=$3
36      grpck=`awk -F: ' $3 == '\"$GID\" /etc/group`
37      if [ -z "$grpck" ]; then
38          echo "Invalid group: $GID"
39          exit 104
40      fi
41  fi
42  # Determine parent of home directory:
43  #
44  if [ $# -gt 3 ]; then
45      USER_PARENT=$4
46  fi
47  # set home directory:
48  #
49  HOMEDIR=${USER_PARENT}/${USER}
50  # Now get the next available user id, where UID >= $MINUID
51  #
52  if [ -n "`awk -F\: '{print $3}' /etc/passwd | fgrep $MINUID`" ];then
53      UID=`sort -nt: +2 -3 /etc/passwd | awk -F\: \
54          'BEGIN{last=0}\
```

```
55                 ($3!=last+1)&&(last>='$MINUID'){print last+1;exit}\
56                 {last=$3}\
57                 END {print last + 1}''
58  else
59      UID=$MINUID
60  fi
61  # Update the passwd file:
62  #
63  if mkdir /etc/ptmp; then
64      echo "$USER::$UID:$GID::$HOMEDIR:$SHL" >> /etc/passwd
65      rmdir /etc/ptmp
66  else
67      echo "Password file busy, try again later"
68      exit 105
69  fi
70  # Install a password:
71  #
72  passwd $USER
73  # If the home directory does not exist, make it now
74  #
75  if [ ! -d $HOMEDIR ]; then
76      mkdir $HOMEDIR
77  fi
78  # Install appropriate shell start-up files and
79  # change ownership of directory and files:
80  #
81  if [ $SHL = /usr/ucb/csh ]; then
82      cp /usr/lib/.login /usr/lib/.cshrc $HOMEDIR
83      chown $USER $HOMEDIR/.login $HOMEDIR/.cshrc
84      chgrp $GID  $HOMEDIR/.login $HOMEDIR/.cshrc
85  elif [ $SHL = /bin/sh ]; then
86      cp /usr/lib/.profile $HOMEDIR
87      chown $USER $HOMEDIR/.profile
88      chgrp $GID  $HOMEDIR/.profile
89  fi
90  chown $USER $HOMEDIR
91  chgrp $GID   $HOMEDIR
92  #
93  echo User $USER is set up - home directory = $HOMEDIR
94  exit 0
```

Note: This shell script first appeared in the December 1986 issue of UNIXWORLD magazine on page 82.

D

Determining the Number

of Floppies

You'll need to determine the allocated disk space and number of files for the file system(s) to be backed up. Then you'll need to find out the capacity of your floppies. A simple division plus a "fudge factor" should give you a good estimate for the required number of floppies.

For the particular example discussed in this appendix, we ascertain the number of floppies required to back up the root file system. You'll need to unmount any other file systems before taking the measurements discussed below.

Determining Allocated Disk Space

To determine the number of allocated blocks on your working disk, you can use one of three programs: **du**, **df**, or **fsck**. Each has its advantages and disadvantages.

Using du.   The **du** (disk usage) utility is the simplest to use. Figure D.1 shows that all you need to type is eight keystrokes. However, this command is slow because it must traverse the directory tree.

Figure D.1 Determining allocated disk space with **du**.

```
# umount /dev/dsk/1s0
# umount /dev/dsk/2s0
# du -s /
34848
# □
```

First, we had to unmount other file systems before running **du** so that only the root file system would be counted. Otherwise, **du** will overestimate the allocated disk space since it will descend the directories of those mounted file systems.

Using df. If you're willing to resurrect your grade school arithmetic in exchange for some speed, use the faster alternative—the **df** (disk free) utility with the total (−**t**) option. Part a of Figure D.2 shows the output we obtained for our sample system after unmounting all other file systems.

When you have the total number of blocks and the free block count, you need to calculate the number of allocated data blocks. However, it's more than one simple subtraction since you also need to account for the blocks occupied by inodes. Part b of Figure D.2 shows these computations for the data obtained in part a.

Figure D.2 Determining allocated disk space with **df**.

a. Running **df** -t:

```
# df -t
/          (/dev/dsk/0s0):    1574 blocks    1056 i-nodes
                    total:   37000 blocks    4624 i-nodes
 # □
```

b. Computing the allocated block count:

```
4624 inodes/8 inodes per 512-byte block = 578 blocks for inodes

37000      total blocks
  578      inode blocks
-----
36422      available data blocks
 1574      free data blocks
-----
34848      allocated data blocks
```

Using fsck. The **fsck** (file system check) program reports the number of allocated blocks before it exits. Of course, if you haven't run **fsck** recently, you won't have an accurate value for this information.

You'll want to run **fsck** using the −**n** (no write) option so that no changes will be made to any file system. This way, you can run the check on mounted file systems, which is necessary since the root file system is always mounted. Also, **fsck** takes some time to complete as, like **du**, it must traverse the file system. However, you can get the summary statistics more quickly if you run a quick check using the −**f** (fast) option, which runs only the Phase 1 and 5 checks. Figure D.3 provides an example of **fsck** run on the root file system.

Figure D.3 The **fsck** program reports the number of allocated blocks.

```
# fsck -n -f /dev/dsk/0s0

/dev/rdsk/0s0 (NO WRITE)

File System: root Volume: 0s0

** Phase 1 - Check Blocks and Sizes
** Phase 5 - Check Free List

3881 files 34848 blocks 1574 free
# □
```

The report at the end of the output shows the number of allocated files, number of blocks used by those files, and the number of free blocks for the file system that was checked.

All three methods gave the same result—34,848 512-byte data blocks being used by files, which corresponds to 17,842,176 characters (just under 17.02 megabytes). The numbers for the allocated data blocks obtained by any method—running **du** −**s**, **df** −**t**, or **fsck** −**f** −**n** should agree. If not, your file system may be corrupted or there may be a bug in one or more of these utilities. Since the former is more likely, run the **fsck** program to repair the file system(s).

Determining the Capacity of Your Floppy Diskette

Next determine the capacity of your floppy diskette either from your system documentation or experimentally. You can use the **dd** command on many systems to ascertain the capacity. Figure D.4 shows the result we obtained on one of our systems.

Figure D.4 Determining floppy diskette capacity with **dd**.

```
# dd if=/dev/flpa of=/dev/null
360+0 records in
360+0 records out
# □
```

Here, a "record" is 1 kilobyte since that's the block size of the file system. So we can write up to 360 1-kilobyte or 720 512-byte blocks on a floppy diskette. We'll use this figure in our calculations. Now to determine the number of floppies needed, divide the disk space to be backed up by the capacity of the floppy, which yields for our example 34,848/720 = 48.4, or 49 floppies after rounding up. That's a lot of floppies. But luckily you don't need to do a full backup that often.

Determining the Number of Files

You'll actually need more than 49 floppies. Why? As mentioned in the simple calculation in Chapter 3, files archived by **tar** are preceded by a 512-byte header, which occupies additional space on the diskette. So let's determine how many ordinary files we need to back up. Figure D.5 shows how to do this using the UNIX **find** command.

Figure D.5 Determining the total number of ordinary files on your system.

```
# find / -type f -print | wc -l
3392
# □
```

Note that this number is smaller than the value reported by **fsck** because **fsck** also counts directories, device files, and FIFOs. The **tar** command doesn't back up those file types.

Computing the Required Number of Floppies

Here are the steps to arrive at the final count:

1. Since each file on a **tar** "tape" requires an overhead of one 512-byte block we'll need at least an extra five diskettes, because $3392/720 = 4.7$.

2. We may need more because **tar** also pads the file out to an even block boundary. So, as a worst case, we would need an additional 3392 blocks or another 4.7 diskettes.

3. If the file isn't split across the diskette boundary you'll need even more diskettes as there will be some wasted space. The average file is $34848 / 3392 = 10.3$ or just over 10 blocks in size. So you'll waste at least 10 blocks per diskette. So for 59 diskettes that's another 590 blocks or another diskette worth.

4. So you should format at least 60 diskettes for backing up the file system discussed in this appendix. At this point you may decide to go ahead and purchase a tape drive.

E

tar, cpio Options, and the tarskip Program

This appendix tabulates the many options and arguments recognized by the **tar** and **cpio** backup utilities. Also, we list the **tarskip** C program described in Chapter 3.

tar Command Line Elements

The general format for the command line used for invoking the **tar** command is shown in Figure E.1.

Figure E.1 General syntax for **tar** command.

tar *key*[*option...*] [*file...*]

The *key* argument, which specifies the operation that **tar** is to do, is required. One or more modifying *option* arguments may be used as well. Any files and directory arguments are listed last on the command line as shown.

Table E.1 lists the key options recognized by the **tar** command.

Table E.2 discusses many of the modifying options recognized by the **tar** command. Note that when an option like **f** or **b** requires an argument, the option arguments are listed after the *key* and other *options* in the same order as the option letter.

TABLE E.1 KEYS RECOGNIZED BY THE **tar** COMMAND

c	Create a new tape—start writing a new backup tape from the beginning. Previous contents are overwritten.
u	Update a tape—add the named *files* to the backup tape if they aren't already present or if they've been modified since they were last written.
r	Append *files* onto the end of the backup tape. Previous contents are not affected.
x	Extract the tape—recover the named *files* from the backup tape. If *file* names a directory, all files and subdirectories of that directory are retrieved. If no *file* argument is given, *all* files are extracted from the backup tape. Any files on your working disk with the same pathname as those on the backup tape will be overwritten.
t	Table of contents—lists the pathnames of all files on the backup tape.

For instance, in **tar cvfb /dev/rflpa 20 .** the **/dev/rflpa** argument belongs to the **f** option and **20** to the **b** option. Any file or directory names are listed last, such as the dot (.) in this example.

TABLE E.2 OPTIONS RECOGNIZED BY THE **tar** COMMAND

f	*devicename*. Use the backup device named *devicename*. If *devicename* is a dash (−), **tar** reads from its standard input file or writes to its standard output as determined by the *key* argument. If this argument is omitted, **tar** attempts to use its default device, usually **/dev/mt0** (before System V Release 2) or **/dev/mt/0m** (System V Release 2 and later versions of AT&T UNIX systems).
ns	Use tape drive number *n*, which is numbered from **0** through **7**, at density *s*, which can be l (low density—800 bpi), **m** (medium density—1600 bpi), or **h** (high density—6250 bpi). The default *ns* combination is **0m** as seen in the default device name, **/dev/mt/0m**, mentioned in the last paragraph.
v	Work verbosely—provide information about each file as it is processed. A function letter that specifies the operation and the pathname of each file is given. When used with the **t** key, this option displays additional information about each file over and above the pathname.
w	Work interactively—**tar** displays the action to be taken followed by the filename and waits for your response. Type a word beginning with **y** to process the file; any other input skips taking action on the named file. You will be queried this way about all the files specified by the command line.
b	*size*. Use block size *size* for reading from and writing to the backup device. The default size is **1** (one) 512-byte block and **20** is the maximum block size. You should only use this option with the "raw" (character) backup device. The block size is determined automatically by **tar** when reading tapes (using the **x** or **t** key letters).
l	Use this option to tell **tar** to complain if it can't resolve all the links to a file being processed. Without this option **tar** doesn't report such problems.
m	Causes **tar** to change the modification time in the extracted file to be the time of extraction; otherwise, it isn't changed.
o	Causes **tar** to reset the user- and group-ID of the extracted file to the user running **tar**; otherwise, they aren't changed.

cpio Command Line Elements

Table E.3 tabulates the options recognized by the System V Release 2 and 3 versions of **cpio**. The asterisk (*) denotes options unique to Release 3 of System V.

TABLE E.3 OPTIONS RECOGNIZED BY THE SYSTEM V **cpio** COMMAND

6	Use this option for copy in of a UNIX Version 6-format file.
a	Don't change the access time of the source file when archiving it. Normally, the access time is updated since you're reading the source file.
B	Transfer data in 5120-byte records instead of the 512-byte records (the default). You should specify the "raw" character backup device with this option. The -cpio action argument of **find** uses this larger record size by default.
b	Swap both bytes and half words when copying in an archive.
Cbsz*	Transfer data in bsz bytes to the record. Only meaningful when data is directed to or from a character special device.
c	Write header information in ASCII format for portability.
d	Create directories as needed to store files taken off the archive or when using pass mode.
f	The "false" option means to copy in all files *except* those in the *pattern* argument to **cpio**. Normally, only those files matching the *pattern* argument are restored.
I$file$*	Use *file* as input. If *file* is a character special device, when first medium has been read replace the medium and type RETURN to continue with new medium. Use only with the −i option.
k*	Ignore errors and seek to files with good headers and read them. Use only with the −i option.
l	Link files copied with pass mode instead of copying them. You can't create links across file systems only within them. Useful when moving directory hierarchies when you can't use the **mvdir** command.
m	Retain previous modification time when restoring a file. However, you can't retain the modification time for directories.
Mmsg*	Define a message, *msg*, to use as a prompt when switching media. Can use %**d** to display sequence number of next medium in a series.
O$file$*	Use *file* as output. If *file* is a character special device, when first medium is full replace the medium and type RETURN to continue with new medium. Use only with the −o option.
r	Rename files after you restore them. You will be prompted with a line **Rename** < *filename* >, where *filename* is the name of the file on the archive. Type a new file name to complete the rename or RETURN to skip the rename for the file you were prompted for.
s	Swap bytes when copying in an archive.
S	Swap half words when copying in an archive.
t	Print a table of contents instead of restoring files in copy in mode. Use with the **v** option to give a "long" listing (analogous to a **ls** −**l** listing).
u	Unconditionally copy a file. Without this option newer files will not be replaced with older files.
v	Report the name of a file as it is processed. Use this option when listing the table of contents to get a more informative "long" listing.
V*	Print a dot (.) for each file encountered.

The tarskip Program Listing

This program can ignore read errors when extracting backup tapes created by **tar**. It sends the contents of the tape to its standard output file.

Figure E.2 Listing of the **tarskip.c** program.

```
1    #include <stdio.h>    /* Use standard I/O library */
2    #include <fcntl.h>    /* Open file control */
3    #include <string.h>   /* String manipulations */
4    #define TARBLKSZ 512 /* Block size on tar disk/tape */
5    #define STDOUT   1    /* Standard output file descriptor */
6    #define FALSE    0    /* Boolean false */
7    #define TRUE     1    /* Boolean true */
8
9    /* Global variables: */
10   char fd;     /* file descriptor for tar device file */
11   char buf[TARBLKSZ]; /* buffer for "tar blocks". */
12   /* Substitute your device name in the next line */
13   char *tardev = "/dev/flpa";
14
15   main(argc, argv)
16   int argc; char **argv;
17   {
18       int c, match;
19       char *pathname;
20       void getblk();
21       match = FALSE; /* Initialize to zero */
22
23       /* Process command line arguments */
24       if (argc == 1 || argc > 3) { /* Correct number of args? */
25           fprintf(stderr, "Usage: tarskip pathname [tardevice]\n");
26           exit(1);
27       }
28       pathname = argv[1]; /* The pattern string to search for */
29       if (argc == 3)
30           tardev = argv[2]; /* Use device different from default */
31       if ((fd = open(tardev, O_RDONLY)) < 0) { /* Open for reading */
32           fprintf(stderr, "tarskip: Can't open %s\n", tardev);
33           exit(2);
34       }
35
36       /* Find block containing desired pathname */
37       do {
38           getblk(tardev);
39           match = strncmp(pathname, buf, strlen(pathname));
```

```
40        } while (match);
41
42        /* Then read and process disk blocks "forever" */
43        while (TRUE)
44        {
45            write(STDOUT, buf, sizeof(buf));
46            getblk(tardev);
47        }
48    }
49
50
51    void
52    getblk(device) /* Read the next block into buffer */
53    char *device; /* The tar disk/tape device name */
54    {
55        int c, done, n;
56    begin:
57        n = (read(fd, buf, sizeof(buf))); /* Read a block */
58        if (n == 0) { /* End of tape */
59            done = query("\nEnd of disk/tape, read another (y/n)? ");
60            if (!done) { /* Not done */
61                close(fd); /* Close previous device */
62                fprintf(stderr, "Insert next disk/tape ");
63                fprintf(stderr, "and press RETURN when ready\n");
64                while ((c = getchar()) != '\n' && c != EOF)
65                    ; /* wait for RETURN */
66                if ((fd = open(device, O_RDONLY)) < 0) { /* Open */
67                    fprintf(stderr, "tarskip: Can't open %s\n", device);
68                    exit(2);
69                }
70                goto begin; /* Get first block from next disk/tape */
71            } else /* Done */
72                exit(0);
73        } else if (n < 0) { /* Tape read error */
74            done = query("\nRead error, ignore (y/n)? ");
75            if (done) {
76                close(fd);
77                fprintf(stderr, "Goodbye...\n");
78                exit(2);
79            }
80        }
81    }
82
83    query(msg) /* Display message and prompt for continuance */
84    char *msg;
```

```
85    {
86         int  c, c2;
87
88         fprintf(stderr, "%s", msg);
89         c = c2 = getchar();
90         while (c2 != '\n' && c2 != EOF)
91              c2 = getchar(); /* Ignore remaining input */
92         if (c == 'y') /* First character was a "y" */
93              return(0); /* Not done */
94         else
95              return(1); /* Done */
96    }
```

Note: This program first appeared in Volume II, Issue No. 8 of UNIXWORLD magazine on page 93.

F

Using fsdb

fsdb stands for file system debugger. Debuggers are programming tools for solving problems (removing bugs). Debuggers require a certain degree of sophistication on the part of the user, and **fsdb** is no exception. **fsdb** allows you to edit file systems without the encumbrance of the operating system. Instead, everything you do is your responsibility. If you do it wrong, **fsdb** won't prevent it. In fact, it may assist you.

You will find **fsdb** only on System V releases, not XENIX or BSD. (Differences between the System V file system structure and the Fast File System and variable-length filenames in BSD make the current version of **fsdb** nonportable to 4.x Berkeley environments.)

You might think that a program as potentially powerful as **fsdb** would have a lot of uses. Actually, most people use it for only one thing—repairing filenames. Beyond changing of filenames, doing anything else with **fsdb** is hazardous. To minimize the dangers, you can do two things. First, practice using **fsdb** on a spare partition or with a file system on a floppy disk. Second, always run **fsck** on a file system after using **fsdb**. **fsck** will probably uncover and possibly repair any damage that you inadvertently cause.

Besides changing filenames, we will show you how to display an inode, change its mode, list directory entries, and list the superblock. If you are an experienced programmer, you can create an annotated superblock listing for your system, or confirm that the notations that we provide accurately reflect your superblock's structure. With this information, you can manage some desperate feats if they ever become necessary.

Invoking fsdb

You start up **fsdb** with the name of a file system partition as the only argument. You can use either the block or the character device name; **fsdb** works equally well with either special device. After invoking **fsdb**, you will get a report based on the contents of the superblock in this partition.

Figure F.1 Invoking **fsdb**.

```
# fsdb /dev/dsk/c0d1s2
68000 UNIX T/S assembly
/dev/dsk/c0d1s2(test): 1K byte Block File System
FSIZE = 10943, ISIZE = 2720
□
```

When **fsdb** is ready, it doesn't present a prompt. It's not user friendly; it's user indifferent. Like **fsck**, you must never operate on mounted file systems with **fsdb**. Unlike **fsck**, **fsdb** does not check to see if a block device contains a mounted file system. The assumption is that you know what you are doing.

   fsdb does perform simple bounds checking, just as **fsck** does. The size of the file system (FSIZE) and the inode region (ISIZE) is checked by examining the superblock and is reported after **fsdb** has been started. If the inode region is larger than the file system size, something is seriously wrong with the superblock. You can force **fsdb** to override the values for these sizes by entering **O** (letter O) followed by a RETURN.

Commands and Addresses

fsdb recognizes command characters or symbols and addresses. We will demonstrate only a few of these command characters and symbols. More commands are available, and we suggest that you read the manual pages for **fsdb** and experiment after you have mastered some of the basics described here.

   fsdb is really a bother in terms of understanding. For instance, the letters b, d, and i can be used in two different ways (each) depending on where in the command they appear. Commands are always terminated by a return or newline. The dot (.) character, which appears in all the examples in the documentation, is there for appearances only. You can leave it out.

   Commands operate on the information at an address. This address may be specified at the beginning of the command, or the current address will be used. The current address is the address after the completion of the last command. If a block is printed, the current address is the beginning of the next block. Maybe.

   fsdb also remembers the address of the current inode set by using the **i** command. The **i** command also displays the inode, unless it is followed by another command character that directs **fsdb** to display something else. See, isn't this confusing?

One nice thing about **fsdb** is that it doesn't write anything to the file system unless you use the " = " (equal sign) operator. But as soon as you do, whatever you changed gets written to the file system immediately, with no questions asked and no undo. So be careful!

Displaying an Inode

Once you have started **fsdb**, displaying an inode is trivial. Simply enter the number of the inode that you want to display, follow it with the letter **i** and a RETURN.

Figure F.2 Displaying a root inode.

```
2i
i#:      2   md: d---rwxr-xr-x   ln:    21   uid:    73   gid:    1   sz:        352
a0:    150   a1:      0   a2:      0   a3:      0   a4:      0   a5:      0   a6:      0
a7:      0   a8:      0   a9:      0   a10:     0   a11:     0   a12:     0
at: Wed Dec   2 09:14:04 1987
mt: Thu Oct   8 14:39:41 1987
ct: Thu Oct   8 14:39:41 1987
□
```

fsdb's inode display shows you all the information contained in the inode. You may have noticed that this display is very similar to the one used in Figure 4.6 (in Chapter 4). Another thing about the display are the two- or three-character abbreviations that label each item. These abbreviations are recognized by **fsdb** and can be used to change the labeled item in the current inode. The one exception is the label **ct**, short for inode change time. Altering the change time is not allowed by **fsdb** because it is a security breach. However, you can change anything else in the inode without **fsdb** updating the inode change time. (So much for security. **fsdb** is a good reason for correctly setting your file systems' access permissions.)

One of the things mentioned in the **fsck** section was that you can use **fsdb** to change the mode of the root directory to be of type directory. Changing the mode to be type directory is a desperate measure, because other things are probably corrupt in the root inode as well. However, it is also a good example of how to use the inode abbreviations, and it might help you sometime.

Figure F.3 Changing the mode of an inode to type directory.

```
md=040755
004100: 040755 (16877)
```

Notice the zero after the equal sign in our command. Starting a number with a zero tells **fsdb** to interpret the number as octal, which is exactly what you want when you are setting the mode and permissions. The last three digits are the octal equivalent of the file's permissions, exactly as used with the **chmod** utility. The fourth digit (counting from the right) is for the set-user-id, set-group-id, and sticky bit. To set an inode's mode, you must supply at least six octal digits. Ordinary files require seven digits. Table F.1 shows the five legal inode types.

TABLE F.1 FIVE LEGAL SYSTEM V INODE MODES

Mode	Inode Type
0100XXX	ordinary files
0060XXX	block special files
0040XXX	directories
0020XXX	character special files
0010XXX	named pipes (fifo's)

When changing an inode's mode, pick the correct type from Table F.1 and follow it by four digits, indicating the file's access permissions. Most often, the fourth digit (from the right) will be zero. After you have made the change, redisplay the inode by using the **i** command. If changing the mode is all you want to do, then quit by entering **q**. The change has already been written out to disk.

Displaying Directory Entries

Displaying directory entries is easy, and is also the necessary before changing directory entries. First, discover the inode number of the directory that you wish to display. This is best done by using the **ls** −**id** command while the file system is mounted (before you invoke **fsdb**). Finding a particular directory by descending the directory hierarchy from within **fsdb** is no fun. Figure F.4 shows the inode number-filename pair for the **Tmp** directory.

Figure F.4 Finding the inode number of the **/mnt/Tmp** directory.

```
# ls -id /mnt/Tmp
    6 /mnt/Tmp
# □
```

Then, unmount the file system, start up **fsdb**, and set the inode number of the directory that you want to display by using the **i** command. The **fd** command will display the first block of this inode formatted as directory entries. Be prepared to hit control-S immediately, or the display will quickly scroll off your screen. Note that you can combine the **i** and **fd** commands by using N**ifd**, where N is the inode number.

Figure F.5 Displaying the first block of an inode formatted as a directory.

```
6ifd
d0:      6   .
d1:      2   .   .
d2:     16   c   h   e   c   k   l   i   s   t
d3:     22   l   i   s   t   0   9   1   6   .   n
d4:     35   t   e   m   p
d5:      0
d6:      0
...
d63:      0
□
```

If the directory inode you are examining has a second block of directory entries (the **a1** field of the inode display has a nonzero entry), you can display the second block by using **a1bp0d**, as suggested by the manual. Or you can use the shorthand form **f1d** to view the second block, **f2d** to see the third block, and so on. If you attempt to go past the end of the directory, **fsdb** will tell you that you've tried to display a "nonexistent block."

Changing Directory Entries

The **fsdb** utility is probably used most for changing directory entries. However, before you can change a single directory entry, you must display the directory entries using the commands given in the preceding section. Once you have located the block with the directory entry you desire to change, **fsdb** provides you with two abbreviations that make the change easy. The first is the label at the beginning of the entry, such as **d0** or **d10**. Think of this label as being *directory entry 0* or *directory entry ten*. The second abbreviation is **nm**, which stands for the *name* part of the directory entry.

The **d**N label allows you to change the inode number associated with an entry. An inode number of zero means that this directory entry has been removed. To change the filename, you combine the directory entry label with **nm** and surround the name with quote marks. Although the double quotes are "optional," we have found it good practice to make a habit of using them. **fsdb** will assume that you are inserting a string if it starts with a letter of the alphabet. But if the name begins with or contains a dot (.), you must use double quotes. So, rather than forget, always use the quotes.

Figure F.6 Changing names or the associated inode number.

```
6ifd
d0:      6   .
d1:      2   .   .
d2:     13   c   h   e   c   k   l   i   s   t
```

```
  . . .
d63:      0
d2=0
d2:       0   c   h   e   c   k   l   i   s   t
d2=13
d2:      13   c   h   e   c   k   l   i   s   t
d2nm="newname"
d2:      13   n   e   w   n   a   m   e
□
```

The main reason for changing a name with **fsdb** is that somehow the filename has gotten a strange or illegal character in it. There are tricks for removing or changing filenames with strange characters in them, but only **fsdb** can easily change a filename containing a slash (/). The slash is a special character to the kernel. It can't be quoted or escaped, and using **fsdb** is the easiest way to change a name containing a slash.

To change a directory entry in the second block of an inode, you can use **fld** to display this block as directory entries, and then use the same abbreviations you used when working with the first block, as shown in Figure F.6. Since **fsdb** "remembers" that you are working with the second block, it will change the correct entry.

Remember that if you set the inode number in a directory entry to zero, you have removed the name. When you run **fsck** later, you can clear the inode if this name was the only link to the inode.

Displaying the Superblock

It's easy to display the superblock using **fsdb** by using the command **512p0e** (start at the 512th byte and print to the end of the block in decimal). But there's a catch. **fsdb** doesn't provide nice labels for any of the parts in the superblock. What you see is a listing of numbers.

The superblock begins at the 512th byte in any file system. Some System V versions maintain a duplicate (shadow) of the superblock starting at the 1024th byte. This shadow version won't be used by the kernel if the real superblock is damaged. But you could use **fsdb** to copy parts of the shadowed superblock and repair the real superblock. By copying only seven values, you can patch up a superblock enough so that **fsck** can finish the repair job. You can also get the values that you need from your logbook if you don't have a shadow superblock.

Figure F.7 Displaying the superblock.

```
# fsdb /dev/dsk/0s8
/dev/dsk/0s8(tmp): 1K byte Block File System
FSIZE = 4080, ISIZE = 1008
4080 1024-byte blocks; 8160 512-byte blocks
512p0e
```

0001000:	65	0	4080	45	0	357	0	401
0001020:	0	355	0	336	0	405	0	384
0001040:	0	99	0	139	0	365	0	364
0001060:	0	120	0	229	0	217	0	359
0001100:	0	370	0	318	0	379	0	268
0001120:	0	267	0	266	0	265	0	261
0001140:	0	258	0	257	0	256	0	512
0001160:	0	511	0	152	0	70	0	161
0001200:	0	171	0	153	0	128	0	121
0001220:	0	66	0	500	0	125	0	72
0001240:	0	505	0	499	0	76	0	114
0001260:	0	109	0	148	0	498	0	497
0001300:	0	506	0	160	0	126	0	501
0001320:	0	5	6	100	99	98	97	96
0001340:	95	94	93	92	91	90	89	88
0001360:	87	86	85	84	83	82	81	80
0001400:	79	78	77	76	75	74	73	72
0001420:	71	70	69	68	67	66	65	64
0001440:	63	62	61	60	59	58	57	56
0001460:	55	54	53	52	51	50	49	48
0001500:	47	46	45	44	43	42	41	40
0001520:	39	38	37	36	35	34	33	32
0001540:	31	30	29	28	27	26	25	24
0001560:	23	22	21	20	19	18	17	16
0001600:	15	14	13	12	11	10	9	8
0001620:	7	4	3	4	3	0	0	8667
0001640:	5695	2	170	0	0	0	3944	1004
0001660:	28020	112	0	29488	56	0	0	0
*
0001760:	0	0	-10214	24178	-744	32288	0	2

□

The command **1024p0e** displays the shadow superblock. As this is an "undocumented feature," you can't count on it being there. The way to check is to look for the magic number. The magic number, actually displayed as two numbers, is designed to identify the superblock uniquely. Given that the odds that the magic number will appear in this location randomly are only one in about 4,295,000,000, you can believe you are looking at the superblock when you see the magic number. Figure F.8 shows an "annotated" superblock with the magic number (as two decimal words) in the last row.

Figure F.8 An annotated superblock from a computer using a Motorola 68020.

	Inode Size	File Sys Size	Free Count	Free blk 0	Free blk 1
0001000:	65	0	4080	45	0	357	0	401
	Free blk 2		Free blk 3		Free blk 4		Free blk 5

```
0001020:        0       355       0       336       0       405       0       384
              Free blk 6        Free blk 7       Free blk 8       Free blk 9
0001040:        0        99       0       139       0       365       0       364
  . . .
              Free blk 46       Free blk 47      Free blk 48      Free blk 49
0001300:        0       506       0       160       0       126       0       501
          Inode Count Inode 0 Inode 1 Inode 2 Inode 3 Inode 4 Inode 5 Inode 6
0001320:        0         5       6       100      99        98      97        96
          Inode 7     8         9        10      11        12      13        14
0001340:       95        94      93        92      91        90      89        88
  . . .
          Inode 87    88        89        90      91        92      93        94
0001600:       15        14      13        12      11        10       9         8
          Inode 95    96        97        98      99                  Date of -
0001620:        7         4       3         4       3         0       0      8667
         Last Sync Blks skip Blk/cyl                   Blocks Free Inodes Free
0001640:     5695         2     170         0       0         0    3944      1004
           File System Name              Volume Name
0001660:    28020       112       0     29488      56         0       0         0
*
                                         Magic Number   File Sys Type
0001760:        0         0   -10214     24178    -744     32288       0         2
```

The reason that Figure F.7 may not correspond exactly to your superblock is that the way machines store information in memory may differ form one processor to another. The example shown here was taken from. a computer with a Motorola 68020 processor. The most common difference between different processors is that the word ordering will be different. For example, an Intel 80286 stores the low word before the high word, the opposite of what is shown in the example for the 68020. The structure for the superblock in the header file **/usr/include/sys/filsys.h** can help programmers in illustrating superblocks for their systems.

Seven Critical Superblock Values

The superblock, in its capacity of master keeper of file system statistics, actually contains two types of information—fixed and changing. The fixed information sets the size of the file system and a number of other things. These fixed values represent six of the seven critical values. The changing information has to do with the free block and free inode lists, which change while the file system is in use. **fsck** rebuilds the free block list whenever it finds a problem with it. The kernel recreates a free inode list whenever the list within the superblock is empty. The seventh critical value is the inode count, which, if set to zero, tells the kernel to rebuild the superblock's free inode list before using it.

The seven critical values are shown in Table F.2. You may copy the values for a particular file system from the shadow superblock or get these values from your system's logbook. The values that you need were the ones used when this file system was created using **mkfs**. The file system size, blocks to skip, and blocks per cylinder (the soft interleave) come directly from the arguments to **mkfs**. The inode size in blocks requires a little calculation.

The inode size in blocks is the block address of the first data block after the inodes. The inodes start after the first two blocks, and there are 16 inodes per 1024-byte block (eight if you are using an old-style 512-byte file system). So take the number of inodes created by **mkfs**, divide this by 16, and add 2, as shown

$$(\text{number of inodes} / 16) + 2 = \text{size of inodes for superblock}$$

If you don't have the number of inodes in this file system recorded, you can sequentially display each block of this file system (using *N*p0o) until you reach a series of blocks that are filled with zeros. These are blocks of unallocated inodes. You want to find the last block of unallocated inodes by locating the first block of data that follows the inode list. The first data block address is the size of the inodes in the superblock. (This method won't work if all the inodes in this file system are allocated.)

TABLE F.2 SEVEN CRITICAL SUPERBLOCK VALUES. ADDRESSES ARE SHOWN IN OCTAL, THE SAME WAY THAT **fsdb** DISPLAYS THEM

Address (octal)	Value (decimal)
001000	(inode size in blocks)
001002D	(file system size in blocks)
001320	0 (next free inode counter)
001642	(number of blocks to skip)
001644	(blocks per cylinder)
001770D	037506077040 (magic number)
001774D	2 (file system type for 1K file systems)

Figure F.9 Example values for a file system that was 4080 blocks long when created, with 1008 inodes, and with 2 blocks to skip and 170 blocks per cylinder.

```
001000=65
001002D=4080
001320=0
001642=2
001644=170
001770D=037506077040
001774D=2
```

After you fill in these seven values using **fsdb** (using the correct values for your file system, not our sample values), run **fsck** on this file system. There will be reports of "Bad counts" in the superblock, and the free list will be salvaged. Then you can mount this file system and try it out.

Summary

fsdb seems like it was designed to be intimidating. Many of the commands could easily win the "Cryptic Command of the Month" on any system. Yet, sometimes using **fsdb** is the only way to fix something, and it's nice that it exists.

There are other tricks you can perform with **fsdb**. We once created a root directory and a **lost+found** directory so that the files on a damaged partition could be recovered. Since the superblock was undamaged, we were able to get two free blocks and a free inode by examining the superblock. The key to using the free block and inode lists is that the count is decremented before it is used to index into the lists. Unfortunately, a full explanation of creating directories with **fsdb** is so esoteric that we don't want to include it here. If you ever need it, write or send e-mail to us.

G

Two Versions of the strings Program

If you've ever tried to display a binary (or object code) file with **cat**, you know the effect—gibberish on the screen or even worse—codes sent to the screen that lock up your terminal. If you're lucky enough to have access to the Berkeley **strings** program, use it to display strings of printing characters in binary files. If not, you might want to enter and compile one of the two versions of the **strings** C programs that follow. The first version will work with versions of the UNIX system before System V Release 2. The second version was written to support COFF (Common Object File Format), which is used in System V Release 2 and later.

Here's how **strings** works. If four or more printing characters end with a newline or a null character, the character string is displayed. **strings** can be used as a filter (reading the standard input) or take filenames as arguments. **strings** is most useful for identifying binary files or displaying the error messages "hidden" in them.

Figure G.1 shows the version of **strings** written by Rik Farrow and published in the "Wizard's Grabbag" column in the September 1986 issue of UNIXWORLD magazine. If you don't have UniSoft's System V, you may have to change the code contained within the conditional compilation directives **#ifdef UniSoft-V** and **#endif**. Look at your include file **/usr/include/a.out.h** for the format of your particular "a.out" header. Even if you eliminate this code entirely, the program will still display the strings in an object file, but you'll get extraneous strings from the code (text) and symbol table regions as well.

Figure G.1 Listing of strings.c for non-COFF files.

```
1    #include <stdio.h>
2    #include <ctype.h>
3
4    #ifdef UniSoft-V
5    #include <a.out.h>
6    struct bhdr header;
7    #define MAGIC(x) (x==OMAGIC)||(x==FMAGIC)||(x==NMAGIC)||(x==IMAGIC)
8    #endif
9
10   main(argc, argv)
11   int argc; char *argv[];
12   {
13       int seen, in, n;
14       long limit = 0;        /* Search limit for a.out files */
15       char c, string[256];
16
17       if (argc > 2) {        /* Too many arguments */
18           fprintf(stderr,"Usage: strings [name]\n");
19           exit(1);
20       }
21       if (argc == 1)         /* No file argument, use standard input */
22           in = 0;
23       else                   /* Otherwise, open file for input */
24           if ((in = open(argv[1], 0)) == -1) {
25               fprintf(stderr,"string: can't open %s\n", argv[1]);
26               exit(2);
27           }
28   #ifdef UniSoft-V
29       if ((n = read(in, (char *) &header, sizeof(header))) < sizeof(header)) {
30           fprintf(stderr,"Can't read header. %d bytes read.\n", n);
31           exit(3);
32       }
33       if (MAGIC(header.fmagic)) {         /* If a.out file */
34           lseek(in, header.tsize, 1);     /* seek past end of text, and */
35           limit = header.dsize;           /* limit display to data area */
36       }
37       else
38           lseek(in, 0L, 0);               /* rewind file to beginning */
39   #endif
40       while ((n = read(in, &c, 1)) > 0 && --limit ) {
41           if (isprint(c))                 /* If c is printable */
42               string[seen++] = c;         /* add to string array. */
43           else {                          /* Otherwise, if array */
```

```
44              if (seen >= 4)            /* is at least four characters long */
45                  if (c == '\0' || c == '\n') { /* and c is null or newline */
46                      string[seen] = '\0';  /* add terminator so */
47                      printf("%s\n",string); /* can display string. */
48                  }
49              seen = 0;                     /* reset array index */
50          }
51      }
52  }
```

b. Compilation formula for pre-Release 2 System V UNIX version using the include file **/usr/include/a.out**:

```
$ cc -DUniSoft-V -o strings strings.c
```

The second version of **strings** was written for System V Release 2 and later UNIX system versions. The format of an executable (**a.out**) file was changed in SVR2, so that the first version of **strings** (Figure G.1) can't recognize the magic numbers for executable files to only print the initialized data sections. This second COFF **strings** program was written by Steve Cabito and originally appeared in the April 1987 installment of the "Wizard's Grabbag" column in UNIXWORLD magazine.

Figure G.2 COFF version of **strings**.

```
 1  #include <stdio.h>
 2  #include <ctype.h>
 3  #include <filehdr.h>
 4  #include <scnhdr.h>
 5  #include <ldfcn.h>
 6  #define USAGE fprintf(stderr,\
 7              "Usage: %s [-o] [-nw] file...\n",\
 8              argv[0]); exit(1)
 9  #define FALSE   0
10  #define TRUE    !FALSE
11
12  /* compile: cc -o strings strings.c -lld */
13
14  static char sccsid[] = "@(#) strings   Steve Cabito 9/86";
15
16  main(argc, argv)
17  int argc;
18  char *argv[];
19  {
20      extern char *optarg;
```

```
21        extern int optind;
22        char *malloc();
23        LDFILE *ldptr = NULL;   /* file header struct */
24        SCNHDR *shptr = (SCNHDR *) malloc(SCNHSZ);
25                                /* section header struct */
26        int
27        c,                  /* command line option */
28        seen,               /* index for string array */
29        n,                  /* number of characters read */
30        offset = FALSE,     /* no offset displayed */
31        width = 4;          /* default width is four */
32        char ch,            /* character read */
33        string[256];        /* storage for string */
34
35        while ((c = getopt(argc, argv, "on:")) != EOF)
36            switch (c) {
37                case 'o': /* prepend decimal offset */
38                    offset = TRUE;
39                    break;
40                case 'n': /* change default string width */
41                    width = atoi(optarg);
42                    break;
43                case '?': /* invalid option */
44                    USAGE;
45            }
46        if (optind >= argc) { /* must specify one or more */
47            USAGE;
48        }
49        for ( ; optind < argc; optind++) {
50            printf(":::::::::::::::\n%s\n:::::::::::::::\n",
51                    argv[optind]);
52            if ((ldptr = ldopen(argv[optind], NULL)) == NULL) {
53                fprintf(stderr, "%s: can't open %s\n",
54                        argv[0], argv[optind]);
55                continue;
56            }
57            if (ldnshread(ldptr, _DATA, shptr) == FAILURE) {
58                fprintf(stderr, "%s: no .data section header\n",
59                        argv[0]);
60                continue;
61            }
62            if (ldnsseek(ldptr, _DATA) == FAILURE) {
63                fprintf(stderr, "%s: no .data section\n",
64                        argv[0]);
65                continue;
66            }
67            while ((n = FREAD(&ch, 1, 1, ldptr)) > 0 &&
```

```
68                         --shptr->s_size) {
69                if (isprint(ch))
70                     string[seen++] = ch;
71                else {
72                  if (seen >= width)
73                    if (ch == '\0' || ch == '\n') {
74                        string[seen] = '\0';
75                        if (offset) /* decimal offset */
76                            printf("%06ld: ",
77                                 FTELL(ldptr) - seen - 1);
78                        printf("%s\n", string);
79                    }
80                  seen = 0;
81                }
82             }
83          ldclose(ldptr);
84        }
85      exit(0);
86  }
```

H

A Restricted Environment
for Guests

The approach to a restricted environment shown in this appendix was published originally in the November 1986 "Wizard's Grabbag" column of UNIXWORLD magazine. It was written by Pat Wood of Pipeline Associates and makes reference to a shell script for downloading files published October 1986 in the same column.

This restricted environment uses the "change root" feature to change the root (/) directory for the guest account to **/usr/restrict**. After someone logs into this account, all pathnames are resolved relative to **/usr/restrict**—their new root directory.

The user of this restricted guest account is effectively "bottled up" in a portion of the UNIX file system and simply cannot access files outside this portion. Because of this confinement, security for this account is tight, since this user may only access those files under the **/usr/restrict** directory tree. As you'll see, aside from the shell scripts used for uploading and downloading text files by the account user, only a few additional support files (mainly commands) are needed in this subfile system.

Part a of Figure H.1 shows a sample password file entry and part b a listing of the **restrict** program that uses the **chroot()** system call to put the user into the **/usr/restrict** subfile system. Parts c and d show the permissions of the various files and directories needed for the guest account. Parts e through j list various shell programs and procedures that are specific to the change root implementation.

The **restrict** program is run when **guest** logs in. First, it checks to make sure that it is actually being run by the **guest** account and not some other user. (Although this check isn't necessary in this particular instance, it is a good practice to make sure that the user performing the change root is authorized to do so. The reasoning behind this is too complex to go into here; however, if you're interested, you can refer to the section on change root in *UNIX System Security*, by Steve Kochan and Pat Wood.)

The **restrict** process then changes directory to **guest**'s home directory (**/usr/restrict/guest**) and changes the root directory to **/usr/restrict**. Finally, it runs the shell as **−sh**. This makes the shell assume it's a log-in shell, so it will execute **/etc/profile**. (It would also run **$HOME/.profile**, if the latter file existed.) Note that since **chroot()** is a privileged system call (only the superuser may use it successfully), **restrict** must be owned by **root** and have its set-user-ID permission turned on.

When the shell starts up, it executes **/etc/profile** in the subfile system (actually, **/usr/restrict/etc/profile** relative to the "real" root directory). This shell startup file sets up the environment and then runs the menu system program **.help**. From this point on, the menu system (also a simplistic bulletin-board) will run as described in the October 1986 "Wizard's Grabbag" column.

Note that the home directory for the restricted guest account shouldn't be on the root file system because some of the old Version 7 UNIX systems crash when the root file system fills up. So a malicious "guest" could keep uploading characters until the file system is full causing it to crash. However, the "auto-logout" feature (line 1 of **profile** file shown in Figure H.1e) will minimize this threat. For example, at most 72 kilobytes could be uploaded at 1200 baud in the 10-minute time span.

The **who** and **grep** commands in **/usr/restrict/bin** contain the one line **exit 1** to disable option 4 of the menu system—namely the ability to **write** to the administrator. Under this option, the exit status of the **who | grep "ˆroot "** pipeline is tested to see if **root** is logged in, and if so, **write root** is executed. **exit 1** causes this pipe to fail so that the menu system thinks **root** is never logged in. (For reasons too complex to go into here, **write** is difficult to implement in a change root environment, so the option is simply disabled.) You could also remove option 4 for a cleaner implementation.

Also, electronic mail won't work for the guest user since **mail** can't deliver a message outside the restricted subfile system. However, one can simulate the mail function by writing the message that the user types to a named pipe, such as **/usr/restrict/dev/MAIL**. A daemon (Figure H.1i) executing outside the restricted subfile system runs **rmail** on the messages coming through the pipe. You could invoke the daemon to run in the background from **/etc/rc** by either specifying the name of the shell script or by placing the "while" loop in a subshell by surrounding it with parentheses and placing an ampersand after the closing parenthesis. Note that when the user finishes the message and types control-D, the **cat** command in the **mail** shell script (Figure H.1h) finishes forcing an end-of-file condition on the other end of the named pipe, causing **rmail** in the daemon to send that message. (It is possible for two users sending mail from the guest log-in at the same time to have their mail jumbled together; however, this is highly unlikely.)

If you're on a system that doesn't support named pipes, you can deliver mail simply by storing the messages in a temporary area (i.e., replace **cat > /dev/MAIL** with **cat > /mail/$$**) and sending them periodically to **root** by executing another shell script (Figure H.1j) periodically with **cron**.

In all other respects, the restricted menu system will work as the one documented in the October 1986 column (except for the timeout feature) and users will not even know that they are running in a subfile system (except perhaps for those that have managed to crack the log-in shell script and get to the shell).

All files in **/usr/restrict/bin**, except for **mail**, **who**, and **grep** and the menu system shell programs, are simply copied from **/bin** and **/usr/bin**. (Newer versions of the Bourne shell may not require **test**, **echo**, and **pwd**, and some systems may not run **expr** from within **basename**. You also may have to use **pg** or **pr** instead of **more**, depending on your UNIX implementation.) Note that except for **/usr/restrict/tmp** and **/usr/restrict/dev/null**, all files or directories should not be writable by the group or others; and except for **/usr/restrict/guest** and **/usr/restrict/dev/MAIL**, all files and directories should be owned by **root**.

Figure H.1 Figure H.1: A secure version of the menu system.

a. A sample password file entry:

```
guest::200:100::/usr/restrict/guest:/usr/local/bin/restrict
```

b. Listing of **restrict.c**:

```
1    #define RESTRICT "/usr/restrict"
2    #define UID 200
3    #define HOME "/usr/restrict/guest"
4
5    #include <stdio.h>
6
7    main()
8    {
9        /* verify that user running this is 200 (guest) */
10       if (getuid () != UID) {
11           fprintf (stderr, "restrict: not valid user\n");
12           exit (1);
13       }
14       /* attempt to change directory to new HOME */
15       if(chdir (HOME) < 0) {
16           fprintf(stderr, "restrict: cannot chdir to %s\n", HOME);
17           exit (2);
```

```
18          }
19          /* attempt to change root to RESTRICT */
20          if(chroot (RESTRICT) < 0) {
21              fprintf (stderr, "restrict: cannot chroot to %s\n", RESTRICT);
22              exit (3);
23          }
24          /* set effective UID and GID to real IDs
25              since restrict is set-user-ID owned by root */
26
27          setuid (getuid ());
28          setgid (getgid ());
29
30          /* exec /bin/sh as "-sh" */
31          execl ("/bin/sh", "-sh", 0);
32          fprintf (stderr, "restrict: cannot exec shell\n");
33          exit (4);
34      }
```

c. Permissions of **/usr/local/bin/restrict**:

```
$ ls -l /usr/local/bin/restrict
-rwsr-xr-x  1 root    root    7000 Aug  4 16:16 /usr/local/bin/restrict
$ ☐
```

d. Permissions of files and directories in **/usr/restrict**:

```
$ ls -ld /usr/restrict /usr/restrict/*
drwxr-xr-x  7 root    root     112 Aug  4 16:46 /usr/restrict
drwxr-xr-x  2 root    root     336 Aug  5 11:58 /usr/restrict/bin
drwxr-xr-x  2 root    root      64 Aug  4 16:51 /usr/restrict/dev
drwxr-xr-x  2 root    root      64 Aug  4 16:56 /usr/restrict/etc
drwxr-xr-x  2 guest   guest     96 Aug  4 16:45 /usr/restrict/guest
drwxrwxrwx  2 root    root      80 Aug  5 12:02 /usr/restrict/tmp
$ ls -la /usr/restrict/bin
total 138
drwxr-xr-x  2 root    root     336 Aug  5 11:58 .
drwxr-xr-x  7 root    root     112 Aug  4 16:46 ..
-rwxr-xr-x  1 root    root     316 Aug  4 16:42 .download
-rwxr-xr-x  1 root    root    1674 Aug  4 16:41 .help
-rwxr-xr-x  1 root    root     538 Aug  4 16:41 .upload
-rwxr-xr-x  1 root    root     431 Aug  4 16:19 basename
-rwxr-xr-x  1 root    root    5652 Aug  4 16:19 cat
-rwxr-xr-x  1 root    root    2740 Aug  4 16:18 echo
-rwxr-xr-x  1 root    root    7668 Aug  4 16:20 expr
```

```
-rwxr-xr-x  1 root    root         7 Aug  4 16:52 grep
-rwxr-xr-x  1 root    root      4708 Aug  5 11:58 kill
-rwxr-xr-x  1 root    root     13124 Aug  4 16:20 ls
-rwxr-xr-x  1 root    root        16 Aug  4 16:47 mail
-rwxr-xr-x  1 root    root     23460 Aug  4 16:21 more
-rwxr-xr-x  1 root    root      4964 Aug  4 16:19 pwd
-rwxr-xr-x  1 root    root     30468 Aug  4 16:18 sh
-rwxr-xr-x  1 root    root      4804 Aug  5 11:58 sleep
-rwxr-xr-x  1 root    root     14660 Aug  4 16:19 stty
-rwxr-xr-x  1 root    root      4420 Aug  4 16:18 test
-rwxr-xr-x  1 root    root      5556 Aug  4 16:19 wc
-rwxr-xr-x  1 root    root         7 Aug  4 16:52 who
$ ls -l /usr/restrict/dev
total 0
prw-------  1 guest   root         0 Aug  4 16:50 MAIL
-rw-rw-rw-  1 root    root         0 Aug  4 16:55 null
$ ls -l /usr/restrict/etc
total 1
-rw-r--r--  1 root    root       104 Aug  5 12:01 profile
$ □
```

e. Contents of **/usr/restrict/etc/profile**:

```
1    (sleep 600; echo timed out!; kill -9 0) &
2    trap "" 1 2 3
3    PATH=/bin
4    HOME=`pwd`
5    export PATH HOME
6    exec .help
```

f. **/usr/restrict/bin/who** and /usr/restrict/bin/grep:

```
exit 1
```

g. Making the named pipe:

```
# mknod /dev/MAIL p
# □
```

h. /usr/restrict/bin/mail:

```
(echo " *** mail from guest login ***"; cat) > /dev/MAIL
```

i. Mailer daemon when using named pipe:

```
while true
do
      rmail root < /usr/restrict/dev/MAIL
done
```

j. Mailer daemon when using temporary mail file:

```
for m in /usr/restrict/mail/*
do
    rmail root < $m
    rm -f $m
done
```

I

Terminal Lock Program

The Berkeley UNIX system provides a **lock** program, which allows a user to protect his or her terminal without having to log out and lose the environment that he or she has established. The following C program also provides a terminal lock function. It was originally published in the "Wizard's Grabbag" column in the April 1986 issue of UNIXWORLD magazine. This particular program was written by Dave Schultz of AT&T-IS.

Figure I.1 Listing of **lock.c**.

```
 1   #include <stdio.h>
 2   #include <pwd.h>
 3   #include <signal.h>
 4   #define PASSWDSZ 10
 5   #define PROMPT "           LOCKED! "
 6   main()
 7   {
 8       int uid;
 9       char *cpass, pass[PASSWDSZ];
10       char *getpass(), *crypt();
11       struct passwd *getpwuid();
12       struct passwd *pwd;
13       endpwent();
14
```

```
15        signal(SIGHUP, SIG_IGN);
16        signal(SIGINT, SIG_IGN);
17        signal(SIGQUIT, SIG_IGN);
18
19        uid = getuid();
20        pwd = getpwuid(uid);
21        endpwent();
22        do {
23            strcpy(pass, getpass(PROMPT));
24            cpass = crypt(pass, pwd->pw_passwd);
25        } while (strcmp(cpass, pwd->pw_passwd) != 0);
26    }
```

Bibliography

Selected Annotated Bibliography

PREPARATORY BOOKS

Morgan, Rachel, and Henry McGilton. *Introducing UNIX System V.* New York: McGraw-Hill, 1987.

> An easy to read, beginners book for learning how to use UNIX System V. It emphasizes text editing and formatting, introduces shell and C programming, and has an introductory chapter on system administration.

Thomas, Rebecca, and Yates, Jean. *A User Guide to the UNIX System.* 2d. ed. Berkeley: Osborne/McGraw-Hill, 1985.

> A well organized, easy to read book for users who wish to learn about the UNIX system. The book is divided into four parts: Part One gives you an overview of the UNIX system. Twelve tutorial sessions make up Part Two. These sessions lead you up the learning curve to become a proficient UNIX system user. Part Three explains 44 of the most commonly used command programs in detail. Finally, Part Four presents additional reference information in seven appendices, one of which provides a good introduction to system administration.

UNIX PROGRAMMING

Aho, Alfred V., Brian W. Kernighan, and Peter J. Weinberger. *The AWK Programming Language.* Reading, Mass: Addison-Wesley, 1988.

> The only book devoted to the **awk** programming language, authored by the people who wrote the program. Includes material on the new version of awk, **nawk**.

Anderson, Gail, and Paul Anderson. *The Unix C Shell Field Guide.* Englewood Cliffs, N.J.: Prentice-Hall, 1986.

> An in-depth study of the C shell as a command interpreter and programming language. The authors discuss the C shell as it runs under 4.2BSD, 4.3BSD, System V, System III, XENIX, and Version 7 UNIX systems.

Campbell, Joe. *C Programmer's Guide to Serial Communications.* Indianapolis: Howard W. Sams & Co., 1987.

> A treatise on serial communications. Part I, "Basics," is must reading for anyone using serial communications.

Kernighan, Brian W., and Rob Pike, *The Unix Programming Environment.* Englewood Cliffs, N.J.: Prentice-Hall, 1984.

> This book helps the reader learn the C language while effectively communicating the UNIX programming philosophy. Rik's favorite guide, but geared more for programmers than nonprogramming users.

Kernighan, Brian W., and Dennis M. Ritchie. *The C Programming Language.* Englewood Cliffs, N.J.: Prentice-hall, 1978.

> The original reference to the C programming language. Defines the original form of the language and provides numerous short program examples.

Kochan, Steven G., and Patrick H. Wood. *UNIX Shell Programming.* Hasbrouck Heights, N.J.: Hayden Book Company, 1985.

> Provides a complete, easy-to-understand introduction to UNIX shell programming. It covers all features of the standard (Bourne) shell, the new System V Release 2 Bourne shell and includes a useful chapter on the Korn shell.

Lapin, J.E.. *Portable C and UNIX System Programming.* Englewood Cliffs, N.J.: Prentice-Hall, 1987.

> This book deals with the writing of portable programs. But most significant is its exhaustive comparision of the programs, system calls, and subroutine libraries, special files, and file formats from all major UNIX system dialects,

including Version 7, 4.1BSD, 4.2BSD, 4.3BSD, System III, XENIX 2.3, 3.0 and 5.0, System V, and AT&T's System V Interface Definition.

Rochkind, Marc. J. *Advanced UNIX Programming.* Englewood Cliffs, N.J.: Prentice-Hall, 1985.

> This book clearly and systematically explains how to program using UNIX system calls. The system calls are organized into I/O on files and terminals, processes, interprocess communication, signals, and a miscellaneous category, which includes calls used for system administration. The author treats Version 7, System III, System V Release 1, 4.2BSD, and XENIX versions of the UNIX system.

Thomas, Rebecca, Lawrence R. Rogers, and Jean L. Yates. *Advanced Programmer's Guide to UNIX System V.* Berkeley: Osborne/McGraw-Hill, 1986.

> A broad brush approach to programming in the UNIX System V environment. This book covers the Bourne and C shells, the **vi/ex** text editors, use of the C compiler and programming tools, such as **make** and library archives, and extends the standard documentation for important system calls and subroutines with many example programs.

Sage, Russell G. *Tricks of the UNIX Masters.* Indianapolis: Howard W. Sams & Co., 1987.

> This book provides tools, tricks, and tips for Bourne shell programmers, giving example solutions to a wide assortment of programming problems.

UNIX SYSTEM INTERNALS

Bach, Maurice J. *The Design of the UNIX Operating System.* Englewood Cliffs, N.J.: Prentice-Hall, 1986.

> This book describes the internal algorithms and structures that form the basis of the operating system (the kernel). Numerous C language-like pseudo code examples of the algorithms and diagrams of the data structures help illustrate the in-depth discussions.

SYSTEM ADMINISTRATION

Campbell, Joe. *The RS-232 Solution.* Berkeley: SYBEX, 1984.

> Describes a simple fool-proof method for interfacing RS-232 peripherals to microcomputers.

Fiedler, David and Bruce H. Hunter. *UNIX System Administration.* Hasbrouck Heights, N.J.: Hayden Book Company, 1986.

> A book for beginning system administrators. It includes information on setting up file systems, adding and removing users, making backups, improving security, connecting serial terminals, printers, and modems, communicating with other systems and a brief discussion of writing shell programs.

Strang, John. *Reading and Writing Termcap Entries.* Newton, Mass: O'Reilly & Associates, 1986.

> A guide to interpreting and writing **termcap** database entries used for describing terminal capabilities.

Todino, Grace. *Using UUCP and Usenet.* Revised by Tim O'Reilly and Dale Dougherty. 4th. ed. Newton, Mass.: O'Reilly & Associates, 1987.

> A comprehensive handbook for using both Version 2 and HoneyDanBer UUCP and Revision 2.11 **netnews** software for accessing the Usenet communication network.

O'Reilly, T. and Grace Todino. *Managing UUCP and Usenet.* Revised by Tim O'Reilly and Dale Dougherty. 5th. ed. Newton, Mass: O'Reilly & Associates, 1988.

> A comprehensive handbook for setting up and managing both Version 2 and HoneyDanBer UUCP and Revision 2.11 **netnews** software for accessing the Usenet communication network.

Wood, Patrick H., and Stephen G. Kochan. *UNIX System Security.* Hasbrouck Heights, N.J.: Hayden Book Company, 1985.

> A practical guide to computer security on the UNIX system for the user, administrator, or programmer. It presents several useful programs for making your system secure and keeping it that way.

REFERENCE MANUALS

The Bell System Technical Journal, Vol 57, No. 6, Part 2, July-August 1978.

> This issue contains many early papers on computer programming at Bell Labs using the UNIX system as a central unifying theme.

AT&T Bell Laboratories Technical Journal, Vol. 63, No. 8, Oct. 1984.

The second issue of the *Technical Journal* devoted exclusively to papers on the UNIX system. Several papers should interest system administrators, including those on security, data encryption, performance, and networking.

Unix System V User Reference Manual. April 1984.

The standard AT&T UNIX system documentation for the user commands (section1) and games (section 6).

Unix System V Administrator Reference Manual. April 1984.

The standard AT&T UNIX system documentation for those who administer a UNIX System (section 1M and 7).

Unix System V Programmer Reference Manual. April 1984.

The standard AT&T UNIX system documentation for the system calls (section 2), subroutine libraries (section 3), file formats (section 4), and miscellaneous facilities (section 5).

Unix System V Basic Networking Utilities 1.0. March 1985.

The standard AT&T documentation for the HoneyDanBer UUCP system.

RESOURCES

UNIX Products Directory. Santa Clara, CA.: /usr/group., 7th. ed., 1988.

Presenting the most comprehensive coverage available on UNIX services and products marketplaces including some usually overlooked market segments, this directory is published annually in conjunction with the /usr/group-sponsored UniForum trade show and conference.

Index